A Complete Course i[illegible]
Accounting

Richard Giles

Stanley Thornes (Publishers) Ltd

First published in 1996 by:
Stanley Thornes Publishers Ltd
Ellenborough House
Wellington Street
Cheltenham
GL50 1YW
UK

96 97 98 99 00 / 10 9 8 7 6 5 4 3 2 1

ISBN 0 7487 2729 9

Typeset by Northern Phototypesetting Co Ltd, Bolton
Printed and bound in Great Britain by
Redwood Books, Wilts

Author's note

I would like to take this opportunity to thank the members of staff of the Business Studies and Computing Department at Bournemouth and Poole College for all their kind assistance and guidance, and to John Capel who often provides me with some very good examination questions. I would also like to acknowledge the reviewers of the text who provided helpful additional material, and to thank Francis Dodds at Stanley Thornes for all his support.

In addition, many thanks to the Examining Boards who have kindly allowed me to use their questions, particularly AAT, ICM, CIMA, ACCA, AEB, CIOB, RSA and GCSE. I would also like to thank Microsoft Ltd for the use of the software programs to illustrate the computer section.

Contents

How to use this book

A Complete Course in Business Accounting is designed to provide a comprehensive and flexible resource to meet the pressures of today's teaching and study. It recognises that:

- class sizes are going up
- lecturers and students have less time to prepare
- lecturers often have less time to spend with students
- students need to learn more independently
- texts need to be flexible enough to fit a range of course needs.

A Complete Course in Business Accounting meets these needs in a variety of ways.

Individual chapter features

Chapters incorporate a number of features designed to promote effective student learning. Each chapter begins with a set of **objectives** which focus the reader on the key issues and skills to learn. These are then rounded off in **summaries** at the end of chapters which allow readers to check what they have learnt. Chapters are divided into **numbered sections** for quick and easy reference – these also play an important role in end-of-chapter questions (see below). Throughout the text **key definitions** are provided and highlighted for quick reference. Given the importance of visual aids to learning, the text places particular emphasis on the use of **diagrams** to help situate particular skills and processes within business accounting systems. Chapters also make very full use of practical **worked examples** to show how skills are used in practice – these are also highlighted for ease of reference.

End-of-chapter questions

A vital element in a text of this kind is the quality and range of questions to help students practise and consolidate their skills. The questions at the end of each chapter are designed to build progesssively from basic to more advanced skills. Where appropriate the chapter makes clear which are basic exercises consolidating essential skills and which are more advanced exercises that extend skills further. Where this is helpful, later exercises also consolidate and integrate skills learnt in earlier chapters. Questions are referenced to the relevant numbered section in the chapter. This allows students to isolate which skills they are learning and where they should look if they need to revise particular areas further, allowing them to work and revise more independently if need be. Brief answers to **all** questions are provided at the back of the book. **Fully worked** answers are provided in the accompanying lecturer's pack together with tips on common sources of error and where students can refer to in filling gaps in their skills and understanding. The lecturer's pack also contains a wealth of **additional practice material** (see below).

There is also a section of **multiple-choice questions** at the end of the book to revise skills and help students practise for this kind of assessment. These are supplemented by a bank of further questions in the lecturer's pack. These are organised by chapter and can be used to revise skills learnt in that chapter. Answers are keyed into the relevant section to allow students to revise outstanding points independently.

Flexible organisation

Whilst the book builds knowledge and skills progressively, to meet the needs of individual courses it has also been designed to provide self-sufficient chapters which can be read separately. Recognising that students often need to read selectively, each chapter starts with a brief **context** section, indicating which previous chapters can be consulted to provide a helpful context in making the most of the chapter.

There are a number of possible routes through the book. This section outlines the role of individual parts and chapters and how they are related as a way of helping lecturers and students choose the most appropriate route. Further guidance on using the text with particular syllabuses is provided in the lecturer's pack.

Parts 1 and **2** provide the essential introduction and context for the rest of the book, introducing the principles of accounting and of business accounting systems. We believe it is important to provide a sound introduction of this kind so that students understand from the start how individual processes and skills fit within the business accounting systems and the basic principles of accounting itself. With such an understanding we believe they will grasp individual skills and the role they play more rapidly, thoroughly and independently.

Parts 3 and **4** then look at how credit and cash transactions are dealt with. **Part 5** then consolidates those skills through Chapter 19, which provides a detailed worked example taking the reader from subsidiary books to trial balance, and looks at broader issues such as computerised accounting.

Part 6 concentrates on the key issues relating to the preparation of final accounts, beginning with the basic issues connected with sole traders, and then taking the reader on to more detailed areas such as adjustments. These then allow a detailed consideration of partnership and limited company accounts in Chapters 26 and 27. With this basic framework established, the reader can look at related issues in Chapters 28 to 32.

Part 7 shifts the focus from preparation to interpretation and decision-making using accounting information. Without providing a detailed consideration of management accounting, Chapters 36 and 37 illustrate how financial accounting links in with cost and management accounting and management decision-making in these areas. Finally, **Part 8** covers a range of further accounting issues such as accounting for incomplete records and payroll.

Learning core skills

Perhaps the most important issue in any foundation accounting text is how effectively it introduces the basic skills on which more advanced skills, such as the preparation of final accounts, depend. As has been mentioned, Parts 1 and 2 concentrate on these skills and building the broader understanding students need to learn most effectively. The following material briefly describes how individual chapters build these essential skills and understanding.

Chapter 1 provides the agenda for the book as a whole, concentrating on the three fundamental processes underlying accounting. It sits alongside Chapters 2 and 3 on business organisations and types of finance in getting the student started.

Chapter 4 uses the themes in Chapter 1 to unlock some of the key principles of business accounting. It explains the accounting equation, the role of journals, accounts, ledgers and final accounts to help students put the individual skills they will be learning in context. It also introduces the basic format of the balance sheet and profit and loss account.

With this context, students can then go on to learning the fundamentals of double-entry in Chapter 5. Whilst we believe students will benefit from the context provided by Chapter 4, Chapter 5 has been designed to be self-sufficient so that it can be read at any point. It takes the reader through the basic rules of double-entry, methods of recording transactions in accounts, balancing accounts, the trial balance and treatment of returns. The following questions revise each step, allowing students to consolidate each skill in turn. Finally, Chapter 6 introduces the structure of business accounting systems in practice and sets the agenda for the rest of the book.

Thereafter, Parts 3 and 4 are designed to use the skills and understanding developed in Parts 1 and 2 to follow differing types of transaction through business accounting systems, beginning with credit and cash transactions respectively. Within each part, introductory chapters (7, 10 and 14) introduce the key principles and documentation while the following chapters explore particular processes and rules in more detail.

Lecturer's pack

To support lecturers, a detailed lecturer's pack is available to adopters. This contains:

- fully-worked answers to questions in the text together with tips on common areas of difficulty and which chapter sections revise relevant skills. If appropriate, these will assist students to consolidate skills independently
- over 100 additional questions plus accompanying documentation and fully-worked answers to enable lecturers to test student knowledge and skills independently
- over 300 multiple-choice and short-answer questions plus answer sheets key into chapter sections to allow independent and in-depth testing of student knowledge, and to direct students to where they can revise for themselves
- a set of assignments designed to allow students to practise a range of skills in a realistic setting
- summaries, key definitions and diagrams for each chapter which can be used as overheads or as components of course packs and handouts. The material has been designed particularly to provide effective revision of key points
- guidance notes on how to use the text with a range of syllabuses.

Samples of the lecturer's pack, and complete packs for adopters of *A Complete Course in Business Accounting*, are available from:

Francis Dodds
Publisher
Stanley Thornes (Publishers) Ltd
Ellenborough House
Wellington Street
Cheltenham
Glos. GL50 1YW

Tel: 01242 228888; fax: 01242 221914

PART I AN INTRODUCTION TO ACCOUNTING

1 What is accounting?

Objectives

On completing this section you should:

- understand the nature of accounting
- recognise why accounting information is needed and by whom
- be aware of the different branches of accounting.

1.1 Defining accounting

If you look in a dictionary you will find that the word 'account' has various meanings. It can refer to identifying and recording something or to measuring or explaining it. Accounting is concerned with all these things. We can see this in the widely-accepted definition of accounting produced by the American Accounting Association:

> the process of identifying, measuring and communicating economic information to permit informed judgements and decisions by users of that information.

All of us do some accounting in our daily lives. We earn money and we spend it. As we do, we identify and record what we are spending, perhaps through a bank statement. We may then try to classify differing kinds of expenditure, for example what we pay out for heating, and then try to measure the impact of these items of expenditure on what we still have in the bank. Finally, we may add up all our expenses and match them up against our income to see if we need to change our spending to avoid getting into debt. In other words we put all the information we have together in a way that allows us to make the right decisions about our financial position. If we were in business we might well ask an accountant to assemble such information on our behalf and communicate it to us in a way which will allow us to make the right decision about what to do with the business.

Throughout the book we will emphasise two key points which come out of our definition of accounting. The **first** is that accounting is a process with stages:

- Identifying and recording
- Classifying and measuring
- Communicating and explaining.

Understanding these stages will help us appreciate how accounting systems work in business, and we will refer to them in later chapters to clarify the role a particular process plays in the accounting system as a whole.

The **second** key point is that accounting exists to help people make decisions. Understanding the kinds of decisions business people need to make and the questions they then ask of accountants will also help you to understand why accounting systems in business operate in the way they do. In the next section we will look at the kinds of questions people in business ask of accountants.

1.2 Who needs accounting information?

Accounting systems in business are set up to provide answers to questions raised by a number of groups. In the following diagram, we list some of the most important of these and the kinds of questions they ask:

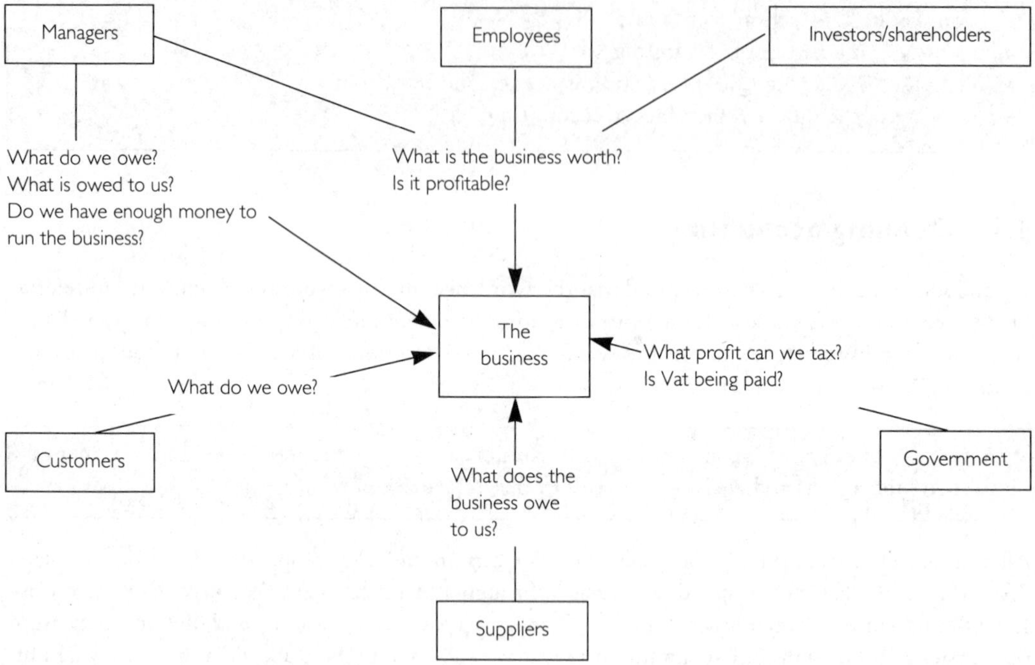

Fig. 1.1 Who needs accounting information?

The **managers** running a business need a wide range of accounting information. They will want to know, for example, if the business is selling enough to cover its costs and make a profit, and how much it might be worth at any one time. They will also want to know what the business is owed by its customers and what it owes to its suppliers, and whether there is enough cash to pay off its debts at any one time. **Employees** also like to be informed of how a business is doing so that, for example, they understand better the challenges a business faces and the targets they need to meet.

Outside the business, its **customers** and **suppliers** will need to know what they owe or what the business owes to them. **Shareholders** and potential **investors** in the business will want to know how well the business is doing and what its worth is so that they can assess what return they will get for their investment.

Government asks businesses a range of questions. As we shall see, many businesses are required by law to publish financial statements for the benefit of their shareholders and potential investors. The taxation authorities will want to assess what profits a business has made in order to assess its liability for tax. Customs and Excise (Vat office) are responsible for ensuring that Vat is being paid and require businesses to keep Vat records (we discuss Vat in Chapter 9).

As we shall see throughout the text, the accounting system is designed to answer these kinds of questions. Those we have listed here represent only some of the most important. In practice, many more are asked. The managers of a business will, for example, want to be able to classify accounting information in a wide range of ways, for example to identify a particular type of expenditure so that they can measure and control it more effectively. The key point is to remember that the accounting system is designed to meet the need to make decisions in business. Understanding the decision needs of potential users of accounting information will help us to see why a particular process is designed as it is and the role it plays in the accounting system as a whole. We will see how the accounting system is designed to answer key questions in Chapter 4.

1.3 The branches of accounting

Understanding the stages of the accounting process and the questions it sets out to answer helps us to understand the differing branches of accounting summarised in Fig. 1.2 below.

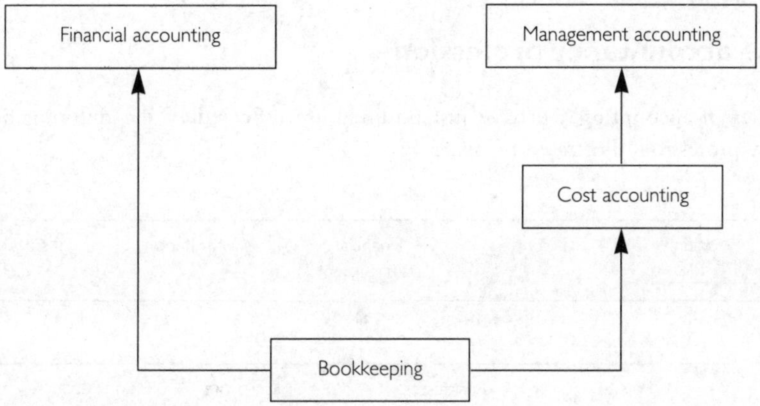

Fig. 1.2 The branches of accounting

Bookkeeping lies at the heart of the recording stage of accounting. It is concerned with ensuring that records of individual transactions are accurate, up-to-date and comprehensive. It makes sure that the rest of the accounting process has all the information it needs and a reliable foundation on which to build. We will deal with individual bookkeeping skills in Parts 3–5 of the book.

Financial accounting uses the information provided by bookkeeping to classify, measure, explain and communicate accounting information to answer the kinds of question we outlined earlier. You may already have seen examples of the annual reports many businesses publish. These will include two key accounting summaries: the profit and loss account (or trading and profit and loss account as it is formally known) and the balance sheet which provide essential information on the company's profitability and what it is worth. Much of a financial accountant's time within a business will be taken up with preparing these statements. Financial accounting skills are discussed in Parts 6–8.

As well as these two branches of accounting, which are covered in some detail in this book, there are two other branches of accounting with a different focus.

Cost accounting, like financial accounting, is concerned with helping managers in their decision-making, particularly with how much things cost to produce. How much does it cost to make something, and what costs should be attributed to it? What costs are involved in making one unit as opposed to 100? Cost accounting provides a way of classifying costs to help managers make decisions about the potential profitability of new products and the profitability of existing products and services.

In the same way that bookkeeping provides a foundation for financial accounting, cost accounting provides the foundation for **management accounting**. Management accounting is designed to provide managers with the information they need to forecast, control and evaluate costs. Management accountants help managers to assess the profitability of new and existing projects and with such areas as forecasting and budgeting for the business as a whole.

This book does not consider cost or management accounting in detail. Aspects of costing and budgeting are dealt with in Chapters 36 and 37 to show the ways in which financial accounting assists management accountants in giving managers the information and tools they need to make the right decisions.

1.4 The accountancy profession

The branches of accounting we have just outlined are reflected in the differing branches of the accountancy profession, illustrated below in Fig. 1.3.

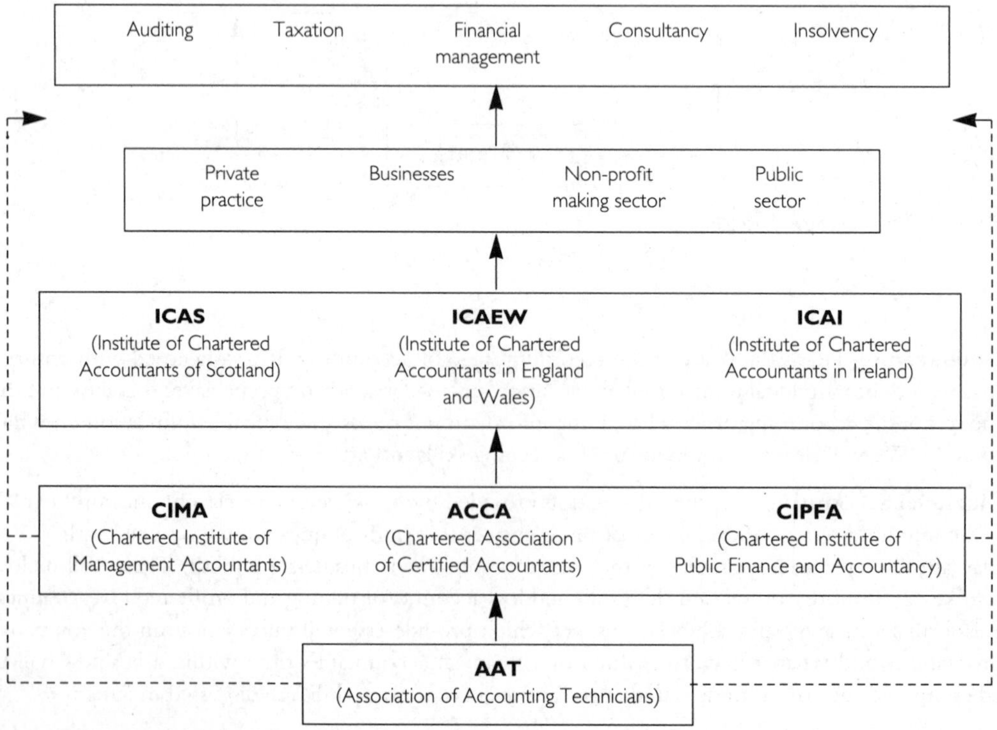

Fig. 1.3 The accountancy profession

The Association of Accounting Technicians (AAT) is sponsored by all the higher bodies (except the Irish Institute) and is responsible for accountancy training broadly up to the level where ACCA, CIMA and CIPFA qualifications begin. These bodies provide courses which allow students to become **certified** accountants. It is only after further training and experience in accountancy practice that accountants can apply for membership of the ICAEW, ICAS and ICAI and become **chartered** accountants.

As the diagram illustrates, a student can choose from a variety of career paths at each level. Specialising in financial accountancy (ACCA courses provide training in both financial and management accounting) would allow the student to pursue a career in private practice. Accountancy firms provide individuals and organisations, including businesses, with a wide range of services. They can advise on legal issues such as taxation or Vat, assist in the preparation of accounts, or, as required by law, audit the accounts businesses are legally obliged to submit to Companies House. Auditing provides an independent review of a company's financial position, and many businesses now use accountants to provide the business with its own audit of internal accounting systems and controls. Accountants also provide advice and support in such areas as mortgages, loans, pensions and investments, overdraft facilities or raising finance, and may act in a broader consultancy role, advising businesses on a range of financial and non-financial issues. Finally, if businesses get into difficulties, insolvency practitioners may be brought in either to help the business recover or, at worst, arrange the disposal of assets to maximise returns for creditors.

Financial and management accountants (CIMA courses specialise in management accounting) may also choose to work within businesses, ensuring the accurate and timely production of the financial information required by Government, shareholders and the management team, helping to arrange finance, sales of assets and acquisitions, managing cash flow or assisting in assessing the viability of new projects and budgeting. Those specialising in financial management would be responsible for the flow of funds into and within organisations, negotiating with lenders for example or assessing the financial needs of differing parts of the business. A similar range of skills is also required in a third potential career path working in non-profit-making organisations, such as charities, and in the public sector (where CIPFA courses are relevant) where recent reforms have greatly increased the need for accounting expertise within the National Health Service and local government, for example.

The addresses of all the major accounting bodies are included in the lecturer's pack.

Summary

You should now have some idea of what accounting is: it is a process which has three basic stages: identifying and recording financial information, classifying and measuring it and communicating and explaining it to those parties which need to know so that they can make the right kind of decisions in business.

Try answering as many questions as you can throughout the text and check your answers with those suggested in the back of the book.

Questions

1 The AAA (American Accounting Association) provides us with a definition of accounting which appears a little complicated. Can you simplify it to make it more meaningful to the person in the street? (1.1)

2 What are the three stages in the accounting process? (1.1)

3 What kind of information does accounting want to identify and record? (1.2)

4 Look at Fig. 1.1 (Who needs accounting information?) and answer the following:
a) Who would wish to know if the business was profitable or not?
b) Who would be concerned with taxes and Vat?
c) Why does management want accounting information? (1.2)

5 What role does the bookkeeping side of accounting play? (1.3)

6 Financial accounting differs from both cost and management accounting. In what way? (1.3)

7 The accounting profession provides many interesting and varied types of career. What kind of jobs would be open to a would-be accountant? (1.4)

8 How would you sum up the role of accounting? (1.1–4)

2 Types of business organisations

Objectives

On completing this section you should:

- understand the distinction between organisations in the private sector and public sector of business
- have an insight into the financial organisation of each type of business
- understand the meaning of the accounting equation.

2.1 Introduction

The United Kingdom is a mixed economy in which the production of goods and services is provided by both the private and public sectors of business. The private sector is defined as 'economic activity in the hands of individuals' as distinct from that of the public sector, described as 'economic activity in the hands of the State'. The private sector is trade conducted by individuals in the form of sole traders, partnerships, and companies, both private limited and public limited companies (plc's). These forms of businesses produce the majority of our goods and services and particularly since the Government has privatised so many of nationalised industries, the public sector's contribution has diminished. Economic activity from the private sector of business will be discussed first.

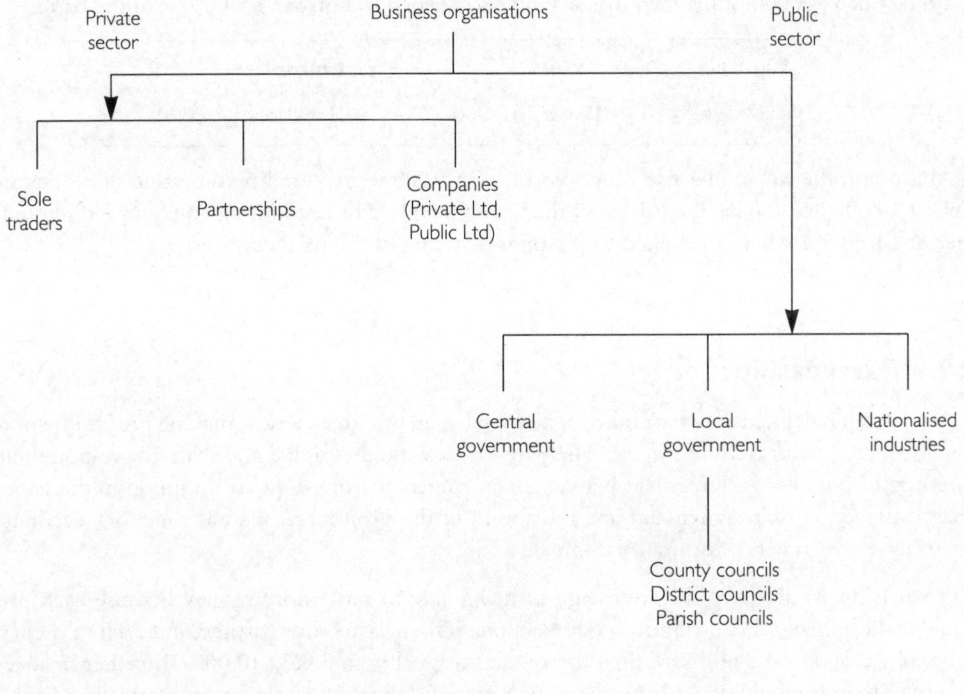

Fig. 2.1 Business organisations

2.2 The sole trader

A very large proportion of our business is conducted by small business organisations. Although their proportion of trade has declined in the last three decades as a result of the growth of public limited companies, they still hold at least one third of the retail trade. It has been the rapid growth of the supermarkets that have expanded the number of their stores into almost all areas of the country which has led to the demise of the small corner shop. Apart from the retail trade, a sole trader could be, for example, a person who provides a service such as an electrician or plumber or window cleaner.

The sole trader will be largely responsible for providing his or her own capital to start the business going and may require additional funds from a bank in the form of a bank loan or overdraft facilities. If the owner could invest £1 000 of his own money, then the bank could lend him any amount depending how viable they considered the business to be and the security he could offer on the repayment of the loan. The amount of money which could be raised in this way will tend to be limited because it would come from the savings of the owner and the banks would only lend up to, say, a maximum of three or four times that of the owner.

The finance raised will then be used to buy assets to get the business going. For example, a small shop may be required, there may be stock to be purchased, equipment to buy, a motor vehicle to run. Finance buys these assets to enable trading to commence.

The accounting equation represents the value of a business's assets and who has financed them (the liabilities). The owner is worth the difference between the assets and liabilities of the business.

Capital = Assets – Liabilities

If a trader had £5 000 of his own money and also needed to borrow £5 000 from the bank:

Capital	=	**Assets**	–	**Liabilities**
£5 000	=	Bank £10 000	–	Bank loan £5 000

At this point, the sole trader has a 'net worth' of £5 000 represented by the value of money in the bank £10 000, less the liability (debt) of the loan £5 000. (The accounting equation is discussed further in Chapter 4 when it is linked to the understanding of the balance sheet).

2.3 Partnerships

A partnership is defined as two or more persons in business with a view to making profits, the number usually limited to a maximum of 20. The partners provide the capital and share the responsibility of running the business on agreement between its members. Partnerships are common in the same services provided by sole traders but are also found in the professions such as solicitors, accountants, estate agents, members of insurance companies etc.

A partnership would have the advantage of being able to raise more money because each partner could make a financial contribution. For example, if there were four partners and each of them contributed £2 500 to the business, then the owners' capital would be £10 000. If further finance was required, then it would come from the same sources as those of a sole trader, normally a bank. For example:

Capital	=	Assets	–	Liabilities
F Brown	£2 500	£80 000	–	£70 000
J Green	£2 500			
D Blue	£2 500			
H Black	£2 500			
	£10 000			

In this case the four partners have a net worth of £10 000, represented by business assets of £80 000 less liabilities of £70 000.

2.4 Companies

A company is owned by its shareholders. It is they who contribute the capital required in the business. Shareholders do not normally interfere in the running of affairs and leave that to the directors who are elected by the shareholders.

There are two distinct types of company: the private limited and the public limited company (plc). **A private limited company**, although having no limit to the number of shareholders it can have, may only sell its shares privately and is therefore restricted in the amount of capital it can raise. On the other hand, the **public limited company (plc)** can invite the public to buy its shares by using a prospectus (an invitation to the public to buy its shares) and therefore has the greatest potential to raise the most capital.

Shareholders of both private or public companies are part owners of their companies. They actually own a proportion of the company in relation to the number of shares they have. The reward for owning shares comes from either dividends (a share of the company profits reserved by the company for its shareholders and paid out to individual shareholders in proportion to the size of their shareholding), or from an increase in the value of their shares (as a result of the increased value of the company as it expands). Limited companies have the advantage of having **limited liability**, a warning to potential creditors that shareholders are only liable up to the value of their nominal capital (i.e. the sum they originally paid for their shares, not their current market value which may be much higher). They are protected against the debts of the company up to the value of issued and paid-up capital.

Companies can also raise capital by various means including the issue of debentures (loan stock) but more often than not, it is the bank that is the most common financial institution for lending (see Chapter 3 on sources of finance).

The accounting equation emphasising the net worth of a company may appear as:

Capital	=	Assets	–	Liabilities
Share capital	£150 000	£385 000	–	£185 000
Reserves	£50 000			
	£200 000			

The shareholders have a net worth of £200 000 made up of their share capital of £150 000 and £50 000 of reserves which are retained profits over the years. This represents the business assets of £385 000 less the liabilities of £185 000.

The essential difference between these organisations is one of size. This is largely determined by the amount of capital invested in the business and also the nature of the goods or services it produces. For example, a small capital sum of £5 000 is not likely to be sufficient to start up a public limited company.

Later in this book, there is a more detailed discussion on both partnerships (Chapter 26) and limited companies (Chapter 27) explaining how these organisations are structured and the legal implications involved.

2.5 Public finance

This refers to economic activity in the hands of the State. Public finance is raised by the Government through taxes and other means, for the purpose of public spending on those goods and services provided by both central and local Government departments. In the 19th and 20th centuries, particularly, large-scale undertakings were organised to provide essential public services like railways, water, gas and electricity supplies. The finance for these came from companies who raised capital by selling shares through public subscription. These were therefore limited companies until, after the Second World War, they became nationalised industries through the various Acts of Parliament under Mr Attlee's Labour Government. We have now come full circle in that only a few nationalised industries are left, most of them privatised by the Conservatives during the 1980s under Mrs Thatcher's leadership. The finances of government are basically divided between central Government finance and local authority finance.

2.5.1 Central Government finance

In the autumn budget speech each year, usually in November, the Chancellor outlines the nation's public expenditure programme and how this is to be financed. Most of the income raised by Government is through direct and indirect taxes of one form or another like income tax, National Insurance contributions, and Vat. Most of this money is spent on health, social security, education, the environment and defence. What the Government cannot raise in taxes must then be borrowed through its PSBR (Public Sector Borrowing Requirement).

2.5.2 Local authority finance

For many years, local authorities raised their finance from rates, a local tax paid by the owner occupiers of land and property. This was supported by central Government in the form of the rate support grant and also other specific grants to help finance local capital expenditure on things like roads, schools and hospitals. In April 1990, the Government introduced the Poll Tax which proved to be immensely unpopular because it was seen as an unfair tax. This meant that a charge was made per head on each adult eligible to pay. The Government got its sums wrong and the charge was at least 30 per cent more than estimated amounting to approximately £350 per head on average throughout the country. It was a very controversial tax and caused chaos in many councils because of lack of payment. Eventually, by April 1993, the Government's Council Tax was introduced, working very much like the old rate system in that a charge is made on the basis of the value of each dwelling. The higher the dwelling's value, the more council tax is paid by the resident.

2.5.3 Government spending

Central Government frequently publishes its spending plans in their Quarterly Reviews and sometimes show how they intend to raise and spend its finances on the basis of each pence in the £.

Study the figures below.

Where money is from		**Where money is spent**	
	Pence/£		Pence/£
Income tax	23	Health & Social Security	48
Corporation tax	11	Education & Science	10
NIC	17	Environment	8
Vat	16	Defence	10
Customs & Excise	12	Government departments	12
Council taxes	11	Interest payments	9
Other receipts	10	Other payments	3
	100		100

Source: The Government's *Quarterly Review 1994*

On the basis of these figures, suppose the Government had to spend £260 billion in the year, how much money would it need to raise through corporation tax? This would be 11 per cent, that is, £28.6 billion. How much would the Government plan to spend on health and social security? This would amount to £124.8 billion, that is, 48 per cent of spending.

Summary

The private sector is defined as business in the hands of private individuals such as sole traders, partnerships and limited companies. This is in contrast to businesses run by the State which is defined as the public sector. The financial structure is based on the provision of capital and this is the major influence on the size of a business organisation.

Questions

1 What is the distinction between economic activity in the private sector as distinct from economic activity in the public sector? (2.1)

2 What type of business organisation do you think the following are:
a) Business A has a capital of £3 000 and provides an electrical service to customers.
b) Business B has a capital of £20 million and manufactures washing machines.
c) Business C has a capital of £150 000 and provides accounting, audit and taxation services. (2.2–4)

3 What advantage(s) does a partnership have over a sole trader? (2.3)

4 What is generally thought to be the most significant factor which determines the size of a business? (2.4)

5 The following data represents the figures of a public limited company:

	£000's
Assets	1 092.90
Liabilities	322.00
Capital and reserves	770.90

a) What is the value of the company's resources?
b) How much are the shareholders worth in the company?
c) How much is the total financing of the company?
d) Why is it unlikely that these accounts are that of a sole trader?
e) Show these figures in the accounting equation, C=A – L. (2.4)

6 From the Government spending table seen on the previous page, based on a spending budget of £300 billion, how much would be spent on education and science? How much would be raised from income tax? (2.5)

7 What is the Council Tax and how is money raised through the use of this system? (2.5)

8 Why has public sector ownership declined in the period of the 1980s and 1990s? (2.5)

3 Sources of finance

Objectives

On completing this section you should:

- understand the various sources of finance in business
- appreciate that these sources are either part of the owners' capital or borrowed capital.

Context

You should have read Chapter 2 as background to this chapter.

3.1 Introduction

As we have already discussed, it takes money to start up a business and also to keep it going. Capital is needed for a business to commence, maintain sufficient liquidity (cash or convertibility to cash) and also to expand. An organisation must be able to plan its resources and this means being able to forecast events ahead of time and to ensure there is enough capital to meet the objectives set by the business. For example, it may want to purchase expensive equipment in six months time; will it have the resources planned to do it?

There are two basic sources of finance: the **owner's capital** and **capital borrowed**. The nature of the organisation will determine what type of finance it needs. The major sources of finance are:

The owner's capital	**owner's** capital
Profits	**owner's** capital
Loan capital	**borrowed** capital
Debenture issues	**borrowed** capital
Leasing/hiring of assets	**borrowed** capital
Factoring	**borrowed** capital
Trade creditors	**borrowed** capital

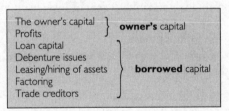

The size of capital is the key to the size of a business. Small business ventures often remain the same size for many years because of their limitations in being able to raise more capital. On the other hand, a plc has the ability to raise large sums and also can exploit more fully the various alternatives to raise further capital. Below is a brief summary of the sources of capital available to business.

3.2 Owner's capital

For a sole trader or partnership, this will be their own personal investment coming from their savings or from assistance from family or friends. The amount raised will be limited because additional sums can be difficult to find.

For a limited company, particularly a plc, the raising of large funds through the selling of shares in the company to new or existing owners, gives them the best potential of raising large sums of capital. Chapter 27 discusses limited companies and types of share capital in more detail.

3.3 Profits

Profits which can be ploughed back into the business are a very important source of finance. Small businesses such as sole traders and partnerships tend to use up most of their profits because of the need for drawing out cash for their day-to-day expenses. Limited companies which make large profits can expand their organisations by retaining funds and use these to finance their objectives.

Very large companies can make substantial profits of £100's millions. Even allowing for payment of corporation tax and dividends to shareholders, the majority of profits can still be retained as reserves, helping these companies to expand and grow even more.

3.4 Loan capital

This represents the borrowed capital for which a business must pay a rate of interest. The most common source for borrowing is from the High Street banks. For short-term funds, it may be that an overdraft facility is adequate to finance day-to-day business, but for specific projects such as purchasing fixed assets, it may be necessary to negotiate a medium or long-term loan over a number of years.

3.5 Debenture issues

Another form of loan capital is a debenture issue. A limited company may attract funds from lenders in return for a fixed rate of interest. The borrowings are 'secured' on the assets of the company, which means that if the company defaults on its payment obligations to the lenders, the debenture holders can force a sale of the assets in order to recover the amounts due to them. Debentures often involve the mortgage of specific company assets and in the event of any default such as non-payment of interest, the specific assets of the company can be sold off to pay the debenture holders what they are due. The charge on the assets may be fixed, as above, or floating, that is, not on any specific assets but on all the company's assets as a whole. Debentures holders are therefore guaranteed interest and the repayment of their loans to the company.

A plc can sell debentures by using the stock exchange and is a form of loan capital. The debentures are marketable, that is, they can be bought and sold on the exchange in the same way as shares. Debentures may be issued for specific periods of time and usually sold in stocks of £100 at a fixed interest rate, for example, 8.5 per cent stock for ten years. This means that a company is prepared to pay 8.5 per cent per annum interest over a ten-year period after which time the stock is said to be redeemable – the company then buys back its stock. Some debentures are irredeemable which means that although the interest is still paid each year, the stock is never 'matured'.

3.6 Leasing/hiring of fixed assets

These are methods whereby a business does not need to purchase its fixed assets (premises, equipment, vehicles etc) but either leases or hires them over a specific time and pays a rental for their use. The maintenance and repairs of fixed assets is usually part of the contract, and this is an additional convenience for the company. Both the leasing or hire-purchase of fixed assets can assist in the cash flow of a business, giving it more funds at its disposal in which to finance other options. In Chapter 33, SSAP 21 discusses different types of leasing in further detail.

3.7 Factoring

A company with a problem receiving payment from its customers (debtors) may use a factoring company to do it for them. Factoring can provide immediate finance for a business because the debts (the invoices outstanding) are taken over and paid by the factors (usually an organisation linked to a bank) who invoice the customers and chase up the debts. Factors either charge a fee for their services or pay the business a proportion of the debt, keeping the remainder they recover. Many types of organisations both large and small employ factoring companies on a more or less continuous basis. They can be a lifeline to them, helping them to overcome cash shortages due to the slow payment of their customers.

3.8 Creditors

This refers to the trade credit given by suppliers and can be very useful to a business, particularly those stores that can purchase huge amounts over a specific period of time. The large supermarkets like Sainsbury's, Tesco and Safeway have the capacity to buy £millions of stock on credit over a period of say several months and take advantage of free finance at nil per cent interest rates!

3.9 Other sources

These can come from the more unusual sources such as the Prince's Youth Business Trust aimed at young entrepreneurs who want grants or low interest loans. There is also the Shell Enterprise and British Coal Schemes, the Arts Council and Rural Development Commission as other possible avenues to obtain finance.

The Government can also provide sources of finance to companies seeking venture capital for projects which may take some time to become profitable. For example, Investors in Industry has been backed by the High Street banks and the Bank of England and has loaned capital to businesses on a long-term basis of up to fifteen years, playing an essential role in helping the development of industry, especially in technology.

There are also funds available from local authorities which can offer a variety of help and financial support by providing grants. The Loan Guarantee Scheme is available for small businesses wishing to obtain loans through the local Business Enterprise Scheme.

In conclusion there is a wide variety of finance available for different types of business organisations. The larger the business, the more money it needs to finance its activities. Note that a major source of external finance is borrowed money from a High Street bank, whether the business is large or small.

Summary

The financial structure of organisations is based on the provision of capital, some of which is provided by the owners of business and some which is borrowed from outside. Finance is essential not only to commence business but to also keep it running. If businesses run short of finance and borrowing from banks or other institutions becomes difficult, a business could find itself facing financial difficulties.

Questions

1 What are the two basic sources of business finance? (3.1)

2 List the finance available under borrowed capital. (3.1)

3 For what purpose would a business obtain a bank overdraft rather than a bank loan? (3.2)

4 What is the difference between buying shares or buying debentures in public limited companies? (3.5)

5 If a debenture holder has £2 500 stock and the rate of interest is 9 per cent for ten years:
a) Calculate the total interest payable over the life of the debenture.
b) If the company fails to make any profit, does the interest still have to be paid?
c) Can the debenture holder sell his stock just like a shareholder? How can stock be sold? (3.5)

6 a) Why would a company wish to lease or hire its assets rather than purchase them? (3.6)
b) What benefit would a company have by 'selling' its invoices? (3.7)

The following questions test your broader understanding of the issues raised by this chapter:

7 Why do you think a sole trader finds it difficult to expand his business?

8 Why is it easier for a public limited company to raise larger sources of finance than other organisations?

4 The basic principles of business accounting systems

Objectives

On completing this section you should:

- understand what a business transaction is
- appreciate the overall picture of an accounting system
- understand the importance of ledgers
- recognise the five major accounting groups (RECAL)
- have an idea of the functions of the profit and loss account and balance sheet.

Context

You should have read Chapter 1 as essential background to this chapter.

4.1 Basic principles

We saw in Chapter 1 that accounting is both a process with stages and that it needs to answer a range of key questions. We can now use these two points to begin to understand some of the basic principles behind the accounting systems we encounter in business, using Fig. 4.1 overleaf.

This diagram of the accounting system is designed to highlight some of the key features to help us understand how the system works as a whole and the way individual processes fit into the system. As we shall see in Chapter 6, in practice accounting systems in business are more complex. At this stage we are more concerned to understand some of the more important principles so that we can understand the detail better when we come to it. On the left-hand side of the diagram we can see the key stages in the accounting process identified in Chapter 1. These help us to separate out the role of key processes in the accounting system outlined in the middle. Finally, on the right we can see how a particular stage and process helps to answer some of the key questions we have identified. Using the key stages, we can now look in more detail at the way the system works.

4.2 Identifying and recording: transactions and journals

Accountants talk about transactions within a business. What is a transaction?

A **transaction** may be defined as any activity involving the exchange of money or value.

As an example, if we go into our local shop to buy a newspaper for 35p, a financial transaction takes place. Every time a sale is made through the cash till a transaction occurs. From the business owner's point of view, he sells a newspaper (earning 35p in sales revenue) and receives 35p in cash (or any

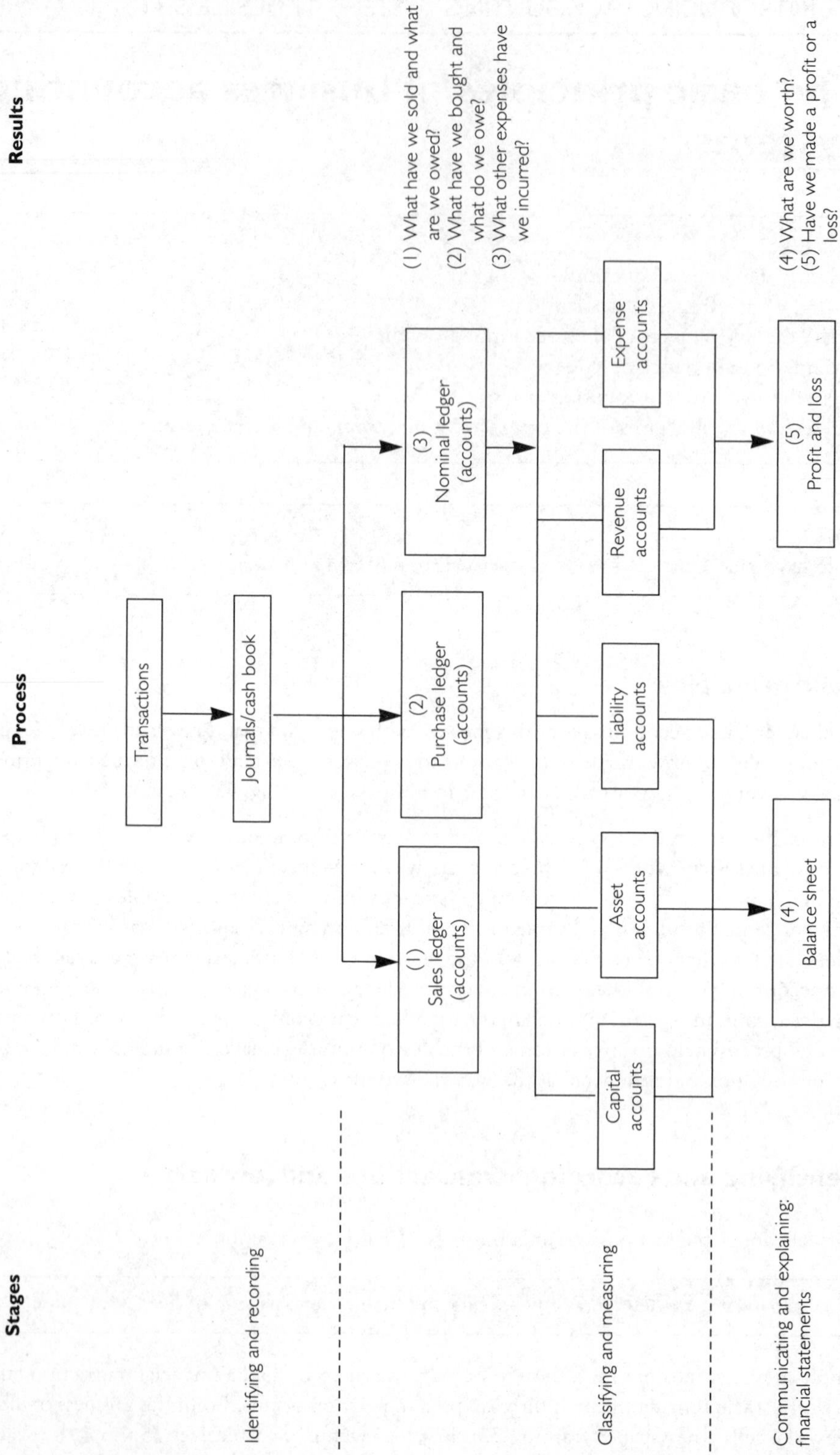

Fig 4.1 The accounting system (1)

other form of payment), which increases his asset, cash. This is the fundamental principle of recording financial transactions in business. Every transaction has a *two-fold* effect, on the one hand giving something and on the other receiving something. Both the receiving and giving aspects of a transaction needs to be recorded in the business accounts. If this were not the case, the business would not have the full information it needs to monitor and control its affairs and the accounts would fail to balance!

Transaction result:	sales	£0.35	(giving)
	cash	£0.35	(receiving)

We will look in more detail at the dual aspect of transactions in Chapter 5.

Accounting is concerned with the financial activities of a business and, particularly, at how money flows in and out of the business as a result of transactions. As we have seen, an example is the purchase of a business's products by a customer. In this transaction a customer agrees to exchange the product for an agreed sum. As we shall see, a transaction like this may not involve money changing hands at the time. The business may offer the customer credit, in other words the chance to take immediate possession of the goods ordered in return for a promise to pay at an agreed point in the future. We would still want to record the transaction and measure the impact of this kind of exchange on the business even though the money might not be paid until later. The same would apply if the business purchased some raw materials on credit from a supplier. The accounting system would be concerned to track the flow of money out of the business to the supplier and the impact of acquiring the raw materials at the time of the transaction. Later on, it would also want to track the actual payment itself once the credit period had expired.

The identifying and recording process begins with entering transactions in the **journals** (or day books) and **cash book**. We will discuss these in detail in Parts 3 and 4. Here the system aims to record each transaction accurately and comprehensively so that it can then be processed effectively through the rest of the system. For example, a sales invoice needs to be checked for correctness before it is entered in the sales journal. Journals have the overall function of classifying and listing transactions of the same type. They form the first stage of recording financial information before being passed to the next stage, that is, the accounts in the ledgers. Once a batch of transactions has been recorded, they are then 'posted' to the relevant accounts in the ledgers.

4.3 Classifying and measuring: accounts and ledgers

Almost any business, even a small one, will process many hundreds or thousands of transactions over a month or a year. If they were not sorted in some way into different types of transaction, they would soon become impossible to manage. To understand their impact on the business and answer some of the key questions we outlined in Chapter 1, a business needs to group similar types of transaction together. The key way is to group them into accounts.

> An **account** is a means of recording similar types of transaction together, for example, a customer's account.

We can illustrate the process by thinking of a number of orders placed by a customer over a period. To be able to find out how much the customer has spent or owes the business in this time, it would make sense to create an account for that customer in which all those transactions would be listed together in one place. We will look in detail at how we create accounts and record transactions in them in Chapter 5. As we shall see, the way we record transactions within accounts also plays a crucial role in helping us to measure the impact of transactions on the business.

Grouping transactions into accounts is one step to classifying them in a way that will help us to measure their impact. On its own, though, it would still make it difficult to answer some of the key questions we saw in Chapter 1. To answer those we need a way of grouping individual accounts together. This next stage involves two overlapping processes.

The first is to group individual accounts into 'ledgers'. Traditionally, once accounts had been created, they were grouped together and written into books called 'ledgers'. Although accounting is now computerised for many businesses, the name is still used.

A **ledger** is the main book of account in which individual accounts are recorded.

For smaller businesses with relatively few accounts, it may be feasible to have one ledger only in which all accounts are recorded. Larger businesses with many hundreds of accounts need more than one ledger. As you can see in Fig. 4.1, larger businesses use three basic types of ledger:

Sales ledger – all customer accounts are recorded here so that the business can access key information on sales and what is owed to it.
Purchase or bought ledger – all supplier accounts are recorded here so that the business can track what it owes.
Nominal or general ledger – this ledger is used to record all accounts relating to revenue and expenses which are then used to complete the profit and loss account. The nominal ledger also records asset, liability and capital accounts to help in putting the balance sheet together. These groups of accounts are discussed below.

As you can see from these definitions, the ledgers are used to answer some of the main questions outlined in Chapter 1 and the nominal ledger plays a key role in the second way accounts are classified.

4.4 The five groups of accounts

Grouping and recording accounts in ledgers helps a business answer some of the many questions it needs to ask. The accounting system answers others by grouping accounts into five fundamental types:

Revenue
Expense
Capital
Assets
Liabilities

} which you can remember by taking the first letter of each as **RECAL**

We can define these types of account as follows:

Revenue – this group of accounts covers all those recording income earned by a business when it sells its goods or services. The majority of revenue comes from sales, whether by cash or credit, though other revenue could come from renting out buildings or equipment, interest on a firm's bank account or investments made by the business.

Expenses – this group of accounts takes in all those costs a business incurs such as wages, rent, heat, lighting and power, the purchase of raw materials, advertising and carriage costs.

Capital – this group of accounts records the owner's personal investment in the business. Capital is needed to start a business off, paying for premises, equipment, staff and raw materials for example. It may grow if the business is successful and makes a profit. The owner's capital is her or his 'net worth' in the business.

Assets – this group of accounts records things of value which a business owns (and which it could sell) such as its premises, equipment, stock, cash and any outstanding debts owed to it. The people who owe money to a business are known as its **debtors**.

Liabilities – this group of accounts includes all the things of value which a business owes to others. These may include what it owes to suppliers, any hire-purchase agreements it has, or its overdraft or loan with the bank. Those people to whom the business owes money are known as its **creditors**.

We will look in more detail at how we decide which account goes to which group in Chapter 5. As we shall see below, grouping accounts in this way allows us to answer two of the most important questions in business: is it making a profit or a loss, and what is the business worth?

4.5 Communicating and explaining (1): introducing the profit and loss account

If you look at the five groups of accounts, you will immediately spot the way we might use the **revenue** and **expense** accounts to help us determine whether a business is making a profit or not. We can simply take one from the other to see if revenue exceeds expenditure or not: if the former, the business has made a profit; if the latter, a loss.

Profit = Revenue – Expenses

Broadly speaking, this is all a profit and loss account is (the full title is the trading and profit and loss account). A simplified example of a profit and loss account is shown below.

J Jones –
Trading and profit and loss account for year ending 1 December

	£	£
SALES		100 000
Cost of sales		50 000
Gross profit		50 000
EXPENSES		
Wages	30 000	
Advertising	5 000	
Heating, lighting	1 000	36 000
Net profit		14 000

The profit and loss account here lists revenue as sales. It then splits up expenses into those directly concerned with producing those sales, such as the purchasing of goods (**cost of sales**), and other costs **(expenses)** which the business must bear when selling its goods or services. These costs might include wages or the costs of renting, lighting and heating for example.

Two figures for profit are given. **Gross profit** measures the profitability of buying or producing the business's goods or services after deduction of cost of sales, whereas **net profit** measures the final profit once all the business's other costs are taken away. We will discuss how the profit and loss account is put together in more detail in Chapter 21.

Unlike the balance sheet, which we discuss below, a profit and loss account may well be produced more than once a year. Although a full profit and loss account meeting Government requirements will only be produced annually, managers often need profit and loss accounts produced more regularly so that they can track how well the business is doing, perhaps on a monthly basis.

4.6 Communicating and explaining (2): introducing the accounting equation and the balance sheet

If the revenue and expense accounts help us answer the key question about whether a business has made a profit or a loss, then the remaining groups of accounts (**capital**, **assets** and **liabilities**) help us to answer the question: what is the business worth?

We encountered capital, assets and liabilities and the accounting equation in Chapter 2 where it helped us to understand types of business. The relationship between capital, assets and liabilities can be best illustrated by looking at an example. If someone starting a business begins with savings of £1 000, this clearly represents her or his capital or personal investment in the business. If, as you might expect, the owner then deposits the money in a bank account for business use, the £1 000 is also an asset, that is something of value that a business owns. Here:

Capital	=	Assets
£1 000	=	£1 000

If the owner also needs to borrow £1 000 from the bank to help start the business, then the business receives more money, increasing its assets to £2 000. However, the £1 000 from the bank is also a loan which needs to be repaid, so it also represents a liability, something which the business owes. Here:

Capital	=	Assets – Liabilities
£1 000	=	£2 000 – £1 000

You can begin to see a very simple rule which links capital, assets and liabilities. A business's worth or capital is represented by the value of its assets, or the things of value which it owns, minus its liabilities, the things of value which it owes to others. This rule is known as the *accounting equation*, and was discussed briefly in Chapter 2:

Capital = Assets – Liabilities

The accounting equation will always balance: as capital increases, so will assets; as assets increase, so will capital; as liabilities increase, capital will be reduced correspondingly. If, for example, the business makes a profit of £500 at the end of the year, the owner would increase his worth or capital, and so would the business increase its assets by the same amount. The equation would then read:

Capital	=	Assets – Liabilities
£1 500	=	£2 500 – £1 000

The accounting equation would also hold if there were changes within assets or liabilities. As an example, if the owner of the business decided to buy a second-hand van for £500 with money from the bank account, as the asset of the bank account was decreased by £500, a new asset of £500 in the form of the van would be created, leaving total assets at £2 500 as before.

Capital	=	Assets	–	Liabilities
£1 500	=	Bank £2 000	–	Bank loan £1 000
		Van £500		

The balance sheet concludes with the business's capital, including the profits the business has made. This information is often presented in the following basic vertical format:

	£	£
ASSETS		
Premises	30 000	
Van	2 000	
Stock	2 500	
Bank	2 500	37 000
LIABILITIES		
Creditors	2 000	
Loan	24 000	26 000
		11 000
CAPITAL	10 000	
Profit	1 000	11 000

Here you can see the accounting equation in action:

Capital	=	Assets	–	Liabilities
£11 000	=	£37 000	–	£26 000

This **vertical** presentation is the format most commonly used in business and will be the one we will use in the text. There are a number of different ways of using this format (a variation is shown in section 4.7, p. 24). You will soon become familiar with the particular type used at work or college. An alternative, which you may come across, is the **horizontal** format:

ASSETS		LIABILITIES	
	£		£
Premises	30 000	Creditors	2 000
Van	2 000	Loan	24 000
Stock	2 500		
Bank	2 500	CAPITAL	10 000
		Profit	1 000
	37 000		37 000

As you can see from this format, the accounting equation can be swapped round to show the value of a company's assets:

Assets	=	Liabilities	+	Capital
£37 000	=	£26 000	+	£11 000

4.7 Changes in the balance sheet

In this section we will bring the strands of the chapter together by looking in more detail at how transactions affect the balance sheet. Please do not worry if you do not grasp all the detail immediately. The main point is to appreciate the two-fold effect of transactions and the way the balance sheet continues to balance in each case, demonstrating the accounting equation at work.

J Jones –
Balance Sheet as at 1 January

	£	£
ASSETS		
Premises	75 000	
Equipment	5 000	
Motor van	8 000	
Stock	6 000	
Debtors	4 500	
Bank	4 000	102 500
less		
LIABILITIES		
Creditors	5 000	
Bills owing	1 000	
Bank loan	14 000	
Mortgage	60 000	80 000
		22 500
FINANCED BY		
Capital	20 000	
+Profit	15 000	
–Drawings	(12 500)	22 500

We have already stated that the balance sheet is a snapshot of the business's financial position. It is simply a list of the business's assets, liabilities and capital at a given period in time. The figures will constantly change in response to the business's trading activities.

Note that drawings under the capital section refers to the amount of money or stock that the owner, Jack, has taken for his own personal use. Indeed, anything of value that the owner takes from the business for his own purposes is seen as a deduction from capital. On the other hand, if the owner introduces more finance into the business from his own personal savings, then this would increase his capital and also increase the business assets.

As transactions occur in the course of day-to-day business, they will have an effect on the accounts. However, irrespective of the number of transactions which may occur, the balance sheet will always balance. Note that in the examples below there is always a dual effect for each transaction. This is the basis of double entry bookkeeping and the principle of recording accounts in the ledgers which will be discussed further in Chapter 5.

Transactions during January in the accounts of Jack Jones:

1 Debtors pay their accounts £2 750 by cheques and cash.
2 Bills of £250 are paid off by cheque.
3 Stock of £2 000 is purchased on credit from suppliers.
4 Creditors are paid £3 000 on account.
5 Jack takes £500 cash for his own use.
6 Equipment of £1 500 is purchased on hire-purchase credit.
7 Stock is sold to debtors for £3 000 having cost £2 000.
8 £500 is paid off the bank loan.

Effect on:

		Assets	**Liabilities**	**Capital**	**Result**	
1	+ Bank	£2 750			Bank	£6 750
	– Debtors	£2 750			Debtors	£1 750
2	– Bank	£250			Bank	£6 500
			– Bills £250		Bills	£750
3	+ Stock	£2 000			Stock	£8 000
			+ Creditors £2 000		Creditors	£7 000
4	– Bank	£3 000			Bank	£3 500
			– Creditors £3 000		Creditors	£4 000
5	– Bank	£500			Bank	£3 000
				+ Drawings £500	Drawings	£13 000
6	+ Equip	£1 500			Equipment	£6 500
			+ Hire-purchase £1 500		H-p finance	£1 500
7	+ Debtors	£3 000			Debtors	£4 750
	– Stock	£2 000			Stock	£6 000
				+ Profit £1 000	Profit	£16 000
8	– Bank	£500			Bank	£2 500
			– Loan £500		Loan	£13 500

What will the balance sheet appear as after these transactions have taken place?

J Jones –
Balance Sheet as at 1 January

	£	£
ASSETS		
Premises	75 000	
Equipment	6 500	
Motor van	8 000	
Stock	6 000	
Debtors	4 750	
Bank	2 500	102 750
less		
LIABILITIES		
Creditors	4 000	
Bills owing	750	
Bank loan	13 500	
H-p finance	1 500	
Mortgage	60 000	79 750
		23 000
FINANCED BY		
Capital	20 000	
+Profit	16 000	
–Drawings	(13 000)	23 000

Note that the balance sheet still balances after all eight transactions have been recorded. If we were to put through hundreds of such transactions, the balance sheet would still represent equality because of the dual aspect of recording. The accounting equation appears as:

Capital	=	Assets	–	Liabilities
£23 000	=	£102 750	–	£79 750

The balance sheet can be prepared with a little more sophistication by breaking down assets into fixed and current categories and liabilities into current and long-term. This will be discussed in more detail in Chapter 21 once you have become more acquainted with the overall concept of the accounting system.

Summary
The recording of accounting information is based on transactions which pass through the accounting system. The ledger plays the prime role because it is the book where all the accounts are recorded. There are five major accounting groups recognised by RECAL. The first two of these (revenue and expenses) is used to prepare the profit and loss account, leaving the remaining three (capital, assets and liabilities) to make up the balance sheet.

Questions

1 What are the 3 basic stages of the accounting system and how does the journal fit into this process? (4.1–2)

2 Look at Fig. 4.1 (The accounting system) and answer the following:
a) What are the 5 accounting groups? (4.4)
b) What type of accounts will go into the 3 distinct type of ledgers? (4.4)
c) Which accounts are used to prepare the profit and loss account? (4.5)
d) Which accounts are used to prepare the balance sheet? (4.6)

3 Complete the following accounting equations (4.6):

	Capital	=	assets	–	liabilities
a)	8 000		96 000		
b)	1 500				22 500
c)	14 700		104 500		
d)			16 740		14 340

	Assets	=	capital	+	liabilities
a)	125 000				122 000
b)	57 800		1 800		
c)			12 740		11 400

4 Irrespective of how many transactions occur in business, the balance sheet should always balance. Why is this the case? (4.7)

5 Show how the accounting equation changes after each of the following transactions: (the first one is done for you) (4.7)
a) commenced business with £5 000 in the bank *
b) bought a van for £750 paying by cheque
c) purchased stock on credit for £2 000
d) the owner draws out £200 for his own use
e) purchased equipment £3 400 on credit from XYY Ltd.
f) paid £500 to XYY Ltd on account
g) paid £750 to suppliers on account.

* Capital = assets – liabilities
5 000 = 5 000 – 0

The following questions consolidate and extend your skills, helping you to interpret and relate the balance sheet and profit and loss accounts, for example. You should try these if you are studying the balance sheet and profit and loss account in more depth at this stage:

6 The following information relates to the accounts of Janet Robertson, as on 31 December:

	£
ASSETS	
Plant and machinery	7 875
Motor van	8 350
Equipment	1 875
Stocks	51 450
Debtors	2 421
Cash	904
LIABILITIES:	
Creditors	20 170
Bank overdraft	14 212

Loan account (five years)	11 460
Hire-purchase finance (five years)	9 293
CAPITAL:	
Capital: J Robertson (1/1)	15 000
Net profit for year	4 000
Drawings	1 260

REQUIRED:

a) Prepare the balance sheet of J Robertson as on 31 December.

b) Note the value of stocks. What could be the significance if the demand for Robertson's goods declined?

7 The following information relates to the financial position of J Jones on 1 January:

	£
Debtors	4 900
Creditors	3 350
Bank overdraft	4 200
Bank loan (ten years)	12 500
Premises	28 000
Equipment and tools	6 500
Motor vehicle	5 200
Stocks	4 950
Cash	500

REQUIRED:

a) Calculate the capital of the owner, J Jones, as on 1 January.

b) Prepare the Balance Sheet of J Jones, as on 1 January. Show the accounting equation from the owner's view, as on 1 January.

8 The financial position of Freddy Smith as on 30 June was as follows:

	£
Premises	60 000
Furniture, fixtures	6 500
Equipment	4 450
Motor van	2 150
Stock	3 800
Debtors	1 225
Creditors	3 540
Bank	1 420
Cash	200
Hire-purchase finance (12 months)	850
Customs & Excise (Vat owing)	355
Mortgage on premises	35 000
Freddy's drawings	5 000
Freddy's profit	10 000
Freddy's capital	35 000

REQUIRED:

Prepare the balance sheet of Freddy Smith as on 30 June.

9 The following figures relate to the financial affairs of Mary Jones as on 1 June:

	£
Premises	58 000
Machinery and equipment	15 000

Motor van	5 500
Office furniture	2 500
Stock	5 000
Debtors	2 500
Cash in hand	500
Creditors	3 475
Bank overdraft	2 525
Bills due	1 000
Mortgage	25 000
Bank loan (five years)	10 000
Capital	40 000
Profits	7 000

REQUIRED:

a) Prepare the balance sheet of M Jones as on 1 June.

b) Show the accounting equation emphasising the owner's net worth.

10 The balance sheet of J Robertson as on 31 December is as follows:

ASSETS	£	CAPITAL	£	£
Plant and machinery	787	J Robertson (l/l)	?	
Motor vans	835	Net loss	385	
Tools and equipment	187	Drawings	291	
Stocks	5 145			
Debtors	242	LIABILITIES		
Cash	90	Loan account (eight years)		1 146
		Hire-purchase finance (three years)		929
		Creditors		2 017
		Bank overdraft		1 421
	7 286			7 286

REQUIRED:

a) Calculate J Robertson's capital on 1 January.

b) Prepare his balance sheet as on 31 December.

11 The accounts of a trader, P Jackson, as on 31 December were as follows:

	£
Sales	48 850
Cost of sales	32 420
Wages	5 280
Motor costs	3 624
Light, heat	2 100
Rates, insurance	3 400
Advertising	456
Telephone	195
Stationery	100
General expenses	485

REQUIRED:

a) Prepare the profit and loss account of the trader for the period ended 31 December.

b) What do you think links the profit and loss account with the balance sheet?

c) If P Jackson had a capital of £10 000 before the profit and loss account was prepared and he withdrew £500 during the period for his own use, what would be the sum of his capital on 31 December?

12 Study the following profit and loss account and balance sheet of R James and then try to answer the questions which follow:

Profit and loss account y/e 30 November

	£	£
SALES		148 000
Cost of sales		73 100
EXPENSES		
Motor expenses	3 150	
Rent, rates	6 250	
Postage, telephone	1 440	
Wages, salaries	28 340	
Insurance	1 210	
Petty cash expenses	990	
Loan interest	1 760	
Accountant's fees	800	
Legal costs	450	
Depreciation	950	
Overheads	2 100	
Advertising	5 100	-----

Balance Sheet as on 30 November

	£	£
ASSETS		
Fixtures, fittings	14 270	
Motor vans	17 100	
Stock	12 800	
Debtors	8 200	
Bank/cash	430	52 800
LIABILITIES		
Creditors	6 300	
Loan	16 000	22 300
		30 500
CAPITAL	20 500	
Profit	22 360	
Drawings	(12 360)	30 500

REQUIRED:

a) State the gross and net profit figures for the period ending 30 November.
b) Which expense after cost of sales, helped to reduce net profit the most?
c) Write the accounting equation using the appropriate figures, from the point of view of the owner, R James.
d) How did R James's capital increase by £10 000?

5 How transactions are recorded in accounts

Objectives

On completing this section you should:

- understand the basic double entry principle of recording accounts
- understand the use of the debit and credit aspects of recording
- appreciate the function of a trial balance
- recognise both the traditional 'T' format of the ledger as well as the running balance method of recording.

Context

You should have read Chapter 4 as context.

5.1 Creating accounts

In Chapter 4 we saw the role of accounts in the classifying and measuring process within accounting. Once transactions have been recorded in the journals or cash book, they can be posted to accounts within the ledgers. Putting transactions in accounts provides a key step in both classifying them and beginning to measure their impact on the business.

There are three key steps in entering transactions into accounts.

1. Put transactions in the right account.
2. Allocate account to the right accounting group.
3. Record the transaction using the debit/credit rule.

The first is to place transactions in the right accounts which we cover in this section. The second step is to allocate individual accounts to the right accounting group, which we discuss in section 5.2. Completing this step allows us, finally, to record the details of the transaction in the account itself using the debit/credit rule. We discuss this in section 5.3.

To illustrate how we select accounts into which to place transactions, let us take some examples of transactions in a business which is just starting up.

Scenario

Paula Jackson has decided she wants to start a business as a retailer, opening a clothes shop. She already has a substantial sum of money having sold her house and bought a smaller home. Her personal investment is £20 000 which she has deposited in the bank.

She has found the premises she wants and has taken up a mortgage from the Abbey Building Society of £10 000 and a further borrowing of £3 000 from the bank to ensure she has all the capital she needs to run the business successfully.

With this finance, she can buy the premises for £14 000 and can pay a deposit of £4 000 along with the £10 000 mortgage she has obtained. She also purchases a motor vehicle, a van, which costs her £8 000 and spends a further £2 000 on fixtures and fittings, doing up the shop (shelving, counters, carpets, blinds, etc). A cash register was already installed on the premises as part of the purchase.

To summarise, her first accounts will include:

Capital
Premises
Building society mortgage
Motor van
Bank loan
Fixtures and fittings.

These are her initial accounts when setting up business and once these are completed, she will be able to buy stock and be ready to commence trade. Like Paula, most businesses start with at least their bank account. They need this to check and monitor what money is going into and out of the business bank account in much the same way as we need to know how much we have in the bank. In theory, they could then create as many or as few accounts as they wish in which to record their transactions.

The more information they have at their finger tips, the better the organisation and control of their business. Most businesses need to measure how much they are spending on stock purchases, advertising, motor expenses etc, and to also keep a track of what has been paid to whom and how much is owed by customers to the business, so will create as many accounts as they need to track these aspects of the business.

5.2 Allocating accounts to the five accounting groups

The next step is to allocate the accounts Paula will use to the five accounting groups we saw in Chapter 4:

Account group	Paula's accounts
Revenue	Cash and customer sales
Expenses	Purchases, rent, wages and stationery
Capital	Her investment in the business
Assets	Bank, premises and van accounts
Liabilities	Loan, mortgage and supplier accounts

5.3 Recording transactions in ledger accounts (1)

We saw in the discussion of the accounting equation in Chapter 4 how the impact of transactions balances out so that the accounting equation always holds. This is a fundamental principle in accounting and helps us to understand how we record transactions in accounts and why. We saw in Chapter 1 that accounting is concerned with tracking how value flows through the business. In looking at the impact of a transaction, the accounting system seeks to track how the transaction affects different parts of the business.

We can illustrate this with an example taken from our discussion of the accounting equation in Chapter 4. We saw that if the business decides to buy a van by drawing on its bank account, it creates a new asset, the van, while decreasing the funds in its bank account. Value moves from one place to another in the business. The way we record transactions in accounts helps us to track where the value is going. In the transaction, one account receives, the corresponding account gives.

The classic way of showing how value moves around in the business is the T account:

Debit	Credit

You should remember the golden rule about the layout of a T account:

Debit	Credit
Left side	Right side

The key thing to remember is that, in recording transactions, debit and credit do not have the same meaning we use in everyday language. They have a particular meaning to help us track transactions. In general terms:

Debit – when the account 'receives' the money or value
Credit – when the account 'supplies' the money or value

If Paula were to buy a van for £8 000, paying by cheque, the van is 'received' by the van account and, therefore, that account is debited. The bank account 'supplies' the money for the van and is, therefore, credited:

Debit: Van account
Credit: bank account

Debit	Van account	Credit
Bank 8 000		

Debit	Bank account	Credit
		Van 8 000

This is the principle of double entry bookkeeping, and is the essence of recording accounts. Now that we have grasped the general principle, we can look at the more detailed rules for deciding when to debit and when to credit. The five accounting groups we discussed in Chapter 4 – revenue, expenses, capital, assets and liabilities (RECAL) – determine when we debit or credit a transaction, as the following table shows:

Account group	To increase the account	To decrease the account
Assets	debit	credit
Expenses	debit	credit
Revenue	credit	debit
Liabilities	credit	debit
Capital	credit	debit

If any transaction involving an asset or expense account is increased in value, the entry is debited. If the value is reduced, the entry is credited. The reverse applies for revenue, liabilities and capital, crediting the account if it increases in value, and debiting it if it decreases in value.

We can now illustrate this process at work with some examples from Paula's asset, liability and capital accounts in Fig. 5.1 followed by examples from her revenue and expense accounts in Fig. 5.2.

Fig. 5.1 Recording transaction in Paula's asset, liability and capital accounts

Transaction	Step 1 Accounts involved	Step 2 Account types	Step 3 Debit/credit rule	Step 4 'T' account format	
				Bank	Capital
Paula starts business with £20 000 in bank	Bank Capital	Asset Capital	increase asset = debit increase capital = credit	20 000 (debit)	20 000 (credit)
				Van	Bank
She buys a van £8 000 paying by cheque	Van Bank	Asset Asset	increase asset = debit decrease asset = credit	8 000 (debit)	8 000 (credit)
				Bank	Bank loan
She borrows £3 000 to place into bank	Bank Loan	Asset Liability	increase asset = debit increase liability = credit	3 000 (debit)	3 000 (credit)
				Premises	Bank
Pays deposit £4 000 for shop premises	Premises Bank	Asset Asset	increase asset = debit decrease asset = credit	4 000 (debit)	4 000 (credit)
				Premises	Mortgage
She borrows £10 000 mortgage for shop	Premises Mortgage	Asset Liability	increase asset = debit increase liability = credit	10 000 (debit)	10 000 (credit)

Transaction	Step 1 Accounts involved	Step 2 Account types	Step 3 Debit/credit rule	Step 4 'T' account format
Pays fixtures for shop £2 000 cheque	Fixtures Bank	Asset Asset	increase asset = debit decrease asset = credit	Fixtures: 2 000 (debit) Bank: 2 000 (credit)

Fig. 5.2 Recording transactions in Paula's revenue and expense accounts

Transaction	Step 1 Accounts involved	Step 2 Account types	Step 3 Debit/credit rule	Step 4 'T' account format
10/6 Purchased stock £2 000 for resale	Purchases Bank	Expense Asset	increase expense = debit decrease assetl = credit	Purchases: 2 000 (debit) Bank: 2 000 (credit)
10/6 Purchased stock £3 000 on credit from E Gray	Purchases E Gray	Expense Liability	increase expense = debit increase liability = credit	Purchases: 3 000 (debit) E Gray: 3 000 (credit)
12/6 Sold goods £1 000 to J Clark on credit	J Clark Sales	Asset Revenue	increase asset = debit increase revenue = credit	J Clark: 1 000 (debit) Sales: 1 000 (credit)
13/6 Sold goods for cash £1 840 into bank	Bank Sales	Asset Revenue	increase asset = debit increase revenue = credit	Bank: 1 840 (debit) Sales: 1 840 (credit)
14/6 Paid garage rent by cheque £400	Rent Bank	Expense Asset	increase expense = debit decrease asset = credit	Rent: 400 (debit) Bank: 400 (credit)
15/6 Paid assistant's wages by cheque £520	Wages Bank	Expense Asset	increase expense = debit decrease asset = credit	Wages: 520 (debit) Bank: 520 (credit)
18/6 Paid stationery by cheque £280	Stationery Bank	Expense Asset	increase expense = debit decrease asset = credit	Stationery: 280 (debit) Bank: 280 (credit)
20/6 Cash sales into bank £1 800	Bank Sales	Asset Revenue	increase asset = debit increase revenue = credit	Bank: 1 800 (debit) Sales: 1 800 (credit)

Transaction	Step 1 Accounts involved	Step 2 Account types	Step 3 Debit/credit rule	Step 4 'T' account format					
				Account	Left	Right	Account	Left	Right
24/6 Purchased goods by cheque £2 600	Purchases Bank	Expense Asset	increase expense = debit decrease asset = credit	Purchases	2 600		Bank		2 600
27/6 Cheque £700 received from J Clark	Bank Clarke	Asset Asset	increase asset = debit decrease asset = credit	Bank	700		Clark		700
29/6 Paid to E Gray cheque £2 000	Gray Bank	Liability Asset	decrease liability = debit decrease asset = credit	Gray	2 000		Bank		2 000
30/6 Paid assistant's wages by cheque £540	Wages Bank	Expense Asset	increase expense = debit decrease asset = credit	Wages	540		Bank		540
30/6 Sold goods £1 320 to J Clark on credit	Clark Sales	Asset Revenue	increase asset = debit increase revenue = credit	Clark	1 320		Sales		1 320

5.4 Recording transactions in ledger accounts (2)

Once you have grasped the three basic steps in recording transactions in ledger accounts, we can consider how we would record the information in practice: a standard format for a 'T' account would be as follows:

Name of the account

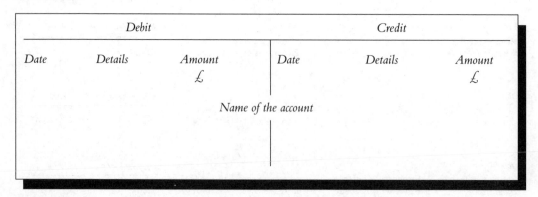

Debit			*Credit*		
Date	*Details*	*Amount* £	*Date*	*Details*	*Amount* £

NOTES

1. The traditional 'T' accounts have two sides, the left is for recording all debit entries, the right for recording all credit entries.
2. The name (or title) of each ledger account is best entered in the centre of the page.
3. In the details column, the name of the corresponding account is recorded as a means of cross-reference.

We can use this format to enter Paula's initial capital, asset and liability accounts into her ledger. Since she is a small business, Paula has opted to have one ledger for her accounts rather than the three used by most larger businesses. These are her ledger accounts when she sets up the business.

The ledger of P Jackson

Debit			*Credit*		
Date	*Details*	*Amount* £	*Date*	*Details*	*Amount* £
			Bank account		
June 1	Capital	20 000	June 5	Equipment	8 000
June 5	Bank loan	3 000	June 5	Premises	4 000
			June 5	Fixtures	2 000
			Capital account		
			June 1	Bank	20 000
			Van account		
June 5	Bank	8 000			
			Premises account		
June 5	Bank	4 000			
June 5	Abbey Bld. Soc.	10 000			
			Abbey Building Society account		
			June 5	Premises	10 000
			Bank loan account		
			June 5		3 000
			Fixtures and fittings account		
June 5	Bank	2 000			

5.5 Balancing off the accounts in the ledger

With this method of recording, it is necessary to periodically 'balance off' each account in order to find the actual balance. In the above example there is a debit balance of £9 000 on the bank account (debits have totalled £23 000, credits have totalled £14 000, a difference of £9 000).

The procedure to be adopted is as follows:

a) Enter 'balance c/d' (carried down) on the lesser value of the two sides.

b) This will make both sides equal in total. The totals should appear on the same horizontal line and be double underscored.

c) Once the totals have been entered, the word 'balance b/d' (brought down) is entered under the total, on the opposite side of the account, i.e. this will be the balance at that time.

As regards the frequency of balancing off much depends on the volume of transactions. Once per month is the acceptable minimum. The balancing of P Jackson's bank account and premises account is as follows:

Bank account

Debit			*Credit*		
		£			£
June 1	Capital	20 000	June 5	Equipment	8 000
June 7	Bank loan	3 000	June 5	Premises	4 000
			June 5	Fixtures	2 000
			June 8	**Balance c/d**	9 000
		23 000			23 000
June 9	**Balance b/d**	9 000			

Premises account

Debit			*Credit*		
June 5	Bank	4 000			
June 5	Abbey Bld. Soc.	10 000			
		14 000			

Note In this case the relevant parts of the account have been highlighted to illustrate the process – they would not normally be highlighted. Where entries appear only on one side of an account as is the case with the premises account these need only be sub-totalled – do not underscore.

We can now see all we've done so far, from entering the transactions into the relevant accounts to balancing off accounts, in Paula's revised ledger, now incorporating the new transactions from Figs. 5.1 and 5.2:

The ledger of P Jackson

Debit			*Credit*		
Date	*Details*	*Amount* £	*Date*	*Details*	*Amount* £
		Bank account			
June 8	Balance b/d	9 000	June 10	Purchases	2 000
13	Sales	1 840	14	Rent	400
20	Sales	1 800	15	Wages	520
27	J Clark	700	18	Stationery	280
			24	Purchases	2 600
			29	E Gray	2 000
			30	Wages	540
			30	Balance c/d	5 000
		13 340			13 340
July 1	Balance b/d	5 000			
		Capital account			
			June 1	Bank	20 000
		Van account			
June 5	Bank	8 000			
		Premises account			
June 5	Bank	4 000			
	Abbey Bld. Soc.	10 000			
		14 000			
		Abbey Building Society account			
			June 5	Premises	10 000
		Bank loan account			
			June 7	Bank	3 000
		Fixtures and fittings account			
June 5	Bank	2 000			

(continued)

(continued)

Purchases account

June 10	Bank	2 000			
11	E Gray	3 000			
24	Bank	2 600			
		7 600			

E Gray account (Creditor)

June 29	Bank	2 000	June 11	Purchases	3 000
30	Balance c/d	1 000			
		3 000			3 000
			July 1	Balance b/d	1 000

Sales account

			June 12	J Clark	1 000
			13	Bank	1 840
			20	Bank	1 800
			30	J Clark	1 320
					5 960

J Clark account

June 12	Sales	1 000	June 27	Bank	700
30	Sales	1 320	30	Balance c/d	1 620
		2 320			2 320
July 1	Balance b/d	1 620			

Rent account

July 14	Bank	400			

Wages account

June 15	Bank	520			
30	Bank	540			
		1 060			

Stationery account

June 18	Bank	280			

5.6 The trial balance

The *trial balance* is an arithmetical check of the double entry system. Have both aspects of each transaction been recorded precisely? Is there a debit entry for every credit? The trial balance may be prepared at any time as a check on the ledger, extracting the **balance** of each account and merely listing the debits and credits.

Example

P Jackson –
Trial balance as on 30 June

	Debit £	*Credit* £
Bank	5 000	
Capital		20 000
Van	8 000	
Premises	14 000	
Abbey Building Society		10 000
Bank loan		3 000
Fixtures and fittings	2 000	
Purchases	7 600	
E Gray (Creditor)		1 000
Sales		5 960
J Clark	1 620	
Rent	400	
Wages	1 060	
Stationery	280	
	39 960	39 960

Are the accounts prepared for P Jackson on the previous pages correct? The total debits £39 960 equals the total credits £39 960. The double entry accuracy of recording appears to look satisfactory. The trial balance will fail to balance if both aspects of each transaction have not been recorded, or there is an arithmetical error in the figures.

The trial balance is not however, a foolproof system. Errors can be made which the trial balance fails to disclose because the debits can equal the credits, yet the entries still be in error. This will be discussed more fully in Chapters 30 and 31.

5.7 Returns

These usually refer to the return of goods or allowances made on a previous invoice. The credit note is the document which is raised to process the return.

There are two returns to consider: *returns inward* (sales returns) from customers, and *returns outward* (purchases returns) to suppliers. Both have the effect of reducing the value of the customer's or supplier's account. The double entry for the former, returns inward is:

> Debit: returns inward account (or debit sales)
> Credit: the customer's account.

To take an example. Brown, a customer, returned £35 goods to us because he considered them unsuitable.

Returns inward account

Debit	£		*Credit* £
Brown	35		

Brown account

		Returns in	35

The double entry for returns outward is:

> Debit: the supplier's account
> Credit: returns outward account (or credit purchases).

To take an example. Returned goods to Smith, a supplier, £25 because they were faulty.

Returns outward account

Debit	£		*Credit* £
		Smith	25

Smith account

Returns out	25		

It is preferable to open separate returns accounts so that at any time the value of either returns in from customers, or returns out to suppliers, can be readily seen. Further examples of returns can be seen on the pages which follow, demonstrating the running balance method of ledger recording. Returns are discussed in more detail in Chapter 12.

5.8 The running balance method of recording

In the traditional style of recording ledger transactions, debit entries were separated from credit entries by the centre line of the page. The balance of each account was determined by finding the difference between the two columns of entries. In the ledger of P Jackson, the bank account had a balance of £5 000 on 30 June as a result of debits of £13 340 and credits of £8 340.

The running balance method adopts a style which is like a bank statement with debit, credit and balance columns *adjacent to* each other. The principal advantage of this style of recording is that, after each transaction, the balance is calculated, revealing an immediate update of the account.

The traditional method, while clearly dividing debits and credits, does not give an immediate balance after each entry. There is the need to go through the balancing procedure at frequent intervals to determine the balance of each account.

P Jackson's bank account in running balance format

		Dr £	*Cr* £	*Balance* £
8/6	Balance			9 000 Dr
10	Purchases		2 000	7 000
13	Sales	1 840		8 840
14	Rent		400	8 440
15	Wages		520	7 920
18	Stationery		280	7 640
20	Sales	1 800		9 440
24	Purchases		2 600	6 840
27	Clark	700		7 540
29	Gray		2 000	5 540
30	Wages		540	5 000

Whichever method of recording is adopted to record ledger transactions makes little difference as long as the double-entry principle is always observed. Students need to be able to record using either method and the running balance format would be useful to know if a computerised accounting package is used.

5.8.1 Example: the running balance method using three ledgers

On 1 January, W Williams had the following balances in his ledgers:

Sales ledger:	J Brown	£200 Dr
	D Jones	£150 Dr
Purchases ledger:	R Smith	£350 Cr
	J Jackson	£400 Cr
Nominal ledger:	Bank	£400 Dr

Transactions occurring during January were:

Jan. 5	Sold goods to Brown, £230.
7	Sold goods for cash £55 into bank.
10	Bought goods from Smith £150.
14	Returned goods to Smith £25 as faulty.
15	Bought goods from Jackson, £280.
17	Sold goods to Jones £300.
18	Brown returned goods to us, £35, as unsuitable.
19	Cash purchases £80 by cheque.
21	Sold goods to Brown £115.
25	Paid Smith £350 by cheque.
	Paid Jackson £300 by cheque.
30	Received cheques from Brown, £200 and from Jones, £150.

You are required to enter all the above information in the books of W Williams for the month of January and extract a trial balance as on 31 January.

Sales ledger

		Debit £	*Credit* £	*Balance* £
Brown account				
1/1	Balance			200 Dr
5	Sales	230		430
18	Returns in		35	395
21	Sales	115		510
30	Bank		200	310
Jones Account				
1/1	Balance			150 Dr
17	Sales	300		450
30	Bank		150	300

Purchase ledger

		Debit £	*Credit* £	*Balance* £
Smith account				
1/1	Balance			350 Cr
10	Purchases		150	500
14	Returns out	25		475
25	Bank	350		125
Jackson account				
1/1	Balance			400 Cr
15	Purchases		280	680
25	Bank	300		380

Nominal ledger

		Debit £	Credit £	Balance £
Sales account				
5/1	Brown		230	230 Cr
7	Bank		55	288
17	Jones		300	585
21	Brown		115	700
Purchases account				
10/1	Smith	150		150 Dr
15	Jackson	280		430
19	Bank	80		510
Returns inward account				
18/1	Brown	35		35 Dr
Returns outward account				
14/1	Smith		25	25 Cr
Bank account				
1/1	Balance			400 Dr
7	Sales	55		455
19	Purchases		80	375
25	Smith		350	25
	Jackson		300	275 Cr
30	Brown	200		75 Cr
	Jones	150		75 Dr

W Williams –
Trial balance as on 31 January

Account	*Debit* £	*Credit* £
Brown	310	
Jones	300	
Smith		125
Jackson		380
Sales		700
Purchases	510	
Returns in	35	
Returns out		25
Bank	75	
	1 230	1 230

Summary

Financial transactions in business are recorded in ledger accounts although in many small businesses traders often have their own unique methods of recording. The important thing is that transactions *must* be recorded in order to monitor and control what is going on. When ledgers are used, recording of transactions is based on the double entry principle: for every debit there must be a corresponding credit. Without this, the accounts would fail to balance and the accounting records would be incomplete.

Questions

1 What 3 steps are involved in entering transactions in accounts? (5.1)

2 Complete the following table by entering either debit or credit (5.3):

Account Group	Increase the a/c	Decrease the a/c
Revenue		
Expenses		
Capital		
Assets		
Liabilities		

3 There are 8 transactions to enter into a table as suggested below (5.2–3). Draw out a table with the 4 columns and then complete for each transaction.The first is completed for you:

1. Commenced business with £5 000 in the bank
2. Purchased equipment by cheque £550
3. Van bought for £2 600 cheque
4. Purchased goods by cheque £850
5. Purchased goods from T Jones on credit £400
6. Cash sales £250 into bank
7. Sold goods to B Baker on credit £220
8. Paid month's rent by cheque £450

Accounts involved	Account group	Dr/Cr rule	T A/C format			
Bank	Asset	+ asset = debit	Bank a/c		Capital a/c	
Capital	Capital	+ capital = credit	5 000			5 000

How much would you have in the bank? (5.5)

4 From the following list of transactions:

- name the two accounts involved (5.1)
- decide whether they should be debited or credited (5.2–3)
- enter them into Jane's ledger (5.4)
- calculate the balance in the bank account (5.5)

a) Jane commenced business with £4 000 in the bank
b) Computer purchased by cheque £550
c) Obtained a short-term bank loan £2 500
d) Purchased a motor van £1 000 from Harry's Garage on credit and paid a deposit of £200 cheque
e) Purchased equipment from Hardwick's £2 000 on credit
f) Placed a deposit on premises paid £2 500 by cheque
g) Obtained a mortgage of £25 000 to buy the premises (total cost £27 500)
h) Paid a cheque for fixtures £150
i) Paid Hardwick £500 cheque on account
j) Bought a second van for £875 paying by cheque
k) Paid £125 against the bank loan
l) Paid Harry's Garage £100 on account.

5 This question continues from number 4, so commence with the same accounts as above and the balance in Jane's bank account. First, name the account to be debited and the corresponding account to be credited and at the end enter them into Jane's ledger:

a) Purchased £1 500 goods from Arrowsmith on credit
b) Cash purchases by cheque £650
c) Purchased £880 goods from E Jones on credit
d) Sold goods to James on credit £420
e) Sold goods to Harris on credit £300
f) Cash sales into bank £365
g) Purchased goods from Arrowsmith £2 000 on credit
h) Paid rent £250 by cheque
i) Paid overheads by cheque £150
j) Paid Arrowsmith £500 by cheque
k) Cash purchases by cheque £850
l) Paid £125 against the bank loan
m) Paid Arrowsmith a further £500 by cheque on account
n) Received from Harris £150 cheque on account.

Balance all the accounts and then prepare a trial balance to check the accuracy of your recording (5.6).

Now, try the following questions which consolidate and extend your skills.

6 Balance the following accounts at the end of the month:

Jack Jones account

		£			£
1/1	Bank	500	1/1	Balance b/d	1 200
31	Bank	1 850	20	Purchases	1 000
			28	Purchases	500

Bank account

1/1	Balance b/d	500	1/1	J Jones	500
7	Sales	750	5	Rent	250
14	Sales	540	7	General expenses	345
21	Sales	650	15	R Green	1 200
28	Sales	535	20	Light and heat	340
			27	J Jones	1 850

Sales account

			1/1	Balance b/d	2 300

7	Sales	750
14	Sales	540
21	Sales	650
28	Sales	535

7 The ledger account balances on 30 June of Hannah Smith were:

	£
Stock	1 500
Bank (Dr)	6 610
Plant and equipment	8 000
Motor vehicle	3 500
Sales	4 190
Purchases	1 760
Wages	2 230
Rent	1 130
General expenses	960
Debtors	1 910
Creditors	2 500
Bank loan	3 120
Interest due on loan	110
Capital account: Hannah Smith	17 680

REQUIRED:
Prepare the trial balance of H Smith as on 30 June.

8 The following information relates to the books of David Novel:

July 1 Commenced business with a capital of £2 000 represented in his bank account.
2 Bought goods on credit from Tom Smith, £2 500.
14 Cash sales into bank, £750.
15 Paid purchases by cheque, £500.
17 Paid rent by cheque, £125.
18 Paid gas, electricity by cheque, £80 (light and heat account).
21 Cash sales into bank, £600.
25 Sold goods to R Baker on credit, £200.
26 Paid cheque to Tom Smith on account, £500.
27 Bought further goods from Tom Smith on credit, £1 000.
28 Cash sales into bank, £625.
30 R Baker paid £100 on account, by cheque.
30 Paid for general expenses, £80 cheque.
30 Paid for advertising, £35 cheque.
30 Bought a second-hand motor van, £500 by cheque.

REQUIRED:
a) Enter the above transactions in David Novel's ledger for the month of July.
b) Extract a trial balance as on 31 July.

9 Mrs J Boddy decided to commence business by opening a small retail shop in the High Street on 1 May. Her finances on that day were: cash £2 500 and a motor van valued £1 500. Hire-purchase still outstanding on the vehicle was £1 000. During her first month's trading, the following transactions took place:

May
1 Deposited £2 000 into the business bank account, retaining £500 in cash.
2 Rented shop premises paying £250 cheque in advance.

4 Cash purchases of goods for resale £300.
5 Purchased £550 goods from Arthur Daley on credit.
7 Paid £40 cash on stationery items.
10 Cash sales £120.
12 Sold goods on credit to Jack Smith £180.
14 Purchased £750 goods on credit from Donna Steele.
16 Paid motor expenses £30 cheque.
17 Cash sales £235 into bank.
18 Returned goods to Arthur £150 as stock damage.
19 Paid £100 cheque on the hire-purchase of van.
20 Bought equipment on credit from Land Supplies Ltd £1 800, paying 25% deposit by cheque, the balance on credit.
24 Cash sales £130 into bank.
26 Paid general expenses by cash £80.
27 Received 50 per cent of the sum due from Jack Smith, by cheque.
28 Sold goods on credit to David Wheelbarrow £330.
30 David Wheelbarrow returned 10 per cent of goods to us as being unsuitable.
31 Cash sales £225 into bank.
31 Paid Donna Steele £500 on account.
31 Paid Land Supplies Ltd on account £270 by cheque.

REQUIRED:
a) Enter all the above information in the ledger of Mrs J Boddy for the month of May.
b) Extract a trial balance as on 31 May.

10 Jack Jones started in his own business on 1 March having the following:

£1 000 in cash which he deposited in his new business bank account.
£1 800 motor van which he will use in the business.
£550 equipment.
£1 150 is on hire-purchase from XYB Garages Ltd over two years.

Your task is to assist Jack set up a ledger to record the day-to-day transactions as they occur. Calculate Jack's capital as on 1 March and enter the above information in the accounts required in the ledger. The following transactions occurred during March:

March
3 Purchased goods on credit from D Guest £350 and J Good £245.
4 Bought some office furniture, paying by cheque £150.
5 Sold goods on credit to M Bright £180.
8 Cash sales £125, into bank.
10 Bought further goods from J Good £300.
11 Sold goods on credit to M Bright £85.
12 Bought goods from Cash & Carry Warehouse, £220 by cheque.
14 Sold goods to C Taylor, on credit £300.
19 Paid general overheads by cheque £115.
20 20 per cent of the goods bought on the 10th, were returned to J Good as unsatisfactory (debit J Good, credit Returns outward).
22 Sold goods on credit to M Bright, £125.
26 Cash sales into bank £190.
27 M Bright returned £40 goods to us which he had purchased on the 22nd (debit returns inward, credit M Bright).
29 Paid general overheads by cheque £135.
29 C Taylor sent a cheque £150 on account.
30 Drew a cheque for £200 for personal use (debit Drawings, credit Bank).

30 Bought goods by cheque £480.
30 Cash sales into bank £400.
31 Purchased further equipment for £1 200, paying a deposit of 20 per cent by cheque. The balance outstanding is on credit from Rawlings Ltd over three years.
31 Paid off the account outstanding to D Guest and paid J Good £250 on account.
31 Received a cheque £225 from M Bright on account.

REQUIRED:
a) Enter all the above information in the ledger of J Jones.
b) Prepare a trial balance as on 31 March.

11 Roger Longbotham started in business on 1 May having the following:

£800 in cash which he deposited in his new business bank account.
£750 motor vehicle which he will use in the business.

Open the appropriate accounts in the ledger.

The following transactions occurred during the month of May:

May
3 Purchased goods on credit from Stan Smith £400.
4 Bought some office equipment, paying by cheque £100.
5 Sold goods on credit to Rita Jones £160.
8 Cash sales £158, into bank.
10 Bought goods from Arthur Hardcastle £550.
11 Sold goods on credit to Rita Jones £120.
14 Bought goods from Cash & Carry Warehouse, £233 by cheque.
16 Sold goods to David Arrowsmith, on credit £300.
19 Paid electricity bill by cheque £135.
21 Goods bought on the 10th from Hardcastle £65, were returned as unsatisfactory (debit Hardcastle, credit Returns outward).
22 Sold goods on credit to David Arrowsmith, £125.
25 Cash sales into bank £130.
27 Rita returned £44 goods which she had purchased on the 11th (debit Returns inward, credit Rita).
29 Paid general expenses by cheque £115.
29 Sent a cheque to Stan Smith £200 on account.
30 Drew a cheque for £160 for personal use.
30 Bought goods by cheque £400.
30 Cash sales into bank £120.
31 Purchased microcomputer for £650, paying a deposit of 20 per cent by cheque. The balance outstanding is on credit from Lansdowne Computers Ltd over 15 months.
31 Paid £250 to Arthur Hardcastle on account.
31 Purchased further goods from Arthur Hardcastle on credit, £385.
31 Received £150 from David Arrowsmith on account.

REQUIRED:
a) Enter all the above information in the ledger of R Longbotham.
b) Prepare a trial balance as on 31 May.

12 The following information refers to the accounts of Ann Rogers, a retailer on the high street:

Balances on 1 May:

		£
Debtors:	R David (Dr)	500
	L Jones (Dr)	230
Creditors:	J Robert (Cr)	150
	G Andrew (Cr)	200
Bank account (Dr)		270
Capital account (Cr)		650

Transactions occurring during the month of May:

May 3	Sold goods to R David £300 on credit.
3	Sold goods to L Jones £250 on credit.
3	Bought goods on credit from J Robert, £600.
5	Bought goods on credit from G Andrew, £850.
10	R David settled his account balance as on 1 May, sending a cheque £500.
12	Sent a cheque £150 to J Robert and £200 to G Andrew.
15	Paid for shop rent, £300 cheque.
17	Paid assistant's wages, £125 cheque.
20	L Jones sent a cheque £200 on account.
25	Sold goods to L Jones on credit, £180.
27	General overheads paid by cheque, £70.
28	Bought goods on credit from J Robert, £50.
30	Sold goods to R David, £280 on credit.
31	Bought some shop equipment on credit from Joe Brown, £750.

REQUIRED:

a) Enter all the above information in the ledger of Ann Rogers for the month of May.
b) Extract a trial balance as on 31 May.

13 The trial balance of Ken Stevens on 30 April was as follows:

Ken Stevens – Trial balance as at 30 April

	Dr £	*Cr* £
Sales		20 750
Purchases	13 170	
General expenses	4 972	
Fixtures	2 500	
K Gibson	1 130	
T Lowe		700
Bank	1 720	
Drawings	2 800	
Capital		7 228
Stock	2 386	
	28 678	28 678

During the month of May the following transactions took place:

1 May	Bought goods on credit from T Lowe, £85.
2 May	Sold goods on credit to K Gibson, £105.
18 May	Banked cash sales £400.
20 May	K. Gibson paid £680 by cheque in part settlement of his account.
26 May	Paid general expenses by cheque, £97. Sent a cheque value £300 to T Lowe in part settlement of his account.

28 May Paid general expenses by cheque, £275.
30 May Withdrew £300 from the bank for his own use.

REQUIRED:

a) Open the accounts at 1 May.
b) Record the transactions directly in the accounts by means of double entries. Do *not* use subsidiary books.
c) Extract a trial balance at 31 May.

14 The following are the balances in the ledger of J Stamp, a sole proprietor, as at 31 July.

	Dr £	*Cr* £
L Brain (Debtor)		200
S Round (Debtor)		400
A Wells (Creditor)	500	
Heating and lighting	600	
Printing and stationery	500	
Rent and rates	900	
Wages		5 400
Vehicle	1 500	
Equipment	600	
Discount allowed and received	300	200
Purchases		8 400
Sales	1 3000	
Bank	500	
Capital	5 600	

REQUIRED:

The accounts clerk cannot think why his trial balance fails to balance. Check the entries and prepare a new trial balance with the necessary corrections inserted. Note: discount allowed £300 is an expense and discount received £200 is revenue.

6 Business accounting systems in practice

Objectives

On completing this section you should:

- understand the difference between recording credit and cash transactions
- appreciate the primary functions of the journals and cash book for feeding into the ledgers
- understand the links in the process of recording accounts and communicating them through the financial statements
- recognise the various jobs found in an accounts office.

6.1 Introduction

Having seen the basic principles underlying the accounting system in Chapters 4 and 5, we can now look at how accounting systems work in practice in businesses. We will use the diagram below to show the basic structure of a business accounting system:

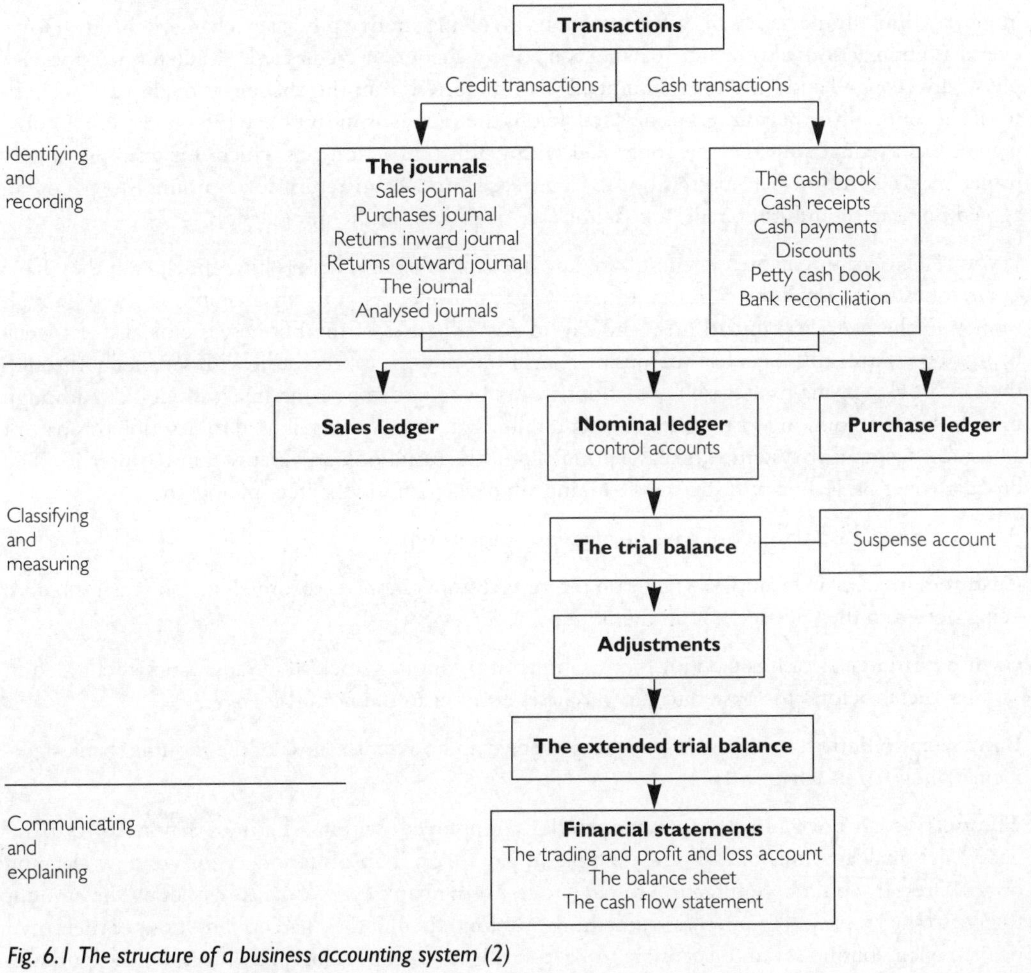

Fig. 6.1 The structure of a business accounting system (2)

The diagram is necessarily simplified, but illustrates some of the key processes at work. You will recognise some of the features of the system which we have already outlined: transactions, journals and cash book, the ledgers, the trial balance and the profit and loss account and balance sheet. Others you will be less familiar with. In this chapter, we will introduce some of the most important which we discuss later in the book. This chapter will provide a context into which to fit later chapters. We will begin by looking at the identifying and recording stage of the system.

6.2 Identifying and recording: credit and cash transactions

You will notice that the key new feature here is the different treatment of credit and cash transactions. In Chapter 1 we identified the importance of businesses keeping track of what they owed and what is owed to them, and ensuring that there is enough cash to run the business. These needs are dealt with by routing cash and credit transactions separately. Let us look at cash transactions first.

6.3 Dealing with cash transactions: introducing the cash book

You may think immediately of cash transactions involving money physically changing hands. However, cash transactions also include payments made by cheque or credit card. While money does not physically change hands, the sum is immediately transferred from the cheque or credit card account to the account of the person or business for whom the money is meant once the transaction is completed. Cash transactions may be contrasted with credit transactions, in which, for example, a customer may take immediate possession of a business's product in return for a promise to pay at an agreed point in the future. Credit transactions are dealt with in the next section.

If you remember in Chapter 1, one of the key questions managers ask is how much cash they have at any one time to run the business: to pay wages, bills etc. As you can imagine, keeping enough money in the bank account to meet the day-to-day expenses of the business is crucial to its well-being. To control this aspect of the business, cash transactions can be dealt with separately through the cash book. At one time, cash transactions would be recorded by hand in a 'cash book'. Although most business accounting systems are now computerised, the term is still used to describe this part of a business accounting system. The basic principles of the cash book are discussed in Chapter 15. The broader issues of dealing with business banking are dealt with in Chapters 14 and 16.

As you can see, cash transactions are divided into various types.

Cash receipts. As an example, when cash is received from sales, it is recorded in cash receipts before being posted to the sales account in the nominal ledger.

Cash payments. If cash is paid out, for example in paying for stock, the transaction is recorded in cash payments before it is posted to the purchases account in the nominal ledger.

Bank reconciliation involves the checking of the cash book with those of the monthly bank statements, discussed in Chapter 16.

The petty cash book. In day-to-day operations, employees within a business may need to spend occasional small amounts of cash, for example to pay for an item of stationery, or window cleaning or taxi fares. It would be impractical to have to go to the bank every time to withdraw the amount to give to the employee to purchase something or refund them if they had bought it out of their own pocket. Many businesses find it sensible to keep small amounts of cash, 'petty' cash, for this purpose.

As with any other aspect of business accounting, transactions involving petty cash need to be properly recorded and measured. This is done through the petty cash book, which is discussed in Chapter 17.

6.4 Dealing with credit transactions: introducing the journals

Similarly, businesses need to keep track of what they owe or are owed. Just as cash transactions need to be dealt with separately, so credit transactions are routed separately through the journals before they are posted to the ledgers. There are a number of journals designed to track differing kinds of credit transaction. These journals are also referred to as **'day books'**.

Sales journal. Businesses will keep a separate record of what they are owed by customers in the sales journal, extracting the information from the invoices they send to customers. These records can then be posted to the relevant accounts in the ledgers. The sales journal is discussed in detail in Chapter 8.

Purchases journal. The purchases journal is used by businesses to record what they owe themselves if they buy something on credit from a supplier. The information is taken from invoices received from suppliers and the information posted to the relevant accounts in the ledgers. The purchases journal is discussed in detail in Chapter 11.

Returns inward journal. Many customers will buy goods on a sale or return basis: if the goods cannot be sold on to the end user, they have the right to return the surplus stock. The value of returned goods needs to be recorded in the returns inward journal before being posted to the relevant ledger accounts. Figures are extracted from the credit notes sent to customers. The returns inward journal is discussed in Chapter 12.

Returns outward journal. Similarly, if the business itself returns goods, it will record the return in the returns outward journal from the supplier's credit notes and adjust the account with the relevant supplier within the purchase and nominal ledgers from the supplier's credit notes to show a credit in its favour. (The returns outward journal is in the same chapter as returns inward).

The journal. The journal is used for those transactions which occur outside the scope of the other journals, for example correcting errors. The journal is discussed in Chapter 31.

6.5 Analysed journals

Analysed journals are adapted from the main journals to allow businesses to analyse more closely what they sell and buy so that, for example, they can order the right levels of stock. Here the journals are used to communicate key information direct to managers to assist in their decision-making. Analysed journals are discussed in Chapter 13.

6.6 Classifying and measuring

There are a number of features at the classifying and measuring stage of business accounting systems which we have not dealt with before.

Control accounts. These accounts are, like the trial balance, used as a way of checking the accuracy of the recording process. Located in the nominal ledger, they summarise the total figures for debtors and creditors, which can then be compared with the sales and purchase ledgers to see if the figures match. Control accounts also help managers see how much is owed to creditors, and how much debtors owe to the business. Control accounts are discussed in Chapter 20.

Suspense account. If, for any reason, the trial balance fails to balance because of a recording error, a suspense account is created temporarily to make up the difference between the total of debits and credits. Creating the account allows the business to put together the profit and loss account. Once the error or errors have been located, the suspense account can be adjusted back. Suspense accounts are discussed in Chapter 31.

Adjustments. When a business needs to compile a profit and loss account or balance sheet, there will usually be outstanding items, for instance an unpaid bill, which needs to be allowed for. Before accounts can be finalised in order to prepare the balance sheet and profit and loss account, such items need to be identified and accounted for. This is done through adjustments. These are discussed in Chapters 22, 23 and 25.

Extended trial balance. As we have seen, the trial balance is a way of testing the accuracy of the double-entry recording process in accounts within the ledgers. The extended trial balance, as the name suggests, is an expanded version of the trial balance with extra columns which take account of adjustments before it can be used in the preparation of final accounts. The extended trial balance is discussed in Chapter 32.

6.7 Communicating and explaining: preparing financial statements

The final stage in business accounting systems is the preparation of the key financial reports: the balance sheet and the profit and loss account. The specific requirements of such reports for the various kinds of business enterprise are discussed in Chapter 21 (sole traders), Chapter 26 (partnerships) and Chapter 27 (limited companies). We have mentioned the importance of businesses managing cash effectively. **Cash flow statements** help to monitor this part of the business: they are discussed in Chapter 28. Chapter 1 discussed the role of cost and management accounting in providing information for managerial decision-making. The use of information from the business accounting system in these areas is discussed in Chapters 35–37.

Given their importance, it is, of course, essential that reports such as the profit and loss account are compiled according to a commonly accepted set of definitions and standards so that any outside party can interpret them with confidence. The accounting profession has developed a range of standards to meet this need, and these are outlined in Chapter 33.

Finally, as we pointed out in Chapter 1, the key role of accounting is to provide the information that managers and others need to make decisions. This can be demonstrated by looking at the balance sheet and profit and loss account to see what it can tell us about the nature, problems and potential of a business. Accounting ratios are a helpful tool in analysing financial statements, and we discuss these in Chapter 34.

6.8 The structure of a business accounting department

Once you understand the basic structure of business accounting systems, it becomes much easier to understand the structure of an accounts department within a business and the roles that individuals within it play. An example of the structure of an accounts department within a large business is shown below:

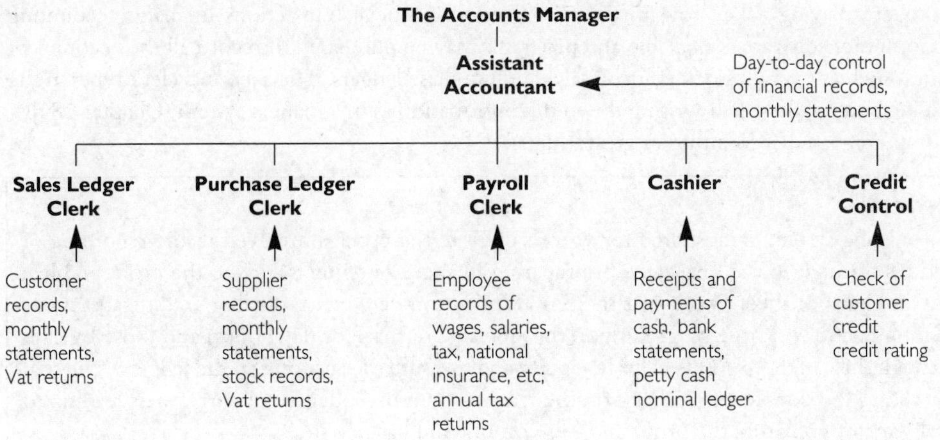

Fig. 6.2 The accounts office

The accurate, day-to-day recording of financial transactions is one of the most important functions of an accounts office.

The sales and purchase ledger clerks are responsible for customer and supplier accounts respectively. Documents such as invoices and credit notes, and evidence of payment will be the 'raw materials' from which the accounting information will be recorded.

The cashier is responsible for banking and cash transactions and also receiving and checking bank statements to see if entries match the business's records. He or she may also be responsible for the nominal ledger which records all accounts except customers' and suppliers' – the responsibility of the sales and purchase ledger clerks. A junior accounts clerk may be delegated with the responsibility of being in charge of all petty cash expenses.

The payroll clerk is responsible for the calculation of the business's wages and salaries paid to its employees. This will include payments for bonuses and overtime, the appropriate deductions for tax and national insurance, and other payments stopped from pay.

Many businesses need to keep accurate records of stock for the purpose of knowing when to reorder the next batch before stocks fall too low. It is important to carry the optimum level of stock because if too much is purchased, it may tie up cash required for other purposes, or if too little is bought, stock levels could soon run out and valuable orders lost.

The credit controller is responsible for ensuring that customers are creditworthy and can pay their bills on time. If customers delay their payments, this can lead to liquidity problems for the business, that is, the business can become short of immediately accessible funds to meet its debts.

The management of the office will have overall control of the accounting staff and be responsible for ensuring that records are maintained accurately and the accounts are thoroughly up-to-date. The accountant and his assistant will be responsible for the preparation of the accounting statements, such as the profit and loss account and the balance sheet. They will also be responsible for coordinating the process of budgeting, that is, planning ahead to ensure that sufficient cash resources will be available to meet future payments and also to help control patterns of expenditure for the departments within the organisation.

Computers are playing a key role in the recording of financial transactions in many accounting offices. Computer software is available and programs may be purchased to record all the accounts of the business such as payroll, stock control, sales and purchase ledgers. The accounts clerk types in the data on a keyboard rather than writing down the information as in a manual system. Chapter 18 discusses computer-based accounting in greater detail.

Summary

The accounting system is illustrated for you to indicate the process involved in the recording of transactions through to the final stage of preparing financial statements such as the profit and loss account and balance sheet. Note that there is a distinction between recording credit transactions and cash transactions. Those on credit pass through the journals (or day books) and those by cash pass through the cash book. This helps to classify and measure the accounts in the ledgers. The trial balance acts as the double entry check on the ledgers to ensure a degree of correctness leading to the final stage of preparing the profit and loss account and balance sheet.

If a computer program was used, the transactions would be input directly to the ledgers and automatically, all the accounts would be updated and printouts taken when required. See Chapter 18 for further information on computer programs.

Questions

1 Take a look at the diagram in Fig. 6.1, where the accounting system is extended, and try to answer the following:
   a) What is the essential difference between recording transactions in the journals with those in the cash book? (6.2–4)
   b) Bank reconciliation is part of the cash book system. What do you think this applies to?
   c) Why could it be beneficial to operate a petty cash book? (6.3)
   d) The four major journals deal with sales and purchases. What is 'the journal's' function? (6.4)
   e) How could analysed journals be of assistance to management? (6.5)
   f) What is the function of the trial and extended trial balance? (6.6)
   g) Why should a suspense account be inserted in the trial balance and be recorded in the nominal ledger? (6.6)
   h) Why may it be necessary to make adjustments to the accounts before the financial statements are prepared? (6.6)

2 You will find that control accounts appear in a number of chapters in the first half of the text. What is their function? Why do they act as a kind of trial balance? (6.6)

3 Communicating information to interested parties usually means preparing financial statements for their use. Who are the 'interested parties' and briefly define financial statements. (6.7)

4 Take a look at the diagram in Fig. 6.2 and try to answer these questions: (6.8)
   a) From what source(s) do you think the sales ledger clerk would obtain information for recording data into the accounts?
   b) Where would the purchase ledger clerk get his information from?
   c) Which accounts assistant would deal with banking transactions?
   d) In larger organisations, it would be unlikely that a manual accounting system would be operated. What advantages has the alternative system?
   e) Customers may fail to pay their debts. What could be done to restrict the amount lost as bad debts?

PART 3 DEALING WITH CREDIT TRANSACTIONS

7 Sales on credit (1): an introduction

Objectives

On completing this section you should:

- understand the meaning of selling terms such as quotations, estimates and tenders as well as the various terms of payment
- understand the function of invoices and statements and be able to prepare them from data provided
- appreciate the importance of credit control.

Context

Chapter 6 puts credit transactions in the context of business accounting systems as a whole. Chapter 4 explains the basic role of journals and ledgers.

7.1 Introduction

Cash sales must clearly be differentiated from credit sales. Cash sales are the ones we associate with most when we go out shopping. We may pay by cash, cheque, or by using a credit card such as Access or Barclaycard. A sale on credit is one where the supplier sells goods on trust. The words *del credere* basically mean 'on trust'. The goods can be taken and payment is deferred until a later date. Buy now pay later.

When businesses trade with each other, it is the accepted practice that the buying and selling of goods is on a credit basis. The invoice will be the bill of sale and used as the contract between the buyer and the seller. Payment is made at an agreed date after receipt of the invoice. The basic process of documenting credit transactions is shown below:

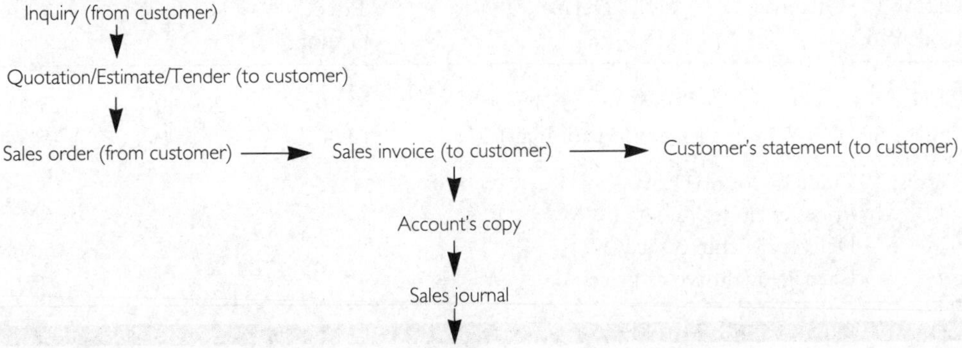

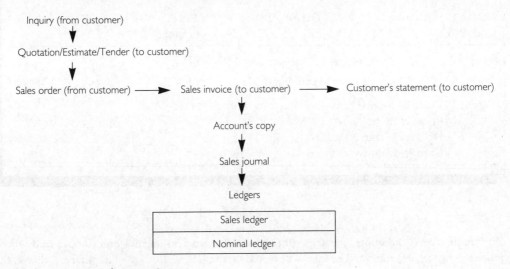

Fig. 7.1 Documenting credit transactions

The documentation procedure illustrated above commences with an initial **customer inquiry** requesting price, terms and availability of goods. A **quotation** is sent to the customer and is accepted. The **sales order** is then recorded and an **invoice** set is raised, including copies of the advice note, delivery note, store and of course, accounts copy.

The customer will receive a **statement** from the supplier of the goods or services, usually once a month, to remind him of the transactions which have occurred during the period and the amount of money which he owes. The **accounts copy**, checked for accuracy, will then be the source document for entry in the accounting books, that is, the sales journal (sales day book) and subsequent posting to the ledgers. The sales journal is discussed in more detail in the following chapter and is used to record the invoices sent out to customers.

The sales ledger is used to record the details of sales and Vat from the invoice to the customer's account. The nominal ledger will be used to record the accounts for sales and Vat.

7.2 Quotations, estimates and tenders

7.2.1 Quotations

Some customers may require a quote for the goods or services they want to buy. They may be important customers who want a specific reduction from the list price because of the quantity they can order, or it may be a customer who wants something different from the normal range of goods listed. The quotation is a letter of response to a customer's inquiry and is an offer to sell its goods at the prices and terms and conditions stated.

Example: quotation to F Smith

In reply to your inquiry, dated 15 January, we are pleased to offer the following:

Cat. Code No.	Quantity	Details	Price per unit	Cost	Vat rate
242Y	50	Norman's cricket balls	4.00	200.00	17.5%
258Y	20	Jackson pads (pair)	12.50	250.00	17.5%

Terms: Trade discount 12.5%
Prices exclude Vat
Delivery within 30 days
Carriage inclusive of price.

If F Smith accepts the quote, the sales office enters the order in its sales order book, ready to be processed by the department. The sales staff would be responsible for raising the invoice, that is, the bill of sale to the customer.

7.2.2 Estimates

Sometimes a customer may want an estimate of the cost of goods or services. For example, you may want an estimate of how much it would cost to paint and decorate your house or to install a central heating system or have an extension put onto the property. The supplier would have to prepare a reasonably accurate estimate of how much the job would cost in terms of labour, materials and anything else including delivery. The following is an example of an estimate to build a small extension:

	£
Materials: tiles, bricks, sand cement, timber etc.	3 450.00
Labour: approx. 35 hours per week, 4 weeks × £15.00 hour	2 100.00
Overheads:	200.00
	5 750.00
Vat 17.5%	1 006.25
Total estimate:	6 756.25

7.2.3 Tenders

If a job requires doing or goods need to be purchased, the customer may want to offer the job to anyone who might be interested in submitting a tender for it. The party interested in applying for the job would generally state:

a) what they will provide in terms of materials, goods, service etc
b) how long it will take to complete the job
c) the price it will cost.

After the closing date of the tender, the customer will then decide which of the offers to choose in terms of price, availability, quality, etc.

Public sector services like the local district corporations often advertise in newspapers inviting suppliers for tenders to be submitted for all kinds of public services including new buildings, maintenance and repair, cleaning and other council services.

A tender, therefore, is inviting a supplier's quotation for specified goods or services, and if it is accepted, a firm contract can be made between the supplier and the customer.

7.3 The sales invoice

In small businesses such as that of a sole trader, the invoice is usually an uncomplicated affair where the customer receives the top copy and the duplicate is retained by the seller. In larger organisations, the invoice may come in sets of say five or six copies, because each copy has a specific function in helping to administer the sale and despatch of goods.

In manufacturing, the invoice procedure may well be very complicated with multiple copies going to different sections such as the contracts office, fabrication shop, computer section, engineering works and so on. In the example below the use of six copies of an invoice is demonstrated to show how they are used and distributed:

Copies	Function
1 **Top copy**:	the customer's bill of sale, showing details of prices and terms of sale.
2 **Sales copy**:	the sales office copy for filing and used to record record of sales etc.
3 **Delivery note**:	usually accompanies the delivery of goods and signed by the customer as evidence of receiving order.
4 **Advice note**:	the customer may be advised when and where the goods are to be despatched to him.
5 **Accounts copy**:	required as evidence of transaction and for recording in sales day book and ledgers.
6 **Stores copy**:	recording the despatch and entering details on a stock record card.

The use of computers can now greatly simplify the amount of paperwork. The essential details can be entered to produce a printed invoice automatically for the customer and a delivery note to accompany the goods. Sales and accounting staff can then refer to the relevant documentation on screen, while stores can amend details on screen to show despatch, automatically updating their own stock details and records in accounts in the process. Chapter 18 discusses the role of computers in accounting. A typical sales invoice is shown on the next page.

7.3.1 Terms of payment

Trade discount: A sum allowed to the buyer of goods off the usual list price. The discount rate varies usually in proportion to the amount of goods purchased. There is no double entry with trade discount, the net sum payable is recorded, not the gross sum.

Cash discount: A sum allowed to the buyer to encourage prompt payment, perhaps 2.5 per cent or 5 per cent if invoice is paid within a specific number of days. Cash discount is recorded as part of the double entry when the payment is received.

Carriage forward: The buyer pays for the delivery of goods. This is referred to as carriage inwards and is part of the cost of sales in the trading account.

Carriage paid: The seller pays for the delivery of goods to the buyer's destination.

Cash on delivery: Payment is made when the goods are handed over.

E&OE Errors and omissions excepted. This indicates that the supplier has every right to correct any error or omission on an invoice.

Ex stock Goods will be supplied from stock.

Ex works The buyer is normally responsible for the delivery cost from the factory.

INVOICE 44572
R PEARCE SPORTS LTD.
77 PENHILL ROAD
POOLE,
BH40 I65

VAT Reg. No. 76 48424 23
Telephone 01202 684120
Date 24 March

To: M Jones
Ashley Stores
14 The Parade
Wareham
Dorset

Your Order No. 1038/93 dated 8 March

Quantity	Details	Code No.	Price/ Unit	Cost	Vat Rate	Vat Amount
20	Empire bats	Z133	14.16	283.20	17.5	
150	Empire balls	Z128	2.28	342.00	17.5	
10	Snr. batting pads	Z342	21.00	210.00	17.5	
				835.20		
	Less trade discount 10%			83.52		
				751.68		131.54
	Add Vat			131.54		
				883.22		

Terms: Net cash within 30 days of above invoice date.
Delivery: Our vehicle to your store, carriage paid.
E&OE

Vat Value added tax charged by the Government's Customs & Excise Department on many of our goods and services. Vat is a charge on goods and services in the UK and represents an indirect source of taxation to the Government. Business people who are Vat registered, that is, they have received a certificate of registration from the Customs & Excise Department, are given their registration number and tax periods. They are obliged to pay output tax (Vat collected on sales) and have the right to deduct input tax (Vat paid on purchases, fixed assets or expenses). The current standard rate is 17.5 per cent. Chapter 9 discusses Vat in much greater detail.

Note that Vat is calculated *after* trade discount has been deducted from the cost of goods. The key figures for recording will be:

Sales	£751.68
Vat	£131.54
M Jones	£883.22

7.4 Customer statements

Statements of account are sent to customers giving details of the current transactions which have occurred between buyer and seller. It is a statement which reminds customers of their outstanding debt. In the example below, R Pearce sends a prepared statement of account to his customer, C Taylor. The final balance due should, of course, cross-check with Taylor's account in the sales ledger.

Statement of account

R Pearce Sports Ltd.
77 Penhill Road
Poole
BH40 I65

Vat Reg. 76 48424 23
Telephone: 01202 684120

To: C Taylor
24 Boscombe Drive
Bournemouth

Account no. S12

Date	*Details*	*Debit* £	*Credit* £	*Balance* £
1/7	Balance b/f			1 058.00
30/7	Cheque – Thank you		500.00	558.00
15/8	C/N 545		105.75	452.25
3/9	Invoice no. 2955	200		
	Vat	35		687.25
5/9	Balance due			687.25

This statement lists the balance in the account from the last statement, any payments made subsequently and any new invoices raised for goods supplied. It may also include credit notes for goods returned (these are discussed in Chapter 12).

When the statement is sent to the customer, the supplier will expect payment or at least part payment of outstanding invoices on the account within a reasonable period of time. Payment is likely to be by cheque or through the banking system such as direct debit or credit transfer. Sometimes it is inevitable that some customers will fail to pay their accounts. If trade becomes slack and the demand for goods and services fall, a recession can linger on for a great length of time as it did in the early 1990s. In many cases, customers found that they were unable to pay because they faced financial difficulties or even went bankrupt.

7.5 Credit control

It is important for a business to try and restrict the total of outstanding debts due from their customers (debtors). A system of control is needed to ensure that all customers pay their accounts on time, and particularly when the economy starts to take a downturn.

It would be foolhardy to allow any customer to buy any amount of goods they wanted without first fully checking how reliable they were. If a customer shows that he can regularly pay his outstanding debts, then trust is built up between the buyer and seller.

Where some customers take their time about paying and their debts are outstanding over a long period of time, say beyond a period of three months, then firm action needs to be taken to recover the debts.

It is essential in business to have an 'aged debtors list', that is, a list which clearly establishes how old the debts of customers are. For example, a business may have £1 770 of debtors three months or more, (see aged debtors list below) and would want to chase these customers up and expedite payment. A business may employ a credit controller with the responsibility of chasing up the older debts. A thorough and continuous system is required to ensure that customers do not exceed their credit limits and that they pay their bills on time.

A credit rating is a device which seeks to inform the controller how good or bad a customer is when paying his bills. For example, a 5-star rating might indicate an absolute top mark rating for those customers showing great reliability. At the other end of the scale, a 1-star rating would indicate that the customer needs close attention and that the value of sales would have to be closely monitored to make sure payment is made.

A credit limit is made on customers which indicates the limit of their purchases. In this way, payment must be made before further sales are made to the customer. Credit ratings of customers can change, depending on whether they become more or less reliable. The credit rating also gives guidance to the value of sales allowed to a customer. It follows that the higher the rating, the higher the sales value a customer is given.

The credit controller can make up the ratings according to past experiences with customers. With new customers, assistance can be gained from organisations like Dun & Bradstreet which makes evaluations on company performance and estimates their ability to pay debts. A new customer would normally be expected to give references from other suppliers or from their bank.

7.5.1 Computer programs

If a computer program is used to record sales on credit (see Chapter 18 on computer-based accounts), the sales ledger program would have a function which would give the aged debtors list automatically.

The list would print out precisely the 'age' of each debtor in months and could also be linked to print out standard letters to late customers such as account numbers S001 and S004 (below) who need reminders to pay their accounts on time.

An aged debtors list:

A/c	3 months	2 months	1 month	Current	Total	Name of Customer
S001	920	190	450		1 560	Chappell
S002		480	210	345	1 035	Mason & Co
S003			150	420	570	Walters Ltd.
S004	850				850	Hardcastles
Totals	1 770	670	810	765	4 015	

Summary

Estimates, tenders and quotations are all part of the buying and selling jargon in business with the object of trying to sell. The invoice is the bill of sale for goods or services usually supplied on a credit basis and is a prime document for entry in the sales journal if selling or purchase journal if buying. Credit control is about checking customers and ensuring that bad debts are strictly limited.

Questions

1 A customer requires an estimate to instal a new kitchen. He has chosen a particular model he likes from your catalogue and has given you details of the number of units he wants and the approximate cost. The following details need an estimate:

12 units code 2475 @ £36.50 each
12 units code 2475/1 @ £8.75 each
12 units code 2475/2 @ £17.80 each
12 units code 2475/3 @ £2.20 each

Laminate top 3 552/1 4.5 metres @ £12.75 per metre.
Stainless steel sink @ £26.80
All the above is subject to 10% trade discount and 17.5% at the standard rate Vat.
Labour cost: 20 hours @ £12.00 per hour and 17.5% Vat.

You are to prepare the estimate clearly specifying separate figures for materials, labour, Vat and total cost. (7.2)

2 If a quotation is accepted by the customer, give a brief outline of the procedure which might follow. (7.2)

3 Differentiate clearly between the following terms:

quotation	sales order	
statement	bank statement	
trade discount	cash discount	
carriage forward	carriage paid	(7.2–4)

4 Explain briefly the function of an invoice and why a number of copies will be required by an organisation. (7.3)

5 The following is an invoice no. 6542 from Stationery People Ltd to R Pearce Sports Ltd.

Customer Order	Despatch Date	Price/Unit	Total
P/234/96	5/1/19XX		
100	Pencils	0.21	21.00
60	Biros	0.30	18.00
100	Pocket files, various	0.10	10.00
25	Writing pads	0.72	18.00
10	Rolls sellotape	1.25	12.50

REQUIRED:
a) Add up the total.
b) Deduct 10% trade discount.
c) Add the standard Vat rate. (7.3)

6 What is the purpose of a customer statement? How often would it normally be sent to a customer? (7.4)

7 Stationery People Ltd have sent R Pearce their statement of account for the end of the month:

Date	Details	Reference	Debit	Credit	Balance
1/1	Balance b/f				300.80
5/1	Invoice	6542	?		?
19/1	Invoice	7444	88.75		?
26/1	Credit note	C32		15.65	?
30/1	Cheque	6544321		300.80	?
	Balance now due				?

Note: debit entries add value, credit entries reduce value.

REQUIRED:
a) Insert the answer to invoice no. 6542 in question 5 (above) in the customer's statement.
b) Enter all relevant figures where there is a ?
c) Explain briefly, each of the details. (7.4)

8 What is credit control? Briefly explain how this function could save a business a great deal of money. (7.5)

9 Explain briefly what an aged debtors's list is and how it can prove to be useful. (7.5)

8 Sales on credit (2): the sales journal

Objectives

On completing this section you should:

- understand why the sales journal is used
- recognise that the invoice is the prime document of entry to the sales journal
- appreciate that Vat is charged on many goods and services at the standard rate
- understand the function of the sales ledger control account
- understand posting procedures from the sales journal to the ledgers.

Context

Chapter 7 introduced the basic documentation involved in credit sales. Chapter 5 covers the appropriate rules for recording transactions in the ledgers.

8.1 Introduction

In this chapter we will concentrate on the sales journal within business accounting systems. The place of the sales journal in the accounting system is summarised below:

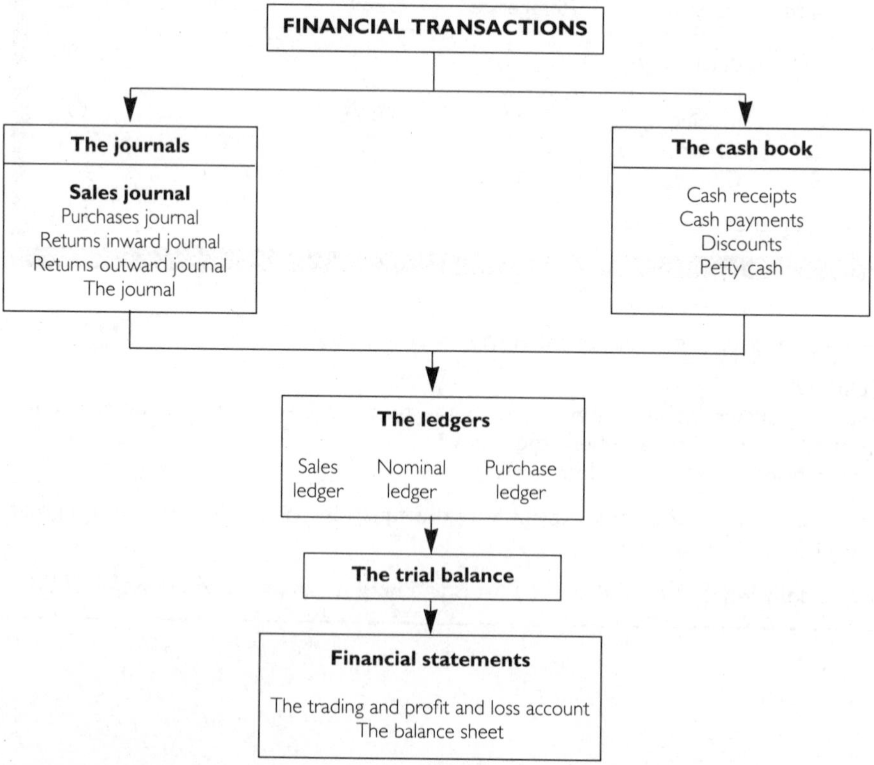

Fig. 8.1 The sales journal in the accounting system.

As we have seen, the major function of journals is to record credit transactions relating to sales, purchases, sales returns (returns inward) and purchases returns (returns outward). The same type of transactions of a daily and routine nature can be recorded together. For example, a batch of sales invoices can be listed in the sales journal by their invoice number and in date order and key information such as customers' names, account numbers, sales values, Vat and total sums due, are extracted. Daily, weekly or even monthly figures (depending on the number) can then be totalled and details posted to the appropriate ledgers.

It may appear that in modern systems of accounting, particularly where computers are used, that the journal's function has become obsolete. This is not really the case. Someone needs to classify a batch of invoices in some sort of order. The invoices must be checked for accuracy and a total of the day's or week's figures should be calculated as a check *prior* to posting to the ledgers. These figures could be entered on a control sheet that goes with the batch of invoices. This is a function called *journalising*, that is, preparing information from business documents before ledger posting.

8.2 Entering details into the sales journal

Details for entry to the sales journal will be extracted from the sales invoice sent to customers. A **control sheet**, showing the key figures of the invoices sent, may in itself, be a form of journal. Generally, the details extracted from the **invoice** are:

- Date of sale
- Customer's name
- Customer's account number
- Invoice number
- The net sales values
- Vat (if charged)
- The total value of the invoice.

This information could be directly fed into a computer system. Chapter 9 will demonstrate the procedure where a computer program is used for the input of invoice data. An example of the layout of a sales journal is given below:

The sales journal of R Pearce

Date	*Customer's name and account no.*		*Invoice no.*	*Net sales account* £	*Vat (17.5%) account* £	*Total value* £
1/6	C Taylor	S12	2801	800	140.00	940.00 Dr
4/6	M Johnson	S08	2802	200	35.00	235.00 Dr
19/6	M Johnson	S08	2803	300	52.50	352.50 Dr
23/6	C Taylor	S12	2804	120	21.00	141.00 Dr
				1 420	248.50	1 668.50
				Cr Sales	Cr Vat	

8.3 Posting to the ledgers

Using these examples, we can demonstrate how information from the sales journal is posted to the ledgers. Remember the double entry rules in Chapter 5. From these, we can derive the following:

Account type	Account group	Increase account	Decrease account
sales	revenue	credit	debit

which gives us the following rule:

Credit the **sales** account
Debit the **debtors** account

To simplify matters, we will assume a 'nil' balance in the customer's account at the beginning of the month, and **exclude Vat**. We would post the journal entries in the following way:

		Debit £	*Credit* £	*Balance* £	
C Taylor account					
1/6	Sales	800		800	Dr
23/6	Sales	120		920	
M Johnson account					
4/6	Sales	200		200	Dr
19/6	Sales	300		500	
Sales account					
30/6	Debtors		1 420	1 420	Cr

If we **include Vat**, the ledger entries would look as follows:

Sales ledger

		Debit £	*Credit* £	*Balance* £	
C Taylor account S12					
1/6	Sales	800.00		800.00	Dr
1/6	Vat	140.00		940.00	
23/6	Sales	120.00		1 060.00	
23/6	Vat	21.00		1 081.00	
M Johnson account S08					
4/6	Sales	200.00		200.00	Dr
4/6	Vat	35.00		235.00	
19/6	Sales	300.00		535.00	
19/6	Vat	52.50		587.50	

Nominal ledger

		Debit £	Credit £	Balance £
Sales account N25				
30/6	Debtors		1 420.00	1 420.00 Cr
Vat account N30				
30/6	Debtors		240.50	248.50 Cr

NOTE

The double entry:

1 *Debit* each debtor's account (in the sales ledger) with sales+Vat.

2 *Credit* the total value of sales (in the nominal ledger) to sales account; the total value of Vat (in the nominal ledger) to Vat account.

We can show how the entries into the ledger then fit into the overall system as follows:

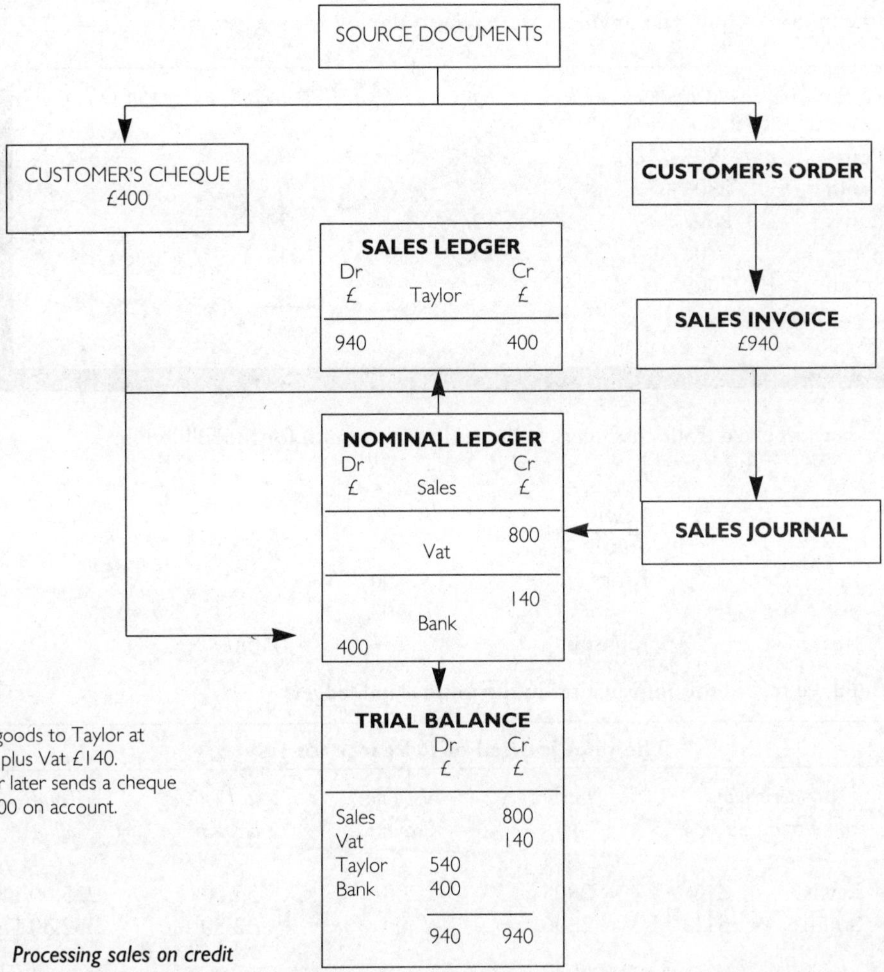

Fig. 8.2 Processing sales on credit

8.4 Sales, Vat and the use of the sales ledger control account

On 1 July, the balances in the books of R Pearce were:

Sales ledger:	£	*Nominal ledger:*	£
Lewis	100 Dr	Sales account	1 420 Cr
Smith	250 Dr	Vat account	213 Cr
Kings	150 Dr	Sales ledger control*	2 133 Dr
Taylor	1 058 Dr		
Johnson	575 Dr		
	2 133		

The sales ledger control account represents a total account of all debtors listed in the sales ledger (£2 133). It may be used as a cross-checking device and as a measure of control, that is, a check can be made to ensure that the individual balances totalled in the sales ledger equal the sales ledger control account balance. Control accounts are discussed in more detail in Chapter 20.

During the month of July, sales invoices were sent to the following customers:

	Invoice no.	*Date*	*Net sales*	*+ Vat (17.5%)*
			£	£
Lewis	2805	4/7	200	
Smith	2806	8/7	300	
Lewis	2807	12/7	120	
Kings	2808	15/7	340	
Smith	2809	21/7	100	
			1 060	

Cheques were received from customers at the end of the month for the following:

	£	£
Lewis	400	
Smith	500	
Kings	100	
Taylor	500	
Johnson	–	1 500

How would we record this information in the journal and ledger?

The sales journal of R Pearce for July

Date	*Customer's name and account no.*		*Invoice no.*	*Net sales account*	*Vat 17.5% account*	*Total value*
				£	£	£
4/7	Lewis	S10	2805	200	35.00	235.00 Dr
8/7	Smith	S11	2806	300	52.50	352.50 Dr

(continued)

(continued)

12/7	Lewis	S10	2 807	120	21.00	141.00 Dr
15/7	Kings	S09	2 808	340	59.50	399.50 Dr
21/7	Smith	S11	2 809	100	17.50	117.50 Dr
				1 060	185.50	1 245.50
				Cr Sales	Cr Vat	Dr Sales control

Sales ledger

		*Folio**	*Debit* £	*Credit* £	*Balance* £
D Lewis account S10					
1/7	Balance				100.00 Dr
4/7	Sales	SJ6	200.00		
	Vat		35.00		335.00
12/7	Sales	SJ6	120.00		
	Vat		21.00		476.00
30/7	Bank	C8		400	76.00
D Smith account S11					
1/7	Balance				250.00 Dr
8/7	Sales	SJ6	300.00		
	Vat		52.50		602.50
21/7	Sales	SJ6	100.00		
	Vat		17.50		720.00
30/7	Bank	C8		500	220.00
B Kings account S09					
1/7	Balance				150.00 Dr
15/7	Sales	SJ6	340.00		
	Vat		59.50		549.50
30/7	Bank	C8		100	449.50
C Taylor account S12					
1/7	Balance				1 058.00 Dr
30/7	Bank	C8		500	558.00
M Johnson account S08					
1/7	Balance				575.00 Dr

*(Folio Cross-refer to the journal or cash book page number.)

The schedule of debtors for July

	£	£
Lewis	76.00	
Smith	220.00	
Kings	449.50	
Taylor	558.00	
Johnson	575.00	1 878.50

The total value of debtors, £1 878.50, must cross-check with the sales ledger control account in the nominal ledger. If the figures do not match, an error has been made either in the sales ledger or the control account. The error must be located and corrected.

Nominal ledger

		Folio	Debit £	Credit £	Balance £
Sales account N42					
1/7	Balance				1 420.00 Cr
30/7	Debtors	SJ6		1 060.0	2 480.00 Cr
Vat account N50					
1/7	Balance				213.00 Cr
30/7	Debtors	SJ6		185.5	398.50
Sales ledger control account N40					
1/7	Balance				2 133.00 Dr
30/7	Sales and Vat	SJ6	1 245.50		3 378.50
	Bank	C8		1 500.0	1 878.50
Bank account (extract from cash book)					
30/7	Debtors		1 500.00		1 500.00 Dr

Summary

The sales journal is used as a prime source of entry to record the transactions on a credit basis to customers. Routine sales transactions can be summarised together and facilitate posting to the sales and nominal ledgers. The function of the control account is to act as a cross-check between the schedule of debtors in the sales ledger and the control account in the nominal ledger.

Questions

1 The following represents the sales invoices of R Jones for the month of June

	Customer's account	*Invoice no.*	*Value £*
2/6	Gibbs, P	4535	360
5/6	Walton, G	4536	400
9/6	Doe, M	4537	700
15/6	Slater, G	4538	420
20/6	Gibbs, P	4539	280
25/6	Doe, M	4540	100

No Vat is charged, the items being wholesale vegetables.

REQUIRED:

a) Prepare the sales journal for the month of June.
b) To which ledger are the above accounts posted? On which side of the customer's account do they appear?
c) Where is the total value for the month posted? On which side of the account does it appear? Why? (8.2–3)

2 On 1 July, the sales ledger balances of G Grant were:

	£
Goldney, P	220 Dr
Woods, B	150 Dr
Capel, J	400 Dr
Carlton, R	300 Dr
	1 070

In the nominal ledger, the sales ledger control account on the same date verified the debtor's schedule of £1 070 Dr.

Sales invoices sent to customers for July were:

	Customer's account	*Invoice no.*	*Value* £	*+ Vat (17.5%)* £
5/7	Goldney	4005	360	
9/7	Capel	4006	160	
14/7	Carlton	4007	100	
18/7	Capel	4008	180	
17/7	Woods	4009	240	
25/7	Carlton	4010	200	

On 30 July, Goldney, Capel and Carlton settled their account balances as on 1 July, by cheque.

REQUIRED:

a) The sales journal for the month of July.
b) The preparation of the sales and nominal ledger accounts (including control) (8.2–4)

3 Invoice 4242 from R Pearce to I Creese is shown on the following page. Answer the questions below from the view of R Pearce, the Sports Ltd proprietor.

R Pearce
Sports Ltd

Invoice
No. 4242

Vat reg. 76 48424 23   Telephone 01202 684120

Area	Customer order details	Fwd	Date	Account no.	Supplier no.	Page no.
16	0/15672 2.MAY		25.5	H1452	184285	

Invoice address	Consignee
I Creese Loxley Dve Broadstone	

Code	Qty	Description	Price	Goods value	Vat rate %	Vat
451	10	Tennis sets	£8.20		17.5	
452	10	Squash racquets	£15.00			
465	150	Master footballs	£8.40			
480	60	Master boots	£11.25			

Total goods
Total Vat

Invoice total

Terms: 20% trade discount

REQUIRED:

a) Calculate the value of the invoice.
b) In which journal would the figures from the above invoice be entered? How are the figures posted to the ledgers?
c) R Pearce uses control accounts. For what purpose are they used? (8.2–4)

4 The following information represents the sales journal of J Durham for May:

Customer account	*Invoice*	*Product 'A'*	*Product 'B'*	*Vat (17.5%)*
		£	£	£
R Jones	3651	60	20	
S Smith	3652	280	40	
T Brown	3653	400	100	
R Jones	3654	100	60	

REQUIRED:

a) Complete the sales journal for May, calculating the appropriate sum for Vat.
b) The opening balances in J Durham's sales ledger were:

		£
1/5	Jones	250
1/5	Smith	345
1/5	Brown	675

Enter these in the sales ledger and then post the above journal entries. Make up your own dates.

c) Post the information above to the appropriate ledgers and use the control account. Prepare separate sales accounts for each product.
d) Prepare a schedule of debtors and ensure the total matches the sales ledger control account. (8.2–4)

5 The following information relates to the accounts of Jenkins Jeans Ltd as on 1 January:

		£	
Debtors:	Davies	800	Debit
	Smith	450	Debit
	Forbes	100	Debit

During January, the following invoices were sent to customers:

January		Invoice number	Amount £	
5	Davies	2334	200	+ Vat 17.5%
12	Smith	2335	80	+ Vat 17.5%
17	Davies	2336	120	+ Vat 17.5%
21	Forbes	2337	400	+ Vat 17.5%
28	Smith	2338	300	+ Vat 17.5%
30	Forbes	2339	160	+ Vat 17.5%
31	Davies	2440	340	+ Vat 17.5%

On 31 January, cheques were received from:

Davies	£1 000
Forbes	£ 250
Smith	£ 544

REQUIRED:

a) Prepare the sales journal of Jenkins Jeans Ltd for January.
b) Record the sales ledger account of each customer.
c) Post the sales, Vat and sales ledger control accounts to the nominal ledger. Assume sales and Vat accounts have a zero balance on 1 January. (8.2–4)

These additional questions consolidate and extend your skills:

6 The following invoices were listed in the sales journal of Ray Jackson for the first week in January:

Date	Customer's account	Invoice number	Sales account	Vat account	Total debtors account
3/1	R James	1142	180	31.50	211.50
4/1	D Simpson	1143	200	35.00	235.00
6/1	G Seymour	1144	100	17.50	117.50
6/1	F Forster	1145	360	63.00	423.00
7/1	R James	1146	160	28.00	188.00

a) Check the standard rate of Vat (17.5%) for accuracy and ensure totals across are correct.
b) Total figures down and cross check for accuracy.
c) These figures will then be transferred to the ledgers. How will you post the above information to the sales and nominal ledgers?

7 The following information represents what is often called a 'columnar' journal day book where analysis columns are used. A business might wish to know how individual items or categories of sales are moving:

This is a columnar day book of RZ Co Ltd which sells three principal products, golf, cricket and tennis items:

Date	Customer account	Invoice number	Golf a/c	Cricket a/c	Tennis a/c	Vat a/c	Total debtors
7/1	Faldo	3364	400		120	94.0	
8/1	Boycott	3365	100	180		49.0	
9/1	Woosnam	3366	580	60	140	136.5	
10/1	Bates	3367		130	110	42.0	
10/1	Gooch	3368	60	440		87.5	
11/1	Castle	3369	100	126	74	52.5	
12/1	Lyle	3370	240		100	59.5	

a) Complete the totals across and check the calculation of Vat at the standard rate.
b) Total the figures down and cross check for accuracy.
c) The customer's accounts will be posted to the sales ledger in the normal way, how do you think the nominal ledger entries will be posted?

Note: Columnar journals (day books) will be discussed in greater detail in Chapter 10.

9 Vat and Vat returns

Objectives

On completing this section you should:

- recognise the various categories of Vat at standard, zero or exempt rates
- understand the difference between Vat inputs and outputs and how these are recorded in the Vat account and the Vat return.

9.1 Introduction

Vat is a charge on most of our goods and services in the United Kingdom and represents an indirect source of taxation for the Government. The collection of this tax, charged between traders in business, eventually falls to the consumer who is purchasing the product. Businesses in effect, are the collectors of Vat along the chain of distribution and consumers are the eventual payers.

Those businesses who are Vat registered, that is, they have received the Certificate of Registration from Customs & Excise (the Government Department responsible for the collection of Vat), are given a Vat registration number and the date of their tax period which in most cases, is a quarterly return. The Vat account is therefore normally settled on a three month basis although other arrangements can be made with the Vat office.

Supplies of goods and services may be at the standard rate, zero rated or exempt. The current standard rate of Vat charged is 17.5 per cent on most of our goods and services. The Chancellor of the Exchequer, responsible to the Government for deciding taxation rates, has over recent years imposed the standard rate on a wider area of products. Under much pressure to raise more revenue in order to cut the budget deficit, he imposed Vat from 1 April 1994, at 8 per cent on all domestic fuel and power.

9.1.1 Zero-rated supplies

Most business transactions are at the *standard rate*, or the *zero rate*, which is nil. Zero-rated supplies include:

- most food (but not catering which includes meals in restaurants, cafes, etc)
- books and newspapers
- young children's clothing and footwear
- the export of goods
- prescription charges
- the construction (or long leasing) of new houses and some other buildings but not existing buildings.

Zero-rated supplies of goods or services cannot charge Vat on sales but a firm can recover its Vat charges on purchases or any other business expenses.

From the date on which a trader is first required to be registered, all taxable supplies, either at the standard or zero rate, are liable for Vat.

9.1.2 Exempt supplies

Exempt supplies are transactions on which Vat is not charged. If a trader is exempt from Vat, he must not charge Vat on the supplies of goods or services to customers. At the same time, the trader is not allowed to reclaim any Vat he may have paid on purchases or other business expenses.

Those traders with a small turnover (below that set by the Chancellor's threshold), are exempt and need not keep Vat records. The taxable turnover is the value of all taxable supplies which are either at the standard rate or zero-rated, made in the UK. Note that the turnover does not include any supplies that are exempt. Exempt supplies also include:

- insurance
- betting, gaming and lotteries (but not gaming machines, club subscriptions and admission to premises)
- certain education and training
- the services of doctors, dentists, opticians
- membership benefits provided by trade unions and professional bodies
- entries to certain sports competitions
- the letting, leasing and sales of most land and buildings (but not hotel and holiday accommodation or garages and parking spaces)
- the provision of credit services including the operation of bank accounts.

If a trader supplies mostly zero-rated goods, he or she may be exempt from Vat registration, particularly if the input tax would normally exceed the output tax. However, once exempted, the trader cannot recover Vat paid on purchases of goods or services.

On the other hand, a trader could still register for Vat even though his or her turnover may be under the required threshold. Before applying, however, a trader needs to think carefully whether registration would gain benefit, because once registered all outputs and inputs of Vat must be accurately accounted for, including the formality of sending Vat returns regularly to the Vat offices. The return is normally on a quarterly basis (on form Vat 100). The period covered by the return is called the tax period and details of supplies made and received in that period will need to be entered on the form.

9.2 Vat calculations

When we purchase goods or services, we do not pay a separate sum for Vat, it is part of the price paid. Businesses charge Vat on goods sold (these are Vat outputs) and are themselves charged on goods purchased (Vat inputs).

The total Vat received in a tax period less the total Vat paid, is completed on the traders form Vat 100, the difference between the two being the balance due to the Vat office. In a simple example:

Sales in the quarter £16 779 (inclusive of Vat)

Purchases in the quarter £15 087 (inclusive of Vat)

How much Vat is due to the Vat office?

Vat outputs (on sales) $= \dfrac{16\,779 \times 7}{47} = £2\,499$

Vat inputs (on purchases) $= \dfrac{15\,087 \times 7}{47} = £2\,247$

difference = £252

The difference between Vat outputs and inputs (2 499–2 247)=the tax due (£252) for the period. This would be payable to the Vat office along with the tax return form Vat 100. If the inputs of Vat had been £2 499 against the outputs of Vat £2 247 because more goods had been purchased in a tax period than sold, then the Vat office would owe the business £252 for that period.

Most tax periods are payable quarterly although some traders prefer to have monthly tax periods, particularly if they are likely to get refunds because they deal with zero rated supplies. Other traders can have annual tax periods.

The cash accounting scheme allows traders the advantage of accounting for their Vat on the basis of receiving and paying cash, rather than on the normal invoice dates which are taken as the date of the tax point. In other words, the Vat return is prepared from the cash receipts (Vat outputs) less the cash payments (Vat inputs) in the given tax period. The turnover threshold of this scheme is currently for those traders whose taxable turnover, not including Vat, is less than £350 000 per annum.

The annual accounting scheme allows businesses to make a Vat return just once per year but again, there is a turnover threshold and is intended for those traders having a turnover (excluding Vat) less than £300 000 per annum. Traders are directed to make payments on account to the Vat office through the year, on the amount due to them.

Businesses who are not registered for Vat because they sell exempt supplies or are under the turnover threshold because they are a small business, do not need to account for Vat or keep records for Vat purposes.

Vat records for those businesses who are registered with the Vat office, must retain records of their transactions for six years (unless Customs & Excise grant permission to destroy records at an earlier date).

Note that SSAP 5 (Accounting for Vat), is the standard dealing with this topic. Accounting standards are covered in Chapter 33.

9.3 Foreign trade

Goods and services imported to the UK are subject to the same rules and regulations when these same goods are available here at home. Since the Single European Market came into force on 1 January 1993, the idea of imports and exports between the member states of the EU has been disbanded. Instead of 'imports' the term is 'acquisition'. When a buyer from the UK acquires goods or services from a member state, he will account for Vat on the form Vat 100 in the normal way under Vat inputs.

If goods are imported from a non-EU country, the importer will have to account for them with the Customs & Excise at the port of entry. Customs will provide a certificate as evidence that goods were imported and this can then be treated as a taxable input on the importer's next return on form Vat 100.

The export of goods from the UK are at the zero rate.

9.4 Input tax

For registered traders, input tax offsets the amount deductible to the Vat office. Most of the business's capital and revenue expenditure is allowable for Vat inputs if they are wholly for business purposes. Not all expenditure items are allowable, however, and these concern the acquisition of:

a) motor cars (unless it is for stock resale by a business buying and selling vehicles, or for taxi, car hire, driving school, or other purposes where the vehicle generates income);
b) on non-business expenses incurred by the organisation on items such as entertainment, meals, private use of facilities etc, where the Vat office does not see these as business-related.

In such cases as these, the full charge for the expense (including Vat) can be made in the annual profit and loss account. If there is any doubt as to what can be claimed as an input, traders must contact their local Vat office.

9.5 Bad debts

If bad debts occur when a trader is registered for Vat, bad debt relief may be claimed as a Vat input in the case where a customer's debt has been owing for a minimum period of 12 months and the debt written off as bad in the accounting books. If at a later point, the customer repays the debt (bad debts recovered), the Vat office must be repaid with the input tax.

9.6 Example of Vat account and return

Assume that you have a business which is registered with the Vat office. Your registration number is: 7648424. The end of your first Vat quarter is on 28 February and the trading details are:

Sales (outputs)	£70 500	(Vat inclusive)
Purchases (inputs)	£47 500	(Vat inclusive)
Allowable expenses	£940	(Vat inclusive)

Your Vat account and Vat form 100 would be as follows:

Nominal ledger

		Debit £	Credit £	Balance £
Sales account				
28/2	balance		60 000	60 000 Cr
Purchases account				
28/2	balance	40 000		40 000 Dr
Vat account				
28/2	debtors		10 500	10 500 Cr
	creditors	7 000		3 500
	expenses	140		3 360

On 28 February the Vat account shows a credit balance of £3 360 which, if no other entries are made, will be payable to the Vat office not later than the 20th day of the following month.

The Vat form 100 is shown below.

Value Added Tax Return

For the period
to

Registration number | Period

You could be liable to a financial penalty if your completed return and all the VAT payable are not received by the due date.

Due date:

For official use DOR only

Your VAT Office telephone number is 0123-4567

Fold | here

Before you fill in this form please read the notes on the back and the VAT Leaflet *"Filling in your VAT return"*. Fill in all boxes clearly in ink, and write 'none' where necessary. Don't put a dash or leave any box blank. If there are no pence write "00" in the pence column. Do not enter more than one amount in any box.

For official use			£	p
	VAT due in this period on sales and other outputs	1		
	VAT due in this period on acquisitions from other EC Member States	2		
	Total VAT due (the sum of boxes 1 and 2)	3		
	VAT reclaimed in this period on purchases and other inputs (including acquisitions from the EC)	4		
	Net VAT to be paid to Customs or reclaimed by you (Difference between boxes 3 and 4)	5		
	Total value of sales and all other outputs excluding any VAT. Include your box 8 figure	6		00
	Total value of purchases and all other inputs excluding any VAT. Include your box 9 figure	7		00
	Total value of all supplies of goods and related services, excluding any VAT, to other EC Member States	8		00
	Total value of all acquisitions of goods and related services, excluding any VAT, from other EC Member States	9		00

Retail schemes. If you have used any of the schemes in the period covered by this return, enter the relevant letter(s) in this box.

If you are enclosing a payment please tick this box.

DECLARATION: You, or someone on your behalf, must sign below.

I, ... declare that the
(Full name of signatory in BLOCK LETTERS)
information given above is true and complete.

Signature.. Date .... 19 ....

A false declaration can result in prosecution.

9.7 Tax invoices

All documents relating to Vat, including credit and debit notes, must be filed and retained in order to reclaim input tax. The invoice date is usually taken as the tax point when the supply is made. A business must comply strictly with the requirements as outlined by Customs and Excise as to the preparation of invoices, including:

- the business's name, address and Vat registration number
- date of supply
- customer's name and address
- the description of the goods or services supplied
- the total cost of the goods or services (excluding Vat charged)
- the rate of any trade or cash discounts offered
- the total Vat payable
- the total amount of the invoice.

9.7.1 A business's Vat details

To provide you with an example of inputs and outputs of Vat, the information in the table below relates to a business's activity for the quarter from January to March inclusive.

Business activity January–March

	£ *(inc. Vat)*	£ *Vat*
Sales (outputs)	61 428.0	9 148.85
Purchases (inputs)	47 700.0	7 104.26
Motor expenses	1 245.0	185.43
Telephone	380.0	56.60
Advertising	587.5	87.50
Accounts fees	493.5	73.50
General expenses	263.2	39.20
Total inputs	50 669.2	7 546.49
	Outputs	9 148.45
	Inputs	7 546.49
Total Vat payable:		1 601.96

Assume that on 1 January the Vat account had a balance of £1 480 credit and this had been settled with the Vat office on the 14th. The Vat account on 31 March would appear as shown.

VAT accounts 31 March

Vat account		Debit £	Credit £	Balance £
1/1	Balance			1 480.00 Cr
14/1	Bank	1 480.00		–
31/3	Outputs		9 148.45	9 148.45 Cr
31/3	Inputs	7 546.49		1 601.96 Cr

The balance owing to the Vat office = £1 601.96.

Summary

Vat is an indirect tax charged on many of our goods and services. Some goods may be zero rated or exempt tax. The Vat account is made up of outputs from sales (credited) and inputs from expenses (debited). The balance of the account will determine whether tax is owed to Customs (credit balance) or tax is owed to the business (debit balance). The Vat return to Customs is normally prepared every quarter and indicates the value of outputs against inputs.

Questions

1 Answer the following questions in brief (9.1–5):

a) Although Vat is normally collected on a quarterly basis, what other methods are allowed by the Vat office?
b) At what date is the tax point normally identified?
c) How would EC imports normally be dealt with if they were taxable items?
d) When can bad debts relief be taken as a taxable input?
e) Are all expenses by a business allowable for taxable input?
f) How does a business, which is exempt from Vat, record Vat when it is charged against them?
g) How does a business which is zero rated deal with Vat in its accounts?

2 The following transactions have been recorded in the company's books during one week's trading:

		£
Trade purchases	(list price)	4 500
Credit sales	(list price)	6 000
Purchase of a van		10 460
Entertaining expenses		360
Purchase of sales representative car		8 600

On the sales, a settlement discount of £300 is available and all figures exclude Vat at 17.5 per cent. If the balance on the Vat account was £2 165 credit at the beginning of the week, what is the balance at the end, after the above transactions took place? (9.2,4)

3 A business registered for Vat incurred the following transactions during the year 31 March:

	£
Taxable sales at standard rate	500 000
Taxable sales at zero rate	25 000

Sales exempt tax	75 000
Expenses subject to input tax	300 000

Included in the expenses figure is the purchase of a motor vehicle for £8 000 and also a delivery van for £10 000. All figures are given exclusive Vat.

How much input tax can be reclaimed by the business? (Note that the input tax that can be reclaimed is in the same proportion of taxable sales/total sales). (9.2,4)

4 Janet Jones provides you with the following information for her last quarter for Vat purposes:

sales (taxable outputs) £393 390 (inclusive of Vat at standard rate);
purchases (taxable inputs) £281 060 (inclusive of Vat at standard rate).

During this period, Janet paid £9 875 in settlement of the previous quarter's return. (Open the Vat account with this as a credit.) Draft the Vat account to record these entries for the quarter. (9.6)

5 The following data refers to the accounts of Susan Brambles Ltd for the Vat tax period April–June. Note that all the figures are *inclusive* of Vat.

	£
Sales	14 570
Purchases	11 327
Credits allowed to customers	940
Credits received from suppliers	799
Equipment purchases	987
New motor car for finance chief	8 850
Operating expenses allowable by Vat office	846

There was also an over-payment made to the Vat office of £62 in the previous period.

Note that credits refer to returns inward and outward.

REQUIRED:

a) The Vat account for the period to 30 June.
b) The sales and purchase figures to June (returns inclusive of these).
c) The amounts which will be posted to equipment, vehicles and operating expenses accounts. (9.6)

6 The following is a more advanced question:
A businessman purchases its goods on credit for £17 500 (net of Vat) and sells goods for £25 000 (net of Vat). At the end of the Vat quarter he pays what is due to Customs & Excise and also pays his creditors £12 000 and his debtors send him £18 250. Vat is at the standard rate.

a) Show all necessary recordings of these transactions in the books of account.
b) The opening stock for the period was £4 200 and the closing figure was 25 per cent higher. You are to prepare the trading account for the period, using the appropriate figures as indicated above.

(Association of Accounting Technicians)

10 Purchases on credit (1): an introduction

Objectives

On completing this section you should:

- understand the documentation procedure and the importance of checking invoices
- be able to calculate Vat including goods with discounts.

Context

Chapter 6 puts credit transactions in the context of business accounting systems as a whole.

10.1 Introduction

The purchasing of stock is of great importance to those business organisations which need to buy and sell goods. The right amount of stock must be bought at the right price, at the right time. If a business spent too much of its money on stock, it could find itself short of money to pay for alternative things such as wages and overheads and be short of working capital. If too much stock was purchased, there may be problems of storage. If too little stock was acquired the business may run out of certain items and valuable orders could be lost. Businesses need, therefore, to pay close attention to the way they record purchases of materials so they can track stock levels and how much they are spending for example. As with sales, most purchases are on a credit basis and businesses need also to keep track of these credit transactions so that they can monitor what they owe.

The basic process of documenting purchases on credit is as follows:

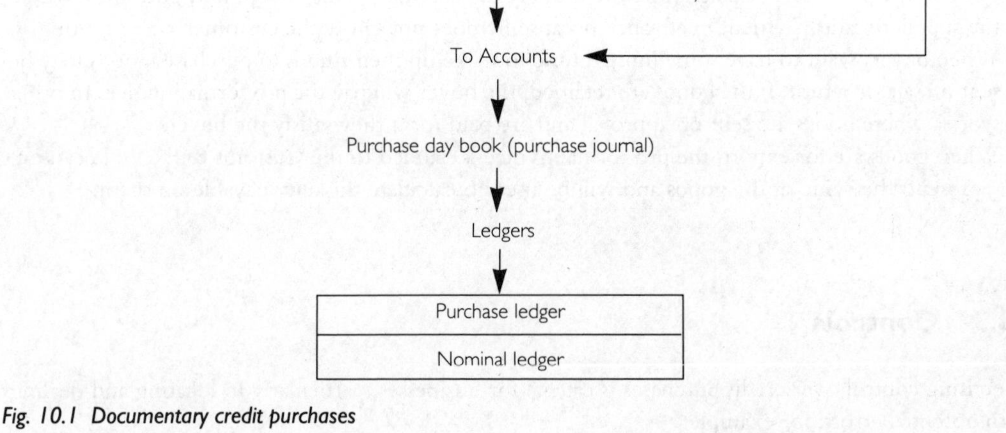

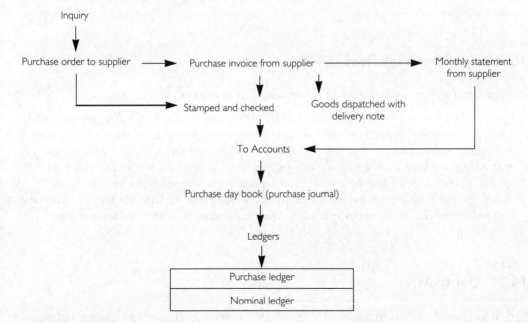

Fig. 10.1 Documentary credit purchases

The documentation procedure illustrated above could commence with an initial inquiry to a prospective supplier about the terms and conditions of their goods. A purchase order would follow if the buyer is satisfied with prices, discounts, etc. A copy of the order is retained in the buying office to check against the supplier's invoice when it arrives to see if it complies with the terms of the order.

When stock is delivered, it must always be thoroughly checked to ensure that the correct items have been received. The driver of the vehicle would have a delivery note to be signed once the goods have been checked in. A copy of the note should be retained by the person receiving and signing for the goods. If there were any discrepancies between the actual goods and the delivery note, the note should state what the discrepancy is, for example, only three parcels checked in, not four.

Many businesses prepare a goods received note which records details taken from the delivery note once the goods have been checked. A copy of the goods received note (grn) would then be sent to the buying office to confirm with the supplier's invoice that the goods charged for had been received in store.

Only correct invoices are passed for payment. This is the key concept for the responsible person or persons who are given the task of checking invoices thoroughly against the purchase order with either the goods received note or the delivery note.

If an invoice agrees with the purchase order and the goods received note, then the invoice is passed to the accounts office for recording and can be authorised for payment. The invoice, checked for accuracy and correctness, will then be the source document for entry in the accounting books, that is, the purchases day book (purchase journal) and subsequent posting to the ledgers.

The purchase ledger is used to record the supplier's account and the nominal ledger for the purchases, Vat and purchase ledger control accounts, corresponding to the purchases on credit.

The buyer of the goods will receive a statement from the supplier, usually once a month, to indicate the transactions which have occurred and the amount of money which is owed.

10.2 Pro forma invoices

Pro forma invoices are used in different circumstances from those of 'normal' invoices:

a) For goods which must be paid for before they are delivered. This may be for new customers where the supplier wants payment in advance because he does not know the customer's credit rating.
b) When buyers want to have some limited time to make up their minds to purchase, goods may be sent on sale or return. If the goods are retained, the buyer will pay the pro forma invoice. In other words, where goods are sent on approval and are paid for if they satisfy the buyer.
c) When goods are for export, the pro forma invoice is handed to the Customs & Excise because it represents the value of the goods and will be used to calculate the duty payable on them.

10.3 Controls

Exercising control over credit purchases is crucial for businesses, particularly in locating and dealing with potential errors, for example:

a) on the invoice itself because it is arithmetically wrong;
b) the invoice fails to agree with the terms of the purchase order, such as incorrect trade discount;
c) the goods received note does not agree with the invoice because there is a discrepancy between quantities received and quantities charged.

Action must be taken to solve discrepancies which may have been found. It may be the firm's policy to return to the supplier any invoice which is incorrect. Alternatively, the buying office may telephone, fax or write to the supplier explaining the nature of the error and come to some mutual agreement in solving the problem, for example, it may be more convenient for the supplier to send the shortfall of goods later, or alternatively, a credit note.

If a computerised system is used to record incoming invoices in the ledgers, it is very important to ensure that any document which is entered in the program is checked and initialled as to its correctness. Once the information is logged in, it is a permanent record and any error will require an adjusting entry to correct it. The responsibility for checking the correctness of the invoice normally lies with either the buying office or the accounts office.

If we delegate this responsibility to the buying office, it would tie in with the copies of the purchase order they raised for the goods in the first place. Copies of the delivery note or goods received note can then be sent to the buying office so that an authorised check can be implemented.

The invoices are then stamped with the date and control grid (see below), to ensure that a full check on each invoice is made. The control grid would have checks for goods received, price terms and calculations. Each check should be initialled by the person authorised to do so.

Example of control grid

CONTROL GRID	**INITIALS**
Date invoice received	
Internal reference no.	
Order price check	
Extensions check	
Goods received check	

CONTROL GRID

	INITIALS
Invoice date	AJ
Internal reference no.	JE
Order price check	WK
Extensions check	CT

Slazenger Sports
Denby Dale
WAKEFIELD
West Yorkshire

Vat Reg. 144 9842 84
Telephone 01204 664555
Telex 669944 88

INVOICE

No. 428754
Date 12 December, 19

R Pearce Sports Ltd
77 Penhill Road
POOLE BH40 165

Your order no. 678/92 Date 03/12/ Tax point 12 December, 19

Quantity	Details	Cat.No.	Price/unit	Goods	Net value
100	Young Master balls	X448	8.40	840.00	642.00
60	Young Master boots	X568	11.25	675.00	540.00
10	Master Goal posts	X442	15.00	150.00	120.00
			Total goods		1 302.00
			Vat		227.85
			Invoice total		1 529.85

Invoice illustrating use of control grid

To summarise an example of procedure when an invoice is received:

1 The invoice is stamped with a control grid for checking purposes.
2 The invoice is dated and given a reference number.
3 The order price check confirms the purchase order details as to price, quantity, discounts, delivery charges etc.
4 The extensions are checked to see if the invoice is arithmetically correct in terms of quantity, price per unit, gross amount, discount etc.
5 A goods received note check is to ensure that the goods actually did arrive in store.
6 Once the grid is initialled and accepted as correct, it is passed to the accounts office for recording and payment.

Any errors arising from these checks could be entered on an invoice action form. The buyer or supervisor can then contact the supplier for any correcting procedure to be followed through. As we shall see in Chapter 18, computerisation can help not only in speeding up the inputting of information and producing appropriate documentation. As the example of Ford's purchase system illustrates, it can also help to simplify the procedures and amount of paperwork involved (page 189).

10.4 The calculation of Vat

The standard rate of Vat charged on goods and services may vary from one year to another depending on the decision made by the Chancellor of the Exchequer when he presents his budget in the Autumn Statement. Often the value of goods and services have the Vat *inclusive* in the amount. If we wanted to extract the Vat from sales or purchases at the rate of 17.5 per cent, the formula is:

$$\frac{17.5}{117.5} = \frac{7}{47} = \text{Vat charged}$$

Example: What is the Vat on sales of £423?

$$\text{sales} \quad \frac{423 \times 7}{47} = \pounds 63.00 \text{ Vat}$$

Therefore goods value excluding Vat = £360.

The Vat is always charged on the net value of the goods, that is, after any trade or cash discounts have been deducted. For example on the following invoice:

	£	£
20 units £6.00 each:	120.00	
less trade discount 25%	30.00	90.00
Vat		15.75
Total		105.75

10.5 Cash discounts and Vat

If the supplier also offered the buyer a cash discount to encourage prompt payment on the invoice, the Vat calculation is adjusted to take this into account for example:

A supplier offers a cash discount of 5 per cent if the bill is paid within 30 days of the invoice date. The invoice for goods is £100 less 10 per cent trade discount.

The 5 per cent discount is deducted from the net purchase for Vat calculation:

	£	£
Net purchase	90.00	
less 5%	4.50	85.50
(or £90 × 0.95)		
Vat 17.5%: £85.50 × 17.5%		= 14.96

The Vat charge is now £14.96 (rather than £15.75).

The value of the invoice would now be:

	£	£
Purchases	100.00	
less 10% trade discount	10.00	
	90.00	
add Vat 17.5%	14.96	104.96

The buyer would only deduct the cash discount of £4.50 if the invoice was paid within the specified period, in this case, 30 days of the invoice date.

Check the invoice from Slazenger on the previous page. Can you calculate the trade discount? How would the Vat change and therefore the total value of the invoice, if a cash discount of 5 per cent was offered?

Check:
Invoice is incorrect, goods X448 net value £672 (not £642)

Trade discount 20%

Goods	£1 332.00
Vat	£221.44
Total	£1 553.44

10.6 The tax point

When companies are registered for Vat they are legally bound to charge Vat on their invoices to their customers on any goods or services levied with Vat, as discussed in the previous chapter.

Because of this, the tax point needs to be clearly indicated on the invoice and is usually the invoice date. The date of the tax point shows when the title for the goods passes from the seller to the buyer. Thus when the Vat return (F100) is completed to the Customs & Excise, the date of the tax point will dictate the period the purchase is made.

For cash sales over the counter, the tax point occurs simultaneously when the goods are paid for and will be the date on the till roll.

Summary
An incoming invoice must always be checked for accuracy and correctness. A control grid stamped on invoices helps to regulate this procedure. If an incorrect document is entered in the accounts, time is wasted making the appropriate adjustments. The Vat tax point indicates the date a sale or purchase goes through and when the title of the goods passes from the supplier to the buyer. When calculating Vat at the standard rate, it is always based on the net value of goods, that is, after discounts are deducted.

Questions

1 Many manufacturers find it essential to complete a goods received note from the delivery note. What is a grn and explain how it could save the business money. (10.2)

2 How is a pro forma invoice different from other invoices? (10.2)

3 A control grid is stamped on incoming invoices. What purpose does it serve? (10.3)

4 The following refers to details of invoices received from suppliers. You are to check the value of the Vat at 17.5 per cent and then add up the totals across and down. The carriage is to be paid by the buyer where stated. (10.4)

	Supplier	Invoice	Value £	Carriage £	Vat £	Total
05	Metro	2483	180	10	33.25	
11	Auto	4933	60		10.50	
15	Slazenger	248375	244		42.70	
22	Metro	2978	125	10	23.62	
25	Dunlop	4735	308	15	56.52	

5 The following supplier's invoice No. 2895 is found to be *inaccurate* when checked. Can you calculate what the real cost should have been?

Qty	Details	Price/Unit	Gross	Net value
300	Auto Sports kits	£4.20	£1 260	£945.00
			Vat	£165.37
				£1 110.37

Terms: 25% trade discount.
5% Cash discounted is deducted if the account is paid within 21 days of the invoice. (10.4–5)

6 Outline what action you would take when you have discovered the discrepancy in Question 5 above. (10.3)

7 A trainee does not clearly understand why the tax point is required on invoices. Briefly explain its significance. (10.6)

11 Purchases on credit (2): the purchases journal

Objectives

On completing this section you should:

- understand why the purchases journal is used
- recognise that the invoice is the prime document of entry to the purchases journal
- understand the function of the purchase ledger control account
- understand posting procedures from the purchases journal to ledgers.

Context

Chapter 10 explains the basic documentation used in credit purchases. Chapter 5 covers the appropriate rules for recording transactions in the ledgers.

11.1 Introduction

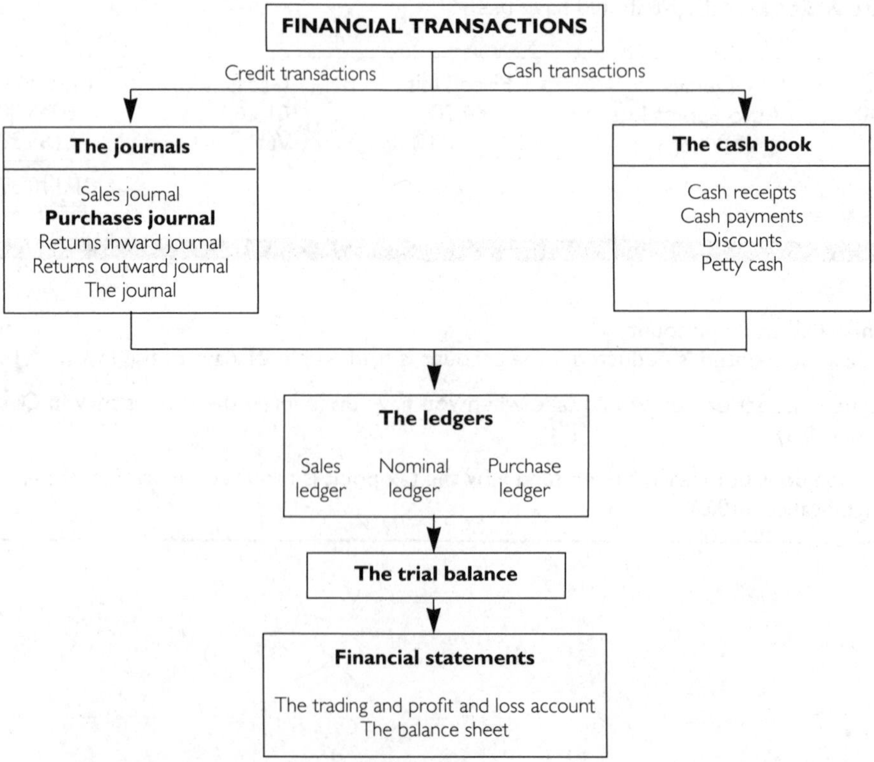

Fig. 11.1 The purchase journal in business accounting systems

As we have seen, when invoices are received from suppliers following the purchase of goods, the purchasing department needs to check the details against the original purchase requisition to ensure that the terms, conditions and price are as agreed.

The goods received in stores also need to be checked to ensure that all aspects are in order in terms of quantity, type and condition of goods. When these details are verified, the invoices received may then be sent to the accounts department for recording in the appropriate ledgers.

Credit notes are used when returns or allowances are made against invoices and have the effect of reducing the balance of a supplier's account. Credit notes from suppliers represent returns outward and details need to be checked against the original invoice to verify value, trade and cash discounts, and Vat. When these are verified, the note is passed to accounts for ledger recording. Returns are discussed in the next chapter.

Monthly statements from suppliers of goods or services, summarise the transactions between the buyers and sellers. Statements received from suppliers (creditors) must be checked against the details of the supplier's account in the purchase ledger, before any payment is made.

An illustration of how a properly checked purchase invoice from a supplier is then processed is shown below. Details are entered into the purchases journal before being posted to the purchase and

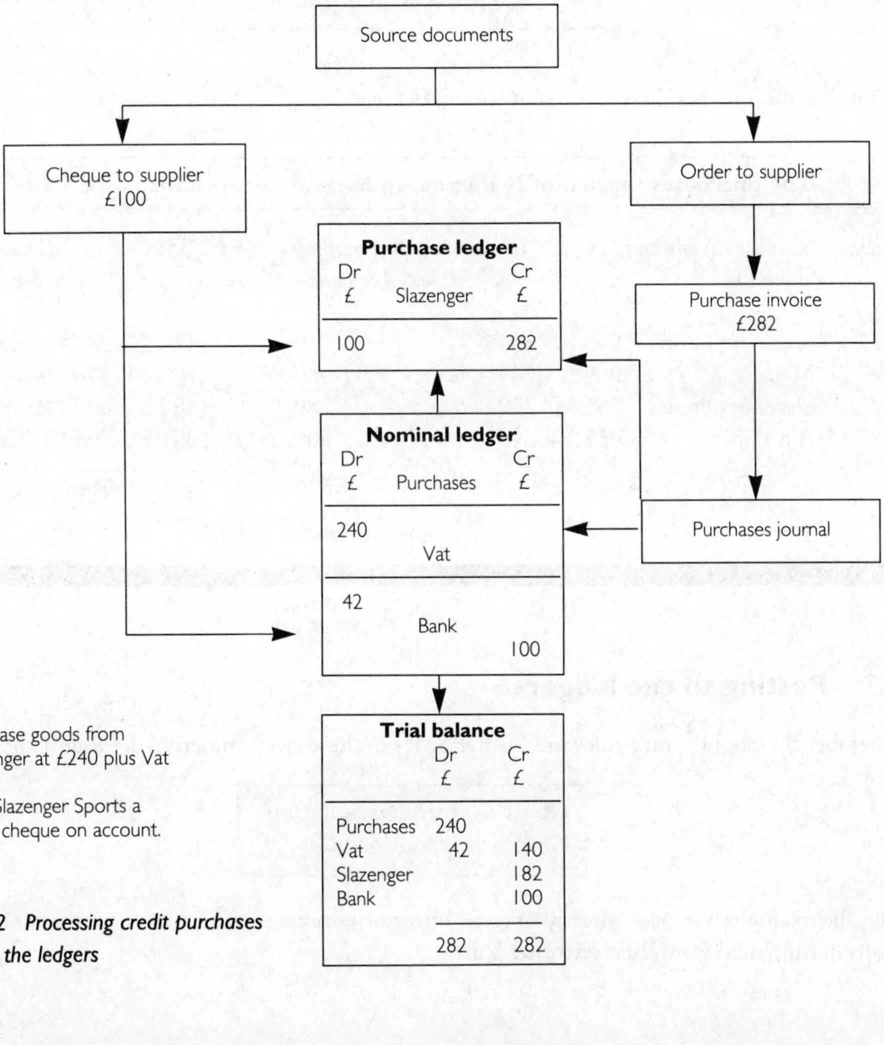

Notes:
a) Purchase goods from Slazenger at £240 plus Vat £42.
b) Paid Slazenger Sports a £100 cheque on account.

Fig. 11.2 Processing credit purchases through the ledgers

nominal ledgers. The illustration also shows how payment to a supplier is dealt with through the ledgers. We will now go through the process in more detail.

11.2 Entering details into the purchases journal

Details for entry into the purchases journal will be extracted from the purchase invoice. Generally, the details are very similar to those for a sales journal:

- Date of purchase
- Invoice no.
- Supplier's name
- Supplier's account number
- The net purchase values
- Vat (if charged)
- The total value of the invoice

A typical layout of a purchases journal is shown below:

The purchases journal of R Pearce, sports shop proprietor (with Vat)

Date	*Supplier's name and account no.*		*Invoice no.*	*Net purchases account*	*Vat 17.5% account*	*Total value*
				£	£	£
12/7	Slazenger Sports	P65	334597	240	42	282 Cr supplier
15/7	Metre	P60	78568	400	70	470 Cr supplier
23/7	Slazenger Sports	P65	379442	280	49	329 Cr supplier
25/7	Auto Sports	P55	2121	600	105	705 Cr supplier
				1 520	266	1 786
				Dr Purchases	Dr Vat	

11.3 Posting to the ledgers

Remember the double entry rules in Chapter 5. From these, we can derive the following:

Debit the **purchases** account
Credit the **creditors** account

Using the examples we have already entered into our purchases journal, we can show the posting process in simplified form, first **without Vat**:

		Debit	Credit	Balance
		£	£	£
Slazenger Sports account				
12/7	Purchases		240	240 Cr
23/7	Purchases		280	520
Metre account				
15/7	Purchases		400	400 Cr
Auto Sports account				
25/7	Purchases		600	600 Cr
Purchases account				
30/7	Creditors	1 520		1 520 Dr

If we **include Vat** and show the full process to the purchase and nominal ledgers, we would see:

Purchase ledger

		Debit	Credit	Balance
		£	£	£
Slazenger Sports account P65				
12/7	Purchases		240.0	
	Vat		42.0	282 Cr
23/7	Purchases		280.0	
	Vat		49.0	611
Metre account P60				
15/7	Purchases		400.0	
	Vat		70.0	470 Cr
Auto Sports account P55				
25/7	Purchases		600.0	
	Vat		105.0	705 Cr

Nominal ledger (N/L)

		Debit	Credit	Balance
		£	£	£
Purchases account N35				
30/7	Creditors	1 520		1 520 Dr
Vat account N30				
30/7	Creditors	266		266 Dr

NOTE

The double entry:

1 Credit each creditor's account (in the P/L) with purchases+Vat.
2 Debit the total value of purchases (in the N/L) to the purchases account (excluding Vat). Debit the total value of Vat (in the N/L) to the Vat account.

11.4 Purchases, Vat and the use of the purchase ledger control account

On 1 August, the balances in the books of R Pearce were:

Purchase ledger:	£	*Nominal ledger:*	£
Slazenger Sports	594.1 Cr	Purchases account	2 840.0 Dr
Metre	460.0 Cr	Vat account	147.9 Cr
Auto Sports	690.0 Cr	*Purchase ledger control	1 744.1 Cr
International	—		
	1 744.1		

The purchase ledger control account represents a total account of all creditors in the purchase ledger (£1 744.10). It is used as a cross-checking device and as a measure of control. A check can be made to make sure that the individual balances of the purchase ledger are verified with the purchase ledger control account. Control accounts are discussed in Chapter 20.

11.5 The journals and ledgers in action

To reinforce what we have learnt so far, let us see how a range of transactions affect the journal and ledger entries we have so far:

During the month of August, purchase invoices were received from the following suppliers:

	Invoice no.	*Date*	*Net purchases* £	(+ *Vat*) 17.5%
Metre	88735	5/8	400	
Metre	88956	10/8	860	
International	444497	21/8	600	
Auto Sports	3765	27/8	200	

At the end of August, cheques were sent to the following:

	£	£
Slazenger Sports	250	
Metre	1 000	
Auto Sports	500	1 750

REQUIRED:

1 Prepare the purchases journal for the month of August.
2 Record all the appropriate details in the ledgers of R Pearce.

The purchases journal of R Pearce for August PJ8

Date	*Supplier's name and account no.*	*Invoice no.*	*Net purchases account*	*Vat 17.5% account*	*Total value*
			£	£	£
5/8	Metre	88735	400	70.0	470.0 Cr supplier
10/8	Metre	88956	860	150.5	1 010.5 Cr supplier
21/8	International	444497	600	105.0	705.0 Cr supplier
27/8	Auto Sports	3765	200	35.0	235.0 Cr supplier
			2 060	360.5	2 420.5
		Dr Purchases	Dr Vat		Cr Purchase ledger control

Purchase ledger

		Folio	*Debit*	*Credit*	*Balance*
			£	£	£
Slazenger Sports account P65					
1/8	Balance				594.1 Cr
30/8	Bank	C9	250		344.1
Metre Sports account P60					
1/8	Balance				460.0 Cr
5/8	Purchases	PJ8		400.0	
	Vat			70.0	930.0
10/8	Purchases	PJ8		860.0	
	Vat			150.5	1 940.5
30/8	Bank	C9	1 000		940.5
Auto Sports account P55					
1/8	Balance				690.0 Cr
27/8	Purchases	PJ8		200.0	
	Vat			35.0	925.0
30/8	Bank	C9	500		425.0
International account P70					
1/8	Balance				—
21/8	Purchases	PJ8		600.0	
	Vat			105.0	705.0 Cr

The schedule of creditors for August:

	£	£
Slazenger Sports	344.1	
Metre	940.5	
Auto Sports	425.0	
International	705.0	2 414.6

Nominal ledger

		Folio	Debit £	Credit £	Balance £
Purchases account N35					
1/8	Balance				1 520.0 Dr
30/8	Creditors	PJ8	2 060.0		3 580.0
Vat account N30					
1/8	Balance				147.9 Cr
30/8	Creditors	PJ8	360.5		212.6 Dr
*Purchase ledger control account N45**					
1/8	Balance				1 744.1 Cr
30/8	Purchases and Vat	PJ8		2 420.5	4 164.6
30/8	Bank	C9	1 750.0		2 414.6
Bank account (extract from cash book)					
30/8	Creditors			1 750.0	1 750.0 Cr

NOTE: The balances between the schedule of creditors and the purchase ledger control account agree (£2 414.6). The double-entry aspect is therefore verified. When the trial balance is prepared, the control account balances will be entered to represent the total of debtors and creditors.

Summary

The purchases journal is used as a prime source of entry to record purchases on credit from suppliers' invoices. Routine purchases can be summarised together as we saw with the sales journal, to facilitate posting to the purchase and nominal ledgers. The function of the control account is to act as a cross check between the schedule of creditors in the purchase ledger and the control account in the nominal ledger. Now try the following questions which consolidate skills learnt in Chapter 10 with those learnt in this chapter.

Questions

1 The following supplier's invoices were received by R Pearce, for September:

		Invoice no.	Value £	Vat 17.5% £
7/9	Slazenger	84552	480	
12/9	Auto	5553	100	
15/9	Slazenger	84995	500	
23/9	Metre	2333	320	
29/9	Auto	6541	400	

REQUIRED (11.2–3):

a) Prepare the purchases journal for the month of September.
b) To which ledger are the individual accounts posted? On which side of the account?
c) How are the totals of this journal posted?

2 The credit purchases of stock for January were as follows:

Date	*Supplier account*	*Invoice no. received*	*Gross purchases*	*Net purchases*	*Vat*	*Total*
		£	£	£	£	£
Jan 5	Underwood Mills Ltd	3046	1 000	800	114.00	
7	Illingworth & Edwards	29851	1 200	960	136.89	
10	Milburn & Harris Ltd	4367	500	425	62.16	
15	Underwood Mills Ltd	4768	380	304	43.32	
20	Illingworth & Edwards	34420	530	424	68.42	
25	Snow Material Supplies	2321	240	204	29.84	

Check the accuracy of the invoices before totalling the columns. Underwood Mills Ltd and Illingworth & Edwards give 20 per cent trade discount and offer 5 per cent cash discounts. Milburn & Harris and Snow Supplies give 15 per cent trade discount and offer 5 per cent cash discounts.

REQUIRED:

a) Total the columns across and down after checking the accuracy of the Vat calculations. Correct any which may be inaccurate. Vat is at 15% in this question. (10.4–5)
b) Which of the above figures would be posted to the nominal ledger and to which accounts? (11.3)

3 The details of an invoice received by R Pearce were as follows:

From: Sports Ltd
10 Cricket bats; Code 55; Unit price £22 each.

Trade discount	25 per cent
Cash discount	5 per cent (if paid within 28 days)
Vat	17.5 per cent

REQUIRED:

a) Calculate the net value of the invoice (including Vat). (10.4–5)
b) If the facts are recorded in the books of R Pearce, which ledgers would be used? (11.3)

4

Purchases day book – ABC Company

Date	*Supplier*	*Invoice no.*	*Men's shoes*	*Women's shoes*	*Children's shoes*	*Vat*	*Total creditor*
		£	£	£	£	£	
3/2	Footwear Ltd	F2236	120			18.00	138.00
6/2	FH&W	08476			95	14.25	109.25
7/2	Country Casual	14279		75		11.25	86.25
14/2	Footwear Ltd	F2239	210			31.50	241.50
16/2	FH&W	08979			190	28.50	218.50
21/2	Footwear Ltd	F2240	525			78.75	603.75
28/2	Jones Leather	26011		270		40.50	310.50
			855	345	285	222.70	1 707.75

How would the following entries be posted to the ledgers? (11.3)
a) Each supplier's account;
b) The total sum of men's, women's and children's shoes
c) Check the accuracy of figures down and across. At what rate is Vat charged?

5 Suppliers' account balances on 1 September in the books of R Pearce were:

	£
Metre	800 Cr
Auto	500 Cr
Dunlop	420 Cr
P/L control a/c	1 720 Cr

In September, Pearce bought on credit:

		Invoice	£
8/9	Metre	2 775	1 200+Vat 17.5%
12/9	Auto	7 884	680+Vat 17.5%
17/9	Auto	8 552	600+Vat 17.5%
23/9	Dunlop	11 447	300+Vat 17.5%

On 30 September, Pearce sent cheques to:

	£
Metre	1 000
Auto	1 000
Dunlop	420

REQUIRED (11.2–4):
a) The purchases journal for September.
b) The purchase ledger accounts for each supplier.
c) The purchase ledger control account, as it would appear in the nominal ledger.
d) The purchases and Vat accounts in the nominal ledger. (Commence each with a zero balance.)

6 The undermentioned credit purchases were made on 1 July

	List price £
Royal Engineering Co	1 400
Preston Builders Ltd	1 700
Edward & Smith Co	1 300

The first two companies give a trade discount of 25 per cent off the list price. Edward & Smith give 20 per cent trade discount. All purchases are subject to 15 per cent Vat.

REQUIRED (11.2–4):
a) Write up the purchases journal showing net price, Vat and the total charged to each customer.
b) When posting to the appropriate ledgers, state how the accounts would be posted from the journal.

(Royal Society of Arts)

The following questions consolidate and extend your skills:

7 The following supplier's invoices were received by R Pearce, for October:

		Invoice no.	*Value £*	*Vat*
10/10*	Slazenger	94555	460	+ 17.5%
14/10	Metre	3342	300	+ 17.5%
17/10	Auto	6553	220	+ 17.5%
22/10	Auto	6589	120	+ 17.5%
24/10*	Slazenger	98993	500	+ 17.5%
27/10	Metre	3873	360	+ 17.5%
29/10	Auto	7541	400	+ 17.5%

REQUIRED:

a) Prepare the purchases journal for the month of October. *Note that Slazenger allows a cash discount of 5 per cent on their invoices and this affects Vat calculations.

b) Post the relevant details to the purchase and nominal ledgers. Commence each account with a zero balance. Open the appropriate control account.

8 The following sales and purchases were made by Smithers during the month of May

5 May	Sold three desks the list price of which was £150 each on credit to Ace Furnishings. Trade discount was given at the rate of 33⅓ per cent.
10 May	Sold two dining suites list price £360 each less trade discount of 25 per cent on credit to Comfy Chair Co.
18 May	Purchased the following goods on credit from The Top Woodworkers: 24 kitchen chairs list price £12 each, trade discount 25 per cent; 12 wall cupboards list price £10 each, trade discount 20 per cent.

All transactions are subject to Vat at 15 per cent and cash discount is neither given nor received. In addition to the above, Smithers *received an invoice* for £110 on 20 May from Jones. This was for shop fittings supplied for use within the business and charged Vat at 15 per cent.

REQUIRED:

a) Calculate the net value of the invoice in each of the four instances mentioned above.

b) Write up the sales account, purchases account, shop fittings and Vat account for the month of May. Your Vat account should show the amount owing to/by the Customs & Excise as at 31 May.

(Royal Society of Arts)

12 The returns journals

Objectives

On completing this section you should:

- understand why the returns inward and returns outward journals are used
- recognise that the credit note is the prime document for the returns journal
- understand posting procedures from the journals to ledgers.

Context

Chapter 6 puts the returns journals in the context of business accounting systems as a whole.

12.1 Introduction

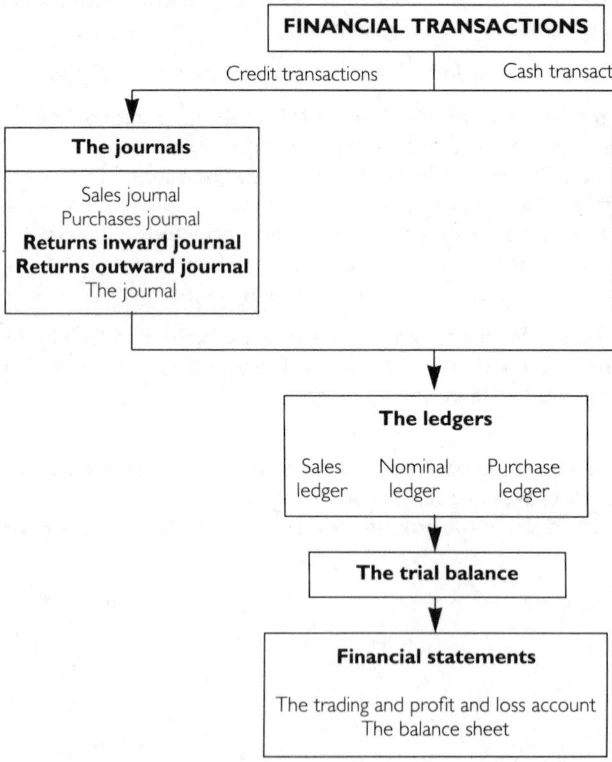

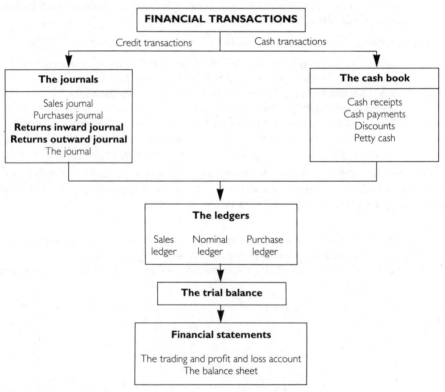

Fig. 12.1 The returns journals

When goods are sent out to customers, some may be returned, perhaps because they are faulty. Similarly, goods purchased may be returned for similar reasons. In these cases, a credit note may be issued by a supplier to the purchaser of the goods. A credit note may also be used to compensate for an error on an invoice where the actual amount to be paid is less than originally stated. A debit note can also be issued where an invoice error results in an underpayment, or where a buyer wishes to compensate a supplier for goods returned. An example of a credit note from R. Pearce in favour of a customer, Slazenger Sports, for goods returned is shown below:

Slazenger Sports

CREDIT NOTE

Denby, Wakefield,
West Yorks

R Pearce
77 Penhill Rd
Penhill
Poole

Vat Reg. 144 9842 84
Telephone 01204 664555
Fax 01204 664544

Credit in respect of

Goods Return ✓
Shortage —
Errors —
Allowances —

Invoice no. 334597
Date 12/7/96

Order no.

Credit note no. C/8957
Date 4/8/96

Quantity	Code no.	Details	Price	Goods value	Trade (20%)	Net value
4	Z238	Tennis R	15	60	12	48.00
	Vat					8.40
		Total credit:				56.40

On the receipt of the credit note, the document should be checked, as always, for accuracy, which would include the same terms and conditions as applied on the invoice such as trade or cash discounts and Vat.

The returns journals (commonly referred to as returns day books) are:

Returns inward journal:	For returns or allowances to customers. Credit note sent to customer.
The double entry:	Debit the returns inward account, (and Vat if applicable); Credit the customer's account.

Returns outward journal:	For returns or allowances from suppliers. Credit note received from supplier or Debit note sent to the supplier
The double entry:	Debit the supplier's account; Credit the returns outward account, (and Vat if applicable).

The credit note has the effect of reducing the value of either a customer's or supplier's account for goods or services which have been returned. On the following pages, the process for returns inward from customers and the returns outward to suppliers is illustrated by diagrams. The credit note in both cases is the originating document.

12.2 Returns inward from customers

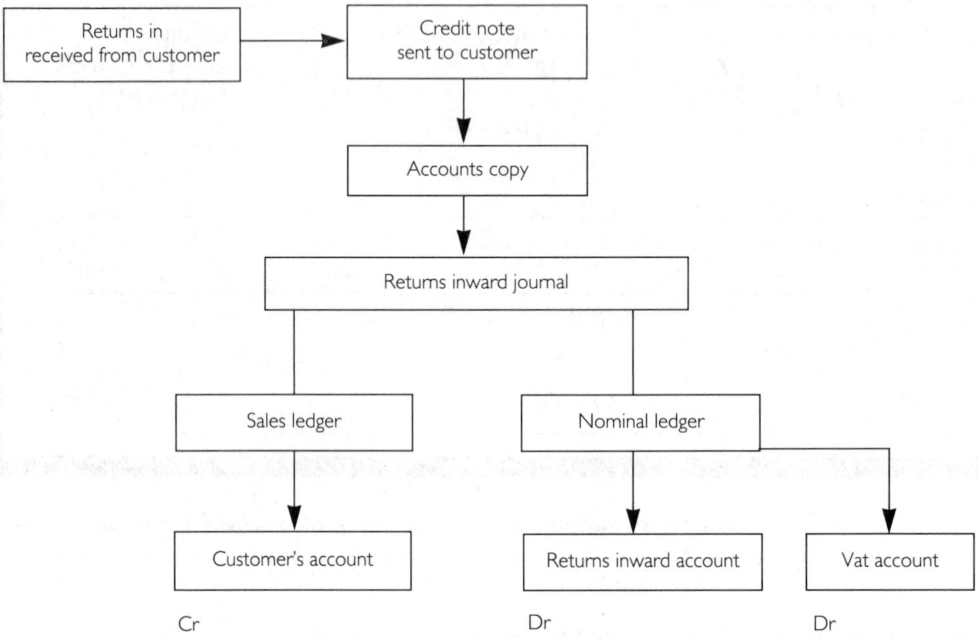

Fig. 12.2 Dealing with returns inward

The documentation procedure for returns inward commences with a credit note raised by the sales office in response to goods returned by a customer. A copy of the credit note is retained in the sales office for the file and a further copy is sent to accounts for recording in the returns inward journal and ledgers.

The credit note will again be the source document for entry in the accounting books, that is, the returns inward journal and subsequent posting to the ledgers. The sales ledger for the customer's account and the nominal ledger for the returns inward and Vat accounts.

12.3 Returns outward to suppliers

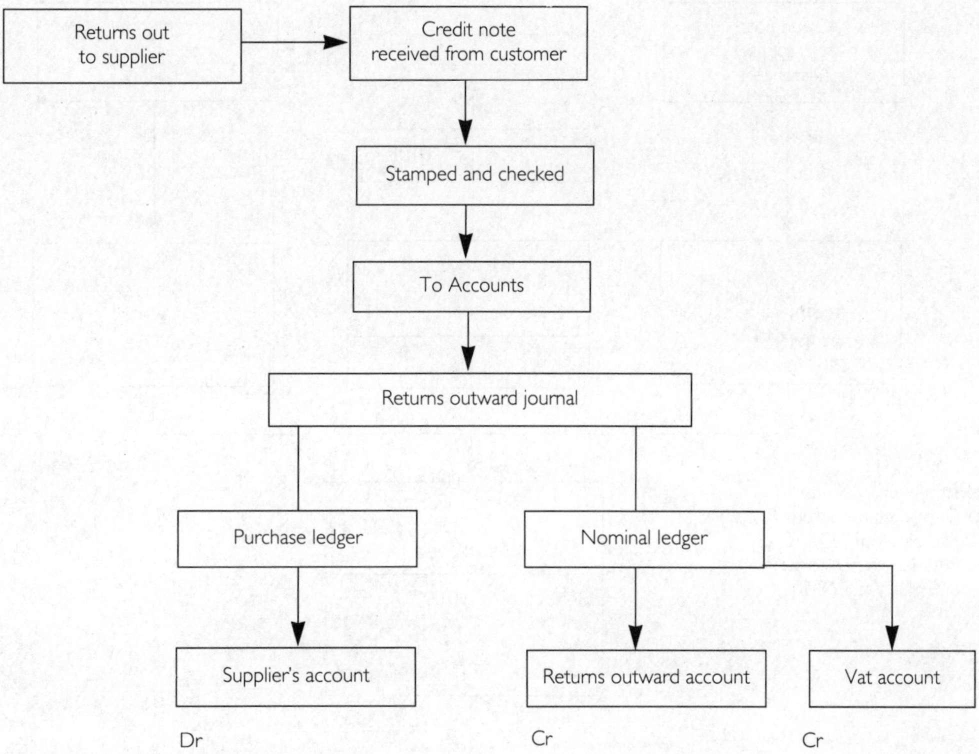

Fig. 12.3 Dealing with returns outward

The documentation procedure for returns outward commences with the return of goods back to the supplier. A credit note is raised by the supplier in response to goods returned by the customer. The credit note is received into the buying office and is stamped and checked for accuracy before it is passed to the accounts office for recording.

The credit note will then be the source document for entry in the accounting books, that is, the returns outward journal and subsequent posting to the ledgers: the purchase ledger for the supplier's account and the nominal ledger for the returns outward and Vat accounts.

The process of entering credit note details into the journals and ledgers are shown overleaf:

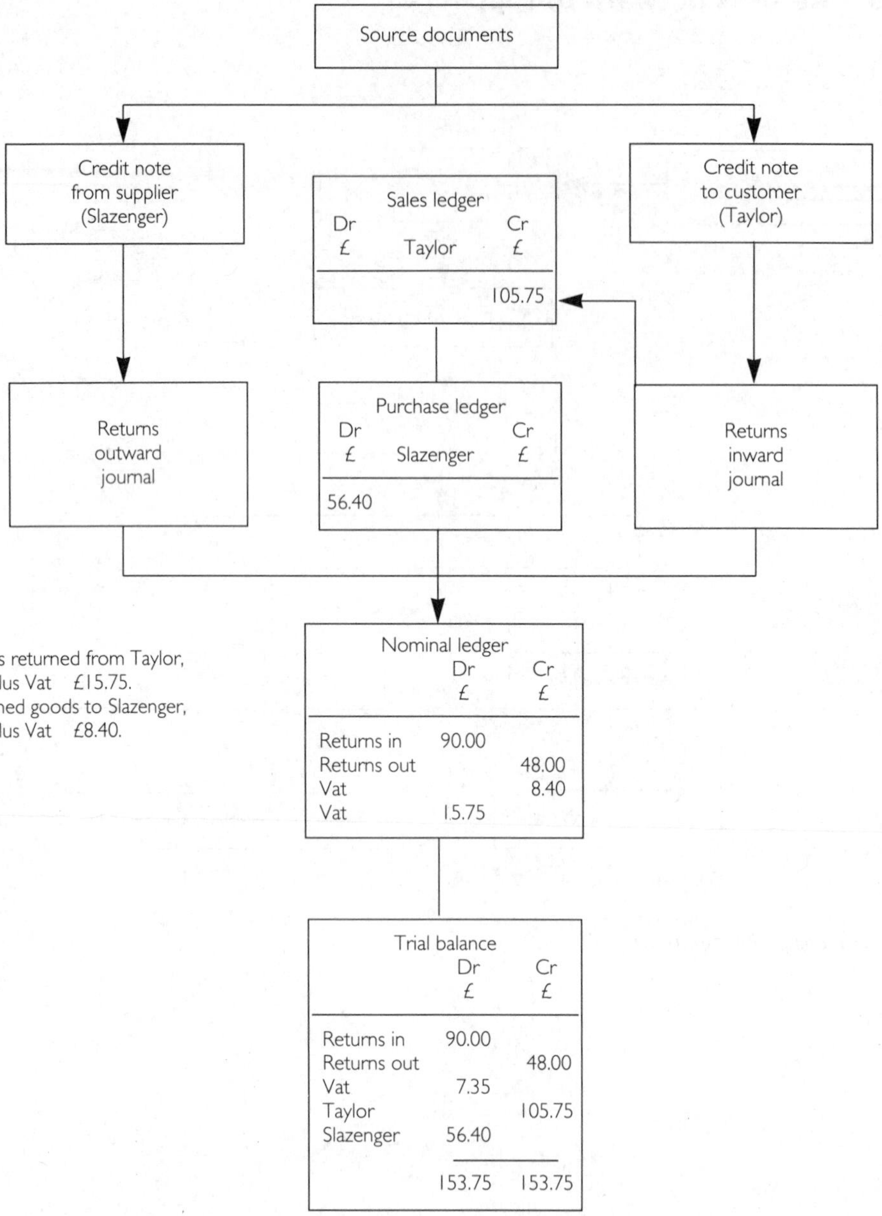

Notes:
a) Goods returned from Taylor, £90 plus Vat £15.75.
b) Returned goods to Slazenger, £48 plus Vat £8.40.

Fig. 12.4 Processing returns through the ledgers

We will now look in more detail at how details are recorded in the journals and ledgers.

12.4 Entering details into the returns outward journal

During the month of August, R Pearce sent goods back to two of his suppliers, Slazenger Sports and

Metre. The returns outward journal recording these returns and corresponding entries in the ledgers are shown below:

Returns outward journal of R Pearce

RO4

Date	*Supplier's account*	*Credit note no.*	*Returns outward account*	*Vat 17.5% account*	*Total value*
			£	£	£
4/8	Slazenger	8 957	48	8.40	56.40 Dr Supplier
25/8	Metre	43 335	50	8.75	58.75 Dr Supplier
			98	17.15	115.15
			Cr Returns out a/c	Cr Vat a/c	Dr Purchase ledger control a/c

Purchase ledger

		Folio	*Debit*	*Credit*	*Balance*
			£	£	£
Slazenger Sports account P65					
1/8	Balance				594.10 Cr
4/8	Returns out	RO4	48.00		
	Vat		8.40		537.70
Metre account P60					
1/8	Balance				460.00 Cr
25/8	Returns out	RO4	50.00		
	Vat		8.75		401.25

Nominal ledger

		Folio	*Debit*	*Credit*	*Balance*
			£	£	£
Returns outward account N44					
1/8	Balance				—
30/8	Creditors	RO4		98.00	98.00 Cr
Vat account N50					
1/8	Balance				147.90 Cr
30/8	Creditors	RO4		17.15	165.05
Purchase ledger control account N45					
1/8	Balance				1 744.10 Cr
30/8	Returns and Vat		115.15		1 628.95

NOTE

The double entry:

1. Debit: each creditor's account with returns and Vat Purchase ledger control account £115.15

2. Credit: returns outward account £98.00 Vat account £17.15

12.5 Entering details into the returns inward journal

During the month of August, R Pearce had goods returned to him from two of his customers, Taylor and Johnson because the goods were flawed. The returns inward journal is prepared from the credit notes raised by Pearce and is shown below:

R12

Date	*Supplier's account*		*Credit note no.*	*Returns outward account*	*Vat 17.5% account*	*Total value*	
				£	£	£	
15/8	C Taylor	S12	545	90	15.75	105.75	Cr Customer
23/8	M Johnson	S08	546	100	17.50	117.50	Cr Customer
				190	33.25	223.25	
				Dr Returns inward a/c	Dr Vat a/c		Cr Sales ledger control a/c

Sales ledger

		Folio	*Debit*	*Credit*	*Balance*
			£	£	£
C Taylor account S12					
1/8	Balance				558.00 Dr
15/8	Returns in			90.00	
	Vat			15.75	452.25
M Johnson account S08					
1/8	Balance				575.00 Dr
23/8	Returns in	R12		100.00	
	Vat			17.50	457.50

Nominal ledger

		Folio	*Debit*	*Credit*	*Balance*
			£	£	£
Returns inward account N41					
1/8	Balance				—
30/8	Debtors	R12	190.00		190.00 Dr
Vat account N50					
1/8	Balance				147.90 Cr
30/8	Creditors	R04		17.15	165.05
30/8	Debtors	R12	33.25		131.80
Sales ledger control account N40					
1/8	Balance				1 852.00 Dr
30/8	Returns in	R12		190.00	
	Vat			33.25	1 628.75

NOTE
The double entry:

1. Credit: each debtor's account with returns and Vat Sales ledger control account £223.25
2. Debit: returns inward account £190.00 Vat account £33.25.

Summary

The function of the returns journal is to provide a prime source of entry for the credit note and to facilitate posting to the ledgers. Returns inward is used for customer returns and returns outward for supplier returns. In some cases, a business which requires a credit note from a supplier will initiate a debit note (a debit against the supplier's account) and then confirm it when the credit note arrives.

Questions

1 **R Pearce received goods which had been returned by his customers during September. He sent them the following credit notes:**

		Credit note no.	*Value* £	*Vat 17.5%* £
14/9	D Lewis	C13	60	
22/9	D Smith	C14	120	
28/9	C Taylor	C15	20	

REQUIRED:

a) Prepare the returns inward journal for September.
b) How are the individual accounts posted?
c) How are the totals of the journal posted? (12.2, 5)

2 **Debtors' balances on 1 October in the books of R Pearce were:**

	£
D Lewis	680 Dr
D Smith	1 020 Dr
C Taylor	420 Dr

Balances found in Pearce's nominal ledger on 1 October were:

	£
Returns inward account	775 Dr
Vat account	224 Cr
Sales ledger control account	2 120 Dr

R Pearce sent credit notes to customers who had returned goods to him during October:

			Credit note no.
4/10	D Smith	£44+Vat 17.5%	C16
13/10	D Lewis	£20+Vat 17.5%	C17
28/10	C Taylor	£36+Vat 17.5%	C18

REQUIRED:

a) The returns inward journal for October.
b) The sales ledger accounts of the three debtors.
c) The nominal ledger accounts as listed above. (12.2, 5)

3 R Pearce returned goods to his suppliers in September and received the following credit notes:

		Credit note no.	Value £	Vat 17.5% £
15/9	Slazenger	C44	60	
22/9	Auto	C80	20	
29/9	Metre	C14	100	

REQUIRED:
a) Prepare the returns outward journal for the month of September.
b) How are the individual accounts posted?
c) How are the totals of the journal posted? (12.3–4)

4 Creditors' balances in the books of R Pearce on 1 October were:

	£
Slazenger	885 Cr
Auto	350 Cr
Metre	638 Cr

Balances in Pearce's nominal ledger on 1 October were:

	£
Returns outward account	980 Cr
Vat account	224 Cr
Bought ledger control account	1 873 Cr

R Pearce received the following credit notes during October:

			Credit note
12/10	Slazenger	£60+Vat 17.5%	C79
25/10	Metre	£30+Vat 17.5%	C185
29/10	Auto	£84+Vat 17.5%	C26

REQUIRED:
a) The returns outward journal for the month of October.
b) The purchase ledger accounts of the three creditors.
c) The nominal ledger accounts as listed above. (12.3–4)

The following questions consolidate and extend your skills learnt from this and earlier chapters:

5 D Withers is a wholesaler. The following *credit* transactions took place during the month of May. Enter each transaction in the appropriate book of original entry, total for the month and post to the purchases, sales, returns and Vat accounts in the ledger.

All amounts given are before the addition of Vat, which is to be taken as 15 per cent. All trade purchases are allowed a trade discount of 20 per cent, not yet taken into account in the figures given below. Trade discount is *not* allowed on any sales.

			£
May	1	Purchased stock from T Smithers Ltd	400
	3	Sold stock to W Wilkin	350
	4	Sold stock to T Wilson	300
	11	Returned stock bought on 1 May to T Smithers Ltd	50
	12	Purchased stationery for office use from Paper Co Ltd	150
	14	Purchased office furniture from Office Supplies Ltd	400
	20	T Wilson returned stock	20
	29	Sold stock to W Wilkin	170
	29	Purchased stock from T Smithers Ltd	150

REQUIRED:

a) The appropriate journals for the month of May.
b) The posting of all relevant accounts to the nominal ledger only.

6 On 1 June personal accounts in J Smith's ledger had the following balances:

	£
R Morton	175 Cr
W Pierce	184 Cr
L Appleby	150 Dr
T Shuttleworth	210 Dr
M Vincent	145 Dr

The following transactions took place during the month of June

			£
June	3	Sold goods on credit to T Shuttleworth	150
	4	Sold goods on credit to M Vincent	210
	8	Bought goods on credit from R Morton	470
		Paid R Morton by cheque	175
	9	T Shuttleworth settled his account to date by cheque	
	11	Bought goods on credit from W Pierce	197
	12	Returned goods to R Morton	10
		Sold goods on credit to L Appleby	240
		Sold goods on credit to T Shuttleworth	160
	15	L Appleby returned goods	10
		Returned goods to W Pierce	15
	19	Paid W Pierce by cheque	184
	25	L Appleby paid by cheque	150
	26	Sold goods on credit to M Vincent	310
	29	Bought goods on credit from W Pierce	180
		Sold goods on credit to T Shuttleworth	160
	30	M Vincent returned goods	14
		Paid W Pierce by cheque	182

From the information given above write up the *personal accounts* in J Smith's ledger. To obtain full marks the accounts should be of the three-column type, with columns headed Dr, Cr and balance. The amount of the balance on each account should be calculated afresh after each entry in the account.

Note Day books and nominal ledger accounts are *not* required.
Vat is not charged.

7 Lesley Dawson commenced business on 1 January with capital of £30 000. She put £28 000 into a business bank account and kept the remainder in a cash account as cash in hand. During the first two weeks in January the following business transactions occurred:

January	1	Credit purchases: Green & Co £4 000; Black & Co £2 500.
	2	Purchased fixtures and fittings £6 200, paying by cheque.
	5	Paid by cheque £56, advertising in the local paper.
	6	Paid rent six months in advance, £6 000 by cheque.
	7	Cash sales, £400. Credit sales: Redhill & Co, £3 500.
	8	Wages paid by cheque, £86.
	9	Paid insurance premium for 12 months £400, by cheque.
	12	Credit purchases: Green & Co, £3 000.

13 Paid postage and stationery by cash, £38.
14 Withdrew cash, £500, for personal use.
15 Paid Green & Co 50 per cent of his outstanding balance.
15 Wages paid by cash, £84.
16 Cash sales, £880. Credit sales: Redhill & Co £4 600; Shaw Ltd £2 100.
17 Redhill & Co send a cheque £5 000 on account.
20 Shaw returned £300 goods as unsuitable.
21 We returned £500 goods to Green.

REQUIRED:

a) Prepare the sales and purchases journals for the period to 21 January. Post to the appropriate ledgers.
b) Open appropriate ledger accounts for the business, recording the above transactions. Extract a trial balance as on 21 January.
c) Why is it necessary to have more than a single ledger system for different types of business organisations?

13 Analysed journals

Objectives

On completing this section you should:

- understand how sales or purchases can be analysed
- recognise the value of analysis to the business for sales and stock control
- understand the posting procedure from analysed journals to ledgers.

13.1 Introduction

Many businesses want to know more specific details about what they sell and what they purchase. An off-licence shop, for example, may want to know the different categories of wines and spirits it sells. This will help it to order the correct levels of stock its customers demand. With larger organisations it is absolutely essential for them to have access to information which tells them which lines are selling and which are slow movers. This is linked to their stock control and purchasing departments so that they can order the optimum levels of stock.

If computer programs are used, then the coding of sales and purchases for different items of stock makes the analysis of figures so much more accessible. This gives the business a far greater range of information and a greater degree of efficiency and control. In the following chapter, you will see a basic example of computerised accounts and the analysis of sales into just four categories. Imagine the codes for both sales and purchases to be in hundreds of categories and you then have an idea of the essential nature and use of the computer.

If a manual system of recording is used, the journals can use extra columns to help give greater analysis of figures. These analysed books of original entry are often referred to as 'columnar' day books because of the extra columns required for analysis purposes.

13.2 The analysed sales journal (or day book)

The sales journal can be adapted to give businesses more information. Extra columns may be added to provide sales data for different types of products.

Large wholesalers and retailers need to know how various categories of goods are moving. It is inadequate for them to merely have one total to represent all of their sales. Stores such as Comet and Curry's want to know for example, how their 'white' goods (washing machines, dishwashers, refrigerators) are selling in contrast with their 'brown' goods (televisions, stereos, videos) because they need to know how much profit each of their major categories is earning. Other large retail stores like Argos, WH Smith and Menzies also need to have stock coding systems to help them identify the volume and type of goods which are selling and need stock replacement.

This type of information helps management in their decision-making. It helps them to keep better control of sales and therefore, purchases and stock levels. If some goods are slow moving, these can be more readily identified and action taken to remedy the situation. Department stores also need to know how sales are moving on each of their floors so that slow-moving goods, or inefficient sections can be recognised more quickly and the necessary action taken.

The analysis of sales and indeed purchases, in the following section, is one of the first steps in creating a 'cost centre', that is, grouping costs to a particular section or department, to see how efficient it is in its control and monitoring of costs and to identify if the section is cost effective and profitable. This is discussed in more detail in Chapter 36.

In the analysis of the sales journal on p. 118, sales are identified into four distinct categories, code numbers S161, S162, S163 and S164. The code numbers represent different categories of goods and shows sales for each of them for the month of March.

13.3 Posting to the ledgers

The details from the analysed journal are posted in the same manner as before, although there are more entries in the nominal ledger because of the individual categories of sales.

Each customer's account is posted to the debit side of their account in the sales ledger in the normal way. Each of the sales accounts and Vat account are credited in the nominal ledger. The total amount is debited to the sales ledger control account. Examples from both sales and nominal ledgers are shown below:

Sales ledger

		Folio	*Debit*	*Credit*	*Balance*
			£	£	£
M Johnson account					
3/3	Sales	SD3	199.15		
	Vat		34.85		234.00 Dr
27/3	Sales	SD3	152.00		
	Vat		26.60		412.60
D Lewis account					
5/3	Sales	SD3	320.00		
	Vat		56.00		376.00 Dr
15/3	Sales	SD3	356.60		
	Vat		62.76		795.36

Nominal ledger

		Folio	*Debit*	*Credit*	*Balance*
			£	£	£
Total Sales account S160					
01/3	Balance				2 410.00 Cr
31/3	Debtors	SD3		2 058.07	4 468.07 Cr

(continued)

(continued)

Sales account S161				
01/3 Balance				850.00 Cr
31/3 Debtors	SD3		499.75	1 349.75
Sales account S162				
03/3 Balance				620.00 Cr
31/3 Debtors	SD3		393.00	1 013.00
Sales account S163				
01/3 Balance				520.00 Cr
31/3 Debtors	SD3		466.00	986.00
Sales account S164				
01/3 Balance				420.00 Cr
31/3 Debtors	SD3		699.32	1 119.32
Vat account N50				
01/3 Balance				112.50 Cr
31/3 Debtors	SD3		360.52	473.02
Sales ledger control account N60				
01/3 Balance				3 200.50 Dr
31/3 Sales, Vat	SD3	2 418.59		5 619.09

13.4 The analysed purchases journal (or day book)

Some businesses will prefer to maintain a purchase journal which records all their outstanding invoices whether for goods or services. All incoming invoices would be entered in the purchase journal in a similar way to that of entering data in the sales journal.

In the example that follows on p. 119, the analysis journal of R Pearce has distinct columns to record purchases, stationery, motor expenses, light and heat, telephone and carriage inwards, as well as a total amount and a Vat column.

The supplier's invoices, whether for goods or services, will be posted to the purchase ledger on the credit side of their respective accounts.

Each of the totals will be posted to the nominal ledger on the debit side of their corresponding accounts, that is, for purchases and each of the expenses. The total amount of the purchase journal will be posted to the credit side of the purchase ledger control account.

Date	A/c No.	Customer's details		Invoice number	Total amount £	Vat a/c £	Sales S161 £	Sales S162 £	Sales S163 £	Sales S164 £	Total Sales S160 £
Mar 3	S08	Johnson, M		2642	234 00	34 85	199 15				199 15
4	S09	Kings, B		2643	232 65	34 65		138 00	36 00	24 00	198 00
5	S10	Lewis, D		2644	376 00	56 00	50 00		270 00		320 00
10	S11	Smith, D		2645	460 60	68 60	34 00	58 00		300 00	392 00
15	S10	Lewis, D		2646	419 36	62 76	192 60	132 00	32 00		356 60
18	S21	Wilson, W		2647	300 00	44 68				255 32	255 32
20	S12	Taylor, C		2648	217 38	32 38		65 00		120 00	185 00
27	S08	Johnson, M		2649	178 60	26 60	24 00		128 00		152 00
					2418 59	360 52	499 75	393 00	466 00	699 32	2058 07
					N/L Dr	N/L Cr	N/L Cr	N/L Cr	N/L Cr	N/L Cr	N/L Cr

SD3

Fig. 13.1 The analysis of the sales journal

Date	A/c No.	Supplier's details	Invoice number	Total amount	Vat a/c	Purchases a/c	Stationery a/c	Motor exps. a/c	Light, heat, telephone	Other exps. a/c
Mar 3	P004	Dunlop Sports	2263	141 00	21 00	120 00				
5	P011	Metre	43875	258 50	38 50	220 00				
6	P024	Southern Gas	209/565	56 40					56 40	
10	P018	Long's Garage	423/X	94 00	14 00			80 00		
12	P027	Strings Stationers	98327	79 90	11 90		68 00			
15	P002	Auto Sports	3353 W	338 40	50 40	288 00				
16	P004	Dunlop Sports	2949	188 00	28 00	160 00				
20	P009	Maintenance Services	442	70 50	10 50					60 00
25	P018	Long's Garage	596/X	126 90	18 90			108 00		
28	P022	Rainbow Suppliers	1536	49 35	7 35		42 00			
30	P023	Sondico	3328/12	146 29	21 79	124 50				
				1549 24	222 34	912 50	110 00	188 00	56 40	60 00
				N/L Cr	N/L Dr	N/L Dr	N/L Dr	N/L Dr	N/L Dr	N/L Dr

PD3

Fig. 13.2 The analysis of the purchases journal

13.5 Posting to the ledgers

Examples from both purchase and nominal ledgers are shown below:

Purchase ledger

		Folio	Debit	Credit	Balance
			£	£	£
Dunlop Sports account					
3/3	Purchases	PD3		120.00	
	Vat			21.00	141.00 Cr
16/3	Purchases	PD3		160.00	
	Vat			28.00	329.00
Metre account					
5/3	Purchases	PD3		220.00	
	Vat			38.50	258.50 Cr
Southern Gas account					
6/3	Light and heat	PD3		56.40	56.40 Cr
Long's Garage account					
10/3	Motor expenses	PD3		80.00	
	Vat			14.00	94.00 Cr
25/3	Motor expenses	PD3		108.00	
	Vat			18.90	220.90 Cr

Nominal ledger

		Folio	Debit	Credit	Balance
			£	£	£
Purchase account N15					
01/3	Balance				1 740.00 Dr
31/3	Creditors	PD3	912.50		2 652.50
Stationery account N20					
01/3	Balance				85.00 Dr
31/3	Creditors	PD3	110.00		195.00
Motor expenses account N21					
01/3	Balance				242.50 Dr
31/3	Creditors	PD3	188.00		430.50
Light and heat account N22					
01/3	Balance				145.60 Dr
31/3	Creditors	PD3	56.40		202.00

(continued)

(continued)

Maintenance services account N25

01/3	Balance				142.00 Dr
31/3	Creditors	PD3	60.00		202.00

Vat account N50

01/3	Balance				112.50 Cr
31/3	Debtors	SD3		362.52	475.02
31/3	Creditors	PD3	222.34		252.68

Purchases ledger control account N45

31/3	Purchases & Vat	PD3		1 549.24	1 549.24 Cr

The journals therefore, in columnar format, can provide useful information to the business by identifying various categories of sales, purchases and expenses. The analysis of these figures may help management make more effective decisions.

Summary

All journals may be customised to suit the needs of a business. Extra columns can be used for analysis purposes and this can provide management with very useful information on how stocks are moving. It is essential for large companies to know how each category of sales is performing because this helps in making important marketing decisions. Computer programs can accommodate a whole range of different categories by using code numbers and instant analysis can be printed by simply pressing the right key.

Questions

1 The following invoices were listed in the sales journal of Ray Jackson for the first week in January:

Date	Customer's Account	Invoice Number	Sales Account	Vat Account	Total Debtors Account
3/1	R James	1142	180	31.50	211.50
4/1	D Simpson	1143	200	35.00	235.00
6/1	G Seymour	1143	100	17.50	117.50
6/1	F Forster	1144	360	63.00	423.00
7/1	R James	1145	160	28.00	188.00
7/1	D Simpson	1146	240	42.00	282.00

a) James and Seymour buy category A class goods. James and Simpson buy category B class goods. Prepare an analysed day book to take these categories into account.

b) How will you post the above to the sales and nominal ledgers? (13.2–3)

2 This is a columnar day book of SQ Co Ltd which buys three principal products, footwear, leisure and sporting items:

Date	Supplier Account	Invoice Number	Footwear a/c	Leisure a/c	Sports a/c	Vat a/c	Total a/c
7/1	Foulks Ltd	48735	850	70			
8/1	Johnsons	564/33		350			
9/1	Foulks Ltd	49822	436	164	80		
10/1	Hardcastle	3388	200		325		
10/1	Johnsons	648/33	236	164			
11/1	Dougas Ltd	4422		346			
12/1	Just Sport	1889	140		825		

a) Complete the totals across including the calculation of Vat at the standard rate.
b) Total the figures down and cross check for accuracy.
c) How do you think the totals might be posted to the nominal ledger? (13.3)

3 This is a columnar day book of ABC Co Ltd which sells three principal products, golf, cricket and tennis items:

Date	Customer Account	Invoice Number	Golf a/c	Cricket a/c	Tennis a/c	Vat a/c	Total Debtors
7/1	Faldo	3371	200		120		
8/1	Boycott	3372	300	180			
9/1	Woosnam	3373	480	160	140		
10/1	Bates	3374	240	100	110		
10/1	Gooch	3375	200	480			
11/1	Castle	3376	180	120	74		
12/1	Lyle	3377	240	140	100		

a) Complete the totals across including the calculation of Vat at the standard rate of 17.5%.
b) Total the figures down and cross check for accuracy.
c) The customer's accounts will be posted to the sales ledger in the normal way, how will the nominal ledger entries be posted? (13.3)

4 Prepare an analysis day book which includes columns for purchases, motor expenses, stationery, light, heat and telephone, advertising, Vat and total amount.
The invoices received in March were as follows:

		Invoice no.	Net amount	Vat Rate (add)
4/3	D Mason Ltd goods,	4421	180.00	17.5%
5/3	J Ball & Son goods,	3378/1	200.00	17.5%
8/3	N Anderson goods,	7578	84.00	17.5%
10/3	British Gas	24589/12	148.60	0

12/3	Andrews Motors	231	104.20	17.5%
15/3	Palmers Stationers	289/55	36.50	17.5%
18/3	D Mason Ltd goods,	5783	142.00	17.5%
20/3	Southern Electric	11258/87	96.40	0
22/3	British Telecom	33890/23	112.80	17.5%
27/3	Southern Echo	8553/21	124.00	17.5%
28/3	Andrews Motors	348	136.70	17.5%
31/3	Palmers Stationers	312/55	54.60	17.5%

On completion of the above entries, explain clearly how the individual suppliers of goods and services will be posted as well as each of the total columns. (13.4–5)

The following question consolidates and extends your skills:

5 The following information represents the Sales Day Book of Dawson's Ltd, a seller of furniture in 3 grades, basic, standard and deluxe models. All sales are charged with the standard rate of Vat 17.5%.

Customer Account	Basic Model	Standard Model	Deluxe Model	Total Sales	Vat a/c	Total Debtors
Jackson	200	420	160			
Thompson	125	500	365			
Illingworth	0	0	660			
Rocastle	280	400	820			
James	320	640	1 040			

REQUIRED:

a) Complete the totals of the Sales Day Book for the week ended 7 April (across and down).

b) The following balances are to be entered in the sales ledger on 1 April:

	£
Jackson	740.50 Debit
Thompson	356.75 Debit
Illingworth	125.50 Debit
Rocastle	1 040.50 Debit
James	1 360.00 Debit

c) Post the transactions from the Sales Day Book for the week ended 7 April to the sales ledger. Cheques received included £1 000 from Jackson and £2 000 from James.

d) Post the sales figures and Vat to the nominal ledger using separate sales accounts for each grade of furniture. Assume balances nil on 1 April.

The S/L control account on 1 April was £3 623.25 Dr.

Cross check the control account with the sales ledger.

14 Banking transactions

Objectives

On completing this section you should:

- recognise the various functions and services of banks
- be able to complete documents like the paying in slip (bank giro credit)
- understand payments through the banking system
- appreciate the relationship between the bank and its customers.

14.1 Introduction

The major deposit, or clearing banks in England and Wales are: Barclays, Lloyds, Midland, National Westminster and the Trustee Savings Bank. In Scotland, the Bank of Scotland, the Royal Bank of Scotland and the Clydesdale Bank are the main banks.

The banks deal mainly with receiving deposits of money on one hand and providing overdrafts and loans, on the other. The clearing banks also provide a numerous list of services for their customers which includes: providing home mortgages, foreign currency, night safe deposit, insurance schemes and pension plans. They also act as trustees, investment brokers, financial consultants and provide a wide range of other services.

Increasingly, they have taken an interest in providing loans for housing and are in direct competition with building societies. The societies too, have been able to provide more intense competition with the banks because of the Financial Services Act 1986, giving them greater scope to provide many banking services to their customers.

The clearing banks provide two major types of accounts: the **deposit** account and the **current** account.

With the **deposit** account (or investment account), money can safely be invested, earning interest at various rates depending on how much is deposited and how much notice is given to the bank on withdrawals of cash.

Current accounts are used for operating cheques and making payments through the bank. By having a cheque account, you can arrange to have your bills paid through the bank. The bank can arrange payments by direct debit or standing order to pay for regular expenses such as insurance premiums, rates, gas and electricity and so forth. Increasingly, the banks are providing current accounts which pay interest on balances that are in credit, making them more attractive to customers.

It is essential for all businesses to have a business current account. Deposits of money and the payment of bills by cheque or through the bank assists the business in organising its finances more professionally and with greater security.

The banks also act as important business advisors and are the first stopping place for overdrafts and loan facilities when money is needed to keep the business afloat or to give it adequate liquidity (money it can use to keep on trading). It is inconceivable to imagine any business conducting its affairs without having a bank account of any kind.

14.2 Bank services

The clearing banks offer a wide range of facilities for their customers, some have been already mentioned. A more comprehensive list is as follows:

- The banks provide a safe place for the deposit of money, encouraging savings and paying interest on deposit, investment and even current accounts.
- Banks provide the current account which operates the cheque system. An essential account for all businesses.
- Night safe deposits allow customers to bank out of business hours enabling them to deposit money for safe keeping.
- Cash dispensers placed just outside the bank, provide customers with cash facilities, day or night.
- The bank will arrange payments on your behalf through the bank, such as standing orders, direct debits and bank giro.
- The bank provides overdraft and loan facilities.
- A bank can arrange for its customers to buy or sell stocks and shares on the Stock Market.
- The bank can offer financial advice both to the individual and to businesses.
- The bank can arrange for foreign currency and travellers cheques for customers going abroad.
- It can arrange insurance schemes and pension plans.
- The bank provides mortgages for homes and businesses.
- It will act as executor, trustee and tax advisor, making financial decisions on the deceased estate.
- It will assist businesses on foreign exchange transactions including arranging and receiving payment for the export and import of goods.
- Credit cards are associated with the banks, particularly Access and Barclaycard.

The banks have increasingly been involved in international banking and have considerably widened their service activities, particularly in lending more money for house purchase. The Financial Services Act 1986 has made competition between banks and building societies more intense, each trying to offer their customers the greatest benefit for depositing and borrowing money and for providing the best all-round banking services.

14.3 Going to the bank

In many businesses, particularly shops, it is important not to hold too much cash on the premises. This can only invite possible theft or burglary. It is not surprising, therefore, to find a large number of traders visiting their banks daily to deposit cash, cheques and other valuables, to be credited to their accounts.

When money is to be transferred to the bank, it should be properly organised into convenient bundles so that the bank assistants can quickly and efficiently count and dispose of it.

Notes should be carefully counted and be in their proper denoninations, the Queen's head preferably appearing on the right hand side. Coins should be placed in the appropriate bags in their right denominations: 50p, 20p, 10p etc. All monies, including cheques and sales vouchers, should be taken in security bags which must not be obviously displayed to the public. You must always be careful and discreet.

For example, if you took the following money to the bank:

	£
10 × £20 notes	200.00
30 × £10 notes	300.00
35 × £5 notes	175.00
42 × £1 coins	42.00
11 × 50p coins	5.50
20 × 20p coins	4.00
28 × 10p coins	2.80
60p bronze	0.60
Total	729.90

You would be carrying over £700 in cash to deposit at the bank. You would therefore try to take alternative routes and not go the same identical way each time. For very large sums of money, the business would need to make security arrangements and may hire a security van to make these deposits.

14.4 Recording procedure

Before going to the bank to deposit money, it must first be recorded in the business's books. The cashier or other person responsible for banking, would count up the takings for the day and enter the figures on a form which may be referred to as a 'Daily Takings Sheet' or other suitable title. The figures below are the takings for the week ending 22 February:

Daily Takings Sheet: week ending 22/02

Date	Cheques/PO	Credit card vouchers	Cash	Bank
18/12	151.65		729.90	881.55
19/2		87.50	325.60	413.10
20/2	195.00	55.00	473.00	723.00
21/2	210.60	21.00	480.00	711.60
22/2		32.60	525.00	557.60
Totals	557.25	196.10	2 533.50	3 286.85

Signed by

The cashier or other person responsible would sign the receipts abstract once it has been checked as correct. A bank paying-in-slip for the cash and cheques and a voucher summary form for the credit card vouchers, would be completed and taken to the bank so that the business bank account can be credited.

In the accounts of the business, these daily entries would be recorded in the bank account or cash book on the debit side (receipts). The cash book is discussed in the following chapter.

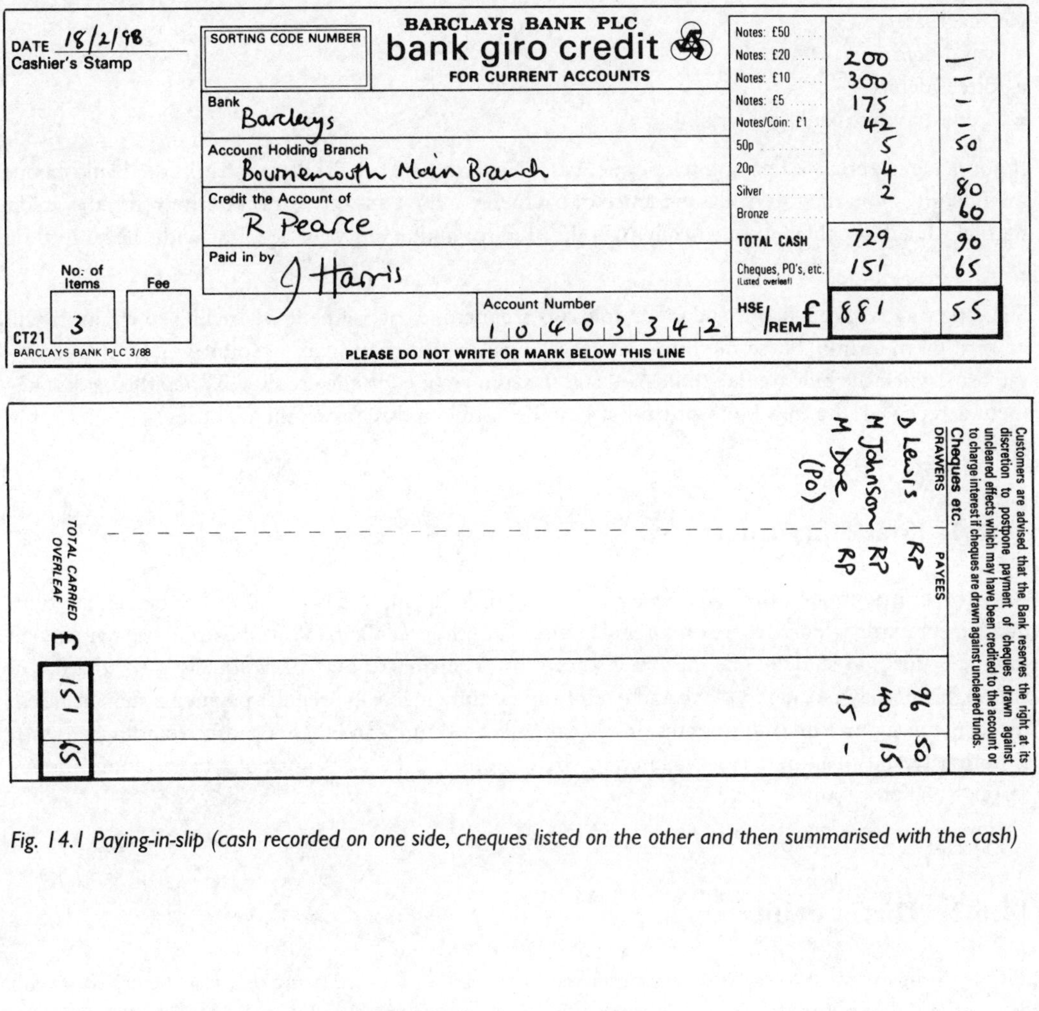
BARCLAYS BANK PLC
bank giro credit
FOR CURRENT ACCOUNTS

DATE 18/2/98
Cashier's Stamp
SORTING CODE NUMBER
Bank: Barclays
Account Holding Branch: Bournemouth Main Branch
Credit the Account of: R Pearce
Paid in by: J Harris
No. of Items: 3
Fee
Account Number: 1 0 4 0 3 3 4 2
CT21
BARCLAYS BANK PLC 3/88
PLEASE DO NOT WRITE OR MARK BELOW THIS LINE

	£	p
Notes: £50		
Notes: £20	200	—
Notes: £10	300	—
Notes: £5	175	—
Notes/Coin: £1	42	—
50p	5	50
20p	4	80
Silver	2	60
Bronze		
TOTAL CASH	729	90
Cheques, PO's, etc. (Listed overleaf)	151	65
HSE / REM £	881	55

Customers are advised that the Bank reserves the right at its discretion to postpone payment of cheques drawn against uncleared effects which may have been credited to the account or to charge interest if cheques are drawn against uncleared funds.

Cheques etc.

DRAWERS	PAYEES	£	p
D Lewis	RP	96	50
M Johnson	RP	40	15
M Doe (PO)	RP	15	-
TOTAL CARRIED OVERLEAF		£ 151	65

Fig. 14.1 Paying-in-slip (cash recorded on one side, cheques listed on the other and then summarised with the cash)

14.5 Authorisation of cheques

When cheques are to be prepared for payment, not just any person can sign a cheque in business. Only those persons authorised to do so. This may be delegated to the cashier or someone with sufficient responsibility to prepare cheques up to a certain figure, for example, £500 or £5 000.

It may be necessary to have two signatures on a cheque for larger sums of money. The greater the value of money, the higher the authorised signature required. It may be that for sums in excess of say, £5 000, that a director of the company needs to also co-sign the cheque before it can be posted to the creditor.

All cheques are now 'crossed', that is they have two vertical parallel lines and the words *Account* or *A/c payee* in the centre. This instructs the receiving bank that the cheque must be paid into a bank account and cannot be exchanged for cash over the counter.

14.6 Payments through the bank

Remember that the bank can arrange a great many payments to suppliers and other creditors. The principal means of payment through the bank, other than by cheque, or special cheque card such as Connect, are:

- standing orders
- direct debits
- credit transfer (bank giro credit).

If you have experienced paying telephone, gas, electricity and other bills at a bank, the bank stamps the bill, gives you the top half as evidence of payment, and retains the tear off bottom slip, the credit transfer. The bank then automatically pays the creditor and debits your account with the sum to be paid.

Standing orders, direct debits and credit transfers are methods of payment where bills to creditors will be paid by the bank. These methods are very similar in that the payers' account will be debited by the bank when the bills are due to be paid and the sum credited to the creditor. When the bank statement is received, the cash book or bank account must be updated with these entries.

14.6.1 Standing orders

A customer may request the bank, using a standing order form, to pay on his or her behalf, any sum due to a creditor which occurs on a regular basis. It authorises the bank to make such payments on the dates due and to debit the customer's account. The sum to be paid is usually a fixed amount although this may be altered on the advice of the customer. Ideally, regular payments such as house mortgage, insurance premiums, rates or any other expenditure can be arranged by standing order. It is both safe and of utmost convenience to the customer as he does not need to send any money through the post to meet these bills.

14.6.2 Direct debits

This is a similar system to the standing order with the main difference being that it is the creditor who claims the amount due from the customer. The supplier initiates the direct debit with the customer by asking him to complete and sign a direct debit form which will instruct the bank to pay the amount agreed on the dates required. The amounts may be fixed or at varying rates, depending on what is agreed between the customer and supplier. Payments for gas, electricity, insurance premiums, rates, goods from suppliers, can all be arranged by this method and is particularly useful when dates or amounts tend to vary. Standing orders are more convenient if the dates and amounts to be paid are on a fixed basis.

The supplier sends the direct debit forms he has agreed with his customers to his bank who will credit his account with the total amount due. The direct debits are sent to the customer's banks where the amounts will be debited against their accounts.

The bank statement will indicate all standing orders, direct debits and bank giro credits that have been placed through the bank for payment.

14.6.3 The credit transfer system

Clearing banks in this country operate the bank giro credit system where payments can be made between debtors and creditors. Many household bills can be paid directly through the bank by completing the giro credit slip which is torn off and retained by the bank. The bank debit your account and credit the account of the payee, British Gas, British Telecom, or whoever it might be.

In business a firm can also pay its employees in this way by sending a list of names to their bank indicating the wages to be paid to each employee, the branch and sort codes of their banks and the time to credit their accounts. Each employee will also receive a payment advice informing them of their gross and net pay and how much will be credited to their bank account. If an employee wishes to be paid through a post office or building society, the same procedure applies.

Trade creditors of the business can also be paid in this way. The firm simply gives the bank a list of its creditors to be paid, indicating the amount, branch and sort codes of their banks. With the list, credit slips are provided for each payment to a supplier so that he will know where the payment is from. This system saves an enormous amount of time and effort because separate cheques will not be required. All that really happens is that the debtor's account is debited with the total amount to be paid, while each creditor's account is credited with the sum due to him. The total debit value equals the total value of credits. The credit transfer system makes for a very safe and convenient way of making payments for staff wages and to suppliers of goods and other creditors.

14.7 The use of eurocheques

Writing a eurocheque is as easy and almost the same as writing an ordinary cheque. The reason for using this type of payment is for buying goods or services abroad. It has the advantage that there is no need to carry large sums of foreign currency before embarking on an overseas trip.

The difference is that when you write out a eurocheque, you do so in the local currency. If in France, you would write francs, in Spain, pesetas, in Germany, deutschmark, etc. As in this country, you need a eurocheque card when presenting the cheque to guarantee the payment. The card number will be written on the reverse side of the cheque. There is also the great advantage of being able to cash a eurocheque at any overseas bank which displays the EC sign.

In most European countries, the local banks do not make an extra charge when cashing a eurocheque. Therefore, if you write a cheque for 600 francs, you receive 600 francs. When the cheque is returned to your own bank for payment, it is converted at the current exchange rate. The cheque for 600 francs at an exchange rate of say, 9.80 would be £61.22 which is debited against your account. In addition, there is a commission charge which varies from bank to bank, of about 1.5 per cent. This would be 92p on £61.22, again debited against your account. There is also a small handling fee for each cheque used. Overall, because of the convenience and relative safety of using eurocheques, the extra fees paid to the bank are well worth it.

14.8 Bank withdrawals

Many banks have attracted their customers to use various cheque cards like 'Connect' or 'Switch' which saves them writing out a cheque when paying for purchases or other bills. All you do is hand over your card, sign the sales voucher or receipt and what you spend is deducted from your current account. Details of the transaction will appear on the sales voucher or receipt and can be checked against the bank statement. When a bill is paid, the sum will be directly debited to the customer's current account.

When a Switch or Connect card is used, tills which are linked to EFTPOS (electronic funds transfer at the point of sale), traders have the payment of goods or services automatically debited to the customer's current account and credited to their own account. The banks usually take within three working days to transfer funds from one account to the other. An instant double-entry in accounting, no money or cheques passing hands, just an immediate transfer of funds between the buyer and seller!

14.9 Bank overdrafts

A trader can apply for a bank overdraft which lets him have money on credit. This means that he can spend more money than he has in his current account. Most banks offer up to £2 000 on a personal current account which enables you to overdraw up to this figure. But beware, interest is charged on a daily basis on the outstanding balance, usually a number of percentage points above the bank's base rate, which can be very expensive.

For business accounts, the bank can arrange for much larger borrowing requirements. Many firms are dependent on overdraft facilities to enable them to meet their day-to-day expenses, without which they would run into serious cash shortages. Overdrafts are simple to arrange but the bank will normally put a limit on the amount of credit. Unauthorised overdrafts could be charged at higher rates of interest or worse, the cheques could 'bounce', that is, they would be stopped by the bank and the payee would not be paid. A serious problem for the business.

14.10 The legal relationship between the bank and its customers

When money is deposited at the bank for safe keeping and to earn interest, the relationship is one of debtor and creditor. The bank owes you the money, you are the creditor, the bank the debtor. On the other hand, if you owe the bank money, the situation is reversed, the bank being the creditor and you the debtor.

However, there is a difference between the normal debtor/creditor relationship. When money is deposited at the bank, the bank has absolute responsibility of it and may do what it likes with your money. The significant points of difference include:

a) The money deposited is only repaid to the customer when demanded.
b) The bank has the responsibility to honour cheques demanded by the customer as negotiated between the customer and the bank (including overdraft limits).
c) The bank has a right to charge interest and commission on customer's accounts for example, in cases of overdrafts, loans and handling charges.
d) The bank has a duty of discretion, that is, it does not disclose customer's banking details to other sources unless given express permission by the customer or there is a legal requirement to do so.

Summary

Banks are financial institutions whose main function is to provide safe keeping for the deposits of money and to be a source of borrowing, offering loans and overdraft facilities. The banks provide a host of various services for their customers and it is inconceivable that a business could do without its bank, particularly for depositing money and processing cheques.

Questions

1 Briefly describe the main functions of a clearing bank (14.1).

2 What is the main difference between a deposit account and a current account (14.1)?

3 Why should you make variations to your journey when going to the bank? (14.3)

4 Make out a paying-in-slip, making up details for the name of the business etc. with the following information (14.4):

Cheques:	Harry Jones	£123.55
	James Last	£23.87
Postal order:	Rod Stewart	£18.50
Cash:	2 × £50 notes	
	7 × £20 notes	
	11 × £10 notes	
	23 × £5 notes	
	8 × £1 coins	
	4 × 50p coins	
	17 × 20p coins	
	14 × 10p coins	
	5 × 5p coins	
	36p bronze	

5 When a cheque is crossed, what does it signify? (14.5)

6 What is the difference between a direct debit and a standing order? (14.6)

7 What advantages are there for a business using the credit transfer system? (14.6)

8 Briefly explain why a bank overdraft can be more than useful to a business. (14.9)

9 What legal relationship exists between a bank and its customers? (14.10)

To extend your understanding, try the following assignment:

10 Find out what you can about today's banking world by visiting your local branch, collect their leaflets and booklets and be aware of the variety of services they can offer.

15 The cash book

Objectives

On completing this section you should:

- understand why the cash book is used
- recognise the use of analysed cash books
- understand the posting procedure from the cash book to ledgers.

Context

Chapter 14 introduces cash transactions. Chapter 6 places the cash book in the context of business accounting systems as a whole.

15.1 Introduction

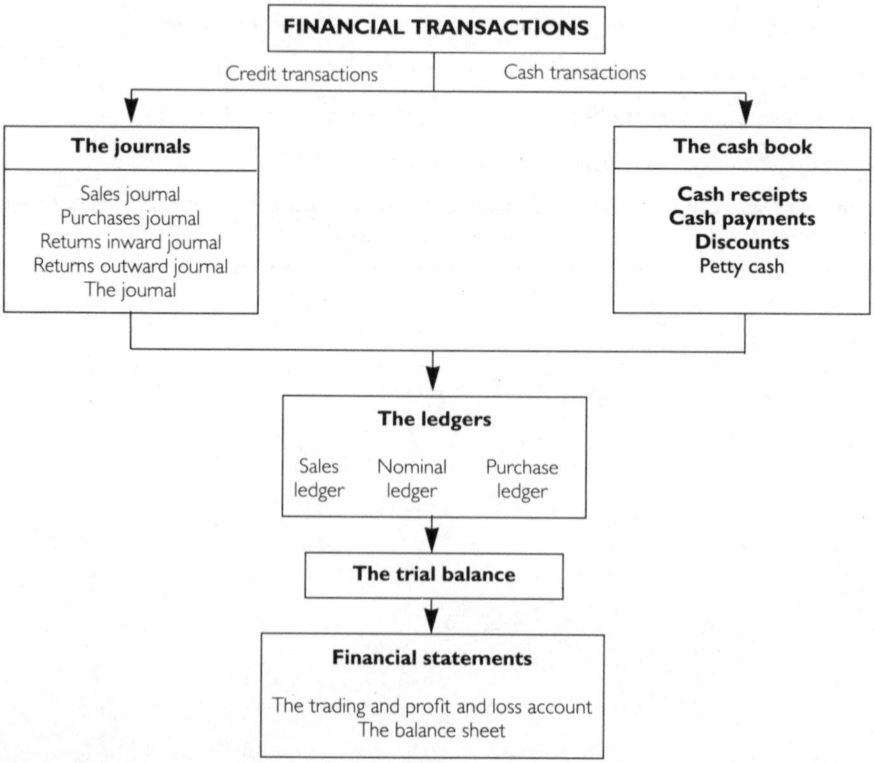

Fig. 15.1 The cash book in business accounting systems.

In Chapter 5 we saw that both cash and bank entries were recorded in the ledger. The cash book now takes over this function and is used to record all transactions relating to cash or bank accounts, whether receipts or payments. Therefore, instead of having a separate bank and cash account in the nominal ledger, a cash book can be used.

There are different designs of cash book. A basic model would have cash or bank receipts on the debit side and cash or bank payments on the credit side. Some businesses want to analyse receipts and payments in the same way as we discussed with analysed journals in the previous chapter, and may have several extra columns used for this purpose. A section on analysed cash books is discussed later in this chapter. The process of entering receipts and payments into the cash book and posting to the ledgers is described below. We begin by looking at the general principles using a single journal (15.2), go on to look at analysed journals (15.3) and the use of separate journals for analysis purposes in section 15.4.

15.2 Recording transactions in the cash book (1): using one journal

Remember the golden rules for posting information from the cash books to the ledgers:

		Cash book	Ledgers
Cash receipts	–	debit (asset increase)	credit
Cash payments	–	credit (asset decrease)	debit

Different rules apply to the posting of discounts – these are discussed on the following page. If a business is using a single journal to record cash transactions, the receipts are entered on the left-hand side of the book (debit) and payments on the right-hand side (credit):

(Dr)	Receipts			Payments		(Cr)
		Cash £	Bank £		Cash £	Bank £

A further facility which can be used in the design of a cash book is to have columns to record cash discounts. If a cash discount is offered to customers to encourage them to pay their accounts more promptly, the discount taken by customers can be recorded at the same time their payment is made.

Example: debit side of cash book

D Smith (debtor) sends a cheque of £200 to settle his account of £210, receiving a £10 discount for prompt payment.

	Discount allowed	*Cash account*	*Bank account*
	£	£	£
D Smith	10		200

Example: credit side of cash book

R Pearce sends a cheque of £675 to International, receiving a £15 discount for prompt settlement of account:

	Discount received	*Cash account*	*Bank account*
	£	£	£
International	15		675

In posting discounts to the ledgers, it is important to remember that the two discount totals remain on the same side because only a tally of the totals are recorded (the double entry is already completed when entries are posted to personal accounts).

From cash book to ledgers: a practical example using one journal

R Pearce recorded the following transactions during the month of August:

1/8	Balances brought forward, cash £200, bank £1 925 (Dr).
5/8	Paid general expenses, cheque £50.
6/8	Cash sales, £420.
6/8	Personal drawings (R Pearce) £120 cash.
7/8	D Smith settles his account, £200 cheque, discount £10.
10/8	Southern Electricity bill paid by cheque, £43.
12/8	General expenses, cheque £50.
13/8	Cash sales, £345.
13/8	Drawings, £120 cash.
15/8	Southern Gas, £85 cheque.
19/8	From B Kings, cheque £420, in settlement of debt, £441.50.
20/8	Drawings, £120 cash.
20/8	Cash sales, £410.
21/8	Paid cash, £800, into bank. (Contra entry, credit cash £800, debit bank £800.)
23/8	Paid for stationery, £25 cash.
26/8	General expenses, cheque £50.
27/8	Cash sales, £450.
27/8	Drawings, £120 cash.
28/8	British Telecom (telephone), £67 cheque.
30/8	Payments to creditors (by cheque): Slazenger Sports £250 Metro Sports £1 000 Auto £500

31/8 Paid International £675 cheque, discount received, £15.
31/8 Drawings, £150 cash.

REQUIRED:

1 Prepare the cash book of R Pearce for the month of August. Bring down the cash and bank balances on 1 September.
2 Post the personal accounts of debtors and creditors to their respective accounts in the sales and purchase ledgers.
3 Post other accounts relating to sales, expenses and drawings to their respective accounts in the nominal ledger.
4 Post the totals of discount allowed and received to the nominal ledger.

The cash book of R Pearce for the month of August

Ref: C9

(*Dr*)		*Receipts*				*Payments*			(*Cr*)
		Discount allowed £	*Cash* £	*Bank* £			*Discount received* £	*Cash* £	*Bank* £
1/8	Balances b/f		200	1 925	5/8	General expenses			50
6/8	Sales		420		6/8	Drawing		120	
7/8	D Smith	10.0		200	10/8	SEB			43
13/8	Sales		345		12/8	General expenses			50
19/8	B Kings	21.5		420	13/8	Drawings		120	
20/8	Sales		410		15/8	SG (gas)			85
21/8	Contra (cash)*			800	20/8	Drawings		120	
27/8	Sales		450		21/8	Contra (bank)*		800	
					23/8	Stationery		25	
					26/8	General expenses			50
					27/8	Drawings		120	
					28/8	BT (telephone)			67
					30/8	Slazenger			250
						Metro			1 000
						Auto			500
					31/8	International	15		675
						Drawings		150	
						Balances c/f		370	575
		31.5	1 825	3 345			15	1 825	3 345
1/9	Balances b/f		370	575					

Note:
*Contra entries: cash £800 has been transferred to the bank by crediting the cash column and debiting the bank. The reverse would occur if £800 cash was withdrawn from the bank.

Sales ledger

		Folio	Debit £	Credit £	Balance £
D Smith account S11					
1/8	Balance				210.0 Dr
7/8	Bank	C9		200.0	
	Discount allowed			10.0	—
B Kings account S09					
1/8	Balance				441.5 Dr
19/8	Bank	C9		420.0	
	Discount allowed			21.5	—

Purchase ledger

		Folio	Debit £	Credit £	Balance £
Slazenger Sports account P65					
1/8	Balance				594.1 Cr
30/8	Bank	C9	250		344.1
Metro Sports account P60					
10/8	Balance				1 909.0 Cr
30/8	Bank	C9	1 000		909.0
Auto Sports account P55					
27/8	Balance				920.0 Cr
30/8	Bank	C9	500		420.0
International account P70					
21/8	Balance				690.0 Cr
31/8	Bank	C9	675		
	Discount received		15		—

Nominal ledger

		Folio	Debit £	Credit £	Balance £
Sales account N42					
1/8	Balance				2 480 Cr
6/8	Cash	C9		420	2 900
13/8	Cash	C9		345	3 245
20/8	Cash	C9		410	3 655
27/8	Cash	C9		450	4 105

(continued)

(continued)

General expenses account N36					
1/8	Balance				380 Dr
5/8	Bank	C9	50.0		430
12/8	Bank	C9	50.0		480
26/8	Bank		50.0		530
Drawings account N31					
1/8	Balance				1 020 Dr
6/8	Cash	C9	120.0		1 140
13/8	Cash	C9	120.0		1 260
20/8	Cash	C9	120.0		1 380
27/8	Cash	C9	120.0		1 500
31/8	Cash	C9	150.0		1 650
Light and heat account N37					
1/8	Balance				280.0 Dr
10/8	Bank	C9	43.0		323.0
15/8	Bank	C9	85.0		408.0
Stationery account N8					
1/8	Balance				20.0 Dr
23/8	Bank	C9	25.0		45.0
Telephone account N39					
1/8	Balance				55.0 Dr
28/8	Bank	C9	67.0		122.0
Discount allowed account N34					
1/8	Balance				70.0
7/8	Bank	C9	10.0		80.0
19/8	Bank	C9	21.5		101.5
Discount received account N35					
1/8	Balance				60.0 Cr
31÷8	Bank	C9		15	75.0

15.3 An analysed cash book

In practice there are many different types of cash book, each designed and adapted to suit the nature of the business. If R Pearce, for example, wanted to bank his cash sales each day and retain a cash float for his change, he may want a different format to analyse his takings and expenses. He may prefer to:

a) show sales and Vat separately;
b) analyse separate debtors' and creditors' totals to facilitate posting to the control accounts in the nominal ledger;
c) use separate columns for general expenses and his drawings;
d) group all his other expenses under the heading 'overheads'.

R Pearce's analysed cash book is shown overleaf.

An analysed cash book – R Pearce

		Discount allowed	Debtors	Sales	Vat	Total	Bank
		£	£	£	£	£	£
1/8	Balance b/f						1 925
6/8	Sales			365	55	420	
7/8	D Smith	10.0	200			200	
13/8	Sales			300	45	345	
19/8	B Kings	21.5	420			420	
20/8	Sales			356	54	410	
27/8	Sales			391	59	450	
		31.5	620	1 412	213	2 245	2 245
							4 170
1/9	Balance b/f						745

		Discount received	Creditors	General expenses	Overheads	Vat	Drawings	Total	Bank
		£	£	£	£	£	£	£	£
5/8	General expenses			50				50	
6/8	Drawings						120	120	
10/8	SEB				43			43	
12/8	General expenses			50				50	
13/8	Drawings						120	120	
15/8	SG (gas)				78.70	6.30		85	
20/8	Drawings						120		
23/8	Stationery				21.28	3.72		25	
26/8	General expenses			50				50	
27/8	Drawings						270	270	
28/8	BT (telephone)				57.03	9.97		67	
30/8	Slazenger		250					250	
	Metro		1 000					1 000	
	Auto		500					500	
31/8	International	15	675					675	
		15	2 425	150	200.01	19.99	630	3 425	3 425
31/8	Balance c/f								745
									4 170

NOTE

The advantage of this cash book format is that:

a) total columns identify group figures;

b) totals facilitate ledger postings which are shown on the next page for the nominal ledger.

Nominal ledger

		Folio	Debit £	Credit £	Balance £
Sales account N42					
1/8	Balance				2 480.00 Cr
31/8	Bank	C9		1 412.0	3 892.00
Vat account N30					
1/8	Balance				147.90 Cr
31/8	Bank	C9	19.99	213.0	340.91
General expenses account N36					
1/8	Balance				380.00 Dr
31/8	Bank	C9	150.00		530.00
Overheads account N37					
1/8	Balance				355.00 Dr
31/8	Bank	C9	200.01		555.01
Drawings account N31					
1/8	Balance				1 020.00 Dr
31/8	Bank	C9	630.00		1 650.00
Bought ledger control account N45					
30/8	Balance				4 113.10 Cr
31/8	Bank	C9	2 425.00		
	Discount received		15.00		1 673.10
Sales ledger control account N40					
30/8	Balance				2 755.50 Dr
31/8	Bank	C9		620.0	
	Discount allowed			31.5	2 104.00
Discount allowed account N34					
1/8	Balance				70.00 Dr
31/8	Bank	C9	31.50		101.50
Discount received account N35					
1/8	Balance				60.00 Cr
31/8	Bank	C9		15.0	75.00

15.4 Recording transactions in the cash book (2): using separate journals

Many business organisations prefer to use separate journals for cash receipts and cash payments because they may want to make use of multi-columns for analysis purposes.

In the examples that follow, the cash book receipts and payments are totalled up weekly. The final bank column must of course, cross check with the individual column totals. Note that the bank totals are posted to the bank account in the nominal ledger, receipts are debited and payments credited to the bank.

There are no balances carried or brought down in these separate cash receipts and payments books. Discounts are recorded separately here as in the discussion of the use of a single journal.

Cash book receipts

Date		Details	Sales Ledger Discount Allowed £		Customer's a/c £		Vat a/c £		Sales S161 £		Sales S162 £		Sales S163 £		Sales S164 £		Total Sales S160 £		Bank a/c £	
Apr	4	Cash sales					85	45	234	84	34	60	58	30	160	55	488	29	573	74
	5	Cash sales					42	37	129	49	27	40	35	65	49	60	242	14	284	51
	6	Cash sales					48	75	138	46	37	85	27	50	74	76	278	57	327	32
	6	D. James	6	50	123	50													123	50
	7	Cash sales					74	36	276	21	54	22	82	50	12	00	424	93	499	29
	8	Cash sales					44	00	132	32	34	28	46	20	38	70	251	50	295	50
	8	D. Lewis	18	80	357	20													357	20
	8	M Johnson	11	70	222	30													222	30
	9	Cash sales					31	12	68	40	23	44	65	00	21	00	177	84	208	96
		Week's Totals	37	00	703	00	326	05	979	72	211	79	315	15	356	61	1863	27	2892	32
			S/L		S/L		N/L	Cr	N/L	Cr	N/L	Cr	N/L	Cr	N/L	Cr	N/L	Cr	N/L	Dr
			Control	Cr	Control	Cr														

Fig. 15.2 Cash book receipts

Cash book payments

Date		CHQ No.	Details	Purchase Ledger Discount Recd £		Suppliers a/c £		Vat a/c £		Mainten. & Repairs a/c £		Salaries a/c £		Stationery a/c £		Sundries a/c £		Bank a/c £	
Apr	4	0631	Dunlop Sports	6		135	00											135	00
	4	0632	Long's Garage			94	00											94	00
	4	0633	Strings Stationers			79	90											79	90
	4	0634	Metre	11	00	247	50											247	50
	4	0635	Auto Sports			250	00											250	00
	5	0636	Petty cash (R)													100	00	100	00
	5	0637	Salaries									3168	50					3168	50
	5	0638	Inland Revenue									892	26					892	26
	6	0639	Smith's Stationers					4	20					24	00			28	20
	7	0640	Rowlands C & C					4	90							28	00	32	90
	7	0641	B & Q stores					9	80	56	00							65	80
	8	0642	Southern Gas			56	40											56	40
	9	0643	Smith's Stationers					3	24					18	50			21	74
			Week's Totals	17	00	862	80	22	14	56	00	4060	76	42	50	128	00	5172	20
				P/L		P/L	Dr	N/L	Dr	N/L	Dr	N/L	Dr	N/L	Dr	N/L	Dr	N/L	Cr
				Control	Dr	Control													

Fig. 15.3 Cash book payments

These transactions in the cash books would be posted to the ledgers as follows:

Sales ledger

		Folio	Debit	Credit	Balance
			£	£	£
D James account					
1/4	Balance				130.00 Dr
6/4	Bank	CB4		123.5	
	Discount			6.5	—
D Lewis account					
1/4	Balance				795.36 Dr
8/4	Bank	CB4		357.2	
	Discount			18.8	419.36
M Johnson account					
1/4	Balance				412.60 Dr
8/4	Bank	CB4		222.3	
	Discount			11.7	178.60

Purchase ledger

		Folio	Debit	Credit	Balance
			£	£	£
Dunlop Sports account					
1/4	Balance				329.00 Cr
4/4	Bank	CB4	135.00		
	Discount		6.00		188.00
Metre account					
1/4	Balance				258.50 Cr
4/4	Bank	CB4	247.50		
	Discount		11.00		—
Auto Sports account					
1/4	Balance				250.00 Cr
4/4	Bank	CB4	250.00		—
Southern Gas account					
1/4	Balance				56.40 Cr
8/4	Bank	CB4	56.40		—
Long's Garage account					
1/4	Balance				220.90 Cr
4/4	Bank	CB4	94.00		126.90
Strings Stationers account					
1/4	Balance				79.90 Cr
4/4	Bank	CB4	79.90		—

Nominal ledger

		Folio	Debit	Credit	Balance
			£	£	£
Sales account S161					
9/4	Bank	CB4		979.72	979.72 Cr
Sales account S162					
9/4	Bank	CB4		211.79	211.79 Cr
Sales account S163					
9/4	Bank	CB4		315.15	315.15 Cr
Sales account S164					
9/4	Bank	CB4		356.61	356.61 Cr
Total sales account S160					
9/4	Bank			1 863.27	1 863.27 Cr
Vat account					
1/4	Balance				141.16 Cr
9/4	Bank	CB4		326.05	467.21
9/4	Bank	CB4	22.14		445.07
Purchases ledger control account					
1/4	Balance				1 549.24 Cr
9/4	Bank	CB4	862.80		
	Discount		17.00		669.44
Sales ledger control account					
1/4	Balance				1 840.00 Dr
9/4	Bank	CB4		703.00	
	Discount			37.00	1 100.00
Salaries account					
9/4	Bank	CB4	4 060.76		4 060.76 Dr
Maintenance and repairs account					
9/4	Bank	CB4	56.00		56.00 Dr
Stationery account					
9/4	Bank	CB4	42.50		42.50 Dr
Sundries account					
9/4	Bank	CB4	28.00		28.00 Dr
Bank account					
9/4	Cash receipts	CB4	2 892.32		2 892.72 Dr
9/4	Cash payments	CB4		5 172.20	2 279.88 Cr
Discounts account					
9/4	Allowed	CB4	37.00		37.00 Dr
9/4	Received	CB4		17.00	20.00

NOTE:
1. The totals of both cash book payments and receipts can be posted to the bank account so that it is convenient to record the balance at the bank. At the moment it is in overdraft because payments are greater than receipts.
2. The discounts have been posted to a single account, the debit balance of £17 indicating net discount allowed.
3. The sales accounts S161, 162, 163, 164 indicate different categories of sales used for analysis purposes.
4. Expenses like Southern Gas £56.40 are debited in the purchase ledger because a creditor's account was opened previously when the bill was received.

Summary

The cash book is used to record cash transactions. This means in cash or through the bank or by use of a credit card. Receipts are debited and payments are credited. When posting to the ledgers, the double entry is completed when receipts are credited to their respective accounts and payments debited. Analysed cash books provide management with further information and facilitate ledger posting.

Questions

1 The following cash/bank transactions occurred during April in the books of G Whitehall:

		£
1/4	Balances brought forward:	
	Cash	250 Dr
	Bank	1 725 Dr
2/4	Cash sales (week).	440
3/4	General expenses, cash.	50
5/4	Drawings (G Whitehall), cash.	125
9/4	Cash sales.	385
10/4	Paid Rawlings (creditor) £975 cheque, having been allowed a 2.5 per cent discount (on £1 000).	
11/4	Assistant's wages, cash.	85
13/4	Insurance premium by cheque.	122
16/4	Cash sales into bank.	400
18/4	General expenses, cash.	50
20/4	Contra – cash to bank.	500
23/4	Cash sales.	410
25/4	Received from Barnes, cheque £390, in settlement of £400 account.	
27/4	General expenses, cash.	50
28/4	Assistant's wages, cash.	85
30/4	Received from Ewing, cheque £585, in settlement of £600 account.	
30/4	Cash sales into bank.	420
30/4	Paid Long (creditor) cheque £780, in settlement of £800 account.	

REQUIRED:

a) Prepare the cash book of G Whitehall for the month of April and bring down the balances on 1 May.

b) Explain how the personal accounts of G Whitehall would be posted to his sales and purchase ledgers. (15.1–2)

2 The following balances were brought down from the cash book of B Kings on 1 June:

Cash	£220 Dr
Bank	£420 Cr (Overdrawn)

The transactions which occurred during June were as follows:

		£
1/6	Paid general expenses, cheque.	75
5/6	Cash sales into bank.	755
6/6	Paid a cheque to P Williams £290, having been allowed a £10 discount.	
12/6	Cash sales.	635
13/6	Paid general expenses, cheque.	80
14/6	Drawings, cash.	150
15/6	Paid for advertising, cheque.	105
15/6	Transferred to bank (contra).	400
19/6	Cash sales into bank.	785
20/6	Paid cheque to J Grant on account.	600
25/6	Received cheque from P Gibbs, £390 in settlement of £400 account.	
25/6	Received cheque from G Walton in settlement of £500 account, less 5 per cent discount.	
26/6	Cash sales into bank.	625
26/6	Drawings, cheque.	180
28/6	Paid general expenses, cheque.	75
30/6	Paid bills for light and heat, cheque.	115

REQUIRED:

a) Prepare the cash book for B Kings for the month of June and bring down the balances on 1 July.

b) Prepare the nominal ledger accounts for sales and general expenses, commencing balances on 1 June with 'nil'. (15.1–2)

3 On 1 May, P Goldney had the following balances in his books:

	£
Cash book:	
Cash	350 Dr
Bank	825 Dr
Sales ledger:	
E Allen	400 Dr
M Doe	360 Dr
Purchase ledger:	
R Baker	875 Cr
V Winch	380 Cr

During the month of May, the transactions of P Goldney were as follows:

Cheques paid:

2/5 Withdrew from bank, for personal use, £150 per week (to 30 May).

3/5 To R Baker in settlement of account, £850.

7/5 To Southern Gas, £184
12/5 To Southern Electricity Board, £95.
18/5 To V Winch, £361 in settlement.

Cheques received:
25/5 From E Allen, £390, in settlement of account.
27/5 From M Doe, in settlement, less 5 per cent discount.
30/5 From Inland Revenue, rebate of £335.

Cash received:
5/5 Cash sales £725, £500 into bank.
12/5 Cash sales £800, all into bank.
19/5 Cash sales £650, £500 into bank.
26/5 Cash sales £735, all into bank.

Cash paid:
5/5 Shop assistant's wages, £80 per week (to 26 May).
7/5 General expenses, £40 per week (to 28 May).
10/5 Petty cash, £100.

REQUIRED:
a) Prepare the cash book for P Goldney for the month of May and bring down the balances on 1 June.
b) Show the personal accounts of P Goldney as they would appear in his ledgers on 31 May. (15.1–2)

4 At 1 May, Jack, a retailer, has the following balances in his cash book: cash in hand £42; overdraft at bank £138.

During the month of May:

Cheques were issued as follows:
2 To Surrey for £95 in full settlement of a debt of £100.
8 To Hampshire who is owed £80 and who is prepared to allow 2.5 per cent cash discount.
19 To Kent RDC £66 in payment of rates.
25 Withdrawn from bank for use as change in the till, £20.
31 Proprietor withdrew for private purposes £100.

Cheques were received as follows:
17 From Mrs Lancashire £26 in payment of a monthly account.
(On 30 May you are advised by the bank that this cheque has been returned marked R/D).

Cash received during the month:
Shop takings for week ending 5 May £125, of which £100 was paid to the bank.
Shop takings for week ending 12 May £144, of which £120 was paid to the bank.
Shop takings for week ending 19 May £159, of which £150 was paid to the bank.
Shop takings for week ending 26 May £148, of which £105 was paid to the bank.

Cash paid out during month:
Wages 5, 12, 19, 26 of month; £28 on each date.
23 Telephone account £15.
29 Delivery charges £8.

You are required to draw up a cash book for the month of May and enter the above transactions in date order. Balance the book as at 31 May and bring down the balances. (15.1–2)

5 Entrepreneur, I Creese, used an analysed cash book in his business. All payments were made by cheque, all shop takings banked each day. He retained an adequate cash float for his 'change'.

On the debit side of his cash book he used columns for:

Discount allowed	*Debtors*	*Sales*	*Bank*
£	£	£	£

On the payments side (credit), he had columns for:

Discount received	*Creditors*	*Drawings*	*Wages*	*Other expenses*	*Bank*
£	£	£	£	£	£

On 1 June, I Creese's bank balance was £485 Dr. During the month, his transactions were:

Money received:

		£
3/6	Cash sales for the week	450
10/6	Cash sales for the week	385
17/6	Cash sales for the week	455
24/6	Cash sales for the week	435

All shop takings are banked on the dates given.

5/6	From Lewis £195, discount £5.
11/6	From Smith £100 on account.
13/6	From Taylor £475, discount £15.
20/6	From Johnson £250 on account.

Cheques issued:

2/6	Drawings, £120 per week (to 30 May).
5/6	Wages, £60 per week (to 26 May).
10/6	To B Woods, £1 250 on account.
11/6	General expenses, £170.
15/6	Rates, £345.
21/6	To R Carlton, £570 in settlement of £600 account.
25/6	General expenses, £150.
27/6	Petty cash, £100.

REQUIRED:
Draw up the cash book (analysed) for I Creese, for the month of June, balancing at the end of the month and bringing down the balance on 1 July. (15.3)

6 On 1 January L Dawson, a retailer, has the following balances in his cash book: cash £42; bank (overdrawn) £150. During January his cash transactions were as follows:

Cheques paid:

January	3	To Smith for £195 in settlement of £200 debt.
	9	To Harrison £76 in settlement of £80 debt.
	17	To Jones £160 on account.
	22	Withdrawn from bank to cash £200 (contra).
	28	Proprietor took for his own use £80 (drawings).

Cheques received:

16	From Bradshaw £95 in settlement of £100 account.
22	From Green £50 on account.

Cash received:

5	Shop takings for the week £125, £100 in bank.
12	Shop takings for the week £180, £125 in bank.
19	Shop takings for the week £124, £100 in bank.
26	Shop takings for the week £130, £100 in bank.

Cash paid:

5	Assistant's wages, £35 per week for the month, to 26 January.
22	Gas bill, £56.
27	Electricity bill, £27. Telephone, £30.

REQUIRED:

a) Prepare a cash book for Dawson for the month ending 31 January and bring down the balances on the next day.

b) What do you think 'returned to drawer' or 'R/D' means marked on a cheque? (15.3–4)

7 A wine shop owned by R Lees kept an analysis cash book using columns for: wine, beer and lager, spirits, other sales, total sales, Vat and bank. The daily takings are banked each day at the local branch. The cash register calculates the Vat separately when a sale goes through the till.

The takings over four days were as follows:

			Wine	*Beer and lager*	*Spirits*	*Other sales*	*Total sales*
			£	£	£	£	£
June	2	Takings	200.0	250.0	80.0	30.0	
		Vat	30.0	37.5	12.0	4.5	
	3	Takings	150.0	200.0	50.0	20.0	
		Vat	22.5	30.0	7.5	3.0	
	4	Takings	180.0	240.0	60.0	24.0	
		Vat	27.0	36.0	9.0	3.6	
	5	Takings	300.0	340.0	100.0	60.0	
		Vat	45.0	51.0	15.0	9.0	

REQUIRED:

a) Prepare a suitable cash book using the above columns to analyse the different sale categories.

b) Post the sales and Vat to the ledger.

c) Why is it sometimes useful to make analysis columns? (15.3–4)

8 J Durham had the following balances in her cash book on 1 July:

	£
Cash	200
Bank	455 Cr (Overdraft)

During the month the transactions were as follows:

Cheques received:		£	Discount allowed: £
2/7	Jackson and Son	186	14.00
3/7	Chappell Ltd	250	18.75
12/7	Clogg and Co	100	–
28/7	Hughes, K	358	17.90

Cheques issued:		£	Discount received: £
2/7	Mitre Sports	500.00	12.50
4/7	Arena	160.00	8.00
22/7	Dunlop	80.50	–

28/7	Slazenger Sport	172.50	7.50

Cash received:

Week ending

6/7	Shop takings	258.75	Paid £200 into Bank
13/7	Shop takings	196.80	Paid £150 into Bank
20/7	Shop takings	220.00	Paid £175 into Bank
7/7	Shop takings	187.75	Paid £150 into Bank

Cash paid out:

6, 13, 20, 27/7	Assistant salaries	£56.75 (each date)
22/7	Advertising	£42.24
23/7	Delivery expenses	£14.75
25/7	Petty expenses	£8.50
29/7	Delivery expenses	£10.50

REQUIRED:

a) Enter the above transactions in *date order* for the month of July.

b) Ledger accounts required – for nominal accounts only. Assume balances are nil on 1 July. (15.3–4)

(Institute of Bankers)

9 Prepare an analysed cash payments book for R Pearce Sports having columns for: discount received, suppliers accounts, stationery, light and heat, telephone, wages, drawings, sundry expenses, Vat and total bank.

All payments are made by cheque. You could include a further column to enter the cheque number if you wish.

The following transactions are for the month of May:

May

4	Paid Dunlop Sports £146.25 (discount received £3.75)
7	Paid Metre Sports £304 (discount received £16)
8	Drawings £150.
8	Paid Smith's Stationers £32 inclusive of Vat.
10	Paid Southern Electricity £124 plus Vat 8%.
11	Paid telephone account to BT £146.50 plus Vat 17.5%.
15	Drawings £150.
17	Repairs to plate glass window paid £36 inclusive of Vat.
20	Paid Auto Sports £400 on account.
21	Balance paid to Southern Gas £56 plus Vat 8%.
22	Drawings £150.
29	Paid Slazenger £399 (discount received £21).
29	Drawings £150.
30	Paid wages £1 946.

Explain how you would post the above entries to the nominal ledger. (15.3–4).

16 The bank reconciliation statement

Objectives

On completing this section you should:

- understand the need to confirm the bank account records with the bank statement records
- be able to prepare a bank reconciliation statement which aligns the statement balance with the updated cash book balance.

Context

Chapter 14 and 15 introduce banking transactions and the cash book respectively.

16.1 Introduction

When the bank statement arrives from the bank giving details of the business's transactions, it very rarely agrees with the bank balance as recorded either in the cash book or as a nominal account in the ledger. The major reason for this is that there is a time discrepancy between recording the business's bank transactions in the cash book and the bank's recording of them.

This is particularly the case with 'unpresented cheques'. When payments by cheque are prepared and recorded in the cash book, it may take a number of days for the bank to clear them and, therefore, the bank records these at a later point in the bank statement.

The banks arrange for many items to be paid directly through the banking systems, such as credit transfers, direct debits and standing orders, and the business may record these items on receipt of the bank statement and usually not before.

The banks also may make charges for handling accounts and interest may either be paid or charged depending on whether the bank account is in credit with the bank or is in an overdraft position. A *credit* in the bank statement balance is, in effect, 'money in the bank' because from the bank's point of view, it owes money to the business. In the cash book, the bank will show a debit entry. On the other hand, a *debit* in the bank statement balance will indicate an overdraft, which, in the cash book, will appear as a credit balance.

When the bank statement is received from the bank, the general practice is to:

a) Check carefully all banking items between the cash book and the bank statement. Those items found in both sets of records may be given a light tick as items agreed. The receipts side of the cash book will be checked with the receipts (credit side) of the bank statement; the payments side of the cash book with the payments side (debit side) of the statement. The opening balance on both records must also be checked.

b) This will leave some items left unticked. Some unticked items may appear both in the cash book and bank statement. Those items left unticked in the bank statement must first be recorded in the cash book, to bring it up-to-date. These may include items such as bank charges, direct debits and standing orders.

c) Once the cash book is brought up-to-date with those unticked items from the bank statement, it is balanced. The reconciliation statement can then be prepared, bringing the adjusted cash book balance into agreement with the bank statement.

d) The reconciliation statement is the verifying check between the bank account in the cash book and the bank statement balance. The procedure in summary is as follows:

1 balance as per bank statement (final balance);
2 add any undeposited cheques (unticked items, debit side of cash book);
3 less any unpresented cheques (unticked items, credit side of cash book);
4 balance as per cash book.

The process can be illustrated as follows:

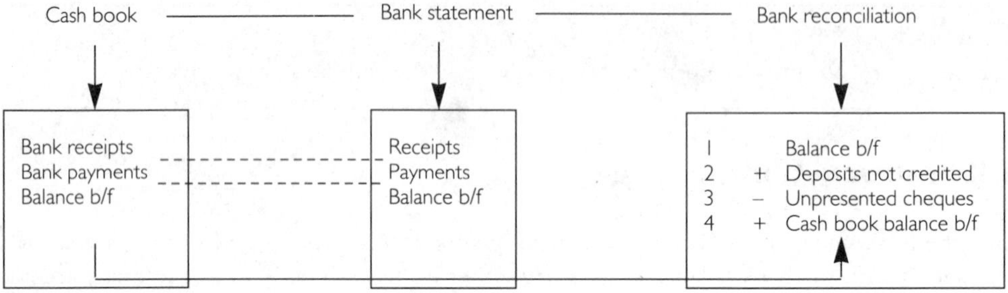

Figure 16.1 Bank reconciliation

16.2 Bank reconciliation: a practical example

Prepare the bank reconciliation statement of Robert Jones for the month of May. Find the balance of the cash book first and include any items unticked from the bank statement. The items on both sets of records have already been ticked.

Cash book of R Jones

Date	*Details (bank)*	£		*Date*	*Details (bank)*	£	
May 1	Balance b/d	93	✓	May 2	Motor expenses	52	✓
4	Sales to bank	88	✓	8	Office costs	24	✓
7	Sales to bank	87	✓	9	Jack Soames	141	
16	Sales to bank	228	✓	10	Light and heat	34	✓
18	Tom Smith	74	✓	12	Ron James	108	✓
21	Sales to bank	255	✓	17	Stationery	46	✓
28	D Marks	54		21	Wages	84	✓
31	Sales to bank	36		30	P Jackson	116	
				31	Balance c/d	310	
		915				915	
	Balance b/d	310					

Bank statement of R Jones for month of May

Date	*Details*	*Debit* £	*Credit* £	*Balance* £
May 1	Balance b/f			93 ✓ Cr
4	Deposit		88 ✓	181
8	Deposit		87 ✓	268
11	100452	52 ✓		
	100453	24 ✓		192
12	STO (rates)	55		137
14	DDR (insurance)	18		119
16	Deposit		228 ✓	347
17	100455	34 ✓		313
18	100456	108 ✓		205
19	Deposit		74 ✓	279
21	Deposit		255 ✓	534
22	100457	46 ✓		488
24	100458	84 ✓		404
29	DIV		16	420

Abbreviations: STO Standing Order, DDR Direct Debit, BGC Bank Giro Credit, DIV Dividend, ATM Cash Dispenser, DR Overdrawn

REQUIRED:

a) Check and tick alike items in both the cash book and bank statement.

b) Bring the cash book up-to-date with those unticked items from the bank statement.

c) Prepare the bank reconciliation statement for the month of May.

Unticked items in the cash book:

Debits	£	*Credits*	£
D Marks	54	Jack Soames	141
Sales to bank	36	P Jackson	116

Unticked items in the bank statement:

Debits	£	*Credits*	£
STO	55	DIV	16
DDR	18		

Cash book updated

			May 31	Balance c/d	310
		915			915
June 1	Balance b/d	310	June 1	STO – rates	55
	Dividend	16		DDR – insurance	18
				Balance c/d	253
		326			326
	Balance b/d	253			

Bank reconciliation statement as on 31 May

	£	£
Balance as per bank statement (29/5)		420 Cr
Add		
Deposits not yet credited: Marks	54	
Sales	36	90
		510
Less		
Unpresented cheques: Soames	141	
Jackson	116	257
Balance as per cash book		253

16.3 Difference in opening balances

In most cases, when a cross-check is made between the cash book entries and those of the bank statement, the opening balances do not agree. This is because transactions are recorded at different times at the bank, as already discussed. Many of the questions will have the opening balances agreeing, but this is only for convenience. In practice, we require the previous bank reconciliation statement to tick off items like unpresented cheques or deposits not yet credited which do become presented at the bank and are recorded in the following bank statement.

Example

Cash book of R Jones

			£
June	1	Balance b/d	253 Dr

Bank statement of R Jones

			Debit	Credit	Balance
			£	£	£
June	1	Balance			420 Cr
	3	credit		90 ✓	510
	7	01295	141 ✓		369
	10	01297	116 ✓		253
	14	01306	180		73
	15	credit		224	297
	16	01308	121		176

Note that the difference between the two opening balances=£167 (£253 debit in the cash book against £420 credit in the bank statement). If 3 entries are ticked off against the previous reconciliation statement for May:

£90 not yet deposited and
£141 and £116 as unpresented cheques,

then the opening balances would agree.

Therefore, in practice, when ticking off the same entries in the cash book and bank statement, the previous reconciliation figures also need to be ticked off against the current bank statement's figures.

16.4 Using previous bank reconciliation statements

On 1 August R Jones had an overdraft of £33.65 in his cash book. The previous bank reconciliation statement as on 31 July showed:

Balance as per bank statement		£149.25	
Add			
Deposits not yet credited		£440.00 ✓	
		£589.25	
Less			
Unpresented cheques:			
05 625	£37.50		
05 634	£133.20 ✓		
05 637	£98.80 ✓		
05 651	£200.00 ✓		
05 653	£153.40 ✓		£622.90
Balance as per cash book			£33.65 (overdrawn)

Cash book of R Jones

Aug 1	Balance b/d		33.65 Cr (overdrawn)

Bank statement to 16 August of R Jones

		Debit	Credit	Balance
		£	£	£
Aug 1	Balance			149.25
2	credit		440 ✓	
3	05634	133.20 ✓		
7	05637	98.80 ✓		253

(continued)

(continued)

10	05651	200.00	✓		73
10	05653	153.40	✓		
11	05654	76.92			
11	05659	123.50			
13	05663	48.00			
14	DDR (Insurance)	3235.00			
16	credit			500	

Have you checked this? The deposits of £440 and all cheques except 05625 from the previous statement, can be ticked off against the same entries on the bank statement above. The figures for August in the cash book can then be cross-checked against the remainder of the bank statement for August in the usual way.

16.5 Cheques dishonoured by the bank

The bank statement may include cheques received from customers that have been lodged as deposits then, at a later date, refused to be paid by the debtor's bank usually because of insufficient funds in the debtor's account. The entry would be first made as a credit at the bank then, once the cheque had been refused payment, a debit entry would be made on the statement.

If this occurs, the customer's account would have to be re-debited with the amount of the cheque and the bank account credited with the same figure: for example, if Mr Soames's cheque for £141 had 'R/D' (refer to drawer) and was therefore dishonoured:

Sales ledger

		Debit	Credit	Balance
		£	£	£
Soames account				
May 1	Balance			141 Dr
9	Bank		141	0
June 10	Bank (R/D)	141		141 Dr

Cash book (extract)

		Payments (credit)
		£
June 10	Soames (R/D cheque)	141

16.6 Overdrafts

Remember that a bank overdraft is shown as a debit balance in the bank statement and is a credit balance in the bank account or cash book.

When preparing the bank reconciliation statement therefore, the additions and subtractions work in the opposite way:

Bank reconciliation as on 31 August:

	£	
Balance as per statement	450 Dr	
Less		
Deposits not yet credited	210	
	340	
Add		
Unpresented cheques	425	
Balance as per cash book	765	(overdrawn)

16.7 Cheques

If a customer sends a cheque, remember that it must be correct in all detail, including signature, date, figures matching with words, etc. A cheque which is over six months old is referred to as a 'stale' cheque and will not be accepted by the bank.

Remember that there may also be arithmetic or other errors in the cash book and the bank itself is not immune to making errors. Therefore, there may be questions which will include all types of omissions and errors as well as the 'run of the mill' unpresented cheques and sums not yet credited.

Summary

The business's bank account must be periodically reconciled with the bank statement to verify that records are correct. The cash book (or bank account if held separately) needs to be brought up to date with those items in the statement such as bank charges, giro credits or direct debits. It also helps to locate errors and may be seen as a form of internal audit for banking transactions.

Questions

1 The following information represents the cash book and bank statement of B Wood, for the month of June:

Cash book (bank only)

		£			£
1/6	Balance b/f	1 407	5/6	Wages	390
8/6	Sales	1 179	8/6	Purchases	189
16/6	Sales	600	19/6	D Smith	876
26/6	Sales	615	26/6	Rent	234
			30/6	Balance c/f	?

Bank statement

		Debit (Payments) £	*Credit (Receipts)* £	*Balance* £
1/6	Balance			1 407 Cr
8/6	Credit		1 179	2 586
12/6	712	390		2 196
18/6	713	189		2 007
20/6	Credit		600	2 607
26/6	Credit transfer: D Lewis		300	2 907
28/6	STO Abbey Build Society	258		2 649
29/6	Bank charges	57		2 592

REQUIRED:

a) Balance the cash book of B Wood on 30/6, bring down the balance.

b) Bring the cash book up to date with those unticked items found in the statement. Bring down the new balance on 1/7.

c) Prepare the bank reconciliation statement as on 30/6. (16.1–2)

2 The following information relates to the banking transactions of L Jones for the month of July:

Cash book (bank only)

		£			£
1/7	Balance b/f	9 200	2/7	Rent	616
3/7	Sales	1 368	3/7	Brown	672
6/7	Birdwood	512	10/7	Wages	872
9/7	Sales	1 736	16/7	Whitehall	2 068
15/7	Peters	900	20/7	Purchases	104
24/7	Sales	716	30/7	Balance c/f	?
		14 432			14 432

Bank statement

		Dr	Cr	Balance
		£	£	£
1/7	Balance			9 200 Cr
3/7	Credit		1 368	10 568
6/7	558	672		9 896
7/7	Credit transfer J Jack		1 740	11 636
7/7	Credit		512	12 148
11/7	559	872		11 276
12/7	STO WDC	500		10 776
12/7	Credit		1 736	12 512
13/7	DD (SEB)	176		12 336
15/7	Credit		900	13 236

REQUIRED:

a) Adjust the cash book with the appropriate entries and balance as on 30/7.

b) Prepare the bank reconciliation statement as on 30/7. (16.1–2)

3 The following information relates to the cash book of R Pearce

The cash book of R Pearce for the month of August

(Dr) Receipts — Payments (Cr) Ref: C9

		Discount allowed	Cash	Bank			Discount received	Cash	Bank
		£	£	£			£	£	£
1/8	Balances b/f		200	1 925	5/8	General expenses			50
6/8	Sales		420		6/8	Drawings		120	
7/8	D Smith	10.0		200	10/8	SEB			43
13/8	Sales		345		12/8	General expenses			50
19/8	B Kings	21.5		420	13/8	Drawings		120	
20/8	Sales		410		15/8	SG (gas)			85
21/8	Contra (cash)			800	20/8	Drawings		120	
27/8	Sales		450		21/8	Contra (bank)		800	
					23/8	Stationery		25	
					26/8	General expenses			50
					27/8	Drawings		120	
					28/8	BT (telephone)			67
					30/8	Slazenger			250
						Metro			1 000
						Auto			500
					31/8	International	15		675
						Drawings		150	
						Balances c/f		370	575
		31.5	1 825	3 345			15	1 825	3 345
1/9	Balances b/f		370	575	1/9	Bank charges			8
	M Johnson			300		WDC – rates			170
						Balance c/f		370	697
			370	875				370	875
	Balances b/f		370	697					

Using the three-column cash book figures for the month of August, *check* R Pearce's bank statement against the bank columns of the cash book. Details from the bank statement were:

		Payments (Dr)	*Receipts (Cr)*	*Balance*
		£	£	£
1/8	Balance b/f			1 925 Cr
6/8	665	50		1 875
6/8	Credit		200	2 075
13/8	666	43		2 032
15/8	667	50		1 982
18/8	668	85		1 897
19/8	Credit		420	2 317
21/8	Credit		800	3 117
28/8	669	50		3 067
30/8	Charges	8		3 059
	Credit transfer – M Johnson		300	3 359
	WDC – rates	170		3 189

REQUIRED:

a) Tick the alike items on both sets of records.
b) The cash book has been brought up to date, but check the items which have been taken from the bank statement.
c) Prepare the bank reconciliation statement for the month of August. (16.1–4)

4 From the following extract from the cash book of D W Lane and the bank statement from his bank, received by him at the beginning of June:

a) Calculate the amount of D W Lane's bank balance on 31 May after making the necessary corrections in the cash book.
b) Prepare a bank reconciliation statement to reconcile the corrected cash book balance with the balance of the bank statement. (16.1–4)

Extract from the cash book of D W Lane:

		Discount	*Bank*			*Discount*	*Bank*
		£	£			£	£
1 May	Balance		300	9 May	P Stone	1	28
7 May	Cash		162	14 May	Alpha Properties – Rent		50
16 May	C Brewster	2	80	29 May	E Deakin		10
16 May	A Kennedy		9				
24 May	Cash		60				
31 May	Cash		40				

Bank statement received by D W Lane at the beginning of June:

Date	*Particulars*	*Payments* £	*Receipts* £	*Balance* £
1 May	Balance			300
4 May	Stone	28		272
7 May	Cash		162	434
10 May	Dividend from investment		63	497
17 May	Insurance premium standing order	5		492
17 May	Cheques		89	581
18 May	Property company	50		531
25 May	Cash		60	591
31 May	Charges	1		590

5 On 31 May the bank columns of R Barker's cash book showed a balance at bank of £850. A bank statement written up to the same date disclosed that the following items had not been entered in the cash book.

i) The sum of £42 paid to White Rose Insurance Company by standing order on 28 May.
ii) Commission received £120 from M Newall had been paid directly into Barker's account by credit transfer on 25 May.
iii) Bank charges of £90 had been charged directly to Barker's account on 29 May.

A further check revealed the following:

i) Cheques drawn in favour of creditors totalling £642 had not yet been presented.
ii) Cash and cheques £210 deposited at the bank on 30 May had been entered in the cash book but did not appear on the bank statement.

REQUIRED:
Write up Barker's cash book on 31 May after taking into account the above matters and prepare a bank reconciliation statement showing the balance appearing in the bank statement. (16.1–4)

6 The following were from the bank columns of the cash book of V White:

Dr		£			*Cr* £
Mar 1	Balance b/f	150	Mar 8	A Roe	30
6	Cash	75	16	T Salmon	15
13	W Wing	17	28	A Bird	29
31	R Nest	39	31	Balance c/f	
		___			___
		___			___

On 31 March she received the following bank statement from her bank:

		Debits	Credits	Balance
		£	£	£
Mar 1	Balance (Cr)			150
6	Cash		75	225
10	A Roe	30		195
13	W Wing		17	212
15	Credit transfer (M Fish)		16	228
18	T Salmon	15		213
31	Charges	10		203

REQUIRED:

a) Bring the cash book up to date, and state the new balance at 31 March.
b) Prepare a statement, under its proper title, to reconcile the difference between the new up-to-date balance in the cash book and the balance in the bank statement on 31 March. (16.1–4)

7 The following represents the cash book and bank statement of George Gershwin for the month of June:

Cash book (bank only)

		£			£
1/6	Balance b/f	180	16/6	Wages	725
14/6	Sales	450	19/6	Purchases	373
18/6	R Hammerstein	375	23/6	D Smith	405
28/6	Sales	528	28/6	Rent	250
30/6	Balance c/f	220			
		1 753			1 753
				Balance b/f	220

Bank statement for June

		Dr	Cr	Balance
		£	£	£
1/6	Balance			380 Cr
2/6	971	200		180
15/6	Credit		450	630
19/6	972	725		95 Dr
19/6	Credit		375	280 Cr
21/6	C/T: R Jones		135	415
23/6	973	405		10
28/6	WDC – Rates	185		175 Dr
29/6	Bank Charges	15		190 Dr

NOTE
C/T = credit transfer.

REQUIRED:
a) Bring the cash book up to date and balance on 30/6, bringing down the balance the next day.
b) Prepare the bank reconciliation statement for the month of June. (16.1–4)

Note: The difference between the two opening balances, £180 in the cash book and £380 in the statement. Cheque number 971 on 2/6 links the two together, an unpresented cheque from the previous period.

8 The following information relates to the cash ledger of A D Robert for the month of June:

		Debit		*Credit*
		£		£
1/6	Balance b/f	2 870	General expenses	2 420
	Debtors	8 755	Creditors	10 455
	Cash sales	6 420	Salaries	2 815
	Other receipts	895	Rental charges	400

The bank statement received by the business on 30 June showed a balance of £1 935 (credit).

When the proprietor checked his records with those of the statement, the following facts were revealed:
a) The bank's commission and other charges amounted to a total of £79.
b) A customer's cheque which had been sent to Robert, had been marked 'R/D' and dishonoured by the bank. The cheque was for £1 353.
c) A receipt of £300 from a customer of Robert, had wrongly been entered as a payment in his cash ledger.
d) The opening cash ledger balance of £2 870 was brought forward in error and should have been £2 780.
e) Several cheques signed by Robert and presented for payment, had not yet been cleared by the bank. The cheques were for: £315, £455, £170 and £595.
f) Wages of £200 had been undercast in error and had not been recorded in the cash ledger.
g) A credit transfer of £420 from a Robert customer had been directly paid into the bank.
h) Other entries in the statement included £122 paid to Robert as a dividend from ACY Ltd and a direct debit relating to an insurance premium for £70.
i) The final paying-in-book deposit of £1 800 had not yet been credited by the bank.

REQUIRED:
a) Reconstruct the cash ledger for the month of June, bringing down the balance on 30 June. Prepare the bank reconciliation statement for the month ending 30 June.
b) Why is there a need to reconcile banking transactions? (16.1–7)

9 The following information refers to a summary of R David's cash book as at the month ended 31 May.

Receipts		£	*Payments*	£
May 1	Balance b/d	2 706	General expenses	7 225
	Cash sales	11 142	Creditors	6 955
	Debtors	3 100	Wages	2 580
	Commission	2 152	Office equipment	1 000

The bank statement dated 31 May received by R David had an overdrawn balance of £893 (Dr).

When checking with the cash book records the following facts were revealed:

a) A payment of £420 to a supplier had been entered as a receipt.
b) Bank commission of £19 and administrative charges and interest payment of £23 had not yet been entered in the cash book records.
c) A cheque of £215 from a customer of R David had been dishonoured by the bank and marked 'R/D'.
d) A credit transfer of £426 from an R David customer had been directly paid through the bank.
e) Cheques of £375, £410, £72 and £95 had not yet been presented to the bank for payment.
f) The opening cash book balance of £2 706 was b/d in error and should have read £2 607.
g) A request to transfer £850 from deposit to current account, and entered in the cash book, had been misinterpreted by the bank and the transfer had been made the opposite way round. Cash book to be corrected.
h) Cash sales of £11 142 were under-cast in error and should have read £11 642.
i) The final paying-in-book deposit of £1 215 had not yet been credited by the bank.

REQUIRED:

a) Reconstruct the cash book incorporating the information above and bring down the balance on 31 May.
b) Prepare the bank reconciliation statement for the month ended 31 May. (16.1–7)

10 Kirsty McDonald has recently received the following bank statement:

National Bank plc

Kirsty McDonald Statement of Account

Date	*Details*	*Debits* £	*Credits* £	*Balance* £
Oct 30	Balance			841
Oct 31	606218	23		818
Nov 5	Sundry credit		46	864
Nov 7	606219	161		703
Nov 9	Direct debit	18		685
Nov 12	606222	93		592
Nov 15	Sundry credit		207	799
Nov 19	606223	246		553
Nov 19	Bank Giro credit		146	699
Nov 20	Bank Giro credit		246	945
Nov 21	606221	43		902
Nov 21	Sundry credit		63	965

Nov 22	Bank Giro credit		79	1 044
Nov 23	Loan interest	391		653
Nov 26	606220	87		566
Nov 26	Deposit A/C interest		84	650
Nov 27	606226	74		576
Nov 28	Sundry credit		88	664
Nov 30	606225	185		479

Her cash book showed the following details:

		£			Cheque No.	£
Nov 1	Balance b/d	818	Nov 2	Rent	219	161
Nov 5	B Mason	46	Nov 5	H Gibson	220	87
Nov 8	K Dean	146	Nov 7	G Wise	221	43
Nov 14	G Hunt	207	Nov 8	T Allen	222	93
Nov 16	C Charlton	79	Nov 12	Gas	223	246
Nov 19	D Banks	63	Nov 15	F Causer	224	692
Nov 26	P Perry	88	Nov 19	M Lewis	225	185
Nov 28	A Palmer	29	Nov 23	G Bridges	226	74
Nov 30	J Dixon	17	Nov 29	L Wilson	227	27
Nov 30	Balance c/d	206	Nov 29	P Brown	228	91
		1 699				1 699

REQUIRED:

a) Bring the cash book balance of £206 up to date as at 30 November.
b) Draw up the bank reconciliation statement as at 30 November. (16.1–7)

11 According to the cash book of John Broadbent Limited, the company's account with the North Regional Bank plc had an overdrawn balance of £1 689 on 30 April. Subsequently, the company received its bank statements for April and the following discoveries were made:

a) The following cheques, recorded in the company's cash book for April were not presented for payment until the following month:

	£
326	223
329	1 137
343	5
364	894

b) A dividend of £142 received from Justyn Tyme plc was credited direct to the company's bank account on 23 April, this is the only information the company has so far received concerning this dividend.
c) A standing order payment on 16 April of £46 in favour of the Central Traders Protection Society has been omitted from the company's cash book.
d) A cheque for £144 received from J Blunt on 21 April was returned on 30 April by North Regional Bank plc endorsed 'refer to drawer'. This coincides with information that J Blunt

has ceased trading and left the country for an undisclosed destination abroad.

e) The following items have been debited to the company on 30 April in the bank statements:

	£
Bank charges	164
Bank interest	310

f) The following items, recorded by John Broadbent Limited as receipts during April were not credited by the bank until 1 May.

	£
Timber Products plc	438
Hedge and Gate Limited	362

g) In the company's cash book for April, discounts received of £8 have been included in the bank payment column.

h) A cheque number 986 drawn by James Broadview for £1 040 has been debited in the company's bank statement on 29 April. The bank has now accepted that this was an error.

REQUIRED:

a) Prepare a corrected cash book (bank columns) to show the balance at 30 April.

b) Prepare a bank reconciliation statement at 30 April. (16.1–7)

17 The Petty Cash Book

Objectives

On completing this section you should:

- recognise that some payments for smaller expenses ought to be paid in cash
- be able to prepare a petty cash book from a given list of payments or from petty cash vouchers
- understand the posting procedure from a petty cash book to the nominal ledger.

Context

Chapter 15 discusses the cash book.

17.1 Introduction

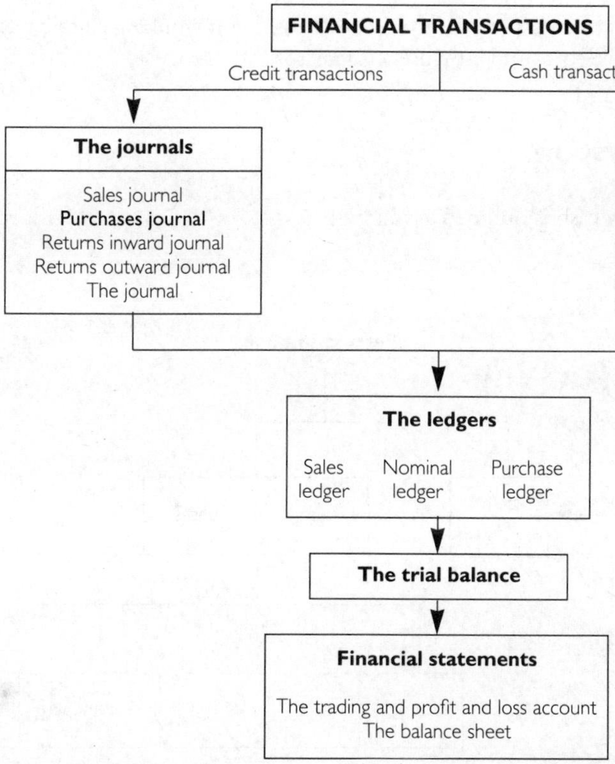

Fig. 17.1

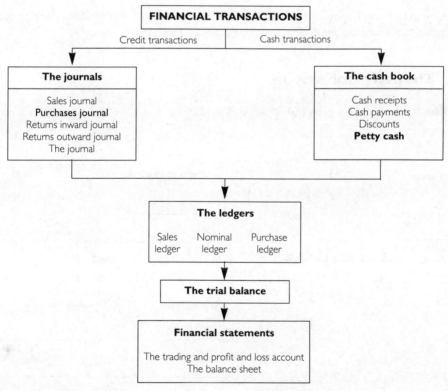

When it comes to spending relatively small sums of cash, for example, if we had to go down the road to buy tea and coffee for office refreshments, it would be convenient to have a ready sum of money available to pay for these items. This is one reason for having a petty cash system where an employee can withdraw cash, sign for it, and pay for the things required, whether it is for office refreshments, postage stamps, items of stationery or any other small expense.

The main advantages of having a petty cash system to record small payments by cash include:

- delegating responsibility to a junior member of staff and allowing more senior staff (cashier) to handle larger receipts and payments of money
- the style of the petty cash book allows for analysis columns to be totalled and posted to the ledger
- it frees the main receipts and payments of money recorded in the firm's cash book, from less significant figures like paying for tea and coffee
- it is always convenient to have some money available to make these kind of payments.

The petty cash system will give accounting assistants experience in:

a) the principles of recording financial transactions;
b) encouraging the checking of documents for correct authorisation;
c) ensuring accuracy and neatness in recording information;
d) totalling and balancing procedures;
e) recording petty cash expenses in the ledger;
f) creating some responsibility for cash and to gain confidence in dealing with other members of staff in an accounting situation.

If you were to be made responsible for keeping control of petty cash, you would need to have a good command of numeracy and be able to confidently use a calculator.

17.2 The petty cash system

The system for dealing with petty cash is outlined as follows:

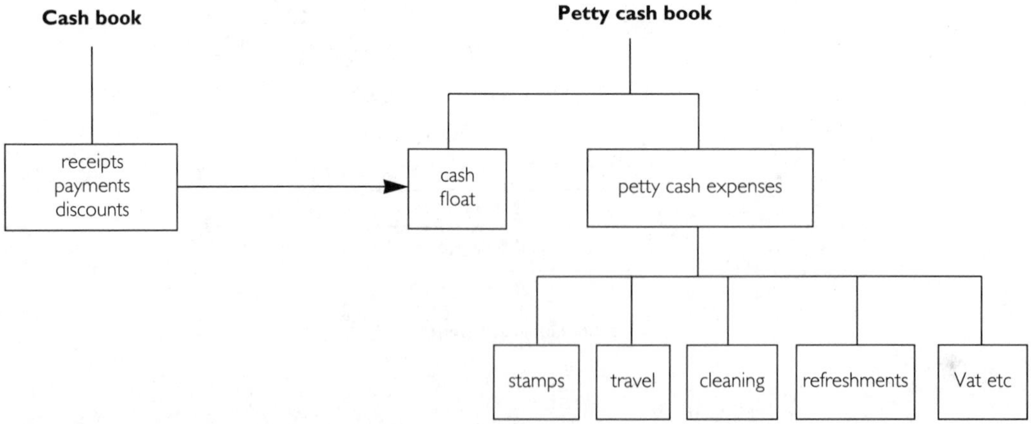

Fig. 17.2 The petty cash system

To begin a system of processing petty cash, a sum of money (float) can be used for petty cash purposes. The business may decide to allocate £100 per month to the junior assistant and make him or her responsible for distributing this money to those persons authorised to spend it. The size of the float depends upon the nature and size of the business. Some firms may require £100 per week while others may find that £100 per month is adequate.

Once a petty cash system has been set up and the junior assistant is given say, £100 per month to finance small expense payments, whatever money has been spent in the month can then be reimbursed back to the original float. For example, if £85 was used for petty cash expenses in the month, the balance remaining is £15. This is then made up (or reimbursed) back to the float of £100 by drawing a further £85 from the firm's cashier. Reimbursements can be made as frequently as required by the business. This is known as the *imprest* system.

Each person requiring cash would need to have an authorised voucher before money could be handed out. A voucher system will help to formalise the handing out of money. It should have details relating to:

a) what the payment is for;
b) the signature of the person authorising payment;
c) the signature of the person who is to take the money.

In this way, control is maintained. Each cash payment should, therefore, be supported by some documentary evidence such as a voucher. Vouchers can be numbered consecutively and the number entered in the appropriate petty cash column. An example of a voucher is shown below:

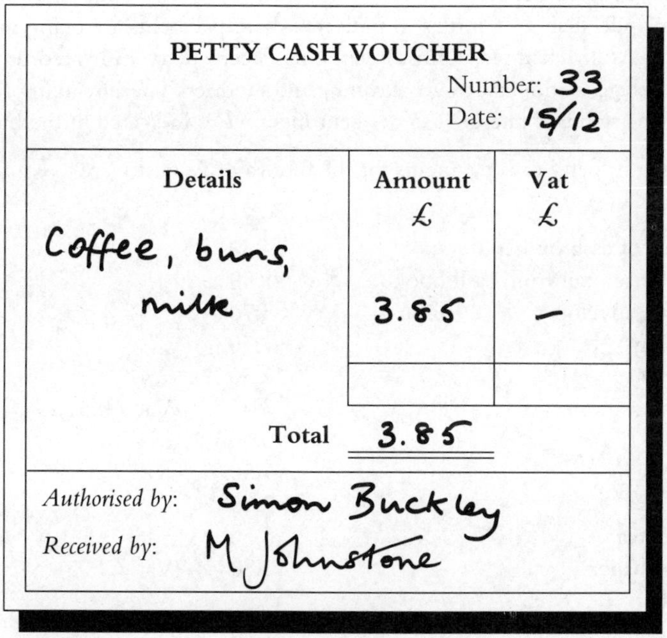

PETTY CASH VOUCHER

Number: 33
Date: 15/12

Details	**Amount** £	**Vat** £
Coffee, buns, milk	3.85	–
Total	3.85	

Authorised by: Simon Buckley
Received by: M Johnstone

Receipts obtained for items could be attached to the voucher as a record that the sum was paid for the intended purpose detailed on the voucher. It may be advisable to retain any receipts particularly for those items where Vat is charged because these may be debited and reclaimed against the Vat account.

Random checks should be made on petty cash payments, just to keep the person responsible for payments alert. The balance of money in hand, added to the vouchers used, should always equal the *imprest sum* (the float). For example:

	£
Cash in hand	27.50
Vouchers used	72.50
Float:	100.00

The double entry required to commence or reimburse the petty cash float is:

Debit:	petty cash book	(receipts)
Credit:	cash book	(payments)

17.3 The petty cash book

Once vouchers had been received and cash handed out, each payment would need to be correctly entered in a petty cash book and balanced when required. Your book would need to match your voucher records and the cash you have in hand at any time. Petty cash books may be designed in various ways. Most include analysis columns to indicate where payments are being made and to facilitate ledger posting. As an example, Christopher Jones keeps petty cash records and uses analysis columns for Vat, postage, stationery, travel, cleaning and sundries. The agreed imprest (float) is £100 per month. Vat at the standard rate of 17.5 per cent inclusive as indicated in the brackets.

Transactions relating to petty cash payments for the month of August were:

		£	
1/8	Balance of cash on hand	4.50	
	Reimbursement from cash book	95.50	
3/8	Postage, envelopes	5.70	
4/8	Cleaning	7.50	
5/8	Bus fares	2.50	
7/8	General stationery	3.45	(Vat £0.51)
9/8	Stamps	3.60	
11/8	Cleaning	7.50	
13/8	Bus fares	2.25	
14/8	Coffee, tea	5.50	
15/8	Typing paper	13.80	(Vat £2.05)
18/8	Cleaning	7.50	
19/8	Paper clips	1.60	
21/8	Postage	2.90	
24/8	General stationery	9.20	(Vat £1.37)
27/8	Bus fares	2.25	
28/8	Parcel post	5.00	
30/8	Gummed paper	2.50	

The petty cash book for the month of August might look as follows:

Petty cash book

August | No. 4

£	Date	Details	Voucher no.	Total £	Vat £	Postage £	Stationery £	Travel £	Cleaning £	Sundries £			
4 50	1	Balance b/f											
95 50		Cash book											
	3	Postage, envelopes	1	5 70		5 70							
	4	Cleaning	2	7 50					7 50				
	5	Bus fares	3	2 50				2 50					
	7	Stationery	4	3 45	51		2 94						
	9	Stamps	5	3 60		3 60							
	11	Cleaning	6	7 50					7 50				
	13	Bus fares	7	2 25				2 25					
	14	Coffee, tea	8	5 50						5 50			
	15	Typing paper	9	13 80	2 05		11 75						
	18	Cleaning	10	7 50					7 50				
	19	Paper clips	11	1 60			1 60						
	21	Postage	12	2 90		2 90							
	24	Stationery	13	9 20	1 37		7 83						
	27	Bus fares	14	2 25				2 25					
	28	Parcel post	15	5 00		5 00							
	30	Gummed paper	16	2 50			2 50						
				82 75	3 93	17 20	26 62	7 00	22 50	5 50			
		Balance c/f		17 25									
100				100									
17.25		Balance b/f											
82.75		Cash book											

The main features are:

1. The balance in hand of £4.50, is entered on the left as a debit. The sum of £95.50 is the reimbursement. The money would have come from an authorised person like the office manager or cashier, making the float to £100.
2. The payments are entered on the right hand side (that is, the credit side). First the total sum is entered, then again in the appropriate analysis column, for example, 3/8 postage and envelopes £5.70 both in the total column and also in the postages column.
3. Each payment should be accompanied by a voucher which acts as a form of receipt for the money every time a sum is paid from the petty cash box. Vouchers should be numbered consecutively.
4. The petty cash book may be totalled as often as is convenient. In this case, each month. At the end of August, £82.75 was spent from the float of £100.00. The balance is £17.25 and this should be the amount of cash left. The totals of the six analysis columns must cross-check with the grand total.
5. The balance c/f of £17.25 is recorded under the total spent. The totals (£100.00) are on the next line, both debit and credit should be level on the same line. This signifies that both receipts (debit) and payments (credit) are equal.
6. Finally, the new balance b/f £17.25, is recorded under the totals on the debit side. The cashier or office manager can then give the petty cashier £82.75 to top up the float back up to £100.00. The double entry:

Debit:	petty cash book	£82.75
Credit:	cash book	£82.75

17.4 The calculation of Vat

Where some items are purchased by petty cash, which include Vat, the amount of Vat included is recorded as a separate sum in the petty cash records because it can be recovered as 'input tax' and must be recorded in the Vat account.

Example:

	£
Envelopes and typing paper	4.40
Add 17.5% Vat	0.77
	5.17
Cleaning materials	8.00
Add 17.5% Vat	1.40
	9.40

The vouchers will need to indicate both the cost of the items and the Vat figure where applicable. When these items are recorded in the petty cash book, the procedure is:

	Total	Vat	Stationery	Cleaning
	£	£	£	£
Typing paper etc	5.17	0.77	4.40	
Cleaning materials	9.40	1.40		8.00

If a payment is given which is inclusive of Vat, it is still necessary to calculate the sum charged. Can you remember how to extract the Vat when it is inclusive?

For example, the cleaning materials were £9.40, how is the Vat calculated when it is included in the cost?

The fraction 7/47 = the Vat charged:

$$\frac{7 \times 9.40}{47} = £1.40 \quad \text{(on cleaning)}$$

$$\frac{7 \times 5.17}{47} = £0.77 \quad \text{(on stationery)}$$

17.5 Posting to the nominal ledger

The totals of the analysis columns are posted to the nominal ledger. To complete the double entry:

Debit: each analysis total (from the petty cash book) to the appropriate expense account
Credit: the petty cash book, already entered.

Cross-check these postings from the petty cash book on p. 169:

Nominal ledger

		Folio	*Debit*	*Credit*	*Balance*
Vat account					
30/8	Petty cash	PC4	3.93		3.93 Dr
Postage account					
30/8	Petty cash	PC4	17.20		17.20 Dr
Stationery account					
30/8	Petty cash	PC4	26.62		26.62 Dr
Travel expenses account					
30/8	Petty cash	PC4	7.00		7.00 Dr
Cleaning expenses account					
30/8	Petty cash	PC4	22.50		22.50 Dr
Sundry expenses account					
30/8	Petty cash	PC4	5.50		5.50 Dr

Summary

The petty cash book is a subsidiary of the cash book or bank account and is used for smaller payments in cash. The petty cash voucher is the documentary evidence for payments and all cash receipts should be attached to vouchers as evidence of payment. The posting procedure from payments in petty cash is to debit the corresponding expense account in the nominal ledger.

Questions

1 Smith & Jones uses a petty cash book system. On 30 April the cash in hand was £0.25 from an imprest of £100. The business uses a voucher system, all vouchers commencing from number 1 on the first of every month.

Analysis headings are used for: cleaning; travel; newspaper/journals; stationery; post office; refreshments; sundries; and Vat.

Transactions for May were as follows:

			Total sum £	*Vat 17.5% inclusive* £
May	1	Cash book reimbursement £99.75		
	3	Office cleaning	11.50	1.71
	4	Stamps, post	8.50	
	7	Pencils, pens, etc.	5.52	0.82
	11	Newspapers, magazines	2.20	
	13	Tea, coffee	4.85	
	14	Envelopes, ribbons, etc.	11.50	1.71
	15	Postage, telegrams	9.50	
	17	General stationery	23.00	3.42
	19	Charity donations	10.00	
	20	Increase of imprest from cash book	25.00	
	23	Taxi fares	8.00	
	24	Office cleaning	11.50	1.71
	27	Stamps	3.50	
	28	Floor polish	0.80	
	30	Newspapers	1.30	

REQUIRED:

a) Prepare the petty cash book for Smith & Jones for the month of May. Bring down the balance on 1 June.

b) Post the analysis totals to the nominal ledger as on 31 May. Commence each expense type, including Vat, with a nil balance.

c) Is the use of vouchers a waste of time? The petty cash book can still be prepared without them, so why bother? Briefly explain your view. (17.2-5)

2 Gilly Jones runs her petty cash on the imprest system, having a float of £200 per month. She uses analysis columns for: Vat, post, travel, cleaning, refreshments, stationery and sundries. At the end of August, she had £28.75 to carry forward to the new month. During the first three weeks of September, the following transactions occurred:

September:

1	Enter the balance brought down from August in the petty cash book.
2	Cashier reimburses Gill to bring up to required float.
3	Purchased stamps £12.50.

5 Rail fares to Bristol, £13.60.
6 Typing paper, biros etc. £14.10 (inc. Vat 17.5%).
8 New kettle and cups £18.80 (inc. Vat 17.5%).
11 Window cleaner £10.50.
12 Postal orders £8.75.
15 Taxi expenses £7.80.
16 Repairs to typewriter £12.80+Vat 17.5%.
18 Window cleaner £10.50.
20 Donation for Poppy Appeal £2.00.
20 Milk money £6.25.
21 Tea, coffee etc. £4.80.

For the remainder of September, there are 8 further vouchers to record.

Petty cash vouchers for question 2

Petty Cash Voucher No. 22 Date 22/9

For what required	Amount £	Amount p
Misc. items of stationery	1	80
VALUE ADDED TAX:		32

Signature David James
Passed by GH

Petty Cash Voucher No. 26 Date 27/9

For what required	Amount £	Amount p
Train fare S'ampton	11	40
VALUE ADDED TAX:		
	11	40

Signature S. Davies
Passed by GH

Petty Cash Voucher No. 23 Date 24/9

For what required	Amount £	Amount p
Coffee, tea, cakes	4	24
VALUE ADDED TAX:		
	4	24

Signature Julie Harris
Passed by GH

Petty Cash Voucher No. 27 Date 28/9

For what required	Amount £	Amount p
Magazines & papers	3	40
VALUE ADDED TAX:		
	3	40

Signature H. Daws
Passed by GH

Petty Cash Voucher No. 24 Date 25/9

For what required	Amount £	Amount p
Milk	8	20
VALUE ADDED TAX:		
	8	20

Signature
Passed by

Petty Cash Voucher No. 28 Date 28/9

For what required	Amount £	Amount p
Stamps	4	65
Envelopes	2	21
Card	1	50
VALUE ADDED TAX:		

Signature Julie Harris
Passed by GH

Petty Cash Voucher	No. 25 Date 27/9	
For what required	Amount	
	£	p
Window cleaner	10	50
VALUE ADDED TAX:	–	
	10	50
Signature David James		
Passed by GG		

Petty Cash Voucher	No. 29 Date 30/9	
For what required	Amount	
	£	p
Stationery		?
VALUE ADDED TAX:		?
	4	98
Signature G. Capes		
Passed by GG		

REQUIRED:

a) Enter the above petty cash transactions in the petty cash book of Gill Graham. Record the remaining 8 petty cash vouchers, calculating the Vat wherever there is no figure in the total.

b) Balance the petty cash book on 30 September, bringing down the balance the next day.

c) Post the individual analysis columns to the ledger. (17.2–5)

3 The following information relates to J Robertson's petty cash. He keeps an imprest of £125 per month. The cash in hand on 1 July was £8.40 and the necessary reimbursement from the cash book was made on the same date. Transactions for July were as follows:

			Voucher no.	*Total sum* £	
June	1	Cash book reimbursement			17.5%
	3	Motor expenses	1	8.05	(Vat inc.)
	5	Stationery	2	4.60	(Vat inc.)
	8	Office cleaning	3	10.00	
	9	Refreshments	4	7.25	
	10	Newspapers	5	1.25	
	11	Postage	6	6.60	
	14	Envelopes, paper	7	16.10	(Vat inc.)
	16	Office cleaning	8	10.00	
	17	Motor expenses	9	12.65	(Vat inc.)
	20	Repair to chair	10	17.25	(Vat inc.)
	23	Coffee, tea	11	8.35	
	26	Parcel post	12	3.65	

REQUIRED:

a) Prepare the petty cash book for J Robertson for the month of July. Use appropriate analysis columns of your choice.

b) Balance as on 31 July, bringing forward the balance on 1 August and showing the appropriate cash book reimbursement. (17.3–4)

4 G Walton uses a petty cash book in her business. She uses the following analysis column headings: cleaning; office refreshments; travel; postage and telegrams; Vat; and sundries.
Her petty cash float is £150 per month. The balance brought forward on 30/6 was £2.75. The transactions for the month of July were:

			Voucher no	*Total sum* £	*Vat 17.5% (inclusive)* £
July	1	Balance b/f		2.75	
		Cash book (reimbursement)		147.25	

3	Office coffee, tea, etc.	1	7.50	
5	Fares – taxi	2	15.00	
7	Cleaning	3	9.20	1.37
8	Bus tickets	4	2.45	
11	Stamps	5	7.50	
12	Crockery (sundries)	6	17.25	2.56
15	Telegrams, parcel post	7	5.25	
17	Journals and newspapers	8	8.55	
22	Cleaning	9	9.20	1.37
23	Bus tickets	10	3.30	
24	Office refreshments	11	6.20	
27	Replacement glass	12	24.15	3.59
28	Fares – taxi	13	14.00	
30	Postage	14	8.40	

REQUIRED:

a) Prepare the petty cash book for G Walton for the month of July.
b) Indicate briefly how the analysis columns may be posted to the ledger. (17.3–5)

5 D Lewis uses an imprest system for the payment of minor expenses. The imprest is £150. Analysis columns are used for: postages & stationery; Vat; travel; office refreshments; and sundries.

On 1/7 his balance brought forward was £9.50. He was reimbursed with the imprest balance on the same day. You are to prepare the petty cash book for D Lewis for July. Transactions for July were as follows:

			Voucher no	*Total sum* £	*Vat 17.5% (inclusive)* £
July	3	General stationery	1	12.65	1.88
	4	Taxi fares	2	5.85	
	5	Stamps	3	7.20	
	7	Typing paper	4	16.10	2.39
	8	Bus fares	5	3.50	
	10	General stationery	6	13.80	2.05
	12	Cleaning materials	7	11.50	1.71
	15	Refreshments	8	6.25	
	18	Bus fares	9	3.20	
	19	Writing materials	10	18.40	2.74
	22	Bus fares	11	3.75	
	23	Newspapers, etc.	12	5.15	
	24	Stamps, parcels	13	8.00	
	27	Refreshments	14	6.20	
	28	Tea tray, cups	15	9.20	1.37
	30	Taxi fares	16	3.25	

REQUIRED:

a) Balance the petty cash book on 31 July, bringing down the balance the next day.
b) Post the totals of the analysis columns to the ledger. (17.3–5)

6 ABC Co uses the bank for all significant receipts and payments of cash. All cash payments under £10 come out of the petty cash. The imprest is £100 and is reimbursed every month by a cheque payment from the cash book.

The headings used by ABC Co are as follows: cleaning; travelling expenses; stationery; post office; refreshments; general; and Vat.

The balance of the petty cash on 30 June was £15.65. The firm uses the voucher system, all vouchers being from number 1 on the first of the month.

The transactions for July were as follows:

			£
July	2	Reimbursement from cash book	
	2	Cleaning materials	1.50
		Vat	0.26
	3	Stamps and parcel post	8.68
	6	Window cleaning	6.00
		Vat	1.05
	8	Pens, pencils, typing paper	10.00
		Vat	1.75
	11	Newspapers	0.85
	12	Tea, coffee and sugar	3.76
	15	Envelopes, ribbons	2.40
		Vat	0.42
	19	Telegrams	4.60
	20	Taxi fares	3.85
	23	Charity donations	1.50
	27	Bus fares	4.50
	28	Window cleaning	6.00
		Vat	1.05
	29	Floor polish and dusters	2.80
		Vat	0.49

REQUIRED:

a) Draw up a petty cash book using the appropriate columns. Bring the imprest balance up to date on 2 July.

b) Enter the above transactions and balance the book on 31 July. Bring down the balance and make the appropriate reimbursement on 1 August.

c) Post the analysis totals to the general ledger on 31 July. (17.3–5)

(BTEC National)

7 The following headings are used to analyse the petty cash columns: Vat, postage, stationery, travel cleaning, sundries and the total.

The agreed imprest is £100 per month. It is the usual policy of the firm to transfer the analysis totals to the ledger (where the accounts are recorded), at the end of the month.

Transactions for January were as follows:

		£
1/1	Balance of cash in hand	4.50
1/1	Reimbursement from cashier	95.50
3/1	Postages	5.70
4/1	Window cleaning	7.50
5/1	Bus fares	2.50
7/1	Stationery (inc. Vat)	3.45
9/1	Postages	3.60
11/1	Window cleaning	7.50
13/1	Bus fares	2.25
14/1	Coffee and tea	5.50
15/1	Typing paper (inc. Vat)	13.80
18/1	Window cleaning	7.50

19/1	Paper clips, etc.	1.60
21/1	Postages	2.90
24/1	Stationery (inc. Vat)	9.20
27/1	Bus fares	2.25
28/1	Parcel post	5.00
30/1	Gummed paper	2.50

REQUIRED:

a) Prepare the petty cash book for the company for the month of January, bringing down the balance and the correct reimbursement for February.
b) Post the analysis totals to the nominal ledger on the debit side of each account.
c) The accountant has asked you to provide a checklist of what you consider important for the security of handling petty cash. (17.3–5)

18 Computer-based accounts

Objectives

On completing this section you should:

- understand some of the terminology used in computer-based programs such as hardware and software
- recognise the advantages of using computer programs in accounting.

Context

Chapter 6 outlines business accounting systems in general.

18.1 Introduction

Computers have revolutionised accounting. Most large businesses now use computerised accounting systems as do many small businesses. There are many advantages in using such systems compared to manual systems:

- data can be processed more quickly
- data can be processed more accurately
- a greater volume of data can be processed
- with just one data entry, other parts of the accounting system can be automatically updated
- data can be accessed more easily
- data can be analysed more quickly and effectively
- reports can be generated more quickly and effectively
- computerised systems can link accounting and other functions in the business more effectively.

There are also a number of problems associated with computerised accounting systems. These include:

- the cost of acquiring and running the relevant hardware and software
- the training and expertise required in operating such systems
- potential inflexibility in adapting systems to individual business requirements

This chapter looks at some of the issues involved in setting up and operating a computerised accounting system.

18.2 Hardware

There are many types of hardware, that is, the computer and its peripheral equipment, available to businesses. Larger companies may well have centralised mainframe systems servicing all the departments within a business. Smaller firms, together with an increasing number of bigger firms, may make more use of one or a network of microcomputers, each with its own software and database. This solution can be more cost-effective and give individual users the chance to develop their own tailormade systems, though it can also create problems of coordination and communication.

An illustration of a microcomputer is shown opposite.

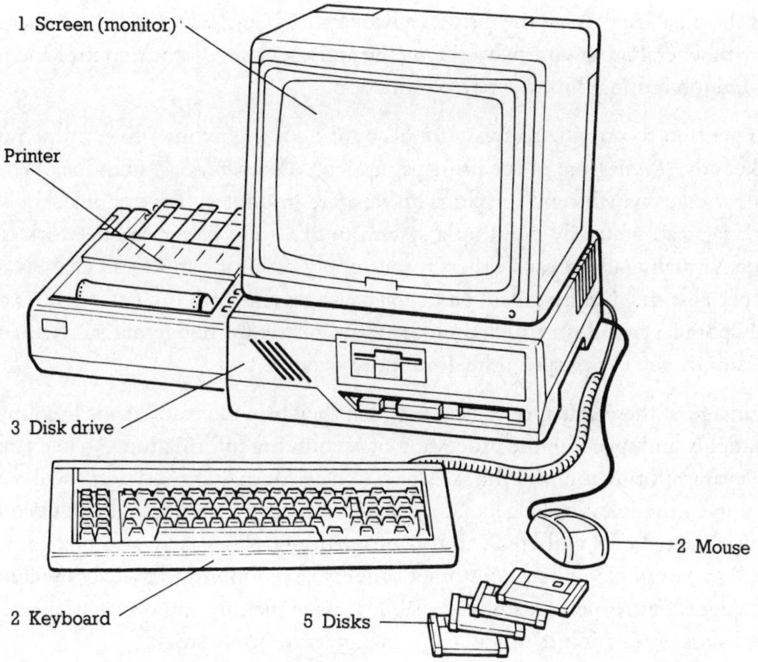

Fig 18.1 The hardware components of a microcomputer

1 The computer screen which provides the visual display of the program and data.

2 The keyboard, very much like that of the typewriter, but having a number of extra keys to provide further computer functions. The keyboard is complemented by a mouse which allows a user to move a pointer around on the screen. Within a windows environment a user can click on commands or icons representing particular functions and access them more quickly and easily than typing instructions into a keyboard.

3 The computer disk drive. This will include a hard disk, usually housed permanently in the computer itself, which has significant storage capacity and a processing speed. The hard disk can be used to store data and software within the computer itself.

4 The printer, which has the obvious function of printing the information (called hard copies) required for business documents such as invoices and customer statements, and also the printouts of individual accounts.

5 Floppy disks with software programs or data. Mostly $3^1/_2''$ in diameter, these disks may provide data to be loaded into the computer or a particular software application. In the latter case, it may be necessary to load the disk to run the software. Alternatively, the software can be copied on to the hard drive, removing the need to have the floppy disk inserted to run the application every time a user needs a particular programme.

18.3 Software

Software provides the instructions for a particular application for use on a computer. The range of software programs tailored specifically to the accountant is large. These include many packages which basically provide the same functions: to improve the recording, storage and retrieval of information.

Many of these packages have the distinct advantage of being fully integrated, that is, the package can link up with several programs such as invoicing and sales ledger, stock control and purchase/sales processing, and job costing with the payroll function.

The competition to provide software for accounting is highly intensive. Some popular packages on the market are *Pegasus* (one of the principal leaders), *Plusmark, Sage* and *Tetra*. These provide a wide range of packages which tend to start with separate 'modules', for example, the sales and purchases ledgers. Users can gradually build up a system until a fully integrated network is developed where computers virtually talk to each other in the supply of information and analysis. *Lotus* and *Microsoft* tend to specialise in what are called *spreadsheet* packages and both the *Lotus 1–2–3* and *Excel* programs are highly popular in industry and commerce particularly for budgeting, analysis and graphics. Chapter 37 examines the use of spreadsheets in more detail.

The advantage of these software programs is that they provide ready made accounting systems which greatly simplify and speed up the processing of accounting information. As an example, once you key in the relevant information into the sales or purchase journal, most systems will automatically update the accounts in the relevant ledgers. Some accounting software packages go even further in producing invoices, statements and credit notes automatically. They may also link into other parts of the business. As an example, when a customer order is keyed in, some packages will not only update the relevant ledgers but also check stock availability, issue picking and dispatch instructions to the warehouse and alert production to any need to manufacture more stock.

Accounting packages will also produce up-to-date reports on a range of issues from Vat to aged debtor lists. Other possible reports may include those answering the following questions:

- How much is owed to creditors and when do they need to be paid?
- How much do customers owe and do they pay regularly?
- Is sufficient cash coming in?
- Which products sell best?
- How much is spent on overheads?
- How much is spent on the payroll?
- Is there sufficient stock available?

18.4 Using accounting software (1): the example of the sales ledger program

An accounting program may either be part of a network system or linked to a mainframe, where it may be conveniently called upon the screen when required, by simply pressing the appropriate command key. Or, it may be necessary to load a program disk which includes the program instructions to run a particular function, such as the sales or purchases ledgers.

If the program is being used for the first time, it will be necessary to set up the relevant ledger and customer accounts. These are generally given a code for automatic recognition. Particular products may also be given particular codes to allow a business to call up reports about the sales performance of a particular product line, for example.

Once a disk is loaded onto the computer, the operator will choose which file or menu is required. There may be several files on an accounting package and the computer may require an identifying letter or number, for example, '1' may be the code for the sales ledger program, '2' for the purchase ledger.

Programs in business usually operate on what is called a *menu* system, that is, the user is given a number of choices or functions to use. The user will choose a particular function and press the relevant key in order to get started. For example, in the programs shown in this section, the Jenkins Jeans Co Ltd displays the following main menu:

1. Sales Ledger
2. Purchase Ledger
3. Nominal Ledger
4. Stock Control
5. Payroll
6. Invoicing
7. Costing
8. Terminate

Select and Press Number Required

The first function we need is the sales ledger, therefore the number 1 would be pressed on the keyboard. The sub-menu of the sales ledger would then be displayed:

MENU: SALES LEDGER

1. Ledger Transactions
2. Period End
3. Analysis of Sales
4. Reports

Select and Press Number Required

The most frequently used function would be number 1, Ledger Transactions, which would give a list of further options to operate such as entering invoices, credit notes and receipts. The function Period End may be used to end a financial period and sales turnover may be zeroed to commence a new period. The customers' balances are not zeroed of course, the balance being brought forward.

The Analysis of Sales function may be particularly useful to those types of businesses which want to know which stocks are moving and which may be slow. They may want an analysis of sales geographically, by department or by sales executives. Sales may easily be coded for this purpose. The fourth function, Reports may be used to indicate batches of sales over periods of time or any other statistical information provided by a particular program.

The general features of a reasonable sales ledger program would include:

a facility to store a large number of accounts;
details of each debtor's records;
individual customer turnover to date;
automatic processing to the nominal ledger, thereby completing the double entry;
sales journal;
Vat analysis;
credit control limits for customers;
aged debtors analysis;
receipts analysis and details of discounts;
customer statements.

Most of the above items would be available for printout and this gives computer-based accounting a further edge. Not only can this information be stored on a small disk, it can be retrieved instantly and a copy output on the printer whenever the information is required – unbeatable over a manual system any time. In large organisations the use of computerised information is essential for management and helps them in their daily decision making.

If the user selected function number 1 of the sales ledger menu, Ledger Transactions, a further menu would appear, giving an additional list of options:

MENU: LEDGER TRANSACTIONS

1. Accounts Up-Date
2. Ledger Posting
3. Invoice & Credit Note Listing
4. Receipts & Adjustments
5. Customer Accounts
6. Customer Statements
7. Aged Debtors List
8. List of Accounts
9. Outstanding Debtors Total
10. Terminate

Select and Press Number Required

The Ledger Transactions function would be used daily to enter details relating to customers. Examples of these functions are shown as hard copies in the exercise relating to Jenkins Jeans Co Ltd on pages 185–88. The facilities that each of the options provide is summarised overleaf:

1 **Accounts Up-Date:** The screen would show information such as:

*ACCOUNT NUMBER	NAME & ADDRESS
S001	J. DAVIES 14 Highfield Road Broadstone

COMMENT	CREDIT LIMIT	CODE
Tele. 554788	4 000	S

*Cursor flashing

The cursor is awaiting an instruction from the user and in this case it is flashing over the account number and is waiting for the operator to enter the relevant number. If the account is new, the computer will state 'New Account' and await further input. If the account is an existing one, all other relevant information will be displayed on screen (as above).

2 **Ledger Posting:** The cursor on the screen would prompt which account was required and then the details of the customer would be displayed automatically:

ACCOUNT NUMBER	DATE	TYPE	REFERENCE	VALUE	VAT/DISC.	PERIOD
S001	1/1/90	A	Open/Bal	800		1
J. DAVIES						

In the above example, the opening balance of a customer, J Davies, has been entered. Under 'TYPE', the letter 'A' signifies the appropriate code to enter an opening balance. The letter 'I' could signify invoice, the letter 'C' credit note, and so forth. Once details of any transaction are entered, the sales ledger file is automatically updated and may be viewed when required.

3 **Invoice & Credit Note Listing:** This function lists the invoice and credit notes for any given period, for example, a day, a week, a month, or longer. In the printout, the month's invoices and credit notes are listed. This detail would be the same as that given in the sales journal:

Sales:	£1 040
Vat	£156
Total Debtors	£1 196

4 **Receipts & Adjustments:** This function allows the operator to list the receipts and adjustments for the period required as with the invoice and credit note listing. In the printout, totals are shown for:

Receipts:	£1 510
Discounts	£40
Adjustments:	£1 250 (opening balances)

5 **Customer Accounts:** This function is used to display, either on screen or printout, the details of each customer's account. All transactions to the debtor are shown, including:

date of entries
invoice and credit note numbers
cheque numbers
discounts given
the age of the debt in months.

This function is used frequently to check records of individual customers and will be an important check on credit control. How much does the customer owe? Account No. S001 (Davies) has a current debt of £299. When did he last pay his account? Does he pay in reasonable time? These are important questions which need answers in order to keep adequate control of customer accounts. The speed of debt collection is vital to a business's cash flow and working capital.

6 **Customer Statements:** If a customer's statement needs to be printed and sent, this function will give details of the account as found in option number 5 above.

7 **Aged Debtors List:** This function may be viewed on screen or as a printout, as shown in the example. The balance of each customer is indicated and 'aged' according to how old the debt is. In the printout, all the debts are listed as 'current', the total debt being £896. This figure should equal the sales ledger control account as in the nominal ledger. The credit limit and telephone numbers of each customer are also printed for convenience.

8 **List of Accounts:** This function gives a list of the customer accounts required. In the printout,

only three accounts of Jenkins Jeans are listed as an example, also indicating the turnover to date, credit limit and telephone number of each customer. Code 'S' can refer to the geographical area the customer comes from.

9 **Outstanding Debtors Total:** This function will display on screen the outstanding debt owed by the total debtors. It should equal the total amount given in option number 7 and is used as a quick check on how much customers owe; it should also equal the sales ledger control account balance.

Total Debtors = £896

10 **Terminate:** This function returns the operator to the main sales ledger menu.

An example of the computer-based accounts of Jenkins Jeans Co Ltd is presented as a set of printouts on the following pages.

If you were using a sales ledger program you would:
A. Enter the invoices below in the sales program of Jenkins Jeans Co Ltd. On 1 January Davies had a balance of £800 and Smith £450 in the sales ledger.

During the month of January, the following invoices were sent to customers:

	Name	*Invoice*	*Amount £*	*Sales code*
5/1	Davies	2334	200 + Vat	S161 (clothing)
12/1	Smith	2335	80 + Vat	S162 (equipment)
17/1	Davies	2336	120 + Vat	S162 (equipment)
17/1	Forbes (new)	2337	400 + Vat	S163 (misc.)
28/1	Smith	2338	300 + Vat	S161 (clothing)

Credit note sent to customer:

24/1	Davies	c/n 42	60 + Vat	S162 (equipment)

Cheques received during January were:

	Name	*Amount (£)*
28/1	Davies	760 (discount allowed £40).
30/1	Smith	500 on account.
30/1	Forbes	250 on account.
31/1	Cash sales	3 220 (into bank). (Vat £420 included)

B. Enter all cheques received in the sales program.

C. Obtain the appropriate hard copies as indicated below.

18.4.1 The sales ledger program printouts

Printouts from ledger transactions are as follows:

a) Option No. 3: Invoices and credit note listing;
b) Option No. 4: Receipts and adjustments;
c) Option No. 5: Customer accounts;
d) Option No. 7: Aged debtors list;

e) Option No. 8: List of accounts; and
f) Option No. 9: Sales analysis.

Option No. 3: Invoice and credit note listing

Jenkins Jeans Co Ltd

01.01. S/L Invoices & Credit Notes (To Date) Page 1

A/c	Date	Type	Reference	Value	Goods	VAT	
S001	05.01	Invce	2 334	230.00	200.00	30.00	J Davies
S002	12.01	Invce	2 335	92.00	80.00	12.00	F Smith
S001	17.01	Invce	2 336	138.00	120.00	18.00	J Davies
S003	01.01	Invce	2 337	460.00	400.00	60.00	B Forbes
S002	28.01	Invce	2 338	345.00	300.00	45.00	F Smith
S001	24.01	Cnote	c/n	–69.00	–60.00	–9.00	J Davies
Total Invoices				1 265.00	1 100.00	165.00	
Total Cr. Notes				–69.00	–60.00	–9.00	
Total				1 196.00	1 040.00	156.00	

Note: acts as the Sales Journal

Option No. 4: Receipts and adjustments

Jenkins Jeans Co Ltd

01.01. S/L Receipts & Adjusts (To Date) Page 1

A/c	Date	Type	Reference	Value	Period	
S001	01.01	Adjust	open/bal	800.00	1	J Davies
S002	01.01	Adjust	open/bal	450.00	1	F Smith
S001	28.01	Recpt	chq345678	–760.00	1	J Davies
S001	28.01	Discnt	chq345678	–40.00	1	J Davies
S002	30.01	Recpt	chq234567	–500.00	1	F Smith
S003	30.01	Recpt	chq234123	–250.00	1	B Forbes
Total Discounts				–40.00		
Total Receipts				–1 510.00		
Total Refunds				.00		
Total Adj – Contras				.00		
Total Adj – Bad Debts				.00		
Total Adj – Write Offs				.00		
Total Adj – Misposts				.00		
Total Adj – Discounts				.00		
Total Adj – Interest				.00		
Total Adj – Sundry				1 250.00		
Total				–300.00		

Option No. 5: Customer accounts

J Davies | Account S001 | 01 Jan
14 Highfield Rd
Broadstone | T/Over 260/Jan | Cr. Lim 4 000
Interest Rate 0.00%

Date	Type	Reference	Status	Debit	Credit	Balance
01.01	Adjust	open/bal	Jan	800.00		
05.01	Invoice	2334		230.00		
17.01	Invoice	2336		138.00		
24.01	Cr. Note	c/n			69.00	
28.01	Receipt	chq345678	Jan		760.00	
28.01	Discnt	chq345678	Jan		40.00	

3 Months+	2 Months	1 Month	Current	Total
.00	.00	.00	299.00	299.00

Note: indicates the turnover (£260) for the month (exc. vat)
Credit Limit £4 000

F Smith | Account S002 | 01 Jan
224 Ashley Rd
Poole | T/Over 380/Jan | Cr. Lim 4 000
Interest Rate 0.00%

Date	Type	Reference	Status	Debit	Credit	Balance
01.01	Adjust	open/bal	Jan	450.00		
12.01	Invoice	2335		92.00		
28.01	Invoice	2338		345.00		
30.01	Receipt	chq234567	Jan		500.00	

3 Months+	2 Months	1 Month	Current	Total
.00	.00	.00	387.00	387.00

B. Forbes | Account S003 | 01 Jan
15 Christchurch Rd
Bournemouth | T/Over 400/Jan | Cr. Lim 4 000
Interest Rate 0.00%

Date	Type	Reference	Status	Debit	Credit	Balance
01.01	Invoice	2337		460.00		
30.01	Receipt	chq234123	Jan		250.00	

3 Months+	2 Months	1 Month	Current	Total
.00	.00	.00	210.00	210.00

Option No. 7: Aged debtors list

Jenkins Jeans Co Ltd

01.01.			Aged Debtors List			Page 1
A/c	3 Months +	2 Months	1 Month	Current	Total	Cr. Limit
S001	.00	.00	.00	299.00	299.00	4 000
.Davies			000 554788*			
S002	.00	.00	.00	387.00	387.00	4 000
.Smith			000 667744			
S003	.00	.00	.00	210.00	210.00	4 000
.Forbes			000 554433			
Total	.00	.00	.00	896.00	896.00	

*Customer's telephone number

Option No. 8: List of accounts

S001	J Davies	000 554788	
	14 Highfield Rd	Code S	
	Broadstone	Type B	
		Cr. Limit	4 000
		T/Over	260/Jan
S002	F Smith	000 667744	
	224 Ashley Rd	Code S	
	Poole	Type B	
		Cr. Limit	4 000
		T/Over	380/Jan
S003	B Forbes	000 554433	
	15 Christchurch Rd	Code S	
	Bournemouth	Type B	
		Cr. Limit	4 000
		T/Over	400/Jan

Note: Code S indicates 'southern' trader
Type B indicates 'balance' brought forward each month
Telephone numbers and credit limits included
Turnover per month excludes Vat

Option No. 9: Sales analysis

Jenkins Jeans Co Ltd

01.01. Sales Analysis Input Page 1

Code	Type	VAT	Value	A/c	Date	Reference
S L697	I	0	30.00	S001	05.01	2334
S S161	I	1	200.00			
S L697	I	0	12.00	S002	12.01	2335
S S162	I	1	80.00			
S L697	I	0	18.00	S001	17.01	2336
S S162	I	1	120.00			
S L697	I	0	60.00	S003	01.01	2337
S S163	I	1	400.00			
S L697	I	0	45.00	S002	28.01	2338
S S161	I	1	300.00			
S L697	C	0	–9.00	S001	24.01	c/n
S S162	C	1	–60.00			

Jenkins Jeans Co Ltd

01.01. Sales Analysis Input Page 1

Cust. Type	Product	Value	
S	L697	156.00	Vat
S	S161	500.00	Clothing
S	S162	140.00	Equipment
S	S163	400.00	Miscellaneous
Total		1 196.00	

Check the sales ledger control account with the aged debtors list:

Sales ledger	Control account	Debit	Credit	Balance
		£	£	£
1 Jan	Balance			1 250 Dr
31	Sales, Vat	1 196		2 446
31	Bank, discount		1 550	896

18.5 Using accounting software (2): the purchase ledger program

This program operates in an almost identical way to the sales ledger program and is used to record the individual suppliers of a business, giving details of purchases, returns, payments, and any other information which relates to creditors.

The control of purchasing is a key management function. All purchases must be bought and paid for at the right time, at the right quantity and quality, and at the right price. Management needs to have up-to-date information about all its suppliers. How long will they wait before payment? What discounts do they offer? Who is the person to contact in the event of queries?

The amount of money a business spends on its stock can be a major expenditure and therefore affects its cash flow and working capital. Has the business sufficient cash resources to pay its creditors on time?

A good computer program can provide the up-to-the-minute information management needs, including:

- a facility to store a large number of accounts;
- details of supplier's records;
- supplier turnover;
- printouts of the purchases journal;
- Vat analysis;
- automatic processing to the nominal ledger;
- analysis of purchases, payments and discounts;
- aged creditors analysis;
- a link-up to stock control.

The options available on the purchases ledger program are virtually the same as those of the sales program and the sub-menu, Ledger Transactions, is the one most frequently in use on a daily basis to record all transactions with suppliers.

18.6 Using computers to improve business systems

As we have seen, the use of accounting software can greatly improve the speed, cost, reliability and flexibility of a manual accounting system. However, it is being increasingly recognised that information technology can do more than just automate existing manual systems in helping business. It can help to transform existing practices, and the organisation lying behind them. A classic example is Ford's reorganisation of its purchasing department.

In the 1980s, Ford employed 500 people to deal with purchase orders within its accounts department. On a visit to a rival manufacturer, Ford discovered that the equivalent department employed only 5! This huge difference prompted them to look more closely at their procedures.

When the purchasing department issued a purchase order a copy went to the accounts department. When the goods themselves were received, stock control would send invoice details to accounts, as would the supplier. If all three matched, accounts would issue payment. Accounts staff spent most of their time dealing with mismatches between these documents, particularly as the invoice had 14 separate items to check off against the supplier's invoice and the goods-received information from stock control.

Ford used computers to help streamline the process. Under its new system, the purchasing department now enters details of a purchase order onto a database using far fewer details than before. When the goods are delivered, stock control checks them off against the database details. If they match, the goods are booked in and the database details updated for accounts to issue payment. If they don't, the goods are rejected and returned to the supplier. In this way, Ford cuts down the paperwork and the amount of cross-checking within the company.

Ford's system could, for example, be applied in Chapter 10 where there is currently a large amount of paperwork in processing within the purchasing department.

Summary

There are many computer-based accounting programs available to help businesses update their accounting systems and to provide instant information to help their decision-making. Computerised accounts provides immediate access to any section of information required including 'up to the minute' analysis of key accounting areas and has the important facility of providing hard copy when required. For the larger organisations, computer-based accounting is seen as an essential aspect of their financial systems.

Questions

1 Briefly explain why more large businesses tend to use computer programs rather than the traditional manual methods of recording financial information (18.1).

2 Briefly describe the parts which make up the computer's hardware (18.2).

3 What is computer software? What kind of software is available in accounting (18.3)?

4 A computer program often works by a menu system. What is a menu in computer language? Give an example to illustrate your answer (18.4).

5 In the printouts of the sales ledger program, check the following:
   a) the function of option 3 (invoice and credit notes) and how it relates to the sales journal;
   b) the function of option 5 (customer accounts) and how the information compares with a manual recording in the sales ledger;
   c) the significance of option 7 (aged debtors) and its usefulness to management;
   d) the function of option 9 (sales analysis) and the importance of having sub-totals for each sales category (18.4).

6 If you have access to a computer system and an accounting program, try to input the data from an appropriate journal question from the previous chapters.

7 Which type of businesses would not really benefit from the use of a business program?

19 The accounting system in action: a worked example from subsidiary books to trial balance

Objectives

On completing this section you should:

- have an improved understanding of the accounting system
- recognise the various parts which make up the whole of the worked example
- use the example as a project by changing the Vat rate.

Context

This chapter assumes you have read and understood Parts 3 and 4.

19.1 Introduction

In this chapter we bring together the skills learnt in Parts 3 and 4, using an extended example from the books of R Pearce. This extended example will illustrate the following:

a) Setting up the ledgers.
b) Preparing the sales journal.
c) Preparing the purchases journal.
d) Preparing the cash book receipts and payments.
e) Preparing the bank reconciliation statement.
f) Extracting a trial balance.

You are to place yourself in the position of R Pearce's accounts assistant responsible for preparing all the necessary entries for the month of January. Please note that, for the purposes of this exercise, Vat is calculated at 15%.

19.2 Setting up the ledgers

The following information represents the accounts of R Pearce on 1 January

	£
Premises (cost)	100 000
Equipment, machinery (cost)	13 500
Motor vehicle (cost)	5 000
Bank (Dr)	455
Petty cash float	150
Sales ledger control (debtors)	2 575
Bought ledger control (creditors)	5 640
Stocks	3 680
R Pearce: Capital	50 000
Mortgage on premises	69 720

R. Pearce also has the following personal ledger accounts already set up.

Sales ledger

	£
D Lewis	1 025 Dr
D Smith	200 Dr
B Kings	600 Dr
C Taylor	285 Dr
M Johnson	465 Dr
	2 575

Purchase ledger

	£
Slazenger Sports	1 975 Cr
Metro Sports	300 Cr
Auto	1 215 Cr
International	2 150 Cr
	5 640

a) Set up the ledger system of R Pearce using sales, purchase and nominal ledgers, from personal ledger accounts and the opening financial position as above. The bank balance of £455 will be recorded in the cash book.

19.3 Credit sales and credit purchases

The credit sales for January were as follows:

Date		*Customer account*	*Invoice no.*	*Net sales*	*Vat*	*Total*
				£	£	£
Jan	5	D Lewis	4219	500		
	18	D Smith	4220	240		
	12	D Lewis	4221	168		
	17	C Taylor	4222	350		
	18	B Kings	4223	450		
	24	D Smith	4224	180		
	25	D Lewis	4225	290		
	27	B Kings	4226	650		
	30	M Johnson	4227	300		

b) Use the above table to record your figures. Calculate Vat at 15 per cent and total the columns. Post the transactions to the ledgers.

The credit purchases of stock for January were as follows:

Date		*Supplier account*	*Invoice no. received*	*Gross purchases*	*Net purchases*	*Vat*	*Total*
				£	£	£	£
Jan	5	International	3046	1 000	800		
	7	Slazenger Sports	29851	1 200	960		
	10	Metro Sports	4367	500	425		
	15	International	4768	380	304		
	20	Slazenger Sports	34420	530	424		
	25	Auto	2321	240	204		

c) Use the above table to record your findings. Check the accuracy of the invoices before totalling the columns. International and Slazenger Sports give 20 per cent trade and 5 per cent cash discounts. Metro Sports and Auto give 15 per cent trade and 5 per cent cash discounts. Calculate Vat at 15 per cent. Post to the ledgers.

19.4 Cash book entries

All cash receipts and payments of money are to be made through the bank. For receipts use separate columns to identify totals for: debtors; cash sales; Vat; and bank. No discount is given to debtors.

Receipts

			£
Jan	8	B Kings	300
	10	C Taylor	200
	12	Cash sales	185+Vat
	15	B Kings	300
	17	D Lewis	500
	18	Cash sales	162+Vat
	20	D Smith	200
	26	Cash sales	425+Vat
	29	M Johnson	465

Use separate columns to identify totals for: discount received; creditors; overheads; general expenses; and bank.

Payments

Jan	1	Overheads	250.0
	5	Slazenger Sports	1 000.0 discount taken £50.00
	8	Auto	500.0 discount taken £12.50
	13	Overheads	250.0
	13	International	1 500.0

16	Metro Sports	292.5	discount taken £7.50
20	Overheads	350.0	
21	Southern Gas	56.0	
24	British Telecom	122.0	
28	Wages	6 025.0	
28	Tax and insurance	215.5	
30	Overheads	250.0	
31	Miscellaneous expenses	121.0	

d) Prepare the company's cash book for January, balancing at the end of the month (31 January). Bring down the bank balance on 1 February.

Post all relevant transactions from the above information to the appropriate ledgers. Ensure that control accounts in the nominal ledgers cross-check with the personal ledgers. Prepare schedules for debtors and creditors to confirm totals with the control accounts.

e) Bank reconciliation statement – from the information given in the bank statement below, cross-check entries made in the cash book. Bring the cash book up-to-date, post any new entries to the ledger and then prepare the bank reconciliation statement on 31 January.

Extract a trial balance for the company as on 31 January.

Statement of account

R Pearce
77 Penhill Avenue
Penhill
Poole
Dorset

Cheque account
104236876

31 January

Details	*Payments* £	*Receipts* £	*Date*	*Balance* £
Balance forward			1/1	455.00 Cr
100197	250.0		1/1	205.00
CC		300.00	8/1	505.00
CC		200.00	10/1	705.00
CC		212.75	12/1	917.75
100198	1000.0		13/1	82.25 O/D
100200	250.0		15/1	332.25
CC		300.00	15/1	32.25
100199	500.0		16/1	532.25
CC		500.00	18/1	32.25
100201	1500.0		19/1	1 532.25
CC		186.30	19/1	1 345.95
CC		200.00	20/1	1 145.95
100202	292.5		20/1	1 438.45
100203	350.0		20/1	1 788.45
CC		488.75	26/1	1 299.70
100204	56.0		27/1	1 355.70

100206	6025.0	30/1	7 380.70
DDR WDC rates	49.5	30/1	7 430.20
Commission			
2 Oct–2 Jan	12.0	30/1	7442.20 O/D

NOTES

Commission – charges by the bank
DDR – direct debit
STO – standing order
O/D – overdrawn balances
CC – deposits to bank

19.5 Solution

Sales journal

Page 1

Date		*Customer account*	*Invoice no.*	*Net sales £*	*Vat £*	*Total £*
Jan	5	D Lewis	4219	500	75.00	575.00
	8	D Smith	4220	240	36.00	276.00
	12	D Lewis	4221	168	25.20	193.20
	17	C Taylor	4222	350	52.50	402.50
	18	B Kings	4223	450	67.50	517.50
	24	D Smith	4224	180	27.00	207.00
	25	D Lewis	4225	290	43.50	333.50
	27	B Kings	4226	650	97.50	747.50
	30	M Johnson	4227	300	45.00	345.00
				3 128	469.20	3 597.20

Purchases journal

Page 3

Date		*Supplier account*	*Invoice no.*	*Net purchases*	*Vat*	*Total*
Jan	5	International	3046	800	114.00	914.00
	7	Slazenger Sports	29851	960	136.80	1 096.80
	10	Metro	4367	425	60.56	485.56
	15	International	4768	304	43.32	347.32
	20	Slazenger Sports	34420	424	60.42	484.42
	25	Auto	2321	204	29.07	233.07
				3 117	444.17	3 561.17

(continued)

(continued)

Sales ledger

D Lewis account			*Folio*	*Dr*	*Cr*	*Balance*
Jan	1	Balance				1 025.00 Dr
	5	Sales	SJ1	500.00		
		Vat	SJ1	75.00		1 600.00 Dr
	12	Sales	SJ1	168.00		
		Vat	SJ1	25.20		1 793.20 Dr
	17	Bank	CB9		500	1 293.20 Dr
	25	Sales	SJ1	290.00		
		Vat	SJ1	43.50		1 626.70 Dr
D Smith account			*Folio*	*Dr*	*Cr*	*Balance*
Jan	1	Balance				200 Dr
	8	Sales	SJ1	240		
		Vat	SJ1	36		476 Dr
	20	Bank	CB9		200	276 Dr
	24	Sales	SJ1	180		
		Vat	SJ1	27		483 Dr
B Kings account			*Folio*	*Dr*	*Cr*	*Balance*
Jan	1	Balance				600.00 Dr
	8	Bank	CB9		300	300.00 Dr
	15	Bank	CB9		300	—
	18	Sales	SJ1	450.00		
		Vat	SJ1	67.50		517.50 Dr
	27	Sales	SJ1	650.00		
		Vat	SJ1	97.50		1 265.00 Dr
C Taylor account			*Folio*	*Dr*	*Cr*	*Balance*
Jan	1	Balance				285.00 Dr
	10	Bank	CB9		200	85.00 Dr
	17	Sales	SJ1	350.00		
		Vat	SJ1	52.50		487.50 Dr
M Johnson account			*Folio*	*Dr*	*Cr*	*Balance*
Jan	1	Balance				465 Dr
	29	Bank	CB9		465	—
	30	Sales	SJ1	300		
		Vat	SJ1	45		345 Dr

Sales ledger

Schedule of debtors as at 31 January

	£
D Lewis	1 626.70
D Smith	483.00
B Kings	1 265.00
C Taylor	487.50
M Johnson	345.00
	4 207.20

Purchase ledger

Slazenger sports account			*Folio*	*Dr*	*Cr*	*Balance*
Jan	1	Balance				1 975.00 Cr
	5	Bank	CB9	1 000		
		Discount received	CB9	50		925.00 Cr
	7	Purchases	PJ3		960.00	
		Vat	PJ3		136.80	2 021.80 Cr
	20	Purchases	PJ3		424.00	
		Vat	PJ3		60.42	2 506.22 Cr

Metro sports account			*Folio*	*Dr*	*Cr*	*Balance*
Jan	1	Balance				300.00 Cr
	10	Purchases	PJ3		425.00	
		Vat	PJ3		60.56	785.56 Cr
	16	Bank	CB9	292.50		
		Discount received	CB9	7.50		485.56 Cr

Auto account			*Folio*	*Dr*	*Cr*	*Balance*
Jan	1	Balance				1 215.00 Cr
	8	Bank	CB9	500.00		
		Discount received	CB9	12.50		702.50 Cr
	25	Purchases	PJ3		204.00	
		Vat	PJ3		29.07	935.57 Cr

International account			*Folio*	*Dr*	*Cr*	*Balance*
Jan	1	Balance				2 150.00 Cr
	5	Purchases	PJ3		800.00	
		Vat	PJ3		114.00	3 064.00 Cr
	13	Bank	CB9	1 500		1 564.00 Cr
	15	Purchases	PJ3		304.00	
		Vat	PJ3		43.32	1 911.32 Cr

Purchase ledger

Schedule of creditors as at 31 January

	£
Slazenger Sports	2 506.22
Metro Sports	485.56
Auto	935.57
International	1 911.32
	5 838.67

Nominal ledger

R. Pearce: Capital account			*Folio*	*Dr*	*Cr*	*Balance*
Jan	1	Balance				50 000 Cr

Mortgage on premises account			*Folio*	*Dr*	*Cr*	*Balance*
Jan	1	Balance				69 720 Cr

Sales account			*Folio*	*Dr*	*Cr*	*Balance*
Jan	1	Balance				—
	31	Debtors	SJ1		3 128	3 128 Cr
	31	Sundry cash sales	CB9		772	3 900 Cr

Vat account			*Folio*	*Dr*	*Cr*	*Balance*
Jan	1	Balance				—
	31	Debtors	SJ1		469.20	469.20 Cr
	31	Creditors	PJ3	444.17		25.03 Cr
	31	Cash sales	CB9		115.80	140.83 Cr

Purchases account			*Folio*	*Dr*	*Cr*	*Balance*
Jan	1	Balance				—
	31	Creditors	PJ3	3 117		3 117 Dr

Discount received account			*Folio*	*Dr*	*Cr*	*Balance*
Jan	1	Balance				—
	31	Sundries	CB9		70	70 Cr

General expenses account			*Folio*	*Dr*	*Cr*	*Balance*
Jan	1	Balance				—
	31	Sundries	CB9	576		576 Dr

Premises account			*Folio*	*Dr*	*Cr*	*Balance*
Jan	1	Balance				100 000 Dr

Equipment, machinery account			*Folio*	*Dr*	*Cr*	*Balance*
Jan	1	Balance				13 500 Dr

Motor vehicle account			*Folio*	*Dr*	*Cr*	*Balance*
Jan	1	Balance				5 000 Dr

Petty cash float account			*Folio*	*Dr*	*Cr*	*Balance*
Jan	1	Balance				150 Dr

Sales ledger control account			*Folio*	*Dr*	*Cr*	*Balance*
Jan	1	Balance				2 575.00 Dr
	31	Sales (inc. VAT)	SJ1	3 597.20		6 172.20 Dr
	31	Bank	CB9		1 965	4 207.20 Dr

Purchase ledger control account			*Folio*	*Dr*	*Cr*	*Balance*
Jan	1	Balance				5 640.00 Cr
	31	Purch. (inc. VAT)	PJ3		3 561.17	9 201.17 Cr
	31	Bank	CB9	3 292.50		5 908.67 Cr
	31	Discounts received	CB9	70.00		5 838.67 Cr

Stock account			*Folio*	*Dr*	*Cr*	*Balance*
Jan	1	Balance				3 680 Dr
Wages account			*Folio*	*Dr*	*Cr*	*Balance*
Jan	1	Balance				—
	31	Sundry	CB9	6 025		6 025 Dr
Overheads account			*Folio*	*Dr*	*Cr*	*Balance*
Jan	1	Balance				—
	31	Sundries	CB9	1 100		1 100 Dr

Dr **Cash book – receipts** Page 9

Date		*Particulars*	*Debtors*	*Cash sales*	*Vat*	*Bank*
Jan	1	Balance				455.00
	8	B Kings	300			300.00
	10	C Taylor	200			200.00
	12	Cash sales		185	27.75	212.75
	15	B Kings	300			300.00
	17	D Lewis	500			500.00
	18	Cash sales		162	24.30	186.30
	20	D Smith	200			200.00
	26	Cash sales		425	63.75	488.75
	29	M Johnson	465			465.00
	31	Balance c/d				7 685.70
			1 965	772	115.80	10 993.50

Cash book – payments

Cr Page 9

Date		*Particulars*	*Discount received*	*Creditors*	*Overheads*	*Wages*	*Expenses*	*Bank*
Jan	1	Overheads			250			250.00
	5	Slazengers Sports	50.00	1 000.00				1 000.00
	8	Auto	12.50	500.00				500.00
	13	Overheads			250			250.00
	13	International		1 500.00				1 500.00
	16	Metro Sports	7.50	292.50				292.50
	20	Overheads			350			350.00
	21	Southern Gas					56.00	56.00
	24	British Telecom					122.00	122.00

(continued)

(continued)

	28	Wages				6 025		6 025.00
	28	Tax and insurance					215.50	215.50
	30	Overheads			250			250.00
	30	WDC rates					49.50	49.50
	30	Commission					12.00	12.00
	31	Miscellaneous					121.00	121.00
			70	3 292.50	1 100	6 025	576.00	10 993.50
Feb	1	Balance b/d						7 685.70

Bank reconciliation as at 31 January

		£	£
Balance per bank statement			7 442.20 O/D
Add	Unpresented cheques:		
	British Telecom	122.00	
	Tax and insurance	215.50	
	Overheads	250.00	
	Miscellaneous	121.00	708.50
			8 150.70
Less	Undeposited cheques:		
	M Johnson		465.00
Balance as per cash book			7 685.70 O/D

R Pearce –
Trial balance as at 31 January

	Dr	*Cr*
	£	£
Premises	100 000.00	
Equipment, machinery	13 500.00	
Motor vehicle	5 000.00	
Petty cash float	150.00	
Sales ledger control (debtors)	4 207.20	
Purchase ledger control (creditors)		5 838.67
Stock	3 680.00	
R Pearce: Capital		50 000.00
Mortgage on premises		69 720.00
Sales		3 900.00
Vat		140.83
Purchases	3117.00	
Discount received		70.00

(continued)

(continued)

Expenses	576.00	
Wages	6 025.00	
Overheads	1 100.00	
Bank		7 685.70
	137 355.20	137 355.20

Summary

The worked example should be seen as a useful device in recognising the main ingredients of recording both cash and credit transactions through the subsidiary (prime) books to the ledgers. The cash book also had to be checked against the bank statement and a reconciliation made. The Vat was calculated at the old rate of 15% and this could now be updated to the standard rate of 17.5% for your own project although you need to ignore the bank reconciliation.

Assignment

Rework this worked example, updating the figures at the current rate of Vat (17.5%).

20 Control accounts

Objectives

On completing this section you should:

- recognise the function of control accounts as discussed in previous sales and purchase journal chapters
- appreciate their use in helping to locate errors and assist management.

Context

Chapter 6 put control accounts in the context of business accounting systems in general. The use of control accounts was also introduced in Chapters 8 and 11.

20.1 Introduction

We have already discussed control accounts in Chapters 8 and 11. The two control accounts are recorded in the nominal ledger and should verify the total balances of debtors and creditors in the sales and purchase ledgers respectively, at any given time. Note that in some examinations these control accounts are referred to as debtors and creditors control.

If an organisation has numerous customers and suppliers it is advisable to use control accounts to confirm the accuracy of recording personal accounts. If a computer program is used, it will give immediate access to the totals of both debtors and creditors. If records are kept manually, the control accounts will also give this information – perhaps not as expediently as a computer but total debtors and creditors will be confirmed.

Total figures for debtors and creditors may also be required for management purposes. How much is owed by debtors? When can the business expect its cash to come in? How much is owed to creditors? How much cash is due to be paid? These questions reflect the future cash flow of the business and the amount of working capital which will be available for trading. It is therefore important to have up-to-date access to these figures at any time.

Once the control accounts have verified the sales and purchase ledger balances, the control balances are listed in the trial balance, not the individual balances for debtors and creditors. This makes the task of balancing the trial balance a little easier because if errors prevent a balance, they cannot be associated with either debtors or creditors. The control accounts have already confirmed the accuracy, being arithmetical proofs of individual debtors and creditors.

If either of the control accounts do not agree with the total balances of the sales and purchase ledgers (that is, the schedules of debtors and creditors), a detailed check will need to be made to locate the errors. Both individual accounts and control accounts will have to be investigated to locate and correct the errors.

20.2 Locating an error

A likely source of error may be due to an incorrect addition or posting from a subsidiary book such as the journals or cash book. In the following case, an error is located in the sales journal:

Sales journal	£	£	£
D Lewis	200	35.0	235.0 Dr
D Smith	420	73.5	493.5 Dr
B Kings	500	87.5	587.5 Dr
	1 120	196.0	1 216.0
	Cr	Cr	Dr
	Sales	Vat	S/L control

Sales ledger posting: Each debtor is posted correctly to the debit side of their respective accounts.

Nominal ledger posting: Sales and Vat totals are posted correctly to the credit side of their respective accounts.

When the sales ledger control account is debited with £1 216 (the figure should be £1 316), an error of £100 is overstated. When cross-checking the sales ledger control account with the sales ledger, there would be a difference of £100. To locate this error, a thorough check of the control account and the sales ledger would need to be carried out.

20.3 Preparing control accounts from given data

Prepare the sales ledger control account from the following information:

	£
Sales ledger control account	
Balance b/f 1 July	21 900 Dr
Credit sales	37 500
Bank/cash from debtors	34 500
Returns inward	1 200
Bad debts written off	800
Discount allowed to customers	840
Cheques dishonoured	100
Cash sales	10 500
Sales ledger Dr balance from debtors schedule: 31 July	22 160

NOTES

1. The control account may be prepared either in the traditional or running balance method of recording. Both methods will be shown.
2. Cash sales is a 'red herring' because it does not affect debtors.
3. The control accounts are part of the double entry principle. The individual personal accounts in the sales and purchase ledgers are subsidiary records.

20.3.1 The sales ledger control account (nominal ledger)

Dr		*Sales ledger control account*			*Cr*
		£			£
1/7	Balance b/f	21 900	31/7	Bank/cash	34 500
31/7	Sales	37 500		Discount allowed	840
	Dishonoured cheques	100		Returns in	1 200
				Bad debts	800
				Balance c/f	22 160
		59 500			59 500
1/8	Balance b/f (as per S/L)	22 160			

20.3.2 The running balance format

		Dr	*Cr*	*Balance*
Sales ledger control account		£	£	£
1/7	Balance b/f			21 900 Dr
31/7	Sales	37 500		59 400
	Bank/cash		34 500	24 900
	Discount allowed		840	24 060
	Returns in		1 200	22 860
	Dishonoured cheque	100		22 960
	Bad debts		800	22 160
	Balance (S/L)			22 160 Dr

NOTE

The balance on 31 July agrees with the debtors' schedule in the sales ledger.

Prepare the purchase ledger control account from the following information:

	£
Purchase ledger control account	
Balance b/f 1 July	37 500
Credit purchases	59 250
Payments to suppliers	54 600
Discounts received	1 435
Returns outward	1 635
Refund received from suppliers due to overcharge	200
Debit note from supplier because of undercharge on invoice	150
Purchase ledger Cr balance from creditors' schedule: 31 July	39 400

20.3.3 The purchase ledger control account (nominal ledger)

Purchase ledger control account

Dr		£			Cr £
31/7	Bank	54 600	1/7	Balance b/f	37 500
	Discount received	1 435	31/7	Purchases	59 250
	Returns out	1 635		Refund	200
	Balance c/f	39 430		Dr Note	150
		97 100			97 100
			1/8	Balance b/f	39 430
				Balance (P/L)	39 400

NOTE

An error has been made and must be located and corrected. This is a difference of £30. Is it a purchase ledger error or control account error? It was found that in the purchase ledger, Vat of £30 had not been posted to a supplier's account, therefore the P/L balance should have read £39 430.

20.3.4 The running balance format

Sales ledger control account		*Dr* £	*Cr* £	*Balance* £
1/7	Balance b/f			37 500 Cr
31/7	Purchases		59 250	96 750
	Bank	54 600		42 150
	Discount received	1 435		40 715
	Returns out	1 635		39 080
	Dr note		150	39 230
	Refund		200	39 430
	Balance (P/L)			39 430 Cr

An important point to remember is that every transaction that affects an individual debtor or creditor, must correspondingly affect the control account. Control accounts represent the totals for debtors and creditors.

It may occur, from time to time, that a debtor is in credit because of an over payment, or that a creditor is in debit because he or she is overpaid. This may also be reflected in the control accounts and both debit and credit balances may be shown at both the commencement and ending of the control account period.

Example

		Dr	*Cr*
		£	£
Sales ledger control account			
Balances b/f	1 July:	21 160	520
	31 July:	21 000	340
Purchase ledger control account			
Balances b/f	1 July:	440	10 500
	31 July:	100	7 000
Credit sales			57 000
Credit purchases		38 400	
Returns in		700	
Returns out			3 300
Receipts from debtors		52 560	
Payments to suppliers			36 960
[1]Bad debts		1 520	
[2]Contra entries £300			
Cash sales			13 855
Interest charges to customers due to overdue accounts		100	
[3]Bills payable			1 000
[3]Bills receivable		2 000	

NOTES

1 Bad debts are customers who have been written off because they have failed to pay their debts. The double-entry is:

Debit: bad debts account (an expense)
Credit: customer's account and S/L control account.

2 Contra entries refer to those accounts which are 'set off' against each other, that is, where a customer may also be a supplier. For example, if a customer owes £300 (debtor) and the business owes the same customer £1 000 (creditor), the contra entry will be:

Debit: the creditor's account £300 (debt now £700)
Credit: the debtor's account £300 (account cleared).

Therefore, with contra entries:

Debit: purchase ledger control account
Credit: sales ledger control account.

3 Bills payable and receivable are like post-dated cheques, payments are made when the dates are due. Bills payable refers to payments to creditors and bills receivable refers to receipts from debtors:

Debit: bills payable to purchase ledger control account
Credit: bills receivable to sales ledger control account.

20.3.5 The control accounts in traditional format

Sales ledger control account

Dr					Cr
		£			£
1/7	Balance b/f	21 160	1/7	Balance b/f	520
31/7	Sales	57 000	31/7	Bank	52 560
	Interest	100		Returns in	700
	Balance c/f	340		Bad debts	1 520
				Contra	300
				Bills receivable	2 000
				Balance c/f	21 000
		78 600			78 000
1/8	Balance b/f	21 000	1/8	Balance b/f	340

Purchase ledger control account

Dr					Cr
		£			£
1/7	Balance b/f	440	1/7	Balance b/f	10 500
31/7	Bank	36 960	31/7	Purchases	38 400
	Returns out	3 300		Balance c/f	100
	Contra	300			
	Bills payable	1 000			
	Balance c/f	7 000			
		49 000			49 000
1/8	Balance b/f	100	1/8	Balance b/f	7 000

NOTE

Cash sales amount (£13 855) is not entered in the control account because there is no effect on debtors. The same applies to cash purchases, there is no effect on creditors.

Summary

Control accounts are used to verify the accuracy of the sales and purchase ledgers. When a business has many customers or suppliers record, the control accounts act as a 'mini trial balance' for debtors and creditors. Management needs to know the total sum owing from customers for credit control purposes just as they need to know how much in total they owe to their suppliers.

Questions

1 The following details were extracted from the books of a company for the month ended 31 March.

		£	£
Mar 1	Purchase ledger (debit balance)	200	
	(credit balance)	12 000	

	Sales ledger (debit balance)	35 000
	(credit balance)	400
Mar 31	Purchase ledger (debit balance)	100
	(credit balance)	23 420
	Sales ledger (credit balance)	200
	(debit balance)	39 050
	Purchases (credit)	24 000
	Sales (credit)	36 000
	Discount received	600
	Discount allowed	500
	Returns inwards	200
	Returns outwards	100
	Cheques received from debtors	30 400
	Cheques paid to creditors	11 400
	Contras	400
	Bills receivable (debtors)	1 000
	Bills dishonoured (debtors)	200
	Cheques dishonoured	100
	Cheques received from creditors	20
	Cheques paid to debtors	50

REQUIRED:

a) Prepare the purchase ledger control account.

b) Prepare the sales ledger control account.

c) Give three reasons why control accounts are used. (20.1–3)

(The Institute of Commercial Management)

2 L Ashurst's sales ledger contains the accounts of many debtors. The information given below relates to the accounts of A Durban and W Elliott, which had been mislaid at the time of preparation of the remaining debtors' accounts.

		£
March 1	A Durban	400 debit
	W Elliott	240 debit

During March the following transactions took place.

March 3	Sold goods to A Durban £925 on credit.
5	Sales on credit to W Elliott £1 200.
8	Sent a credit note to A Durban for £23 relating to damaged goods.
16	Received a cheque from A Durban in settlement of his account at 1 March, less 5 per cent cash discount.
17	Sold goods to W Elliott, on credit, list price £1 000 less 15 per cent trade discount.
20	A Durban complained that the credit note issued on 8 March should have been £32. Correct this error.
31	L Ashurst also bought some goods from W Elliott. The credit balance of £168 on Elliott's account in the purchase ledger was transferred to his account in the sales ledger.

REQUIRED:

a) The accounts of A Durban and W Elliott, as they would appear in Ashurst's sales ledger for the month of March.

b) Ashurst's sales and returns inwards accounts for the month ended 31 March.

The following total figures relate to the debtors' accounts in C Nelson's sales ledger for the month ended 31 January.

	£
Opening debit balances (at 1 January)	42 606
Sales	160 000
Cheques received	142 220
Discounts allowed	7 321
Bad debts	1306
Returns inward	621

c) Preparation of the sales ledger control account of C Nelson for the month of January.
d) A comment on the main purpose of control accounts.
e) Where, and under what headings does the balance of the sales ledger control account appear in the final accounts? (20.1–3)

(Associated Examining Board)

3 As a member of the accounting team of ABC Co Ltd you are asked to prepare the control accounts of both the sales ledger and purchase ledger for the month ended 31 March.

The following were balances taken from the books of ABC Co Ltd for the month of March.

		£
1 March		
Purchase ledger	Cr balance	12 860
Purchase ledger	Dr balance	225
Sales ledger	Dr balance	34 755
Sales ledger	Cr balance	372
31 March		
Purchases journal		23 805
Sales journal		37 215
Discount received		621
Discount allowed		558
Cheques received from customers		29 950
Cash/cheques to suppliers		22 140
Contra entries between debtors and creditors		420
Cash purchases		1 285
Bad debts written off		470
Returns outward journal		950
Dishonoured cheques from customers		155
Interest charged to customers on overdue accounts		85
Returns inward journal		1 472
Received from creditor in respect of over payment		25
Bills receivable		1150
Cash refund to customer		50
Provision for bad debts		750

The balances extracted from the personal ledgers of ABC Co Ltd on 31 March were:

		£
Purchase ledger	Cr balance	12 484
Purchase ledger	Dr balance	150
Sales ledger	Dr balance	38 124
Sales ledger	Cr balance	456

REQUIRED:

a) Prepare the purchase ledger control account and the sales ledger control account for the month ended 31 March.

b) From the figures you have prepared for task a) what conclusions can you draw?
c) Briefly explain, by means of memorandum to the junior accounts clerk, why in some business enterprises, there is a need to keep control accounts. (20.1–3)

(Institute of Bankers)

4 The financial year of Handile plc ended on 31 March 19-8. A trial balance extracted as at that date reveals a difference of £100 in the books. It is decided to draw up a sales ledger control account and a purchase ledger control account to help locate any errors. The trial balance figures for debtors and creditors were £16 940 and £23 188 respectively. These represent the totals of the balances on the individual debtors' and creditors' accounts in the sales and purchase ledgers.

The following information is obtained from the books of original entry

Cash book:	£
Discounts allowed	3 112
Cash and cheques from customers	125 050
Discounts received	2 097
Cash and cheques paid to suppliers	139 830
Refunds given to customers	231
Customers' cheques dishonoured	55
Journal:	
Balances in the purchase ledger set off against balances in the sales ledger	460
Bad debts written off	661
Decrease in the provision for bad debts	51
Sales book	130 411
Purchases book	155 603
Returns in book	3 150
Returns out book	3 227

According to the audited accounts for the previous year, debtors and creditors as at 1 April 19-7 were £18 776 and £13,199 respectively.

REQUIRED:
a) Draw up the relevant control accounts.
b) Suggest where an error might have been made. (20.2–3)

(The Association of Accounting Technicians)

5 The following information relates to the accounts of E Gibbs for the month of July:

	£ Dr	£ Cr
Balance b/f from sales ledger (1/7)	41 220	
Credit sales, July		37 350
Returns inward	500	
Receipts from debtors	27 800	
Bad debts written off	950	
Discounts allowed	675	
Cheques from customers marked R/D – insufficient funds		790
Cash sales		21 500
Interest charged to customers		40

Debit note sent to customer (account undercharged)		300
Contra entry between sales and purchase ledgers, £800		
Balance b/f from sales ledger (31/7)	48 975	

REQUIRED:
Prepare the sales ledger control account of E Gibbs for the month of July. The opening balance on 1 July confirms with the control account. (20.3)

6 The following information has been taken from the accounts of G Grant for the month of July:

	£ *Dr*	£ *Cr*
Balance b/f from purchase ledger (1/7)		6 432
Credit purchases, July	81 360	
Payments made to suppliers		58 200
Discounts received		2 450
Returns outward		11 285
Received from a supplier due to an overpayment	125	
Cash purchases	2 455	
Balance b/f from purchase ledger (31/7)		15 982

REQUIRED:
Prepare the purchase ledger control account of G Grant for the month of July. The opening balance on 1 July confirms with the control account. (20.3)

7 The following details were extracted from the books of a company for the month ended 28 February.

		£
February 1	Purchase ledger	9 000 Cr
	Sales ledger	5 000 Dr
February 28	Credit purchases for the month	72 000
	Credit sales for the month	103 000
	Cash paid to creditors	74 000
	Cash received from debtors	81 000
	Discounts received	1 200
	Discounts allowed	1 500
	Returns outwards	600
	Returns inwards	400
	Bad debts written off in month	200
	Dishonoured cheque from debtor	300

On 28 February the balances extracted from the ledgers were:

Purchase ledger	£5 200
Sales ledger	£25 110

REQUIRED:
a) Prepare the sales ledger control account.
b) Prepare the purchase ledger control account.
c) Briefly comment on the control accounts prepared in a) and b) above. (20.3)

(The Institute of Commercial Management)

8 The figures below are for the financial year for Albright Trading Company ended on 31 December. You have been asked to prepare the total debtors and creditors account in order to produce the end of year figures for the draft financial statements.

	£
Sales – credit	249 124
– cash	112 345
Purchases – credit	445 320
– cash	12 840
Total receipts from sales	300 470
Total payments on purchases	403 970
Discounts given (credit sales)	4 480
Discounts received (credit purchases)	2 850
Refunds given to cash customers	4 020
Contra entries between sales and purchase ledgers	1 235
Bad debts from customers written off	800
Increase in the provision for bad debts	20
Credit notes received from suppliers	1 285
Credit notes sent to customers	3 200
Credit suppliers paid from petty cash	85

The balances on 1 January for debtors and creditors were £35 740 and £28 480 respectively.

REQUIRED:
Draw up the relevant debtors and creditors control accounts as at the end of the year, 31 December. (20.3)

(Association of Accounting Technicians)

9 The following sales ledger control account has been prepared by an inexperienced member of staff from the accounting records of HAC plc at 30 September:

Sales ledger control

	£		£
Balance b/fwd	92 580.23	Returns outward	11 376.19
Sales	318 741.90	Debtor receipts	299 878.43
Discount allowed	12 702.18	Discount received	10 419.76
Decrease in provision for doubtful debts	10 429.61	Bad debts written off	5 318.23
Purchase ledger contras	49 516.27	Balance c/fwd	160 387.70
Returns inwards	3 410.12		
	487 380.31		487 380.31

The total of the individual balances in the sales ledger (net of credit balances) has been calculated to be £86 476.15 on 30 September.
An investigation revealed the following:

1. A credit balance of £4 381.22 on an individual account within the sales ledger was included in the calculation of the total of the individual balances as though it were a debit balance.
2. One of the pages of the sales daybook had been incorrectly totalled. The total calculated was £2 291.18 more than the correct sum of the individual entries.
3. A credit note issued to a customer for £742.37 had been entered in the returns inwards daybook as £472.37.
4. No entries had been made in the individual accounts to record
   i) the purchase ledger contras; or
   ii) the decrease in the provision for doubtful debts.
5. A bad debt of £421.33 previously written off was recovered in September: the correct entries have been made in the individual customer account.

REQUIRED:
Make any entries that you consider necessary in the sales ledger control account, commencing with the closing balance given, and reconcile the listing of the individual debtor balances to the closing balance shown on the control account (as amended).

(Chartered Institute of Management Accountants)

21 Introducing final accounts: sole traders

Objectives

On completing this section you should:

- understand that final accounts refer to the financial statements
- recognise how the five accounting groups (RECAL) are used in preparing the financial statements
- be able to extract and format final accounts from the trial balance
- understand the significance of working capital as part of the balance sheet
- recognise that revenue and expense accounts are 'zeroed' at the end of the accounting period.

Context:

Chapter 2 introduced sole traders; Chapter 4 introduced the basics of final accounts

21.1 Introduction

Financial statements were first introduced in Chapter 4. The two basic financial reports refer to the **trading and profit and loss account** and the **balance sheet**. These statements (or reports) are commonly referred to as the **final accounts** because, at the end of a financial period, the final balances listed in the trial balance are used to prepare the accounting reports. These reports help to determine the performance of a business in terms of profit or loss and its financial position.

The purpose of the trading and profit and loss account is to determine the business's profit or loss in the accounting period under review. This accounting period is at the end of the financial year for most sole traders. For larger business organisations, the determination of profit or loss may be required more frequently for management purposes.

The preparation of the balance sheet represents the business's financial position in terms of its assets, liabilities and capital, listing its resources (assets) and the financing of these resources (capital and liabilities).

When preparing the final accounts of sole traders (people who own and control businesses by themselves) the accountant is likely to prepare these at the end of the financial year, giving the trader a picture of his or her business performance and also to prepare the necessary figures for the Inland Revenue for the purpose of assessing the trader's personal tax liability.

Profit or loss is basically the difference between revenue and expenses. If revenue is greater, a profit is made. The reverse is true if expenses exceed revenue. Therefore, from the five accounting groups:

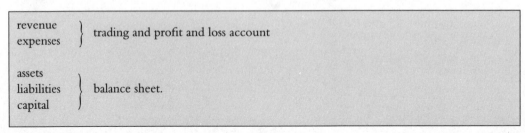

revenue expenses	trading and profit and loss account
assets liabilities capital	balance sheet.

The link between the two statements is that, in the event of a profit or loss, capital is either increased or decreased respectively, because profit or loss is transferred to the owner. If capital is affected, by the same token, net assets (assets less liabilities), must be affected equally by the same sum.

Example

Capital	=	Assets	– Liabilities
£10 000	=	£60 000	– £50 000

Profit for year: £2000, the accounting equation after adding profit:

Capital	=	Assets	– Liabilities
£12 000	=	£62 000	– £50 000

If a loss of £2000 was made in the year, capital would be reduced to £8000, the net assets equalling £8000.

It is the usual practice to prepare the financial statements from a set of accounts listed in the business's trial balance. At the end of a financial period, all revenue and expense accounts are transferred to the trading and profit and loss account and in so doing, their balances are *zeroed*. In the new financial period, revenue and expense accounts will commence with a nil balance. Assets, liabilities and capital accounts are not affected in this way and their balances are carried forward from one accounting period to the next.

21.2 The preparation of final accounts

At the end of the accounting period, a trial balance would be extracted from the accounts in the nominal ledger. Any adjustments to the accounts such as the value of closing stock, would be included as footnotes to the trial balance. The final accounts would then be prepared from these figures. An illustration of this is shown below:

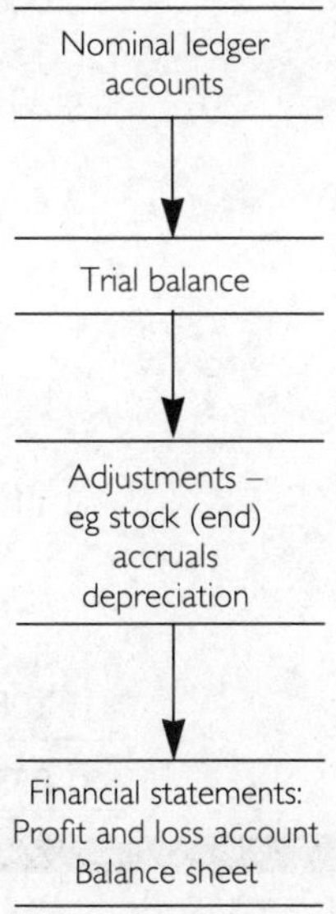

Fig 21.1 The preparation of final accounts

21.3 The accounts of R Pearce

The preparation of final accounts for different types of organisations usually follow after the trial balance has been prepared. The same procedure applies for sole traders, partnerships, limited companies and clubs and societies which are all in this section of the text.

The following figures have been taken from the trial balance of R Pearce which concluded with the worked example in Chapter 19. The unsold stock as at 31 January had an estimated value of £5200. The closing stock is an important figure because it is deducted from the cost of sales and therefore affects the calculation of gross profit. We discuss how stock is valued more fully in Chapter 39.

Page 217 illustrates the trading and profit and loss account of R Pearce. The trading account part matches sales with the cost of sales for the purpose of calculating the gross profit. Gross profit is about selling prices less cost prices:

Gross profit	=	Sales	–	Cost of sales
£2 303	=	£3 900	–	£1 597

The profit and loss account is the part which is used to calculate net profit by deducting all other expenses from gross profit. Any other income such as interest or discount received is added to profit:

Net profit	=	Gross profit	–	Other expenses	+	Other income
£172	=	£2 303	–	£2 201	+	£70

Note that the closing stock at 31 January, £5 200, is deducted from cost of sales and is also entered as a current asset in the balance sheet because it is still available to be sold.

R Pearce –
Trial balance as on 31 January

	Dr	*Cr*
	£	£
Premises	100 000.0	
Equipment, machinery	13 500.0	
Motor vehicle	5 000.0	
Petty cash (float)	150.0	
S/L control (debtors)	4 207.2	
P/L control (creditors)		5 838.67
Stock (1/1)	3 680.0	
Capital: R Pearce		50 000.00
Mortgage on premises		69 720.00
Bank (overdraft)		2 185.70
Vat		140.83
Sales		3 900.00
Purchases	3 117.0	
Discount received		70.00
Expenses	576.0	
Wages	525.0	
Overheads	1 100.0	
	131 855.2	131 855.20

NOTE
At 31 January unsold stock was valued at £5 200.

R Pearce –
Trading and profit and loss account, month ended 31 January

	£	£
Sales		3 900
Cost of sales:		
Stock (1 January)	3 680	
Purchases	3 117	
	6 797	
Stock (31 January)	(5 200)	1 597
Gross profit		2 303
Expenses:		
General expenses	576	
Wages	525	
Overheads	1 100	2 201
		102
Other revenue:		
Discount received		70
Net profit		172

R Pearce –
Balance sheet as at 31 January

	£	£	£
FIXED ASSETS			
Premises	100 000.00		
Equipment, machinery	13 500.00		
Motor vehicle	5 000.00		118 500
CURRENT ASSETS			
Stock	5 200.00		
Debtors	4 207.20		
Bank	0.00		
Cash	150.00	9 557.2	
less			
CURRENT LIABILITIES			
Creditors	5 838.67		
Vat	140.83		
Bank overdraft	2 185.70	8 165.2	
Working Capital			1392
Capital employed			119 892
less			
LONG TERM LIABILITIES			
Mortgage on premises			69 720
			50 172

21.4 Presentation of the balance sheet

The financial statements were first introduced in Chapter 4. In this section, they are presented with a little more sophistication. For example, in the trading and profit and loss account, the cost of sales is not merely a single figure, but a combination of opening and closing stocks and the value of purchases.

The balance sheet shows a breakdown of **assets**:

Fixed assets represent the more permanent assets of the business and are not usually for resale (although they are when they are disposed of). Premises, fixtures and fittings, equipment, plant and machinery, vehicles, are the common type of fixed assets which can be seen in most balance sheets.

Different types of fixed assets may include long-term investments in financial institutions or stocks and shares purchased in other companies. All these are seen as the 'tangible' assets of a business.

Current assets are the type of assets which are used for day-to-day trading and constantly change in value, circulating between buying **stock** and selling it for cash or to customers on credit (**debtors**)

Current assets are also referred to as **trading** or **circulating** assets. They are more liquid than fixed assets because they can be converted to cash more quickly.

There are also 'intangible' types of assets because they are not 'physical' in the same way as owning premises. Goodwill is an example and represents the value of the good name or reputation of a business when it is bought or sold.

The 'marshalling' of assets in the balance sheet should represent a liquidity order where the less liquid assets like premises are entered first and the most liquid asset, cash, entered last.

The balance sheet also shows a breakdown of its **liabilities**:

Current liabilities represent the debts of a business which are repayable within 12 months such as trade creditors, bank overdraft, Vat and other bills outstanding.

Long term liabilities are those debts which can be repaid over a longer period of 12 months. They are also known as 'deferred' liabilities. Examples include mortgages, specific loans, hire purchase agreements, and debentures.

Working capital is calculated by deducting current liabilities from current assets:

Working capital	=	Current assets	–	Current liabilities
£1392	=	£9557.20	–	£8165.20

Every business needs to have adequate working capital to be in a position to trade comfortably and meet day-to-day running costs. A business does not want to be pressed by its creditors to meet payment on demand. It should have sufficient **liquidity** to pay bills when they become due.

Working capital is also referred to as the 'net current assets' of a business. If current liabilities were in excess of current assets, the business would have negative working capital or 'net current liabilities'.

The working capital ratio is calculated by dividing current assets by current liabilities:

$$\text{Working capital ratio} = \frac{\text{Current assets}}{\text{Current liabilities}}$$

$$= \frac{9557.2}{8165.2} = 1.17 : 1$$

The minimum working capital ratio should not fall below 1 : 1, otherwise the business would not have sufficient funds to meet its current debts. This is discussed more fully in Chapter 34.

Capital employed refers to the fixed assets added to working capital and indicates the business's employable assets (total assets less current liabilities).

21.5 The transfer of revenue and expense accounts

At the end of a financial period, when revenue and expense accounts are extracted from the trial balance to prepare the trading and profit and loss account, the ledger account balances for these are transferred from the nominal ledger to the trading and profit and loss account. This procedure, in effect, allows the double entry to be completed and effectively zeroes the balances. In the following accounting period, revenue and expense accounts will therefore normally commence with nil balances. The stock account is also adjusted to record the value of the unsold stock at the period end.

For the following example, we will assume that the period end of R Pearce is 31 January.

Nominal ledger

		Dr	*Cr*	*Balance*
		£	£	£
Sales account				
31/1	Balance			3 900 Cr
31/1	Trading account	3 900		—
Purchases account				
31/1	Balance			3 117 Dr
31/1	Trading account		3 117	—
Stock account				
31/1	Balance			3 680 Dr
31/1	Trading account		3 680	—
31/1	Trading account	5 200		5 200 Dr
*1/2	Balance			5 200 Dr

(continued)

(continued)

General expenses account

31/1	Balance		376 Dr
31/1	Profit and loss account	376	—

Wages account

31/1	Balance		525 Dr
31/1	Profit and loss account	525	—

Overheads account

31/1	Balance		1 100 Dr
31/1	Profit and loss account	1 100	—

NOTE

*The value of unsold stock on 31 January (£5200) is brought into the account and therefore, the stock end of one period becomes the stock beginning of the next period on 1 February.

Example

The following accounts represent the business of R Pearce at the end of the financial year, 31 December:

	Dr £	*Cr* £
Capital: R Pearce		50 000
Drawings: R Pearce	5 600	
Premises	100 000	
Equipment, machinery	17 150	
Motor vehicle	4 000	
Mortgage on premises		69 200
Stock (1/1)	3 680	
Petty cash	200	
Debtors, creditors	4 650	5 950
Sales		62 900
Returns inward	850	
Purchases	35 800	
Returns outward		1 350
Wages	7 480	
Light and heat	970	
Telephone	480	
Printing and stationery	385	
Carriage inwards	220	
Carriage outwards	300	
Advertising	675	
Overheads	12 640	
Discount allowed	100	
Motoring expenses	1 370	
Interest payable	210	
Commission received		300

Discount received		850
Vat (owing)		1 320
Bank (O/D)		4 890
	196 760	196 760

NOTE
The value of unsold stock on 31 December was £5500.

REQUIRED:
a) Prepare the trading and profit and loss account of R Pearce for the year ended 31 December.
b) Prepare the balance sheet of R Pearce as on 31 December in vertical format, showing clearly his net current assets and the working capital ratio.
c) Comment briefly on R Pearce's working capital.

R Pearce –
Trading and profit and loss account for year ended 31 December

	£	£
Sales	62 900	
Returns inward	(850)	62 050
Cost of sales:		
Stock (1 January)	3 680	
Purchases	35 800	
Returns outward	(1 350)	
Carriage inwards	220	
	38 350	
Stock (31 January)	(5 500)	32 850
Gross profit		29 200
Expenses:		
Wages	7 480	
Light and heat	970	
Printing and stationery	385	
Telephone	480	
Carriage outwards	300	
Advertising	675	
Overheads	12 640	
Discount allowed	100	
Motor expenses	1 370	
Interest charges	210	24 610
		4 590
Other revenue:		
Commission received	300	
Discount received	850	1 150
Net profit		5 740

NOTE

Carriage inwards refers to the cost of delivery for purchases and is therefore a trading expense. Carriage outwards refers to the cost of delivery to customers and is regarded as a profit and loss expense.

R Pearce –
Balance sheet as on 31 December

	£	£	£
FIXED ASSETS			
Premises	100 000		
Equipment, machinery	17 150		
Motor vehicle	4 000		121 150
CURRENT ASSETS			
Stock (31/12)	5 500		
Debtors	4 650		
Bank	—		
Petty cash	200	10 350	
less			
CURRENT LIABILITIES			
Creditors	5 950		
Vat	1 320		
Bank (O/D)	4 890	12 160	
Net current liabilities (0.85 : 1)			(1 810)
Capital employed			119 340
LONG-TERM LIABILITIES			
Mortgage on premises			69 200
			50 140
FINANCED BY			
Capital: R Pearce	50 000		
+ Net profit	5 740		
	55 740		
– Drawings	(5 600)		50 140

NOTES

1 The value of unsold stock on 31 December is included in the balance sheet as a current asset.

2 Net profit is added to capital, increasing the owner's net worth. Personal drawings reduces net worth.

3 R Pearce has insufficient working capital because his current assets are less than his current liabilities, a working capital ratio (current ratio) of less than 1. This is known as an 'insolvent position' and R Pearce will need to be aware that his creditors can press for payments and demand their

debts to be honoured. He may need to reduce his expenses or increase his sales to be in a better liquidity position.

Summary

The final accounts of a business refers to the financial statements: the trading and profit and loss account and the balance sheet. They represent the final accounts because they are the end product of the accounting system. Revenue and expenses provide the answer to profit or loss. Assets, liabilities and capital provide the financial position of the business illustrated by the accounting equation: capital = assets – liabilities. Revenue and expense accounts are zeroed to the profit and loss account so that in the new financial period, their balance commence with zero.

Questions

1 The following accounts relate to the business of P Jackson as at the month ended 31 January:

P Jackson –
Trial balance as on 31 January

	Dr	*Cr*
	£	£
Bank	2 855	
Premises (cost)	12 000	
Fixtures and fittings (cost)	2 000	
Equipment (cost)	3 000	
Mortgage on premises		8 000
Bank loan (long-term)		2 000
Capital: P Jackson		10 000
Drawings: P Jackson	100	
Wages	375	
Light and heat	220	
General expenses	20	
Purchases	2 370	
Sales		3 085
Commission received		30
Debtors	875	
Creditors		1 435
Stock (1 January)	735	
	24 550	24 550

NOTE
The value of unsold stock on 31 January is £805.

REQUIRED:
a) Prepare the trading and profit and loss account of P Jackson for the month of January (21.2)
b) Prepare a balance sheet as on 31 January and show working capital as part of the format. Calculate the working capital ratio. (21.4)

2 The following represents the trial balance of D Smith for the month ended 30 June:

	Dr £	*Cr* £
Capital: D Smith		20 000
Drawings: D Smith	540	
Fixtures, fittings	2 100	
Motor vehicle	4 450	
Bank/cash	155	
Debtors	2 440	
Creditors		1 180
Premises	56 600	
General expenses	390	
Wages	665	
Purchases	2 000	
Stock (1 June)	1 900	
Sales		8 070
Mortgage on premises		40 000
Returns inward	60	
Returns outward		50
Loan from bank (4 years)		2 000
	71 300	71 300

NOTE
The value of stock on 30 June was £2 125.

REQUIRED:
a) Prepare the trading and profit and loss account of D Smith for the month ended 30 June (21.2).
b) Prepare the balance sheet of D Smith as at 30 June. Show the net current assets and capital employed as part of your answer. Calculate the current ratio (working capital ratio). (21.4)

3 The following information relates to the accounts of D Balfour as on 31 December:

D Balfour –
Trading and profit and loss account as on 31 December

	Dr £	*Cr* £
Capital: D Balfour		16 600
Drawings: D Balfour	10 200	
Sales		209 200
Returns inward	200	
Purchases	104 350	
Returns outward		50
Stock (1 January)	38 500	
Wages	28 000	
Rent, rates	5 600	

(continued)

(continued)

General expenses	2 150	
Insurance	1 850	
Advertising	980	
Postage and stationery	2 150	
Debtors	11 800	
Creditors		4 230
Plant and equipment	42 600	
Fixtures, fittings	6 000	
Motor vehicle	7 900	
Bank loan (long-term)		38 000
Bank	5 300	
Cash	500	
	268 080	268 080

NOTE
The value of unsold stock on 31 December was £42 100.

REQUIRED:
a) Prepare the trading and profit and loss account of D Balfour for the year ending 31 December (21.2)
b) Prepare the balance sheet of D Balfour as on 31 December, clearly showing working capital. Calculate the current ratio. (21.4)

4 The following information relates to the accounts of E Mitton for the year ended 31 March 19–8:

E Mitton –
Trial balance as on 31 March 19–8

	Dr £	*Cr* £
Bank	1 532	
Petty cash	150	
Fixtures and fittings (cost)	2 200	
Motor vehicle	4 025	
Stock (1/4/19–7)	3 700	
Debtors, creditors	1 943	3 580
Vat	127	
HP loan (3 years)		4 050
Capital: E Mitton		11 000
Drawings: E Mitton	4 100	
Sales		21 360
Returns	400	350
Purchases	13 500	
Carriage inwards	75	
Carriage outwards	250	
Rent	2 500	
Wages	4 150	
General overheads	1 546	
Discount	142	
	40 340	40 340

NOTE
The value of unsold stock on 31 March was £3500.

REQUIRED:
a) Prepare the trading and profit and loss account of E Mitton for the year ended 31 March 19–8 (21.2)
b) Prepare the balance sheet of E Mitton as on 31 March 19–8 (21.4)
c) Make a brief comment relating to the working capital of the owner. (21.4)

5 Prepare from the following accounts, a trial balance for B Jackson, as on 1 January.

	£		£
Bank overdraft	300	Sales	48 475
Cash	200	Purchases	35 450
Motor van	2 420	General expenses	2 485
Debtors	515	Motor expenses	850
Creditors	1 225	Rent received	840
Capital	10 500		
Bank loan	3 400		
Premises	25 300		
Mortgage	8 950		
Equipment	6 570		

Trial balance of
B Jackson as on 1 January

	Dr £	*Cr* £
Bank overdraft		300
Cash	200	
Motor van	2 420	
Debtors	515	
Creditors		1 225
Capital: P Jackson		10 500
Bank loan		3 400
Premises	25 300	
Sales		48 575
Purchases	35 450	
General expenses	2 485	
Motor expenses	850	
Rent received		840
Mortgage		8 950
Equipment	6 570	
	73 790	73 790

REQUIRED:
a) Check that the list of accounts are entered correctly in the trial balance. (21.2)
b) There are no opening/closing stocks. Estimate *your own* value of closing stock on 31 January, say *under* £1000, and proceed to the preparation of the final accounts for the period ending to 31 January. The author has used a closing value of £800. (21.5)

6

Trial balance of
Jenkins Jeans Co Ltd
31 March 19–8

	Dr £	*Cr* £
Premises	53 150	
Equipment and machines	4 000	
Motor vehicle	4 750	
Stocks (1/4/19–7)	3 680	
Bank		8 022
Petty cash	200	
Debtors, creditors	4 050	4 785
Mortgage on premises		32 450
Bank loan (5 years)		4 725
Sales		11 850
Purchases	5 600	
Vat		248
Gross wages	5 025	
Light and heat	72	
Telephone, insurance	105	
Petty cash expenses	148	
General overheads	800	
Directors' fees	500	
Share capital		20 000
	82 080	82 080

NOTE
On 31 March 19–8 stocks were valued at £4580.

REQUIRED:
a) Prepare the trading and profit and loss account of the company for the month ending 31 March 19–8. (21.2)
b) Prepare a balance sheet as on that date. Show working capital as part of the presentation. (21.4)
c) Calculate the appropriate accounting ratio to measure working capital. (21.4)

7 The trial balance of J Robert as on 30 April is indicated below:

J. Robert –
Trading and profit and loss account as on 30 April

	Dr £	*Cr* £
Capital: J Robert		18 000
Drawings	2 800	
Bank overdraft		725
Premises	15 700	

(continued)

(continued)

Motor van	1 000	
Equipment	1 400	
Debtors	2 900	
Creditors		3 850
Stock (beg.)	3 500	
Purchases	28 400	
Sales		42 650
Rent received		750
Wages	8 500	
Rates and insurance	270	
Light and heat	195	
Administrative expenses	325	
Selling and distribution costs	500	
Vat	275	
Returns inward	400	
Returns outward		190
	66 165	66 165

NOTE: Stock unsold on 30 April was valued £5 280. Vat is not an expense. Customs & Excise owe the money to J Robert and is entered in the balance sheet.

REQUIRED:

a) The trading and profit and loss account for the year ended 30 April. (21.2)
b) A balance sheet as at this date.(21.4)

8 The trial balance of G Chappell on 31 March was as follows:

	Dr £	*Cr* £
Bank loan (2 years)		402.77
Cash	48.00	
Bank	1 532.80	
Stock (beg.)	700.00	
Fixtures and fittings	200.00	
Motor van	1 025.00	
Sales ledger control	941.50	
Purchase ledger control		1 580.23
Vat	145.41	
Capital		4 050.00
Drawings	600.00	
Sales		1 867.00
Purchases	1 562.12	
Discount	42.15	
Overheads	546.25	
Wages	154.00	
Motor expenses	303.77	
Petty cash expenses	99.00	
	7 900.00	7 900.00

NOTE: Stock on 31 March still unsold, £1 300.

REQUIRED:

a) The trading and profit and loss account for the year ended 31 March. (21.2)
b) A balance sheet as at that date, showing working capital. (21.4)

22 Adjustments to final accounts

Objectives

On completing this section you should:

- understand what is meant by the 'accounting period'
- recognise and use adjustments for accruals, prepayments and owners' drawings both in the ledger and final accounts.

Context

Chapter 21 put adjustments in the overall context of preparing final accounts. Chapters 23 and 25 discuss other types of adjustment.

22.1 Introduction

An accounting period can be of any duration of time. In large organisations, it may be necessary for management purposes to prepare final accounts every month in order to keep a check on the pulse of the business, whether or not profits are going to plan. With smaller organisations this is often not possible or even desirable and the preparation of the financial statements is the normal period of one year. A financial period commences at the time the business commenced trading. This could be the first of any month of the year and ending 12 months later, for example, starting 1 June 19–7 and finishing 31 May 19–8.

Adjustments to the final accounts are required because any transaction which specifically belongs to an accounting period, whether paid or incurred (due to be paid), must be included within the accounts of that period. This is part of what is called the 'accruals' concept in accounting. For example, if wages of £2500 were owing to staff during the last month of the year, 31 May, the cost would still need to be included for the year to 31 May, even though as yet unpaid.

22.2 Types of adjustments

In this section, we will look at four major adjustment types:

1	**Accruals**	(expenses still owing)
2	**Prepayments**	(expenses paid in advance)
3	**Revenue accrued**	(income owed)
4	**Owners drawings**	(anything of value taken for personal use).

Other adjustments include provisions for bad and doubtful debts, provision for cash discounts (Chapter 23) and the provision for depreciation of fixed assets. Each of these adjustments will have a double effect on the final accounts:

a) they are included in the trading and profit and loss account, thereby affecting the profit or loss for the period,

b) they are included in the balance sheet because they affect the value of assets and liabilities.

A summary of major adjustments used in final accounts

Type of adjustment		The effect on final accounts	
		Trading and profit and loss	Balance sheet
1	**Accrued expense**	**increase expense**	**current liability**
2	**Prepayment**	**reduce expense**	**current asset**
3	**Accrued revenue**	**increase revenue**	**current asset**
4	Provision for bad and doubtful debts (increase)	increase expense	reduce debtors
5	Provision for cash discounts (increase)	increase expense	reduce debtors
6	**Stock drawings**	**reduce cost of sales**	**reduce capital**
7	Provision for depreciation of fixed assets	increase expense	reduce fixed asset

Note: If provisions for bad debts and cash discounts were reduced for the period, then the effect would be reversed, the expense would be reduced and the provisions in the balance sheet would also be reduced. Adjustments in **bold** are discussed in the following sections.

22.3 Accrued expenses

We may define these as follows:

Accrued expenses are expenses incurred during the financial year but not yet paid for.

Any outstanding expenses must be charged to the profit and loss account for the year in which they were used. Even if an invoice for the telephone, gas or electricity account, has not yet been received for the period, an estimate of the cost can still be included in the accounts. This could mean looking at previous figures for the same quarterly bills or estimating the number of units consumed in the period. The estimated charge due to be paid would be included in the profit and loss account and also as a current liability in the balance sheet.

Example

The following accounts represent the business of R Pearce at the end of the financial year, 31 December:

	Dr	*Cr*
	£	£
Capital: R Pearce		50 000
Drawings: R Pearce	5 600	
Premises	100 000	
Equipment, machinery	17 150	
Motor vehicle	4 000	
Mortgage on premises		69 200

Stock (1/1)	3 680	
Petty cash	200	
Debtors, creditors	4 650	5 950
Sales		62 900
Returns inward	850	
Purchases	35 800	
Returns outward	1 350	
Wages	7 480	
Light and heat	970	
Telephone	480	
Printing and stationery	385	
Carriage inwards	220	
Carriage outwards	300	
Advertising	675	
Overheads	12 640	
Discount allowed	100	
Motoring expenses	1 370	
Interest payable	210	
Commission received		300
Discount received		850
Vat (owing)		1 320
Bank (O/D)		4 890
	196 760	196 760

NOTE

The value of unsold stock on 31 December was £5500.

Using these figures assume that on 31 December, footnotes included the following accounts:

a) Wages due to an employee, £150.
b) A gas bill of £85 was still unpaid.
c) Interest charges from the bank £35, had to be included under interest payable.

The effect on trading and profit and loss account as on 31 December:

	£	£
Wages	7 480	
Accrued	150	7 630
Light and heat	970	
Accrued	85	1 055
Interest payable	210	
Accrued	35	245

The effect on the balance sheet as on 31 December:

	£
CURRENT LIABILITIES	
Accrued expenses (150 + 85 + 35)	270

NOTES
1 An accrued expense is *added* to the appropriate expense paid.
2 An accrued expense is included under *current liabilities* because they represent short-term debts still unpaid.

Accounts as marked in the nominal ledger as follows:

Nominal ledger

		Debit	*Credit*	*Balance*
		£	£	£
Wages account				
31/12	Balance			7 480 Dr
31/12	Accrual	150		7 630
31/12	P&L account		7 630	00
1/1	Accrual		150	150 Cr
5/1	Bank	150		00

NOTES
1 The accrual is brought down in the new accounting period, 1 January, because the wages are still to be paid.
2 When they are paid by cheque on 5 January, the account is cleared.

22.4 Prepayments (prepaid expenses)

We may define these as follows:

> Prepayments are expenses which are paid in advance of the current financial period.

Some expenses may be likely to be paid in advance including rent, rates, insurance premiums and advertising. Unused stocks of stationery or packing materials etc. are also classified as prepaid if the value of them is material enough. (If there was only £ 10 stationery it may not be a sufficiently material enough figure to bother about). Any payment for expenses which has been made in advance of the financial period needs to be deducted from the appropriate expense in the profit and loss account and that figure also included as a current asset in the balance sheet.

Example
Using the trial balance figures of R Pearce as on 31 December, the following prepayments were included as footnotes:

a) There was £150 for advertising, already paid, which was for press releases in January.
b) There was still £100 of stationery still in stock, to be used in the next financial period.

The effect on trading and profit and loss account as on 31 December:

	£	£
Advertising	675	
Prepaid expense	(150)	525
Printing and stationery	385	
Prepaid expense	(100)	285

The effect on the balance sheet as on 31 December:

	£
CURRENT ASSETS	
Prepayments (150 + 100)	250

NOTES

1 A prepaid expense has the effect of *reducing* the expense because that portion is part of the next period.

2 The prepayment is regarded as a *current asset* because some value of the expense is still to be used in the next period.

Prepayment would be recorded in the nominal ledger as follows:

Nominal ledger

		Debit	*Credit*	*Balance*
		£	£	£
Advertising account				
31/12	Balance			675 Dr
31/12	Prepayment		150	525
31/12	P&L account		525	00
1/1	Prepayment	150		150 Dr

NOTE

The prepaid expense is brought down as a debit in the new accounting period to indicate that £150 has already been spent on advertising in the new period, 1 January.

22.5 Accrued revenue

This may be defined as follows:

> **Accrued revenue** is income owing to the business (apart from normal sales) at the end of the financial period.

If any income is owing to the business (other than normal sales which are already listed as debit entries in the relevant customers' accounts) at the end of the financial period, then this must be included in the same way as in the previous adjustments. If, for example, a trader owed us money for commission because we sold his goods in our shop, the sum owing must be added to the income already earned on commission during the period. Other income could come from rent received from tenants or interest receivable due from the bank. Accrued revenue (or accrued income) is therefore added to the appropriate revenue account in the profit and loss and is also included as a prepayment in the balance sheet.

Example
Using the figures of R Pearce again, the following accrued revenue was included in the footnotes:

a) £120 was due to be paid on commission,
b) £240 was owing on sub-let of premises as rent received – this was the first sum due to be paid by the tenant.

The effect on trading and profit and loss account as on 31 December:

	£	£
Commission	300	
accrued revenue	120	420
Rent received accrued		240

The effect on the balance sheet as on 31 December:

	£
CURRENT ASSETS	
Prepayments	250
+ Accrued revenue (120 + 240)	360

We would record in the nominal ledger as follows:

Nominal ledger

		Debit	Credit	Balance
		£	£	£
Commission received account				
31/12	Balance			300 Cr
31/12	Revenue accrued		120	420
31/12	P & L account	420		0
01/01	Revenue accrued	120		120 Dr
10/01	Bank		120	0

NOTE
The revenue accrued is brought down as a debit entry in the new financial period to indicate that this sum is still outstanding. When it is actually received on 10 January, the account is cleared. Any further commission will then be credited to the account in the normal way.

22.6 Owner's drawings

We may define this as follows:

> **Drawings** are money or returns of value taken out of the business by the owner for personal use.

We have already noted that when the owner of the business takes out cash for his own benefit, the sum withdrawn is debited to the drawings account and the bank or cash account is credited.

The same principle applies if the owner takes anything of value away from the business for his own personal use. This could include any value in stock, anything that benefits him by way of using his motor vehicle for personal use, or insurance, telephone bills, repairs or building on his personal premises. Indeed, any value that is personal as distinct from any business value. This is the principle of the owner being a separate entity from that of the business. The double entry would be:

Debit:	drawings
Credit:	the corresponding account.

For example, if R Pearce were to take £500 stock for his own use and £100 of the telephone account were categorised as private calls, then:

Debit:	drawings	£600	
Credit:	purchases		£500
	telephone		£100

The effect on trading and profit and loss account:

Cost of sales:	£	£	£
Stock	3 680		
Purchases	35 800		
Returns outward	(1 350)		
Carriage inwards	220	38 350	
Stock drawings		(500)	
		37 850	
Stock (31 December)		(5 500)	32 350
Expenses:			
Telephone	480		
Drawings	(100)	380	

The effect on the balance sheet as on 31 December:

		£	£
FINANCED BY:			
Capital			50 000
less Drawings	(cash)	(5 600)	
	(stock)	(500)	
	(telephone)	(100)	(6 200)
			43 800

22.7 Practising adjustments

The following examples are questions which have been taken from examinations and focus on adjustments to the accounts.

Example 1
A company makes its accounts up to 31 December 19–7. The following information relates to the telephone account:

	£
Charges paid to date for 19–7	2 144.56
Rental charges paid 15 November 19–7 to 15 February 19–8	428.60
and incurring dialled calls 1 December 19–7 to 1 March 19–8	856.24

Prepare the telephone account for the period ended 31 December 19–7.

Telephone account

		£			£
31/12	Balance	2 144	31/12	Prepaid	214
	(rental)	428		Profit & loss	2 643
	Accrued (calls)	285			
		2 857			2 857
1/1	Prepaid b/d	214	1/1	Accrued b/d	285

In this case half the rental is paid in advance to 15 February and one third of the calls are still to be charged for to the year ended 31 December.

Example 2
The light and heat account had a balance to profit and loss of £ 1520 but this included an electricity accrual of £375 which in error had been treated as a prepayment. What effect did this have on the account? What would be the entry to correct the error?

The account would have appeared as:

Light and heat account

		£			£
31/12	Balance b/d	1895	31/12	Accrued	375
			31/12	Profit & loss	1 520
		1 895			1 895
1/1	Accrued b/d	375	1/1	Profit & loss	750

Because the accrual had been entered as a credit entry and brought down as a debit in the new period, we need to double the £375 as a credit entry of £750 to provide the correct balance of £375 credit. The correct figure to profit and loss account would then be £2270. The account should have read:

Light and heat account		£			£
31/12	Balance b/d	1 895	31/12	Profit & loss	2 270
	Accrued	375			
		2 270			2 270
			1/1	Accrued b/d	375

Example 3

The financial period for ABC Co Ltd runs from 1 June to 31 May and it maintains separate accounts for rent and rates in the nominal ledger.

Rent is payable quarterly in advance and was £4 800 pa, year ended 31 December 19–7 and £6 000 pa year ended 31 December 19–8.

The following quarterly payments have been made by cheque:

19–7		£
1/1	Balance b/f	2 800
5	January	1 200
4	April	1 200
3	July	1 200
5	October	1 200
19–8		
4	January	1 500
6	April	1 500

Rates are assessed by the local council (DCC) annually, year ending 31 March. The assessment for rates was £4 080 for the period ended 31 March 19–7 and £4 560 for the period ended 31 March 19–8. The rates are recorded in the purchase ledger when the bill is received from DCC on 10 April each year and the expense account debited. The balance brought down in the rates account on 1 April 19–7 was £3 200.

REQUIRED:

Prepare the Rent Account and Rates Account for the periods ended 31 May 19–7 and 19–8. Show the appropriate figures to be recorded in the profit and loss account and the balance sheet for the period 31 May 19–8.

Rent account		£			£
19–7			19–7		
1/1	Balance b/d	2 800	31/5	Prepaid	400
5/1	Bank	1 200		Profit & loss	4 800
4/4	Bank	1 200			
		5 200			5 200
19–7			19–8		
1/6	Prepaid b/d	400	31/5	Prepaid	500
3/7	Bank	1 200		Profit & loss	5 100
5/10	Bank	1 200			

19–8					
4/1	Bank	1 500			
6/4	Bank	1 500			
		5 600			5 600
1/6	Prepaid b/d	500			

Rates account

		£			£
19–7			19–7		
1/1	Balance b/d	3 200	31/5	Prepaid	3 400
10/4	DCC	4 080		Profit & loss	3 880
		7 280			7 280
19–7			19–8		
1/6	Prepaid b/d	3 400	31/5	Prepaid	3 800
19–8					
10/4	DCC	4 560		Profit & loss	4 160
		7 960			7 960
1/6	Prepaid b/d	3 800			

Profit and loss account 31 May 19–8:

Rent £5 100
Rates £4 160

Balance sheet as on 31 May 19–8:

Prepaid rent £ 500
Prepaid rates £3 800

Summary

Adjustments to the final accounts are those which at the financial period end, need to be included because they belong to that period. Their entry will provide a more 'true and fair' financial position. Each adjustment has a dual effect in that one aspect affects profit and the other affects an item in the balance sheet.

Questions

1 The following information represents the accounts of A Land on 31 December:

Trial balance as on 31 December

	Dr £	Cr £
Capital: A Land		18 000
Drawings	5 500	
Bank	4 250	
Cash	200	
Office equipment	5 800	
Motor van	2 575	

(continued)

(continued)

Stock (1/1)	4 250	
Debtors	3 930	
Creditors		2 185
Sales		37 800
Purchases	22 400	
Returns inward	945	
Returns outward		350
Rent	800	
Discount		225
Stationery	580	
Assistant's wages	4 855	
General overheads	2 800	
Rates, water	115	
Vat (Customs & Excise)		440
	59 000	59 000

NOTES

As on 31 December:

a) Unsold stock valued £4875.
b) Rates paid in advance, £30.
c) Assistant's wages unpaid, £85.
d) Unused stationery, £140.

REQUIRED:

a) A trading and profit and loss account for the period ending 31 December
b) A balance sheet as at that date. (22.1–4)

2 The following accounts were taken from the books of H Smith at the financial year ended 31 December:

	Dr £	*Cr* £
Capital: H Smith		16 000
Drawings	4 200	
Stock (1/1)	12 890	
Purchases	22 430	
Sales		32 300
Premises	12 000	
Equipment	760	
Motor van	2 250	
Debtors	23 220	
Creditors		33 600
Returns inward	250	
Returns outward		540
Rates and water	850	
Wages	4 480	
Advertising	250	
Office expenses	280	
Discount received		350
General expenses	820	
Bank overdraft		1 890
	84 680	84 680

NOTE
At 31 December:
a) The value of stock £10 500.
b) Wages owing £42.
c) Rates prepaid £30.
d) An invoice for office stationery still unpaid £55.

REQUIRED:
Prepare the trading and profit and loss account of H Smith for the year ended 31 December and a balance sheet as at that date. (22.1–4)

3 The following balances remain in John Wild's books after compilation of his trading account for the year ended 30 June:

	Dr £	*Cr* £
Capital		80 000
Gross profit		10 000
Shop premises	73 000	
Stock (30/6)	9 000	
Trade creditors		2 500
Rates	700	
Insurance	350	
Postage and stationery	270	
Proprietor's drawings	6 000	
Cash in hand and bank	2 380	
Heating and lighting	800	
	92 500	92 500

NOTE
The following additional information is available as at 30 June:
a) Rates paid in advance, £140.
b) Insurance paid in advance, £150.
c) Heating and lighting account due but unpaid, £170.

REQUIRED:
Prepare John Wild's profit and loss account for the year ended 30 June and a balance sheet as on that date. (22.1–4)

(Royal Society of Arts)

4 George Price is the proprietor of a small business. He keeps his financial records on double-entry principles and extracted the following trial balance on 31 May 19–6:

	£		£
Stock 1 June 19–5	7 000	Capital 1 June 19–5	85 000
Cash at bank	8 000	Creditors	3 700
Furniture and fittings	7 500	Sales	40 000
Premises	65 000		
Rates	1 600		
Purchases	30 000		
Heating and lighting	1 500		
Cleaning	1 700		
Packing materials	1 400		
Drawings	5 000		
	128 700		128 700

You are required to take the following into consideration on 31 May 19–6:

	£
i) Stock on hand	9 500
ii) Rates paid in advance	400
iii) Stock of packing material	300

and prepare a trading and profit and loss account for the year ended 31 May 19–6 and a balance sheet at that date. (22.1–4)

(Royal Society of Arts)

5 On 31 December 19–7, the accounts of a company show accrued rent to be paid of £250. During the financial period for 19–7, the company had paid rent bills totalling £1275, including one bill for £375 in respect of the quarter ending 31 January 19–8. Prepare the rent account and indicate the charge to the profit and loss account for the year ended 31 December 19–7. (22.3–6)

6 The following balances remain on the books of S Davis after completion of his trading account for the year ended 30 October 19–5:

	Dr £	*Cr* £
Gross profit		29 500
Debtors and creditors	2 400	3 600
Premises	50 000	
Bank loan to be repaid over 10 years		21 000
Stock of goods for resale	2 400	
Stationery	1 560	
Rates	350	
Loan interest	300	
Insurance	290	
Cash in hand and cash at bank	1 700	
Proprietor's drawings	5 450	
Wages and salaries	10 500	
Capital		20 850
	74 950	74 950

The following information is available as at 31 October 19–5:
i) There is a stock of unused stationery valued at £150.
ii) £50 of the insurance refers to the period 1 November 19–5 to 31 January 19–6.
iii) There is £300 loan interest outstanding.

PREPARE:
The profit and loss account for S Davis for the year ended 31 October 19–5 and a balance sheet as at that date clearly showing fixed and current assets, long-term and current liabilities and capital. (22.3–6)

(Royal Society of Arts)

7 The following trial balance was extracted from the books of R Colebrook on 31 May 19–6. You are required to prepare the trading and profit and loss account for the year ended 31 May 19–6 and the balance sheet as at that date. Your trading account should clearly show the cost of sales.

Trial balance as at 31 May 19–6

	Dr	Cr
	£	£
Capital		29 250
Drawings	4 600	
Bank and cash	9 200	
Salaries and wages	23 000	
Purchases and sales	35 000	68 000
Debtors and creditors	12 350	18 000
Office expenses	2 500	
Light and heat	1 700	
Rates	1 400	
Premises	15 000	
Fixtures and fittings	2 300	
Vehicles	4 200	
Stock (1/6/85)	4 100	
Sales and purchase returns	400	500
	115 750	115 750

The following information as at 31 May 19–6 is also available:

i) Stock on 31 May 19–6 was £3900.
ii) Wages owing but not yet paid £100.
iii) Light, heat and rates are to be apportioned –
 1/4 to trading account
 3/4 to profit and loss account.
iv) Included in the office expenses is an insurance prepayment of £50. (22.3.6)

8 The light and heat account had a balance to profit and loss of £3550 but this included an electricity prepayment of £750 which in error had been treated as an accrual. Prepare the light and heat account and include how it would be corrected. (22.3–6)

9 A business, commencing trade on 1 December 19–7, had the following transactions relating to its insurance premiums:

1 December 19–7 Took cover on public liability.
Annual premium £1000
1 February 19–8 Took cover on buildings
Annual premium £1200
1 May 19–8 Took cover on stock
Annual premium £800

Write up the insurance account in the ledger clearly showing the sum to be transferred to profit and loss account for the period ending 30 November 19–8. (22.3–6)

10 A company makes its accounts up to 31 December 19–7. The following information relates to the telephone account:

Charges paid to date for 19–7 £2256
Rental charges paid 1 November 19–7 to 1 February 19–8 £390
Dialled calls outstanding 1 November 19–7 to 1 February 19–8 £840

Prepare the telephone account for the period end 31 December 19–7. (22.3–6)

23 Bad debts and provisions for debtors

Objectives

On completing this section you should:

- know how to write off a customer as a bad debt
- understand how to make a provision for bad debts against debtors
- understand how to make a provision for discounts against debtors.

Context

Chapter 22 introduced the various types of adjustment; Chapter 21 put adjustments into the wider context of preparing final accounts.

23.1 Introduction

Accounting tends to be a very cautious profession and will always provide for any possible losses which may occur. This is referred to as the concept of *conservatism* or prudence. On the other hand, accounting will rarely be optimistic and make a provision for a future gain.

A possible loss is likely to be associated with debtors, particularly if the control of credit sales is poor. An accountant is likely to set a sum aside and charge it against profits if it is considered that a proportion of debtors may fail to honour their debts. It may be that some debts will never be paid and these will have to be written off as bad.

A **bad debt** is one a business is not able to collect.

23.2 Writing off a bad debt

The double entry to write off a debtor's account is:

1 Debit – bad debts account (expense).
2 Credit – Customer's account (and sales ledger control account).

We can see this in the following example:

One of R Pearce's customers, D Lewis, has fallen on hard times and gone bankrupt and has had to be written off. The appropriate ledger entries are:

Sales ledger

		Debit	Credit	Balance
		£	£	£
D Lewis account				
31/12	Balance			260 Dr
31/12	Bad debts		260	—

Nominal ledger

		Debit	Credit	Balance
		£	£	£
Bad debts account				
31/12	D Lewis	260		260 Dr
31/12	P&L account		260	—

23.3 Provision for bad and doubtful debts

The accountant has decided to make a provision of 10 per cent of the debtors taken from R Pearce's sales ledger:

	£	
Balance of debtors (31/12)	4 650	
Less bad debt	260	
10% provision:	4 390	× 10%
	= 439	

The effect on trading and profit and loss account at 31 December:

	£	£
Bad debts	260	
Provision for bad debts	439	699

The effect on the balance sheet as on 31 December:

	£	£
CURRENT ASSETS		
Debtors	4 390	
– Provision for bad debts	439	3 951

NOTES

1 A sum of £699 is charged against profits for the year (£260 writing off a bad debt and £439 set aside as a provision against possible future bad debts).

2 The debtors in the balance sheet, net £3951, is what is considered a realistic sum customers will pay.

We would record this information in the nominal ledger as follows:

Nominal ledger

		Debit	Credit	Balance
		£	£	£
Provision for bad debts account				
31/12	P&L account		439	439 Cr
1/1	Balance			439 Cr

In his new accounting period, R Pearce has set aside £439 to catch any future possible bad debts. Any further debtors who go bad will be written off and debited to the bad debts account (as previously with D Lewis). The total bad debts account can then be transferred to the provision for bad debts account.

Let us assume that R Pearce writes off debtors worth £325 as bad. These are recorded in the provision for bad debts account. The debtors' final balance as on 31 December is £5780 and the accountant wishes to make a further 10 per cent provision against bad debts:

Nominal ledger

		Debit	Credit	Balance
		£	£	£
Provision for bad debts account				
1/1	Balance			439 Cr
31/12	Bad debts	325		114
31/12	P&L account		464	578
1/1	Balance			578 Cr

The effect on trading and profit and loss account as on 31 December:

	£
Provision for bad debts (expense)	464

The effect on the balance sheet as on 31 December:

	£	£
CURRENT ASSETS		
Debtors	5 780	
– Provision for bad debts	578	5 202

NOTES

1 £464 is charged against profits in the profit and loss account to make the provision up to equal 10 per cent of debtors, £578. (£114 credit was already in the provision account).
2 If a provision for bad debts was reduced instead of increased, the effect would be to debit the provision account and credit 'other revenue' in the profit and loss account.
3 The balance sheet shows the 10 per cent provision against the current debtors balance.

23.4 The recovery of bad debts

In the event of a customer paying back a debt which had previously been written off, either in part-payment or in full, the debt must first be reinstated in the customer's sales ledger account. It is important to do this because the record will then show that the customer did, in effect, honour the debt at some future point in time. Once the cheque has been received and banked, the posting to the ledger account clears the debt. The procedure for this type of transaction is therefore as follows:

1 Reinstate the debt

Debit: the customer's account (and sales ledger control account) with amount recovered;
Credit: the bad debts account (or alternatively a bad debts recovered account)

2 Banking the amount received

Debit: bank account
Credit: customer's account (and sales ledger control account).

Example

A customer of R Pearce, Arthur Harrington, had been previously written off as a bad debt £115. In November 19–7, a cheque for the full amount had been received from the solicitors of Harrington, in settlement of the old account. In Pearce's ledgers:

Sales ledger

		Debit	*Credit*	*Balance*
		£	£	£
A Harrington account				
19–6				
30/6	Balance			115 Dr
	Bad debts		115	0
19–7				
30/11	Bad debts	115		115 Dr
	Bank		115	0

Sales ledger

		Debit	*Credit*	*Balance*
		£	£	£
Bad debts account				
19–7				
1/11	Balance			420 Dr
30/11	A Harrington		115	305 Dr

(continued)

(continued)

Sales ledger control account

19–7				
1/11	Balance			6 840 Dr
30/11	Harrington	115		6 955
30/11	Bank		115	6 840

Bank account

19–7				
1/11	Balance			742 Dr
30/11	Harrington	115		857

NOTES

Remember that the sales ledger control account must reflect, in total, what affects the individual accounts in the sales ledger. Both the debt recovered and received in Harrington's personal account must also be recorded in the control account, otherwise the schedule of debtors would not reconcile with the sales ledger control account. In effect, it makes no difference to the sales ledger control balance, but the record must still show the reinstatement and clearance of the debt.

23.5 The provision for debtors' discounts

If it is the policy of a business to allow customers to have cash discounts on their sales, (discount allowed) it may be seen as prudent to make an appropriate provision for it in the same way as providing for bad and doubtful debts. The double entry for the provision for discounts is:

Debit: profit and loss account (an expense)
Credit: provision for discounts allowed account (reduction of asset).

The provision for discounts must always be calculated on the net value of debtors, that is, after deducting the provision for bad debts.

The balance sheet will then indicate the gross debtors figure, less both provisions for bad and doubtful debts and discounts.

The provision for discounts allowed to customers may then be adjusted each year in relation to the amount of discounts allowed and the provision for bad debts.

Example

A trader has £800 credit as the opening balance, 1 January 19–7, in the provision for bad debts account. He decides to provide a 2.5 per cent provision for discounts at the year end. The following figures relate to the two years ended 31 December 19–7 and 19–8:

19–7	Debtors	£16 800	Bad debts written off £785
19–8	Debtors	£18 000	Bad debts written off £700.

Provision for bad debts 5 per cent
Provision for discounts 2.5 per cent

The relevant accounts for both these years are as follows:

		Debit	Credit	Balance
		£	£	£
Provision for bad debts account				
19–7				
1/1	P & L a/c			800 Cr
31/12	Bad debts	785		15
	P & L a/c		825	840
19–8				
1/1	Balance			840 Cr
31/12	Bad debts	700		140
	P & L a/c		760	900
Provision for discounts allowed account				
19–7				
31/12	P & L a/c		399	399 Cr
19–8				
31/12	P & L a/c		29	428

They would appear in the final accounts as follows:

Profit and Loss Account year ended 31 December

19–7	Provision for bad debts	825	
	Provision for discounts	399	
19–8	Provision for bad debts	760	
	Provision for discounts	29	

Balance sheet as on 31 December

19–7	Debtors		16 800
	Less Prov. for bad debts	840	
	Prov. for discounts	399	(1 239)
			15 561
19–8	Debtors		18 000
	Less Prov. for bad debts	900	
	Prov. for discounts	428	(1 328)
			16 682

Summary

If a business finds that a customer cannot repay a debt it will need to write it off, either in part or the whole sum. An asset thereby becomes an expense. A provision for bad debts is a sum set aside from profits to cover those debtors which may be unreliable. The older the age of the debt, the more likely it is that a provision needs to be made. This concept was first introduced in Chapter 7. Where discounts are offered to customers, a similar provision can be made against debtors because the business can expect less receipts. This provision is made before the provision for bad debts.

Questions

1 The accounts of Harry Smith as at 31 December were as follows:

Account	*£*
Capital:	8 000
Drawings	2 500
Cash	100
Bank	400
Equipment	400
Motor vehicle	1 500
Stock (1/1)	4 800
Debtors	2 500
Creditors	3 130
Sales	12 200
Purchases	7 000
Returns outward	250
Rent	160
Discount received	20
Stationery	90
Wages	3 000
General expenses	1 000
Rates	150

Adjustments: 31 December

1 Stock unsold £4 300.
2 Rates pre-paid £38.
3 A provision for bad debts is to be made to equal 5 per cent of debtors.
4 Wages outstanding £120.
5 Stationery unused £40.

REQUIRED:
a) A trading and profit and loss account for the year ended 31 December.
b) A balance sheet as at that date. (23.2–3)

2 You work for a firm of accountants and have to prepare the final accounts for a client, S Waugh. The following trial balance was extracted on February 19–5.

	Dr £	*Cr* £
Capital		60 000
Loan from A Boarder (repayable 2001)		25 000
Premises	39 000	
Drawings	15 000	
Stock at 1/3/19–4	26 500	
Motor vans (at cost)	35 000	
Carriage outwards*	4 000	
Fixtures (at cost)	15 000	
Purchases and sales	173 200	319 200
Debtors and creditors	21 400	14 200
Returns inwards and outwards	1 200	800
Discounts allowed and received	4 000	2 100
Motor expenses	9 200	

Rent and rates	12 400	
Postage and telephone	3 100	
Wages and salaries	49 800	
Insurance	6 100	
Interest paid	2 000	
Advertising	4 200	
Bank/Cash	200	
	421 300	421 300

*Profit and loss expenses.

Notes at 29/2/19–5:

1 Stock at cost £31 000.
2 A provision for bad debts is to be created to equal 4 per cent of debtors.
3 Rent is prepaid (£850).
4 There is £140 still outstanding on interest payments.
5 Advertising paid in advance is £146.

REQUIRED:
a) Prepare the trading and profit and loss account for the year ended 28 February 19–5.
b) Prepare the balance sheet as at 28 February 19–5. (23.2–3)

(Institute of Commercial Management)

3 During the financial period ending 31 December, Charcoal Ltd wrote off bad debts totalled £6 420. The company rather surprisingly, also received £850 from a customer previously written off as a bad debt a few years ago.

On 31 December its debtors were 'aged' as follows:

No. of days outstanding	*Debtors* £	
Over 90 days	4 210	
90 days	7 560	
60 days	20 800	
30 days	56 400	89 010

The company had an opening provision for bad and doubtful debts of £6 400.

When the customers of over 90 days' debt were investigated, it was decided to write off £800 as bad.

The company's policy concerning the provision for bad debts is to use a percentage sliding scale off:

Over 90 days	75%
90 days	50%
60 days	10%
30 days	0%

REQUIRED:
On 31 December:
a) The bad debts account.
b) The provision for bad debts account. (Bad debts to be transferred to this account.)
c) The figure to be transferred to the profit and loss account and the debtors' presentation in the balance sheet.
d) Explain briefly the double-entry procedure when a bad debt is recovered. (23.3–4)

(Association of Accounting Technicians)

4 The following trial balance was extracted from the accounts of A Farney on 30 November 19–5:

	Dr £	*Cr* £
Bad debts written off in year	400	
Cash in hand	250	
Cash at Bank	6 250	
Purchases/sales	23 500	80 000
Motor vehicles	12 500	
Rent and rates	1 250	
Light and heat	600	
Carriage outwards*	350	
Opening stock	18 750	
Commissions received		1 350
Capital		75 740
Drawings	8 500	
Returns	1 650	2 000
Office salaries	25 000	
Debtors and creditors	23 600	5 650
Provisions for bad debts		1 860
Fixture and fittings	8 000	
Land and buildings	46 000	
Bank loan (repayable 1999)		10 000
	176 600	176 600

* Profit and Loss expense

Notes at 30 November 19–5:

1 Closing stock £19 500.
2 £800 owing on office salaries.
3 Rates had been paid £150 in advance.
4 £100 is owed for heating.
5 Provision for bad debts is to be increased to 10 per cent of the debtors.
6 Interest on loan of £1 000 is still outstanding.
7 It was decided to create a provision for discounts for customers at a rate of 1.25 per cent pa.

REQUIRED:

a) Prepare the trading and profit and loss account for the year ended 30 November 19–5.
b) Prepare the balance sheet as at 30 November 19–5. (23.3–5)

(Institute of Commercial Management)

5 Bradshaw Limited produced the following aged debtor analysis as at end of the financial year:

	Balance £	*Current* £	*One month* £	*Two months* £	*Three months and over* £
Debtors at 31/12/19–4	120 000	50 000	30 000	30 000	10 000
Debtors at 31/12/19–5	180 000	90 000	60 000	25 000	5 000

In both years the provision for bad debts account is made up by providing for bad debts at:

20% on debtors over 3 months
10% on debtors aged 2 months

2% on debtors aged 1 month
0.5% on current debtors

REQUIRED:

a) (i) Calculate the provision for bad debts as at 31/12/19–4.
   (ii) Calculate the provision for bad debts as at 31/12/19–5.
b) Prepare the provision for bad debts account over the two years; note provision as at 1/1/19–4 was £4 900 Cr).
c) Briefly state with reasons if you think Bradshaw's credit control has improved over the two years.
d) If a provision for discount allowed was created to equal 2 per cent of net debtors, show how the debtors would be shown in the balance sheet as on 31/12/19–5. (23.3–5)

(Institute of Commercial Management)

6 The trial balance as at 31 May 19–5 Tip Top Dealers Limited included the following:

	Dr £	*Cr* £
Purchases ledger control account	654.00	7 348.00
Sales ledger control account	12 360.00	716.00
Provision for doubtful debts		410.00
Bad debts recovered (received from K L Blaney)		970.00

Additional information:

1 K L Blaney's bad debts were written off in the accounts for the year ended 31 May 19–5.
2 It had now been decided to write off the following debts due to the company, as irrecoverable.
   L Pink £210.00
   G Slack £50.00
3 The provision for doubtful debts account is not used for actual bad debts written off or for bad debts recovered.
4 The company's continuing policy is to maintain a provision for doubtful debts at 2 per cent of outstanding debtors at each accounting year end.

REQUIRED:

a) Prepare the provision for doubtful debts account for the year ended 31 May 19–5 in the books of Tip Top Dealers Limited.
b) Prepare the entry for debtors and creditors which will be included in the balance sheet as at 31 May 19–5 of Tip Top Dealers Limited. (23.3–4)

(Association of Accounting Technicians)

24 Capital and revenue expenditure

Objectives

On completing this section you should:

- understand the difference between capital and revenue expenditure
- recognise the effect of capital and revenue expenditure in the profit and loss account and the balance sheet.

Context

Chapter 4 introduced the capital and revenue accounts in the context of the five groups of accounts.

24.1 Introduction

A business spends money on two types of expenditure: (1) when it purchases fixed assets such as premises, vehicles and equipment, and (2) when it spends money on running the business on expenses such as purchases of stock, wages and salaries, light and heat, stationery, etc.

24.2 Capital expenditure

Capital expenditure is money which is spent on improving and adding value to fixed assets.

For example, if a second-hand vehicle is purchased for £5000 and later, it required a brand new engine costing £1000 to replace it (improving on the original second-hand motor) then the value of the vehicle under fixed assets should be £6000. This is capital expenditure rather than revenue expenditure. If however, a second-hand engine was purchased as the replacement, this would not be seen as **improving** the value of the vehicle. It would not be classified as capital but as revenue expenditure.

24.3 Revenue expenditure

Revenue expenditure is expenditure required for the day-to-day running of the business.

As this definition suggests, all aspects of expenditure in running the vehicle for business purposes including petrol, repairs and maintenance, car tax and insurance, depreciation of the vehicle, replacement tyres, etc would all be treated as revenue expenditure, that is, it would be seen as part of the day-to-day expenses of running the business.

Capital expenditure on fixed assets must also include any costs which is involved in bringing their value to the business. For example, if premises were purchased, the value capitalised would include solicitor's and estate agent's fees, land registry fees and any other cost involved with the purchase. If new plant and machinery were to be installed in a factory, the capital cost would include the carriage of it to the premises and all costs in the installation. Even the cost of training staff to operate the new plant would be seen as capital expenditure. Once the plant was up and running, then the cost of running it would be revenue expenditure.

24.4 The distinction between capital and revenue expenditure

In the financial statements all capital expenditure is listed in the balance sheet under fixed assets, whereas all revenue expenditure appears as expenses in the trading and profit and loss account. It is extremely important, therefore, to make the distinction between these two expenditure types, otherwise serious errors will arise when the financial statements are prepared.

For example, if machinery was purchased for £5000 and it was wrongly treated as purchases under revenue expenditure, this would have the effect of understating the value of fixed assets and overstating the value of chargeable expenses. Result: profits are understated and fixed assets are understated. The Inland Revenue would also be displeased and would demand an adjustment to the accounts because it would reduce the tax payable on profits.

An article published in one of the major newspapers titled '*The roof falls in and upsets the taxman*' is a case in point. The problem concerned the repairing of a roof and whether or not it was an expense under repairs, or a capital item as an improvement to the roof, the subtle difference being that it can cost companies many more thousands of pounds in the payment of tax.

According to the Inland Revenue, repairs to fixed assets are allowable expenses against tax whereas improvements to fixed assets are not. A company called Cableduct fell foul of the Tax Office when they had part of their factory roof replaced. In this case, the old roof was made of asbestos and corrugated iron and its replacement was a profile metal sheeting. The Tax Office said that this was an improvement in roof covering because the roof had a different covering from that of the original. In other words, it should have been treated as a capital item, rather than a revenue item.

This would have been a big blow to Cableduct because the roof cost £55000. It was very old and although they had temporary repairs, the lot had to come down and be replaced. This was the problem, the Tax Office regarding something to be replaced in its entirety as improvement and therefore a capital cost.

At the time, the company was struggling hard to break-even and the Tax Office's decision was an additional burden it could have done without. The accountants of the company argued that a roof was only part of a building and that profile metal sheeting was not available when the original roof was built.

Fortunately for Cableduct, their accountants won the case, saving the company £13750 in tax. The company survived and continued trading.

The purchase of fixed assets is made on the assumption that it will benefit the business over a number of accounting periods, whereas when money is spent on day-to-day expenses their value is consumed within the accounting period. There are some exceptions to this such as painting or repairs and maintenance of buildings which could last far longer than the financial period. However, as a general rule, this is treated as revenue expenditure.

Check the following table to see how capital and revenue expenditure are treated:

	Transaction	*Revenue expenditure (P & L a/c)*	*Capital expenditure (balance sheet)*
		£	£
1	New computer £2500		2 500
2	Installation of computer £1000		1 000
3	Staff training on computer £500		500
4	Computer software £200		200
5	Stationery for computer £125	125	
6	Computer operators' wages £1300	1 300	
7	Gas and electricity £450	450	
8	Modernisation of premises £8000		8 000
9	Office buildings painted (every 5 years) £6 000	6 000	
10	Wages and salaries £17500	17 500	
11	New vehicle for manager £9500		9 500
12	Stock for resale £3200	3 200	
13	Motor expenses £800	800	
14	Modernisation of offices £20000	5 000	15 000
15	Upgrading the computer £800		800

In the last two transactions, the office modernisation could have had some element of repairs in the cost, say £5000 and therefore, this sum would have been apportioned to revenue expenditure rather than the whole amount capitalised. The upgrading of the computer with say greater memory and more functions would be seen as an improvement and therefore capital expenditure.

24.5 The distinction between capital and revenue income

When fixed assets are sold, the sale value of them is referred to as capital income. The profit or loss from the disposal of them will depend on how much they are sold for against their net book value. For example, if a motor van is sold for £2800 and has a net book value of £2400, then a 'profit' of £400 has been made in the books. This is discussed in further detail in the following chapter. The profit and loss account would record:

Other revenue:
Profit on sale of fixed asset £400 or, if it had sold for only £2200.

Expenses:
Loss on sale of fixed asset £200.

Revenue, however, refers to the normal trading activities of the business when it sells its goods or services and recorded under sales. Further income from rent, interest, commission received, etc. is recorded under 'other revenue'.

Summary

It is important to make the distinction between capital and revenue expenditure because the former affects the balance sheet and the latter the profit and loss account. If these expenditures are confused then distortions of profit and balance sheet items will occur and the accounts will not provide a 'true and fair' financial position.

Questions

1 An accounting clerk has produced two lists of expenditure which she has categorised into capital and revenue. Unfortunately, they are not all correct:

Group A	*Group B*
Revenue expenditure:	Capital expenditure:
Carriage inwards	Carriage outwards
Rent and rates	Equipment
Filing cabinet	New tools
Insurance	Unsold stock of goods
Pocket calculators	Advertising
Salaries and wages	Word processor
Postage and telegrams	New staples and gun
Purchases of goods	Painting of office building
Petty cash	Payment of dividends
Office desk and chair	Transfer to reserves
Packing materials	Second-hand motor van
Drawings	New light bulbs

REQUIRED:

a) List the errors you believe are listed in the wrong group or should not be in either group.

b) What effect would it have in the final accounts if these groups were not amended? (24.2–4)

2 R Smith bought a motor van for use in his business. Classify the following under either capital or revenue expenditure:

	£
Cost of vehicle	1 800
Additional fittings	450
Motor tax	100
Insurance premium	95
Petrol and oil	400
Service and maintenance	80
New car seats and covers	225
New front tyre	30
Exhaust replacement	100

Those items you have considered as capital expenditure, record them in the nominal ledger under 'Motor vehicle account'. Are there any items which could be recorded as either capital or revenue expenditure? Briefly comment. (24.2–4)

3 Why is it important to distinguish clearly between capital and revenue expenditure? Illustrate your answer by using examples and show their effect in the final accounts.

4 Classify the following items as to whether they are capital or revenue expenditure:

a) The purchase of a new IBM computer for the office. (24.2–4)

b) Cost of software for the use of the new computer.

c) Cost of computer paper.
d) A refit of the stockroom with new shelving.
e) The payment of gas and electricity bills.
f) The purchase of stock for resale.
g) Discounts allowed on the sale of stock.
h) The acquisition of a new motor vehicle for the supervisor's use.
i) The road tax and insurance of the vehicle.
j) The repairs and maintenance of the motor vehicle.
k) The cost of new floppy disks for the use of the computer.
l) The complete decoration of the offices to last a number of years. (24.4)

5 In the setting up of a new business for Jack Ramsgate, classify the following between capital and revenue expenditure:
a) The purchase price of premises.
b) The estate and solicitor's fees.
c) The cost of a computer system.
d) The cost of delivery charges and installation fees of the new computer.
e) The training of personnel costs on the computer system.
f) Running repairs to the computer.
g) Oil and petrol for the motor vehicle.
h) An extension is built on the premises.
i) The extension is painted on completion.
j) The extension is repainted six months later.
k) Improved roofing of the premises is installed two years later.
l) The cost of an advertising campaign which is expected to benefit a number of accounting periods. (24.4)

6 a) Why is it important to make the distinction between capital and revenue costs as those stated in the two previous questions?
b) If the cost of a computer, £2800, was recorded in the purchases account and the cost of the vehicle insurances £480 was recorded in the motor vehicles account, what effect, if any, would it have on the final accounts? (24.4)

25 The depreciation of fixed assets

Objectives

On completing this section you should:

- understand the meaning of depreciation and its effect on fixed assets
- recognise the various methods of depreciation
- prepare the ledger accounts for depreciation including any disposal of fixed assets
- understand the effect of depreciation in the final accounts
- recognise the guidance of SSAP 12
- recognise the use of fixed asset registers.

Context:

Chapter 22 introduced adjustments to final accounts such as depreciation.

25.1 Introduction

Fixed assets lose their value over time. The continuous use of them from one financial period to the next means that some of their value will be lost. For example, if a motor vehicle was purchased in January for £10000 would it be worth the same sum a year later? At the end of the year, it may only be worth £8000 and therefore its value would have diminished by £2000. This is the concept of depreciation. Fixed assets lose their value over periods of time and that loss is an expense charged to the business.

Depreciation is a measure of the declining value of an asset.

Two key points to note:

1 Depreciation is a measure of the wearing out of fixed assets through use, time or obsolescence as stated in SSAP 12 (see below)

2 Depreciation charges should be made as equitably as possible over the useful life of the asset.

There are various reasons why a fixed asset should lose its value. Fixtures, fittings, equipment and motor vehicles all wear out over periods of time due to the continuous use of them.

Equipment, particularly in computer technology, can soon become obsolete or out of date and need replacement. This is because competition in the market place often demands that the business with the most cost effective goods and services will win a larger share of the market. Therefore equipment needs to be replaced even though it could still be relatively new.

Other fixed assets deplete in value because their resources are used up. Quarries and mines become exhausted due to output of minerals etc. The extraction of the resource in effect becomes the charge for depreciation as we will demonstrate later on in the section.

Depreciation is therefore a charge against the purchase of fixed assets spread over their 'useful life'. It represents the annual revenue expenditure against the capital expenditure of the asset when it was purchased. The measurement of the actual charge each year is not an exact science because it is too subjective. To calculate how much is to be charged on an annual basis will depend upon:

1 The method chosen to depreciate.
2 The estimation of how long the fixed asset will last.
3 The estimation of how much the residual (or scrap) value of the fixed asset will be when it is eventually disposed of.

Nevertheless, fixed assets must be depreciated in each financial period and should be calculated on an equitable and consistent basis. In other words, as fairly as possible and once a method has been adopted, to consistently apply that same method each time the depreciation charge is made. Although there are a number of various ways to depreciate fixed assets there are two major methods:

1 The straight line (or fixed installment) method.
2 The reducing balance method.

25.2 The straight line (or fixed instalment) method

This method charges the same depreciation sum each year against profits. Many organisations use this type of depreciation on fixed assets such as furniture, fittings, plant, machinery and equipment. The cost of these assets is simply divided by the estimated time the assets are expected to last, less any residual value.

For example, the equipment of R Pearce (valued at £17 150) may be expected to last an estimated five years and have a scrap or residual value of say £500. How much should be charged against profits in the profit and loss account? The formula is as follows:

$$\frac{\text{Cost} - \text{Residual value}}{\text{Estimate life (years)}}$$

So

$$\frac{£17\ 150 - £500}{5 \text{ years}} = £3330 \text{ per year.}$$

The profit and loss account will be charged with £3330 depreciation each year for five years as an expense.

The balance sheet will show the cumulative sum of depreciation over the life of the asset, thereby reducing its value over the five years. In its fifth year, the book or net value of the asset should show it is only worth £500, its residual value.

Fixed assets	*Cost*	*Depreciation*	*Net value*
	£	£	£
Year 1 Equipment	17 150	3 330	13 820
Year 2 Equipment	17 150	6 660	10 490
Year 3 Equipment	17 150	9 990	7 160

Year 4 Equipment	17 150	13 320	3 830
Year 5 Equipment	17 150	16 650	500

25.2.1 Recording depreciation in the nominal ledger

The double entry for the recording of depreciation is:

Debit: the profit and loss account with the expense (£3330).
Credit: the provision for depreciation of fixed asset account (the cumulative depreciation).

The fixed asset account is recorded at its cost value and although the depreciation charge each year could be credited against its cost, a separate provision for depreciation is preferred to indicate the cumulative (or total) depreciation charged against the asset over its estimated life.

Nominal ledger

			Debit £	*Credit* £	*Balance* £
Equipment account					
Year 1	1/1	Bank	17 150		17 150 Dr
Provision for depreciation of equipment account					
Year 1	31/12	P&L account		3 330	3 330 Cr
Year 2	31/12	P&L account		3 330	6 660
Year 3	31/12	P&L account		3 330	9 990
Year 4	31/12	P&L account		3 330	13 320
Year 5	31/12	P&L account		3 330	16 650

Each year, using the fixed instalment method, £3330 would be charged as an expense in the profit and loss account. The balance sheet would indicate the *cumulative* depreciation each year and show the asset's book value at the time. For example, in year 5:

Balance sheet

	Cost £	*Depreciation* £	*Net value* £
FIXED ASSETS			
Equipment	17 150	16 650	500

After five years the asset's net value of £500 is in line with its estimated residual value.

25.3 The reducing balance method

An alternative method of depreciation of fixed assets is to ensure that the depreciation charge each year diminishes as the asset gets older and is of less value. The argument for using this method assumes that the newer the asset, the more should be charged against profits because presumably more value is lost in the earlier years rather than in the later.

Irrespective of the method of depreciation that is adopted, one of the major concepts in accounting is that of consistency and therefore once a certain method is used, it should be consistently applied throughout the expected life of the asset.

The reducing balance method may be applied by using a fixed percentage rate on the asset's net value each year, thereby effecting a lower depreciation charge each year. For example, using this method to depreciate equipment:

Cost:	£17 150
Fixed percentage rate:	50 per cent
Estimated life:	five years

Formula for rate percentage: n = number of years
r = rate % applied
rv = residual value
c = cost of fixed asset

$$r = 1 - \sqrt[n]{\frac{rv}{c}}$$

$$= 1 - \sqrt[5]{\frac{500}{17150}}$$

$$= 1 - \sqrt[5]{0.029} = 1 - 0.49 = 0.51$$

= approximately 50 per cent depreciation each year on the net value of the asset. The net book value is the cost less the total depreciation to date.

25.3.1 To check the percentage rate

Year	*Reduced balance*	*Profit and loss account Depreciation @ 50 per cent*	*Balance sheet Net book value (NBV)*
	£	£	£
1	17 150	8 575	8 575
2	8 575	4 288	4 287
3	4 287	2 143	2 144
4	2 144	1 072	1 072
5	1 072	536	536 (residual value)

Note that with the fixed instalment method, £3330 was charged each year as an expense in the profit and loss account (the same charge for each financial year). After two years, the charge would be £6660 using this method and £12 863 using the reduced balance. A large difference in the first two years. However, after five years, the total depreciation charge is virtually the same for either method, only a small variance in the residual value being the result.

25.4 Which method to depreciate?

The most equitable charge should be made. This would allocate the cost of depreciation in the fairest way over the useful life of the asset in relation to the benefits it brings. If the benefit is highest in the earlier years and less in the later years, then depreciation should be greater during those earlier periods. The reducing balance method would probably be the most appropriate.

On the other hand, if the asset brings benefit more or less equally throughout its useful life, then depreciation charges should reflect this and the straight line method adopted.

The cost of some fixed assets notably motor vehicles, plant, machinery and equipment, includes not only depreciation charges but also the cost of maintenance and repairs. As these fixed assets become older and more wear and tear occurs, it is argued that they will cost more to service and maintain. Reducing depreciation in the latter years will then allow for further costs on repairs, making the overall cost of operating the asset more evenly throughout its useful life.

Both methods of depreciation are used commonly in practice. A business could use the straight line method to depreciate its furniture, fixtures and fittings, while adopting the reducing balance method for its vehicles and equipment.

Other methods of depreciating certain types of fixed asset are discussed in a later section in this chapter.

25.5 The disposal of a fixed asset

When a fixed asset is finally disposed of, either sold or scrapped, it may be transferred to a disposal of asset account. Any provision for depreciation of the asset is also transferred to the disposal account thereby removing it from the accounts of the business.

If an asset is sold for more than its net book value, the gain may be transferred to the profit and loss account as 'other revenue'. If it is disposed of at less than its net value, the loss may be charged against profits as a further expense to the business.

If, for example, R Pearce decided to sell his equipment in year 4 for £3000 (see nominal ledger on p. 261), the accounts would show:

Nominal ledger

			Debit £	*Credit* £	*Balance* £
Equipment account					
Year 1	1/1	Bank	17 150		17 150 Dr
Year 4	31/12	Disposal account		17 150	—
Provision for depreciation of equipment account					
Year 4	31/12	Balance			13 320 Cr
		Disposal account	13 320		—
Disposal of fixed asset account					
Year 4	31/12	Equipment	17 150		17 150 Dr
		Provision for depreciation		13 320	3 830
		Bank		3 000	830
		P&L account		830	—

NOTE

The asset was sold for £3000 in year 4, having a net value of £3830 at the time. This would represent a loss on the book value of £830 which would be a charge against profits in the profit and loss account. If £4000 had been the selling price of the asset, a book profit of £170 would have been credited as a gain in the profit and loss account, as other revenue.

25.6 Accounting for depreciation: SSAP 12

Statements of standard accounting practice (SSAPs) represent the profession's accounting standards (these are discussed in Chapter 33). They are prepared for the purpose of standardising the preparation of business accounts. SSAP 12 is the accounting profession's guideline of how to deal with depreciation.

In this statement the SSAP states:

> 'Depreciation is defined as the loss in value of fixed assets over periods of time, that is, the measure of the wearing out, consumption or other reduction in the useful life of a fixed asset through use, time, obsolescence or market changes. Depreciation should be allocated so as to charge a fair proportion of the cost of the fixed asset to each accounting period expected to benefit from its use'.

The standard is to provide depreciation of all fixed assets having a finite life. However, there are some exceptions such as investments, goodwill and freehold land. Buildings should be depreciated even though their market value may have increased. It is still prudent to depreciate them because they do deteriorate with time and need repairs and maintenance.

The straight line method is seen as the most common depreciation type although it may not be the most appropriate for all types of assets. The standard indicates that a change of method (or base) is only acceptable if this is thought to give a better or fairer allocation of cost in the final accounts.

The standard recognises that goodwill (the value of a business in terms of its custom and reputation) should be written off as soon as is practicable, particularly if this is the cost arising from the purchase of a business.

The term '**amortisation**' means the same as depreciation in that something is written off over its useful life. This can apply to the leasing of fixed assets whereby a bank or a finance house provides finance under a lease contract which will enable a business to acquire the use of a fixed asset over a fixed contractual period of time, usually over the greater part of its useful life. The business can then treat this acquisition as a fixed asset and amortise the writing off of it in the profit and loss account and balance sheet as in the case of depreciation.

Some fixed assets, namely land and buildings, may well appreciate in value over periods of time. A business, however, may ignore the increased value because of the concept of prudence (a cautious approach to the valuation of assets) and merely retain the value of their premises at the cost of purchase.

Example
A business depreciates its equipment at the rate of 20 per cent per annum, based on the straight line method, applied on a month by month basis. The residual value is nil. Its financial period commences 1 January.

Note that when a question informs you of the date of purchase or sale of a fixed asset, it is usual to calculate the charge for depreciation on a monthly basis. If no dates have been given, it is assumed that a full year's depreciation charge will be made, unless otherwise stated. For example, 'a full year's depreciation is to be taken in the year of purchase but no charge to be made on the year of sale'. In this example, the depreciation charge is to be taken on a month by month calculation.

The following information relates to the purchase, depreciation and disposal of the equipment over a period of three years:

19–4	Purchased equipment code A300 costing £4800 on 1 January.
	Purchased equipment code A310 costing £3600 on 1 October.
19–5	Purchased equipment code A320 costing £2400 on 1 July.
19–7	On 1 October, traded in the equipment bought on 1 January, 19–4 for £1500 and purchased new equipment coded A330 for £8000 from Jackson & Turner Ltd on credit, on the same date.

It was decided that the remaining economic life of the equipment code A320 purchased in July 19–5 should be reduced and written off in total by 30 June 19–8.

REQUIRED:

a) Prepare the equipment account, provision for depreciation of equipment account and disposal of equipment account over the four years, ending 31 December 19–7.
b) Show the appropriate journal entries which are required for 19–7.
c) Prepare an extract of the profit and loss account for each of the four years for the period ending 31 December.
d) Prepare an extract of the balance sheets as at the end of each of the four years as on 31 December.

SOLUTION

Equipment account

		Debit	*Credit*	*Balance*
		£	£	£
19–4				
1/1	Bank A300	4 800		4 800 Dr
1/10	Bank A310	3 600		8 400
19–5				
1/7	Bank A320	2 400		10 800
19–7				
1/10	Disposal A300		4 800	6 000
1/10	Disposal A300	1 500		
	J & T Ltd A330	6 500		14 000

Provision for depreciation of equipment account

			Debit	*Credit*	*Balance*
			£	£	£
19–4					
31/12	Profit & Loss	A300		960	
		A310		180	1 140 Cr
19–5					
31/12	Profit & Loss	A300		960	
		A310		720	
		A320		240	3 060
19–6					
31/12	Profit & Loss	A300		960	
		A310		720	
		A320		480	5 220
19–7					
1/10	Disposal*	A300	3 600		1 620
31/12	Profit & Loss	A300		720	
		A310		720	
		#A320		1 120	
		A330		400	4 580

* Calculation: £960 pa × 3 = £2880
+ £960 × (3/4) = £720 £3600

\# Calculation: £1680 depreciation left for 1.5 years, therefore 1 year: 2/3 × £1680 = £1120

Disposal of fixed asset account

		Debit	*Credit*	*Balance*
		£	£	£
19–7				
1/10	Equipment A300	4 800		4 800 Dr
	Provision for Depreciation		3 600	1 200
	Trade-in J & T		1 500	300 Cr
31/12	Profit & Loss	300		0

25.7 Recording the purchase and disposal of fixed assets and depreciation: the journal

In this section the journal is used for:

a) The purchase or sale of fixed assests
b) The profit or loss on the disposal of fixed assets
c) The transfer of depreciation to the profit and loss account at the period end.

The journal is used as a book of original entry in the same way as other journals but is used to record transactions outside the scope of other prime records of entry. The journal is discussed in greater detail in Chapter 31. In this case it is used to record the disposal and purchase of a fixed asset and the depreciation figures for the year which fall out of the scope of the sales, purchases and returns journals or cash book. The debit and credit columns indicate which accounts will be debited and credited. By tradition the credit entry is slightly indented.

Journal

Date	*Details*	*Folio*	*Debit*	*Credit*
			£	£
19–7				
1/10	Equipment A330		8 000	
	Disposal A300			1 500
	J & T Ltd			6 500
	Being purchase of new equipment using A300 as part-exchange			
1/10	Disposal A300		4 800	
	Equipment A300			4 800
	Provision for Depreciation		3 600	
	Disposal			3 600
	Being disposal of old equipment, A300			
31/12	Disposal		300	
	Profit & Loss			300
	Being profit on disposal of A300			
31/12	Profit & Loss: depreciation of equipment		2 960	
	Provision for depreciation of equipment			2 960
	Being depreciation of equipment for the year.			

Extract of profit and loss account for years ended 31 December:

	Expenses:		
19–4	Depreciation of equipment	1 140	
19–5	Depreciation of equipment	1 920	
19–6	Depreciation of equipment	2 160	
19–7	Depreciation of equipment	2 960	
	Other revenue:		
19–7	Profit on disposal of fixed asset		300

Extract of balance sheet as at years ended 31 December:

Fixed assets		*Cost*	*Depreciation*	*NBV**
		£	£	£
19–4	Equipment	8 400	1 140	7 260
19–5	Equipment	10 800	3 060	7 740
19–6	Equipment	10 800	5 220	5 580
19–7	Equipment	14 000	4 580	9 420

*NBV net book value

25.8 The use of a fixed assets register

The purchase of capital transactions can cost a business large sums of money. It may have a fleet of motor vehicles or extensive factory equipment, plant and machinery, office equipment, etc. The journal, as we have already pointed out, can be used as a book of prime entry to record the buying of these fixed assets. Yet is this sufficient to record and control what happens to them? There could be a whole list of valuable fixed assets housed in various departments or factory floors and occasionally, some of these would be scrapped or sold off and replaced by new ones. What is required therefore, is a fixed asset register which lists all these assets of a business, together with other important facts about each of them, such as:

- the date of purchase
- description of the asset
- internal control number or other number for identification
- the location of the asset
- the cost of the asset
- the method of depreciation used
- the estimated scrap/sale value
- the estimated useful life of the asset
- its disposal date and authorisation of disposal
- the proceeds, if any, on disposal.

The fixed asset register is not part of the double entry system, it is simply used for the purpose of internal control. The register can be used to make physical checks for the location of fixed assets and which person, the supervisor or manager, is in charge of them. The register should also be reconciled with the fixed asset accounts in the nominal ledger to ensure that all aspects match. In other words, if an asset is sold off, this should be properly authorised, the asset released, the register completed and the necessary entries made in the journal and ledger accounts.

If any discrepancies do arise as a result of checks between the ledger accounts and the register, these must be investigated to find out why there are differences. It could be that there is a delay in sending the appropriate authorisation form when an asset has been disposed of. It could of course, be far more serious in that theft could have occurred. Whatever the cause of any discrepancy, a solution should be found and the appropriate action taken. It may also arise that some assets may require an adjustment in their expected life due to excessive wear and tear. Again, the proper authority to change any estimations to the life of an asset, must have the correct authorisation and the information communicated to the accounts department who will need to make the right adjustments in the journal and ledger.

The type of register for fixed assets will vary from one business to another. Some may have an individual page devoted for each type of fixed asset. Others may have columns across the page for various headings and list the assets in an organised way, for example, by department, or by the type of asset it is. Have a look at the following example:

Fixed assets register

Fixed asset register – equipment account no. N210
Jackson and Walker Co Ltd 31 December 19–7

Title of asset:	IBM Word Processor, 4432
Date of purchase:	12 June 19–3
Internal control no.	377342/95
Location:	Personnel office
Cost/Supplier	£2800 + Vat Computer Services Ltd
Nominal ledger account No.	N210
Method of depreciation:	20% per annum straight line
Estimated residual value:	£200.00
Estimated life:	5 years
Cumulative depreciation:	£560.00
Depreciation account:	N220
Proceeds from sale:	
Date of disposal:	
Disposal authorisation number:	
Comments:	

To be disposed of January 19–8 and replaced by updated IBM model to be decided

25.9 Alternative methods of depreciation

Apart from the main two methods already outlined, the **straight line** and the **reducing balance**, there are other ways in which to depreciate which may be more appropriate for certain types of fixed assets. These other methods are:

1 Revaluation
2 Machine hour rate
3 Depletion rate

25.9.1 Revaluation

This method could be suitable for fixed assets which may not have a high unit value. The hotel, catering and tourism industry could adopt this method against such items as crockery, cutlery, bedding, kitchen utensils etc, whereby an appraisal of their annual worth at the end of the financial period helps to calculate the depreciation charge for the year. For example:

Hotel Splendour

		£
1 January	Value of kitchen equipment	3 250
	+ Cost of new equipment during period	850
		4 100
31 December	Valuation of kitchen equipment	3 350
	– Depreciation charges for the year	750

25.9.2 Machine hour rate

Where plant and machinery is used, the number of operative or productive hours a machine can perform could be the basis of adopting this method. For example, if a machine costing £40 000, having a scrap value estimated at £5 000, had the capacity to operate for a total of 2500 hours and is expected to use 750 hours in its first year, the depreciation charge would be:

$$\frac{(\text{Cost of fixed asset} - \text{Scrap value}) \times \text{Number of period hours used}}{\text{Estimated total number of hours operated}}$$

$$= \frac{(£40\,000 - £5\,000) \times 750}{2500}$$

= £10 500 depreciation for the year.

The balance sheet would indicate:

Equipment £40 000 – Depreciation £10 500 NBV £29 500

How much would we depreciate in the second year if 500 hours were used? (Check £7 000)

This method is virtually identical to the unit rate which uses the number of units of output a machine could produce. Instead of the number of hours operated, substitute the number of units produced.

$$\text{Unit Rate} = \frac{(\text{Cost} - \text{scrap value}) \times \text{Number of period units}}{\text{Estimated total output (units)}}$$

For example, if a machine cost £30 000 with nil scrap value and was capable of producing a total of 150 000 units, if in year one it produced 40 000 units, what is the depreciation charge for the year? (Check £8 000)

25.9.3 Depletion rate

Again a similar method is used. For example, if a quarry was purchased on lease for £800 000 and it was estimated that a total of 10 000 tons of a resource could be extracted from it and 1 500 tons taken in the first year:

$$\frac{\text{Cost of fixed asset} \times \text{Tonnage taken in period}}{\text{Total tonnage expected}}$$

$$= \frac{£800\ 000 \times 1\ 500}{10\ 000}$$

= £120 000 depreciation charge for the year.

The balance sheet would indicate:
Quarry £800 000 – Depreciation £120 000 NBV £680 000.

If the quarry was to be used for a further five years with even extraction each year, how much would we depreciate per annum? (Check £13 600)

To recap the methods of depreciation which may be used. A business could use any of the methods discussed in this chapter. The key point is that the method should be the most equitable for a particular fixed asset, depreciation being in proportion to the benefit given by the asset over its useful life.

Summary

Depreciation refers to the loss in value of fixed assets due to reasons such as time, wear and tear etc. It is a chargeable expense in the profit and loss account and its cumulative total is deducted from the cost of fixed assets in the balance sheet. There are various methods by which assets can depreciate but the most equitable method should be adopted which provides the most appropriate benefit over the life of the asset.

Questions

1 The following is a trial balance of John Smith Sports Shop proprietor, as at year ended 31 December 19–6:

	Dr £	*Cr* £
Capital		170 350
Drawings	14 240	
Stock (1/1/)	12 890	
Purchases and sales	122 430	132 370
Returns	5 210	2 470
Premises	110 000	
Fixtures and fittings (at cost)	12 760	
Van (at cost)	7 200	
Trade debtors and creditors	23 270	33 690
Rent	7 850	
Wages and salaries	24 480	
Advertising	1 350	
Discount	450	1 260
Office expenses	1 160	
Cash	1 020	
Bank overdraft		4 170
	344 310	344 310

You are required to prepare a trading and profit and loss account for the year 31 December 19–6 and a balance sheet as at that date, taking the following items into consideration:

i) Stock at 31 December was valued at £15 477.
ii) Depreciation at 31 December: fixtures and fittings 25 per cent of cost; vans have a market value of £5750. (25.3)

(BTEC National)

2 The following figures have been extracted from the ledgers of Frances Mitchell:

Trial balance as at 30 June 19–7

	Dr £	*Cr* £
Sales		276 156
Purchases	164 700	
Carriage inwards	4 422	
Carriage outwards	5 866	
Drawings	15 600	
Rent and rates	9 933	
Insurance	3 311	
Postage and stationery	3 001	
Advertising	5 661	
Salaries and wages	52 840	
Bad debts	1 754	
Debtors	24 240	
Creditors		25 600
Returns outwards		131
Cash	354	
Bank	2 004	
Stock (1/7/19–6)	23 854	
Equipment (cost)	116 000	
Capital, F Mitchell		131 653
	433 540	433 540

The following additional information was available on 30 June 19–7:

a) Wages are accrued by £420.
b) Rates have been prepaid by £1400.
c) Stock of unused stationery valued £250.
d) A provision for bad debts is to be created to equal 5 per cent of debtors.
e) Unsold stock at the close of business valued at £27 304.
f) Depreciate equipment at 10 per cent of cost.

REQUIRED:

a) Prepare the trading and profit and loss account for the year ended 30 June 19–7 and a balance sheet as at that date.
b) Advise F Mitchell on the position of the working capital of the business. (25.3)

(Institute of Bankers)

3 The following trial balance has been extracted from the ledger of M Yousef, a sole trader:

Trial balance as at 31 May 19–6

	Dr	*Cr*
	£	£
Sales		138 078
Purchases	82 350	
Carriage	5 144	
Drawings	7 800	
Rent, rates and insurance	6 622	
Postage and stationery	3 001	
Advertising	1 330	
Salaries and wages	26 420	
Bad debts	877	
Provision for bad debts		130
Debtors	12 120	
Creditors		6 471
Cash on hand	177	
Cash at bank	1 002	
Stock (1/6/19–5)	11 927	
Equipment		
at cost	58 000	
accumulated depreciation		19 000
Capital (1/6/19–5)		53 091
	216 770	216 770

The following additional information as at 31 May 19–6 is available:

a) Rent is accrued by £210.
b) Rates have been prepaid by £880.
c) £2211 of carriage represents carriage inwards on purchases.
d) Equipment is to be depreciated at 15 per cent per annum using the straight line method.
e) The provision for bad debts to be increased by £40.
f) Stock at the close of business has been valued at £13 551.

REQUIRED:

Prepare the trading and profit and loss account for the year ended 31 May 19–6 and a balance sheet as at that date. (25.2)

(Association of Accounting Technicians)

4 The following information is taken from the accounts of Mary Walker, a businesswoman selling science equipment to colleges:

Trial balance of M Walker as at 30 June 19–7

	£	£
Stock (1/7/19–6)	6 855	
Motor vehicle (cost)	8 750	
Premises (cost)	36 900	

Accumulated depreciation of vehicle		1 750
Purchases	55 725	
Sales		120 344
Discounts	855	1 044
Returns	548	738
Salaries (assistants)	18 346	
Overheads	14 385	
Creditors		6 755
Debtors	7 400	
Bank		2 045
Cash	400	
Drawings	10 420	
Capital		?

On 30 June, the following additional information was also available:

a) Stock in hand valued at £7455.
b) The motor vehicle is depreciated on the straight line principle and is now three years old.
c) Of the overheads, £240 is prepaid and £600 is accrued.

REQUIRED:
Prepare M Walker's trading and profit and loss account for the year ended 30 June 19–7 and a balance sheet as on that date. (25.2)

5 Davy Jones owns a small business. At the close of trading on 31 May 19–6 the following balances were extracted from his books:

	£
Stock (1/6/19–5)	11 000
Purchases	52 000
Sales	84 000
Carriage inwards	150
Sales returns	650
Purchase returns	400
Insurance	250
Heating and lighting	2 500
Stationery	1 500
Rates	1 200
Motor expenses	1 600
Carriage outwards	100
Discounts allowed	140
Discounts received	110
Wages	4 200
Telephone	180

You are required to take the following into consideration on 31 May 19–6:

i) Stock in hand £12 000
ii) Insurance paid in advance £50
iii) Stock of stationery £100
iv) Heat and lighting accrued £150

v) Rates prepaid £300
vi) Depreciation – the motor vehicle valued at £4000 cost was depreciated by 20 per cent on reducing balance. It is now three years old.

and prepare a trading and profit and loss account for the year ended 31 May 19–6 showing clearly in your trading account the cost of sales. (25.3)

Note: a balance sheet is not required.

(Royal Society of Arts)

6 The following trial balance was extracted from the books of Gina Chappell a retailer, at 30 June 19–6. You work as her assistant and are to prepare the final accounts.

	£	£
Capital (1/7/19–5)		127 500
Drawings	25 000	
Fixtures and fittings (cost)	100 000	
Delivery van (cost)	25 000	
Sales		500 000
Purchases	400 000	
Discount received		2 500
Wages	25 000	
Rent and rates	12 000	
Carriage inwards	1 000	
Insurance	1 500	
Stock (1/7/19–5)	101 000	
Provision for depreciation: fixtures and fittings		25 000
Provision for depreciation: vehicles		5 000
Creditors		81 500
Debtors	34 000	
Balance at bank	15 000	
Cash in hand	2 500	
Provision for bad debts		500
	742 000	742 000

NOTES (30/6/19–6)
Stock £132 000
Wages owing £3000
Accrued rent £2000
Prepaid insurance £100
Depreciation is provided at 20 per cent per annum for the van and 25 per cent per annum for fixtures and fittings both on a straight line basis. The provision for bad debts is to be increased to £2500.

REQUIRED:
a) Prepare the trading and profit and loss account for the year ended 30 June 19–6.
b) Prepare the balance sheet as at 30 June 19–6 (25.2)

7 The following information relates to the fixed assets of Rockbourne Company Limited on 1 January 19–7:

	Cost	Depreciation to 31/12/19–6
	£	£
Premises	1 200 000	–
Plant and machinery	950 000	413 500
	2 150 000	413 500

The company depreciates plant and machinery at the rate of 10 per cent per annum on a straight line basis. A full year's depreciation being provided in the year of purchase, but none in the year of sale.

During the year ending 31 December 19–7 the following took place:
i) The directors decided to revalue the premises to £1 500 000.
ii) Plant and machinery purchased in 19–3 for £200 000 was sold in October 19–7 for £130 000. Depreciation to date was £80 000.
iii) New plant was purchased in July 19–7 for £150 000.

REQUIRED:
a) Provide relevant ledger accounts including an asset disposal account as they would appear on 31 December 19–7.
b) Prepare a schedule of fixed assets for inclusion in the accounts to be published for the year ended 31 December 19–7.
c) Provide any details you think are relevant to accompany the accounts to be published for the year ended 31 December 19–7.

(Please note that zero scrap value is assumed for plant.) (25.7)

(Institute of Bankers)

8 A company depreciates its plant at the rate of 20 per cent per annum on the straight line method for each month of ownership. The following details relate to the purchase and sale of plant for the years 19–4, 19–5, 19–6 and 19–7 – the company draws up its final accounts on 31 December of each year.

19–4 Bought plant costing £1000 on 1 January
Bought plant costing £500 on 1 July
19–6 Bought plant costing £4000 on 1 October
19–7 Sold plant which had been bought on 1 January 19–4 for the sum of £300 on 1 January 19–7.

REQUIRED:
a) Draw up the plant account for the above transactions.
b) Draw up the plant depreciation account for the above transactions.
c) Draw up a plant disposal account.
d) Show the extract from the balance sheet as at 31 December 19–7.
e) State two *other* methods of depreciation. (25.2–7)

The following are advanced questions:

9 Three of the accounts in the ledger of B Clough have the following balances at 31 December 19–6: stationery debit £110; rent credit £96 and provision for bad debts credit £249.

During 19–7 Clough paid for stationery £406 and rent £768 by cheque (rent is payable at £48 per month). At 31 December 19–7 there was a stock of stationery valued at £125. On the same day debtors amounted to £4000 and the provision was adjusted to 5 per cent of that figure.

REQUIRED:
a) Preparation of the stationery, rent and provision for bad debts accounts for the year ended 31 December 19–7 showing year-end transfers.

b) Preparation of a profit and loss account extract showing clearly the amounts transferred from each of the above accounts for the year ended 31 December 19–7.

   An explanation of the effect (if any) on the calculation of the net profit of each of the year-end transfers.

c) An explanation of the effect on, and significance to, final accounts of accounting for accruals and prepayments at year-end.

(Associated Examining Board)

10 a) Identify the factors which can cause fixed assets to depreciate. Using these factors which depreciate fixed assets, which of them do you consider significant in the following:
   - a new high-tech machine capable of increased productivity;
   - the purchase of a motor vehicle;
   - the mining of minerals;
   - the purchase of land;
   - a new long-term lease of a fleet of vehicles.

b) What do you think are two important points which can be taken from SSAP 12 as regards the application of depreciation to various fixed assets.

c) Outline the need for a business to maintain a fixed asset register.

d) What purpose does the use of the journal serve as regards capital transactions?

11 Jim Barlow is the owner of a taxi business and his financial year runs from 1 July to 30 June. On 1 July 19–7 he had two vehicles, one a Ford purchased on 10 January 19–5 for £10 000 and the other, a Toyota, purchased on 12 August 19–5 for £8 000. During November 19–7, Jim Barlow decided to replace the Ford and trade it in for a new Mercedes costing £15 500. Jim took delivery of the new car on 5 November 19–7. The garage accepted the Ford together with a cheque for £9 500 in payment.

Vehicles are depreciated at 10 percent per annum on the reducing balance method (alternatively known as diminishing balance), with a full year's depreciation charged in the year of purchase and no depreciation charged in the year a vehicle is disposed of.

REQUIRED:

a) Calculate the value of the Ford and Toyota vehicles as on 1 July 19–7.

b) Write up the journal entries and draw up the appropriate ledger accounts for motor vehicles, provision for the depreciation of motor vehicles and the disposal of motor vehicles accounts for the year ended 30 June 19–8. Show clearly any transfers to the profit and loss account and the balance sheet.

c) If depreciation was applied on a month by month basis (in the final year only), how would it affect the ledger accounts on the trade-in and purchase of the new Mercedes in November 19–7? How would the final accounts be affected?

d) When a fixed asset is purchased, a business will use depreciation as a means to set aside cash each year so that it eventually has the funds to purchase a replacement when it becomes necessary. Comment briefly on this statement.

(Association of Accounting Technicians)

12 a) Prepare a report to a departmental manager, explaining the reasons for providing depreciation, with special reference to the measurement of income, capital maintenance, and the effect of changing price levels.

b) ABC Limited had the following balances on its motor vehicles accounts at 30 September 19–7:

	£
Motor vehicles at cost	10 000
Provision for depreciation of motor vehicles	4 000

During the year to 30 September 19–8, the following transactions occurred:

31 January 19–8	Bought a motor van (plant number MV11) costing £9 000.
24 April 19–8	Sold a motor van (plant number MV05) for £500 which had originally cost £4 000 in January 19–5.

During the year to 30 September 19–9, the following transactions occurred:

20 February 19–9	Bought a motor van (plant number MV12) costing £12 000.
31 August 19–9	Traded-in van bought on 31 January 19–8 (plant number MV11) for a new van (plant number MV13) costing £14 000. The trade-in allowance was £7 400.

ABC Limited provides for depreciation on its motor vehicles at a rate of 25 per cent per annum using the reducing balance method. It is company policy to make a full year's charge against all assets held at the end of its financial year (30 September).

REQUIRED:

Show the ledger accounts necessary to record the above transactions. The form of presentation should clearly show the values which will be transferred to the company's profit and loss account and balance sheet at the end of **each** of the financial years to 30 September 19–8 and 19–9.

(Chartered Institute of Management Accountants)

26 Accounting for partnerships

Objectives

On completing this section you should:

- understand the terms of a partnership agreement
- be able to prepare a partnership appropriation account and partners' current accounts
- understand how goodwill affects the partners' capital accounts and share of profits.

Context

Chapter 2 introduced the basic principle of a partnership in the context of other forms of ownership.

26.1 Introduction

A partnership may be described as a business having at least two owners, with a view to making a profit. The maximum number allowed in this type of organisation is normally 20 partners, although in professional partnerships, such as solicitors, accountants, estate agents and members of the Stock Exchange, this number may be exceeded on request to the Registrar of Companies.

Although many partnerships convert their businesses to limited companies, in the case of professional partnerships this is against their standard practice and therefore it is exceedingly unlikely to find a group of solicitors bearing the word 'limited' after the title of their business.

As far as legal requirements are concerned, there is little constraint in setting up a partnership and there is no need for complicated documentation. For partnerships, the 1890 and 1907 Partnership Acts apply, the first to all partners and the second to limited partners. A limited partner is one who has relinquished any ideas concerning control or decision making in the business. Only the general partners have the right to control. Limited partners may have once been general partners who have retired from the business, but may still wish to be associated with it by virtue of leaving their capital in the enterprise. However, by applying to the Registrar for limited status, they then become protected against unlimited liability and are only liable to the amount of capital they have in the business. General partners are all unlimited and therefore liable to the debts of the business, even to the extent of their personal wealth.

It is advised that all partners have some form of written agreement between them – a contract which binds them together in law. In the event of any disagreements, the contract can be referred to and upheld in a court of law. A Deeds of Partnership is such an agreement, where the partners draw up a contract which outlines the conditions they have consented to. Agreements usually include items such as:

a) The venue of the business premises and the name of the accountant, solicitors and bank, acting on behalf of the business.
b) How the profits and losses of the business are to be shared by the partners.
c) How salaries or drawings are to be arranged.
d) Whether interest is to be paid on capital accounts.
e) Whether interest is to be charged on any drawings.

f) The rate of interest to be paid on any loans provided by partners.
g) Any aspects concerning control and responsibilities by partners.
h) The procedure in the event of admittance of a new partner or the departure of an existing partner.
i) The procedure in the event of *dissolution* (the partnership being wound up).

In the event of disagreement between partners and where a Deeds of Partnership does not exist, the 1890 Partnership Act applies. In particular, Section 24 of the Act states:

a) Any profit or loss is to be borne *equally* between partners.
b) No interest is to be paid on partners' capital accounts.
c) No interest is to be charged on drawings by partners.
d) No partnership salaries are to be paid from profits.
e) Loans by partners will be entitled to interest at 5 per cent per annum.

26.2 Dissolution of a partnership

The decision concerning how the partnership may be dissolved (terminated) may be laid down in the Deeds of Partnership. However, many partnerships may be dissolved in a number of different ways:
a) It may be for a fixed length of time and therefore by the expiration of that time.
b) If the partnership is for an unspecified term, *any of the partners* can give notice to terminate their agreement and therefore dissolve the partnership. A new partnership can be reformed by the existing partners.
c) By the death or bankruptcy of any partner.
d) By an unlawful act which forces the partnership to dissolve.
e) At the conclusion of a venture if the partnership was formed for such a venture.

Once the partnership is dissolved, partners must ensure that all unfinished transactions are wound up and the payments for all outstanding debts are made. Any surplus assets will be due to the partners in proportion to their share of capital and current accounts.

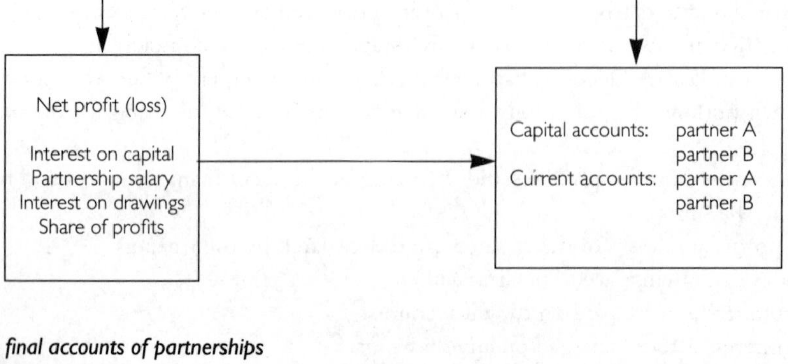

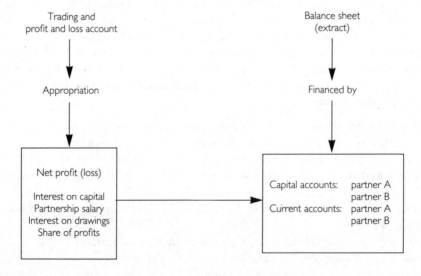

Fig. 26.1 The final accounts of partnerships

26.3 Partners' current accounts

A current account is a record of a partner's personal finances in the partnership. Items recorded in this account will include profit share, interest paid on capital or loans, salary awarded from profits, interest charged on drawings and the total drawings for the period, either in cash, stock or any other items.

The partners' appropriation account which shows how profits (or losses) are to be divided, acts as the double entry between each partner's current account and the appropriation account.

A partner who has a debit balance in his current account has 'overdrawn' on the account, that is, his drawings are more than his earnings. The current account must not be mistaken for the bank current account which is altogether different. A partner's current account is the business's record of the personal finances of the partner. If a partner has a credit balance, this is in his favour, meaning that he could make further drawings.

Some partnership agreements have insisted that any partner being in debit on his current account at the end of the financial period, must make it 'good' by depositing a sum in the business finances which clears the debit. For example:

Harry's current account

		Debit	*Credit*	*Balance*
		£	£	£
31/12	Balance			420 Dr
31/12	Bank		420	0

Harry was overdrawn on his current account on 31 December and had to deposit £420 to clear the debit balance at the year end.

The partners' current account balances at the financial year end are listed in the balance sheet under the 'financed by' section, along with their capital accounts:

Harry and Sally –
Balance sheet extract as at 31 December

	£	£
Capital accounts		
Harry	15 000	
Sally	20 000	35 000
Current accounts		
Harry	(500)	
Sally	1 500	1 000
		36 000

Note that Harry's balance is in debit by £500 and their combined current accounts are £1 000. The partners' net assets must also equal £36 000.

It is normal practice to keep the partners' current accounts separate from their capital accounts, their capital accounts are then not subject to fluctuations in value. With separate currrent accounts, it is easier to see each partner's balance and therefore to monitor those who become in debit.

26.3.1 Interest charges on drawings

Drawings are the cash, stock and other benefits taken by the partners. Most drawings of course would be in cash because these are in effect, the wages of the partners. The amount of drawings will be decided by the mutual agreement between partners and can be adjusted at partnership meetings according to circumstances.

Interest charges on drawings is basically a penalty for drawing resources out of the business. The partner drawing the most could then be expected to pay the most interest. It is better for the business to keep drawings to a minimum and keep the resources within the firm. The partnership agreement could indicate a certain percentage to be charged. This could be made on a monthly, quarterly, half yearly or even on the total balance at the year end. It is up to the partners to agree. The interest charged has the effect of increasing the profit share between the partners and the sum debited to their current account, as you will gather from the example which follows.

26.3.2 Interest on capital

Interest on capital accounts may be agreed by the partners at a certain annual percentage rate for example, 5 per cent. Where capital contributions are not the same, this has the effect or rewarding those partners who may have contributed more capital than others. The amount of interest is deducted from the net profit before the profit-sharing ratio.

26.3.3 Partners' salaries

Partners may in their terms of agreement, decide to award themselves salaries from profits at the year end. These could be for partners working longer hours or for taking on greater responsibilities. Salaries would be deducted from profit before the agreed profit-sharing ratio and rewards partners without having to 'rejig' the profit ratio. The salaries are then credited to the partners' current accounts. Note that salaries awarded are not cheques or sums of cash but salaries credited to their current accounts to offset their drawings in the financial period.

26.3.4 The partners' appropriation account

This is the account which immediately follows the net profit (or loss) and shows how the profits are to be divided between the partners. The appropriation could be quite straightforward and simply be a division of profit equally or in proportion to capital, or some other fraction decided upon by the partners. Often for exam purposes, the appropriation account will include a number of items including salaries, interest on capital and interest on drawings. Note that a double entry occurs between the appropriation account and the partners' current accounts. For example, if a salary is awarded, net profit is deducted with the sum (a debit) while the partner's current account is credited. For example:

Debit:	appropriation account	£8 000
Credit:	current account (salary)	£8 000

26.3.5 Partners' loans

Any partner may make a loan to the business at an agreed interest rate per cent. The loan is recorded under long-term liabilities and the interest paid will be credited to the partner's current account and debited as an expense in the profit and loss account.

An example of partnership accounts

The preparation of the final accounts of a partnership are almost identical to those of other business organisations. Partnerships do have, however, the appropriation account to show the division of profits or losses between partners.

In the 'financed by' section of the balance sheet, each of the partner's capital accounts will be listed as well as each of their current accounts. The total sum of the partners' capital and current accounts will equal the partners' net worth in the business (that is, the same as the net assets).

The following information relates to the partnership between Graham and Rod who, in their Deeds of Partnership, have stated that profits or losses are to be borne equally. Figures related to 31 May 19–6:

	Graham	*Rod*
	£	£
Capital accounts	10 000	12 000
Current accounts	800 Cr	400 Dr
Drawings for the year	14 500	13 500
Salaries to be credited	8 000	6 000
Rod's loan account (10% p.a.)		3 000
Interest charged on drawings	350	250

Interest is to be paid on capital accounts at 8 per cent per annum. The net profit for the period ended 31 May was £28 500 before interest was charged on Rod's loan account.

REQUIRED:

a) Prepare the partnership appropriation account for the year ended 31 May 19–6.
b) Prepare each of the partner's current accounts for the same period.
c) Prepare a balance sheet extract which will indicate the partner's 'financed by' section.

Profit and loss appropriation account
Graham and Rod, year ended 31 May 19–6

	£	£	£
Net profit (before loan interest)			28 500
Interest on loan: Rod		300	28 200
Deduct:			
Salaries: Graham	8 000		
Rod	6 000	14 000	
Interest on capital: Graham	800		
Rod	960	1760	15 760
			12 440

(continued)

(continued)

Add:			
Interest on drawings: Graham	350		
Rod	250	600	
			13 040
Share of profit:			
(Residue) Graham	6 520		
Rod	6 520		13 040

NOTE
The residue of profit (£13 040) is the sum *after* items such as partners' salaries, interest on capital, and interest on drawings have been taken into consideration. The residue is then divided as per the partnership agreement. In this case, equally.

Partners' current accounts

These are the personal finances of the partners and recorded in the nominal ledger.

Nominal ledger

Current accounts		*Debit* £	*Credit* £	*Balance* £
Graham's account				
31/12	Balance			800 Cr
	Salary		8 000	8 800
	Interest on capital		800	9 600
	Interest charged	350		9 250
	Profit share		6 520	15 770
	Drawings	14 500		1 270
Rod's account				
31/12	Balance			400 Dr
	Salary		6 000	5 600 Cr
	Interest on capital		960	6 560
	Interest charged	250		6 310
	Profit share		6 520	12 830
	Interest, loan		300	13 130
	Drawings	13 500		370 Dr

NOTE
A debit balance in the partner's current account indicates that the partner has overdrawn on his account.

Balance sheet extract

In the 'financed by' section, the partners' capital and current accounts are both recorded to represent the partners' net worth in the business:

	£	£	£
FINANCED BY			
Capital accounts:			
Graham	10 000		
Rod	12 000	22 000	
Current accounts:			
Graham	1 270		
Rod (Dr)	(370)	900	22 900

Although Rod's loan to the business could be entered in this section of the accounts, it is a long-term liability and should be listed after net current assets, *before* the 'financed by' section.

26.4 Goodwill

The term *goodwill* may arise in a business for several reasons. Its meaning is concerned with the good name or reputation of an enterprise, built up over a certain period of time. Its assessment and calculation may be based on a proportion or percentage of average sales or profits over a number of years. For example, if the average sales over five years is £70 000, the figure for goodwill may be arrived at say 15 or 20 per cent of this sum.

When a partner leaves the business, or a new partner is admitted, an assessment of goodwill may become necessary. In the former case, a partner retiring from the business will want his proper share of the business's value. In the latter case, a new partner may be expected to pay some portion or premium to come into an already established business.

When a business is sold or taken over, or two businesses amalgamate, the value of goodwill often needs to be assessed. A business may not simply be worth its net asset value alone, some consideration needs to be given to its *reputation* in terms of its customers and turnover, and its potential profits. It is finally up to the buyer and seller to come to some agreement about the value of goodwill.

If a new partner is admitted to an existing business, he is likely to contribute his share of capital and to pay an agreed sum for goodwill. If the goodwill is assessed to be valued at £4000 and the new partner is able to pay in cash, the double entry is:

Debit:	Bank account £4000
Credit:	Existing partners' capital accounts, £4000 (shared as per the *profit sharing ratio*).

Alternatively, if the new partner has insufficient resources to pay goodwill in cash or other assets, a goodwill account is debited:

Debit:	Goodwill account £4000
Credit:	Existing partners' capital accounts, £4000.

It is usually prudent of the partners to write off the amount of goodwill as soon as is practicable because it is only an intangible asset (not a physical thing) and its value is only realistic in terms of changes in the business's circumstances, such as admitting a new partner or the selling of the business. Writing off goodwill is usually based on the partner's profit sharing ratios.

Accounting for goodwill has always been rather a contentious aspect, the main problem being that it is an intangible asset and incapable of being separated from the business as a whole. The basis for its calculation is also very subjective and is likely to change over financial periods.

Example

Diane and Bert are in partnership and have agreed to share profits and losses on the basis of their capital input. At the financial year end 30 June 19–6, the following information relating to their accounts revealed:

			Debit £	*Credit* £
Capital accounts:	Diane			10 000
	Bert			20 000
Current accounts:	Diane		500	
	Bert		350	
Drawings for the year:		Diane	7 500	
		Bert	12 750	
Fixed assets (net)			48 000	
Stock			3 000	
Debtors			5 500	
Creditors				6 000
Bank overdraft				2 600
Bank loan (five years)				15 000
Net profit for year:				24 000
			77 600	77 600

Jane is to join the partnership at the start of the new financial period, 1 July 19–6. She will bring £7000 in cash as her contribution to capital.

Goodwill is considered at a value of 50 per cent of the net profit for the year ended 31 May 19–6 and a goodwill account is to be opened. Profits and losses are to be shared in proportion to the members' capital in the new partnership agreement.

Other information is as follows:

a) Interest charged on drawings is at 10 per cent per annum based on the average drawings for the year:
   Diane £5000
   Bert £6400
b) Interest is to be paid on capital at 6 per cent per annum.
c) No partners' salaries are awarded.

REQUIRED:

a) Prepare the partnership profit and loss appropriation account for the year ended 30 June 19–6.
b) The partners' current accounts for the period to 30 June 19–6.
c) The partnership balance sheet as at 30 June 19–6.
d) The balance sheet of the new partnership as it would appear in the new financial period, 1 July 19–6.

Profit and loss appropriation account for Diane and Bert, year ended 30 June 19–6

	£	£	£
Net profit b/f			24 000
Deduct:			
Interest on capital (6%):			
Diane	600		
Bert	1 200		1 800
			22 200
Add:			
Interest on drawings (10%):			
Diane	500		
Bert	640		1 140
			23 340
Share of profit (1 : 2):			
Diane	7 780		
Bert	15 560		
			23 340

Current accounts of Diane and Bert – Nominal ledger

Current accounts		*Debit* £	*Credit* £	*Balance* £
Diane's account				
30/6	Balance			500 Dr
	Interest on capital		600	100 Cr
	Interest charged	500		400 Dr
	Profit share		7 780	7 380 Cr
	Drawings	7 500		120 Dr
Bert's account				
30/6	Balance			350 Dr
	Interest on capital		1 200	850 Cr
	Interest charged	640		210
	Profit share		15 560	15 770
	Drawings	12 750		3 020

Balance sheet of Diane and Bert as on 30 June 19–6

		£	£	£
FIXED ASSETS (net)				48 000
CURRENT ASSETS				
Stock		3 000		
Debtors		5 500		
Bank/cash		—	8 500	
CURRENT LIABILITIES				
Creditors		6 000		
Bank overdraft		2 600	8 600	
Net current liabilities:				(100)
Capital employed:				47 900
LONG-TERM LIABILITIES				
Bank loan				15 000
				32 900
FINANCED BY:				
Capital accounts:	Diane	10 000		
	Bert	20 000	30 000	
Current accounts:	Diane	(120)		
	Bert	3 020	2 900	
				32 900

The calculation of goodwill:

This is agreed by the partners to be 50 per cent of net profit:

Net profit $\frac{£24\,000}{2} = £12\,000$

Shared as per profit ratio:

Diane 1
Bert 2 $\frac{£12\,000}{3} = £4\,000$

= Diane £4000, Bert £8000

Double entry: Debit – goodwill account £12 000
Credit – capital accounts £4000 (Diane)
£8000 (Bert)

Balance sheet of Diane, Bert and Jane as on 1 July 19–6

	£	£	£
FIXED ASSETS (net)			48 000
Intangibles			
Goodwill			12 000
			60 000
CURRENT ASSETS			
Stock	3 000		
Debtors	5 500		
Bank (+ £7000)	4 400	12 900	
CURRENT LIABILITIES			
Creditors		6 000	
Net current assets:			6 900
Capital employed:			66 900
LONG-TERM LIABILITIES			
Bank loan			15 000
			51 900
FINANCED BY:			
Capital accounts:			
Diane	14 000		
Bert	28 000		
Jane	7 000	49 000	
Current accounts:			
Diane	(120)		
Bert	3 020		
Jane	–	2 900	
			51 900

26.4.1 The writing off of goodwill

It has been standard practice to write off the value of goodwill arising from the purchase or the commencement of a new business partnership. SSAP 22 (Statements of Standard Accounting Practice), recognises that it is difficult to separate goodwill from the business as a whole and is largely a subjective valuation agreed by the partners. It has not been the practice to recognise goodwill in published accounts, therefore, if a value has been placed on a business, or partners come together with previous experience/clientel etc. which is given an agreed sum for goodwill, it ought to be written off as soon as practicable on the basis of the agreed partnership profit-sharing ratio. If this is not stated, it will be assumed that it is written off equally. Accounting standards are discussed in Chapter 33.

If goodwill is to be written off either immediately or over a period of time, the partners' capital accounts will be debited and the goodwill account credited in relation to their **new** profit-sharing ratio.

Example

Tom, Dick and Harry were separate traders for a number of years and now have decided to form a partnership bringing their assets and liabilities into the new business. Their capital accounts at the time, 1 January, were:

Capital:	£	£
Tom	18 000	
Dick	12 000	
Harry	6 000	36 000

It has been recognised by Tom, Dick and Harry, that a sum for goodwill should be included in the accounts, valued at £24 000. The share of this was:

Goodwill:	£	£
Tom	6 000	
Dick	8 000	
Harry	10 000	24 000

If the goodwill was to remain in the current year's accounts, then the partners would have these sums credited to their capital accounts and the goodwill account would be debited with the total, that is, £24 000, as an intangible fixed asset.

However, if the partners wanted to write off the goodwill immediately, then it would be written off in relation to their agreed profit-sharing ratio at the time the goodwill was introduced. If the partners, Tom, Dick and Harry, had agreed to share profit and losses in the ratio of 3: 2: 1 respectively:

	Capital introduced	*Goodwill introduced*	*Goodwill written off*	*New balances*
	£	£	£	£
Tom	18 000	6 000	(12 000)	12 000
Dick	12 000	8 000	(8 000)	12 000
Harry	6 000	10 000	(4 000)	12 000
	36 000	24 000	(24 000)	36 000

Goodwill is credited to the partners' capital accounts at the time it was introduced. When it is written off, the goodwill is debited against the partners' capital accounts in relation to the partners' profit-sharing ratio at the time it is written off.

What has occurred here is that Harry has benefitted the most by introducing a greater value of goodwill (he may have brought in more trading customers) and because of the profit-sharing ratio, only loses 1/6 of total goodwill to be written off (24 000/6). On the other hand, Tom has most capital to lose because he takes half the profit share and therefore must apportion half the value of goodwill against his capital account. By coincidence, their capital accounts are now equal!

26.5 Revaluation of assets

When anything affects the constitution of the partnership such as a new partner being admitted or an old partner retiring or the partners decide to change their profit-sharing ratio, it may become necessary to make a revaluation of the business assets. For example, if a partner retires, the partnership must be re-constituted and new profit-sharing ratios established. The retiring partner would want to take what was rightly due to him. He may have been in the partnership for a considerable period of time and helped to build up the business. He would want his fair share of the business to take with him.

Example

Jack, Tom and Jill have been in partnership for a number of years and Tom now wishes to retire from the practice. The profits are shared in the ratio of 2: 2: 1. The balance sheet at the time Tom was to retire was:

Jack, Tom and Jill –
Balance sheet as at 31 December

	£	£	£
FIXED ASSETS (NBV)			
Premises	25 000		
Equipment	5 000		
Motor vehicles	8 000		38 000
CURRENT ASSETS			
Stock	5 600		
Debtors	1 400		
Bank	6 500	13 500	
CURRENT LIABILITIES			
Creditors		9 500	
WORKING CAPITAL			4 000
			42 000
FINANCED BY			
Capital accounts:			
Jack	18 000		
Tom	12 000		
Jill	8 000	38 000	
Current accounts:			
Jack	2 500		
Tom	2 000		
Jill	(500)	4 000	42 000

On Tom's retirement, it was agreed that the value of goodwill was to be £15 500, based on an average figure of profits over the last three years. At the same time, the premises were to be revalued to £50 000 in line with the current market valuation and the stock was to be reduced to £5 100.

Tom was to take £2 500 in cash and his vehicle in the business, also at a net book value of £2 500. The balance due to him was to be retained in the business as a loan to the partnership at an agreed 8 per cent interest per annum.

Prepare the new partnership balance sheet immediately after Tom's retirement, as on 1 January. Jack and Jill want to eliminate the goodwill from the books. Their new profit sharing ratio has been agreed at 3:2 in favour of Jack.

SOLUTION

a) The effect of goodwill and revaluation:

	£	£
Goodwill	15 500	
Increase in value:		
premises	25 000	
Decrease in value:		
stock	(500)	40 000

The division of this is in relation to the old profit sharing rate of 2:2:1 which is then credited to their capital accounts:

Jack $\frac{£40\ 000 \times 2}{5} = £16\ 000$

Tom $\frac{£40\ 000 \times 2}{5} = £16\ 000$

Jill $\frac{£40\ 000 \times 1}{5} = £8\ 000$

b) Tom, on his retirement, is then entitled to:

Capital (12 000 + 16 000)	£28 000	
Current account	£2 000	£30 000

He takes with him:

Cash	£2 500	
Motor vehicle	£2 500	
Loan to partnership	£25 000	£30 000

c) The goodwill is written off between the existing partners in the new profit sharing ratio of 3:2. 3/5 of £15 500 Jack and 2/5 of £15 500 Jill.

Jack and Jill's capital accounts:

	Jack	*Jill*
	£	£
Balances	18 000	8 000
+ Goodwill and revaluation	16 000	8 000
– Goodwill written off	(9 300)	(6 200)
	24 700	9 800

d) The new partnership balance sheet would appear as:

Jack and Jill –
Balance sheet as at 1 January

	£	£	£
FIXED ASSETS (NBV)			
Premises	50 000		
Equipment	5 000		
Motor vehicles	5 500		60 500
CURRENT ASSETS			
Stock	5 100		
Debtors	1 400		
Bank	4 000	10 500	
CURRENT LIABILITIES			
Creditors		9 500	
WORKING CAPITAL			1 000
			61 500
Long-term liabilities			
Partner's loan 8%			25 000
			36 500
FINANCED BY			
Capital accounts:			
Jack	24 700		
Jill	9 800	34 500	
Current accounts:			
Jack	2 500		
Jill	(500)	2 000	36 500

26.5.1 Profit calculation

When Tom has retired, he would also be entitled to a share of the profits for the period. If he had retired half-way through the year, he would be entitled to receive his share based on half the year's profits which would then be added to his current account. If a loss was made in the period, then his current account would be reduced by the loss.

Therefore, if a change in the constitution of the partnership occurs in say, the middle of the accounting period, the profit and loss appropriation needs to be divided into two distinct parts:

a) profits earned up to the change in terms of the old partnership agreement;
b) profits earned after the change in terms of the new partnership agreement.

Unless otherwise specified, the profits are assumed to be earned on a more or less even basis throughout the period. The partners may agree to wait until the year end before profits are calculated and then divide it up as up to the change in constitution and after the change. For example, if Jack, Tom and Jill had made an annual profit of £36 000 and Tom had retired at mid-way through the year, it is assumed that £18 000 profit was made to the half year.

The partners' share of profit (2 : 2 : 1) in the old ratio:

	£	£
Jack	7 200	
Tom	7 200	
Jill	3 600	18 000

The new partner's share of profit (3 : 2) in the new ratio:

	£	£
Jack	10 800	
Jill	7 200	18 000

However, if the net profit of £36 000 was calculated before loan interest was charged, the calculation of profit for the new partner's share must take this into consideration as part of the post-change period. The old profit share still stands however for the first half year's share.

Post calculation of Jack and Jill's profit:

£		
Net profit		18 000
Less interest on 8% loan (half year)		
1/2 (25 000 × 8%)		1 000
		17 000
Jack	£10 200	
Jill	£6 800	17 000

Note that the interest charged on the loan (£1000) would be debited to the profit and loss account as an *accrued expense* until it was paid to the retiring partner.

26.6 Share of losses

Losses are shared in the same way as profits, that is, according to the partnership agreement. This may be equally, or in the proportion to capital, or in any other way as mutually agreed.

In the event of bankruptcy, where the partnership is to be wound up, any surplus in net assets will be divided in the proportion to the partners' capital and current accounts.

Note that general partners are liable up to their own personal wealth. In the event of a partner having a debit balance in his capital account and who is also insolvent (not in a position to pay off debts), the remaining partners are unfortunately liable for their partner's insolvency.

At the turn of this century, the partnership of Garner, Murray and Wilkins was dissolved, Wilkins ending up with a debit capital account balance and also insolvent. In the 1903 case Garner *v* Murray, it was the opinion of the court that the indebtedness of Wilkins should be borne by Garner and Murray *in proportion to their last capital account balances* and not their profit sharing ratio.

It is therefore held, that in the absence of any written partnership agreement, the case of Garner *v*

Murray applies, and any debt by an insolvent partner is to be borne by the other partners as per their last capital ratios. Any losses prior to bankruptcy are to be shared as per the partners agreed profit sharing ratio.

Summary

Partnerships are common in both the professions and trades. A Deed of Partnership is a written contract between partners outlining their mutual agreements in relation to the business including how to share profits or losses and the amount of personal drawings each partner can make. The preparation of the accounts is the same as sole traders although the addition of the appropriation account indicates how profits or losses are distributed. Goodwill is an intangible asset and its value based on reputation is rather subjective. It can influence the partners' capital accounts and their profit sharing ratio if a new partner is admitted or an existing partner leaves.

Questions

1 The following information relates to the accounts of Trevalyn & Curtis in partnership and who, in their contract, have agreed to share profit and losses equally:

	Trevalyn	*Curtis*
	£	£
Capital account balances 31/12	20 000	25 000
Current account balances 31/12	720 (Cr)	180 (Dr)
Drawings for the year:	9 725	10 800
Salaries to be credited	2 500	2 000
Interest to be charged on drawings	360	420

Interest paid on capital accounts is at 5 per cent per annum. The net profit for the year ended 31 December was £26 800.

REQUIRED:

1a) Prepare the partnership appropriation account for the year ended 31 December.
b) Prepare the partners' current accounts for the year ended 31 December.
c) Prepare a balance sheet extract to show the partners' 'financed by' section as on 31 December.

2 Explain briefly the difference between a general and limited partner. What advantage will the latter have in the event of bankruptcy of the business? (26.1–3)

2 Robert, Susan and Thomas are in partnership. The capitals they have invested in the partnership are £50 000, £40 000, and £20 000 respectively. During the financial year ended 30 September 19–6 the partnership earned a net profit of £42 000. The partners have agreed the following appropriation scheme:

i) interest to be allowed on capital at 12 per cent per annum,

ii) Susan and Thomas are to receive salaries of £4000 and £5000 respectively, and

iii) profits are to be shared in the ratio 4:3:1 respectively.

The partners had the following balances on their current accounts as at 1 October 19–5

	£	
Robert	121	(credit)
Susan	105	(debit)
Thomas	197	(credit)
	213	

During the year ended 30 September 19–6 the partners withdrew the following amounts from the partnership:

	£
Robert	15 940
Susan	16 020
Thomas	10 400
	42 360

REQUIRED:

a) Show the appropriation account for the partnership for the year ended 30 September 19–6 under the scheme.

b) Prepare the partners' current accounts for the year ended 30 September 19–6. (26.1–3)

(Association of Accounting Technicians)

3 Alan, Bill and Charles are in partnership in a very successful firm. The partners have agreed to share profits and losses in the ratio of Alan 3, Bill 2 and Charles 1. At the year end, on 30 June 19–5, the following trial balance was extracted from the books of the firm:

	£	£
Capital accounts:		
Alan		60 000
Bill		40 000
Charles		20 000
Current accounts:		
Alan		5 000
Bill		3 000
Charles		4 000
Drawings:		
Alan	10 000	
Bill	10 000	
Charles	10 000	
Commission		150 000
Property (at cost)	100 000	
Vehicles (at book value)	10 000	
Fixtures (at book value)	2 000	
Bad debts	3 000	
Provision for bad debts		3 500
Bank	27 000	
Debtors and creditors	20 000	20 500
Cash in hand	700	
Sundry expenses (including rent, insurance and depreciation for the year to 30 June 19–5)	113 300	
	306 000	306 000

REQUIRED:

The partnership profit and loss account (including the appropriation account) for the year ending 30 June 19–5, and a balance sheet, in net asset form, as at that date, after taking the following into account:

i) The provision for bad debts is to be reduced to £1000.

ii) At the year end £700 insurance has been paid in advance and rent – £900 – is still owing. (26.1–3)

(Institute of Commercial Management)

4 Fairway and Rough, partners in a consultancy business have the following balances in their books at 31 December 19–4 (after extraction of the trading and profit and loss accounts):

	£
Capital accounts (1 January 19–4)	
Fairway	20 000
Rough	25 000
Current accounts (1 January 19–4)	
Fairway	4 200 Cr
Rough	2 060 Dr
Drawings (for the year ended 31 December 19–4)	
Fairway	12 000
Rough	15 000
Motor van at cost	6 000
Provision for depreciation on motor van	4 500
Premises	50 000
Cash at bank	3 298
Wages accrued	1 968
Debtors	3 210
Bank loan (repayable in 19–6)	15 000
Interest on bank loan owing	600
Net trading profit	20 300
Interest on drawings:	
Fairway	200
Rough	900

The partners had agreed to allow 8 per cent interest on capital and to share remaining profits equally.

REQUIRED:

a) For the year ended 31 December 19–4:
   i) the profit and loss appropriation account of the partnership;
   ii) each partner's current account.

b) The balance sheet of the partnership as at 31 December 19–4. (26.1–3)

(Associated Examining Board)

5 Smith and Jones are in partnership, sharing profits and losses in a ratio to their capital accounts. The trial balance as on 31 December was as follows:

		Dr	Cr
		£	£
Premises		23 500	
Furniture and fittings		2 750	
Motor van		2 000	
Provision for bad debts			115
Carriage in		142	
Returns		288	343
Purchases		11 665	
Sales			21 429
Discounts		199	146
Stock (1/1)		3 865	
Debtors, creditors		2 355	3 569
Salaries		5 055	
Rates and insurance		645	
Light and heat		162	
Bank		522	
Capital:	Smith		18 000
	Jones		12 000
Current accounts:	Smith	625	
	Jones	540	
Drawings accounts:	Smith	2 303	
	Jones	1 500	
Rent received			2 514
		58 116	58 116

NOTES

31 December

1 The value of unsold stock £4200.
2 Gas bill due for payment £66.
3 Rates paid in advance £30.
4 Provision for bad debts to be increased to £250.
5 Depreciation: furniture and fittings by 20 per cent motor van revalued £1800.
6 Jones is awarded a salary of £1000 for extra responsibilities.
7 Interest charged on drawings: Smith £210
Jones £160.

REQUIRED:

a) Prepare the trading, profit and loss appropriation accounts for the year ended 31 December and balance sheet as at that date.
b) Show the current accounts as they would appear in the ledger. (26.1–3)

(Institute of Bankers)

6 J Stevenson and S Little, partners in a consultancy business, had the following balances in their books at 31 December 19–6 (after the extraction of the profit and loss account):

	£
Capital accounts (1 January 19–6):	
Stevenson	35 000
Little	25 000
Current accounts (1 January 19–6):	

Stevenson (credit)	6 200
Little (debit)	4 060
Drawings (for year ended 31 December 19–6):	
Stevenson	12 000
Little	15 000
Motor van	2 500
Premises	61 290
Cash at bank	3 498
Light and heat accrued	964
Debtors	3 510
Net profit	34 694
Interest on drawings:	
Stevenson	350
Little	940

The partners had agreed to allow 8 per cent per annum on capital, and to award salaries to Stevenson of £12 500 per annum and to Little of £14 200 per annum. Remaining profits to be shared equally.

REQUIRED:

a) For the year ended 31 December 19–6:
   i) the profit and loss appropriation account of the partnership;
   ii) each partner's current account.
b) The balance sheet of the partnership as at 31 December 19–6.
c) An explanation of the treatment of employees' salaries in a partnership's final accounts. Why is this treatment different from the treatment of partners' salaries? (26.1–3)

(Associated Examining Board)

7 You work as accountant for Wooldridge & James, a partnership, and have to prepare their final accounts for the year ended 31 May 19–7.

	£ *Dr*	£ *Cr*
Capital account balances: 1/6/19–6		
Wooldridge		50 000
James		30 000
Current account balances: 1/6/19–6		
Wooldridge		1 000
James		2 000
Drawings on 30/11/19–6		
Wooldridge	5 000	
James	8 000	
Drawings on 31/5/19–7		
Wooldridge	8 000	
James	10 000	
Fixed assets (net) 31/5/19–7	114 000	
Current assets 31/5/19–7	80 650	
Deferred liabilities 31/5/19–7		29 000
Current liabilities 31/5/19–7		75 000
Profit for the year		38 650
	225 650	225 650

The partnership agreement between Wooldridge & James stipulates:
i) Profits and losses to be shared 60 per cent Wooldridge and 40 per cent James.
ii) Salaries to be received Wooldridge £9 000, James £12 000.
iii) Interest to be paid on capital and current account balances as on 1/6/19–6 at 10 per cent per annum.
iv) Drawings also to be subject to interest at a rate of 10 per cent per annum.

REQUIRED:
a) Prepare the partnership profit and loss appropriation account for the year ending 31/5/19–7. Prepare the partners' current accounts after completion of the profit and loss and appropriation account.
b) Prepare the partnership balance sheet in its abbreviated form as on 31/5/19–7.
c) Write a memorandum to the partners explaining the situation under Section 24 of the Partnership Act 1890 if no partnership agreement existed.
d) Prepare a statement, to be sent with the above memorandum, showing how the profits would be divided if Section 24 of the Partnership Act 1890 applied. (26.1–3)

(BTEC National)

8 The following is the trial balance of Dick and Tom who trade in partnership, at 31 March 19–5:

	£	£
Capital account balances 1 April 19–4		
Dick		15 000
Tom		15 000
Current account balances 1 April 19–4		
Dick		1 500
Tom		2 500
Sales		75 000
Stock (1 April 19–4)	15 000	
Wages	7 250	
Rent	2 500	
Expenses	1 500	
Heat and light	600	
Debtors/creditors	7 000	5 750
Delivery costs	2 650	
Drawings:		
Dick	3 500	
Tom	4 500	
Cash	2 250	
Fixed assets	13 000	
Purchases	55 000	
	114 750	114 750

NOTES
1 Stock at 31 March 19–5 was valued at £19 480.
2 Depreciation of £1 750 is to be written off the fixed assets for the year to 31 March 19–5.
3 At 31 March 19–5 wages accrued amounted to £250, and rent of £500 was prepaid.
4 On 1 February 19–5 the partnership ordered and paid for goods costing £350. These were recorded as purchases but were never received as they were lost by the carrier responsible for their delivery. The carrier accepted liability for the loss during March 19–5 and paid full

compensation of £350 in April 19–5. No entries had been made in the books in respect of the loss or claim.

5 Dick took goods which had cost the firm £170 for his own use during the year. No entry has been made in the books to record this.

6 The partnership agreement provided that profits and losses should be shared equally between the partners after:

a) allowing annual salaries of £1000 to Dick and £2000 to Tom.

b) allowing interest of 5 per cent per annum on the balance of each partner's capital account; and

c) charging Dick £210 and Tom £290 interest on drawings.

7 The balances on the capital accounts shall remain unchanged, all adjustments being recorded in the current accounts.

REQUIRED:

a) Prepare the trading, profit and loss and appropriation accounts for the Dick and Tom partnership for the year to 31 March 19–5.

b) Prepare the balance sheet at 31 March 19–5 showing working capital.

c) Write a brief statement to the owners of the enterprise outlining the profit return for the year.(26.1–3)

(Royal Society of Arts)

9 The following information refers to the accounts of Smith, Jones & Rogers who are in partnership and according to their deeds, share profits and losses in the ratio of 2 : 2 : 1 respectively.

During the financial period ended 31 May 19–7, the net profit of the business was £7 300 and the partners' drawings for the year were:

	£
Smith	2 000
Jones	1 900
Rogers	1 500

Interest on partners' drawings has been calculated as follows:

	£
Smith	65
Jones	55
Rogers	45

As far as the partners' capital accounts are concerned, the agreement states that 6 per cent will be allowed as interest payment. The partners had agreed that Smith should withdraw £1000 from his capital account on 1 December 19–6 and that Rogers should contribute the same amount on that date. Jones is awarded a salary of £900 for extra responsibilities.

The balances on the partners' accounts on 1 June 19–6 were:

	Capital accounts	*Current accounts*
	£	£
Smith	9 000	600 Cr
Jones	8 000	400 Dr
Rogers	7 000	300 Dr

Other balances on 31 May 19–7 were as follows:

	£
Fixed assets (net)	30 700
Stocks	12 750
Debtors	4 655

Cash	500
Bank (Cr)	2 995
Creditors	14 560
Accruals	300
Bank loan (5 years)	4 950

REQUIRED:

a) Prepare the partnership profit and loss appropriation account and the partners' current accounts for the year ended 31 May 19–7.

b) Prepare the partners' balance sheet as at 31 May 19–7 and show net current assets as part of its construction.

c) Make a brief comment on the partners' financial position as at 31 May 19–7. (26.1–3)

(Institute of Bankers)

10 French & Saunders run a business consultancy and have the following account balances in their books on 31 March 19–4:

	£
Capital accounts:	
French	20 000
Saunders	25 000
Current accounts:	
French	4 200 Cr
Saunders	2 060 Dr
Drawings for the year:	
French	12 000
Saunders	15 000
Premises	60 000
Vehicles	6 000
Depreciation of vehicles	5 000
Bank	3 800
Debtors	3 210
Creditors	6 970
Bank loan 11% (19–9)	20 000
Net trading profit for year	19 800
Interest accrued on loan (6 months)	

NOTES

1 The partners have agreed on equal sharing of profits/losses.

2 The partners have agreed 8 per cent interest on capital accounts.

3 Interest charges on drawings amount to: French £200, Saunders £600.

REQUIRED:

As an assistant to a group of accountants who have French & Saunders as one of their clients, you have been asked to prepare in draft form:

a) The profit and loss appropriation account of French & Saunders for the year ended, 31 March 19–4 and the current accounts of each partner.

b) The balance sheet of the partnership as on 31 March 19–4.

c) A brief memorandum, addressed to the partners, commenting on the partnership liquidity and suggesting how it could be improved.

d) French has used her own premises for the business partnership and £500 has been agreed for running costs. No entries have been made. What effect would this have on the preparation of the above accounts?

11 Bell, Ring and Gong, who traded separately for several years, decided to form a partnership on 1 April 19–4 and transferred all the assets and liabilities of their individual businesses to the partnership at that date.

Whilst the assets and liabilities brought into the partnership have been recorded in the partnership books of account at agreed valuations, it has now been discovered that recognition has not been given in the partnership books for the goodwill as at 1 April 19–4 of the businesses transferred to the partnership:

Bell	£8 000
Ring	£12 000
Gong	£16 000

At the same time, it must be noted that the partners do not want a goodwill account to be maintained in the partnership books.

The partnership agreement provides for partners to be credited with interest on their capital account balances at the rate of 10 per cent per annum, Ring and Gong to be credited with partners' salaries of £10 000 and £13 000 per annum respectively, and the balance of profits and losses to be shared between Bell, Ring and Gong in the ratio 5 : 3 : 2 respectively.

The following trial balance as at 31 March 19–5 has been extracted from the partnership accounts:

	£	£
Freehold land and buildings: at valuation	50 000	
provision for depreciation		1 250
Plant and machinery: at valuation	21 000	
provision for depreciation		2 100
Motor vehicles: at valuation	12 000	
provision for depreciation		3 000
Stock	9 000	
Debtors	4 000	
Balance at bank	600	
Creditors		5 250
Capital accounts: Bell		40 000
Ring		20 000
Gong		14 000
Drawings: Bell	13 000	
Ring	11 000	
Gong	9 000	
Net profit for the year ended 31 March 19–5		44 000
	£129 600	£129 600

Additional information:

1) It is agreed that a current account be opened for each partner.
2) On 1 October 19–4, by agreement between the partners, Ring acquired from the partnership a motor vehicle at a valuation of £2,000 – this vehicle was valued at £2,400 [cost] at 1 April 19–4. Entries have not yet been made in the partnership books for this transfer which is to be debited to the partner's drawings account.

3) There have been no additions to any fixed assets since the commencement of the partnership.
4) The partners have decided that depreciation is to be provided on the straight-line basis as follows:

	% per annum
Freehold land and buildings	2½
Plant and machinery	10
Motor vehicles	25

REQUIRED:
a) The partnership's profit and loss appropriation account for the year ended 31 March 19–5
b) The partnership's balance sheet as at that date. (26.1–4)

(Association of Accounting Technicians)

12 Owing to staff illnesses, the draft final accounts for the year ended 31 March 19–8 of Messrs. Stone, Pebble and Brick, trading in partnership as the Bigtime Building Supply Company, have been prepared by an inexperienced, but keen, clerk. The draft summarised balance sheet as at 31 March 19–8 is as follows:

			£	£
Tangible fixed assets: At cost less depreciation to date				45 400
Current assets			32 290	
Less: Trade creditors			6 390	25 900
				71 300
Represented by:	*Stone*	*Pebble*	*Brick*	*Total*
	£	£	£	£
Capital accounts: at 1 April 19–7	26 000	18 000	16 000	60 000
Current accounts:				
Share of net profit for the year ended 31 March 19–8	12 100	12 100	12 100	
Drawings year ended 31 March 19–8	(8 200)	(9 600)	(7 200)	
At 31 March 19–8	3 900	2 500	4 900	11 300
				71 300

The partnership commenced on 1 April 19–7 when each of the partners introduced, as their partnership capital, the net tangible fixed and current assets of their previously separate businesses. However, it has now been discovered that contrary to what was agreed, no adjustments were made in the partnership books for the goodwill of the partners' former businesses now incorporated in the partnership. The agreed valuations of goodwill at 1 April 19–7 are as follows:

	£
Stone's business	30 000
Pebble's business	20 000
Brick's business	16 000

It is agreed that a goodwill account should not be opened in the partnership's books. It has now been discovered that effect has not been given in the accounts to the following provisions in the partnership agreement effective from 1 January 19–8:

1) Stone's capital to be reduced to £20 000 the balance being transferred to a loan account upon which interest at the rate of 11% per annum will be paid on 31 December each year.
2) Partners to be credited with interest on their capital account balances at the rate of 5% per annum.
3) Brick to be credited with a partner's salary at the rate of £8 500 per annum.
4) The balance of the net profit or loss to be shared between Stone, Pebble and Brick in the ratio 5 : 3 : 2 respectively.

NOTES:
1) It can be assumed that the net profit indicated in the draft accounts accrued uniformly throughout the year.
2) It has been agreed between the partners that no adjustments should be made for any partnership goodwill as at 1 January 19–8.

REQUIRED:
a) Prepare the profit and loss appropriation account for the year ended 31 March 19–8.
b) Prepare a corrected statement of the partners' capital and current accounts for inclusion in the partnership balance sheet as at 31 March 19–8. (26.1–4)

(Association of Accounting Technicians)

27 Accounting for limited companies

Objectives

On completing this section you should:

- recognise how companies are formed
- be aware of the classes of shares and debentures
- prepare the company appropriation account
- understand the various company terms such as authorised and issued capital and revenue and capital reserves
- be aware of the 1985 and 1989 Companies Act
- recognise the contents or a company's annual and corporate reports.

Context

Chapter 2 introduced the basic principles behind limited companies.

27.1 Introduction

There are basically two types of limited company – private limited or public limited. Both belong to the private sector of business as distinct from public ownership, which refer to the Government's business enterprises, such as British Rail.

There is no restriction as to the number of shareholders who may contribute capital to a company. However, the private company can only sell its shares privately as its title suggests, and cannot resort to publishing a prospectus, inviting the public to buy its shares. A public limited company (plc) may do this, having no such binding restriction as that of the private company. A public company may offer its shares to the public by issuing a prospectus, thereby advertising its share issue to the public, inviting it to purchase its shares. Merchant banks like Hambros, Rothschilds or Barings are part of the 60 issuing houses in the UK, whose interest is to organise and arrange for the public issue of shares. The success of the new share issue will, to a large degree, depend upon the reputation and good name of the issuing house.

By the issue of shares to the public, very large sums of capital can be raised and public companies can take credit for stimulating the growth of share capital investment over the last 100 years or so.

For a public company, at least £50 000 of share capital must be registered with the company, of which a minimum of 25 per cent must be issued and paid for before it can commence business operations.

Shareholders of both private or public companies are part owners of their companies. They are not creditors. They actually own a proportion of the company in relation to the number of shares they have. The reward for owning shares comes from either dividends (a share of the company profits), or from an increase in the value of their shares (capital gain). Dividends are paid on the basis of the nominal value of shares, that is, their face value, not their market value. Dividends are usually expressed in terms of so many pence per share. For example, 10p per share. They may also be determined as so much in the pound, so that 10p per £ would gain £10 per 100 shares.

Limited companies have the advantage of having *limited liability*, a warning to potential creditors that shareholders are only liable up to the value of their nominal capital. They are protected against the debts of the company up to the value of issued and paid-up capital.

Most private companies are relatively small business ventures having a limited number of members as shareholders and being restricted to selling its shares to family and friends or business acquaintances. Public limited companies can often be very large business concerns like ICI plc, Barclays Bank plc and Fords plc, which have thousands of shareholders and employees.

The shares of the plcs may be listed on the Stock Exchange once they have been vetted by the Stock Exchange Council and been given an official market quotation. When this has been granted, the shares (or securities) may be included in the Exchange's Official List and therefore be quoted on the Stock Market. To become a listed company, the Exchange can ensure that the company is providing all the relevant information which is necessary to enable investors to assess their securities fairly and squarely and that they comply with all the necessary standard practice of companies. Private limited company shares are not listed.

27.2 Formation of limited companies

A limited company must prepare two important documents which are sent to the Registrar at Companies House, in order to become a registered limited company. All companies are regulated by the 1985 Companies Act which consolidates all previous Acts, 1948 to 1981.

The principal document is the Memorandum of Association which attempts to give the *external* view of the company to the public, including such details as the company's name, address, registered office, share capital and, most significantly, its objectives which set out what it proposes to do. In the final part of the Memorandum comes the *association clause* which is a declaration signed by the founder members of the company, stating that they desire to form themselves into a company (a corporated body).

The second document is the Articles of Association which gives the *internal* view of the company in the form of a list of regulations which will serve as a guideline to the general conduct of running the company. This includes its organisation and control, voting rights, conduct at directors' meetings, power of directors, the rights attached to the different classes of shares and also meetings between shareholders and directors such as the annual general meeting. The Articles must be signed by the founder members. A model form of Articles are to be found in Schedule A of the Companies Act.

Once approval is confirmed by the Registrar, a company is issued with its Certificate of Incorporation, which gives it the status of an incorporated body having a separate legal entity from the owners of the company (its shareholders). The company attains the right of its own identity and can proceed and act under its own name. It has its own existence.

A company is under the control of its board of directors who *direct* the company on behalf of its shareholders – directors control, the shareholders own.

On receipt of a Certificate of Incorporation, a private company may commence trading operations. However, a plc must first issue its prospectus to sell its shares and acquire the minimum share capital it needs to commence operations, as stated in its prospectus. The prospectus must also give details concerning the underwriting of the issue which will ensure that the minimum capital is raised. Once the minimum capital is raised, the Registrar will issue the new company its Certificate of Trading. The plc can then commence trading.

27.3 Classes of shares

There are two distinct classes of shares:

a) **Ordinary shares**. These are also referred to as **equities**. They represent the most common type of share and are considered the true shares of a company, taking the greater risk compared to preference shares. The rate of dividend will depend on the profits of the company, and how much the board is willing to distribute and how much it would like to retain. These shares have voting rights, one share, one vote. In the event of the company being liquidated (wound up), these shares are paid last from any surplus of net assets.

b) **Preference shares**. These shares are considered a little less of a risk than equities. They are paid at a **fixed rate of dividend** and are entitled to be paid before any dividend to ordinary shares. They do not however, have any voting rights. Some preference shares are **cumulative** in that any dividend which is not paid in one year, can be claimed in other years. These shares are suitable for those investors who want an assurance of a certain fixed dividend rate from one financial period to the next. Participating preference shares allow the holder to receive a further amount from profits in addition to their fixed rate of dividend, once other shareholders have been provided for.

27.4 Loan stock

A company may issue **debentures** as well as shares if it wishes to raise finance. This stock is not part of the share capital but represents loan capital and is recorded under long-term liabilities rather than the 'financed by' section.

Debenture holders, who are creditors of the company, are paid at a **fixed rate of interest** over the specified period of the loan. The interest is an expense to be paid and recorded in the profit and loss account. **Redeemable debentures** are those which are redeemed (or paid back) when the stock matures. For example, 9 per cent debentures, 1995, 2005 refers to the earliest and latest dates the stock may be redeemed.

The share and loan capital are both marketable securities and may be bought and sold on the Stock Exchange, if they are officially listed.

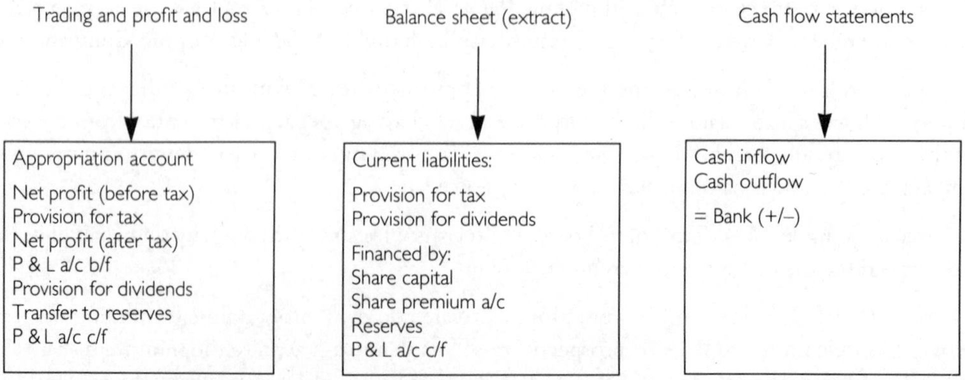

Fig 27.1 The final accounts of limited companies

Note:
1 The appropriation account indicates the division of profits or losses
2 Provisions for tax and dividends are transferred to current liabilities in the balance sheet
3 Reserves and P & L a/c c/f are transferred to the 'Financed by' section of the balance sheet
4 The P & L a/c is any residue of profit still in balance carried forward to the next accounts period
5 Cash flow statements are discussed in Chapter 28.

Example of distribution of dividends and interest

Allied Components plc have made a profit before interest payments and tax provision of £80 000. It has a registered capital of:

200 000 @ £1 ordinary shares
100 000 @ £1 8 per cent preference shares and
50 000 @ £1 debenture stock at 11 per cent.

Taxation is to be provided for £25 000 and the board has recommended an ordinary share dividend of 10 per cent. Show how the profit is to be distributed.

Allied Components plc

	£	£
Profit (before interest and taxation)		80 000
Interest payable:		
11% debenture stock		5 500
Profit (before tax)		74 500
Provision for tax		25 000
Profit (after tax)		49 500
Provision for dividends:		
8% preference shares	8 000	
Ordinary shares (10%)	20 000	28 000
Retained profits (P&L balance)		21 500

Notes

1 The interest payable of £5500 is an expense which must be paid irrespective of profits and is part of the company's profit and loss account.
2 The provision for taxation and dividends is part of the company appropriation account, that is, how the company distributes its profits *after* taxation.
3 The retained profits are either transferred to what are known as **revenue reserves** which are merely profits retained over the years, or simply retained in the profit and loss balance.

27.5 The divorce between ownership and control

Limited companies are owned by their shareholders. The more shares owned by a shareholder, the greater the ownership in the company. If a shareholder owns the majority of shares, that is over 50 per cent, he or she can take control because the combined number of remaining shares cannot upset the balance of power. In effect, in some circumstances, power can be held by a small number of shareholders owning less than 50 per cent.

The shareholders have the responsibility of electing a board of directors to manage the company on their behalf. In this way the shareholders own a company, the board take control of it. The shareholders can hire or fire their directors at annual general meetings although this rarely occurs in practice.

The board of directors may include both executive and non-executive directors. An executive director takes responsibility for the day-to-day running of his particular department, for example the sales or managing director. Non-executive directors may be invited to join the board for various reasons, for example to give specialist consultation.

The board of directors are responsible for appointing managers to run various departments and to delegate authority and responsibility to them in order that they can carry out the decisions made by the board.

27.6 The company appropriation account

The appropriation account always commences at net profit before taxation and immediately follows the trading and profit and loss account of the company. The account shows how profit is divided much in the same way as we saw in partnership accounts in the previous chapter. The account may be credited with any balance of profit brought forward from the previous period. Deductions would be made for dividends either proposed or already paid for and any transfers to reserve (retained profits over a number of accounting periods). Any final balance is carried forward to the next accounting period.

Many exam questions often ask for the appropriation account and balance sheet only, so make sure you start at the correct point of the question.

Example

Argyle & Company Ltd –
Profit & Loss Appropriation Account year ended 31 December:

	£	£
Net Profit before tax		80 000
–provision for taxation		20 000
Net Profit after tax		60 000
+Profit & Loss balance (1/1)		18 000
		78 000
Provision for Dividends		
8% Preference paid	8 000	
8% Preference due	8 000	
Ordinary shares	40 000	56 000
		22 000
Reserves		20 000
Profit & Loss balance (31/12)		2 000

Balance sheet extract:

		£
CURRENT LIABILITIES:		
Provision for tax		20 000
Provision for dividends		48 000
FINANCED BY:		
8% £1	Preference shares	200 000
£1	Ordinary shares	800 000
	Reserves	115 000
	Profit & loss	2 000

NOTE:

1 A preference dividend may have been paid during the year (interim) and is shown separately from that still due for payment.
2 The profit and loss account (1/1) is that profit b/f from the previous period.
3 The profit and loss account (31/12) is the final figure which is transferred to the balance sheet and also carried forward to the next financial period.
4 The provision for dividends and tax are current liabilities because they are due to be paid in the following financial period.
5 The reserves total £115 000 with the transfer of £20 000 in this period. This means that there was £95 000 in reserves already. The reserves and final profit and loss balance are part of the 'financed by' section, referred to as the shareholders' funds.

The appropriation account, therefore, shows what happens to the company's profits. If a company wanted to write off any goodwill, it can be deducted from the appropriation account and the goodwill account credited to complete the double entry.

27.7 The capital of limited companies

Unlike the capital of sole traders and partners, there are a number of terms relating to a limited company's capital and you need to be able to distinguish each of them. These terms refer to authorised (or nominal), issued, called up and paid up capital.

Authorised capital is also the nominal capital of the company and is normally the maximum amount of capital it can issue. It is the company's registered capital and is that sum stated in the company's Memorandum of Association. A company may set up with share capital of £1 million pounds, some of which may be preference shares (as in the above example). However, it is far more likely that they will be ordinary shares, easily the most common shares in limited companies.

The **issued capital** is that nominal capital issued to shareholders and cannot be in excess of authorised capital. If all the authorised capital is issued, then authorised and issued capital will equal the same sum. For example, if the nominal capital was £1 million and £500 000 was issued, there would be a further £500 000 unissued shares that the company could still issue at a later date.

The **called up capital** refers to when shares have been allotted to shareholders and have only called up part of the sum due on the shares and wait until a later date to call up the rest. For example, if a company allots £500 000 £1 shares and only calls up 50p a share, it will receive £250 000. This means that although it has issued £500 000 of share capital, it has only called up half of it. The remainder is uncalled capital.

The **paid up capital** refers to the issued capital paid for by shareholders. If some shareholders have not yet paid for their shares, they would be debtors to the company until they have paid for them. For example, if only £245 000 had been received for the called up capital, then £5 000 represents unpaid.

Example

	£	
Authorised capital:		
1 million £1 ordinary shares	1 000 000	
Issued capital:		
500 000 £1 ordinary shares	500 000	
Called up capital:		
500 000 50p ordinary shares	250 000	
Paid up capital	245 000	
Called up unpaid capital	5 000	250 000

The issued and paid up capital equals £245 000 plus the unpaid called up capital equals £250 000 representing the capital of the company at that time of the floating of the shares. On the asset side, the current assets would show the £245 000 banked *plus* the £5 000 as debtors still to pay for their shares.

27.8 Revenue reserves

Revenue reserves are amounts which are retained from the profits of a company and may be available for distribution as dividends to shareholders. The reserves will increase as more profits are retained from year to year. Reserves will help a company to expand and grow, and transfers to reserve may be used for specific purposes like building up fixed assets or held for general financing. Retained profits are an important source of capital for company growth.

27.9 Capital reserves

Capital reserves are retained profits which have not been created from what has been considered normal trading. The share premium account is such a reserve where a company has sold its shares above the par value (face value) and retained the extra money it has received. The revaluation of fixed assets is another example. If land and buildings have increased in value fairly substantially, the amount of the increase could be debited to the asset and the same amount credited to the capital reserve account. These capital reserves are not available for shareholders' dividends and they are shown with other general reserves as part of the shareholders' funds in the balance sheet of the company.

Example 1

On issuing its prospectus, a company sold all its shares: 500 000 @ £1 ordinary shares at £1.25 each.

Balance sheet (extract)

	£
Shareholders' funds:	
Issued and paid-up capital	
500 000 @ £1 ordinary shares	500 000

Share premium account	125 000
	625 000

Example 2

A company decided to revalue its property to bring it into line with current prices. Premises were recorded at a cost of £80 000 and were now to be revalued to £150 000.

Balance sheet (extract)

	£	£
Fixed assets:		
Premises	80 000	
+ Revaluation	70 000	150 000
Shareholders' funds:		
Revaluation reserve account		70 000

27.10 Accounting requirements of the 1985 Act

Under Part VII of the 1985 Companies Act and particularly, sections 221 and 222, the main points state:

1. Every limited company must keep accounting records, with reasonable accuracy, to disclose the financial position of the company.
2. Financial records must be kept daily including receipts and payments of money, the assets and liabilities of the company, including stock-taking at the year-end. These records must be kept for a period of three years for a private company and six years for a public company.
3. The final accounts of the company must be kept in accordance with the formats laid down in *Schedule 4 of the Act*. This must include:
   - a profit and loss account
   - a balance sheet, as at the same period
   - an auditors' report
   - a directors' report.

Public companies must have at least two directors and a private company, one. Every company must have a secretary. The directors of a company must make a report as part of the annual accounts and must present a fair view of the business's development in its financial year. The directors must also indicate the dividend they wish to recommend and also the amount they propose to withold as reserves.

Annual reports must be filed with the Registrar at Companies House. For companies registered in England and Wales, there is an address in London and Cardiff. For companies registered in Scotland, there is an address in Edinburgh.

A company must show its account to its members for each accounting period at its annual general meeting. It must ensure that a copy of its accounts is sent to the Registrar within a period of ten months following the end of the financial period for a private company and seven months for a public company.

27.11 The Companies Act 1989

The Companies Act 1989, is a supplementary Act and does not replace the 1985 Companies Act, which in effect, consolidated all previous Acts from 1948–81. The 1989 Act amends and adds to the existing legislation of the 1985 Act. It is expected that the accounting provisions relating to Part I are likely to be effective in respect to accounting periods beginning on or after 1 January 1990.

The new Act came about as a result of the UK's obligation to implement the European Community's Seventh Directive on consolidated accounts and its Eighth Directive on the regulation of company auditors. At the same time, the Government had an opportunity to take stock of its company law and to bring in desired amendments such as the power to investigate and obtain information, to make provision for the safeguarding of certain financial markets and to amend the Financial Services Act 1986 and the Company Securities Act 1985 (Insider Dealing).

As far as company accounts go, the provisions of the Act under sections 221 and 222 (Part VII), emphasise the duty of all companies to keep accounting records. Some of the 1989 Act's interesting sections are outlined below:

221:(1) Every company shall keep accounting records, sufficient to show and explain the company's transactions with reasonable accuracy at any time, the financial position of the company and to enable the directors to ensure that the balance sheet and profit and loss account complies with the requirements of the Companies Act.

A company's accounts shall be kept at its registered office or such other place where the directors think fit and shall at all times be open to inspection by the company's officers.

221:(2) Accounting entries shall contain day-to-day records of all sums of money received and spent as well as a record of its assets and liabilities.

221:(3) If a company deals with goods for resale, the accounts must contain statements of the value of stock held at end of the financial year and to show sufficient details of buyers and sellers, except by way of ordinary retail trade.

226: It is the duty of the directors to have individual, as well as group company accounts prepared for each financial period, a balance sheet as at the last day of that period and a profit and loss account for that period. Both these financial reports must give a 'true and fair' view of the state of affairs of the company for the financial period under review.

227: Where a company acts as a parent company and has subsidiary companies, the directors must prepare individual accounts for each company and also consolidated accounts for the group, as a whole.

238: The persons entitled to receive copies of the annual accounts and directors' and auditors' reports are:

a) every member of the company,
b) every holder of the company's debentures,
c) every person entitled to receive notice of general meetings (not less than 21 days before the meeting is held).

242: Directors must send to the Registrar at Companies House, a copy of the company's annual accounts and also a copy of the directors' and auditors' reports. Penalties for not complying within the stated specified time (within ten months of the financial period end for a private company and seven months for a public company) will be fined according to the length of time the accounts are delayed. For a public company, the fine will range between £500 and £5000 and for a private company, the fine will range between £100 and £1000.

Other sections of the 1989 Companies Act deal with aspects outside the scope of this publication. These include matters relating to the following:

a) investigations and power to obtain information,
b) the eligibility for the appointment of company auditors,
c) various amendments to company law,
d) mergers and related matters,
e) financial markets and insolvency,
f) the Financial Services Act 1986 – amendments,
g) the transfer of securities.

27.12 The preparation of company accounts

The 1985 (Consolidated) Companies Act gives guidance as to the preparation of final accounts of companies, that is, the trading and profit and loss account and the balance sheet. The trading and profit and loss account is sometimes referred to as the profit and loss statement, or the revenue statement.

The 1985 Act outlines the presentation for the profit and loss statement. The expenses may be subdivided into two major categories, that is, sales and distribution costs and administration expenses. There is also a separate category for listing interest payable. Net profit is shown before and after tax. Financial Reporting Statement 3 (FRS 3) provides further guidance on how the profit and loss account should be presented.

The company appropriation account is part of the profit and loss statement and shows how the profits are divided. Some profits may be retained and will not be available for distribution. Retained profits may be held in the profit and loss account or in revenue reserves, or in both.

In a company balance sheet, the Companies Act outlines a choice of two formats. The first format of presentation will be used because it is in the vertical form as already followed in this text. The alternative method is often adopted by banks and is represented in horizontal format.

Company accounts may be prepared either for internal use or for publication. Accounts for internal use represent a full version of the accounts as is generally prepared for sole traders or partnerships, that is, full details of revenue and expenses may be indicated. Accounts for external use only need indicate the sub-totals for each of the major headings. When preparing the profit and loss statement, only the external version needs to be sent to the Registrar to be filed. A full version of the balance sheet is normally prepared, either for internal or external use, the Registrar requiring the full version to be filed.

The following information illustrates the final accounts for internal use of Allied Components plc, for the year ended 31 December:

Allied Components plc –
trial balance as at year ended, 31 December

	£000	£000
Land, buildings	1 800	
Equipment, machinery	650	
Motor vehicles	450	
Investments	600	
Provision for depreciation:		
Land, buildings		20
Equipment, machinery		140
Motor vehicles		110
Debtors, creditors	280	50
Bank/cash	330	
Prepayments, accruals	5	10
Bank loan (10 years)		123
Issued and paid-up capital:		
Ordinary shares		1 000
8% preference shares		1 000
Share premium account		100
Profit and loss balance (1/1)		5
Purchases, sales	1 200	3 500
Stock (1/1)	85	
Sales and distribution costs:		
Sales salaries	85	
Warehouse costs	150	
Advertising, publicity	250	
Motor expenses	150	
Administration expenses:		
Office salaries	80	
General overheads	255	
Rates, insurances	15	
Light, heat	11	
Telephone	12	
Interest paid	60	
Dividends received		10
Reserves		400
	6 468	6 468

Other information as on 31 December:

a) Stock valued at £65 000.
b) Depreciation charges for the year:
Equipment, machinery £230 000
Motor vehicles £300 000.
c) The board of directors recommend that the preference shareholders be paid their dividend and that 10 per cent should be provided for ordinary shares.

d) A sum of £200 000 is to be set aside for corporation tax and £300 000 is to be transferred to reserves.

REQUIRED:

a) For internal use: a trading, profit and loss account for Allied Components plc, for the year ending 31 December.
b) A balance sheet for Allied Components plc as on 31 December.

NOTE

The final accounts are to follow Format 1 of the 1985 Companies Act. There is £2 million of authorised ordinary shares. All preference shares have been issued.

Allied Components plc – trading and profit and loss account, year ending 31 December

	£000	£000	£000
Turnover (net sales)			3 500
less			
Cost of sales			
Stock (1/1)	85		
Purchases	1 200		
	1 285		
Stock (31/12)	65		1 220
Gross profit			2 280
Sales and distribution costs:			
Sales salaries	85		
Warehouse costs	150		
Advertising, publicity	250		
Motor expenses	150		
Depreciation, motor vehicles	300	935	
Administration expenses:			
Office salaries	80		
General overheads	255		
Rates, insurances	15		
Light, heat	11		
Depreciation, equipment	230		
Telephone	12	603	1 538
			742
Other income			
Dividends from other companies			10
			752

(continued)

(continued)

Interest payable		(60)
Net profit (before tax)		692
Corporation tax (provided)		(200)
Net profit (after tax)		492
Profit and loss balance (1/1)		5
		497
Provision for dividends:		
8% preference shares	80	
Ordinary shares	100	(180)
		317
Reserves		(300)
Profit and loss balance (31/12)		17

NOTES

1 The profit and loss balance is the residue of profit after the appropriations to dividends and reserves. The balance at the end of one financial period becomes the opening balance in the next.

2 The provision for dividends were based on:
1 000 000 8% preference (£80 000)
1 000 000 ordinary, 10% recommended, (£100 000).

3 The provision for both taxation and dividends will also be listed as current liabilities in the balance sheet, funds not to be distributed from calculated profits.

4 The retained profits will be listed under shareholders' funds, in the 'financed by' section of the balance sheet.

Allied Components plc –
Balance sheet as at
year ending 31 December

	£000	*£000*	*£000*
FIXED ASSETS			
Intangibles			—
Tangibles			
Land, buildings	1 800	20	1 780
Equipment, machinery	6 650	370	280
Motor vehicles	450	410	40
Investments	600		600
	3 500	800	2 700

(continued)

(continued)

CURRENT ASSETS			
Stock (31/12)	65		
Debtors	280		
Bank/cash	330		
Prepayments	5	680	
less			
CREDITORS FALLING WITHIN 12 MONTHS			
Creditors	50		
Accruals	10		
Provision for taxation	200		
Provision for dividends	180	440	
Net current assets			240
Total assets less current liabilities			2 940
less			
CREDITORS FALLING AFTER 12 MONTHS			
Bank loan (10 years)			123
			2 817
	Authorised capital £000	*Issued and paid-up capital £000*	
FINANCED BY:			
Shareholders' funds			
Ordinary shares	2 000	1 000	
8% preference shares	1 000	1 000	
	3 000	2 000	
Share premium account		100	
Reserves		700	
Profit and loss balance (31/12)		17	2 817

NOTES

1 Creditors falling within 12 months and after 12 months relate to current and long-term liabilities. Total assets less liabilities refers to the capital employed.

2 The authorised capital is the sum as stated in the company's Memorandum of Association. A public limited company must have at least £50 000 worth of registered (authorised) capital. It is the issued and paid-up capital which are the relevant figures for balancing.

3 The share premium account relates to the company's capital reserves and represents the sum received in excess of the nominal value of the shares issued. In the above case, the ordinary shares sold at £1.10 each, a premium of 10p per share.

27.13 An example of financial statements prepared for private limited companies

The Rafael Private Co Ltd

The following information relates to the documents prepared for filing with the Registrar at Companies House, London. Rafael is a small manufacturing company, producing nothing for the home market. Its financial period runs from 1 January to 31 December.

It is a typical, small, private company, held in ownership by the Jones and Smith families who have an equal number of shares between them. Its four directors have 250 shares each, a total of 1000 ordinary shares. It employs fewer than 20 in its workforce.

The financial statements attached are the type of external reports which are sent to the Registrar. The cash flow statement is not included and information concerning this account is found in the following section.

Note that the previous year's financial figures (19–7) are always included with the current year as a matter of standard practice. The company made a loss of £14 350 in the current year, having made a profit of £9524 in the previous period. This was largely due to diminishing sales and costs which did not fall in proportion.

Study the figures as to the general presentation and content of the accounts, prepared in accordance with the Companies Act 1985.

By law, limited companies must produce statements other than the profit and loss account and the balance sheet. These are of a non-financial nature and are part of a company's annual report.

The *chairman's report* is normally the first item in the annual report and conveys the chairman's overall views of the company, including the financial results for the year, special events, the economic and political events which may have affected the company's performance and what the future may hold for the company.

The *directors' report* provides information concerning the company's operations and the number and type of shares held by its directors.

The *auditors' report* is an external, independent report on the financial statements of the company. The Companies Act states that all companies must appoint external auditors who report to the members of the company and state, in their opinion, whether the annual accounts of the company represent a 'true and fair view'. External auditors are appointed by the company to examine their accounts but are not employees.

Internal auditors, on the other hand, are employees of the company and many larger companies do set up their own internal audit systems for the purpose of checking, monitoring, investigating and analysing its own accounting systems. This service may help to improve the recording and reporting of accounting data and also to detect any fraud or malpractice which may have occurred.

The financial statements for the year ended 31 December 19–8

The financial statements for the year ended 31 December 19–8 include:

the directors' report
the auditors' report
the profit and loss account
the balance sheet.

27.13.1 The directors' report

The directors present their report together with financial statements for the year ended 31 December 19–8.

Principal activities: the company is principally engaged in the production of clothing, mainly men's and children's.

Results: The company's results reflect both the move to the new premises in the year and the recruitment of two sales staff who proved unsuccessful. As a result a small loss was recorded. The directors are confident that the company will shortly revert to profitability. The directors consider the position at the year-end to be satisfactory.

The loss for the year after taxation amounted to £10 850. The directors do not recommend payment of a dividend and the loss has therefore been deducted from reserves.

Directors: the directors in office at the end of the year are listed below. All served on the board throughout the year.

The interests of the directors in the shares of the company at 1 January 19–7 and at 31 December 19–8 as recorded in the register maintained by the company in accordance with the provisions of the Companies Act 1985, were as follows:

	19–8 and 19–7 ordinary shares
T Jones	250
R Jones	250
D Smith	250
L Smith	250

27.13.2 The auditor's report

REPORT OF THE AUDITORS TO THE MEMBERS OF THE RAFAEL PRIVATE CO LTD
We have audited the financial statements of the company on the following pages in accordance with auditing standards.

In our opinion, the financial statements have given a true and fair view of the state of the company's affairs at 31 December 19–8 and of its result and sources and application of funds for the year ended. These have been properly prepared in accordance with the Companies Act, 1985.

Rosenthal & Rosenthal
Chartered Accountants

25 February 19–9

Rafael Private Co Ltd – Profit and loss account for the year ended 31 December 19–8

	19–8	*19–7*
	£	£
Turnover	458 227	553 586
Cost of sales	(313 377)	(369 800)
Gross profit	144 850	183 786
Distribution costs	38 000	42 094
Administrative expenses	118 400	131 606
	(156 400)	(173 700)
Operating loss/profit	(11 550)	10 086
Interest receivable and similar income	600	638
Interest payable and similar charges	(3 400)	(1 200)
(Loss)/profit (before taxation)	(14 350)	9 524
Tax on (loss)/profit on ordinary activities	3 500	(3 324)
Retained profits (after taxation)	(10 850)	6 200
Statement of retained profits		
At 1 January 19–7	36 760	30 560
Transfer to reserves	(10 850)	6 200
At 31 December 19–8	25 910	36 760

Rafael Private Co Ltd – Balance sheet at 31 December 19–8

	19–8	*19–7*
	£	£
FIXED ASSETS		
Tangible assets	45 762	35 270
CURRENT ASSETS		
Stocks	48 810	70 187
Debtors	102 462	88 651
Cash at bank and in hand	133	25 965
	151 405	184 803
CREDITORS: AMOUNTS FALLING DUE WITHIN ONE YEAR	(161 397)	179 701
Net current (liabilities)/assets	(9 992)	5 102

(continued)

(continued)

Total assets less		
current liabilities	35 770	40 372
CREDITORS FALLING DUE AFTER MORE		
THAN ONE YEAR	7 560	1 286
PROVISIONS FOR LIABILITIES		
AND CHARGES		
Deferred taxation	1 300	1 326
	(8 860)	(2 612)
	26 910	37 760
CAPITAL AND RESERVES		
Called-up share capital	1 000	1 000
Profit and loss account	25 910	36 760
	26 910	37 760

The financial statements were approved by the board of directors on 25 February 19–9.

27.13.3 Statutory books

These are the registers which by law a company must keep:

a) a register of members, that is, the company's shareholders. Their names, addresses and the type of shares they have as well as the transfer of shares from one person to another. For shareholders who have more than a 5 per cent shareholding, a separate register is used. A shareholder is obliged to inform the company if he has more than a 5 per cent holding.
b) A register of debenture holders, their names, addresses etc, as in the case of shareholders.
c) A register of charges, that is, the company borrowing money from its debenture holders or any other financial institution and the assets whereupon the borrowing has been secured.
d) A register of directors and company secretaries to indicate who they are.
e) A register of directors' interests, that is, the holding of shares or debentures they may have in the company.

27.13.4 The corporate report

Why does a business enterprise prepare financial statements? A business should produce information concerning its activities because different groups of people want to know a variety of information, primarily concerning the financial performance of the business. There may well be other areas of information which they may be interested in, such as future developments, customer service, staff satisfaction and the relationship of the company with that of its environment, that is, its social responsibility.

The corporate report is basically concerned with the company's financial activities. Shareholders will want to know how well their investment is doing. Is the company maximising profits? Is it financially secure? Will it continue to trade confidently in the future? Should the shareholder hang on to his stock or sell it?

Financial reports do not profess to tell the whole story, but at least there is an attempt to relate the financial facts to those parties who have an interest in their content. Various groups of people, such as shareholders, management, creditors and other providers of finance, the tax authorities and staff members, all have a right to know of the activities of a business enterprise. Is the business going in the right direction? Is its future looking bright or are there distinct clouds looming over the horizon?

A corporate report, prepared by the company's management, is primarily about the company's financial activities concerning past, current and forecasted figures. Corporate aims and objectives may not always be the same for every type of company, each corporate body chooses its own goals to achieve. However, the general consensus of most organisations is to:

a) Provide goods or services which are marketable and can reliably earn revenue for the enterprise.
b) Be efficient and productive, to eliminate waste in terms of labour, materials and capital. In other words, to maximise the resources of the enterprise as efficiently as possible.
c) As a consequence of a) and b) above, to maximise the profit potential of the business. To achieve greater profits in real terms each financial year (taking into account inflation), increasing the earnings per share of its shareholders and the return of profit on the company's capital employed. In the daily newspapers, when financial results are published by companies, they always emphasise, often by graphs or tables, the details of profit growth and earnings. For example:

   Sales up by 40 per cent
   Pre-tax profits up by 20 per cent
   Earnings per share up by 25 per cent
   Dividends up by 50 per cent.

   Thus a company will advertise its success for the year and hope to keep the confidence of its shareholders and also the market for its products or services.

   A company's profit may be described as *trading* or *operating* profit which refers to profits made from trading operations, excluding taxation and interest payments. *Pre-tax profits* refer to profit before taxation is provided for, but after the payment of interest (if any). *Profit after tax* is profit after taxation has been provided for and is the net income available to the enterprise which is available for distribution – some as dividends to shareholders and some as retained profits in the business.
d) Take care of its staff, that is, to provide opportunities for them to achieve their goals, good rates of pay, job satisfaction, employee participation, training, promotion, and generally motivating them to achieve their best for themselves and for the company.
e) Be aware of its social responsibilities in that an organisation not only has a duty to its shareholders and staff, but to the social community as a whole in terms of enterprise, jobs, careers, welfare, sports and the general well being of the environment.

Therefore, the corporate reports' aims and objectives are to ensure a good level of profit returns, growth of markets, employee satisfaction and also a degree of social responsibility to the community.

Summary

A limited company is an incorporated body and a separate legal entity from its owners, the shareholders. Ordinary shares make up the bulk of share capital and are known as 'equities'. Preference shares are not true shares because they do not carry voting rights like equities. The appropriation account indicates how profits are distributed after providing for taxation: a proportion may go as dividends and the remainder retained in reserves. The Companies Act regulates the activities of limited companies and lays down the guidelines for the preparation of accounts.

Questions

1 You work for the financial accountant of Compton Ltd, manufacturers of cosmetics, and are working on the annual accounts.

The following balances remain in the ledger of Compton Ltd after the preparation of the profit and loss account for the year ended 31 March 19–6.

	£
Stocks and work in progress	98 000
Debtors	87 000
Provision for bad debts	4 000
£1 ordinary shares [authorised £600 000]	400 000
10% preference shares of £1 each [authorised £200 000]	100 000
Creditors	74 000
Balance at bank	4 000
Accruals	3 500
Prepayment	2 500
General reserve account	14 000
Share premium account	20 000
Net profit for the year ended 31/3/–6	108 000
Profit and loss account balance 1/4/–5	22 000
Premises (at cost)	300 000
Plant and equipment (at cost)	310 000
Vehicles (at cost)	200 000

The directors propose the following:

i) To transfer £20 000 to general reserve.
ii) To propose an ordinary dividend of 12 per cent and to pay the preference dividend.
iii) To provide for corporation tax of £30 000, payable in October 19–7.

Depreciation of fixed assets has been calculated as follows:

i) Plant and equipment has a residual value of £30 000 and a 'life' estimated at ten years. It is five years old and depreciation is based on the straight-line method.
ii) The vehicles are valued at current market price of £84 000.
iii) There is no depreciation on premises.

REQUIRED:
A profit and loss appropriation account for the year ended 31 March 19–6 and a balance sheet as at that date. (27.6)

2 The following information relates to an electrical components manufacturing company, Hardcastle Co Ltd. Its cost of production (factory cost) is transferred to the cost of sales in the profit and loss statement. The figures are for the financial year end of 31 December 19–8:

	£	£
Turnover		327 000
Stock (1/1/)	58 750	
Cost of production	201 500	
Sales and distribution	44 800	
Administration expenses	38 700	
Interest charges	5 500	
Fixed assets (net)	135 100	
Debtors and creditors	76 750	89 400
Bank overdraft		10 800

Accruals		4 900
Prepayments	500	
Loans (15 years)		52 000
Issued and paid up ordinary shares (£1)		50 000
Share premium account		10 000
Reserves		17 500
	561 600	561 600

NOTES

As on 31 December 19–8:

1 Stock value £68 750.
2 A proposed dividend of 5p per share.
3 To provide £14 500 for corporation tax.
4 To transfer £25 000 to reserves.

REQUIRED:

Prepare the profit and loss account of the company for the period ending 31 December 19–8 and a balance sheet as on that date. Use Format 1 of the 1985 Act. (27.6–12)

(BTEC National)

3 You work as an assistant to the accountant for Jason Ltd which has an authorised capital of £500 000, divided into 800 000 ordinary shares of 50p each and 200 000 8 per cent preference shares of 50p each. The following balances remained in the accounts of the company after the trading and profit and loss accounts had been prepared for the year ended 30 November 19–6.

	Debit £	*Credit* £
General reserve		5 000
Ordinary share capital: fully paid		100 000
8% preference shares: fully paid		30 000
Premises at cost	140 000	
Light and heat owing		840
Profit and loss account balance (1/12/–5)		19 200
Bank		8 200
Debtors and creditors	5 800	1 120
Net profit (for year ended 30/11/–6)		40 600
Machinery and plant at cost	50 000	
Provision for depreciation on machinery and plant		25 000
Stock	33 340	
Insurance prepaid	820	
	229 960	229 960

Information as on 30 November 19–6

The directors of Jason Ltd have recommended:

1 A transfer of £10 400 to reserve.
2 An ordinary dividend of 12 per cent.
3 To provide payment of the year's preference dividend and also to provide for corporation tax of £10 000.

REQUIRED:

a) Prepare the profit and loss appropriation account for the year ended 30 November 19–6.

b) Prepare the balance sheet as at 30 November 19–6 showing clearly the shareholders' funds and the working capital. (27.6–10)

4 Hurley Ltd had a registered capital of £250 000, divided into 400 000 ordinary shares of 50p each and 100 000 8 per cent preference shares of 50p each. The following balances remained in the accounts of the company after the trading and profit and loss accounts had been prepared for the year ended 31 May 19–6.

	Debit £	*Credit* £
Ordinary share capital: fully paid		50 000
8% preference shares: fully paid		15 000
Premises at cost	65 000	
Light and heat		420
Profit and loss account balance (1/6/–5)		9 600
Bank		4 100
Debtors and creditors	2 900	560
Net profit (for year ended 31/5/–6)		10 300
Machinery and plant at cost	25 000	
Provision for depreciation on machinery and plant		15 000
Stock	11 670	
Insurance	410	
	104 980	104 980

The directors have recommended:

1 a transfer of £12 000 to general reserve;
2 an ordinary dividend of 12 per cent; and
3 to provide for payment of the year's preference dividend.

REQUIRED:

a) The profit and loss appropriation account for the year ended 31 May 19–6.
b) The balance sheet as at 31 May 19–6, in a form which shows clearly the shareholders' funds and the working capital.
c) An explanation of the term 'interim dividend' and two differences between an ordinary share and a preference share. (27.6–10)

(Associated Examining Board)

5 You work in the financial accounts department of the ABC Trading Co Ltd which is registered with an authorised capital of £2 000 000 divided into 800 000 10 per cent preference shares of £1 each and 1 200 000 ordinary shares of £1 each.

After completion of the trading and profit and loss account for the year ended 31 May 19–6 the following balances remain in the books:

	£000	*£000*
Preference share capital (fully paid)		500
Ordinary share capital (fully paid)		900
Profit and loss account balance brought forward		10
General reserve		50
Net profit for the year ended 31/5/–6		300
Premises (at cost)	1 250	
Delivery vans (at cost)	125	
Provision for depreciation of delivery vans		35
Fixtures and fittings (at cost)	60	
Provision for depreciation of fixtures and fittings		20

Cash in hand and at bank	314	
Trade debtors	27	
Provision for doubtful debts		1
Creditors		12
Stocks	50	
Payments in advance	2	
	1 828	1 828

The directors propose to pay the preference dividend, a dividend of 20 per cent to the ordinary shareholders and transfer £40 000 to general reserve, and to provide for taxation of £10 000.

REQUIRED:

a) Prepare the profit and loss appropriation account for the year ended 31 May 19–6.
b) Prepare the balance sheet as at 31 May 19–6.
c) State the amount of working capital.
d) State the total equity (or ordinary shareholders') funds. (27.6–10)

6 The accounts of Robertson & David Co Ltd were extracted from the books on 30 June 19–8:

Trial balance as on 30 June 19–8

	Dr £	*Cr* £
Issued and paid-up capital:		
160 000 ordinary shares @ £1		160 000
40 000 8% preference shares @ £2		80 000
P&L account (1/7/–7)		7 780
General reserve		25 000
7% debentures		40 000
Premises cost	287 910	
Motor vehicles (cost)	32 000	
Plant, equipment (cost)	16 880	
Provision for depreciation of motor vehicles		4 800
Stock (1/7/–7)	49 600	
Bank		11 752
Cash	1 558	
Purchases	535 600	
Sales		696 500
Returns	500	1 600
Wages	65 460	
Rates, water, insurance	3 600	
General expenses	22 536	
Preference dividend paid (31/12/–7)	3 200	
Debtors, creditors	63 380	53 944
Bad debts	2 150	
Provision for bad debts		3 120
Discount allowed	122	
	1 084 496	1 084 496

NOTES

Additional details as at 30 June 19–8:

a) Stock value £39 400.
b) Rates pre-paid £1000. Wages still outstanding £3360.
c) Invoice unpaid for general expenses £30.
d) Depreciation: motor vehicles 20 per cent on book valuation
   plant and equipment 25 per cent on cost.
e) Adjust the provision for bad debts to equal 5 per cent of debtors.
f) The Directors of the company propose a dividend of 10 per cent for ordinary shares. Preference shares to receive their final dividend.
g) No interest has been paid on the debentures.
h) A transfer of £4000 is to be made to general reserve.
i) A provision of £19 200 is to be made for taxation.

REQUIRED:

Prepare the trading, profit and loss appropriation accounts for the year ended 30 June 19–8, and a balance sheet as at that date. (27.6)

(Institute of Bankers)

7 The following balances, at 1 January 19–7, were taken from the books of Seaham plc, which had an authorised capital of 250 000 ordinary shares of £1 each and 100 000 9 per cent preference shares of £1 each:

issued share capital £100 000 in ordinary shares of £1 each, fully paid; premises £75 000; fittings and equipment £18 900; debtors £10 600; creditors £5300; stock £7861; balance at bank £8079; profit and loss account, credit balance £7640; proposed ordinary dividend for 1986, £7500.

During the month of January 19–7, some of the company's transactions were:

1 sold an item of equipment, book value £4600, for £5600 by cheque;
2 bought goods on credit £5000;
3 sold goods on credit £8000, which had been marked up by 33⅓ per cent on cost.

REQUIRED:

a) The balance sheet of Seaham plc at 31 January, assuming there were no other transactions in January, in a form which shows clearly the shareholders' funds and the working capital.

   Your balance sheet must include the three transactions occurring in January. Where a balance sheet figure has changed as a result of these transactions, you are advised to indicate the direction and amount of the change in brackets, next to the item concerned, within the balance sheet.

b) The main danger to a firm of:
   i) holding too little working capital;
   ii) holding too much working capital.

(Associated Examining Board)

8 The following balances appeared in the books of Carlos Ltd at 31 December:

	£
Premises	62 000
Equipment	18 000
Fittings	7 904
Gross profit (for year ended 31/12)	25 300
Authorised and issued capital (in ordinary shares of £1 each)	60 000
Directors' fees	4 000

10% debentures	30 000
Stock in trade	6 200
Debenture interest	1 500
Profit and loss account credit balance at 1/1	3 200
Cash at bank	18 070
Sundry expenses	5 816
Debtors	1 600
Creditors	5 110
Auditors' remuneration	1 620
Commission received	850
Discount allowed	250
Discount received	700
Profit on sale of motor van	1 800

The following additional information is also available:

equipment and fittings are to be depreciated by a total of £5000;
debenture interest for the final six months of the year remains outstanding;
£2000 is to be transferred to general reserve;
a dividend of 12 per cent has been proposed on the ordinary shares.

REQUIRED:

a) Preparation of a profit and loss account, including the appropriation section, for Carlos Ltd for the year ended 31 December.
b) Preparation of the liabilities section of the balance sheet of Carlos Ltd as at 31 December. This section should be set out to show clearly shareholders' funds, long-term and current liabilities.
c) An explanation of the meaning of the terms:
   i) 'limited liability';
   ii) 'authorised capital';
   iii) 'issued capital';
   iv) 'working capital';
   v) 'current assets'. (27.6–7)

(Associated Examining Board)

9 The following information relates to an electrical components manufacturing company, Arrowsmith Co Ltd. Its cost of production (factory cost) is transferred to the cost of sales in the profit and loss statement. The figures are for the financial year end of 31 December:

	£	£
Turnover		356 000
Stock (1/1)	62 000	
Cost of production	256 500	
Sales and distribution	28 100	
Administration expenses	44 400	
Interest charges	4 000	
Fixed assets (net)	156 500	
Debtors and creditors	84 200	86 500
Bank/cash	4 800	
Accruals		500
Prepayments	—	
Loans (15 years)		40 000
Issued and paid-up ordinary shares (£1)		100 000

Share premium account		20 000
Reserves		37 500
	640 500	640 500

NOTES

As on 31 December:

1 Stock value £84 000.
2 A proposed dividend of 9p per share.
3 To provide £15 500 for corporation tax.
4 To transfer £20 000 to reserves.

REQUIRED:

a) Prepare the profit and loss account of the company for the period ending 31 December and a balance sheet as on that date. Use Format 1 of the 1985 Act. These accounts are for *external* use.
b) Calculate the company's current ratio and comment briefly on its adequacy.

10 You are an assistant to the accountant at J P Davies plc, which has been in business for several years. The trial balance on 30 June 19–8 was as follows:

J P Davies plc –
Trial balance as on 30 June 19–8

	Debit £	*Credit* £
£1 preference shares (15%) (authorised £200 000)		100 000
£1 ordinary shares (authorised £500 000)		200 000
Revenue reserves		45 000
Debenture stock (12.5%), 19–5		100 000
Profit for year ending 30/6/–8 (before debenture interest)		80 000
Profit and loss balance (1/7/–7)		40 000
Stocks	200 000	
Premises	200 000	
Plant and machinery	180 000	
Vehicles	50 000	
Office equipment	90 000	
Provisions for depreciation:		
Premises		10 000
Plant and machinery		70 000
Vehicles		30 000
Office equipment		55 000
Debtors	220 000	
Creditors		190 000
Cash	500	
Provision for bad debts		11 000
Prepayments	9 500	
Accruals		21 000
Bank overdraft		5 500
Interim preference dividend paid	7 500	
	957 500	957 500

NOTES

1 A full year's debenture interest is still to be charged.
2 Corporation tax is to be provided for, payable in March 19–9, £20 000.
3 The final dividend on preference shares is to be provided for.
4 To propose an ordinary dividend of 20 per cent.
5 To transfer £25 000 to revenue reserves.

REQUIRED:

a) You are to draw up, in draft form, for the accountant of the company, the profit and loss appropriation account for the year ended 30 June 19–8 and a balance sheet as at that date. The accounts are for internal use but should follow Format 1 as per Companies Act 1985.
b) Your accountant has also asked you to prepare a brief memorandum, suitable for trainees in the office, explaining the importance of SSAP 2 when preparing accounting statements. You may use any examples from the accounting statements prepared in Task A to illustrate your answer.

(BTEC National)

11 ABC Limited has the following trial balance at 31 March 19–8

	Dr £	*Cr* £
Freehold land at cost	60 000	
Buildings at cost	50 000	
Plant and equipment at cost	120 000	
Motor vehicles at cost	32 000	
Provisions for depreciation:		
Buildings		20 000
Plant and equipment		74 000
Motor vehicles		16 800
Stock at 1 April 19–7	74 000	
Debtors and creditors	122 500	99 800
Cash at bank	3 500	
Sales (all on credit)		249 760
Purchases (all on credit)	134 630	
Returns	12 900	4 875
Discounts allowed and received	3 200	1 850
Administration expenses	22 150	
Selling and distribution expenses	6 900	
Ordinary shares of £1 each, fully paid		100 000
Profit and loss reserve		69 695
Suspense		5 000
	£641 780	£641 780

NOTES:

1 The balance on the suspense account represents the proceeds from the disposal of a motor van which had originally cost £14 000 and had a net book value of £6 000 on the date of disposal. The proceeds have been correctly entered in the bank account but no other entries have been made.
2 The closing stock of finished goods was valued at £124 875.
3 A review of the year-end ledger accounts shows that the following accruals and prepayments are required:

	Accruals	*Prepayments*
	£	£
Administration expenses	4 500	12 000
Selling and distribution expenses	5 300	8 000

4 Depreciation is to be provided in full on all assets held at the end of the year using the following rates:

Buildings	4% per annum on cost
Plant and equipment	20% per annum on cost
Motor vehicles	25% per annum reducing balance

5 The directors propose a dividend of five pence per ordinary share.

6 The company's liability to corporation tax on the profit for the year is estimated to be £15 000.

REQUIRED:

Prepare in vertical form,

a) the company's trading and profit and loss and appropriation account for the year ended 31 March 19–8

b) the company's balance sheet at 31 March 19–8

(Chartered Institute of Management Accounts)

12 In general accounting practice there is a distinction between reserves and provisions and also between accruals and creditors.

Define each of these terms and explain their effect on the preparation of final accounts.

(Chartered Association of Certified Accountants)

28 Cash flow statements

Objectives

On completing this chapter you should:

- recognise the significance of FRS 1
- understand the function of a cash flow statement
- recognise why it is included as part of a company's final accounts.

Context

Part 4 looked at how cash transactions are handled in a business.

28.1 Introduction

Historically, the balance sheet and the profit and loss account were always the most important financial statements of a business organisation. However, during the late 1960s and the early 1970s, it was considered necessary by the Accounting Standards Committee (ASC) representing the accounting profession, to try and highlight a business's cash flow position and they produced SSAP 10, *The Statement for Sources and Application of Funds*, in 1975. SSAPs are discussed in greater detail in Chapter 33.

SSAP 10 attempted to indicate where the sources of funds (profits, issues of shares or loans, etc) came from and where the funds went (purchase of fixed assets, payment for tax and dividends, etc). It was a link between the profit and loss account and the balance sheet and attempted to explain the movement of resources and the effect these had on the working capital of a business.

In August 1990, the ASC was taken over by a new independent body responsible for setting standards, the Accounting Standards Board (ASB). In the September of 1991 they produced their first statement, Financial Reporting Standard No. 1 (FRS 1), the cash flow statement, replacing SSAP 10, which has now become obsolete.

The major purpose of FRS 1 is basically the same as the old funds flow statement and that is to emphasise a business's inflow and outflow of cash during the financial year. The cash flow statement is described as the **link** between

a) two balance sheets in the financial period, that is, one at the beginning of the year and one at the end; and
b) the profit and loss account for the year,

which is basically the same purpose of the previous funds flow statement.

The cash flow statement is prepared under five separate sections which are:

1 Net cash inflow/outflow from operating activities:
 a) Net profit on normal trading activities (before taxation)
 b) Non-cash flow expenses (depreciation)
 c) Adjustments in movements in working capital.

2 Returns on investments and servicing of finance:
 a) Interest received

b) Interest paid
c) Dividends paid.

3 Taxation

4 Investing activities:
a) Purchases of tangible fixed assets/investments
b) Sales of tangible fixed assets/investments.

5 Financing activities:
a) Issuing shares/debentures.
b) Redemption of shares/debentures.
c) Repayment of loans

From these headings, the statement should then balance off in relation to the increase or decrease in the **cash/bank** for the period. Interested parties such as owners, managers, shareholders, etc should be able to see the major inflows and outflows of funds through the financial year. Questions which could be raised are, for example:

- Is enough cash being raised to finance the business's spending?
- Were profits sufficient to pay for tax, interest and dividends?
- How did the large overdraft occur in the bank?
- Why was so much spent on fixed assets when funds looked short?

Example

Duran Ltd – Balance sheet as at 31 December

	19–4		*19–5*	
	£	£	£	£
FIXED ASSETS				
Cost	60 000		100 000	
Less cumulative depreciation	20 000		34 000	
		40 000		66 000
Investments at cost		40 000		20 000
		80 000		86 000
CURRENT ASSETS				
Stock	40 000		120 000	
Debtors	44 000		96 000	
Bank	2 000		6 000	
	86 000		222 000	

(continued)

(continued)

CURRENT LIABILITIES				
Tax owing	12 000		28 000	
Dividend owing	8 000		10 000	
Creditors	14 000		20 000	
	34 000	52 000	58 000	164 000
		132 000		250 000
LONG TERM LOANS		20 000		28 000
		112 000		222 000
FINANCED BY:				
Ordinary shares		80 000		100 000
Share premium account		–		20 000
Profit/loss account balance		32 000		102 000
		112 000		222 000

Duran Ltd – abbreviated profit and loss accounts for year ended 31 December

	19–5
	£
Sales	1 500 000
Cost of sales	(1 200 000)
Gross profit	300 000
Total expenses (inc. depn)	(196 500)
Operating profit for year	103 500
Add profit on sale of investments	8 000
Less interest payable	(3 500)
	108 000
Less tax provision	(28 000)
	80 000
Net profit before tax	
Add retained profits	32 000
	112 000
Less proposed ordinary dividend	(10 000)
Retained profits c/f	102 000

NOTE: No fixed assets were disposed of during the year.

REQUIRED:
Prepare a cash flow (FRS 1) Statement for the year ended 31 December, 19–5.

SOLUTION:

Duran Ltd – Cash flow statement for the year ended 31 December

		£	£
1	Net cash inflow/outflow from operating activities*		(8 500)
2	Returns on investments and Servicing of finance		
	Interest received	0	
	Interest paid	(3 500)	
	Dividends paid	(8 000)	
	Net cash outflow from returns on investments and servicing		(11 500)
3	Taxation		(12 000)
4	Investing activities		
	Purchases of tangible fixed assets	(40 000)	
	Sale of tangible fixed assets	28 000	
	Net cash outflow from investing activities		(12 000)
	Net cash outflow before financing		(44 000)
5	Financing activities		
	Issue of shares	20 000	
	Share premium account	20 000	
	New loan	8 000	
	Net cash inflow from financing		48 000
	Net increase in cash and cash equivalents		4 000

*Calculation of No. 1:

Operating profit	103 500	
+Depreciation charges	14 000	
Working capital:		
+ stock	(80 000)	
+ debtors	(52 000)	
+ creditors	6 000	(8 500)

NOTES

1 The net increase in cash £4 000, corresponds with the balance sheet increase (2 000–6 000) under the bank figures.

2 The movements in working capital indicate that increased spending on current assets is an outflow of cash, reductions would be an inflow. Increase in creditors would increase the inflow of cash, a reduction in creditors would decrease it.

3 Outflows of funds are in brackets, indicating deductions – payment for interest, tax, dividends and fixed assets.

4 Inflows of funds for Duran come from the issuing of shares and an increase in the loan.

Other key facts

a) Dividends and taxation paid. Because these are provided for in one period and actually paid in the next, it is the previous year's figures, (in Duran Ltd 19–4) which will be entered in Section 2, Returns on investments and servicing of finance.

b) Fixed assets. When fixed assets are purchased and entered in Section 4, Investing activities, we need to know how much they cost, therefore the difference between the two periods is taken (£60 000 to £100 000, indicating £40 000 cost of new assets acquired.
If the assets were given at their net values (that is, after depreciation has been deducted), you must remember to add on any depreciation charges in order to arrive at the cost of purchase. The net asset value of the two periods (£40 000 to £66 000) indicates an increase of £26 000, add depreciation charges of £14 000 = £40 000 cost of fixed assets.

c) Disposal of fixed assets. In the event that some fixed assets are disposed of during the financial period, any gain or loss in their disposal is not recorded as part of the inflow of cash in Section 1. The actual sum received for the sale of the fixed assets is recorded in Section 4, Investing activities (sale of tangible assets). £20 000 of the investments had been sold off (£40 000 down to £20 000) under fixed assets and the profit and loss account stated a profit of £8 000, therefore the assumption being that the actual sale of investments brought an inflow of cash of £28 000.

d) Reserves and profit and loss balances. These figures only represent internal transfers of funds and therefore play no part in the entry of figures in the cash flow statement. Ignore them.

28.2 Cash flow and profits

The survival of any business does not just depend upon how much profit is made. The significant question is: can it meet its financial commitments? By this we include both capital and revenue expenditure and also repayments of loans or debentures on top of the interest payments charged. Therefore a company's performance is led by its ability to pay off its debts. That is why a business tries to forecast its liquidity position as can be seen in Chapter 37 'Budgets'.

A cash flow statement however, can assist users to:

a) assess the business's ability to generate positive net cash flows in the future:
b) assess its ability to meet its financial commitments;
c) assess possible reasons for differences between the reported profit and cash flows;
d) assess the effect on its finances from its main transactions in the year such as the purchase of fixed assets.

The cash flow statement should show changes in cash inflows and outflows rather than just changes in a company's working capital. Note that any non-cash transactions such as financing fixed assets through leasing, should be reported separately.

It is important to distinquish between a cash flow statement showing the sources and uses of cash over a period of time, in contrast to a cash budget showing expected sources and uses of cash ahead of time. Both these assist management in their decision making.

Example of cash flow statement taken from accounting records:
Flail Ltd commenced trading on 1 January with a medium-term loan of £21 000 and a share issue which raised £35 000. The company purchased fixed assets for £21 000 cash, and during the year to 31 December entered into the following transactions.

a) Purchases from suppliers were £19 500 of which £2 550 was unpaid at the year end.
b) Wages and salaries amounted to £10 500 of which £750 was unpaid at the year end.
c) Interest on the loan of £2 100 was fully paid in the year and a repayment of £5 250 was made.
d) Sales turnover was £29 400 including £900 debtors at the year end.
e) Interest on cash deposits at the bank amounted to £75.
f) A dividend of £4 000 was proposed as at 31 December.

REQUIRED:
Prepare a cash flow statement for the year ended 31 December 19–8.

SOLUTION:

Flail Ltd –
Statement of cash flows for the year ended 31 December 19–8

	£	£
1 OPERATING ACTIVITIES		
Cash received from customers (£29 400 – £900)	28 500	
Cash paid to suppliers (£19 500 – £2 550)	(16 950)	
Cash paid to and on behalf of employees (£10 500 – £750)	(9 750)	
2 Interest paid	(2 100)	
Interest received	75	
		(225)
4 INVESTING ACTIVITIES		
Purchase of fixed assets	(21 000)	
5 FINANCING ACTIVITIES		(21 000)
Issue of shares	35 000	
Proceeds from medium-term loan	21 000	
Repayment of medium-term loan	(5 250)	
Cash flow from financing activities		50 750
Net increase in cash and cash equivalents		29 525

NOTES:
The dividend is only proposed and so there is no related cash flow in No. 2.

There is no taxation paid, therefore there is no No. 3.

28.3 Deriving the figures for a cash flow statement

In studying the example of Flail Ltd, you may have wondered how in practice the figures would have been derived. For example, how do we know that the figure of purchases from suppliers was £19 500, and that £2 550 of this was unpaid at the year end? This kind of detailed information would not be disclosed in the company's published accounts. The answer is that such figures could only be derived from the accounting records. Two methods of preparing a cash flow statement, therefore, may be obtained from accounting records (direct method) or from a set of published accounts (indirect method), the most common being the latter. A simple example below reveals that the results should be the same.

Direct:

	£
Cash received from customers	12 000
Cash paid to suppliers	(8 000)
Cash paid to and on behalf of employees	(2, 300)
Other cash payments	(630)
Net increase in cash	(970)

Indirect:

	£
Operating profit	3 500
Depreciation	470
Increase in stocks	(2 800)
Decrease in debtors	1 000
Decrease in creditors	(1 200)
Net increase in cash	(970)

Summary

The cash flow statement is a link between the profit and loss account and the balance sheet at the beginning and end of a financial period. Its purpose is to focus attention on incoming funds matched against outgoing funds, the result being either an increase or decrease in the bank account. From this, a company could assess if enough money had been generated to finance its spending and whether it had sufficient liquidity to pay off its debts. Was sufficient profits made to finance its activities?

Questions

1 The final accounts of Wexford & Co Ltd for the year ended 31 December 19–8 were as follows:

Balance sheet as at 31 December

	19–7	*19–8*
	£	£
FIXED ASSETS (COST)	16 600	21 000
Depreciation	1 020	1 600
	15 580	19 400
CURRENT ASSETS		
Stock	1 950	3 555
Debtors	2 140	3 000
Bank	1 750	2 170
	5 840	8 725
CURRENT LIABILITIES		
Creditors	400	2 095
Provision for tax	160	400
Provision for dividends	30	50
	590	2 545
Net current assets	5 250	6 180
Capital employed	20 830	25 580
LONG-TERM LIABILITIES		
Bank loan	600	5 000
	20 230	20 580
FINANCED BY		
Issued and paid-up capital	20 000	20 000
P&L balance	230	580
	20 230	20 580

Profit and loss statement, year ended 31 December 19–8

	£	£
Net profit		800
(after charging depreciation £580)		
P&L balance (1/1)		230
		1 030
Provisions for: tax	400	
dividends	50	450
P&L balance (31/12)		580

REQUIRED:
A cash flow statement for the year ended 3' December 19–8.

2

Rock Ltd – Cash flow statement year ended 31 December

	19–8	19–7
	£	£
Balance sheet		
Fixed assets (cost)	9 000	2 500
Depreciation	1 000	800
	8 000	1 700
CURRENT ASSETS:		
Stock	2 500	2 000
Debtors	1 000	800
Bank		500
Cash		50
	3 500	3 350
CURRENT LIABILITIES:		
Creditors	1 000	700
Bank (overdraft)	250	
Tax provision	350	250
Dividends provision		100
	1 600	1 050
Working capital	1 900	2 300
Capital employed	9 900	4 000
– Loan capital	(5 450)	
	4 450	4 000
FINANCED BY:		
Issued and paid-up capital	3 000	2 800
P&L balance (31/12)	1 450	1 200
	4 450	4 000

Profit and loss account, year ended 31 December 19–8

	£
Net trading profit (after £200 depreciation charges)	600
Provision for tax	350
	250
+ P&L balance (1/1)	1 200
P&L balance (31/12)	1 450

REQUIRED:
Prepare a cash flow statement for Rock Ltd for the year ended 31 December 19–8.
(Institute of Bankers)

3 The following information refers to the accounts of P Jackson & Co Ltd. Prepare a cash flow statement for year ended 31 December 19–8.

		19–7	*19–8*
		£	£
ASSETS			
Premises (cost)		35 000	45 000
Machinery*		20 000	21 500
Stock		15 000	20 580
Debtors		8 450	12 375
Bank/cash		2 255	1 835
		80 705	101 290
LIABILITIES			
Creditors		10 150	12 755
Accruals		1 125	955
Taxation due		5 100	6 530
		16 375	20 240
CAPITAL			
Issued @ £1 ordinary shares		50 000	60 000
P&L account		14 330	21 050
		64 330	81 050
MACHINERY*			
		Cost	*Depreciation*
Net			
		£	£
£			
Balance (31/12/19–7)	25 000	5 000	20 000
Additions 19–8	6 000		
	31 000		
Sale of old stock	(3 000)	(2 000)	
Depreciation 19–8		3 500	
Balance (31/12/19–8)	28 000	6 500	21 500

Profit and loss account year ended 31 December 19–8

	£
Net trading profit	12 750
+ Gain on sale of machinery	500
	13 250
Corporation tax	6 530
Retained to P&L account	6 720

NOTE
Any gain or loss on the sale of a fixed asset is *not* included in the net profit although the actual sum received *is* included.

(Institute of Bankers)

4 You work in the accounts department of Maxpax Ltd and are assisting in the preparation of the annual accounts. The summarised balance sheets of Maxpax Ltd at 31 May are as follows:

	19–7		19–8	
	£	£	£	£
FIXED ASSETS				
Premises		100 000		100 000
Plant at cost	80 000		120 000	
Less cumulative depreciation	(48 000)	32 000	(60 000)	60 000
		132 000		160 000
CURRENT ASSETS				
Stocks	24 000		50 000	
Debtors	16 000		12 000	
Bank	8 000		14 000	
	48 000		76 000	
CURRENT LIABILITIES				
Creditors	14 000		17 000	
Proposed taxation	14 000		15 000	
Proposed dividends	16 000		8 000	
	44 000	4 000	40 000	36 000
		136 000		196 000
FINANCED BY:				
£1 ordinary shares		100 000		140 000
Shares premium account		24 000		40 000
P&L account		12 000		16 000
		136 000		196 000

NOTES

1 There have been no asset disposals during the year ended 31 May.

2 An interim dividend for the year of £10 000 has been paid in December 19–7.

REQUIRED:

a) Calculate the net profit for the year ending 31 May 19–8. Note: you will need to reconstruct the P&L appropriation account.

b) Prepare a cash flow statement for the year ended 31 May 19–8.

(BTEC National)

5 You work for a small limited company and are assisting in the preparation of the annual accounts for the year ending 30/5/19–8. The details are as follows:

Aspen Ltd balance sheet as at 30 May, 19–8

	19–7			19–8		
	£	£	£	£	£	£
Fixed assets at cost		173 000			243 400	
Less depreciation		57 800	115 200		78 100	165 300

(continued)

(continued)

CURRENT ASSETS						
Stock		74 400			72 080	
Debtors		97 920			100 020	
Bank		10 880			—	
		183 200			172 100	
CURRENT LIABILITIES						
Creditors	41 440			37 080		
Overdraft	—			2 320		
Provision for tax	17 120			12 400		
Proposed dividend	10 000	68 560	114 640	12 000	63 800	108 300
			229 840			273 600
FINANCED BY:						
£1 ordinary shares			200 000			220 000
Reserves			29 840			53 600
			229 840			273 600

Aspen Ltd profit and loss account for year ended 30/5/19–8

	£
Profit for the year	48 160
Provision for tax	12 400
	35 760
Undistributed profits from last year	29 840
	65 600
Proposed dividend	12 000
Undistributed profits carried to next year	53 600

REQUIRED:

a) Prepare the cash flow statement of Aspen Ltd for the year ended 30/5/19–8.
b) Compute the current ratio for both years.
c) Compute the return on capital employed for the year ended 30/5/19–8.

(Institute of Commercial Management)

6 As an assistant to the financial accountant you have been asked to assist in the preparation of the following company's figures relating to cash flow:

The balance sheets of John Francis Enterprises Ltd as on 31/3/19–8

	19–7	*19–8*
	£	£
*Fixed assets (net)	86 000	94 400
Stocks and work-in-progress	32 800	35 600
Debtors	27 200	32 000
Bank	4 000	—
	150 000	162 000
Creditors	24 000	26 000
Provision for tax	12 000	8 000
Bank —	2 000	
	36 000	36 000
Loan (5 years)	4 000	3 000
	110 000	123 000
Issued and paid-up capital	60 000	70 000
P&L balance	50 000	53 000
	110 000	123 000

NOTE:
*Fixed asset movements to 31 March 19–8.

	Cost	*Depreciation*	*Net value*
	£	£	£
Balance (31/3/19–7)	110 000	24 000	86 000
Additions during the year	20 000		
Depreciation provided during the year		8 000	
	130 000	32 000	
Disposals during the year	8 000	4 400	
Balance (31/3/19–8)	122 000	27 600	94 400

The profit and loss statement summary for 31 March 19–8

	£
Operating profit	10 400
+ Gain on fixed asset sale	600
	11 000
Taxation provision	8 000
Retained profits	3 000

REQUIRED:

a) Draw up a statement of sources and application of funds for the year ended 31 March 19–8.
b) Calculate the current ratios for each year.
c) From the figures you have prepared, write a brief report to the client with your assessment of working capital position on 31 March 19–7 and 31 March 19–8.

(BTEC National)

7 You work in the accounts office of XYZ Ltd and the accountant has provided you with the following information at the end of the financial period, 31 March 19–8.

Balance sheets of XYZ Ltd at 31 March 19–8

	19–7	19–8		19–7	19–8
	£	£		£	£
Freehold property			Issued share capital	30 000	30 000
at cost	25 000	25 000	Profit and loss account	27 000	33 000
Equipment (see note)	18 000	22 200	Corporation tax due:		
Stock in trade	16 400	17 800	1 January 19–7	6 000	–
Debtors	13 600	14 000	1 January 19–8	–	4 000
Bank	2 000	1 000	Creditors	12 000	13 000
	75 000	80 000		75 000	80 000

NOTE:
Equipment movements during the year ended 31 March 19–8 were:

	Cost	*Depreciation*	*Net*
	£	£	£
Balance at 31 March 19–7	30 000	12 000	18 000
Additions during year	9 000		
Depreciation provided during year		3 800	
	39 000	15 800	
Disposals during year	4 000	3 000	
Balance at 31 March 19–8	35 000	12 800	22 200

The company's summarised profit calculation for the year ended 31 March 19–8, revealed:

	19–7	*19–8*
	£	£
Sales	95 000	100 000
Gain on sale equipment		2 500
Less		102 500
Cost of sales and other expenses	84 800	92 500
Net profit	10 200	10 000
Corporation tax on profits of the year	6 000	4 000
Retained profit of the year (after tax)	4 200	6 000

REQUIRED:

a) From the information given above prepare a cash flow statement for the year ended 31 March 19–8.

b) What is the purpose of preparing such a statement. Give a brief answer only.

29 Accounting for clubs and societies

Objectives

On completing this section you should:

- recognise the type of accounts prepared for clubs or societies
- understand that the same principles of accounting apply.

29.1 Introduction

In every town and village, there is virtually always some sort of social organisation, either a club or society, which has been set up for a specific purpose. It may be a sports club, to run cricket, football, netball or tennis, or an amateur society to put on dramas or operatic events. These organisations are not normally profit motivated and are run for the benefit and enjoyment of their members.

The finance required to run these social clubs comes from the annual subscriptions paid by their members. Other sources of finance may come from fund raising activities or donations from sponsors. Finance is needed to pay for the running expenses and upkeep of the club including any new equipment.

A club treasurer is normally appointed by the members to take charge of their finances. All monies coming in and going out should be controlled and properly accounted for to safeguard the interests of the members. It is therefore necessary for the treasurer to keep basic records of the receipts and payment of monies and to take charge of the club's bank account.

29.2 Accounting reports

It would be rare to find a full accounting system operating ledgers and trial balance in a club or society. The treasurer may not have the time or expertise to record the accounts in a formalised way. However, the position demands that a reasonably tight control of cash and other resources ought to be made and that at committee meetings, the treasurer would be expected to advise members of the club's financial position.

The treasurer is expected to produce some form of financial reporting to the members at the end of the club's social year. These usually consist of:

- the **receipts and payments account**
- the **income and expenditure account**
- the **balance sheet**.

29.2.1 The receipts and payments account

This statement is the equivalent of a simple cash book. It is a summary of all the receipts and payments of the club for the year. Its purpose is to show the club's members where the cash has come from and where it has gone and the balance in hand at the year-end.

29.2.2 The income and expenditure account

This statement is the equivalent of a business's trading and profit and loss account. The principles of the matching of revenue with expenses, including adjustments, apply exactly in the same way. It will not be unusual therefore to find accruals, prepayments and depreciation in this account. A club does not usually use the words 'profit' or 'loss' to indicate the difference between revenue and expenses. The adopted wording is '*surplus or deficit*'.

Some clubs operate a bar or refreshment counter for the use and benefit of their members and visitors and the treasurer can prepare a special *bar account* to indicate whether it has made either a surplus or deficit in the social year.

29.2.3 The balance sheet

This statement is prepared in the same way as any other type of organisation. The capital of the club is generally known as its *accumulated funds*, representing its assets less liabilities. Any surplus or deficit from the income and expenditure account is transferred to this account.

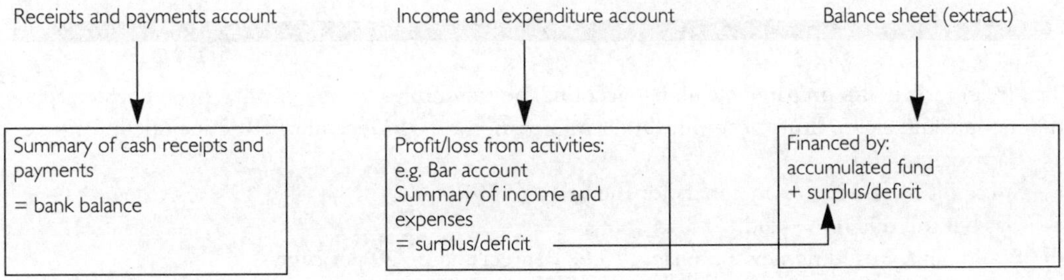

NOTES
1 The bank balance is transferred to the balance sheet as either a current asset or current liability
2 The profit/loss from the bar or other accounts is transferred to either income or expenditure
3 Income would include subscriptions from members
4 The accumulated fund is the capital account of the club/society.

Fig. 29.1 Final accounts of clubs and societies

Example
Broadstone Bowls Club begins its financial year on 1 January. Its accumulated funds on 1 January 19–8 were £29 200:

Assets	£	Liabilities	£
Club house	25 000	Creditors	500
Bank account	2 300	(bar)	
Stock (bar)	800		
Equipment	1 600		
	29 700		

The treasurer at the financial year end, 31 December 19–8, prepared the receipts and payments account for the year, for the benefit of the members as follows:

Broadstone Bowls Club –
Receipts and payments account year ended
31 December 19–8

	Receipts	£		*Payments*	£
1/1	Balance (bank)	2 300		Equipment	900
	Members' subscriptions	1 500		Hire of courts	280
	Subscriptions in advance	50		Hire of halls	1 000
	Bar sales	2 185		Light and heat	135
	Dances	425		General expenses	255
	Donations	150		Bar purchases	1 160
	Tournament fees	270		Club house extension	1 850
			31/12	Balance (Bank)	1 300
		6 880			6 880
	Balance (bank)	1 300			

The treasurer has also prepared a club bar account and the surplus for the year has been transferred to the income and expenditure account. Other information on 31 December 19–8 included:

a) Bar stock, £290.
b) Subscriptions owing by members for the year, £150.
c) Gas bill still due to be paid, £85.
d) Equipment, including new purchases, to be depreciated by 20 per cent.
e) Bar purchases still to be paid, £350.

Broadstone Bowls Club –
Bar Account, year ended 31 December 19–8

	£	£
Sales		2 185
– Cost of sales:		
Stock (1/1)	800	
+ Purchases	1 160	
	1 960	
– Creditors due (1/1)	500	
	1 460	
+ Creditors due (31/12)	350	
	1 810	
– Stock (31/12)	290	1 520
Bar account surplus for year (Transferred to income side of income and expenditure account)		665

NOTE
Creditors due on 1 January (accrual) is deducted from cost of sales because the expense related to last year's bar account. The creditors due on 31 December for bar stock is added as an accrual in the normal way.

**Broadstone Bowls Club –
Income and expenditure account year ended
31 December 19–8**

Expenditure		£	*Income*	£
Hire of courts		280	Subscriptions	1 500
Hire of halls		1 000	Subscriptions owing	150
Light and heat	135		Bar surplus	665
+ Accrued	85	220	Dance receipts	425
General expenses		255	Donations	150
Deprecation of equipment		500	Tournament fees	270
Surplus		905		
(income – expenditure)		3 160		3 160

NOTES
1 The Surplus of £905 is transferred to the accumulated funds (in the balance sheet).
2 Subscriptions owing from members is revenue accrued, which belongs to the current financial year and is added to income.
3 Subscriptions in advance £50, in the receipts and payments account are not included because they belong to the next accounting period, 19–9.

**Broadstone Bowls Club –
Balance sheet year ended
31 December 19–8**

	£ *Cost*	£ *Depreciation*	£ *Net*
FIXED ASSETS			
Club house	25 000		
+ Extension	1 850		26 850
Equipment	1 600		
+ New purchases	900	500	2 000
			28 850
CURRENT ASSETS			
Bar stock	290		
Subscriptions owing	150		
Bank	1 300	1 740	

(continued)

(continued)

– CURRENT LIABILITIES			
Subscriptions in advance	50		
Accruals (350 + 85)	435	485	
Working capital			1 255
			30 105
ACCUMULATED FUNDS			
Balance (1/1)	29 200		
+ Surplus	905		30 105

Example (Institute of Bankers)
The following information has been submitted by the Corfe Mullen Social Club, for the year ended 31 March 19–8:

Corfe Mullen Social Club –
Receipts and payments account, year ended
31 March 19–8

Receipts		£	*Payments*		£
1/4/–7	Balance (bank)	2 000		Insurance, rates	480
	Subscriptions	5 575		Wages	5 650
	Surplus (bingo)	850		Bar purchases	6 500
	Bar takings	10 225		General expenses	275
				Light and heat	480
				New furniture	500
				Club repairs, maintenance	1 275
			31/3/–8	Balance (bank)	3 490
		18 650			18 650

Other information:

1/4/–7	£	*31/3/–8*	£
Club premises at cost	25 000	Bar stock	850
Furniture and equipment	2 000	Subscriptions: in arrears	480
Bar stock	1 600	in advance	50
Bank balance (as above)	2 000	Furniture and equipment	
Subscriptions: in arrears	150	valued	1 950
in advance	100	Bar purchases owing	500
Insurance prepaid	80	Insurance prepaid	35
Light and heat owing	130	Light and heat owing	50

REQUIRED:

a) The club's bar account for the period ended 31 March 19–8.
b) The club's income and expenditure account for the same period.
c) The club's balance sheet as at 31 March 19–8.

a)

Corfe Mullen Social Club – Bar account, year ended 31 March 19–8

	£	£
Sales		10 225
– Cost of sales:		
Stock (1/4/–7)	1 600	
+ Purchases	6 500	
	8 100	
+ Purchases due	500	
	8 600	
– Stock (31/3/–8)	850	7 750
Surplus t/f to income and expenditure account		2 475

b)

Corfe Mullen Social Club – Income and expenditure account, year ended 31 March 19–8>

Expenditure	£	£	*Income*	£	£
Insurance and rates	480		Surplus from bar		2 475
+ Prepaid (1/4/–7)	80		Surplus from bingo		850
	560		Subscriptions	5 575	
– Prepaid (31/3/–8)	35	525	+ In advance (1/4/–7)	100	
Wages		5 650		5 675	
Light and heat	480		– In arrears (1/4/–7)	150	
– Owing (1/4/–7)	130			5 525	
	350		+ In arrears (31/3/–8)	480	
+ Owing (31/3/–8)	50	400		6 005	
General expenses		275	– In advance (31/3/–8)	50	5 955
Maintenance and repairs		1 275			
Depreciation of furniture and equipment		550			
Surplus t/f to accumulated fund		605			
		9 280			9 280

c)

Corfe Mullen Social Club – Balance sheet as at 31 March 19–8

	£	£		£	£
FIXED ASSETS			Accumulated fund		
Premises	25 000		(1/4/–7)	30 600	
Furniture and equipment	1 950	26 950	+ Surplus	605	31 205
			Stock creditors	500	
CURRENT ASSETS			Light and heat (accrual)	50	
Stock (bar)	850		Subscriptions (advance)	50	600
Subscriptions (arrear)	480				
Bank	3 490				
Insurance (prepaid)	35	4 855			
		31 805			31 805

NOTES

1 The Accumulated fund on 1 April 19–7 was calculated as:

	Assets	–	*Liabilities*
	£		£
Premises	25 000		
Furniture and equipment	2 000		
Bar stock	1 600		
Bank account	2 000		
Subscriptions: arrears	150		
advance			100
Insurance (prepaid)	80		
Light and heat (owing)			130
	30 830	–	230

Accumulated fund was £30 830–£230 = £30 600.

2 Adjustments at the beginning of the accounting year as well as at the end.
When accruals and prepayments appear at the beginning of an accounting year (1 April 19–7) they are treated in the reverse way as to how they are treated at the end (31 March 19–8). Therefore:

	1/4/–7	*31/3/–8*
Accrued expenses	deducted	added
Prepaid expenses	added	deducted
Subscriptions: arrears	deducted	added
advance	added	deducted

3 The balance sheet has been presented in the horizontal format with assets on the left and capital and liabilities on the right.

Summary

Clubs and societies are set up for the benefit of their members and are usually non-profit motivated. Accounting records tend to be informal and prepared by the club's treasurer whose task is to look after the finances and at least prepare a bank summary for the year. The same principles of accounting apply and revenue and expenses should be matched correctly in relation to the accounting period, therefore adjustments are made in the normal way.

Questions

1 From the following receipts and payments account of the Mid-Town Golf Club and the further particulars provided below prepare an income and expenditure account for the year ended 31 March 19–6 and a balance sheet as at that date.

Receipts and payments account for the year ended 31 March 19–6

Receipts	£	*Payments*	£
Balance from last year	640	Wages	1 080
Entrance fees	400	Payment for new lockers	140
Subscriptions:		Printing and stationery	145
Current year	820	Postages	135
In advance	40	Lighting and heating	280
Profits from refreshments	165	Insurances	140
Locker rents	75	Balance c/d	280
Interest on deposit account	60		
	2 200		2 200
Balance b/d	280		

Additional information

i) £50 is owing for subscriptions for the year, to March 19–6.
ii) £15 is owing by members for locker rents.
iii) Printing and stationery, value £28, is still unpaid.
iv) £1000 is on deposit at the bank, from 1 April 19–5.
v) The club house and equipment appear in the books on 1 April 19–5 at a value of £10 000. (29.2)

(Royal Society of Arts)

2 The following statement has been submitted to you by the Keyworth Bowls Club whose financial year ended on 31 March 19–8.

Receipts and payments account

	£		£
Balance b/f	2 000	Rent and rates	460
Subscriptions	5 600	Wages	2 650
Profit from dances	825	Light and heat	240
Bar takings	10 200	Bar purchase	6 400
		Sundry expenses	185
		New furniture	200
		Club maintenance	270
		Balance c/f	8 220
	18 625		18 625

You are asked to prepare an income and expenditure account for the year under review and a balance sheet at 31 March 19–8. Your enquiries produce the information:

i) £400 subscriptions are still in arrear.
ii) £60 of the rent is in advance.
iii) At the end of the previous year the furniture and equipment was valued at £2000. £400 of this amount is to be written off.
iv) The bar stock was valued: on 1 April 19–7 at £600; on 31 March 19–8 at £800.
v) £600 was owed for bar purchases.
vi) Of the subscriptions received, £80 were for the 1 April 19–8 season. (29.2)

(Royal Society of Arts)

3 The following were the assets and liabilities of the Fitorama Sports Club on 1 July 19–3:

	£
ASSETS	
Premises at cost	28 000
Fittings and equipment	4 200
Deposit in building society	2 700
Cash and bank balance	2 027
LIABILITIES	
Electricity bill outstanding	168

The club's cash book for the year to 30 June 19–4 showed the following:

Receipts	£	*Payments*	£
Balance b/f	2 027	Rates	1 250
Subscriptions for year	4 870	Groundsman	2 200
Competition entry fees	2 700	Purchase of sports equipment	1 650
Sale of dance tickets	450	League entry fee	20
		Dance expenses	300
		Prizes for competitions	3 050
		Electricity	740
		Balance c/f	837
	10 047		10 047

REQUIRED:

a) Calculate the accumulated fund at 1 July 19–3.

b) Prepare the club's income and expenditure account for the year ended 30 June 19–4, and a balance sheet on that date after taking into account the following points:
   i) An electricity account of £194 was outstanding at the end of the year.
   ii) The amount paid for rates included £200 paid in advance.
   iii) During the year interest of £107 had been received from the building society. The inter est has been reinvested in the society. (29.2)

(Royal Society of Arts)

4 On 1 November 19–4 The Kingsley Bowling Club had the following assets and liabilities.

ASSETS	£
Club house	12 500
Fixtures and fittings	1 750
Sports equipment	340
Bank and cash	1 195
LIABILITIES	
Sundry creditors	235

During the year ending 31 October 19–5 the following amounts were received and paid.

Receipts	£	*Payments*	£
Subscriptions	760	Postage and stationery	175
Sales of refreshments	1 575	Groundsman's wages	550
Dance tickets	240	Purchase of refreshments	960
Competition fees	375	Repairs to equipment	100
		Sundry creditors	100
		Purchase of lawn mower	140
		General expenses	150
		Competition expenses	360

REQUIRED:
a) Calculate the accumulated fund as at 1 November 19–4.
b) Prepare the club's receipts and payments account for the year ending 31 October 19–5.
c) Prepare the club's income and expenditure account for the year ending 31 October 19–5 and a balance sheet as at that date. The following points are to be taken into consideration:
   i) The general expenses included rates, insurance and electricity. At 31 October 19–5 there was an unpaid electricity account of £50 and a payment in advance of £25 for rates.
   ii) There was an unpaid invoice for competition expenses £10.
   iii) Equipment revalued to £200 (excluding lawn mower). (29.2)

(Royal Society of Arts)

5 The following is a summary of the receipts and payments of the Miniville Rotary Club during the year ended 31 July 19–6.

Miniville Rotary Club –
Receipts and payments account for the year ended 31 July 19–6

	£		£
Cash and bank balances b/f	210	Secretarial expenses	163
Sales of competition tickets	437	Rent	1 402
Members' subscriptions	1 987	Visiting speakers' expenses	1 275
Donations	177	Donations to charities	35
Refund of rent	500	Prizes for competitions	270
Balance c/f	13	Stationery and printing	179
	3 324		3 324

The following valuations are also available:

As at 31 July	*19–5*	*19–6*
	£	£
Equipment (original cost £1 420)	975	780
Subscriptions in arrears	65	85
Subscriptions in advance	10	37
Owing to suppliers of competition prizes	58	68
Stocks of competition prizes	38	46

REQUIRED:

a) Calculate the value of the accumulated fund of the Miniville Rotary Club as at 1 August 19–5.
b) Reconstruct the following accounts for the year ended 31 July 19–6:
   i) the subscription account,
   ii) the competition prizes account.
c) Prepare an income and expenditure account for the Miniville Rotary Club for the year ended 31 July 19–6 and a balance sheet as at that date. (29.2)

(Association of Accounting Technicians)

6 The following is a summary of the receipts and payments of the Technicians Club during the year ended 31 December 19–6.

**Technicians Club –
Receipts and payments account for the year ended 31 December 19–6**

	£		£
Cash and bank balances b/f	358	Secretary's expenses	150
Sales of disco tickets	632	Rent	800
Members' subscriptions	2 108	Meeting expenses	722
Donations	250	Heating and lighting	269
		Disco expenses	515
		Purchase of equipment	400
		Stationery and printing	287
		Cash and bank balances c/f	205
	3 348		3 348

The following valuations are also available as at 31 December:

	19–5	*19–6*
	£	£
Equipment written down value	1 300	1 460
Subscriptions in arrears	80	110
Heating and lighting accrued	37	41
Stocks of stationery	54	46
Rent pre-paid	200	240

REQUIRED:

Prepare an income and expenditure account for the Technicians Club for the year ended 31 December 19–6 and a balance sheet as at that date. (29.2)

(Association of Accounting Technicians)

7 The following figures were taken from the records of the Riverside Club for the year ended 31 December.

	£
Receipts	
Members subscriptions	690
Sale of refreshments	2 021
Sundry receipts	140
Payments	
Suppliers of refreshments	1 424
Wages	650
Rent, rates, and insurance	250
Repairs and renewals	213
Purchase of new furniture for lounge	205
Sundry expenses	129

NOTE
All receipts and payments were passed through the club's bank account.

Other information:

	£
Members' subscriptions in arrear at 1 January and paid during the year	60
Members' subscriptions in arrear at 31 December	35
Cash at bank, 1 January	131
Rates paid in advance at 31 December	26
Estimated depreciation on club furniture and fixtures for the year	72
Purchases of refreshments during the year	1 540
Stocks of refreshments at 1 January	138
Stocks of refreshments at 31 December	156

REQUIRED:

a) A receipts and payments account and a refreshment account for the year ended 31 December.

b) An income and expenditure account for the year ended 31 December and a balance sheet as at that date. (29.2)

(Associated Examining Board)

8 Wentworth Cricket Club had the following assets and liabilities at 1 January 19–4:

	£
Ground and pavilion	250 000
Equipment	2 300
Fixtures and fittings	3 900
Subscriptions in arrears (from 19–3)	92
Subscriptions received in advance (for 19–4)	106
Light and heat owing	81
Insurance prepaid	209
Bar stocks	943
Members' long-term (interest free) loans	50 000
Accumulated fund	210 549

Wentworth Cricket Club –
Receipts and payments account for year ending 31 December 19–4

	£		£
Balance b/d	3 292	Bar purchases	7 306
Subscriptions	809	Equipment	860
Bar sales	10 243	Lottery tickets and prizes	821
Sales of monthly lottery tickets	4 391	Ground maintenance	4 202
Net proceeds from fruit machines	5 002	Light and heat	320
Loans from members	5 000	Insurance	609
		Extension to pavillion	11 500
		Affiliation fees	30
		Balance c/d	3 089
	28 737		28 737

At 31 December 19–4, the following matters were outstanding:

1 subscriptions in arrears (for 19–4) £23 and subscriptions received in advance (for 19–5) £86;
2 subscriptions still outstanding for 19–3, £22 were to be written off;
3 equipment, including additions, had depreciated by 10 per cent;
4 insurance prepaid £220 and light and heat owing £90;
5 bar stocks at 31 December 19–4 were valued at £1 100.

REQUIRED:

a) An income and expenditure account of the Wentworth Cricket Club for the year ended 31 December 19–4, including a bar account.
b) A balance sheet as at 31 December 19–4. An explanation of the difference, in accounting treatment at year end, between: (i) subscriptions in arrears and light and heat owing; and (ii) subscriptions in advance and insurance prepaid. (29.2)

(Associated Examining Board)

9 The accounts of the local golf club are shown below:

Redbridge Golf Club – Balance sheet as at 30 June 19–5

	Cost £	*Depreciation* £	*Net* £
FIXED ASSETS:			
Club property	120 000	24 000	96 000
Fixtures and fittings	22 000	6 600	15 400
	142 000	30 600	111 400
CURRENT ASSETS:			
Bar stock		1 420	
Subscriptions in arrears		2 140	
Bank		4 780	
		8 340	

(continued)

(continued)

CURRENT LIABILITIES:			
Creditors for bar supplies	575		
Subscriptions in advance	1 165		
		1 740	
Working capital			6 600
			118 000
FINANCED BY:			
Accumulated Fund:			
Balance as at 1 July 19–4			113 800
Surplus for the year			4 200
			118 000

Redbridge Golf Club – Receipts and Payments Account for the year ended 30 June 19–6

Receipts	£	*Payments*	£
Bank balance b/d	4 780	Bar purchases	7 248
Subscriptions	18 220	Bar steward's salary	4 926
Bar takings	12 435	General expenses	2 674
		Maintenance expenses	3 749
		Heating and lighting	788
		Bank Balance c/d	16 050
	35 435		35 435

NOTES

1 The following balances were available at 30 June 19–6.

Bar stock	£1 540
Subscriptions in arrears	£1 875
Subscriptions in advance	£1 450
Creditors for bar supplies	£638

2 The club's policy is to provide depreciation annually on fixed assets at the following rates:

Club property	2.5% of cost
Fixtures and fittings	10% of cost

REQUIRED:

a) Showing clearly the profit or loss made on the bar, prepare the club's income and expenditure account for the year ended 30 June 19–6.

b) Explain the difference between the receipts and payments account and the income and expenditure account of a club or association. (29.2)

(Association of Accounting Technicians)

10 The following account has been prepared by the treasurer of the Phoenix Model Engineering Society:

Receipts and payments statement for the year ended 31 March 19–5

	£		£
1 April 19–4 Opening balance b/fwd	894	Purchase of building land	8 000
Subscriptions received	12 000	Purchase of machinery and tools	17 500
Sales of machinery and tools	21 000	Rent of temporary office and meeting room	600
Sale of wooden hut	1 100	Printing, stationery and postages	860
Sales of tickets for annual national exhibition	300	Deposit in building society investment account	7 500
		Secretary's honorarium	150
		Coach to annual national exhibition	110
		Admission charges to annual national exhibition	220
		31 March 19–5 closing balance c/fwd	354
	£35 294		£35 294

The following additional information has been obtained from the Society's records:

a) In addition to the balances at bank shown in the above receipts and payments statement, the Society's assets and liabilities were:

As at	*1 April 19–4*	*31 March 19–5*
	£	£
Stocks of machinery and tools at cost	1 200	600
Subscriptions due to the Society	150	250
Wooden hut at valuation	1 300	—
Subscriptions pre-paid by members	300	To be determined
Outing to annual national exhibition	—	See note below

b) The annual subscription for the year ended 31 March has been £50 per member since 1 April. All subscriptions due at 1 April 19–4 have now been paid. The Society's membership was 238 during the year ended 31 March 19–5.

c) All sales of machinery and tools are to members on a strictly cash basis.

d) *Annual National Exhibition*, £40 for tickets was owing by a member to the Society on 31 March 19–5 and at that date the Society owed £45 for the purchase of exhibition programmes distributed to members without charge.

e) Since preparing the above receipts and payments statement, the treasurer has received a bank statement showing bank charges of £14 debited in the Society's bank account on 30 March 19–5; no adjustment was made for these charges in the above statement.

f) Since the sale of the wooden hut on 1 July 19–4, the Society has rented a temporary office and meeting room at an annual rent of £600 payable in advance.

REQUIRED:
Prepare an income and expenditure account for the year ended 31 March 19–5 and a balance sheet as at that date for the Society. (29.2)
(Note: The income and expenditure account should show clearly the overall result of the trade in machinery and tools and the profit or loss of the visit to the annual national exhibition.)
(Association of Accounting Technicians)

30 The trial balance and its limitations

Objectives

On completing this section you should:

- understand the function of the trial balance
- recognise that it is not a fool proof system and that certain errors are not disclosed
- understand how errors may be corrected.

Context

Chapter 5 introduced the trial balance.

30.1 Introduction

In Chapter 5 the trial balance was seen as a checking device of the ledger system. It is not an account in itself, merely a listing of all the relevant ledger accounts in their respective debit and credit balances. If the totals should agree, then it may be assumed that ledger recording has been correct. Yet it is not a foolproof system. Are the ledger accounts 100 per cent correct? If a computer program is used, the input of transactions are virtually certain to have a built-in double-entry system to ensure that the trial balance does balance. Yet even so, errors can still be made within the system and the trial balance will still balance, failing to disclose any discrepancy between the total debits and credits. As a checking device, the trial balance has its limitations.

30.2 Errors in the accounting system

Essentially, there are five basic types of error which the trial balance fails to disclose. These are:

an error of original entry
an error of omission
an error of principle
an error of commission
an error of compensation.

30.2.1 An error of original entry

This refers to an error which may have been made in an original document such as an invoice or credit note. For example in the sales invoice to J Jack:

	£
Sales (net)	350.00
Vat (17.5%)	42.50
	392.50

Error: Vat should be £61.25, total invoice £411.25

The invoice has been sent, the entry is already recorded.

Double entry:

Debit	J Jack (debtor)	£392.50	
Credit	Sales		£350.00
	Vat		£42.50

Both debit and credit entries equal the same value and therefore the trial balance could not disclose the error in Vat.

If a person such as an auditor, cross-checking the accounts, found the error in Vat, the correction in the ledgers would be:

Double entry:

Debit	J Jack (debtor)	£18.75	
Credit	Vat		£18.75

Ledger

		Debit £	*Credit* £	*Balance* £
J Jack account				
5/7	Sales	350.00		350.00 Dr
5/7	Vat	42.50		392.50
21/7	Vat (error)	18.75		411.25
Sales account				
5/7	J Jack			350.00 Cr
Vat account				
5/7	J Jack		42.50	42.50 Cr
21/7	J Jack (error)		18.75	61.25

30.2.2 An error of omission

This type of error is quite similar to that of the above example. It refers to a transaction that has been omitted altogether, neither the debit nor credit entries being made. Suppose for example, a credit note to a customer had somehow been misplaced and no entry had been made. Subsequently, by examining the sequence of credit note numbers, it was revealed that a credit note had not been recorded, and on investigation the note was discovered. In the credit note to H Smith:

	£
Goods returned (damaged)	20.0
Vat (17.5%)	3.5
	23.5

This information now needs to be recorded because no transaction has been entered in the books and the trial balance could not have disclosed it.

Double entry:

Debit	Returns inward	£20.0	
	Vat	£3.5	
Credit	H Smith		£23.5

Ledger

		Debit	*Credit*	*Balance*
		£	£	£
Returns inward account				
22/7	H Smith	20.0		20.0 Dr
Vat account				
22/7	H Smith	3.5		3.5 Dr
H Smith account				
22/7	Returns in	20.0		
	Vat		3.5	23.5 Cr

30.2.3 An error of principle

This is a type of error concerning posting a transaction to the wrong group of accounts. The double entry is correct as far as debit and credit goes, but the choice of accounts is in error. For example:

	£
Purchased equipment from Office Services Ltd	500.0
Vat 17.5%	87.5
	587.5

The entry was posted to the purchases account instead of the office equipment account. An *expense account* instead of an *asset account*.

Double entry:

Debit	Purchases	£500.0	
Credit	Vat	£87.5	
Credit	Office Services Ltd		£587.5

On cross-checking the accounts, the accountant located the error and made the necessary correcting entry. The error of principle was that an expense (purchases) was wrongly debited with £500 which clearly should have been debited to an asset account (office equipment). The correction would be:

Double entry:

Debit	Office equipment	£500	
Credit	Purchases		£500

Ledger

		Debit £	Credit £	Balance £
Purchases account				
5/7	Office Services Ltd	500.0		500.0 Dr
15/7	Office equipment		500.0	—
Vat account				
5/7	Office Services Ltd	87.5		87.5 Dr
Office Services Ltd account				
5/7	Purchases		587.5	587.5 Cr
Office equipment account				
15/7	Purchases	500.0		500.0 Dr

30.2.4 An error of commission

This is a similar error to that of an error of principle, with the exception that, although the transaction has been posted to the wrong account, it has been posted within the same group. For example:

A gas bill of £75, paid by cheque, has been wrongly posted to the stationery account.

Double entry:

Debit	Stationery	£75	
Credit	Bank		£75

Again, both debit and credit entries record the same value and the trial balance would fail to disclose the error. On finding such an error, the correcting entry would be:

Double entry:

Debit	Light and heat	£75	
Credit	Stationery		£75

Ledger

		Debit £	Credit £	Balance £
Stationery account				
10/7	Bank	75		75 Dr
22/7	Light and heat		75	—
Light and heat account				
22/7	Stationery	75		75 Dr
Bank account				
10/7	Stationery		75	75 Cr

30.2.5 An error of compensation

This type of error refers to the *same* mistake made on *both* sides to the transaction, thereby ensuring that both debit and credit sides are equal. For example:

A cheque was sent to H Brown (creditor) in settlement of his account, £359, but was entered incorrectly as £395, an error of £36.

Double entry:

Debit	H Brown (creditor)	£395	
Credit	Bank		£395

Because both debit and credit entries are equal, the trial balance could not disclose this 'compensating' error. To correct this mistake, the entry is:

Double entry:

Debit	Bank	£36	
Credit	H Brown		£36

Ledger

		Debit	*Credit*	*Balance*
		£	£	£
H Brown account				
1/7	Balance			359 Cr
7/7	Bank	395		36 Dr
21/7	Bank		36	—
Bank account				
7/7	H Brown		395	395 Cr
21/7	H Brown	36		359

All these five basic types of error will not be disclosed by the trial balance. It is therefore not a foolproof system and cannot guarantee the absolute accuracy of the ledger.

Example

The following information relates to the accounts of George Ralston on 28 February 19–8:

George Ralston –
Trial balance as on 28 February 19–8

	Dr	*Cr*
	£	£
Bank	3 010	
Premises	12 000	
Equipment	3 000	
Mortgage		9 500

(continued)

(continued)

Vat		215
Capital		10 000
Wages	125	
Light and heat	115	
Purchases	750	
Sales		1 035
Creditor: J Jones		250
Debtor: R Smith	2 000	
	21 000	21 000

The accountant, checking the figures at the end of the month, located a number of errors which the trial balance has failed to disclose:

a) The purchase of goods for resale £800, had wrongly been posted to the equipment account.
b) A sales invoice to R Smith had omitted to charge £15 Vat.
c) A telephone bill £35, had in error been posted to light and heat.
d) A purchase invoice to J Jones £200 + Vat 17.5 per cent had not yet been entered in the books.
e) Wages on the paysheet were £152 and were entered as £125 in the ledger.
f) A gas bill of £45, paid by cheque, had not been recorded.

REQUIRED:

1) For each of the above, state the type of error which was located by the accountant.
2) Make the necessary correcting entries in the ledger.
3) Extract a new trial balance, incorporating the corrections, as on 28 February 19–8.

SOLUTION:

1 *Type of error located*

a) An error of principle.
b) An error of original entry.
c) An error of commission.
d) An error of omission.
e) An error of compensation.
f) An error of omission.

2

Ledger entries

		Debit £	*Credit* £	*Balance* £
Purchase account				
28/2	Balance			750 Dr
	Equipment	800		1 550
	J Jones	200		1 750

(continued)

(continued)

Equipment account				
28/2	Balance			3 000 Dr
	Purchases		800	2 200
Vat account				
28/2	Balance			215 Cr
	R Smith		15	230
	J Jones	35		195
R Smith account				
28/2	Balance			2 000 Dr
	Vat	15		2 015
J Jones account				
28/2	Balance			250 Cr
	Purchases		200	
	Vat		35	485
Wages account				
28/2	Balance			125 Dr
	Bank	27		152
Light and heat account				
28/2	Balance			115 Dr
	Telephone		35	80
	Bank	45		125
Telephone account				
28/2	Light and heat	35		35 Dr
Bank account				
28/2	Balance			3 010 Dr
	Wages		27	2 983
	Light and heat		45	2 938

3

Trial balance as on 28 February 19–8 (reconstructed)

	Dr	*Cr*
	£	£
Bank	2 938	
Premises	12 000	
Equipment	2 200	
Mortgage		9 500
Vat		195
Capital		10 000

(continued)

Wages	152	
Light and heat	125	
Telephone	35	
Purchases	1 750	
Sales		1 035
Creditor: J Jones		485
Debtor: R Smith	2 015	
	21 215	21 215

Summary

The function of the trial balance is to check the arithmetical accuracy of the double-entry system. However, even if it balances, it is not a guarantee that all accounts are correct because certain errors, such as an omission, are not disclosed. This is why a business needs to have an internal audit system where accounts can be regularly checked for accuracy.

Questions

1 The following errors have been found in the books of K Jackson on 31 March:

a) A sum of £550 has been included in the wages account for repairs to the owner's property, not the business's.
b) The purchase of an office typewriter for £180 has been posted to the purchases account.
c) A cheque from R Smith (debtor) £200 has been posted to the account of J Smith, another customer.
d) An invoice from the Wessex Water Authority for £85 has just been discovered and no entries have yet been made.
e) A purchase invoice from K Welland had £7.50 Vat included but this had been excluded in both supplier's and Vat accounts.

REQUIRED:

a) List the type of errors which have been found.
b) Explain briefly why the trial balance would have failed to disclose them.
c) State the relevant double entries required to correct the above errors. (30.1–2)

2 What is the role of the trial balance? Why is it not a foolproof system? Explain your answer by using your own examples to clarify your meaning. (30.1)

3 The following errors have been discovered by J Jones on 31 July:

a) Purchases of £180 + 17.5 per cent Vat had been posted to David Brown Ltd instead of Joe Brown Ltd in the purchase ledger.
b) New office equipment costing £2250 bought on credit from Nelson's Ltd has been entered in the purchases journal and included in the purchases account.
c) Sales totalling £185 had been posted in error as £158 both to the customer's and sales accounts.
d) An electricity bill for £36, paid by cheque, had not gone through the books.

REQUIRED:

Make the necessary correcting entries in the ledger of J Jones. (30.2)

4 The following errors have been located in the books of Jack Jones as on 31 March:

a) A supplier in the returns outward day book, Jane Rawlins, £20 + 17.5 per cent Vat, had not yet been entered in the ledgers.
b) A sales invoice of £220 + 17.5 per cent Vat had been misplaced, no entries having been made. It was addressed to Sam Jones.
c) A purchase invoice of £317 from Rebecca Smith had in error been posted as £371.
d) A private purchase of £435 by the owner, had been included as a business purchase.
e) A commission of £42 received by Jack Jones had not yet been recorded.
f) A purchase of equipment of £200 had been entered under purchases.
g) A sale of office furniture, £300 had been entered in the sales account.

REQUIRED:

a) Show the correcting entries for the above entries.
b) Although all the entries are not disclosed by the trial balance would any of these affect profit? Comment on your findings. (30.1–2)

31 The journal and use of the suspense account

Objectives

On completing this section you should:

- understand the use and function of the journal
- recognise why the suspense account is used
- understand how errors may be corrected and the suspense cleared
- prepare a corrected profit and loss account.

Context:

The suspense account was introduced in Chapter 6.

31.1 Introduction

The function of the **journal** is to provide an original entry for those type of transactions which do not readily 'fit into' the other subsidiary books such as the sales and purchases journal and the cash book. In the early days of accounting, the journal was the only book of prime entry in use. All financial transactions were entered in the journal prior to posting to the ledger system. As accounting developed and was applied to different kinds of business organisations, the use of the journal alone was inadequate. Many repetitious types of entry such as sales and purchases required separate journals to be used.

31.2 The use of the journal

There is still a place for the journal as a record of prime entry even though direct entries could be made to the ledger. The more common uses of the journal include the following:

- the correction of errors,
- the opening entries in a new accounting period,
- the purchase and sales of fixed assets on credit,
- the transfer of balances between accounts, for example, writing off a bad debt or transferring revenue and expense accounts to trading and profit and loss account,
- the making of balance-day adjustments to the final accounts, for example, providing for depreciation or for bad debts.

The presentation of the journal reflects the double-entry principle; that for every debit entry there is a corresponding credit entry. Thus the journal has two columns, precisely to emphasise this point. The debit entry is always recorded first and the credit entry, on a separate line, second. The credit entry is also slightly indented for effect. A brief comment usually accompanies a transaction, offering some very limited explanation why the entry has been made.

Example

Bought £5000 of plant and machinery on credit from Dave McKee Ltd.

Journal

		Debit	Credit
		£	£
1/7	Plant and machinery,	5 000	
	Dave McKee Ltd		5 000
	Bought fixed asset on credit over five years		

Example using the journal

In Chapter 30 a number of errors were not disclosed by the trial balance. These errors could have all been *journalised* first, as a record of prime entry, prior to ledger posting. The errors disclosed in the books of George Ralston, 28 February were:

a) The purchase of goods for resale £800, had wrongly been posted to the equipment account.
b) A sales invoice to R Smith had omitted to charge £15 Vat.
c) A telephone bill £35, had in error, been posted to light and heat account.
d) A purchase invoice to J Jones £200 + Vat 17.5 per cent, had not yet been entered in the books.
e) Wages entry on the paysheet was £152 and was entered as £125 in the ledger.
f) A gas bill of £45, paid by cheque, had not been recorded.

REQUIRED:

Make the necessary journal entries to correct the above errors. Posting to the ledger has already been made in Chapter 30.

Journal – G Ralston

		Debit	Credit
		£	£
Feb 28	Purchases	800	
	Equipment		800
	(Error of principle, an expense posted as an asset)		
28	R Smith (debtor)	15	
	Vat		15
	(Error of original entry, invoice omitted Vat)		
28	Telephone	35	
	Light and heat		35
	(Error of commission, telephone bill charged to light and heat)		
28	Purchases	200	
	Vat	35	
	J Jones		235
	(Error of omission, invoice from supplier temporarily mislaid)		

(continued)

(continued)

28	Wages	27	
	Bank		27
	(Error of compensation; wages £152 misread as £125)		
28	Light and heat	45	
	Bank		45
	(Error of omission, gas bill temporarily mislaid)		

Further examples using the journal in the books of G Ralston are:

a) On 1 February, G Ralston had the following accounts in his books: Premises, £12 000; Bank £2500; Equipment £2200; Stock £500; Debtors £1800; Mortgage £9500; Creditors £500. Make the appropriate journal entry, showing the capital of G Ralston.
b) On 28 February, G Ralston decided to write off £1000 of R Smith's account as 'bad' in response to Smith's financial difficulties.
c) On 28 February, G Ralston decided to depreciate his equipment by 20 per cent.

Journal – G Ralston

		Debit £	*Credit* £
1/2	Premises	12 000	
	Bank	2 500	
	Equipment	2 200	
	Stock	500	
	Debtors	1 800	
	Mortgage		9 500
	Creditors		500
	Capital: G Ralston		10 000
	(Being assets, liabilities and capital of G Ralston at commencement of year)		
28/2	Bad debts	1 000	
	R Smith		1 000
	(£1000 written off as 'bad')		
28/2	Profit and loss account	440	
	Provision for depreciation of equipment		440
	(Equipment depreciated by 20 per cent)		

31.3 The use of the suspense account

The purpose of using a suspense account is to ensure that the trial balance *will agree* until the error or errors have been located and corrected. When errors produce an incorrect trial balance, where total debits fail to agree with total credits, the suspense account may be used to make up the difference between the two sides.

In computer-based accounts, there is usually a suspense account written into the trial balance in the event that the program cannot find an appropriate debit or credit account to enter.

If a suspense account is necessary, it is entered in the nominal ledger, with the balance taken from the trial balance. The account is written off when the errors are located, using the journal to make the relevant entries. If errors are not found before final accounts are prepared the suspense account balance is included in the balance sheet.

The following is an example of using the suspense account in conjunction with the trial balance and journal. It also shows how to correct the profit and loss account and balance sheet, if these had already been prepared. If the final accounts were prepared from these figures, the credit balance in the suspense account would be listed under liabilities in the balance sheet.

Example
The following represent the accounts of G Balfour as on 30 June:

Trial balance as on 30 June

	Debit	*Credit*
	£	£
Bank	1 245	
Stock (1/6)	3 400	
Premises	20 000	
Furniture and fittings	900	
Wages and salaries	5 400	
Office expenses	1 060	
Purchases	23 900	
Sales		31 900
Drawings	3 800	
Debtors	2 600	
Creditors		3 230
Capital (1/6)		24 900
Suspense account		2 275
	62 305	62 305

The net profit for the month of June was £1540 before it was subsequently discovered that the following errors had been revealed on 30 June:

a) The bank account was overdrawn by £1245.
b) £200 drawn by G Balfour for his personal expenses had been charged to office expenses.
c) Purchases of £1000 on credit had not yet been recorded in the books.
d) The balance of £160 discount allowed had been omitted.
e) £2400 included under wages and £600 included under purchases represented, in error, figures which should have been included in premises.
f) The balance of £55 in cash, had also been omitted from the list of accounts.

REQUIRED:

1 Journal entries to make the necessary corrections to the above errors.

2 A suspense account in the ledger to show the effect of these entries.

3 A corrected profit and loss account and a balance sheet as on 30 June.

NOTE

The closing stock value on 30 June was £3 400, the same as the opening stock.

1

Journal entries

			Dr	*Cr*
			£	£
June	30	Suspense account	2 490	
		Bank account		2 490
	30	Drawings account	200	
		Office expenses account		200
	30	Purchases account	1 000	
		Creditors' account		1 000
	30	Discount allowed account	160	
		suspense account		160
	30	Premises account	3 000	
		Wages and salaries account		2 400
		Purchases account		600
	30	Cash account	55	
		Suspense account		55

2

Suspense account

		Dr			*Cr*
		£			£
June 30	Bank	2 490	June 30	Trial balance	2 275
				Discount allowed	160
				Office cash	55
		2 490			2 490

3

Profit and loss month ended 30 June correction

	£	£
Net profit (before errors)		1 540
Add		
Increases to profit:		
Office expenses	200	
Wages	2 400	
Purchases	600	3 200
		4 740
Less		
Decreases to profit:		
Purchases	1 000	
Discount allowed	160	1 160
Net profit (adjusted)		3 580

Balance sheet as at 30 June

	£	£	£
FIXED ASSETS			
Premises	23 000		
Fixtures and fittings	900		23 900
CURRENT ASSETS			
Stock	3 400		
Debtors	2 600		
Bank	—		
Cash	55	6 055	
Less			
CURRENT LIABILITIES			
Creditors	4 230		
Bank overdraft	1 245	5 475	
Working capital			580
			24 480
FINANCED BY:			
Capital	24 900		
+ Net profit	3 580	28 480	
– Drawings		4 000	24 480

31.4 The location of errors

If the trial balance fails to balance the first thing to do is to find out the difference between the total debits and total credits. It is then a matter of checking all the relevant places. Remember that the trial balance has its limitations and that some errors could have been made which the trial balance could not have disclosed.

If control accounts are used and these have been cross-checked with the personal ledgers (sales and purchases ledgers), it may then be assumed that all debtors' and creditors' accounts are correct.

It will then be necessary to comb through the nominal ledger to check for any arithmetical inaccuracies or any obvious errors in double entry. For example, a cheque from a customer posted on the debit side instead of the credit, in his account, or a discount received posted on the debit side instead of the credit, etc.

It may be necessary to look back to the subsidiary books such as the journals and cash book to ensure that the correct figures were posted to the relevant accounts in the ledgers. It may have been an incorrect addition to the columns of figures. Some item in the cash book may have been entered on the wrong side, for example, a payment for a receipt or vice versa.

Therefore, before the entry of any figures to the accounting system, they should be absolutely arithmetically correct and then the precise debit and credit entries made to the relevant accounts. Remember, if the trial balance fails to balance, the suspense account temporarily enables debits to equal credits and the final accounts could still be prepared. However, once all errors have been found the suspense account is cleared. Note that not all errors affect the suspense account.

Summary

The journal is a book of prime entry and is used to record transactions outside the scope of other journals. One of its uses is to correct errors and the debit and credit columns facilitate this. The suspense account should be seen as a temporary device to focus on the discrepancy between debits and credits and cleared once the errors have been located. Profit or loss figures may also have to be adjusted if the final accounts have been prepared.

Questions

1 Draft the journal entries required to correct the following errors discovered on 12 July:

a) Purchases of £170 credited in error to W Brown instead of Willis & Brown.

b) New office equipment costing £2000 had been bought on credit. The item was entered in the purchases journal and included in the purchases total.

c) J Elliot, a customer, had paid his account taking £7 cash discount which he was not entitled to do. This had been entered in the books.

d) An account of £20 for repairs to the owner's car (private use) had been posted to delivery expenses account.

e) An electricity bill for £42 had not yet been entered in the books and had been paid by cheque the previous month. (31.1–2)

(Royal Society of Arts)

2 The following information has been extracted from the trial balance of J Smith as on 30 June:

	Dr	*Cr*
	£	£
Suspense account		247

Subsequently the following errors were found:

a) Goods £285 to R Smith had been posted to J Smith in error.
b) Accounting equipment sold for £600 credited to sales account.
c) Cash discount of £8 allowed to J Jones and credited to him, but no entry was made to the discount account.
d) The addition of the sales day book was undercast by £200.
e) Salaries accrued £55 at the end of the previous year had not been brought forward to the new accounting period.
f) A sales invoice of £275 had been misplaced. No entries had been made.
g) A standing order £55 for insurance had been omitted from the cash book.

REQUIRED:

a) Journal entries necessary to correct the books.
b) The suspense account entries. (31.2–3)

(Institute of Bankers)

3 The following trial balance relating to Len Shackleton's business, failed to agree. One of the major causes of this disagreement appeared to be the failure to post the following day book totals to the ledger: purchases £1562; sales £2941; returns inward £98; and returns outward £46. In addition, the petty cash balance £18 was omitted and some of the items inadvertently placed on the wrong side of the trial balance.

Trial balance of Len Shackleton as at 31 May 19–3

	Debit £	*Credit* £
Premises	25 000	
Purchases	1 398	
Sales		3 975
Bank overdraft	621	
Discount allowed		45
Rates	91	
Lighting and heating	96	
Bank charges	14	
Stock at 1 May 19–3	823	
Debtors	960	
Creditors		840
Capital		21 682
	29 003	26 542

REQUIRED:

a) Preparation of a corrected trial balance as at 31 May 19–3.
b) i) Two types of error which would not prevent trial balance totals from agreeing.
   ii) An explanation, using an example in each case, why the trial balance totals would still be in agreement, despite the existence of such errors. (31.4)

(AEB)

4 D McForan's trial balance, extracted at 31 October 19–4, failed to agree and the difference was recorded in a suspense account. In early November the following errors were discovered:

1 The sales day book had been overcast by £220;
2 Goods valued at £121 returned by A Wilkinson had been correctly recorded in the returns inward account but had not been entered in the personal account;
3 A payment for repairs to the motor van £41 had been entered in the vehicle repairs account as £14;
4 When balancing the account of B Heath in the ledger, the credit balance had been brought down in error as £32 instead of £23;
5 The total of the discounts received column of the cash book £120 had been incorrectly debited to the discounts allowed account and no entry had been made in the discounts received account.

REQUIRED:

a) i) Journal entries to correct each of the above errors (narrations are *not* required).
   ii) A suspense account indicating the nature and extent of the original difference in the books.

b) Name and explain *four* types of error that would not affect the agreement of the trial balance. Illustrate your answer by giving an example of *each* type of error. (31.2–4)

(AEB)

5 The draft trial balance of James McLippie and Son as at 30 April 19–6 did not agree and the difference was posted to a suspense account. Subsequent investigation of the accounts revealed the following errors of £1352 debit.

1 The discount received column in the cash book had been overcast by £100.
2 J Stanley, a customer, had not been credited with £8 discount although this had been correctly entered in the cash book.
3 The sales book had been overcast by £900.
4 An invoice made out (correctly) for £45 in respect of sales made to H Purcell had been recorded in the sales book as £54. (This is quite apart from the error in the sales book referred to above.)
5 The purchases book had been undercast by £360.
6 Goods returned from J Blow, a customer, had been recorded in the returns inward book as £108. In fact, the value of the goods returned had been subsequently agreed with the customer at £88 but no adjustment had been made in the accounting records.
7 Value added tax (at 17.5 per cent) amounting to £17.50 collected on cash sales of £100 had not been entered in the Vat column in the cash book. Instead the sales had been recorded in the cash column as £117.50.

REQUIRED:

a) Prepare journal entries to show how the above errors would be corrected.
b) The suspense account entries.
c) If the profit had been calculated at £13 564 before the errors were disclosed, what is the profit for the year after correcting the above errors? (31.2–4)

(AAT)

6 XYZ Co had prepared its trading, profit and loss account and balance sheet which included a suspense account of £188.

The balances were as follows on 31 December 19–5:

	Dr £	Cr £
Equipment	1 406	
Furniture and fittings	826	
Stock	1 218	
Debtors, creditors	1 548	1 200
Bank	145	
Capital		5 339
Drawings	2 000	
Profit		792
Suspense	188	
	7 331	7 331

On checking the records, your researches reveal:

a) A purchase invoice for £64 had not been entered in the books.
b) A desk valued £82 had been wrongly debited to repairs of fittings account instead of furniture and fittings.
c) The bank account should have been entered as a credit balance.
d) Interest charges of £50 had not been included in the cash book and no posting had been made to the ledger.
e) The sales account balance had been overstated by £378 in error.
f) A credit note from a supplier of £110 had been entered correctly in the returns book but as £10 in the supplier's account.

REQUIRED:

a) Journal entries to correct each of the above errors (no need for narration).
b) A suspense account showing the appropriate correcting errors.
c) A statement showing the revised profit for the year ended 31 December 19–5.
d) A brief comment regarding the effectiveness of the trial balance as a testing device. (31.2–4)

(Institute of Bankers)

7 The trial balance of J Sharp, a retailer, does not balance. You are asked to look through his accounts and subsequently you do find the errors below. The trial balance of the proprietor on 30 June was as follows:

	Dr £	Cr £
Premises	20 000	
Motor van	500	
Equipment	2 100	
Stock	1 860	
Debtors	675	
Creditors		1 155
Capital, J Sharp		12 500
Bank		455
Sales		35 750
Purchases	20 195	
General expenses	1 250	
Wages	3 970	
Suspense		690
	50 550	50 550

Errors found:
a) A piece of equipment £500 had wrongly been posted to purchases account.
b) A gas bill of £85 had been paid but had not gone through any of the books.
c) Discount allowed £68 had not been posted to the ledger.
d) Sales were undercast by £800.
e) A cheque from a debtor (R Smith) £150 had been recorded as £105 in his account but correctly in the corresponding account.
f) The total from the returns inward account £87 had not been posted to the ledger.

REQUIRED:
a) Prepare suitable journal entries to correct the above errors and write up the suspense account.
b) Prepare a corrected trial balance for J Sharp as on 30 June.
c) State which of the above errors were not found by the trial balance and explain briefly to J Sharp why such a device has its limitations. (31.2–4)

(AEB)

8 An extract of the trial balance was taken from the books of Simon Buckley on 30 June:

	Dr	*Cr*
	£	£
Premises	13 000	
Sales		38 600
Purchases	22 500	
Equipment	4 200	
General expenses	150	
Discounts	40	85
Returns	130	420
Suspense		915
	40 020	40 020

The following errors were located:
a) Sales were undercast by £315 in the sales journal.
b) General expenses £85 had been overlooked when posting from the cash book.
c) Purchases had been overcast in the purchases journal by £500.
d) Discount from suppliers £90 had not been posted to the relevant discount account.
e) Returns to suppliers £95 had been posted to the personal accounts but not the nominal account.

REQUIRED:
a) Prepare the appropriate journal entries to correct the above errors.
b) Prepare the suspense account.
c) If the calculated net profit was £12 420 before the above errors were located, compute the corrected net profit. (31.2–4)

(Institute of Bankers)

9 The trial balance as at 31 March of Allsquare Engineers Limited did not balance and therefore a suspense account was opened showing a credit balance of £549. Unfortunately, the errors in the accounts were only traced after the completion of the draft final accounts for the year ended 31 March which showed the following results:

	£
*Profit on manufacturing	12 760
Gross profit	23 410
Net profit	9 746

*Manufactured goods are transferred to the trading account at wholesale prices.

The following errors were discovered:

1 2 January Credit sales to T Sparkes of £1 200 not recorded in the sales day book.

2 15 January A receipt of £500 from K Dodds, debtor, was recorded in the cash book only.

3 February Discounts received of £376 have been recorded correctly in the purchases ledger control account and then debited in the discounts allowed account. Discounts allowed of £224 have been recorded correctly in the sales ledger control account and then credited in the discounts received account.

4 31 March Payments to suppliers totalling £21 257 have been debited in the purchases ledger control account as £21 752.

5 Depreciation for the year ended 31 March on manufacturing equipment was correctly recorded in the provision for depreciation account but not posted to the manufacturing account. The correction of this error cleared the suspense account.

REQUIRED:

a) The suspense account as it would appear after the correction of all the accounting errors.

b) A statement showing the effects on net profit if any, of the correction of the errors upon each of the following results in the draft accounts for the year ended 31 March.

(Association of Accounting Technicians)

32 The extended trial balance

Objectives

On completing this section you should:

- understand the use and function of the ETB (extended trial balance)
- recognise its value as a worksheet in preparing the final accounts.

Context

Chapters 5 and 30 discussed the trial balance, Chapter 6 introduced the ETB.

32.1 Introduction

The trial balance is an indication or test of arithmetical accuracy of the double-entry system as was discussed in the chapter concerning the ledger system.

At the end of a financial period, the trial balance is extracted from the accounts of the nominal ledger in readiness for the preparation of the final accounts. All adjustments relating to the end of the period must also be taken into account to ensure the correct matching of revenue with expenses and to correspond with SSAP 2 Disclosure of Accounting Policies, discussed in greater detail in the following chapter.

The extended trial balance (ETB) is a form of a worksheet where extra columns are provided alongside the trial balance figures in order to accommodate any adjustments or changes which may be required for the preparation of the final accounts. Indeed, the final two columns of the ETB are the profit and loss account and the balance sheet. The worksheet is then used to type up the formal financial statements for the client or the party requesting them. The ETB may be displayed in a number of various formats.

In accounting practice there are often a number of extra columns to include bank and cash transactions. In examination questions the common format is to have columns for the trial balance, adjustments, the profit and loss account and the balance sheet. An abbreviated example of the layout of the ETB is as follows:

The extended trial balance format

Details	*Trial*	*Balance*	*Adjustments*		*Profit and loss*		*Balance Sheet*	
	Dr	*Cr*	*Dr*	*Cr*	*Dr*	*Cr*	*Dr*	*Cr*
	£	£	£	£	£	£	£	£
Sales		35 000						
Purchases	22 150							
Telephone	325							
Light, heat	542							
Stationery	190							
etc.								
← basic format →			← extended format →					

a) The trial balance column lists all figures concerning the trial balance at the year end. Further adjustments can be added beneath the trial balance totals.
b) The adjustments column is used for making the balance day adjustments including the correction of errors disclosed, writing off bad debts, making provisions for depreciation, bad debts or discounts and for adjusting any figures for Vat etc.
c) The final two columns are used to extend the figures from the trial balance, adjustments, accruals/prepayments, across to either the profit and loss account or the balance sheet.

The difference between the columns in the profit and loss account will indicate either profit or loss which is then transferred to the balance sheet.

- A net profit is debited in the profit and loss column and credited in the balance sheet column.
- A net loss is credited in the profit and loss column and debited in the balance sheet column.

In some formats, the ETB has separate columns for accruals or prepayments as we have in the example that follows. If we used the abbreviated format as above, they would be recorded under the adjustments column along with other entries for closing stock, depreciation etc.

32.2 Example

The following accounts relate to Arthur Jones, a local businessman, as at the year ended 31 December.

You are required to prepare the extended trial balance and from this worksheet, the trading and profit and loss account for the year ended 31 December and a balance sheet as at that date.

(See if you can follow the figures. Note the profit of £11 125 debited in the profit and loss column and credited in the balance sheet).

From this worksheet, the final accounts of the business can be extracted and typed up for the client, Arthur Jones.

Example

Trial balance as on 31 December

	Dr	*Cr*
	£	£
Capital – A S Jones		71 000
Premises	57 500	
Equipment	23 000	
Provision for depreciation of equipment		6 000
Motor van	8 000	
Provision for depreciation of motor van		2 000
Stock (1/1)	8 300	
Purchases and sales	30 800	66 600
Returns inward	700	
Returns outward		900

(continued)

(continued)

Wages	16 500	
Carriage inwards	500	
Carriage outwards	400	
Commission received		500
Bank interest	350	
Lighting and heating	1 650	
Postage and stationery	600	
Insurance	1 200	
Telephone	500	
Rent receivable		750
Debtors, creditors	7 000	11 750
Bank	1 950	
Discount	100	
Bad debts	450	
	159 500	159 500

Adjustments to be taken into account 31 December:

a) Unsold stock valued at cost £9 500.
b) Wages due to be paid £550.
c) Jones, the proprietor, takes goods for own use valued at cost £800.
d) Pre-paid stationery – unused stock valued £95.
e) Rent receivable still outstanding £180.
f) Depreciation: Motor van revalued to £4 500.
   Equipment depreciated 20 per cent on net value.
g) Provision for bad and doubtful debts to equal 10 per cent of debtors.

Solution

The ETB of Arthur Jones

Folio	Description	Trial balance Dr	Trial balance Cr	Adjustments Dr	Adjustments Cr	Creditors/ Accruals	Debtors/ pre-payments	Profit and loss account Dr	Profit and loss account Cr	Balance sheet Dr	Balance sheet Cr
	Premises	57 500								57 500	
	Equipment	23 000								23 000	
	Prov. for depn		6 000		3 400						9 400
	Motor van	8 000								8 000	
	Prov. for depn		2 000		1 500						3 500
	Stock (1/1)	8 300			9 500			8 300	9 500		
	Purchases	30 800			800			30 000			
	Sales		66 600						66,600		
	Returns inward	700						700			
	Returns outward		900						900		
	Wages	16 500				550		17 050			550
	Carriage inwards	500						500			
	Carriage outwards	400						400			
	Commission received		500						500		

Folio	Description	Trial balance Dr	Trial balance Cr	Adjustments Dr	Adjustments Cr	Creditors/ Accruals	Debtors/ pre-payments	Profit and loss account Dr	Profit and loss account Cr	Balance sheet Dr	Balance sheet Cr
	Bank interest	350						350			
	Lighting, heating	1 650						1 650			
	Postage, stationery	600					95	505		95	
	Insurance	1 200						1 200			
	Telephone	500						500			
	Rent received		750				180		930	180	
	Debtors	7 000								7 000	
	Provision for bad debts				700						700
	Creditors		11 750								11 750
	Bank	1 950								1 950	
	Discount allowed	100						100			
	Bad debts	450						450			
	Capital account		71 000	800							70 200
	Depreciation – eqpt			3 400				3 400			
	Depreciation – van			1 500				1 500			
	Bad and doubtful debts			700				700			
	Stock (31/12)			9 500						9 500	
	Profit and loss a/c							11 125			11 125
		159 500	159 500	6 400	6 400	550	275	78 430	78 430	107 225	107 225

NOTES:
1. The adjustments column imposes the double-entry principle; for example, depreciation is debited to profit and loss as an expense and the provision for depreciation is credited in the balance sheet. The totals must agree.
2. The accruals and pre-payments columns simply list those items to be adjusted and are totalled.
3. The profit and loss account indicates debits for expenses and credits for revenue. The difference between these equals the net profit (£11,125). Totals must agree.
4. The balance sheet has assets as debits and liabilities, capital and profit as credits. Totals must agree.

If the accruals/prepayments column was omitted, the adjustments column would be used instead. For example, the £550 for wages owing would be a debit and a credit in the adjustments column. A debit for the accrued expense against wages and a credit entry to signify that this is to be carried across to the credit side of the balance sheet.

If we were to prepare a draft copy of the financial statements, that is, the profit and loss account and balance sheet, from the ETB, it should be relatively straightforward. See if you can prepare it yourself then check it with the suggested solution:

Arthur Jones – Trading and profit and loss account
Year ended 31 December

	£	£
SALES		66 600
Returns inward		(700)
		65 900
COST OF SALES		
Stock (1/1)	8 300	
Purchases	30 800	
Carr. inwards	500	

(continued)

(continued)

Returns out	(900)	
Stock drawings	(800)	
Stock (31/12)	(9 500)	28 400
Gross profit		37 500
EXPENSES		
Wages	17 050	
Carriage out	400	
Bank interest	350	
Light and heat	1 650	
Postage and stationery	505	
Insurance	1 200	
Telephone	500	
Discount	100	
Bad debts	450	
Depreciation	4 900	
Bad and doubtful debts	700	27 805
		9 695
OTHER REVENUE		
Rent received	930	
Commission received	500	1 430
Net profit		11 125

Arthur Jones –
Balance sheet as on 31 December

	£ *Cost*	£ *Depreciation*	£ *NBV*
FIXED ASSETS			
Premises	57 500		57 500
Equipment	23 000	9 400	13 600
Motor Van	8 000	3 500	4 500
	92 250	12 900	75 600
CURRENT ASSETS			
Stock	9 500		
Debtors	6 300		
Bank	1 950		
Prepayments	95		
Accrued revenue	180	18 025	

(continued)

(continued)

CURRENT LIABILITIES			
Creditors	11 750		
Accruals	550	12 300	
Working capital			5 725
Capital employed			81 325
FINANCED BY			
Capital	71 000		
Profit	11 125		
Stock drawings	(800)		81 325

The ETB is used widely in accounting practice particularly for client's accounts. As a worksheet, it summarises all the relevant figures which have been calculated either from ledger accounts, or more likely for small traders, from their various business documents provided by the client for the financial year. Although it looks a little complicated by its multi-columns, once it has been used a number of times, it provides an appropriate record of calculations in readiness for the preparation of the year end accounts.

Summary

The extended trial balance is a useful worksheet where the appropriate figures for the preparation of final accounts can be recorded. There are different formats in use and for examination purposes the columns for adjustments, profit and loss account and balance sheet, tend to be used the most. Once the trial balance figures are entered, all year end adjustments such as accruals, prepayments and provisions are recorded. All accounts are then extended across into the profit and loss account or balance sheet or both. The balance between the debit and credit columns of the profit and loss account will result in either profit or loss which is transferred to the appropriate balance sheet column, credit side if its a profit, debit side if it is a loss.

Questions

1. The trial balance of ABC Co as on 31 December was as follows:

Account	*Dr* £	*Cr* £
Premises (cost)	24 000	
Fixtures and fittings (cost)	4 000	
Motor vehicle (cost)	5 000	
Bank	3 305	
Stock	5 750	
Debtors	20 500	
Creditors		24 220
Loan (3 years) 10% p.a.		15 500
Capital: ABC Co		18 000

(continued)

(continued)

Sales		21 274
Commission received		485
Discount		557
Salaries	2 864	
Light and heat	122	
Petty cash expenses	44	
General expenses	268	
Purchases	14 090	
Returns outward		484
Returns inward	577	
	78 520	78 520

The following information is to be taken into account as on 31 December:

1 The value of unsold stock £6 259.
2 Gas bill still outstanding £42.
3 Under general expenses, stationery unused was £70.
4 The owner took stock for his own use £2 100.
5 Depreciation: Furniture and fittings 10 per cent on cost.
Motor vehicle revalued to £3 750.
6 Provision for bad debts 5 per cent of debtors.
7 6 months interest on loan unpaid.

REQUIRED:

a) Prepare the ETB of ABC Co for the year ended 31 December.
b) Prepare a trading and profit and his account and a balance sheet or the year ended 31 December.

2 The following figures have been extracted from the ledgers of Frances Mitchell:

Trial balance as at 30 June

	Dr £	*Cr* £
Sales		276 156
Purchases	164 700	
Carriage inwards	4 422	
Carriage outwards	5 866	
Drawings	15 600	
Rent and rates	9 933	
Insurance	3 311	
Postage and stationery	3 001	
Advertising	5 661	
Salaries and wages	52 840	
Bad debts	1 754	
Debtors	24 240	
Creditors		25 600
Returns outwards		131

(continued)

(continued)

Cash	354	
Bank	2 004	
Stock	23 854	
Equipment (cost)	116 000	
Capital E Mitchell		131 653
	433 540	433 540

The following information was available on 30 June:

1 Wages are accrued by £420
2 Rates have been pre-paid by £1 400
3 Stock of unused stationery valued £250
4 A provision for bad debts is to be created to equal 5 per cent of debtors
5 Unsold stock at the close of business valued at £27 304
6 Depreciate equipment 10 per cent of cost

REQUIRED:

a) Prepare an extended trial balance for F Mitchell as on 30 June.
b) Prepare the trading and profit and loss account for the year ended 30 June and a balance sheet as at that date.
c) Advise F Mitchell on the position of the working capital of the business.

(Institute of Bankers)

3 The following trial balance has been extracted from the ledger of M Yousef, a sole trader:

Trial balance as at 31 May

	Dr £	*Cr* £
Sales		138 078
Purchases	82 350	
Carriage	5 144	
Drawings	7 800	
Rent and rates and insurance	6 622	
Postage and stationery	3 001	
Advertising	1 330	
Salaries and wages	26 420	
Bad debts	877	
Provision for bad debts		130
Debtors	12 120	
Creditors		6 471
Cash on hand	177	
Cash at bank	1 002	
Stock (opening)	11 927	
Equipment		
at cost	58 000	
accumulated depreciation		19 000
Capital		53 091
	216 770	216 770

The following additional information as at 31 May is available:

1 Rent is accrued by £210
2 Rates have been pre-paid by £880
3 £2 211 of carriage represents carriage inwards on purchases
4 Equipment is to be depreciated at 15 per cent per annum using the straight-line method
5 The provision for bad debts to be increased by £40
6 Stock at the close of business has been valued at £13 551

REQUIRED:

a) Prepare an extended trial balance for M Yousef as at 31 May.
b) Prepare the trading and profit and loss account for the year ended 31 May and a balance sheet as at that date.

(Association of Accounting Technicians)

4 The following information is taken from the accounts of Mary Walker, a businesswoman selling science equipment to colleges:

Trial balance of M Walker as on 30 June

	£	£
Stock (opening)	6 855	
Motor vehicle (cost)	8 750	
Premises (cost)	36 900	
Accumulated depreciation of vehicle		1 750
Purchases	55 725	
Sales		120 344
Discounts	855	1 044
Returns	548	738
Salaries (assistants)	18 346	
Overheads	14 385	
Creditors		6 755
Debtors	7 400	
Bank		2 045
Cash	400	
Drawings	10 420	
Capital		27 908
	160 584	160 584

On 30 June, the following additional information was also available:

1 Stock in hand valued at £7 455
2 The motor vehicle is depreciated on the straight-line principle and is now three years old
3 Of the overheads, £240 is pre-paid and £600 is accrued

REQUIRED:

a) Prepare an extended trial balance for M Walker as at 30 June.
b) Prepare M Walker's trading and profit and loss account for the year ended 30 June and a balance sheet as on that date.

(BTEC)

5 The following trial balance was extracted from the accounts of Freddy Smith on 30 June:

	Dr £	*Cr* £
Sales		27 615
Purchases	16 470	
Returns	205	315
Stock (opening)	2 355	
Carriage inwards	442	
Carriage outwards	580	
Drawings	2 560	
Maintenance and rates	1 998	
Insurance, telephone	334	
Light, heat	546	
Postage, stationery	350	
Bad debts	175	
Motor expenses	560	
Wages	5 285	
Provision for bad debts		65
Cash	200	
Bank overdraft		2 005
Equipment (cost)	11 600	
Prov. for depreciation of equipment		1 160
Motor van (cost)	2 500	
Prov. for depreciation of van		1 500
Debtors, creditors	2 420	2 560
Bank loan (deferred)		4 500
Capital: F Smith		8 860
	48 580	48 580

The following additional information was available on 30 June:

1 Unsold stock was valued at £2 895
2 Accrued expenses: wages, £185; electricity bill, £90
3 Pre-payments: stock of unused stationery, £110; insurance, £80
4 The bad debts provision is to be adjusted to equal 5 per cent of debtors
5 Depreciation: the van at 25 per cent on the reducing balance method; equipment at 10 per cent of cost

REQUIRED:
a) Prepare an extended trial balance for F Smith as on 30 June.
b) Prepare the trading and profit and loss account of F Smith for the period ended 30 June
c) Prepare the balance sheet of F Smith as on 30 June, showing net current assets. Calculate the current ratio.

(BTEC)

6 You work for a firm of accountants, Carter & Cutler, and are asked to prepare a draft of the end of year accounts for a client, P Jackson.

The following trial balance was extracted from the accounts of P Jackson on 30 June.

	Dr £	Cr £
Suspense account		549
Bank		6 500
Purchases/sales	46 000	75 250
Motor vehicle	12 500	
Provision for depreciation (Motor vehicles)		5 000
Rent and rates	1 400	
Light and heat	700	
Carriage inwards	500	
Discounts (balance)	400	
Opening stock	6 300	
Commissions received		1 500
Drawings	9 611	
Returns	1 800	1 500
Office salaries	16 000	
Debtors/creditors	24 000	16 000
Provisions for bad debts		2 000
Fixtures and fittings	8 000	
Provision for depreciations (Fixtures and fittings)		2 400
Land and buildings	65 000	
Bank loan (repayable long-term)		10 000
Interest on loan (12½% pa)	938	
Capital		72 450
	193 149	193 149

NOTES: as on 30 June

1. Closing stock £5 300
2. During the financial year P Jackson took goods for own use from the business which cost £2 000
3. Revenue accrued: £426 still to be received on commission
4. Rates had been paid £200 in advance
5. £312 is owed for interest on the bank loan and £540 is due on salaries
6. Provision for bad debts is to be increased to 10 per cent of the debtors
7. Provision for depreciation of 10 per cent p.a. on cost is to be made on fixtures and fittings
8. The motor vehicles are to be revalued to £6 000

The trial balance as on 30 June, did not balance, so a suspense account had to be opened with a credit balance of £549.

However, the following errors were revealed shortly after the accounts had been further scrutinised:

1. Credit sales of £1 200 had been omitted from the books (a sales invoice had been found relating to June)
2. A receipt of £500 from a debtor had been recorded in the cash book only, the posting being omitted
3. Discounts received (£376) had been recorded correctly in the purchase ledger, but had in error been posted to the debit side of the discounts account
4. Discounts allowed (£224) had also been recorded correctly in the sales ledger, but had in error been posted to the credit side of the discounts account

5 Payments made to the firm's supplier totalling £21 257 had been debited as £21 752 in the purchase ledger control account
6 Finally, the accountant's bill of £750 had been paid and recorded in the cash book but no further entry had been made

REQUIRED:
a) Prepare the necessary journal entries to record the above errors and show the suspense account as it would appear after the correction of all the accounting errors.
b) Adjust the relevant accounts in the trial balance affected by the errors.
c) Prepare an extended trial balance for P Jackson as at 30 June.
d) Prepare the trading and profit and loss account of P Jackson for the year ended 30 June.
e) Prepare the balance sheet of P Jackson as on 30 June, showing net current assets and the current ratio (in brackets).

33 Accounting standards

Objectives

On completing this section you should:

- be aware of significant SSAPs and FRSs in use
- recognise the adopted accounting principles when preparing final accounts.

33.1 Introduction

Statements of Standard Accounting Practice (SSAPs), and Financial Reporting Statements (FRSs), represent the profession's accounting standards. These statements are prepared for the purpose of standardising the preparation of the final accounts of a business and all accountants are expected to conform to these standards. The statements strongly oblige the accounting profession to accept what is considered the norm for accounting practice. The provisions laid down must be carried out and if they are not, accountants quite clearly need to state why they have not been adopted.

The preparation and publication of the SSAPs had been the responsibility of the six major accounting bodies of the UK (the ASC, Accounting Standards Committee) and provided both guidance and greater reliability to accountants in preparing the financial statements of a business. One of the principal statements is SSAP 2 (Disclosure of accounting policies) issued in 1971, which outlines the basic accounting concepts and could be said to be at the very heart of accounting theory.

Largely due to these published statements, there has been far greater conformity in accounting practice and therefore less variation in preparing final accounts. The financial statements are then more objective and reliable, rather than subjective and more open to controversy.

Up to 1988 there were some 24 statements which had been published by the ASC, although a number of them have been withdrawn or revised. SSAPs appear in many courses and examinations and included for discussion here are the following:

SSAP 2 (Disclosure of accounting policies)
SSAP 5 (Vat)
SSAP 9 (Stocks and work-in-progress)
SSAP 12 (Depreciation)
SSAP 13 (Research and development)
SSAP 17 (Post-balance sheet events)
SSAP 18 (Contingencies)
SSAP 21 (Leases and hire-purchase)
SSAP 22 (Goodwill).

On 1 August 1990 the Accounting Standards Committee gave way to a new body, the Accounting Standards Board (ASB). The ASB commenced operations on this date and is an independent body responsible for setting standards, taking over the functions of the ASC. The new board agreed to adopt the existing SSAPs although it is giving them a fresh overhaul, that is, modifying and changing them for the purpose of improving even further, the accounting standards of the profession. In time they become the generally accepted accounting practice (GAAP).

33.1.1 GAAP

What is the generally accepted accounting practice? This is governed by the rules which are handed down to the accounting profession from the accounting bodies and company law, such as the 1985 Companies Act. When these rules, mandatory or otherwise, become consistently adopted by different business organisations, they then become the accepted practice by the accounting profession. GAAP is not something which is static, but is always in flux, changing to new circumstances, primarily imposed by the profession itself or by the Government.

33.1.2 Exposure drafts

The ASB also agreed that its future agenda was to consider the overall fundamental concepts of accounting and also the exposure drafts (EDs) issued by the ASC. An exposure draft is all the research and preparation required for the purpose of issuing a future accounting standard. For example ED 51 (The accounting for fixed assets and revaluations) defined a fixed asset as:

> 'that held by an enterprise for use in the production or supply of goods and services, for rental to others, or for administrative purposes and may include items held for the maintenance or repair of such assets, with the intention of being used on a continuous basis and not intended for resale in the ordinary course of business'.

It stated that fixed assets were to be valued at their purchase price or production cost, unless shown at valuation, less any provisions for depreciation. There is, however, no legal obligation to apply to the terms of an exposure draft. With an accounting standard, the accounting profession is obliged to adopt it. With SSAP 2, limited companies are legally obliged to adopt it as it comes under the 1985 Companies Act.

The Board's first standard was published in September 1991 and was given the new title of Financial Reporting Standard (FRS replacing the letters SSAP).

FRS 1 (Cash flow statements) was published by the ASB and provides a standard for cash flow reporting as was discussed in a previous chapter. It superceded SSAP 10 (Statements of sources and application of funds) which is now obsolete.

33.1.3 SORPs

Apart from exposure drafts and accounting standards, there are also Statements of Recommended Practice (SORPs) which advises the profession on the most suitable practices which could be adopted although they are not obliged to do so. These statements were set up by the ASC in the mid 1980s and made it clear that although companies ought to consider adopting such practices, they were clearly not obliged to do so.

Is it all too much? Perhaps the new Accounting Standards Board can simplify some of the procedures with further issues of their financial reporting standards. Whether they succeed or make the rules for preparing financial statements even more complicated or controversial, only time will tell.

33.1.4 International Accounting Standards Committee

The aim of this committee (IASC) established in 1973, was to attempt to eliminate most of the choices of accounting treatment permitted under International Accounting Standards (IAS) in order to promote greater standardisation in the preparation of financial statements in many areas of the world. Less choice would mean better comparability of statements and more objectivity. A balance sheet therefore, prepared in Europe or in Far East Asia, or the USA, should look like a balance sheet prepared here in the UK and follow the same principles.

33.1.5 Financial statements

The major financial statements are the final accounts, that is, the trading and profit and loss account and the balance sheet. These two statements are a result of a business's financial transactions over a period of time. For a small business, this would probably be at the financial year end. For large businesses such as plc's, the statements could be prepared monthly for management purposes. Management need far more detailed statements at frequent intervals in which to monitor and control the business. For legal and tax requirements, the statements must be prepared at the financial year end.

33.2 Accounting principles

In the preparation of these statements certain accounting principles are adopted by the profession. Four of the major principles are referred to as the accounting concepts of going concern, accruals, consistency and prudence and are discussed in more detail in SSAP 2 which follows. Other significant principles to consider are:

33.2.1 The entity concept

This describes the business as a separate entity from that of its owner or owners. Even for a sole trader, his personal affairs must be made distinct from that of his business. Therefore, if the owner has personal cash drawings, or stock drawings, these are deducted from his capital to make them distinct from business transactions.

33.2.2 The concept of money measurement

This implies that only transactions which can be attributed with a monetary value can be recorded. For example, the value of a business's assets or liabilities. The human values of, say, an excellent workforce or brilliant marketing manager cannot be accounted for in monetary terms and therefore will not appear in the accounts.

33.2.3 The concept of cost

The recording of accounts is traditionally on a historical cost basis which means that the recording of transactions through time is made in relation to what the business paid for them. The advantage of recording at cost is that it does not interfere with more subjective aspects such as 'values', that is, what value should we put on stock or motor vehicles, etc. It is much easier and less controversial to record at the cost price of something. For example if we were to value a computer or other asset, what are some of the possibilities?

- at original cost
- at cost less depreciation
- at net realisable value
- at current replacement value
- at present value
- at current purchasing power
- at current cost accounting

Cost price: To value an asset at historical cost price simplifies the recording process. Whatever something cost on invoice or on a cash basis would be recorded at that price at that time.

Cost less depreciation: We have already witnessed in the chapter concerning depreciation that this is how fixed assets are recorded. Each fixed asset group would have a sum calculated as a charge towards depreciation. The difference then, between cost and depreciation becomes the net book value of the asset. This is the generally accepted accounting practice. Variations do occur of course, due to the estimations involved in applying the different depreciation methods (or accounting bases) that companies may adopt.

Net realisable value: This estimates the value of an asset, usually to stock values, although it can apply to a fixed asset, to the estimate of what it would sell for less selling expenses involved such as advertising, freight charges, etc. For example, if stock cost £100 and later it was found that it could only sell for £80, the stock should be valued at £80 rather than at its cost. SSAP 9 discusses this concept further.

Current replacement cost: This, as it suggests, is the current or market cost of replacing an asset in order to acquire the same service from it. Current replacement prices may come from catalogues or quotations from suppliers. (If an asset is purchased second hand, it would have a second-hand replacement value.)

Present value: This applies to different investment opportunities with the returns an asset could provide. The earnings from its future production is discounted at the going rates of interest which could be earned. One asset then could be compared with others as to its income or earnings potential, discounted to present day values. For example, if interest rates were 10 per cent, something purchased for £100 today would only be worth £90 next year and approximately £82 the year after. Therefore the asset with the greatest present value, discounted over a number of given years could be the best potential investment.

Current purchasing power (CPP). This is related to the cost concept but adjusting the purchasing power to take into account changes to the 'buying power of money' by using an index like the retail price or consumer price index. For example, if the cost of an asset was £1500 and since the date of purchase, the retail price index had risen to 120, then the use of current purchasing power would indicate that to buy the asset again would cost £1800.

In times of rising prices or high inflation, the index could rise steeply and the use of current purchasing power would markedly increase the value of assets. However, this aspect of inflation accounting was thought to be controversial because of the inconsistencies that could occur by the use of different indices on different types of assets by different types of business organisations.

The government set up a committee to investigate CPP and to enquire as to its merits. The Sandilands Report (1975) was the outcome of the committee's enquiries at a time when inflation was a serious problem in the United Kingdom. In short, the report stated that CPP 'is complicated and likely to be misunderstood unless it is very carefully interpreted by the company'.

This of course cast shadows of real doubt as to whether consistent standards could be maintained. The report also criticised CPP that it was conceptually the most difficult method of inflation accounting to implement and therefore had its limitations, particularly as to the unit of measurement to use to bring figures up-to-date.

Current cost accounting (CCA). This is a combination of using historical cost and the effect of price changes (due to changes in the retail price index) on the level of profit.

For example, if net assets (assets less liabilities) on 1 January were £30 000 and this had increased to £50 000 on 31 December, the profit for the year would be £20 000 if no other factors were involved like addition to or withdrawing of capital.

1 January:	Net assets	£30 000
31 December:	Net assets	£50 000
Net profit		£20 000

On a historical cost basis the profit is £20 000. If, however, inflation for the period was 8 per cent then the profit of £20 000 is affected in real terms:

1 January:	Net assets + 8%	£32 400
31 December:	Net assets	£50 000
Net profit		£17 600

This method brings us to the important concept of what is termed 'capital maintenance'.

Capital maintenance is about comparing the value of net assets in one period to their value in the next and to see how well off or otherwise a business is at the end of that period.

As we have already discussed under the section of depreciation, it is essential to charge fixed assets with depreciation for the period otherwise profit will be overstated. Profit is really not only about revenue less expenses, it is also how we *value the assets* of a business. How we value stocks and fixed assets will have a profound effect on the outcome of profit.

The theory of capital maintenance is also linked to that of inflation. On a historical cost basis, the calculation of profit does not take into account rising prices or the replacement cost of assets or indeed anything else. Therefore if prices rise due to inflation, we can say again that profits will be overstated by the rate of inflation at the time.

Historical cost is a basic measure of what something costs at the time of purchase. It is simple to use and clearly the most objective method. Historical cost accounting is widely recognised as the generally accepted accounting practice. However, it is not a perfect system, but what is a perfect system? The only difficulty with it, is in times of sharply rising prices. Is it an adequate method to use when preparing financial statements? Will a profit of £25 000 be sufficiently objective if inflation has risen by 20 per cent in the period in which it was earned? The real danger lies in the distribution of profit. If a company paid most of its profits as dividends, its capital and reserves would diminish in real terms because the net value of its capital would have fallen.

The following sections briefly outlines the SSAPs of interest.

33.3 SSAP 2 Disclosure of accounting policies

This was issued in the November of 1971 and outlined fundamental accounting concepts, policies and bases:

> 'It is fundamental to the understanding and interpretation of financial accounts that those who use them should be aware of the main assumptions on which they are based. The purpose of this statement is to assist such understanding by promoting improvement in the quality of information disclosed. It seeks to achieve this by establishing as standard accounting practice the disclosure in financial accounts in clear explanations of the accounting policies followed in order to give a true and fair view'.

A clear and brief description of the accounting policies used by a business should be provided with the final accounts. The SSAP makes it obligatory to disclose the accounting policies to be adopted. The four basic accounting concepts are:

1 *Going concern concept*: It is assumed that the business will continue its operations from one accounting period to the next, thus the value of its assets are based on the business carrying on trading. For example, the fixed assets are valued at cost less depreciation but if there was some reason to suggest that the business was to be sold or fall into bankruptcy, then the assets would have to be valued differently to reflect the circumstances. The value of stock may also be affected and may have to reflect net realisable values well below cost.

2 *Accruals concept*: This concept matches revenue with expenses and it is firmly assumed that the final accounts will incorporate all expenses paid or incurred as well as all the income earned. If a wages bill of say £10 000 was still due to be paid at the end of the accounting period, it would be taken for granted that this would be charged to the profit and loss account and also listed as a current liability, until paid.

3 *Consistency concept*: It is assumed that similar accounting items are treated on a consistent basis, otherwise distortions to profits may easily occur. For example, inconsistencies relating to the methods adopted for depreciation or stock valuation could have unfair distortions to profit. As indicated previously in SSAP No.12 Depreciation, a change in method may only be permitted if it gives a *fairer* representation to the accounts. Any material effect on the charge for depreciation must be explained clearly in the notes to the accounts.

4 *Prudence (conservatism) concept*: It is the standard to adopt a conservative view in the preparation of final accounts so that revenue must be reasonably certain before it is to be recognised and recorded. At the same time, the accountant is expected to provide for any unexpected losses such as providing for bad debts or writing the value of stock down in the event that demand is likely to fall. Thus the accountant is seen to be rather pessimistic rather than overtly optimistic and is likely to be cautious in the valuation of a business's assets.

In addition to the four basic concepts outlined above, there are a number of other concepts which may be included in a business's accounting policies:

Materiality: This concept relates to the view that small or insignificant items may be excluded from the final accounts. For example, to omit pence from the figures is quite a normal practice. The size of the business organisation will influence what is considered material or not. A large business may consider a valuation of a fixed asset under say £500 as relatively insignificant and treat it as an expense item, charged to profit and loss in the year purchased. A smaller organisation may consider a sum of £500 as significant and treat it as capital expenditure and include it as a fixed asset.

Dual aspect This concept recognises the fact that the business is represented by its assets, and that these assets are financed by the owner or owners, and the liabilities. The accounting equation reflects the dual aspect:

Assets (the business)	=	Capital + Liabilities (claims on the business)

Realisation This concept recognises the importance of both prudence and the matching between income and expenditure. Only when a definite sale has been transacted can it be recorded and therefore realised. A sale should not be recorded on the basis of an order, rather on the issue of the sales invoice or the signing of a contract.

33.3.1 Accounting bases

These bases refer to the methods adopted by businesses when they apply the basic concepts in accounting in the preparation of their final accounts. As there are alternative methods available, for example, in the valuation of stock or the depreciation of assets, the accounting policies must disclose which bases are being used and that such bases are consistently applied. Accounting policies help those interested parties to know how certain fundamental items are being dealt with.

An example of an accounting policy

'The company adopts the accrual concept in the preparation of its accounts with the exception of items where, in the opinion of the directors, the inclusion would have no material effect on the profits of the organisation.

The company has a policy where it capitalises the cost of additions and major works to premises at the cost price.

The company adopts a straight-line basis when providing for depreciation of machinery and equipment. Revaluation is adopted for the depreciation of the company's motor vehicles. These policies will continue until the assets are disposed of.

Stocks are valued at the "lower of cost or net realisable value" computed on the basis of selling price after the deduction of all relevant overheads.

Land and buildings are recorded at cost and a 5 per cent depreciation will be charged annually on the straight-line basis.'

33.3.2 The concepts to be indentified

It is important to realise that an organisation would naturally accept that the four basic concepts would be adopted in the preparation of their final accounts:

a) Going concern: the accounts are valued on the basis that the company will continue trading.
b) Accruals: line 1, revenue is matched against expenses relating to the financial period.
c) Consistency: charges for depreciation and stock are using the same method (or base) from one period to the next.
d) Prudence: stock valuation at the lower of cost.
e) Other concepts: materiality and cost.

33.4 SSAP 5 Accounting for Vat

This standard aims to achieve uniformity in the treatment of Vat in published accounts. Vat is currently charged at the rate of 17.5 per cent standard rate on a wide variety of goods and services. There is also zero-rated Vat and exempt Vat. The Chancellor (Mr Clark) made himself unpopular when he wanted to increase the Vat on power and fuel bills from 8 per cent to the standard 17.5 per cent as was planned by his predecessor Mr Lamont. This, however, was also unpopular with some of his own party members and the Vat remains at the time at 8 per cent, the Bill being defeated in the Commons.

Businesses which are registered for Vat (those listed with HM Customs & Excise) are collectors of this indirect form of tax, on behalf of the Government. Traders collect Vat on their sales, (output tax), offset by what they pay on purchases and other expenses, (input tax). The balance between these two figures in the Vat account will either indicate whether a sum is owing to the Vat Office or whether the Vat Office owes the business money because inputs are greater than outputs. Traders who need not register for Vat either because they are below the turnover threshold or they sell exempt goods or services, cannot charge Vat on sales and neither can they recover any Vat charges on inputs.

In the preparation of the final accounts, SSAP 5 states that those businesses registered with Customs & Excise should exclude Vat on all taxable inputs and taxable outputs. In other words, sales, purchases, taxable expenses and fixed assets, are recorded net (excluding Vat). The Vat charges are recorded in a Vat account. At the end of the financial period, any Vat owing to Customs would be listed as a current liability (a credit balance), or a current asset (a debit balance) in the balance sheet.

Expenditure which is not Vat deductible such as tax on motor vehicles or for expenses which the Vat Office will not allow recovery, the full amount will appear in the profit and loss account and balance sheet. The same will apply to those non-registered businesses which are exempt Vat, all their expenditure will include Vat charges in the recording of their accounts as well as in their final accounts.

33.5 SSAP 9 Stocks and work-in-progress

> 'No area in accounting has produced wider differences in practice than the computation of the amount at which stocks and work-in-progress are stated in the financial accounts. This statement seeks to define the practices and to narrow the differences and variations in those practices and to ensure adequate disclosure in the accounts'.

This standard seeks to establish a broad band of generally accepted accounting techniques in the valuation of stock. There are a number of different ways that stocks can be valued and this statement was written with a view to limiting the number of options open in valuation. Stocks may comprise finished goods, raw materials and partly finished goods and SSAP 9 states that 'stock be valued at the lower of cost or net realisable value'.

Net realisable value has already been mentioned earlier in the chapter under valuation of assets and is referred to as the selling price of stock less any expenses involved in the selling process. In other words, stock should be valued as a general rule, at the cost price, but if for any reason (such as a recession), the selling price were to fall lower than that of cost, then the net realisable value should be used. This is the conservatism or prudence concept generally accepted in accounting practice. To be able to foresee possible losses and not recognising profits until realised.

The statement, in defining *cost*, states that the purchase cost would include any import duties, carriage inwards, handling charges or other cost in the procurement of goods, less any trade discount which may be offered. In the manufacturing cost, this should include the cost of direct labour and materials plus factory overheads as a result of what is considered 'normal' output levels. (Any idle or slack production affecting overheads should not be considered as part of the stock valuation.)

A system of costing stocks should be consistently adopted and once a method or base in valuation has been used, the same system should be adopted, otherwise distortion of profits will occur and the final accounts may not be accepted by the firm's auditors as being 'true and fair'. More details concerning the valuation of stocks and work-in-progress is in Chapter 38 of the text.

33.6 SSAP 12 Accounting for depreciation

This statement has already been discussed in Chapter 23 and is only briefly mentioned here. Depreciation is defined as the loss of value in fixed assets over periods of time. The standard defines that 'depreciation is the measure of the wearing out of a fixed asset through use, time, or obsolescence and that charges of depreciation should be spread fairly over the fixed asset's life'. The depreciation charges for the period are written off to profit and loss account as expenses and the cumulative depreciation to date is deducted from the cost value of fixed assets in the balance sheet. The concept of consistency must apply and once a method of depreciation has been adopted, the same method should be used until the asset is finally disposed of. Again, if this were not the case, distortion of profits would occur and incorrect figures would be recorded in the profit and loss account and the balance sheet. If it were necessary to make revaluations in fixed assets which involved changing the method of depreciation, reasons to why this should occur must accompany the final accounts. For example, if premises were to be revalued, the date this occurred, the valuers names, the reason for valuation and other specific details must be noted in the balance sheet.

This SSAP does not apply to all fixed assets and those excluded are those which concern investments (SSAP 19), goodwill (SSAP 22) and research and development (SSAP 13).

33.7 SSAP 13 Accounting for research and development

This standard concerns itself with the costs which are incurred by those companies spending money for research and development purposes. The key point is that of defining the type of expenditure incurred, that is, whether it is classed as capital or revenue expenditure.

Research falls into two basic categories: pure and applied. Pure research is classified as that research into new scientific or technological principles and is seen as original research. Applied research infers a more practical nature, building upon the work classed as original.

Research, whether pure or applied, is generally seen as revenue expenditure because it is of an ongoing nature, part of the day-to-day costs of a business, often trying to stay ahead of its competitors in the manufacture of a wide range of products. Because one accounting period may not benefit substantially more than another from reseach, it is appropriate to see it as revenue expenditure, the costs written off to the profit and loss account as they occur.

The standard defines development as the use of existing scientific or technical knowledge, in order to produce improved products. Development could involve the manufacture of prototype models, testing them, modifying them, for the purpose of earning future income. The development of a new type of car or a new medicine, therefore, could benefit a number of future accounting periods. If future revenues are to be affected, some developmental costs could be spread over a number of financial periods and be capitalised in the same way as other fixed assets. Research is classified therefore as revenue expenditure whilst its 'inseparable twin' development, is more likely to be seen as capital expenditure.

The 1985 Companies Act states that research costs should not be capitalised and should be written off as and when they occur. The Act states that development costs may be capitalised under fixed assets if, in the balance sheet, notes to the accounts explain the reasons why development is being capitalised and the period of time involved when the capitalisation is to be written off as future charges in the profit and loss account.

A development project should be seen as technically feasible and have commercial potential over future accounting periods, otherwise there is little point in making it a capital project and treating it as any other fixed asset.

33.8 SSAP 17 Accounting for post-balance sheet events

Once the balance sheet has been approved by the board of directors in a limited company it is difficult to change the content of the value of assets and liabilities. However, since the publication of this SSAP in 1980 if, after the balance sheet date, certain items are seen to bear significance on the valuation of certain accounts, then their values may be adjusted as long as the additional evidence is seen as influential. For example, if there is evidence available that some fixed assets such as premises or investments are to lose their value.

Under current assets there may be evidence to support that some stocks may have to be adjusted because their net realisable value has fallen. The same applies to liabilities where their valuation may also be under question because of further evidence which has subsequently arisen.

The standard also gives information concerning non-adjusting items where there could exist influential evidence relating to the balance sheet, but figures cannot be adjusted to take account of them. Nevertheless, their disclosure is still required as notes to the balance sheet accounts. Examples of these concern the future issues of shares and debentures, mergers with other companies and the closure of some of the business's trading activities.

33.9 SSAP 18 Accounting for contingencies

Contingent liabilities are probable losses a company may have to pay for in the future and therefore must be included in the balance sheet.

For example, if a company was due to appear in court to defend an action like polluting the environment, and it was most likely going to lose the case and have to pay costs, a sum would have to be set aside as an accrued expense in the profit and loss account and appear as a contingent liability in the balance sheet. If however, it believed that it would not lose the case, a note to the accounts of the contingent liability would be sufficient.

The Companies Act 1985 as well as this statement make it a legal requirement for companies to disclose its contingent liabilities. The concept of prudence, as stated earlier in SSAP 2 indicates that if there is any concern about future losses (as in the case of bad and doubtful debts), then provision must be made in the accounts to cover such possible losses.

33.10 SSAP 21 Accounting for leases and hire purchase contracts

This standard attempts to regularise the accounting treatment and disclosure of assets which are held under lease or hire purchase agreement. The lease or hire purchase of fixed assets is an alternative method of financing assets rather than paying for them outright or by alternative credit terms.

When goods are sold on credit, the legal title of them are immediately passed to the buyer but if they are sold on a hire purchase agreement, the title of the goods does not pass to the buyer until the last instalment has been paid. If fixed assets are acquired under a lease, there is no provision for the title to be passed to the lessee (the person who acquires the asset) under the terms of a lease contract.

If a fixed asset is acquired under a hire purchase agreement it is treated as capital expenditure, even though the legal title of the goods is not passed to the buyer until the final instalment. The cost price of hire purchase is debited to the fixed asset account and the interest calculated in the period is charged to profit and loss account.

The amount owing to the creditor will be the cost price of the asset plus interest charges, less any repayments made. Depreciation of the fixed asset should be dealt with in the normal way, irrespective of how it is financed and will be based on the cost price of the asset (excluding interest charges).

Under the terms of a lease, the lessor (the party offering the lease) retains legal ownership of the asset and only hires it out to the lessee (the hirer), for an agreed length of time. SSAP 21 recognises two basic categories of lease: finance leases and operating leases.

A finance lease (similar to a hire purchase agreement) are offered by finance companies, banks and other organisations, provides either the finance of the asset or the asset itself, for the use by the lessee, normally on a fixed long term contract. The lessee acquires the ownership of the asset without actually having the legal title to it. This is to be treated as acquiring a fixed asset by the lessee, therefore debiting the asset account and crediting the lessor (long term liability) account. In other words, the transaction is capitalised and any interest payment is charged as an expense to profit and loss account.

Depreciation or amortisation (for leasing of premises) is calculated in the normal way and recorded both as an expense in the profit and loss account and cumulative depreciation in the balance sheet. From the lessor's point of view, the financing of the lease will be seen as debiting the lessee (as a debtor) and crediting sales.

An operating lease is acquired more on a rental basis rather than a fixed long term contract as in a finance lease. It is therefore viewed as a rental agreement and payment is charged against profits in the profit and loss account. The lessor would normally be expected to take the responsibility for repairs, maintenance, insurance or any other costs in ensuring the asset is operable. The payment of rental by the lessee will normally be made up of interest charges on the finance provided by the lessor and a repayment charge which covers the capital cost of the asset.

To summarise this standard, hire purchase and finance leasing are both capitalised and recorded as fixed assets, with appropriate charges for interest and depreciation in the profit and loss account. The balance owing to the supplier/lessor is recorded as a long term liability. The operating lease is seen more as a rental charge and is treated as revenue expenditure in the profit and loss account.

33.11 SSAP 22 Goodwill

Goodwill is defined as an intangible fixed asset normally arising from the surplus or excess price of a business over the net asset value, because of the good name or reputation which a business has built up or the value of any concessions or patents which it may have as part of the business. The standard recognises that it is difficult to separate goodwill as a whole from the other business assets and its calculation is both subjective and can fluctuate in value over periods of time.

Therefore the purchasing of a business with a value for goodwill should normally eliminate the goodwill portion immediately upon the acquisition of a business.

In the case of a partnership where goodwill is brought in by the partners, it should be written off on the basis of the partners' profit sharing ratio at the time the partners agree to it being written off.

In the case of a company, the purchase of goodwill may be written off immediately against identifiable reserves (or even some suitable as yet unrealised reserves until realised reserves are obtained). Where in some cases there is 'negative goodwill' where the purchase price of the business is less than the net asset value, then reserves can be credited with the negative balance.

The standard however, does allow the purchase of goodwill to be depreciated (or amortised) over its useful economic life. In this case, it is depreciated over time, the charge being made against the profit and loss appropriation account and then the cost, accumulated depreciation (amortisation) and net book value, is shown in the balance sheet. The following statements have been prepared by the former Accounting Standards Committe (ASC):

The list of existing SSAPs

SSAP 1	Associate companies
SSAP 2	Disclosure of accounting policies
SSAP 3	EPS (earnings per share)
SSAP 4	Government grants
SSAP 5	Vat
SSAP 6	Extraordinary items
SSAP 7	Changes in the purchasing power of money
SSAP 8	Taxation
SSAP 9	Stocks and work in progress
SSAP 10	Funds statement (withdrawn, now FRS 1, Cash Flow)
SSAP 11	Withdrawn
SSAP 12	Depreciation
SSAP 13	Research and development
SSAP 14	Group accounts
SSAP 15	Deferred taxation
SSAP 16	Current cost accounting
SSAP 17	Post balance sheet events
SSAP 18	Contingencies
SSAP 19	Investment properties
SSAP 20	Foreign currency
SSAP 21	Leasing and hire purchase contracts
SSAP 22	Goodwill
SSAP 23	Acquisitions and mergers

At the time of publishing, these Financial Reportings Statements (FRS) have been published by the ASB:

FRS 1	Cash flow statements
FRS 2	Accounting for subsidiary undertakings
FRS 3	Reporting financial performance.
FRS 4	Capital instruments
FRS 5	Reporting the substance of transactions

Summary

SSAPs and FRSs are the accounting standards provided by the accounting profession for the purpose of achieving some conformity in the preparation and presentation of final accounts. This has provided a measure of objectivity to published accounts. The ASB (Accounting Standards Board) is currently responsible for the revision and updating of all SSAPs, in effect, giving them a spring-clean so that they become the accepted accounting practice. Accounting principles are those concepts in accounting which when adopted, affect the computation of the final accounts. The concept of cost, for example, can be a complex matter, particularly if prices rise during an accounting period. Do we use the cost price or a price modified by inflation? An accounting base refers to the method adopted by business when it applies an accounting concept. Once adopted, it should be consistently used otherwise distortion of profit may occur.

Questions

1 If the accounting profession had not drawn up a set of SSAPs, what could have been the effect on the preparation of final accounts for different business organisations? (33.1)

2 What is meant by:
a) the concept of entity
b) the concept of money measurement? (33.2)

3 Suggest three different methods which may be attributed to the value of an asset in the balance sheet. (33.2)

4 Present value takes into consideration the future estimated returns. Explain what this actually means. (33.2)

5 An historic cost basis is traditionally used in preparing final accounts. In times of inflation, it has been said that these final accounts may mislead users of financial information.
a) Explain the alternative approaches in the preparation of inflation-adjusted accounts;
b) Explain the likely effect on the measurement of profits and fixed assets when these alternatives are adopted. (33.2)

(Chartered Institute of Management Accountants)

6 SSAP 2 is seen to be of fundamental importance to the accounting profession. Why is this the case? (33.3)

7 The accounting policies of Renton Industries plc, year ended 30 April is as follows:
'The accounts are prepared under the historial cost convention modified to include the revaluation of investments which are included at their market value. Other fixed assets are valued at cost less accumulated depreciation.
Stock is valued at the lower of cost and net realisable value. Sales will only be accounted for

from the actual date of the invoice. Interest payments and other accruals are to be charged to profit and loss as incurred and if sufficiently material'.
Identify and briefly discuss the underlying concepts of the above accounting policy. (33.3)

8 Under SSAP 5, if a trader is not registered for Vat, yet has to pay Vat on purchases of goods and expenses, how does this affect his final accounts? (33.4)

9 If a trader is registered and charges the standard rate of Vat, how are his accounts affected? (33.4)

10 What do you consider the significant accounting concepts are in relation to SSAP 9? (33.5)

11 How are SSAPs 13 and 21 concerned with capital and revenue expenditure? Briefly explain your answer. (33.7,10)

12 Once the board of directors have approved the final accounts, in which circumstances can they include adjusting values? (33.8)

13 If an imminent loss seems probable to a limited company, how can this be recorded in its balance sheet? (33.9)

14 If a limited company wished to write off any sums for goodwill or preliminary expenses when it was set up, how could it do this in the final accounts? (33.11)

34 Evaluating business performance: accounting ratios

Objectives

On completing this section you should:

- understand why accounting ratios are used
- understand how accounting ratios are calculated
- recognise the various categories of ratios
- recognise their use to management for evaluation and interpretation.

34.1 Introduction

Accounting ratios can assist both the owners and managers in business to improve their decision making. The performance of every business organisation is related to its **aims and objectives**. Whether the results look good or not, will largely depend upon the objectives of the business. If a firm wanted a 30 per cent return of profit on its capital invested and the results showed only a 15 per cent return, then the report on its performance will be disappointing. On the other hand, if the aim was to achieve a 10 per cent return, then the result would be received far more differently.

Accounting ratios help owners and managers in business to compare figures over periods of time and also to compare them with their competitors and with industries in the same field as themselves. It will help them appreciate the levels of financial performance being achieved. From preparing these ratios, key questions about the business can be analysed: **profitability**, **liquidity** and **efficiency** being particularly significant. Is the business becoming more successful or less so? What factors might be identified to help management decide what to do for the best?

34.2 Grouping accounting ratios

A business's accounting ratios can be analysed into various groups and text books are never consistent about this. The reason why they are not is because:

a) there are so many different types of businesses producing a wide variety of different goods or services;
b) accounting ratios are devised to be adapted to meet this wide variety of different business organisations.

However, the important thing is to be *consistent* from one financial period to the next and businesses must try to use the same formula for their calculations within their industry. The comparison of results will be far more accurate as a result. The following are some of the accounting groups to be considered. Each of these will be discussed in the following sections (investment ratios in section 34.7):

1 Profitability
2 Efficiency
3 Liquidity (short-term solvency)
4 Structure (long-term solvency)
5 Investment

There are other groupings too and these should not confuse your basic understanding of how to calculate the ratios and what they are meant to be used for. In accounting, there are always different ways to say and mean the same thing. For example, asset usage ratios can be expressed as asset turnover, solvency ratios are another way of stating liquidity, the rate of stock turnover is also the stock holding period, etc.

By reducing the absolute figures taken from financial statements to accounting ratios, comparisons from one year to another, or with different organisations becomes easier and more meaningful. By using ratios to evaluate financial information, it is possible to compare the performance and structure of different organisations and sizes. A ratio in itself may not provide all that much information about a company, but if a number of years were taken, a trend or pattern emerges, or if one company is compared to others, then ratios do become more useful.

The commercial banks and other financial institutions provide annual performance comparisons with which to analyse key financial ratios for companies in different sectors of industry, for example, business and professional services, retail and distribution, heavy and light manufacturing. They tend to group the ratios into two basic categories:

1 performance ratios which give an indication of a company's profitability and efficiency;
2 financial status ratios (structure) which indicate the overall financial position of a company.

These ratios are defined clearly as to how they are calculated and what they are used for and do provide a valuable yardstick to both owners and managers for *financial planning* purposes.

Example of accounting ratios and evaluation
To illustrate the 5 groups of accounting ratio at work, we will use a specific example. The following information relates to G Johnson-Smith, an entrepreneur in sporting goods. At the financial year end 30 June 19–9 his final accounts were as follows:

Trading and profit and loss statement

	£	£	£
Sales			210 000
Cost of sales			
Stock (1/7/–8)	8 700		
Purchases	124 600		
	133 300		
Returns out	(2 000)		
	131 300		
Stock (30/6/–9)	(5 300)		126 000
Gross profit			84 000
Sales and distribution costs			
Motor expenses	5 870		
Advertising	580		
General expenses	1 650		
Salesmens' wages	18 900	27 000	

(continued)

(continued)

Administration expenses			
Rent and rates	9 005		
Wages, office	20 200		
Printing and stationery	495		
Interest	4 500		
Light and heat	1 800	36 000	63 000
Net profit			21 000

Balance sheet as at year end 30 June 19–9			
	£	£	£
FIXED ASSETS			
Equipment, tools		55 000	
Motor vans		17 400	72 400
CURRENT ASSETS			
Stock	5 300		
Debtors	4 800		
Bank/cash	2 430		
Pre-payments	310	12 840	
CURRENT LIABILITIES			
Creditors	6 000		
Accruals	740	6 740	
Net current assets			6 100
Capital employed			78 500
DEFERRED LIABILITIES			
9% loan			50 000
Net assets			28 500
FINANCED BY:			
Capital		20 000	
Profit		21 000	
Drawings		(12 500)	28 500

REQUIRED:

Using the final accounts of Johnson-Smith, calculate the accounting ratios which will test profitability, efficiency, liquidity and structure. Make brief comments relating to performance for the financial year. There are no previous figures for comparison purposes, therefore the evaluation will tend to be limited and not show the trends of the business.

34.3 Profit ratios

a)

$$\text{Gross profit \%} = \frac{\text{Gross profit} \times 100}{\text{Net sales}}$$

$$= \frac{£84\,000 \times 100}{£210\,000} = 40\%$$

b)

$$\text{Net profit \%} = \frac{\text{Net profit} \times 100}{\text{Net sales}}$$

$$= \frac{£21\,000 \times 100}{£210\,000} = 10\%$$

These two ratios indicate the gross and net margins of profit to sales. Is a 40 per cent gross margin adequate? Is it a more or less constant figure compared with previous years? The gross percentage tells us the difference between cost and selling prices. Every £100 of sales should bring in £40 gross profit. If the gross percentage falls, it could be due to a number of reasons, including:

- increase in cost of purchases which have not been passed on to customers;
- loss of stock from breakages, damage, stealing, or obsolete stock marked down in price;
- poor buying policy, not taking advantage of bulk purchases and discounts.

The net profit margin indicates profit after all expenses have been taken into account. Therefore a 10 per cent return means that for every £100 of sales, £10 is net profit. How does this compare with previous years or with the type of business as a whole (in this case sporting goods)? If the net return was to fall, say to 8 per cent, this would need to be investigated to find out the reason for the decrease. Are the overheads more expensive? Have sales declined in recent years? If they have, what is behind the decrease? Is it a single cause, or are there a number of reasons which can explain what has happened?

c)

$$\text{ROCE (Return on Capital Employed)} = \frac{\text{Net profit} \times 100}{\text{Capital employed}}$$

$$= \frac{£21\,000 \times 100}{£78\,500} = 26.75\%$$

d)

$$\text{ROCE (Return on Capital Invested)} = \frac{\text{Net profit} \times 100}{\text{Capital invested (beginning)}}$$

$$= \frac{£21\,000 \times 100}{£20\,000} = 105\%$$

e)

$$\text{ROTA (Return on Total Assets)} = \frac{\text{Net profit} \times 100}{\text{Total assets}}$$

$$= \frac{£21\,000 \times 100}{£85\,240} = 24.64\%$$

These ratios relate profit or loss to the balance sheet and they are significant because profit is expressed in terms of returns on investment, either on the business or the owners.

The return on capital employed is one of the most fundamental and important accounting ratios measuring profit in relation to the available capital employed (fixed assets plus working capital). A ratio of 26.75 per cent appears to be a very adequate return indeed, but it needs to be compared with previous years to see if it is a constant return or whether, in fact, it is improving or falling. What could the business earn if it invested its capital elsewhere? What effect has inflation had on the figures? Could the business expect a higher return if it was to invest on the Stock Exchange or in property?

The return on capital invested indicates that Johnson-Smith had a capital of £20 000 at the beginning of his financial period and had made a profit of £21 000 at the period end, an admirable return of 105 per cent – a very impressive profitable investment on any terms. It would be difficult to have a similar return in any form of investment, perhaps with the exception of property during times of rising prices.

The return on the total assets of the business recognises profit to all assets and is a very similar ratio to that of capital employed. Profit ratios and interest are also discussed in section 34.7 on p. 423.

34.4 Efficiency ratios

a) Expense percentages

$$\text{Cost of sales (per cent)} = \frac{\text{COS} \times 100}{\text{Net sales}}$$

$$= \frac{£126\,000 \times 100}{£210\,000} = 60\%$$

$$\text{Sales and distribution (per cent)} = \frac{\text{Sales and distribution} \times 100}{\text{Net sales}}$$

$$= \frac{£27\,000 \times 100}{£210\,000} = 12.9\%$$

$$\text{Administration (per cent)} = \frac{\text{Administration} \times 100}{\text{Net sales}}$$

$$= \frac{£36\,000 \times 100}{£210\,000} = 17.1\%$$

Total expenses (per cent) = 90%

Net profit (per cent) = 10%

Total = 60 + 12.9 + 17.1 + 90 + 10 = 100%

A breakdown of expenses may be indicated in relation to pence in the pound:

	Pence / £	
Cost of sales	60p	
Sales and distribution	13p	
Administration	17p	90p
Profit		10p
		100p

Is 10p/£ an adequate return? Could it be improved by a reduction in any one of the above costs? Could any of the selling prices be increased, thereby improving the margin of profit? Perhaps the administration costs could be more efficient – particular aspects to look at are office wages and interest payments which takes up about 60 per cent of administration. Again, comparisons need to be made with previous performances. (See the pie chart on the next page to show expenses/profit.)

Any individual expense could provide a ratio to sales. The office wages to sales ratio for example is 9.6 per cent, representing nearly 10p in the £.

b)

$$\text{The rate of stock turnover} = \frac{\text{Cost of sales}}{\text{Average stock}}$$

$$= \frac{£126\,000 \times 100}{{}^{\star}£7\,000} = 18 \text{ times per annum}$$

$$= \frac{52}{18} = \text{Every 2.88 weeks}$$

⋆Stock (beginning)	£8 700	
Stock (end)	£5 300	$\frac{£14\,000}{2} = £7\,000$

Breakdown of expenses to the number of pence profit in the £

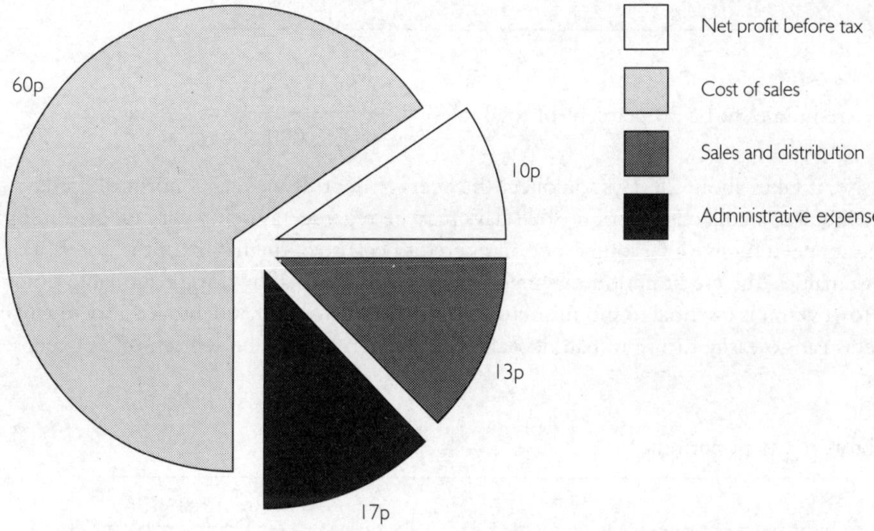

The speed of a business's stock turnover is a very important efficiency ratio, testing how fast a firm can sell its stock. The rate of turnover is dependent on the nature of goods sold. A supermarket selling the essential day-to-day consumables is expected to have a fast turnover, whereas a furniture store would have a much slower rate. The faster the rate of turnover, the greater the potential profit is likely to be. It could be that a reduction to selling prices, reducing the margin of profit, could achieve a faster turnover and therefore greater profits in absolute terms. In this case, Johnson-Smith takes almost three weeks to move his stock which is a relatively fast turnover. Is this a constant figure or has it changed from previous years?

For example, which is best considering units which cost 80p each:

A	100 units	@ selling price £1.00 each; or
B	200 units	@ selling price £0.95 each?

	A	*B*
	£	£
Sales	100	190
– Cost of sales	80	160
Gross profit	20	30

The gross profit percentage in A is 20 per cent and in B it is only 16 per cent. Clearly there is £10 more profit in B even though the margin of profit is less. Therefore, a reduction to selling price could increase profit in absolute terms because a higher turnover is achieved.

A higher stock turnover may also lead to more effective and economic buying, taking advantage of bulk purchasing and better trade discounts, thereby increasing the profit potential even more.

c)

$$\text{The rate of debt collection} = \frac{\text{Debtors} \times 365}{\text{Credit sales}}$$

$$\text{(Assume credit sales to be 30 per cent of total sales)} = \frac{£4\,800 \times 365}{£63\,000} = 27.8 \text{ days}$$

In this case, it takes about 28 days to collect the average debt. If we take a norm of 45 days to pay a monthly invoice, a collection period of 28 days may be regarded as being very efficient. Some types of businesses need to give a far longer period of credit because of the nature of the goods. For expensive consumables, the credit period may need to be extended to allow for a reasonable time for payment. However, it is essential to monitor credit control and ensure that debtors do try to pay on time. Long debts can so easily turn into bad debts and assets then have to be written off as expenses to the business.

d) Creditors payment period

$$\text{Rate of credit from suppliers} = \frac{\text{Creditors} \times 365}{\text{Credit purchases}}$$

$$\text{(Assume credit purchases to be 40 per cent of total purchases)} = \frac{£6\,000 \times 365}{£49\,840} = 43.94 \text{ days}$$

The average payment to creditors works out at about 44 days. On an average 30 day invoice therefore, it takes a further period of 2 weeks to pay. The longer the period of debt repayment, the better for the business because the creditors are providing an extra source of funds to use. As long as there is a mutual understanding and agreement between debtors and creditors of how long the payment period should be, then reliability and trust can grow. If the period becomes too long and creditors repeatedly need to demand payment, then reliability and trust diminishes and further trading may become unacceptable.

34.4.1 Asset usage

a)

$$\text{Sales/fixed assets} = \frac{\text{Sales}}{\text{Fixed assets}}$$

$$= \frac{£210\ 000}{£72\ 400} = 2.9{:}1$$

b)

$$\text{Sales/current assets} = \frac{\text{Sales}}{\text{Current assets}}$$

$$= \frac{£210\ 000}{£12\ 840} = 16.35$$

c)

$$\text{Sales/capital employed (asset turnover)} = \frac{\text{Sales}}{\text{Capital employed}}$$

$$= \frac{£210\ 0005}{£78\ 500} = 2.68{:}1$$

These ratios relate turnover to asset use. It takes £1 of fixed assets to generate £2.90 sales or £1 of current assets to generate a relatively high £16.35 sales. The key figure however, is the sales to capital employed (asset turnover) which is generally recognised as the most significant because it relates the return on capital employed (ROCE) as the product between the net profit percent and asset turnover.

The net profit percent (or margin) of the business is 10 per cent:

ROCE	=	Net profit%	×	Asset turnover
26.75%	=	10%	×	2.68

A company with a higher rate of ROCE therefore, has either a higher margin of net profit or is able to generate more sales from its asset base. G Johnson-Smith could measure this key financial ratio with the average for his industry to see the level of his own business's performance.

34.4.2 Productivity ratios

a)

$$\text{Sales/employee} = \frac{\text{Sales}}{\text{No. of employees}}$$

$$= \frac{£210\,000}{4} = £52\,500$$

b)

$$\text{Profit/employee} = \frac{\text{Net profit}}{\text{No. of employees}}$$

$$= \frac{£21\,000}{4} = £5\,250$$

The business has assumed to have four employees either as full-time or full-time equivalents. Productivity has always been seen to be another key figure in the efficiency of an organisation. The greater the productivity, the greater the profit available for distribution. An average profit of just over £5 000 per employee may or may not be sufficiently adequate to award an increase in productivity pay. A business can only offer to pay its workforce more money if their productivity increases through sales and profits. If productivity falls, then the labour force is seen to be less efficient and instead of extra pay and bonuses, redundancies may be the only alternative on offer.

34.5 Liquidity ratios (short-term solvency)

a)

$$\text{Current (working capital) ratio} = \frac{\text{Current assets}}{\text{Current liabilities}}$$

$$= \frac{£12\,840}{£6\,740} = 1.9{:}1$$

b)

$$\text{Acid test (quick asset) ratio} = \frac{\text{Current assets (– stock)}}{\text{Current liabilities}}$$

$$= \frac{£7\ 540}{£6\ 740} = 1.2{:}1$$

The current ratio has already been explained in Chapter 21. It tests the ability of the business in paying its short-term debts and is essentially the relationship between current assets and current liabilities. Liquidity ratios are also referred to as 'solvency' ratios, meaning the ability to pay creditors. They may be either short or long term.

Fundamentally, a current ratio of 1 : 1 is seen by the accounting profession as the minimum required to be in a position to meet creditors. Any figure less than this means that the business, in effect, is trading whilst insolvent, that is, it is not in a position to meet its current debts. When a business is trading insolvently, it is always more vulnerable to the demand of creditors and is therefore more likely to stretch its resources in attempting to meet payments. It may be in a more risky and precarious financial position and creditors can get very annoyed when their bills are not paid on time. They may refuse to allow further stock sales and may take legal action to reclaim their debts. Bankruptcy proceedings could then be the next stage.

The acid test tends to be a more immediate test of liquidity. The business is being tested to see whether it can be in a position to meet payment for debts without resorting to stock sales. The significance of this ratio is linked to the rate of stock turnover. It follows that, in the majority of cases, the greater the turnover, the less important is the acid test. Sainsbury's, the supermarket, for example, has a very high rate of stock turnover and most of its current assets are stocks. It has a low acid test, well below the value of 1 : 1, but because the stock is almost like cash, due to its high turnover, its significance is diminished.

On the other hand, a business which has a low stock turnover, would be anxious if its acid test was also low, because if any immediate demands for payment were to be made by creditors, these may be difficult to satisfy with sales of stock being slow.

Johnson-Smith's liquidity position appears to be sound in that, even without resorting to stock sales, he could satisfy the demands of creditors. Ideally, a business should have at least a 1 : 1 ratio as its acid test and something like 2 : 1 for its current ratio. However, each business should be fully aware of what its own liquidity position must be in order to trade with reasonable comfort. It should monitor closely its position to ensure it stays within its own set of acceptable parameters.

34.6 Structure ratios (long-term solvency)

a)

$$\text{Proprietor's ratio (owner's stake)} = \frac{\text{Current assets}}{\text{Current liabilities}}$$

$$= \frac{£28\ 500}{£85\ 240} = 0.33{:}1$$

b)

$$\text{Liability ratio} = \frac{\text{Total liabilities}}{\text{Capital}}$$

$$= \frac{£56\,740}{£28\,500} = 2{:}1$$

c)

$$\text{Gearing} = \frac{\text{Debt (fixed interest)}}{\text{Capital}}$$

$$= \frac{£50\,000}{£28\,500} = 1.75{:}1$$

These solvency ratios relate the owner's capital to liabilities. The basic purpose of this is to recognise the extent of external financing against the proprietor's financing.

The proprietor's ratio, or owner's stake in the business, indicates that Johnson-Smith has a 33 per cent stake (or claim) on his business assets. The remaining 67 per cent is in the hands of the business's liabilities. In effect, the business owes Johnson-Smith $1/3$ and the liabilities $2/3$. In the event that the business was closed or sold off, the creditors would have to be satisfied to the extent of £56 740.

The liability ratio is virtually stating the same information. A 2 : 1 ratio indicates that the external financing by creditors is twice that of the owner's financing. A ratio of parity, 1 : 1, would indicate equal financing between the owners and liabilities. A ratio of less than 1 would indicate that financing is more in the hands of the owners relative to its creditors.

Capital gearing relates to the proportion of fixed interest capital (for limited companies this would include preference share capital), to that of the owner's capital. In Johnson-Smith's case, a gearing of 1.75 indicates relatively high gearing, where the proportion of fixed interest capital is high relative to the owner's capital. Low gearing refers to a situation where there is a greater proportion of the owner's capital to that of fixed interest capital. For example, if Johnson-Smith's capital was £200 000, gearing would be 0.25, which would indicate a relatively low dependency on external fixed interest funds.

Where liquidity ratios emphasise the need to have sufficient working capital to meet short-term debts, the long-term solvency ratios indicate longer term financing, taking into account creditors falling after 12 months. If a business ties up too much of its funds in fixed capital (fixed assets), it may be in danger of becoming over-capitalised and may need to resort to borrowing, whether on overdraft with the bank, or on a fixed interest loan over longer periods. In times of high interest rates, this could put a great deal of pressure, particularly on small businesses, to meet their debt commitments.

34.7 Profit ratios and interest

Accounting ratios can be calculated in a variety of different ways because there are different formulas used to measure the same criteria. The important thing is to be consistent (concept of consistency) and use a standard guideline which can bear comparison from one financial period to the next otherwise profits will become distorted and an unfair view of performance will be the outcome.

For example, when companies pay interest on long-term borrowings (debentures or other long-term liabilities), the interest charges can be added back to the net profit figure in order to calculate the net profit per cent and the return on capital employed (ROCE). The purpose of this is to give the ratios more consistency, so that comparisons with other industries are more accurate regarding the profit derived from business activity (without interest payable on long-term loans).

Example

		Company A	*Company B*
		£	£
Turnover (sales)		360 000	540 000
Net Profit (before tax and interest)		24 000	48 000
Interest charges		6 000	12 000
Net Profit (after interest charges)		18 000	36 000
Net Profit %		24 000	48 000
(before interest charges)		360 000	540 000
	=	6.67%	8.89%

What would the net profit percent be with interest charges not added back?

Net Profit %		18 000	36 000
		360 000	540 000
	=	5%	6.67%

It is therefore important to be consistent in the use of accounting ratios, particularly if you are trying to compare businesses in the same industry. If it is generally accepted that interest charges are to be added back to net profit in order to calculate the net profit per cent or the return on capital employed, then this formula should be consistenly applied.

34.8 Interest cover

Interest cover indicates the number of times the profit of the business could pay off interest charges. The generally accepted formula is:

$$\text{Interest cover} = \frac{\text{Net Profit} + \text{Interest}}{\text{Interest}}$$

In our example of Company A and Company B:

		Company A	*Company B*
		£	£
Net Profit + Interest	=	24 000	48 000
		6 000	12 000
		4 times	4 times

The interest cover focuses on the business's ability to meet its interest commitments out of its profits. It is a long-term solvency ratio and also measures the 'gearing' of a company. As a coincidence, both businesses have the ability to cover interest charges 4 times over from profits. The higher the ratio, the better. A company with a low ratio of say 1.5: 1 will find it difficult to meet its debt commitments especially if trade began to fall.

In the following example, relating to the final accounts of Robert Andrew plc, accounting ratios will be calculated over two financial periods, including investment ratios.

34.9 Using ratios: a worked example

The following represents the accounts of Robert Andrew plc for the years ended 31 December:

Trading and profit and loss statement

	19–8	*19–9*
	£	£
Turnover (sales)	500 000	600 000
Cost of sales	300 000	390 000
Gross profit	200 000	210 000
Sales and distribution costs	50 000	70 000
Administration expenses	40 000	60 000
Net profit (before tax)	110 000	80 000
Provision for tax	34 000	22 000
Net profit (after tax)	76 000	58 000
Profit and loss account balance (1/1)	20 000	60 000
	96 000	118 000
Provision for dividends:		
Ordinary shares	20 000	12 000
8% preference shares	16 000	16 000
Profit and loss account balance (31/12)	60 000	90 000

Balance sheet as at 31 December

	19–8	19–9
	£	£
FIXED ASSETS	412 000	472 000
CURRENT ASSETS	209 000	240 000
	621 000	712 000
CURRENT LIABILITIES	101 000	185 000
LONG-TERM LIABILITIES	60 000	37 000
	161 000	222 000
	460 000	490 000
ISSUED AND PAID-UP CAPITAL		
200 000 @ £1 ordinary shares	200 000	200 000
200 000 @ £1 preference shares (8%)	200 000	200 000
Profit and loss account balance	60 000	90 000
	460 000	490 000

REQUIRED:

a) Use the appropriate accounting ratios for both 19–8 and 19–9 to help evaluate financial performance.

b) Compare the financial performance of the company over the two periods. Note that the market value of the company's shares as quoted on the Stock Exchange was 225p in 19–8 and 180p in 19–9.

a) *Robert Andrew plc – accounting ratios*

	19–8	19–9
1 *Profit ratios*:		
Gross profit	40.0%	35.0%
Net profit (before tax)	22.0%	13.3%
ROCE (before tax)	21.2%	15.2%
2 *Efficiency ratios*:		
Cost of sales	60%	65.00%
Sales and distribution	10%	11.67%
Administration	8%	10.00%
	78%	86.67%
Net profit	22%	13.33%
3 *Liquidity ratio*:		
Current ratio	2.1 : 1	1.3 : 1
4 *Structure ratios*:		
Proprietor's ratio	0.74 : 1	0.69 : 1
Liability ratio	0.35 : 1	0.45 : 1
*Capital gearing	*1.00 : 1	0.82 : 1

$$\frac{\text{*Fixed interest debt + preference shares}}{\text{Ordinary shares + profit and loss account}} = \frac{260\,000}{260\,000}$$

5 *Investment ratios:*

Earnings per share (EPS) (ordinary shares)

$$= \frac{\text{Net profit (after tax)} - \text{Pref dividend}}{\text{Number of ordinary shares}}$$

$$= \frac{76\,000\ (-16\,000)}{200\,000} \qquad \frac{£42\,000}{200\,000}$$

$$= 25\text{p/share (19–8)} \qquad 21\text{p/share (19–9)}$$

Dividend per ordinary share

$$= \frac{\text{Amount paid to ordinary shares}}{\text{Number of ordinary shares}}$$

$$= \frac{£20\,000}{200\,000} \qquad \frac{£12\,000}{200\,000}$$

$$= 10\text{p/share (19–8)} \qquad 6\text{p/share (19–9)}$$

Cover

$$= \frac{\text{Net profit (after tax)} - \text{Pref dividend}}{\text{Dividend paid to ordinary shares}}$$

$$= \frac{£60\,000}{£20\,000} \qquad \frac{£42\,000}{£12\,000}$$

$$= 3\text{ times (19–8)} \qquad 3.5\text{ times (19–9)}$$

Yield %

$$= \frac{\text{Dividend per share} \times 100}{\text{Market value per share}}$$

$$= \frac{10\text{p} \times 100}{225\text{p}} \qquad \frac{6\text{p} \times 100}{180\text{p}}$$

$$= 4.4\%\text{ (19–8)} \qquad 3.3\%\text{ (19–9)}$$

Price/earnings ratio

$$= \frac{\text{Market price per share}}{\text{Earnings per share}}$$

$$= \frac{225\text{p}}{25\text{p}} \qquad \frac{180\text{p}}{21\text{p}}$$

$$= 9\text{ times (19–8)} \qquad 8.6\text{ times (19–9)}$$

b) Evaluation of performance

The profit ratios in 19–8 were all superior to 19–9. The basic reason for this is that costs have increased from 78 per cent to 86.6 per cent over the year, the most notable increase being the cost of sales, up by 5 per cent. Perhaps sale prices were marked too low in an effort to generate more sales. Sales did increase but perhaps not sharply enough to gain more gross profit – it could be that the buying of stock was simply not economic enough. The other expenses also increased and were not controlled sufficiently, with the result that the net margin fell by almost 9 per cent, a rather wide margin.

Liquidity has suffered at the same time, the current ratio falling from a respectable 2:1, to a more marginal 1.3:1. Creditors have increased rather substantially perhaps because of over-trading and this has weakened the company's ability to meet its short-term debts.

The long-term solvency ratios indicate that the company's shareholders finance the business by about 70 per cent although this has also fallen from the previous year (74 per cent). Company gearing is slightly on the high side because the preference share capital is grouped with long-term liabilities as part of the fixed interest capital.

The investment ratios indicate a deterioriation of performance over the year. One of the most common and significant indicators to a business's performance is the earnings per share and this has fallen by 4p in the year, or by 16 per cent, not a good sign of success. The shareholders ordinary dividend has been reduced by 4p per share (40 per cent) in an effort to retain funds in the company. This is reflected by the *cover* which indicates the number of times ordinary shareholders could have been paid from the available profits. The greater the cover, the more is retained in the business.

The price to earnings ratio is also very significant to the financial markets because it indicates the market value of the company's shares in relation to profits. A price to earnings ratio of 9 means that the current market price would take about nine years of profit and that the market is willing to pay the sum for the shares. Generally speaking, the higher the rate, the better the share prospects. This has marginally fallen over the year from 9 to 8.6 times. Is the company a good investment or not? Should shares be retained or sold? Although the Stock Exchange is a reliable source as far as reporting financial figures, nothing is ever certain as to which shares will be the most successful.

34.10 The limitations imposed by accounting ratios

Accounting ratios are only really useful if they can be compared with a business's past performances, with its competitors or with a given norm for its particular industry. Ratios used in isolation may not be of any value at all.

When making a study of performance comparisons, it is of critical importance to ensure that there is a consistent use of bases, for example, when measuring capital gearing it needs to be established exactly what items must be included in both debt and equity. By equity, are we to assume all organisations use the total of shareholders' funds (excluding preference share capital)?

Accounting ratios are unlikely to provide any really useful information unless several years of figures are calculated and trends can be observed. If these are compared with trends of companies in the same line of business, evaluation can become much more meaningful.

In some cases, accounting ratios may not reveal the true or realistic situation. For example, a company could have a very sound looking 2:1 current ratio yet, because of either stock or debtors being incorrectly accounted for, the real position could be that the business is close to insolvency.

Accounting ratios also fail to reveal the human side of business. What do they say of the company's employees? Are they reliable? Is the atmosphere at work positive? Are workers satisfied? What may appear good on paper, may be far from the case at the workplace.

Nevertheless, accounting ratios do have their value if they are measured on a consistent basis and there is an opportunity to study trends. The analysis of figures can give clues as to the business's profitability, liquidity, stability and general efficiency. This information could be of great importance to both owners and management and help them make better, more informed decisions.

Summary

Accounting ratios can assist management in their decision making. Instead of relying on absolute figures from year to year, ratios can indicate significant trends in profits, liquidity and efficiency. By analysing and interpreting these figures, an evaluation of business performance can be built up. However, ratios cannot tell the whole story about business performance. They cannot illustrate the human factor such as the morale of workers or the level of effectiveness of individual managers; therefore we need to be aware of their limitations.

Questions

1 The following information relates to the final accounts of Henry R David Co Ltd for the years ending 31 December 19–8 and 19–9.

Profit and loss account of Henry R David Co Ltd for years ending 31 December

	19–8	*19–9*
	£	*£*
Retail sales	132 500	159 000
Net profit	19 875	23 850
Corporation tax	6 000	7 155
Net profit (after tax)	13 875	16 695
Provision for dividends:		
Ordinary shares	6 250	9 000
Retained profits	7 625	7 695

Balance sheet of Henry R David Co Ltd as at years ending 31 December

	19–8	*19–9*
	£	*£*
FIXED ASSETS (net)	65 000	79 735
CURRENT ASSETS		
Stock	8 750	12 150
Debtors	4 950	8 680
Bank	3 150	–
Cash	500	500

(continued)

(continued)

CURRENT LIABILITIES		
Creditors	4 350	4 875
Accruals	580	170
Taxation	6 000	7 155
Dividends	6 250	9 000
Bank	—	500
DEFERRED		
Loan ($1\frac{1}{2}$ years)	5 000	1 500
	60 170	77 865

REQUIRED:
From the information provided, prepare the appropriate accounting ratios which will test the company's profitability and liquidity over the two accounting periods. (34.2)

(Institute of Bankers)

2 a) Give the definition of *working capital* and then describe its components.

b)

Balance sheet of Economy Ltd
as at 30 September 19–5

	£		£
Ordinary shares	75 000	Land and buildings at cost	110 000
Reserves	25 700	Plant (book value)	24 000
		Vehicles (book value)	4 200
Long-term loan	60 000	Stock	18 600
Trade creditors	6 350	Debtors	15 700
Bank overdraft	9 600	Short-term investment	10 000
Taxation	4 100	Cash in hand	2 000
Dividend	3 750		
	184 500		184 500

Use this simplified balance sheet to calculate the value of working capital for Economy Ltd as at 30 September 19–5. Also calculate the current working capital ratio and the liquidity ratio and comment on their values. (34.2)

Note: Liquidity ratio is taken as the acid test ratio.

(Institute of Commercial Management)

3 a) Explain the meaning of the terms, 'profitability' and 'liquidity'.
b) Give two accounting formulae used to measure a firm's profitability.
c) Give one accounting formula used to measure a firm's liquidity.
d) Compare the figures given below, for two separate businesses taken over the same time period, in terms of profitability and liquidity. (34.2)

Business A:		*Business B:*	
	£000		*£*
Capital	100	Capital	80
Net profit	10	Net profit	20
Creditors	20	Creditors	40
Equipment	90	Premises	70
Bank	20	Debtors	5
Stock	10	Motor van	30
Debtors	10	Stock	10
		Equipment	20
		Bank	5

(Associated Examining Board)

4 The following information relate to two companies, both supermarkets, for the year ended 31 March 19–7:

	Company Big Ltd	*Company Spiv Ltd*
	£000	*£000*
Revenue statement		
Sales	750	500
Cost of sales	450	325
Other costs	210	100
Net profit	90	75
Taxation	32	25
Net profit (after tax)	58	50
Balance sheet		
Issued and paid-up capital:		
Ordinary shares	180	60
8% preference shares	20	—
Profit and loss account	30	10
10% debentures	—	80
	230	150
Bank overdraft	—	20
Other liabilities	105	50
	335	220
Fixed assets	146	129
Stocks	140	80
Debtors	29	11
Bank	20	—
	335	220

REQUIRED:

a) Calculate for both companies (to one decimal place) the following:
current ratio
liquid (or acid) ratio
capital gearing
net profit percentage to sales
earnings (after tax) as a percentage to ordinary shares
return on capital employed (after tax).

b) From the information gathered in a) above, briefly comment on the performance of the two supermarkets and state, giving reasons, which you consider is financially the safer investment of the two. (34.2)

(Institute of Bankers)

5 Bourne Park commenced business 1 January, and the company's accounts for the following four years made up annually to 31 December were as follows:

Year ended December 31	*Turnover*	*Purchases*	*Stock*	*Selling and distribution costs*	*Fixed costs*
	£	£	£	£	£
19–3	45 000	42 500	12 500	5 500	6 500
19–4	54 000	35 800	12 300	7 000	6 500
19–5	72 000	57 500	15 800	9 000	7 500
19–6	96 000	68 600	15 400	11 500	7 500

The directors have asked you, as the company's accountant, to provide an evaluation of profitability for the last four years.

REQUIRED:

a) Draw up in columnar form, the trading and profit and loss accounts of Bourne Park for each of the four years to 31 December.

b) Prepare a brief report outlining the implications of these figures and using any analysis ratios which may influence your findings. (34.2–3)

(BTEC)

6 Rocco Bank Ltd and Ball Bearings Ltd are two independent companies in the type of business activity their names suggest. As a young financial adviser, you are asked to assess the situation of both companies, by studying the figures given below:

	Ball Bearings Ltd		*Rocco Bank Ltd*	
	£000		*£000*	
Fixed assets (net)	39 000		4 000	
Intangibles	4 000		—	
Investments (long-term)	2 000	45 000	9 000	13 000
Stocks	27 000			
Debtors	25 000			
Advances			21 000	
Cash, liquid assets	—		59 000	
Investments	3 000	55 000	7 000	87 000
		100 000		100 000
Creditors	48 000			
Taxation	1 000		1 000	
Current and deposit accounts			91 000	
Bank	7 000	56 000		92 000
10% debenture stock		33 000		500

Shareholder's funds				
Ordinary shares @ £1	10 000		2 000	
Reserves	1 000		5 500	
		11 000		7 500
		100 000		100 000
Net profit (before tax)		2 500		2 600
Proposed ordinary dividends		700		400

REQUIRED:
Choose accounting ratios which you consider will reveal the differences between the two companies. Discuss your calculations from the point of view of profitability and financial stability. (34.2–3)

(Institute of Bankers)

7 The following figures relate to a retailing organisation which has expanded its business operations. Its premises were converted into a self-service style during the year 19–7:

	19–6	*19–7*	*19–8*
	£	*£*	*£*
Net sales	120 000	150 000	200 000
Gross profit (%)	30%	33⅓%	35%
Fixed expenses:	20 000	25 000	30 000
Variable expenses: (12% of sales)	?	?	?
Average stock held (cost):	8 000	8 500	10 000
Capital employed:	60 000	105 000	160 000

REQUIRED:

a) Prepare the trading and profit and loss accounts for each trading year, preferably in columnar format.
b) In tabular form, prepare the appropriate business profit returns and also the rate of stock turnover for each of the above years.
c) Briefly evaluate the business's progress over the three years in terms of its efficiency and profits.(34.2–3)

(Institute of Bankers)

8 Andrew David plc intends to expand its business activities and the board of directors are in agreement that an extra £500 000 will be required to meet their plans.

The schemes which have been put forward are:

Scheme A: To issue £500 000 10% preference shares @ £1 per share at par.
Scheme B: To issue £500 000 ordinary shares @ £1 per share at par.
Scheme C: To issue £500 000 10% redeemable debenture stock at par.

The company's current share capital consists of 3 000 000 @ £1 ordinary shares, issued and paid-up. Next year, it is estimated that a dividend of 12 per cent will be declared by the board.

The accountant of the company has estimated that the profit for the budget year ended 31 December 19–9, will be £700 000, *before* the payment of interest or taxation. This year's interest payments on the company's overdraft is £5000 and it is estimated that the same payment will be made in 19–9.

Corporation tax on the company's profits is at a rate of 35 per cent.

REQUIRED:
As the assistant to the accountant, you have been asked to prepare the following:
a) An estimated profit and loss appropriation account for each of the three schemes, in tabular form, relating to next year's figures 19–9. Commence your account with net profit *before* interest payments and taxation.
b) Calculate, for each of the three schemes, the earnings per share and capital gearing and state which scheme, in your view, is likely to be the most appropriate.

(Institute of Bankers)

9 The following trading results refer to the accounts of P Jackson & Co during the last three years, year ending 31 December.

	Year 1	*Year 2*	*Year 3*
	£	£	£
Trading and profit and loss account			
Sales:			
Cash	5 000	6 000	8 000
Credit	25 000	30 000	37 000
Cost of sales	20 000	24 000	31 950
Distribution costs	3 000	3 200	4 100
Administration expenses	3 150	3 750	4 275
Stock:			
1 Jan	1 950	2 050	2 950
31 Dec	2 050	2 950	5 050
Balance sheet (extract)			
Debtors	5 000	6 000	9 000
Capital invested (1 Jan)	26 500	30 000	31 750

REQUIRED:
a) The trading and profit and loss account of P Jackson & Co for each of the three years ending 31 December.
b) Accounting ratios to indicate:
gross profit (%)
net profit (%)
expense (%'s)
rate of stock turnover
credit taken by debtors
return on capital invested.
c) Brief comments using the accounting ratios to give some indication of the firm's performance over the three years. What limitations do the ratios impose? (34.2–3)

(Institute of Bankers)

10 Business X and Y are both retail organisations. According to the figures below, they appear to have a different approach to trade:

Accounting ratio	*Business X*	*Business Y*
Gross profit %	40	25
Net profit %	12.5	12.5
ROCE (%)	35	56.25
Current ratio	1.75	1.25
Acid test ratio	1.2	0.6
Stock turnover	60 days	20 days
Debtors debt collection	55 days	16 days
Creditors payment period	65 days	30 days
Asset turnover	2.8	4.5

REQUIRED:

a) Briefly describe what this information reveals about the differences between the two businesses.

b) A major concept in accounting is that of consistency. Explain what this means and how it may apply to the above information. (34.1–3)

(Chartered Association of Certified Accountants)

11 The following information relates to two limited Companies as at 31 December:

	Premier Building	*G Bailey*
	£000	*£000*
Stocks and work in progress	8 000	600
Creditors	4 000	400
Ordinary Share Capital	10 000	1 600
15% Debentures (2009)	—	2 200
Premises	6 900	2 600
Vehicles	1 100	200
Debtors	4 000	400
Bank	2 000	(200)
Plant and Equipment	2 000	800
Retained Profit (at 31/12/)	8 000	200
Share Capital (10% prefs)	2 000	—

You are further advised that the profit before tax for the two companies was as follows:

Premier Building plc	£4 000 000
G Bailey Ltd	£200 000

REQUIRED:

a) Prepare the balance sheet for each of the two companies as at 31 December.

b) Calculate the two major liquidity ratios for each of the two companies.

c) Calculate the return on shareholders funds for each of the two companies.

d) Calculate the gearing percentage for each of the two companies.

e) Briefly explain based on financial information only which of the two companies appear to have the more stable position. (34.2–3)

(Chartered Institute of Purchasing and Supply)

12 The following information is available from the accounts of a trading company named Tristart plc.

	£000
Provision for taxation	160
Turnover	1 800
Distribution costs	220
Income from investments	40
Interest paid	80
Transfers to reserves	120
Cost of sales	640
Administration expenses	380
Ordinary dividend proposed	100
Retained profits from last year	440

REQUIRED:

a) Prepare the profit and loss account from the above figures.
b) If the issued ordinary share capital of Tristart plc is 500 000 shares of £1 each:
i) Calculate the dividend payable per share
ii) Calculate the earnings per share.
c) If the current market price of one ordinary share is £3.20 calculate the dividend yield.(34.2–3)

(Chartered Institute of Purchasing and Supply)

13 The summarised trading and profit and loss accounts for the three years ended 30 September and the balance sheets as at 30 September T Carr Limited are as follows:

Trading and profit and loss accounts

Years ended 30 September	*Yr 1*		*Yr 2*		*Yr 3*	
	£ 000	*£ 000*	*£ 000*	*£ 000*	*£ 000*	*£ 000*
Sales		120		180		270
Less: Cost of sales		80		135		216
Gross profit		40		45		54
Less: Overhead expenses						
Variable	18		27		27	
Fixed	10	28	10	37	20	47
Net profit		12		8		7

Balance sheet

As at 30 September						
	£ 000	*£ 000*	*£ 000*	*£ 000*	*£ 000*	*£ 000*
Fixed assets		30		60		80
Current assets						
Stock	24		25		40	
Debtors	26		40		55	
Balance at bank	20		10		—	
	70		75		95	
Less: Current liabilities						
Creditors	20		35		45	
Bank overdraft	—		—		10	
	20	50	35	40	55	40
		80		100		120

(continued)

Share capital:			
Ordinary shares of £1	50	62	75
Retained earnings	30	38	45
	80	100	120

The major objective of the company in each of the last two financial years has been to increase turnover by 50 per cent on the immediately preceding year.

REQUIRED:

a) Prepare a table of four accounting ratios, each ratio showing a distinctly different aspect of changes in the company during the past three years.
(*Note*: The ratios may be expressed as percentages.)

b) A brief, but reasoned, report addressed to James and Henry Carr concerning the advisability of the company continuing to concentrate on increasing turnover by 50 per cent each year. (34.2–3)

(Association of Accounting Technicians)

14 Jane Winters is currently considering which of two companies she should choose for the investment of a legacy from her late father's estate. The choice lies between purchasing all the share capital of A Limited or purchasing 40 per cent of the share capital of B Limited. While neither A Limited nor B Limited has paid any dividends in recent years, it is anticipated that the companies will resume dividends in the next year or two.

The summarised final accounts of the companies for their last completed financial year are as follows:

Trading and profit and loss accounts

A Limited £	A Limited £		B Limited £	B Limited £
	160 000	Sales		240 000
		Cost of sales:		
10 000		Opening stock	70 000	
140 000		Purchases	160 000	
150 000			230 000	
30 000		Closing stock	50 000	
	120 000			180 000
	40 000	Gross profit		60 000
		Less:		
10 000		Establishment expenses	14 000	
12 000		Administrative expenses	18 000	
6 000		Sales and distribution expenses	9 500	
3 000		Financial expenses	500	
	31 000			42 000
	9 000	Net profit		18 000

Balance sheet

A Limited £	A Limited £		B Limited £	B Limited £
	80 000	Fixed assets		180 000
		Current assets:		
30 000		Stock	50 000	
6 000		Debtors	20 000	
4 000		Balance at bank	10 000	
40 000			80 000	
		Creditors: Amounts falling due within one year		
10 000		Trade creditors	20 000	
	30 000			60 000
	110 000			240 000
		Creditors: Amounts falling due after more than one year		
	30 000	10% loan stock		5 000
	80 000			235 000
		Represented by:		
	60 000	Ordinary share capital		160 000
	20 000	Retained earnings		75 000
	80 000			235 000

REQUIRED:

a) Prepare a schedule of appropriate accounting ratios or financial ratios utilising the information given on the two companies, A Limited and B Limited, to permit a comparison to be made between these companies in each of the following areas: profitability; effective use of resources; short-term solvency; long-term solvency.
Answers should include 8 ratios or other statistics, each one of which should be stated at 2 decimal places. Taxation is to be ignored.

b) A report to Jane Winters drawing attention to the comparative strengths and weaknesses of each of the companies A limited and B Limited as revealed in the answer to (a) above and making reference to other significant matters which should be borne in mind by Jane Winters when making her investment decision.
Note: Assume that the report is from a financial adviser. (34.2–3)

(Association of Accounting Technicians)

35 Accounting for manufacturing organisations

Objectives

On completing this section you should:

- understand the purpose of preparing a manufacturing account
- recognise the link between the manufacturing and trading account
- know how to calculate the unit cost
- understand the difference between the mark up and margins of profit
- be aware of forecasting manufacturing costs.

35.1 Introduction

The manufacturing account is prepared by those type of businesses which make their own products rather than purchasing them for resale. For example, Ford Motor Company makes their own cars to sell, it does not buy cars from another company like Nissan.

The purpose of preparing a manufacturing account is to find out how much it costs the company to produce their products, that is, its factory cost as distinct from other profit and loss costs such as selling and administration expenses. The factory cost of making the product is transferred to the trading account, recorded under the cost of sales.

- direct costs
- indirect costs
- work-in-progress.

The manufacturing account is basically in three parts:

35.1.1 Direct costs

These costs are directly related to the making of the product, including factory labour, materials and direct expenses.

a) Direct labour: this represents the factory wages directly related to the workers making the product, such as assembly workers and machinists.

b) Direct materials: these represent the raw materials and component parts specifically used to make the product, such as the wheels, engine and brakes of a car.

c) Direct expenses: these include items such as direct power, which may be measured directly for producing the goods, the hiring or leasing of equipment or plant for production, or the payment of royalties for the use of patents or trade marks. Most expenses of the factory tend to be indirect and related to overheads.

Total direct costs = Prime cost of production

35.1.2 Indirect costs

These costs refer to the factory overheads. They are part of the factory cost, but not directly related to the actual making of the product. As in the case of direct costs, they include indirect labour, materials and expenses.

a) Indirect labour: these refer to the wages of factory workers who are not directly involved in making the product. Factory staff such as supervisors, foremen, production controllers, progress chasers, engineers and draftsmen are some examples.
b) Indirect materials: these are materials used in the factory although they are not the materials used in the product. Factory cleaning fluids, lubricants, stationery and safety clothing may be categorised as indirect.
c) Indirect expenses: these refer to the general class of expenses which come under factory overheads. Factory rates, rent and insurance, factory general expenses, depreciation of factory plant and equipment are some examples.

Note that indirect costs include distribution and administration overheads listed in the profit and loss account.

35.1.3 Work-in-progress

This relates to the stock of goods which are incomplete and therefore classed as *partly finished*. The stock of any work-in-progress at the beginning of the financial period is added to the factory cost as being part of the manufacturing expense, whilst any stock of work-in-progress at the end of the period is deducted from the factory cost because it will be used in the following financial period.

35.2 The presentation of the manufacturing account

The account is represented as:

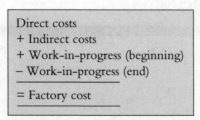

Direct costs
+ Indirect costs
+ Work-in-progress (beginning)
– Work-in-progress (end)
= Factory cost

The *factory cost* is also commonly known as the *production cost* or the *manufacturing cost*. Some manufacturing organisations do not have any significant value for work-in-progress because there is little involvement in the assembly process or specific stages in production. The production of food or paints, for example, is more like a flow of production rather than stages production as in the manufacture of cars, therefore such organisations would have no material figure for partly finished goods.

Example 1 of the manufacturing account layout

	£	£	£
DIRECT COSTS:			
Direct materials:			
Stock of RM* (1/1)	12 000		
+ Purchases of RM	44 200		
+ Carriage inwards	800		
	57 000		
– Stock of RM* (31/12)	(13 000)	44 000	
Direct labour			
Factory wages (direct)	29 000		
Accrued wages (direct)	1 000	30 000	
Direct expenses			
Direct power		1 000	
Prime cost:			75 000
INDIRECT COSTS:			
Indirect materials		2 000	
Indirect factory wages		15 000	
Indirect expenses:			
Factory rates and insurance	3 500		
Factory maintenance	14 000		
Depreciation of plant and equipment	2 500		
Factory general expenses	3 000	23 000	
Factory overheads:			40 000
			115 000
WORK-IN-PROGRESS:			
+ Stock (1/1)			8 800
			123 800
– Stock (31/12)			7 800
Factory cost:			116 000

NOTE
*RM = Raw materials.

COST PER UNIT

If we assume that the factory produced 4000 units in the financial period, calculation of the unit costs are as follows:

a)

$$\text{Prime cost per unit} = \frac{\text{Prime cost}}{\text{Number of units (output)}}$$

$$= \frac{£75\,000}{4\,000} = £18.75 \text{ per unit}$$

b)

$$\text{Factory overheads per unit} = \frac{\text{Factory overheads}}{\text{Number of units}}$$

$$= \frac{£40\,000}{4\,000} = £10.00 \text{ per unit}$$

c)

$$\text{Factory cost per unit} = \frac{\text{Factory cost}}{\text{Number of units}}$$

$$= \frac{£116\,000}{4\,000} = £29.00 \text{ per unit}$$

Therefore (per unit):	Prime cost	= £18.75
	Factory overheads	= £10.00
	Adjustments for work-in-progress	= £ 0.25
	Factory cost	£29.00

Factory cost does not include the business's profit and loss expenses, such as distribution and administration which may also be classified as a type of indirect costs. The factory cost is a guideline to indicate whether the business is cost effective in terms of manufacturing its products in relation to its competitors and the line of industry it is in.

Example 2

Davies & Green Ltd is a small manufacturing company producing electrical components for the computer industry. From the following details, prepare the manufacturing, trading and profit and loss account for the period ending 31 December 19–8:

	£
Stock (1/1):	
Raw materials	4 200
Work-in-progress	5 455
Finished goods	7 525

Stocks (31/12):	
Raw materials	4 875
Work-in-progress	5 855
Finished goods	9 675
Purchases of raw materials	45 750
Wages: Factory direct	27 855
Factory indirect	10 440
Office	15 640
Rent, rates, insurance:	3 600
($^4/_5$ factory, $^1/_5$ office)	
Sales of finished goods	121 565
Manufacturing general expenses	4 380
Selling and distribution expenses	3 895
Administration expenses	1 675
Depreciation: Factory machinery	4 500
Office equipment	1 850
Factory wages (direct) accrued	270

Based on an output of 10 000 units manufactured during the year, calculate:

1 The prime cost per unit.
2 The factory overheads per unit (adjust for work-in-progress).
3 The factory cost per unit.

Davies & Green Ltd –
Manufacturing account, year ended 31 December 19–8

	£	£	£
DIRECT COSTS:			
Direct materials:			
Stock of RM (1/1)	4 200		
+ Purchases of RM	45 750		
	49 950		
– Stock of RM (31/12)	(4 875)	45 075	
Direct labour			
Wages (direct)	27 855		
Accrued	270	28 125	
Prime cost:			73 200
INDIRECT COSTS:			
Indirect labour			
Wages (indirect)		10 440	

(continued)

(continued)

Indirect expenses			
Rent, rates and insurance	2 880		
Manufacturing expenses	4 380		
Depreciation of machinery	4 500	11 760	
Factory overheads:			22 200
			95 400
WORK-IN-PROGRESS:			
+ Stock (1/1)			5 455
			100 855
– Stock (31/12)			5 855
Factory cost:			95 000

Trading and profit and loss account, year ended 31 December 19–8

	£	£	£
Sales			121 565
– Cost of sales:			
Stock of FG* (1/1)	7 525		
+ Factory cost	95 000	102 525	
– Stock of FG (31/12)		9 675	92 850
Gross profit			28 715
– Expenses:			
Selling and distribution expenses		3 895	
Administration expenses		1 675	
Office wages		15 640	
Depreciation of office equipment		1 850	
Office rent, rates, insurance		720	23 780
Net profit			4 935

NOTE
*FG = Finished goods.

Costs per unit based on an output of 10 000 units:

	£	
Prime cost per unit	7.32	$\frac{73\,200}{10\,000 \text{ units}}$

Factory overheads per unit	2.22	$\frac{22\,200}{10\,000 \text{ units}}$
	9.54	
Adjustment for work-in-progress	(0.04)	
	9.50	
Factory cost per unit	9.50	$\frac{95\,000}{10\,000 \text{ units}}$

35.3 The calculation of manufacturing profit

To see if the business is cost effective in its manufacturing process, an assessment of *profit* can be determined if it is possible to obtain a market value of the goods produced. In the example of Davies & Green Ltd, if the company could have purchased the finished goods from another producer at say, £13 per unit, of which £10 could be attributed to the factory cost, is the business cost effective in manufacturing? The answer must be 'Yes'.

		£
10 000 units produced × £10 per unit	=	100 000
Davies & Green's factory cost		95 000
Profit		5 000

If the manufacturer wanted to show the profit made on the production side of the factory, the manufacturing account would need to show the market value of its goods:

	£
Market value	100 000
Factory cost	95 000
Manufacturing profit	5 000

In the trading account, the market value is shown in the cost of sales instead of the factory cost. This will then emphasise both the manufacturing profit, as well as the trading profit:

Davies & Green Ltd –
Trading account, year ended 31 December 19–8

	£	£	£
Sales			121 565
– Cost of sales:			
Stock FG (1/1)	7 525		
Market value of factory cost	100 000	107 525	
– Stock FG (31/12)		9 675	97 850
Trading profit			23 715
Manufacturing profit			5 000
Gross profit			28 715

35.4 The calculation of stock of finished goods

In some examination questions, the value of any unsold stock of finished goods may not be given directly. Instead, the candidate may have to calculate its value on the basis of either its prime cost or its factory cost.

In the example above, the value of stock of finished goods on 31 December was £9675. If this figure was not given and the question asked 'Calculate unsold stock at factory cost', it would need to give:

a) the number of units left in stock
b) the basis of valuation (in this case at factory cost).

Suppose the number of units left in stock was 1000 calculated from:

Number of units manufactured during year:	10 000
Number of units in stock on 1 January:	750
	10 750
Number of units sold during year:	9 750
Number of units in stock (finished goods)	1 000

Stock FG on 31/12 valued at factory cost: 1000 × £9.50 per unit
= £9500

or Stock FG on 31/12 valued at prime cost: 1000 × £7.32 per unit
= £7320

Once a method of stock valuation has been adopted by the business, it should apply consistently that base from year to year in order to avoid any profit distortions (as required in SSAP 2, Concepts in accounting). Note that SSAP 9 (stocks and work-in-progress) states that finished goods should be valued at prime cost and factory overheads at normal output levels.

35.5 The mark-up and margins of profit

The mark-up is usually given as a percentage based on the cost of the goods, and added on in order to arrive at a selling price.

Example

If the total cost of Davies & Green's product (per unit) came to £12 and they sold at £15 per unit, the profit is £3:

$$\text{Mark-up (\%)} = \frac{\text{Profit} \times 100}{\text{Cost price}}$$

$$= \frac{£3 \times 100}{£12} = 25\% \text{ mark-up}$$

Once a mark-up percentage is established by the company, it becomes a guideline to selling price. How much should an organisation mark-up the cost of their products? How much is the market willing to pay? How does their selling price compare with that of their competitors? If the market is willing to pay £15 per unit, the mark-up may well be adequate, but if competition becomes more intense, the company will have to review its prices in line with market forces.

$$\text{Margin (\%)} = \frac{\text{Profit} \times 100}{\text{Selling price}}$$

$$= \frac{£3 \times 100}{£15} = 20\% \text{ margin}$$

The margin percentage is the company's guideline to profits based on sales. Davies & Green should make £20 profit on every £100 sales, £200 on £1000 sales and so on. The margin percentage is an indicator of profit based on sales volume and may be compared with past performances in order to evaluate the company's profitability over periods of time, or with the margins of profit set by their competitors.

35.6 Fixed and variable costs

All the costs of a business may be classified in a variety of different ways. In the field of cost accounting where the emphasis lies in how things cost in relation to labour, materials and overheads, there is a need to differentiate between fixed and variable costs because they influence profit margins in relation to sales volume (or output). Chapter 36 discusses costs in further detail.

35.6.1 Fixed costs

This type of cost is not sensitive to output change. For example, administration expenses would tend to be the same even if production levels fluctuated. Many of the company's overheads tend to be relatively fixed, regardless of levels of production. Factory rent and rates is another good example of a fixed cost.

35.6.2 Variable costs

This cost type does vary with output change because the cost is more sensitive to different levels of production. It refers to the *extra* costs incurred in producing one or more units over and above a given plan of production (or one or more fewer units). Direct materials and direct labour could be examples of variable costs.

For example, using the figures of Davies & Green Ltd, the costs may be classified as:

Variables:	Direct materials		£4.50	per unit
	Direct labour		£2.81	per unit
	Factory overheads (power)		£0.24	per unit
		Total:	£7.55	per unit
Fixed:	All other costs:			
	Factory overheads		£20 000	
	Profit and loss expenses		£24 500	
			£44 500	

Example 3 of a manufacturing account illustrating the production of two major products
Tandem Co Ltd manufacture two major computer products for the electronics industry having an output of 10 000 units for ROM 'A' and 5000 units for ROM 'B'. The trial balance for the year ended 31 December 19–8 was as follows:

Tandem Co Ltd –
Trial balance as on 31 December 19–8

	£	£
Stocks of RM (1/1):		
ROM 'A'	8 000	
ROM 'B'	7 200	
Purchases of raw materials	80 000	
Direct wages	58 500	
Indirect factory wages	24 000	
Manufacturing expenses	18 600	
Provision for depreciation:		
Factory plant, equipment		6 000
Office equipment		3 000
Sales:		
ROM 'A'		108 000
ROM 'B'		120 000
Rent, rates and insurance:		
Factory	4 200	
Office	2 800	
Debtors	18 200	
Creditors		16 800
Bank overdraft		12 200
Sales and distribution costs	8 400	
Administration expenses	18 900	
Plant and equipment (factory)	60 000	
Equipment (office)	10 000	
Capital:		
Issued and paid-up ordinary shares		20 000
Reserves		42 800
Stocks of finished goods (1/1):		
ROM 'A'	6 000	
ROM 'B'	4 000	
	328 800	328 800

NOTES
On 31 December 19–8:
1 Stocks of RM: ROM 'A' £8200
ROM 'B' £6800
There were no stocks of work-in-progress.

2 Stocks of finished goods: value at factory cost per unit. There were 200 units of ROM 'A' and 400 units of ROM 'B' in stock.
3 Of the raw materials purchased, £44 000 was apportioned to ROM 'A'.
4 £1500 was owing for direct wages.
5 Direct wages are to be apportioned to each product, based on the number of production hours:
ROM 'A' 6000 hours
ROM 'B' 9000 hours.
6 Depreciation of all plant and equipment, including office equipment, is 10 per cent of cost.
7 Of all factory overheads, including indirect wages, $^{2}/_{3}$ is apportioned to ROM 'A' and $^{1}/_{3}$ to ROM 'B'.
8 The directors of the company have decided to provide a dividend of 12p per share and a provision for tax of £700 should also be made.

REQUIRED:

a) Prepare the manufacturing account of Tandem Co Ltd for the year ended 31 December 19–8 showing clearly the factory cost of each product in columnar form, as well as the total factory cost.
b) Prepare the company's trading and profit and loss account for the year ended 31 December 19–8, showing the gross profit for each product in columnar form, as well as total gross profit.
c) Prepare the company's balance sheet as on 31 December 19–8, in vertical format.

Tandem Co Ltd –
Manufacturing account, year ended 31 December 19–8

		Products		*Total*
		ROM 'A'	*ROM 'B'*	
		£	£	£
DIRECT COSTS				
Direct materials:				
Stock of RM (1/1)		8 000	7 200	15 200
+ Purchases of RM		44 000	36 000	80 000
		52 000	43 200	95 200
– Stock of RM (31/12)		8 200	6 800	15 000
		43 800	36 400	80 200
Direct labour:				
Direct wages		24 000	36 000	60 000
	Prime cost	67 800	72 400	140 200
INDIRECT COSTS				
Indirect wages		16 000	8 000	24 000
Indirect expenses:				
Manufacturing expenses		12 400	6 200	18 600
Depreciation of plant		4 000	2 000	6 000
Rent, rates, insurance		2 800	1 400	4 200
	Factory overheads	35 200	17 600	52 800
WORK-IN-PROGRESS				
		–	–	–
	Factory cost	103 000	90 000	193 000

NOTES

Factory cost per unit:	103 000 / 10 000	90 000 / 5 000 units
	= £10.30	£18
Stock value of finished goods (31/12)	× 200	× 400
	= £2 060	£7 200

Tandem Co Ltd –
Trading and profit and loss account,
year ended 31 December 19–8

	Products ROM 'A'	ROM 'B'	*Total*
	£	£	£
Sales	108 000	120 000	228 000
Cost of sales:			
Stock of FG (1/1)	6 000	4 000	10 000
Factory cost	103 000	90 000	193 000
	109 000	94 000	203 000
– Stock of FG (31/12)	2 060	7 200	9 260
	106 940	86 800	193 740
Gross profit	1 060	33 200	34 260
Sales and distribution costs			8 400
Administration expenses			18 900
Rent, rates, insurance			2 800
Depreciation of equipment			1 000
			31 100
Net profit (before tax)			3 160
Provision for tax			700
Net profit (after tax)			2 460
Provision for dividends (12p share)			2 400
Profit and loss balance c/f			60

Owing to the far greater profitability of ROM 'B' would it be better for the company to concentrate its resources in favour of this product? Is this just a poor year for ROM 'A'? Directors would need to investigate and decide the outcome.

Tandem Co Ltd –
Balance sheet as at 31 December 19–8

	Cost	Depreciation	Net
	£	£	£
FIXED ASSETS			
Plant and equipment	60 000	12 000	48 000
Office equipment	10 000	4 000	6 000
	70 000	16 000	54 000
CURRENT ASSETS			
Stocks:			
Raw materials	15 000		
Finished goods	9 260		
Debtors	18 200		
Bank/cash	—	42 460	
CREDITORS FALLING WITHIN 12 MONTHS			
Creditors	16 800		
Bank overdraft	12 200		
Accruals	1 500		
Provision for tax	700		
Provision for dividends	2 400	33 600	
Net current assets			8 860
Total assets less current liabilities			62 860
FINANCED BY:			
Issued and paid-up capital		20 000	
Reserves		42 800	
Profit and loss account		60	62 860

NOTES

1 There was no profit and loss balance at the beginning of the year, only £60 residue from the profit and loss appropriation account.

2 Working capital (or current ratio) = 1.26:1.

3 All stocks on 31 December, raw materials, work-in-progress and finished goods, entered as current assets. No stock of work-in-progress in this example.

Example 4

The following information relates to the finances of Davies & Smith Ltd, a small manufacturing enterprise, for the year ended 31 December 19–8:

	Budget year: 19–9
Sales target:	52 000 units
Production schedule:	50 000 units
Finished goods carried forward to 1/1/–9	7 000 units @ £8 each

Costs per unit:	
Direct materials	£5.0
Direct labour	£3.0
Factory variables	£1.0
Sales and distribution variables	£1.5
Fixed costs	£180 000

The unsold stock of finished goods on 31/12/19–9 is to be valued at factory cost. The selling price per unit is to be based on a 40 per cent *margin* on the factory cost.

REQUIRED:

a) A forecast of the manufacturing account for the year ended 31 December 19–9.
b) Calculations to show how the mark-up and margin percentage is arrived at, based on the factory cost.
c) A forecast trading and profit and loss account for the year ended 31 December 19–9.

Forecast of manufacturing account for the year ended 31 December 19–9

	£	£
DIRECT COSTS		
Direct materials (50 000 × £5)	250 000	
Direct labour (50 000 × £3)	150 000	
		400 000
INDIRECT COSTS		
Factory variables (50 000 × £1)		50 000
FACTORY COST =		450 000

Mark-up and margins of profit

$$\text{The factory cost per unit} = \frac{\text{Factory cost}}{\text{No of units produced}}$$

$$= \frac{£450\,000}{50\,000 \text{ units}}$$

$$= £9 \text{ per unit}$$

What is the selling price based on a *margin* of 40 per cent? (Margin is based on selling price, not cost.)

Call the selling price:	100
Deduct margin	40
Cost price	60

Therefore 'profit' is £40 on a cost price of £60.

$$\textit{The mark-up percentage} = \frac{\text{Profit} \times 100}{\text{Cost price}}$$

$$= \frac{40 \times 100}{60}$$

$$= 66^2/_3\%$$

Selling price = Factory cost + $66^2/_3\%$

= £9 + £6 = £15

SALES = 52 000 units × £15

= £780 000

If the question stated that the selling price is £15 per unit and the *mark-up percentage* is $66^2/_3$, how is the margin percentage found?

Call the cost price:	100
Add mark-up	$66^2/_3$
Selling price	$166^2/_3$

Therefore 'profit' is £$66^2/_3$ on a selling price of £$166^2/_3$.

$$\textit{The margin percentage} = \frac{\text{Profit} \times 100}{\text{Selling price}}$$

$$= \frac{£66^2/_3 \times 100}{166^2/_3}$$

= 40% (Check: £15 – 40% = £9).

Davies & Smith Ltd –
Forecast trading and profit and loss account
31 December 19–9

	£	£
Sales (52 000 × £15)		780 000
– Cost of sales:		
Stock (1/1) (7 000 × £8)	56 000	
Factory cost (50 000)	450 000	
	506 000	
– Stock (31/12)		
(5 000 × £9)	45 000	461 000
Gross profit		319 000
– Expenses:		
Sales and distribution costs		
(52 000 × £1.5)	78 000	
Fixed costs	180 000	258 000
Net profit		61 000

Summary

The manufacturing account is prepared for those organisations which make products and need to know the factory cost of production. It is made up of direct and indirect factory costs plus the value of work-in-progress for the period. The value of closing stock is usually based on the factory cost per unit. The markup of profit is based on the cost price of goods whereas the margin is based on the selling price. It is important to make this distinction because the markup will provide the selling price and the margin will indicate profit on the value of sales.

Questions

1 From the following information, prepare the manufacturing and trading accounts of J Mason's Ltd for the year ended 31 December 19–8:

	£
Stock: (1 January)	
Raw materials	5 850
Work-in-progress	1 500
Finished goods	10 570
Purchases of raw materials	95 000
Stocks: (31 December)	
Raw materials	6 250
Work-in-progress	1 400
Finished goods	11 200
Factory direct wages	24 550
Factory indirect wages	15 200
Factory general maintenance	2 500
Factory power, light and heat	1 750
Depreciation of plant	800
General factory expenses	2 550
Sales (finished goods)	185 000

NOTES

On 31 December 19–8:

1 £250 was owing for factory power.

2 Rates of £150 were prepaid under general factory expenses.

REQUIRED:

If the factory had an output of 5000 units in the year, calculate the prime cost and factory cost per unit. (35.2–6)

2 Harry is a manufacturer. From the following details relating to his business, prepare separate accounts to show:

i) the factory cost of goods

ii) the manufacturing profit

iii) the trading profit

iv) the net profit,

for the year ended 31 December.

	£
Stocks (1 January)	
Raw materials	6 757
Finished goods	10 560
Stocks (31 December)	
Raw materials	5 583
Finished goods	12 565
Wages: factory (direct)	15 500
office	12 765
Rent, rates and insurance ($^4/_5$ factory; $^4/_5$ office)	4 580
Sales of finished goods	101 500
Purchases of raw materials	40 875
Manufacturing expenses	5 945
Selling expenses	12 855
Administrative expenses	7 400
Depreciation: machinery	2 150
office furniture	500
accounting machines (office)	150

Other information

a) (1/1) Stocks of work-in-progress, nil.
   (31/12) Stocks of work-in-progress, nil.

b) The market valuation of the cost of production is £78 000.

c) Calculate: on the basis of 2000 units produced in the year:
   i) Direct labour cost per unit.
   ii) Direct material cost per unit.
   iii) Factory overheads per unit.
   iv) Production costs per unit.

c) Was manufacturing cost effective? Compare the market value per unit cost with production cost per unit. (35.2–6)

(Institute of Bankers)

3 You work in the accounts department of Georges Ltd, a manufacturing company. The following were some of the balances appearing in the books at 31 December 19–5.

	£
Ordinary share capital	100 000
Stocks at 1 January 19–5:	
Raw materials	22 000
Work-in-progress	32 000
Finished goods	40 180
Stocks at 31 December:	
Raw materials	34 000
Work-in-progress	36 810
Finished goods	36 080
Wages:	
Direct manufacturing	406 160
Factory supervisors	26 650
General office	59 000
Direct factory power	190 000
Heating and lighting	18 000

Purchase of raw materials	512 000
Carriage outwards	1 972
Plant and machinery	160 000
Premises	240 000
Returns inward	840
Office equipment	30 000
Rates	12 000
Administrative expenses	3 668
Debtors	28 000
Creditors	24 000
Cash in hand	7 324
Sales	1 600 580

NOTES
1 Heating and lighting rates are to be apportioned $^2/_3$ factory and $^1/_3$ office.
2 Depreciate plant and machinery by 5 per cent and office equipment by 10 per cent.
3 The total number of units completed in the year was 30 000.

REQUIRED:
a) Prepare the manufacturing account.
b) Prepare the trading and profit and loss account.
c) Compute the production cost of one item. (35.2–3)

(Institute of Commercial Management)

4 Lindop Co Ltd is a small manufacturing company producing 12 000 units per annum. The accounts on 31 December were:

	£
Stocks (1 January):	
Raw materials	4 250
Work-in-progress	1 875
Finished goods (2050 units)	10 245
Purchases of raw materials	32 550
Sales (10 800 units)	86 400
Returns inward	105
Factory:	
Wages (direct)	14 242
Power	1 540
Indirect wages	4 250
Rent and rates	700
Indirect materials	4 480
Lighting and heating	590
Depreciation of plant and machinery	1 875
Office:	
Sales and distribution costs	4 875
Rent and rates	1 500
Administration expenses	4 950

NOTES
At 31 December:
1 Stocks:
Raw materials £5 155
Work-in-progress £1 722
Finished goods: units in balance to be valued at production cost.

2 Wages owing: £625 (direct).
3 Depreciation of office equipment by 20 per cent of cost (cost £2 500).
4 Create a provision for bad and doubtful debts to equal 5 per cent of debtors (debtors £7 000).
5 Rent of office in advance £175. Factory in advance £100.
6 Bank charges accrued £300 (administration expenses).

REQUIRED:

a) The preparation of the company's manufacturing account for the year ended 31 December. Calculate the cost of production per unit.

b) The preparation of the company's trading and profit and loss account for the year ended 31 December. Stock of finished goods to be calculated at production cost.

c) Based on the production capacity of 12 000 units, calculate:

i) The prime cost per unit.

ii) The production overheads per unit.

iii) The mark-up percentage on cost of production given a selling price of £8 per unit. (35.2–6)

(BTEC)

5 The following information is taken from the accounts of Penny Jackson, a businesswoman producing science equipment to colleges:

Trial balance of P Jackson as on 30 June 19–8

	£	£
Stocks (1/7/19–7):		
Raw materials	6 885	
Finished goods	3 500	
Motor vehicle (cost)	8 750	
Premises (cost)	36 900	
Accumuled depreciation of vehicle (2 years)		1 750
Purchases (raw materials)	55 725	
Direct wages	45 780	
Sales		180 344
Discounts	855	1 044
Returns	548	
Salaries (assistants)	18 346	
Overheads (factory)	14 385	
Overheads (office)	7 044	
Creditors		6 755
Debtors	7 400	
Bank		2 045
Cash	400	
Drawings	10 420	
Capital		?

On 30 June, the following additional information was also available:

a) Stocks in hand were valued:
   raw materials £7432
   finished goods £4200
b) The motor vehicle is depreciated on a straight-line basis and is now three years old.
c) Of the factory overheads, £240 is prepaid and £600 is accrued.

REQUIRED:
Prepare the manufacturing account, trading and profit and loss account for the year ended 30 June 19–8 and a balance sheet as on that date. (35.2)

(BTEC)

6 ACE Co Ltd is a company which manufactures electrical components for the car industry. Production is planned for 50 000 units in the financial year ended 31 December.
The trial balance extracted from the ledgers on 31 December is as follows:

Trial balance of Ace Co Ltd as on 31 December

	£	£
Authorised and issued share capital:		
70 000 @ £1 ordinary shares		70 000
Share premium		7 000
Premises (cost)	86 000	
Plant (cost)	12 000	
Provision for depreciation of plant		6 000
Debtors	10 498	
Creditors		58 409
Stock (1 Jan):		
Raw materials	5 892	
Finished goods (2500 units)	8 500	
Provision for bad debts		200
Bad debts	528	
Bank/cash	2 910	
Direct wages	56 804	
Raw materials, purchases of	156 820	
Sales (48 000 units)		204 000
General expenses (½ factory)	2 944	
Profit and loss balance (1 Jan)		5 830
Rates and insurance (½ factory)	610	
Office wages	5 220	
Delivery charges	2 400	
Discount	313	
	351 439	351 439

Further information available at 31 December:

a) Stocks: raw materials unused £20 893.
   50 000 units of finished goods were produced.
   the unsold stock to be valued at production cost/unit.

b) The provision for bad debts to be increased to £750.
c) The plant is to be depreciated 10 per cent on net value.
d) A taxation provision of £750 is to be made.
e) The directors have recommended a 5 per cent dividend on the share capital. A reserve is to be created of £3000.

REQUIRED:
Prepare the company's manufacturing, trading, profit and loss and appropriation account for the period ended 31 December, and a balance sheet as at that date. (35.2)

(Institute of Bankers)

7 The following list of balances as at 31 July 19–6 has been extracted from the books of Jane Seymour who commenced business on 1 August 19–5 as a designer and manufacturer of kitchen furniture.

	£
Plant and machinery at cost on 1 August 19–5	60 000
Motor vehicles at cost on 1 August 19–5	30 000
Loose tools at cost	9 000
Sales	170 000
Raw materials purchased	43 000
Direct factory wages	39 000
Light and power	5 000
Indirect factory wages	8 000
Machinery repairs	1 600
Motor vehicle running expenses	12 000
Rent and insurances	11 600
Administrative staff salaries	31 000
Administrative expenses	9 000
Sales and distribution staff salaries	13 000
Capital at 1 August 19–5	122 000
Sundry debtors	16 500
Sundry creditors	11 200
Balance at bank	8 500
Drawings	6 000

Additional information for the year ended 31 July 19–6:

1 It is estimated that the plant and machinery will be used in the business for 10 years and the motor vehicles used for four years. In both cases it is estimated that the residual value will be nil. The straight-line method of providing for depreciation is to be used.
2 Light and power charges accrued at 31 July 19–6 amounted to £1000 and insurance prepaid at 31 July 19–6 totalled £800.
3 Stocks were valued at cost at 31 July 19–6 as follows:
raw materials £7000
finished goods £10 000
4 The valuation of work-in-progress at 31 July 19–6 included variable and fixed factory overheads and amounted to £12 300.
5 Two-thirds of the light and power and rent and insurance costs are to be allocated to the factory costs and one-third to general administration costs.
6 Motor vehicle costs are to be allocated equally to factory costs and general administration costs.
7 Goods manufactured during the year are to be transferred to the trading account at £95 000 as the market value.
8 Loose tools on hand on 31 July 19–6 were valued at £5000.

REQUIRED:
Prepare a manufacturing, trading and profit and loss account for the year ended 31 July 19–6 of Jane Seymour. (35.2)

(AAT)

8 WJ & G Ltd of Wakefield, manufacture cricket bats in three qualities, one star, two star and three star. The following information relates to the company's financial year end 31 December 19–8:

	£
Stock of raw materials (1/1/19–7)	4 200
Stock of finished goods (1/1/19–7)	
One star	2 200
Two star	3 000
Three star	5 500
Purchase of raw materials	228 200
Carriage of raw materials	1 200
Returns out raw materials	400
Factory direct wages:	
One star	28 400
Two star	36 300
Three star	42 300
Factory light and heat	2 800
Factory rent and rates	1 800
Factory general expenses	5 400
Depreciation of plant	2 000
Sales:	
One star	120 000
Two star	160 000
Three star	190 000
Stock on 31 December 19–8	
Raw materials	4 000
Finished goods:	
One star	1 600
Two star	2 300
Three star	1 000

The factory records show that of the raw materials actually consumed in production are, one star £64 000, two star £76 000 and the rest allocated to three star.

All factory costs are to be allocated $^1/_4$ each to one star and two star and $^1/_2$ to three star.

REQUIRED:
On 31 December 19–8:

a) A manufacturing account to show the prime cost and factory cost of each product.
b) A trading account showing the gross profit of each product.
c) The gross margin percentage of each product. (35.2,5)

(AEB)

9 The following list of balances as at 31 December has been taken from the books of Fairdeal Manufactures Ltd which started business on 1 January:

	£
Factory plant and machinery at cost 1 January	120 000
Motor delivery vehicles at cost 1 January	25 000
Purchases of raw materials	41 000
Factory labour: machine operatives	36 000
supervisory	7 000
Factory plant and machinery repairs	8 710
Heat, light and power	24 750
Rates and insurance	2 550
General administrative expenses	9 400
Administrative salaries	12 090
Trade debtors	12 000
Trade creditors	7 100
Bank overdraft	4 900
Sales	136 500
Ordinary shares of £1 each, fully paid	120 000
Share premium account	30 000

Additional information:

1 Raw material stocks, at cost, at 31 December were valued at £3 000

2 Work in progress at 31 December was valued at £24 000

3 Depreciation is to be provided on fixed assets at the following rates on cost:

	% per annum
Factory plant and machinery	10
Motor delivery vehicles	25

4 Rates and insurances pre-paid at 31 December amounted to £600; heat, light and power accrued due at 31 December was £2 300

5 Rates and insurances and heat, light and power charges are to be apportioned three quarters to manufacturing and a quarter to the profit and loss account

6 Manufactured goods are to be transferred from the manufacturing account to the trading account at wholesale prices; the wholesale price of goods manufactured during the year ended 31 December was £100 000*

7 Finished goods stock at 31 December, at wholesale prices, was valued at £10 000*

REQUIRED:

a) Prepare the manufacturing, trading and profit and loss account for the year ended 31 December for Fairdeal Manufacturers Limited. (35.2)

b) Prepare the balance sheet as at the same date for Fairdeal Manufacturers Limited. (35.2)

*The finished goods at wholesale (market value) prices is 10 per cent of the value of the wholesale price of manufactured goods $\left[\frac{10\,000}{100\,000}\right]$

It is assumed a provision for unrealised profit is made to equal 10 per cent of the 'profit' on manufactured goods (£540 – check answer).

The double entry is:

Debit: profit and loss account (provision for unrealised profit) £54

Credit: stock of finished goods £54.

(Association of Accounting Technicians)

36 Aspects of costing

Objectives

On completing this section you should:

- recognise the different terms used in costing
- understand the use of a cost centre
- recognise the importance of coding
- recognise the main uses of absorption and marginal costing.

36.1 Introduction

In our commercial system, there is a wide diversity of businesses which require all kinds of information. Even the sole trader operating a small business, must have knowledge of how sales are moving and the type and amount of costs that his business incurs. In larger organisations and particularly in factories making a whole range of products, it becomes even more important to feed management with the type of information they will need in order to assist them in making the right decisions.

In the manufacturing account, discussed in Chapter 35, we needed to find out the different types of direct and indirect costs which made up the cost of production. From these figures we calculated the factory unit cost, which is essential for management to know because it assists them in deciding what the selling price should be. There is also a need to break down costs into fixed and variable categories in order to make further calculations such as the break-even point.

36.2 Costing

Management need to have all kinds of information at its fingertips and costing is a basic essential. For example:

How much does the new product cost?
How many do we need to sell to break even?
Is it possible to reduce the selling price and still make a profit?
How much do we need to sell to cover the advertising campaign?
Can we afford to employ more labour?
Can we sell a special order at 25 per cent less than normal selling prices?

Where managers need information, costing helps to provide it. It is not surprising therefore, that cost accounting is sometimes referred to as management accounting because of the information it supplies to help management make better, more informed decisions.

One of the most common costing questions which arises is simply 'How much does it cost to make?' This involves costing principles and the techniques or methods used to find out that information.

For example, if management wanted to know the full cost of making a specific unit, the technique of absorption costing will be used. If it wanted to know the break-even point of the product, then marginal costing would be used. If management wanted information concerning the future plans of the business in terms of what the costs are planned to be and be able to compare them with what actually happens, then this is the technique of what is called budgetary control. Therefore, whatever the question, costing principles exist to supply the answers. Let us define clearly each costing technique.

36.2.1 Absorption costing

A product or service absorbs all the costs in terms of labour, materials and a charge for overheads. Both fixed and variable costs are included in absorption. The distinction between these types of cost is important to understand:

Fixed costs are insensitive to output change such as rent, rates and insurance costs. No matter how many units may be produced or sold, fixed costs do not change with the level of activity.

Variable costs are those that are sensitive to output change and do vary with the level of activity. Direct materials and direct labour and other variables such as power will increase if there is greater output. Note that these cost types were introduced in the last chapter.

36.2.2 Marginal costing

This refers to variable costs and is really seeking to answer 'How much *extra* cost is involved?' Under this system the cost of a product is treated as including only the variable costs of its production, that is, direct materials, direct labour and any other costs directly changing with output.

The relevance of such an approach is seen, for example, if a decision is to be made whether or not to accept a special order at a lower selling price than normal. The fixed costs should not be affected, only the variable costs and a special price may well be acceptable.

36.2.3 Budgeting

This is the topic for the next chapter and may be described as a management tool to help them form future plans and to be able to assist them in comparing a forecast of results with actual results when they occur. In this way, a yardstick is provided to see if things go according to plan and if not, to find out why and then do something about it. This gives management what is called its 'budgetary control'.

36.2.4 Standard costing

This assists management in providing pre-determined costs and is linked to budgeting. The standard cost for a product can be estimated in advance and when the actual costs are measured, these can then be compared with the standard costs in order to monitor the progress of costs and to exercise the control of them. For example:

	Standard cost per unit	Actual cost per unit	Variance per unit
Direct labour	2.40	2.50	10p +
Direct materials	5.25	5.00	(25p)
Factory overheads	8.75	9.35	60p +
Administration overheads	12.55	12.90	35p +

For reasons of budgetary control, managers will want to know why the variances (or differences) occurred. Labour and overheads were more than planned but materials were less. In this way, costs become more accountable and any corrective or appropriate action can be taken.

36.3 The classification of costs

The nature of the business will influence the categories of cost used.

For example, a bank or an insurance company is not going to use the same classification and coding of costs as, say, the manufacturers of motor cars or washing machines. The principle of classifying costs is to find out how much and where money is being spent. Which areas of the business are using up its resources?

If a bill for £4000 was received for electricity and power which areas of the business (cost centres) should be charged with a share of its cost? If the factory used 60 per cent of it, then the factory overhead cost would be charged with £2400. If the sales office used 10 per cent of it, then it would incur £400 of cost.

In this way, if each section's or cost centre's share of the expense is shown, then the operating costs of a business can be identified and controlled. Chapter 41 also discusses the apportionment of costs between different departments.

36.4 Cost centres

When costs are charged to a specific product, section or department, it is desirable to break up or divide the organisation into identifiable parts which can then be used for making charges against it. For example, a college can operate cost centres through its various departments. In this way, it is easier to monitor the progress of costs and maintain better control of them. A cost centre can be defined as a location, person or unit, in respect of any cost which can be attributed to it. A cost centre can also be a service cost centre to act as the provision of a service such as canteen or administrative facilities, to 'service' other cost centres. By using this system of costing, a manager in charge of a cost centre becomes more aware of the costs his section incurs.

The Chartered Institute of Management Accountants have defined a cost centre as:

> 'a production or service location, function, activity or item of equipment whose costs may be attributed to cost units'.

Direct costs can normally be traced quite easily to a cost centre. For example, direct labour or materials allocated to a centre should present no difficulty. However, indirect costs such as rent, rates, insurance, may not be so easily traceable to each cost centre. Therefore a sound basis of fairly apportioning these costs needs to be identified and adopted.

Example

Rates of £24 000 are charged to a company which operates three production and one service centre. It was decided to apportion the cost in relation to their respective floor areas:

Production centre 1	1400 sq metres
Production centre 2	2600 sq metres
Production centre 3	1000 sq metres
Service centre 4	3000 sq metres

How much should we apportion each centre its share of rates?

		£
Centre 1	1 400/8 000 metres = 17.5% × £24 000:	4 200
Centre 2	2 600/8 000 metres = 32.5% × £24 000:	7 800
Centre 3	1 000/8 000 metres = 12.5% × £24 000:	3 000
Centre 4	3 000/8 000 metres = 37.5% × £24 000:	9 000
		24 000

There are other bases of apportionment which include:

Type of cost	*Bases of apportionment*
Rent, rates	Floor area
Insurance (premises)	Floor area
Insurance (staff)	Number of staff
Light, heat, power	Floor area or metered units
Canteen costs	Number of staff
Depreciation of assets	Value of fixed assets
Distribution costs	Value of sales

NOTE

Apportionment of costs applies when an expense is incurred for the benefit of two or more cost centres and is divided on some equitable basis as above.

Allocation of costs applies where the costs incurred can be traced directly to a cost centre. Direct costs should be easily allocated as well as some indirect costs such as indirect wages or materials.

36.5 Coding of costs

In modern industry where the use of computers are widespread, all costs have a number which is used to code and classify the item of expenditure. The type of system used will be determined by the type of organisation which uses it. For example, UNIPART would use an extensive coding system for its stock of materials, having literally thousands of parts to classify. Almost all coding is based on a numerical system whereby the breakdown of numbers relate to a specific element of the location, type and description of the item coded. For example:

Code No. 7445501	07 =	Cost Centre – Administration Dept: Pumps Division
	44 =	Administration cost – stationery
	55 =	A4 photocopying paper
	01 =	Revenue expenditure

This code number identifies that the expense of photocopying paper has been charged to the administration department of pumps division. Although this appears to look somewhat tedious, once various costs have been coded then each cost centre can be charged with the appropriate figures.

The principles behind coding include:

Simplicity: in terms of structure – codes must be logical and easy to follow
Flexibility: capable to meet changes and additions to the system when required
Unambiguity: any duplication of numbers and meanings should be prevented
Controllability: coding structure must be properly documented and authorised.

Example of absorption and marginal costing
A business, Jake Ltd, has the following costing figures based on a monthly output of 500 units:

Planned output:	500 units per month
Selling Price:	£20 per unit

Variable costs of production

Direct labour	£4 per unit
Direct materials	£8 per unit
Power	£0.20 per unit
Fixed overhead costs are	£2500 per month

CALCULATE:
a) the monthly profit using absorption costing
b) the monthly profit using marginal costing
c) the estimated profit/loss if only 450 units are produced
d) the estimated profit if 550 units were produced
d) the monthly break-even point

Profit per month based on absorption costing

		× 500 units	× 450 units	× 550 units
		£	£	£
Sales (500 × 20)		10 000	9 000	11 000
Less variable costs:	12.20 unit			
fixed costs	5.00 unit			
Absorption per unit:	17.20	8 600	7 740	9 460
Estimated profit		1 400	1 260	1 540

(Any stock unsold would be valued at the absorption cost of £17.20 per unit)

Profits based on marginal costing

	× 500 units	× 450 units	× 550 units
	£	£	£
Sales	10 000	9 000	11 000
Less			
Variable costs:			
12.20 × 500 units	6 100	5 490	6 710
Contribution	3 900	3 510	4 290

Less			
Fixed overheads	2 500	2 500	2 500
Estimated profit	1 400	1 010	1 790

(under marginal costing any unsold stock would be valued at £12.20 per unit)

The importance of contribution

This is an important technique of marginal costing and is defined as:

Contribution	=	Sales	−	Variable costs
7.80 per unit	=	20.00	−	12.20

In full, the term means 'contribution towards covering fixed costs and making a profit'. Here the value of contribution per unit is £7.80 and the formula is commonly used to solve a variety of costing problems.

NOTE:

1 If production falls below the planned output using absorption costing, the estimated profit is higher than the marginal figure because fixed costs of £2500 per month have not been fully recovered (450 units at £5 instead of 500 units at £5). This is an under-recovery of fixed overheads. In marginal costing, the planned fixed costs are always recognised.

2 When output increased to 550 units, absorption costing stated less profit compared to marginal costs because it charged an extra 50 units with the fixed costs (over-recovery of fixed overheads). In marginal costing the same £2500 overheads is used because irrespective of output changes, the fixed costs are relatively insensitive and generally, only variable costs change with output.

3 Costing formula:

Contribution per unit (as above)

Estimation of profit/loss = (contribution × output) − fixed costs

Jake Ltd on 500 units = (7.8 × 500) − 2 500 = £1 400

Break-even point $= \dfrac{\text{Fixed costs}}{\text{Contribution per unit}}$

Jake Ltd break-even $= \dfrac{2500}{7.8}$ 321 units

How much profit on 10 units above break-even? 10 × contribution = £78

Check: (331 units × 7.8) − £2500 = £81.8

(answer slightly more because we rounded up the break-even)

If output was 10 units below break-even, the loss would be? (£78 loss, or more precisely £74.2).

Summary

All organisations are dependent on information systems to help management make better decisions. Costing can be of essential importance to management because they need to know what it costs for different levels of output. Costs can be categorised and coded for computerisation and cost centres used to attribute costs to a specific section or activity of the business thereby recognising how and where costs have occurred so that they can be monitored and controlled. In absorption costing, the cost of units produced includes not only variable but also a share of fixed costs. In marginal costing, focus is on the variable costs and the level of output, where fixed costs are not apportioned per unit but rather deducted in total from the total contribution earned.

Questions

1 Why is there a need for cost accounting? (36.1–2)

2 Basically, how would you explain the difference between absorption and marginal costing? (36.1–2)

3 The following information concerns a small manufacturing business:

	£
Direct wages	40 000
Direct materials	60 000
Business rates	1 800
Advertising	1 500
Administration	18 500
Rent and insurance	6 200

a) If it was estimated that 8000 units were to be produced, calculate the absorption cost per unit.
b) Which of the above would you consider as being the variable costs?
c) What would be the total fixed costs?
d) Can you calculate the contribution and break even point if the selling price per unit was £20? (36.2–3)

4 A company estimates an annual output of 50 000 units and its costs are expected to be:

	£
Direct labour	48 000
Direct materials	55 000
Factory overheads	22 500
Distribution costs	15 000
Other overheads	17 500

The variable costs have been agreed as:

Direct labour 75%
Direct materials 100%
Factory and distribution overheads 10% of each.
All other costs are fixed overheads.
The selling price per unit is to be £4.00

REQUIRED:
a) Under absorption costing, calculate the estimated profit for the year and the absorption cost per unit.
b) Use marginal costing to calculate the variable cost per unit.
c) Find the contribution per unit.
d) If the business were to produce 51 500 units, using marginal costing, calculate the estimated profit.
e) If the business produced only 48 000 units, using marginal costs, what would be the estimated profit?
f) Calculate the break-even point.

g) If there were 500 units of unsold stock at the year end, how would it be valued under absorption costs and alternatively, under marginal costs? (36.2–3)

5 A company has two production departments, A and B and one service department, C. Some of its overheads have already been allocated in the cost table below. You are to apportion the remaining overheads on a fair basis on the given criteria:

	A	B	C
Floor areas (sq metres)	150	100	50
Value of plant, equipment	8000	4000	4000
No. of employees	50	30	20
Metered units	3000	2000	1000
Ouput (volume)	12000	8000	

Cost analysis

	A	*B*	*C*	*Total*	*Notes*
Indirect materials	1800	750	450	3000	Allocated
Indirect labour	27400	23100	18500	69000	Allocated
Power				3000	
Rent and rates				60000	
Insurance				1500	
Distribution costs				8000	
Administration			10000	10000	Allocated
Canteen Costs				4500	

The total value of overheads in the service centre is to be apportioned as 60 per cent to centre A and 40 per cent to centre B primarily on the basis of output capacity.

Complete the table by apportioning the overheads to their appropriate cost centres. (36.4)

37 Budgets

Objectives

On completing this section you should:

- be able to define what a budget is
- understand why budgets are prepared
- calculate the cash and operating budgets
- recognise the use of spreadsheets in preparing budgets.

37.1 Introduction

The purpose of preparing a well planned budget is to make the best possible use of business resources. It is concerned with where funds are going to come from, how funds are going to be allocated and how performance will be measured. Budgets are a management device to assist in decision making.

At the national level, the Chancellor of the Exchequer plans the Government's income and expenditure for the year in the preparation of his budget to the nation. How much in taxes must he raise and from which sources? How is this income to be spent? How are the funds to be allocated to the various Government departments? The budget is not all about raising funds and spending money. Budgets can influence the major policy decisions of an organisation. The Chancellor, for example, can use his budget to influence the economy by way of regulating the demand for goods and services. He can make it easier or more difficult for us to buy the things we want. Look at what the level of interest rates can do or the reduction/increase in taxes.

A business can use its budget to plan its objectives. A budget can help to optimise the use of business resources by forecasting what can be done and establishing objectives. For example, can a sales target of £50 000 per week be achieved? What plan of action will be needed? How much marketing and sales promotion will be required? Are production and manpower facilities adequate? Plans are then made and objectives agreed. A yardstick for management to achieve objectives is established.

Once targets for both revenue and expenditure have been set, profits can be estimated for the financial period (or periods) ahead. The budget will provide management with some means by which to measure business performance. Will the actual results match the budgeted plan? How much difference (or variance) will occur between these figures?

Management will be able to use the information by comparing the budget with actual results to help them to make better decisions about how to use the resources of the business. Will they have to increase production to meet a higher than expected demand or will they have to scale down activities because targets have not been met? Budgets should help management decide what plan of action to take.

37.2 Stages of the budget

1 Management objectives should be stated clearly. How should the resources of the business be used?

2 Plans are drawn up and the appropriate budgets prepared. Targets for sales and expenditure are drafted.
3 All personnel should be aware of budgets; they need to know what the plans and forecasts are and the targets which have been set.
4 Actual results should then be regularly checked with budget figures, identifying any differences between them and analysing the possible reasons for the variances.
5 Any amendments or modifications to the budget can be taken into consideration and new initiatives can be taken by management if changes to plans are required.

Realistic objectives should be set by management otherwise staff morale may suffer. Careful consideration in setting targets is essential. If targets are too optimistic, staff may soon give up or be put under severe stress. If they are set too low, staff motivation may diminish once the targets have been achieved.

37.3 Types of budget

There are a number of different types of budget which may be used by management. Smaller businesses may not prepare any budget and simply conduct their affairs in direct response to the market, without planning too much ahead. Larger organisations however, may adopt one or more of the following types of budget:

- sales budget
- production budget
- manpower budget
- cash budget
- operating budget.

37.3.1 Sales budget

The sales aspect is the life-blood of any organisation and therefore an accurate assessment of future sales is required because this provides the basic framework of what the business activity is going to be. Sales provides income by which expenditure can be met. Expenditure plans can then be prepared. If a 20 per cent increase is predicted, management will need to ensure that the business is ready in every respect to meet this target.

37.3.2 Production budget

The production budget must ensure it has the resources in terms of labour, materials and equipment to meet the sales target. It would be of little use predicting a 20 per cent increase in sales if production is unable to meet this demand because it is under-resourced.

37.3.3 Manpower budget

The manpower (personnel) budget must ensure that the organisation has the right labour force at the right time. Manpower planning is essential, particularly in larger organisations, to prepare for management, educational and training needs. The labour force must be efficiently and effectively employed, and given the right opportunities to motivate them to their best efforts. If there is a labour shortage and staff are overworked or there is under-financing of training needs, morale will decline and staff will fail to produce their best. Any organisation is only as good as its staff.

37.3.4 Cash budget

The cash budget is an essential budget because it predicts the future cash flow of the business. Will it have sufficient cash resources to meet payments at the right time? Will any overdraft or specific loans be required? All other budgets will be involved because the cash budget must include all aspects concerning the receipts and payments of monies. The business must have adequate cash resources to meet its day-to-day needs otherwise it can soon be in financial difficulties. A cash shortage can lead to disaster if creditors cannot be paid on time. The business needs to know, month by month, the cash it requires so that it can organise the finances well ahead of time.

37.3.5 Operating budget

The operating budget (sometimes referred to as the financial budget), is the culmination of all the other budgets. It represents the forecast of the trading and profit and loss account and the balance sheet. Profit is the key figure in management thinking. Will the business improve its performance? Will return on capital be satisfactory?

Profit can be broken down into monthly periods, so that actual results can be measured against those of the budget. Variances (differences) can then be analysed and evaluated which will help management in their decisions. Budgets need not be static or inflexible in their use. They can be modified to meeting changing events. They can be updated to suit new circumstances as these arise.

37.4 Some worked examples

The following examples will illustrate accounting's two significant budgets: the cash budget and the operating budget.

Example 1 Cash and operating budgets
The following information relates to a businessman, D Balfour, who has started business on 1 January with £5000. He has made a forecast for the next six months concerning receipts and payments of cash:

a) Production will involve the making of an electrical component for the computer industry. His plan is to produce 500 units per month in the first six months.
b) Sales: each unit has a selling price of £12.50. The sales estimate for six months to 30 June is:

Jan	Feb	Mar	Apr	May	June	
400	480	480	560	640	400	(Units)

c) Variable overheads (based on output), will be £1.50 per unit, payable in the month of production
d) Fixed costs will be £1000 per month payable *after* the month of production.
e) Production wages (direct) will be £3 per unit payable in the month of production.
f) Salaries will be £500 per month until April, but expected to rise by 10 per cent in the following months.
g) Equipment costing £8000 will be purchased in March. A 25 per cent deposit will be paid in March, with the balance to be paid equally in April and May.
h) Materials will cost £2 per unit and suppliers will be paid in the month *after* the purchase.

All unit sales are on credit. Debtors are expected to pay in the month *following* their purchase. £5000 was deposited in the business bank account on 1 January.

REQUIRED:

a) A schedule of payments for the six months to 30 June and a cash budget covering the same period.
b) A brief analysis of the cash budget.
c) An operating budget which will show the trading and profit and loss forecast for the six months to 30 June and a forecast balance sheet as on that date.

a) **The schedule of payments**

	Jan	*Feb*	*Mar*	*Apr*	*May*	*June*	*Total*
	£	£	£	£	£	£	£
Fixed costs	–	1 000	1 000	1 000	1 000	1 000	5 000
Variable overheads (500 × £1.5)	750	750	750	750	750	750	4 500
Production wages (500 × £3.0)	1 500	1 500	1 500	1 500	1 500	1 500	9 000
Salaries	500	500	500	500	550	550	3 100
Materials (500 × £2.0)	–	1 000	1 000	1 000	1 000	1 000	5 000
Equipment			2 000	3 000	3 000		8 000
	2 750	4 750	6 750	7 750	7 800	4 800	34 600

The cash budget

	Jan	*Feb*	*Mar*	*Apr*	*May*	*June*	*Total*
	£	£	£	£	£	£	£
Bank balance b/f	5 000	2 250	2 500	1 750	–	(800)	5 000 (1/1)
+ Receipts	–	5 000	6 000	6 000	7 000	8 000	32 000
(£12.5 unit)	5 000	7 250	8 500	7 750	7 000	7 200	37 000
– Payments (above)	2 750	4 750	6 750	7 750	7 800	4 800	34 600
Bank balance c/f	2 250	2 500	1 750	–	(800)	2 400	2 400
(to next month)							

b) Analysis of the cash budget

From the forecast of cash flow, it appears that D Balfour may be a little short of liquidity in the months of April and May. This is not surprising because part of his expenditure is capital expenditure, purchasing equipment in March of £8000 and finishing the payment for it in May. He could ask the bank to tide him over during these months by arranging for an overdraft facility. He could, if he wanted, finance the asset purchase in other ways, probably by simply extending the period of credit over 12 months or even longer.

In June, however, the cash flow is back in surplus and certainly appears sound. Cash flow forecasts a business's liquidity. Can sales generate sufficient receipts of money to be able to finance labour, materials, overheads and capital expenditure?

Budgets are an important management tool if they are taken seriously. They can help plan and control the business because they assist in management decision making. When actual results are recorded, they can be carefully monitored against the budget forecast. How will D Balfour's budget compare with his first six months trading? Will he have about £2500 in the bank in June? If he has not, what factors have occurred to have caused the difference? These are the questions which help make accounting more dynamic; a little more involved in making things happen and not just recording what has already happened.

c) The operating budget

The operating budget relates to the forecast of the trading and profit and loss account and the balance sheet. The sales forecast for the six months to June was:

Total of 2960 units × £12.5 per unit = £37 000 (Sales)

The first six production months at 500 units per month would cost:

			£
Wages	£3.0 per unit × 3000	=	9 000
Variable overheads	£1.5 per unit × 3000	=	4 500
Materials	£2.0 per unit × 3000	=	6 000
	£6.5	Total cost:	19 500 (Production)

There was no opening stock because it was a new business and therefore there will be no closing stock carried forward from the previous period. If the closing stock was to be valued at production cost per unit then:

Units produced:	3 000 units
Units sold:	2 960 units
	40 units in stock × production cost per unit
Value of closing stock:	40 × £6.5 per unit = £260

As far as any adjustments are concerned, D Balfour decided to depreciate the equipment by 20 per cent per annum and a full 10 per cent for the six months, even though it was to be purchased in March.

D Balfour –
Budgeted trading and profit and loss account
for six months ending 30 June

	£	£	£
Sales			37 000
– Cost of sales:			
Stock (1/1)	–		
Production cost	19 500		
Stock (30/6)	(260)		19 240
Gross profit			17 760

(continued)

(continued)

Expenses:			
Fixed costs	5 000		
+ Accrued (1 month)	1 000	6 000	
Salaries		3 100	
Depreciation of equipment		800	9 900
Net profit			7 860

D Balfour –
Budgeted balance sheet as on 30 June

	£	£	£
FIXED ASSETS			
Equipment	8 000	800	7 200
CURRENT ASSETS			
Stock	260		
Debtors			
(400 × £12.5)	5 000		
Bank	2 400	7 660	
CURRENT LIABILITIES			
Creditors			
(500 × £2)	1 000		
Accruals	1 000	2 000	
(1 month fixed cost)			
Working capital			5 660
			12 860
FINANCED BY:			
Capital (1/1)	5 000		
+ Net profit	7 860		12 860

D Balfour's prospects look very sound for a period covering the first six months' trading. It may be that his sales forecast is a little optimistic and his expenditure may be greater than predicted. He will be able to compare his actual trading results with the budget and see if his targets have been met. Will the demand for his product be maintained? Has he arranged any firm contracts with clients? Can he hold his own against other competitors? These are the type of questions D Balfour will need to answer.

Example 2 Cash budgets and spreadsheets
You work as an assistant to a firm of accountants who deal with a wide variety of financial and management accounts. One of their clients, a partnership called Smith & Jones, have submitted data for

your preparation. The information has been placed with you to prepare the draft documents before they are passed on to the client.

Smith & Jones wish to form a new private limited company in the name of S & J Co Ltd. The new company is to commence its operations with effect from 1 July. The data estimated for the period from 1 July to 31 December is as follows:

1 Smith is to put £50 000 into the business bank account on 1 July and will be issued with 50 000 £1 ordinary shares.
Jones will put £100 000 into the business bank account on the same date and will be issued with 50 000 £1 ordinary shares and £50 000 of debenture stock at 12 per cent interest.

2 The sales will be on a credit basis and are estimated to be:

July	£25 000	Oct	£50 000
Aug	£45 000	Nov	£45 000
Sep	£65 000	Dec	£60 000

All debtors are expected to settle their accounts two months after the month in which the goods are bought.

3 The purchases will be on a credit basis and are estimated to be:

July	£65 000	Oct	£45 000
Aug	£35 000	Nov	£30 000
Sep	£50 000	Dec	£45 000

Creditors payments are arranged to be paid in the month following the purchase.

4 Wages and salaries are estimated to be £1750 per month payable on the last weekday of each month.

5 Smith and Jones will each draw directors' fees of £1000 per month payable on the same date as in 4 above.

6 Debenture interest is to be paid half-yearly, the first payment is due in December.

7 Premises are to be purchased for £85 000 and paid for in August.

8 Fixed costs are estimated to be £1500 per month for the first three months of business and then increase by 20 per cent thereafter. These costs are payable one month in arrears.

9 Equipment is to be purchased on 1 July for £30 000, half of which is to be paid in July and the other in October. It is also to be depreciated by 20 per cent per annum on the straight-line basis.

10 Stock is estimated to be valued at £40 000 on 31 December.

REQUIRED:

a) Prepare a cash flow budget for the period July to December (inclusive).

b) Prepare a budgeted profit and loss account and a balance sheet for the half year to 31 December.

c) (To be used in conjunction with spreadsheet p. 480)
  i) Using a disk with spreadsheet software, input your data as presented in Task A and obtain a printout of the result.
  ii) Assume that a change has occurred in your estimated cost of the equipment from a value of £30 000 to £40 000 (as in **9** above) and also an increase of £100 in wages for November and December. Input this data in your budget program for the purpose of producing a further print-out indicating the changes it will effect.

SOLUTION

TASK A

S & J Co Ltd

Schedule of payments	*July*	*Aug*	*Sep*	*Oct*	*Nov*	*Dec*	*Total*
	£	£	£	£	£	£	£
Creditors	–	65 000	35 000	50 000	45 000	30 000	225 000
Wages and salaries	1 750	1 750	1 750	1 750	1 750	1 750	10 500
Directors' fees	2 000	2 000	2 000	2 000	2 000	2 000	12 000
Premises		85 000					85 000
Debenture interest						3 000	3 000
Fixed costs	–	1 500	1 500	1 500	1 800	1 800	8 100
Equipment	15 000			15 000			30 000
	18 750	155 250	40 250	70 250	50 550	38 550	373 600
Cash budget	£	£	£	£	£	£	£
Bank balance b/f	150 000	131 250	(24 000)	(39 250)	(64 500)	(50 050)	150 000 (1/7)
+ Receipts	–	–	25 000	45 000	65 000	50 000	185 000
	150 000	131 250	1 000	5 750	500	(50)	335 000
– Payments	18 750	155 250	40 250	70 250	50 550	38 550	373 600
Bank balance c/f	131 250	(24 000)	(39 250)	(64 500)	(50 050)	(38 600)	(38 600)

NOTE

The company will need substantial overdraft facilities or a fixed long-term loan from the bank in its first six months and possibly through to the next six. This was caused by the delay in the receipt of debtors' payments; debtors enjoy two months' credit. In the second six months, the receipts should be flowing in each month to help diminish the overdraft or loan facility.

TASK B

S & J Co Ltd –
Budgeted trading and profit and loss account
six months ending 31 December

	£	£	£
Sales			290 000
– Cost of sales:			
Stock (1/7)	—		
Purchases	270 000		
Stock (31/12)	(40 000)		230 000
Gross profit			60 000
– Expenses:			
Wages and salaries		10 500	
Directors' fees		12 000	
Debenture interest		3 000	

(continued)

(continued)

Fixed costs	8 100		
+ Accrued	1 800	9 900	
Depreciation (equipment)		3 000	38 400
Net profit			21 600

Budgeted balance sheet as on 31 December

	£	£	£
FIXED ASSETS			
Premises	85 000		85 000
Equipment	30 000	3 000	27 000
			112 000
CURRENT ASSETS			
Stock	40 000		
Debtors (Nov/Dec)	105 000		
Bank	—	145 000	
CURRENT LIABILITIES			
Creditors (Dec)	45 000		
Bank O/D	38 600		
Accruals	1 800	85 400	
Net current assets			59 600
			171 600
LONG-TERM LIABILITIES			
Debentures			50 000
			121 600
ISSUED AND PAID-UP CAPITAL			
100 000 @ £1 ordinary shares			100 000
Profit and loss account			21 600
			121 600

37.5 Computer-based accounts: the use of a spreadsheet

A spreadsheet program contains a matrix or grid, which displays a series of rows and columns. A program would normally display around 60 columns across (not all visible on screen at the same time of course) and about 250 rows down.

The matrix is often referred to as a *worksheet* which may be used as a tool to solve a range of business problems. Once a spreadsheet has been set up, for example, to prepare cash budgets, it can be used over and over again, incorporating any changes which may be required. Figures can be changed to try out different ideas and to see their effect on the overall plan, assisting management to make their decisions.

37.5.1 The matrix

← Columns →

		A	B	C	D	E	F	G	H
	1	*Income*	*July*	*Aug*	*Sept*	*Oct*	*Nov*	*Dec*	*Total*
	2	Debtors	500	500	600	600	700	800	3 700
↑	3	Other (cash)	100	150	150	200	200	400	1 200
	4	Total:	600	650	750	800	900	1 200	4 900
	5	*Payments*							
Rows	6	Creditors	400	500	500	500	600	700	3 200
	7	Wages	80	80	85	85	85	85	500
	8	Overheads	100	100	100	100	100	100	600
↓	9	Fixed assets			40		40		80
	10	Total:	580	680	725	685	825	885	4 380
	11	*Balance* b/f	50	70	40	65	180	255	50
	12	+ Total (4)	600	650	750	800	900	1 200	4 900
	13	– Total (10)	580	680	725	685	825	885	4 380
	14	*Balance c/f*	70	40	65	180	255	570	570

Commands: Copy/Delete/Edit/Format/Insert

NOTE

If it was decided to change debtors, for example, in July and August to 600 in each month, all relevant figures on the grid would instantly be updated, ending with a final balance of 770 in December.

37.5.2 Cells

The columns across and the rows down form cells. These are the locations on the grid. For example, B2 locates the cell for the receipts of debtors in July (500) and F8 locates the overheads in November (100). Each individual cell is identified by its column and row position in the same way as a grid reference on an ordinance survey map. Columns in this example are all identified by a letter and rows by a number.

The cells may be used to enter three distinct types of information:

1 The text: the headings for rows and columns.
2 Numbers: whole numbers, decimals or currency.
3 Formulae: relating to numbers for adding, subtracting, multiplying, dividing, etc.

The size of a cell may vary, but will normally hold about 8 to 10 characters. This can be modified if more spaces are required by using a command such as Format.

Formulae may be set up in any of the cells to instruct the computer to do the necessary calculations. For example, in cells B across to G, a total of these must be made in column H, for each of the rows from 2 to 3, 4, 6, 7, 8, 9, 10, 12 and 13.

Method:	+ Sum [B2:G2]	to be entered in column H2
	+ Sum [B3:G3]	to be entered in column H3, etc.

The same principle is applied to the columns down. The totals of income in row number 4 must be calculated for each month including the final total in column H. The same applies to payments in column 10 for each of the months across, including the final total.

Method:	B2 + B3	to be entered in B4 (income)
	C2 + C3	to be entered in C4, etc.
	+ Sum [B6:B9]	to be entered in B10 (payments)
	+ Sum [C6:C9]	to be entered in C10, etc.

This procedure may sound a little tedious, although a command such as Replicate has the facility of making the same formulae across a number of cells and does save time. However, once the formulae are in place, any figures may be entered and calculations are instantly updated!

The symbols for the use of formulae are:

+ Add
– Subtract
* Multiply
/ Divide

By using these basic symbols, any row or column can be totalled, subtracted, divided, averaged, multiplied, percentaged, etc. Once a formula is set to a particular cell, it will calculate the relevant figures. Formulae can also be changed to suit the circumstances. It is then a straightforward matter of entering the appropriate figures in the appropriate cells, entering the calculation command and all figures are instantly updated.

37.5.3 Moving from cell to cell

The arrow keys on the keyboard allow the movement from cell to cell, either across or down. The cell cursor identifies the cell to be used. If the arrow keys are held down, the cursor moves across or down more rapidly. If the cursor is moved beyond the column visible on the screen (in our case, H), then the worksheet automatically scrolls past the screen window to the next section, I onwards, so that the cursor is always on view. If the cursor was moved down beyond row 14, the worksheet would scroll past the screen window to the next section, that is, from 15 downwards.

The prompt line is at the bottom of the screen and allows the operator to select the option required. For example, commands may be entered to copy, delete, calculate, etc. The prompt line lists the set of options for the operator to choose from.

37.5.4 Uses of the spreadsheet

The spreadsheet has a wide range of uses in all sorts of different organisations. A wide spread of calculations can be performed automatically within the basic framework of the matrix. An operator can test any number of variations to check on the outcome, in order to discover what the effects of these changes might be. For example, if another £50 000 was spent on equipment, payable in March and June, what effect would it have on cash flow in the budget period?

In business, the spreadsheet is particularly useful in the preparation of all types of budgets for the purpose of forecasting cash flow, profits, sales, production costs, stocks, etc. Mistakes can be corrected quite easily and new figures inserted. A wide range of calculations can be performed instantly and the operator may try out a number of different variables to see what the effects might be. Spreadsheets may be stored on disks and called up when needed. Printouts of the spreadsheet may also be obtained. Some spreadsheet packages are integrated with other programs and can provide graphics to produce charts and diagrams.

The following is an example of a spreadsheet being used to calculate a cash flow budget: it refers to Task C of S & J Co Ltd on page 476.

Task C: The spreadsheet of S & J Co Ltd

Details	July	August	Sept	Oct	Nov	Dec	Total
INCOME							
Debtors	0	0	25000	45000	65000	50000	185000
S.Cap	150000	0					150000
TOTAL	150000	0	25000	45000	65000	50000	335000
PAYMENTS							
Creds.	0	65000	35000	50000	45000	30000	225000
Wages	1750	1750	1750	1750	1750	1750	10500
Dir.Fees	2000	2000	2000	2000	2000	2000	12000
Deb.Int	0					3000	3000
Premises	0	85000					85000
F.Costs	0	1500	1500	1500	1800	1800	8100
Eqpt.	15000			15000			30000
Sundries							
TOTAL	18750	155250	40250	70250	50550	38550	373600
Bal.b/f	0	131250	–24000	–39250	–64500	–50050	0
+Income	150000	0	25000	45000	65000	50000	335000
	150000	131250	1000	5750	500	–50	335000
Payments	18750	155250	40250	70250	50550	38550	373600
Bal.c/f	131250	–24000	–39250	–64500	–50050	–38600	–38600

Task C: The spreadsheet of S & J Co Ltd showing the effect of changes in wages and equipment costs

Details	July	August	Sept	Oct	Nov	Dec	Total
INCOME							
Debtors	0	0	25000	45000	65000	50000	185000
S.Cap	150000	0					150000
TOTAL	150000	0	25000	45000	65000	50000	335000
PAYMENTS							
Creds.	0	65000	35000	50000	45000	30000	225000
Wages	1750	1750	1750	1750	1850	1850	10700
Dir. Fees	2000	2000	2000	2000	2000	2000	12000
Deb.Int	0					3000	3000
Premises	0	85000					85000
F.Costs	0	1500	1500	1500	1800	1800	8100
Eqpt.	20000			20000			40000
Sundries							
TOTAL	23750	155250	40250	75250	50650	38650	383800
Bal.b/f	0	126250	–29000	–44250	–74500	–60150	0
+Income	150000	0	25000	45000	65000	50000	335000
	150000	126250	–4000	750	–9500	–10150	335000
Payments	23750	155250	40250	75250	50650	38650	383800
Bal.c/f	126250	–29000	–44250	–74500	–60150	–48800	–48800

Summary

A budget is a forecast of a business's resources and a management tool to help them in setting their objectives and making decisions. Budgets need to be well planned and communicated to all key members of staff so that they are part of the planning and monitoring process. Actual results need to be compared with the budget to check on any variances which may occur and to provide any possible plan of action. A spreadsheet is a convenient method of recording budget information because any changes can be easily updated.

Questions

1 The following information relates to Downing & Co Ltd concerning the preparation of its six-monthly budget:

	Mar £	*Apr* £	*May* £	*June* £	*July* £	*Aug* £	*Sept* £	*Oct* £
Sales on credit	20 000	30 000	35 000	34 000	36 000	25 000	26 000	27 000
Purchases on credit	20 000	22 000	23 000	17 000	18 000	19 000	22 000	20 000

Rent, rates	Paid half yearly, in advance; first payment in March; £12 000 per year.
Salaries	£2 000 per month, payable in the same month.
Wages	£1 000 per month, payable in the same month, but having a 10 per cent increase in September.
Fixed costs	£1 000 per month, payable in the same month.
Depreciation on equipment	£75 per month.
Bank balance	1st April £5 000.
Debtors	To pay in the *following* month of sale.
Creditors	To be paid in the month *after* the purchase.
Corporation tax	£12 000 to be paid in June.

REQUIRED:

a) Prepare a schedule of payments for the months April to September, inclusive.
b) Prepare a cash budget for the same period.
c) Make any brief comment on your findings.(37.1–3)

2 You work for a firm of accountants, who have just taken on a client, Small & Co. In addition to the year-end accounts the client requires a cash forecast and has supplied various data.

Information

i) Opening cash (including bank) balance £2000.
ii) Production in units:

April	*May*	*June*	*July*	*Aug*	*Sept*	*Oct*	*Nov*	*Dec*
480	540	600	640	700	740	760	680	620

iii) Raw materials used in production cost £10 per unit, payable in the month of production.
iv) Direct labour costs of £17 per unit are payable in the month of production.
v) Variable expenses are £3 per unit, payable 2/3 in month of production and 1/3 in the month following production.
vi) Sales at £40 per unit:

Mar	*April*	*May*	*June*	*July*	*Aug*	*Sept*	*Oct*	*Nov*	*Dec*
520	400	640	580	800	600	700	800	780	800

Debtors to pay their accounts in the month following the sale.

vii) Fixed expenses of £1200 per month payable each month.
viii) Machinery costing £21 000 to be paid for in August.
ix) Receipt of an investment grant of £7000 is due in November.
x) Drawings to be £800 per month.

REQUIRED:
a) Prepare a schedule of payments for the six months from 1 July to 31 December.
b) Prepare a cash budget for the six months from 1 July to 31 December.
c) Prepare a draft memorandum to the client commenting on the results of your cash budget.
(BTEC)

3 You are employed by a consultancy firm and are working on the cash flow budget of a new client, Forbes & Co Ltd, from 1 April to 30 September 19–8.
i) On 1/4 Forbes plan to set up in business by depositing £120 000 in the business bank account.
ii) On 2/4 to buy and pay for premises £80 000; shop fixtures £10 000; and a motor van £8000.
iii) To employ three sales assistants – monthly wages £1500 (total) payable at the end of each month (ignore tax and insurance).
iv) To buy the following goods:

	April	*May*	*June*	*July*	*Aug*	*Sept*
Units	1000	600	600	700	700	700

v) To sell the following goods:

	April	*May*	*June*	*July*	*Aug*	*Sept*
Units	400	500	500	600	700	700

vi) Units will be sold for £30 each and customers will be expected to pay their accounts in the month following that in which they buy the goods.
vii) Units will cost £17 each and suppliers expect to be paid in the same month as supply.
viii) General expenses are estimated at £600 per month payable in the month following.
ix) The directors will draw monthly salaries totalling £2000 per month-but they will *not* draw such salaries in the first two months.
x) Variable costs are £5 per unit for sales distribution payable in the month following.

REQUIRED:
a) A schedule of payments for the six months ending 30 September 19–8.
b) A cash budget for the same period. (37.1–3)

4 You are employed by a small firm of accountants and one of their clients, P Jackson & Co Ltd requires a four month cash flow forecast leading up to the financial year ending 31 March 19–7.

Information available
Client: P Jackson & Co Ltd

Number of units produced per month:	*Oct*	*Nov*	*Dec*	*Jan*	*Feb*	*Mar*
	650	700	550	500	450	400

a) Direct materials cost £4 per unit paid for one month after production.
b) Direct labour costs are £2.50 per unit paid in the same month of production.
c) Sales revenue is £15 per unit. All production is sold but debtors pay in the second month following production.
d) Variable overheads are £2 per unit paid half in the month of production and the other half in the following month.
e) Fixed overhead costs are £1000 per month paid by the month.

f) Other wages are £600 per month payable in the month.
g) Taxation due to be paid in March 19–7 is £3500.
h) New machinery costing £35 000 in January 19–7 is to be paid by a 20 per cent deposit in January and followed by equal instalments over 14 months commencing in February.
i) The bank balance on 1 December 19–6 is estimated at £1000 rounded up in Jackson's favour.

REQUIRED:
a) Produce a cash flow plan for P Jackson & Co Ltd for the final four months of their financial year (December-March).
b) Prepare a memorandum to the client commenting on the basic difference between fixed and variable costs. (37.1–3)

(Institute of Bankers)

5 The following information relates to a businessman, E Allan, who will be starting his enterprise on 1 July 19–8 with £10 000. He has made a forecast for the next six months concerning his cash flow:
a) Production will concern the making of an electrical component for the computer industry. His plan is to produce 600 units (output) per month in the first six months.
b) Sales: each unit has a selling price of £20.00. The sales estimate for six months to 31 December is:

July	*Aug*	*Sept*	*Oct*	*Nov*	*Dec*	
300	680	680	600	540	400	(units)

c) Variable overheads (based on output), will be £2.50 per unit, payable in the month of production.
d) Fixed costs will be £2000 per month payable *after* the month of production.
e) Production wages (direct) will be £5 per unit payable in the month of production.
f) Salaries will be £700 per month until October but expected to rise by 20 per cent in the months following.
g) Equipment, to cost £12 000 will be purchased in September. A 25 per cent deposit will be paid in September with the balance to be paid equally in October and November. Depreciation is 25 per cent per annum.
h) Materials will cost £4 per unit and suppliers will be paid in the month *after* the purchase.

All unit sales are on credit. Debtors are expected to pay in the month *following* their purchase. £10 000 was deposited in the business bank account on 1 July.

REQUIRED:
a) A schedule of payments for the six months ending 31 December and a cash budget to cover the same period.
b) An operating budget which will show the trading and profit and loss forecast for the six months ending to 31 December and a forecast balance sheet as on 31 December

Note: Closing stock to be valued at £11.50 per unit.

c) A statement which briefly analyses the cash budget. (37.3)

(BTEC)

6 Clare Jones must submit a six month cash budget plan and forecast final accounts for her bank manager. The details are as follows:
a) Opening cash balance £12 000 to be used as her business bank account. She also has a motor van valued £5000 to be used in the business.
b) Her production (in units) per month is as follows:

July	*Aug*	*Sept*	*Oct*	*Nov*	*Dec*
700	720	760	680	700	750

c) Direct materials used in production will cost £10 per unit, payable in the month of production.
d) Direct labour will cost £18 per unit payable in the month of production.
e) Variable overheads will cost £5 per unit payable half in the month of production and half in the following month.
f) Sales per unit will be £50. Estimates sales are:

July	*Aug*	*Sept*	*Oct*	*Nov*	*Dec*
300	700	720	750	800	800

Debtors are expected to pay in the month after the sale.
g) Fixed costs are estimated at £1250 per month, payable each month.
h) Machinery costing £20 000 is to be paid for, 50 per cent in August and 50 per cent in September.
i) The bank loan expected, £10 000 over five years, should be through in August.
j) Personal drawings to be £600 per month.
k) Depreciation of machinery at 25 per cent per annum, the van is revalued to £2000. The interest of £175 per month is accrued from 1 September.

REQUIRED:
a) A schedule of payments and a cash budget for the six months to 31 December. The closing value of stock is to be calculated on the factory cost of £33 per unit.
b) A budgeted profit and loss account for the period of six months to 31 December and a balance sheet as at that date. (37.1–3)

The following are advanced questions:

7 The following information relates to a forecast for Jim Smith, of revenue and costs for the year ending 31 December:

Sales target is expected to reach 35 000 units.
Selling price per unit, £8.00

Costs forecast:	£
Direct materials	1.50 per unit
Direct labour	2.00 per unit
Factory variables	1.25 per unit
Distribution variables	1.75 per unit
Factory fixed cost	28 500 per annum
Administrative fixed cost	15 000 per annum

Stock of finished goods at 31 December to be valued at the factory cost per unit.

The production target is 38 000 units.

REQUIRED:
a) A forecast of the manufacturing cost based on 38 000 units produced in the year to 31 December.
b) A forecast of the trading and profit and loss account for the year ending 31 December.
c) The mark-up and margins of profit based on the factory cost on 31 December (as percentages).

(AEB)

8 Jones is a teacher of accounting and he has decided to produce a book of accounting exercises. He has enlisted the help of his senior class and the headteacher has kindly agreed to the use of school typing and duplicating facilities.

For the first year target production is 5000 books and target sales 4900 books. The senior class agreed to be responsible for sales in return for a fixed fee of £80 and a further 5p for each book sold.
The additional forecasts covering the year ending 31 May 19–8 were:

Materials
Paper and stencils £500 for the 5000 books.
Cover 3p per book.
Binding 10p per book.

Direct labour
Typing of stencils 50p each (50 stencils required, first year).
Duplication 10p per book.
Binding 15 p per book.

Fixed expense of £75 to be paid to the school fund for use of typewriters, duplicating and binding equipment used in producing the books.

Estimated stock on 31 May: 100 books to be valued at factory cost. The selling price per book is to be determined by adding 50 per cent to the factory cost of finished output.

REQUIRED:
a) the forecast manufacturing account showing both prime cost and factory cost of goods manufactured;
b) the forecast trading and profit and loss account.

(AEB)

9 Julie Watt has started her own factory producing toy trains. Her production target for the year is 20 000 and she hopes to achieve a sales target of 90 per cent of her output.

The additional forecasts she has made are as follows:

	£
Direct materials	2.5 per unit
Direct labour	2.0 per unit
Factory variables	0.5 per unit
Fixed factory cost	12 000 per annum
Variable selling and distribution costs	1.75 per unit
Office overheads	4 500 per annum

Julie will determine a selling price by a *margin* of $33^1/_3$ per cent (one third), based on her factory cost.

REQUIRED:
a) A forecast manufacturing account for the year. Stock unsold is to be valued at factory cost per unit.
b) A forecast trading and profit and loss account for the year.
c) A statement to clearly define the difference between fixed and variable costs and its importance to business.

(Associated Examining Board)

38 The sale and purchase of a business

Objectives

On completing this section you should:

- be aware of the accounts involved when a business is disposed of
- understand why the role of the journal is significant
- recognise how goodwill plays a part in the purchase price.

38.1 Introduction

The journal may be usefully employed as a book of original entry to record the sale of a business in the vendor's books and also to record the purchase of a business, from the vendor, in the buyer's books.

The sale price of a business is dependent on, and influenced by, a number of factors including the market value of the assets for sale, the demand for the particular type of business, the general economic conditions prevailing at the time and a price agreed for goodwill (the good name and reputation of the business).

The prospective buyer will want to make a study of the financial accounts of the business he wishes to purchase. He would want to study the final accounts of the vendor over a number of years and certainly the last three financial periods. Is the business a profitable venture? Has it got potential? How keen is the purchaser to buy? These are significant questions which will help determine the final purchase price.

Estate agents normally act on behalf of a vendor's business, particularly where an assessment of property values are concerned. The agents assess the value of the business's assets and in conjunction with the seller, calculate a suitable figure for **goodwill**. A further consideration concerns the liabilities of the business. Will the buyer take on the liabilities, or will the seller settle the accounts himself?

Over recent years, the demand for certain type of businesses has been high. Post offices have sold well because there is usually a good level of demand for them. On the other hand, some small high street businesses have suffered because of the stiff competition from the large retail organisations and consequently their value has fallen.

38.2 The sale of a business in the vendor's books

Mike Walker, owner of a small business selling gifts and general items, decided to sell and retire. On 1 June his balance sheet showed his financial position to be as follows:

M Walker –
Balance sheet as on 1 June

	£	£	£
FIXED ASSETS			
Premises	50 000		
Equipment	2 000	52 000	
CURRENT ASSETS			
Stock	5 000		
Bank	3 000		
Debtors	1 000	9 000	
CURRENT LIABILITIES			
Creditors		5 000	4 000
			56 000
LONG-TERM LIABILITIES			
Mortgage			14 000
			42 000
CAPITAL: M Walker			42 000

The estate agents, Goadsby & Harding, had already updated the value of the property to £50 000 and the net assets, *excluding the bank account of £3000*, had a value of £39 000. This represented the net worth of M Walker, less his bank account.

The purchase was negotiated and M Walker agreed to sell the business to P Jackson for a sum of £50 000. The value of *goodwill* was therefore assessed at £11 000, (£50 000 – £39 000).

All the accounts in the books of M Walker would be closed off against the *realisation account*, except for the bank and capital accounts. This took place on 21 June.

M Walker's (the vendor's) Journal

		Debit	Credit
		£	£
21/6	Realisation account*	58 000	
	Premises		50 000
	Equipment		2 000
	Stock		5 000
	Debtors		1 000
	Assets closed off on sale of business to P Jackson	58 000	58 000
21/6	Creditors	5 000	
	Mortgage	14 000	
	Realisation account		19 000

(continued)

(continued)

	Liabilities closed off on sale of business to P Jackson		
21/6	P Jackson (buyer)	50 000	
	Realisation account		50 000
	(Being the agreed sum to be paid by the buyer)		
21/6	Realisation account	11 000	
	Capital account		11 000
	(Being price agreed for goodwill)		

Note

*The realisation account is used to close off the accounts of the business against the price it will sell for.

Ledger – M Walker

		Debit £	*Credit* £	*Balance* £
Premises account				
1/6	Balance			50 000 Dr
21/6	Realisation		50 000	—
Equipment account				
1/6	Balance			2 000 Dr
21/6	Realisation		2 000	—
Stock account				
1/6	Balance			5 000 Dr
21/6	Realisation		5 000	—
Debtors' account				
1/6	Balance			1 000 Dr
21/6	Realisation		1 000	—
Creditors' account				
1/6	Balance			5 000 Cr
21/6	Realisation	5 000		—
Mortgage account				
1/6	Balance			14 000 Cr
21/6	Realisation	14 000		—
Bank account				
1/6	Balance			3 000 Dr

(continued)

(continued)

Capital account: M Walker				
1/6	Balance			42 000 Cr
21/6	Realisation		11 000	53 000
P Jackson (Buyer)				
21/6	Realisation	50 000		50 000 Dr
Realisation account				
21/6	Premises	50 000		
	Equipment	2 000		
	Stock	5 000		
	Debtors	1 000		
	Capital (profit)	11 000		69 000 Dr
	P Jackson		50 000	
	Creditors		5 000	
	Mortgage		14 000	—

NOTES

1 All the accounts in M Walker's books have been closed off to realisation account, except the bank and capital accounts. £11 000 has been credited to his capital account as the 'profit' from goodwill.
2 The realisation account acts something like 'the disposal of the business accounts', closing off the relevant assets and liabilities, using the realisation as the corresponding double entry.

38.2.1 Final payment by the buyer

When the buyer eventually settles the purchase on completion day, his cheque will be debited to the bank account and credited to the buyer's account, thereby clearing the debt.

The cheque for £50 000 was settled on 30 June. The final closing off of the accounts would be:

Ledger

		Debit £	*Credit* £	*Balance* £
Bank account				
1/6	Balance			3 000 Dr
30/6	P Jackson (buyer)	50 000		53 000
P Jackson account				
21/6	Realisation	50 000		50 000 Dr
30/6	Bank		50 000	—

Ledger

		Debit	Credit	Balance
		£	£	£
Bank account				
1/6	Balance			3 000 Dr
30/6	P Jackson	50 000		53 000
30/6	Capital		53 000	—
Capital account: M Walker				
1/6	Balance			42 000 Cr
21/6	Realisation		11 000	53 000
30/6	Bank	53 000		—

The final double entry would be to withdraw the £53 000 from the business bank account and debit this to the capital account. This last transaction effectively closes off the business.

NOTE
Walker received a total of £53 000 by selling his business. His net worth in the balance sheet was £42 000. He profited by £11 000 because of the goodwill value.

38.3 The purchase of a business in the buyer's books

When Peter Jackson bought the shop from his old friend, Mike Walker, for the sum agreed, £50 000, he added to his property, equipment, stock and debtors. He also took over the responsibility for the payment of debt to creditors and the outstanding mortgage on the property. Part of the agreed price was the sum of £11 000 for goodwill.

Peter Jackson already had a business and with this new acquisition, he will be able to merge the values of the two businesses together.

The following figures relate to his balance sheet as on 21 June:

P Jackson –
Balance sheet as on 21 June

	£	£	£
FIXED ASSETS			
Premises	85 000		
Equipment	3 500		
Motor vehicle	6 500		95 000
CURRENT ASSETS			
Stock	8 600		
Debtors	3 750		
Bank	42 500		
Cash	250	55 100	

(continued)

(continued)

CURRENT LIABILITIES		
Creditors	4 700	
Net current assets		50 400
LONG-TERM LIABILITIES		145 400
Mortgage		48 400
		97 000
CAPITAL: P Jackson		97 000

On 21 June, when the buyer and seller exchanged contracts on the purchase of the business, P Jackson would enter the details in his journal. M Walker would be credited with £50 000 because this would represent the sum owing to him until the sum was paid. The journal entry is as follows:

P Jackson's (the buyer's) journal

		Debit £	Credit £
21/6	Premises	50 000	
	Equipment	2 000	
	Stock	5 000	
	Debtors	1 000	
	Goodwill	11 000	
	Creditors		5 000
	Mortgage		14 000
	M Walker (vendor)		50 000
		69 000	69 000
	(Being the purchase of a business from M Walker)		

Before P Jackson enters these in his books, he may decide to revalue some of the above items. On 30 June, the completion date of the purchase, when he hands over the £50 000 to M Walker, Jackson decided to:

a) Mark-down the value of the equipment to £1500 and the stock to £4000.
b) Increase the value of the property to £60 000.

How would this affect the value of goodwill?

P Jackson's (the buyer's) journal

		Debit	Credit
		£	£
30/6	Premises	60 000	
	Equipment	1 500	
	Stock	4 000	
	Debtors	1 000	
	Goodwill	2 500	
	Creditors		5 000
	Mortgage		14 000
	M Walker		50 000
		69 000	69 000
	(Being the revaluation of assets on acquisition)		
30/6	M Walker	50 000	
	Bank		50 000
	(Settlement of purchase of business)		

NOTE

The new figure for goodwill is simply the total of the revaluation of the assets less the liabilities and purchase price agreed, (£69 000 – £66 500).

The journal entries would be posted to the relevant accounts in P Jackson's ledger, merging the two businesses together. The balance sheet extracted on 30 June would appear as follows:

P Jackson –
Balance sheet as on 30 June

	£	£	£
FIXED ASSETS			
Premises	85 000		
+ New	60 000		145 000
Equipment	3 500		
+ New	1 500		5 000
Motor vehicle	6 500		6 500
			156 500
Goodwill			2 500
			159 000

(continued)

(continued)

CURRENT ASSETS			
Stock	8 600		
+ New	4 000	12 600	
Debtors	3 750		
+ New	1 000	4 750	
Bank		—	
Cash		250	
		17 600	
CURRENT LIABILITIES			
Creditors	4 700		
+ New	5 000		
	9 700		
Bank overdraft (£42 500 – £50 000)	7 500	17 200	
Net current assets			400
			159 400
LONG-TERM LIABILITIES			
Mortgage	48 400		
+ New	14 000		62 400
			97 000
CAPITAL: P Jackson			97 000

38.4 Purchase by a partnership

If a **partnership** or indeed a **limited company** took over the assets and liabilities of a business, the same principles would apply. You still need to calculate the goodwill figure and prepare a balance sheet after the business has been acquired. Let us assume that P Jackson accepts £100 000 for his business from the partnership of Ted and Alice in July.

Example

Ted and Alice, wanting to expand their business widely, decide to take over Jackson's business on 15 July for the agreed sum of £100 000. Jackson is to retain his motor vehicle, the bank overdraft and his remaining cash.

The partnership will revalue the premises to £150 000 but downgrade the equipment to £4 000 and the stock to £10 325. In addition, they decide to make a 10 per cent provision against Jackson's debtors. To finance the purchase, the partners will pay £20 000 in cash and the balance on a long-term business loan.

Calculation of goodwill

		£	£
	Premises	150 000	
	Equipment	4 000	
	Stock	10 325	
	Debtors (4750–475)	4 275	168 600
less			
	Creditors	9 700	
	Mortgage	62 400	72 100
	Net assets =		96 500
	Goodwill =		3 500
	Purchase price =		100 000

The partnership's balance sheet before and after the acquisition on 15 July was:

			BEFORE		AFTER
			£		£
Premises			175 000	325 000	
Equipment			4 750	8 750	
Motor vehicles			10 000	10 000	
Goodwill				3 500	
			189 750		347 250
Stocks	12 500			22 825	
Debtors	4 250			8 525	
Bank	23 500	40 250		3 500	34 850
Creditors		4 500			14 200
Net current assets			35 750		20 650
			225 500		367 900
Mortgage				62 400	
Business loan				80 000	142 400
					225 500
Capital accounts:					
Ted	100 000				
Alice	100 000		200 000		200 000
Current accounts:					
Ted	18 500				
Alice	7 000		25 500		25 500
			225 500		225 500

NOTE

The capital and current accounts are the same after the acquisition. The goodwill is expected to be written off against their capital accounts as soon as it is practicable to do so, as discussed in SSAP 22 (Goodwill) and in the chapter concerning partnership accounts. The debtors of £8 525 was £9 000 less the provision for bad debts of £475.

In the event that the new valuation of a business was less than the purchase price, then no goodwill figure arises. The difference must be listed under the 'financed by' section as a capital reserve. For example, if the purchase price had been only £90 000, then the capital reserve would have been £6 500 (net assets £96 500 – purchase £90 000).

Summary

When a business is disposed of, the final accounts need to be assessed on the grounds of profitability and financial position in terms of asset valuation. The more successful a business is, the greater its value, particularly in goodwill. The realisation account is used to dispose of the asset and liability accounts and any excess received above the value of net assets can be seen as 'profit' or goodwill. The journal is used to record the details of a sale or purchase in both the seller's and buyer's books. If a buyer already has an existing business, the assets and liabilities acquired will merge with those held, at a valuation decided by the buyer.

Questions

1 On 1 April, J Jackson purchased the business of J Davies. It was agreed that Jackson should take over all the assets of the business with the exception of the bank account.

It was also agreed that the debtors should be allowed a 10 per cent provision against bad and doubtful debts. The equipment and motor vehicle should be depreciated by 20 per cent respectively.

An additional figure to be paid for goodwill was to be based on 10 per cent of the average annual sales over the last three years, which were: £65 000, £63 000 and £68 500.

Jackson was to finance the purchase by providing 50 per cent of the purchase price from his own personal funds and the balance from the bank as a fixed loan over a number of years.

The balance sheet of J Davies, on 1 April, before negotiation, was as follows:

	£	£	£
FIXED ASSETS			
Premises	30 000		
Equipment	5 000		
Motor vehicle	1 000		36 000
CURRENT ASSETS			
Stock	4 500		
Debtors	3 500		
Bank	3 000	11 000	
CURRENT LIABILITIES			
Creditors		7 000	4 000
			40 000
FINANCED BY:			
Capital: J Davies			40 000

REQUIRED:

a) Show the journal entries in the books of the *buyer* as on 1 April.
b) If the completion date of the purchase was on 20 April, show the journal entry in the books of the *buyer* on this date.
c) Prepare the opening balance sheet of J Jackson as on 20 April. (38.3)

2 A Donald, a sole trader, has arranged to sell his business to D Smith, already in business as a sole trader. The balance sheet of A Donald, on 1 January was as follows:

	£	£	£
FIXED ASSETS			
Premises	50 000		
Equipment	8 000		
Motor van	2 000		60 000
CURRENT ASSETS			
Stock	12 000		
Debtors	7 500		
Bank/cash	8 500	28 000	
CURRENT LIABILITIES			
Creditors		8 000	20 000
			80 000
FINANCED BY:			
Capital: A Donald			80 000

D Smith has agreed to purchase the business for a sum of £85 000, although this does not include the bank/cash balance.

For the purpose of Smith's own records, she valued the premises at £65 000, equipment at £5000 and stock at £9000.

To finance the purchase, D Smith took out a loan at a fixed rate of interest for ten years for 80 per cent of the agreed purchase price. The balance is financed by her own business funds. The completion date was settled on as 25 January.

The balance sheet of D Smith on 1 January was as follows:

	£	£	£
FIXED ASSETS			
Premises	20 000		
Equipment	5 000		25 000
CURRENT ASSETS			
Stock	5 000		
Debtors	2 000		
Bank	18 000	25 000	
CURRENT LIABILITIES			
Creditors		5 000	20 000
			45 000
CAPITAL: D Smith			45 000

REQUIRED:

a) The journal entries to show the purchase of the business in the books of D Smith both on 1 January and 25 January.

b) The balance sheet of D Smith as on 25 January, after she has acquired the purchase. (38.3)

3 This question relates to the details found in Question 2 above, where the sole trader, A Donald (the vendor), has sold his business to D Smith (the buyer). Details are required in the books of the vendor.

REQUIRED:

a) In the books of the vendor, A Donald, prepare the journal entries as to the sale of the business, as completed up to 25 January

b) Prepare the realisation account as on 1 January

c) Show the capital account of A Donald on 25 January when the business was wound up. (38.2)

4 *The amalgamation of two sole traders*

Johnson and Taylor had agreed to amalgamate their businesses (mutual joining) into a partnership where they had agreed to share profit or loss equally, irrespective of their final capital account balances.

Before the amalgamation took place, they decided on 5 January:

a) To depreciate all their fixed assets by 25 per cent.

b) To make a provision against their debtors of 5 per cent for possible loss of debts.

c) That Taylor should inject money from his own personal funds to clear his bank overdraft and provide the same bank balance as Johnson on 1 January.

The balance sheets of the two sole traders, on 1 January, were as follows:

	Johnson	*Taylor*
	£	*£*
FIXED ASSETS		
Plant and equipment	8 000	6 000
Motor vans	2 000	4 000
	10 000	10 000
CURRENT ASSETS		
Stocks	3 590	2 980
Debtors	1 800	1 600
Bank/cash	1 500	—
	6 890	4 580
CURRENT LIABILITIES		
Creditors	2 800	1 500
Overdraft		500
	2 800	2 000
Working capital	4 090	2 580
CAPITAL ACCOUNTS	14 090	12 580

REQUIRED:

a) Show the capital account of each partner as on 1 January, using the accounting equation.

b) Prepare the amalgamated balance sheet of the new partnership as on 5 January. (38.4)

39 Stock valuation

Objectives

On completing this section you should:

- recognise the documentation used when stock is purchased
- prepare a stock bin card
- calculate stock order levels
- recognise the different bases to value stock
- recognise how stock value affects profit.

39.1 Introduction

In many business organisations the three major elements of cost are labour, materials and overheads.

The purchase of stock is of great importance particularly in manufacturing or in the distribution industry which needs to buy and sell goods. Acquiring the optimum level of stock is the key to good purchasing. If too much stock is purchased, there may be problems of storage and some of it may become obsolete and depreciate in value. If too little stock is purchased, the business may run out of certain material items, a bottle-neck in production could occur and valuable orders could be lost if deadlines are not met.

When stock is delivered, it should always be carefully checked to ensure that it corresponds with the driver's delivery note. If there is anything which does not strictly correspond with what is stated on the delivery note, be it the number of units or parcels etc., the document needs to be endorsed to say what was missing or that some items were unsatisfactory. Once the items of stock have been checked into store, it is the usual practice to prepare a goods received note, indicating what stock has been received.

39.2 Documentation

A control system should be in operation to ensure that stock is:

a) properly ordered
b) properly inspected and received
c) stored in appropriate places
d) issued to production or other departments on request
e) accompanied by the appropriate documentation.

If stock levels fail to be managed properly, it can be very expensive for the business, for example, a sudden shortfall of materials holds up production, labour is idle, machine time is wasted and potential profits soon lost.

39.2.1 Source documents

The main documents to consider are:

Purchase requisition: This is the internal request for materials to be purchased by the chief buyer or purchasing manager and proper authorisation must be made before a requisition is signed and goods purchased. The storekeeper in respect of materials, would send requisitions when stock is approaching re-ordering levels.

Purchase order: The buying or purchasing department will be responsible for sending the purchase order to the suppliers. Price, delivery dates, reliability, quality, are all significant elements the buyer must consider before placing orders. However, most orders will tend to be routine and sent to the usual suppliers. Copies of the order may also go to the section which made the requisition, the goods inward section to await the goods and one for the file.

The goods received note (GRN): Once materials have been checked in by the storeman and the delivery note signed, the GRN is raised as evidence that the materials have arrived and been placed in stock. The GRN is an essential source document because a company must only pay for materials it actually receiveds. When the purchase invoice arrives from the supplier, the GRN will be checked against it. A copy of the GRN must go to the buying department and the section which made the requisition will receive a copy.

The stores issue voucher: When materials are issued to production, a voucher is raised to authorise the transfer of materials to a specific job or contract. The appropriate stock bin card will record in the issue column, the materials released from store.

The stores returns voucher: This form reverses the procedure given with the stores issue voucher. If materials are returned to store, the voucher indicates what has been sent back, perhaps because of surplus or wrong stock, and the appropriate stock bin card will enter details in the receipts column.

Bin cards: The storeman needs to show movements of individual stock receipts and issues. The bin card (or stores card), is a simple record of stock movements and is kept with each category of stock. Physical checks can be made against the records maintained by the stores or cost office (the stock record card) and a system of control is provided.

The bin card should be designed to give all the information we need concerning each item of stock. This includes at the top of the card, its description, code number if applicable, unit of storage such as boxes, packages, of single units and the level of stock required, including maximum, minimum and re-order levels.

Bin Card

BIN CARD

ITEM 50 mm strips
CODE No. 4221

MAXIMUM STOCK 6500
MINIMUM STOCK 2000
RE-ORDER LEVEL 4500

RECEIPTS			ISSUES			
Date	GRN No.	Quantity Received	REQ No.	Quantity Issued	Stock Balance	Notes
1/3					3250	c/forward
5/3	G 928	3000			6250	
6/3			5100	850	5400	
7/3			5138	755	4645	
8/3			6200	400	4245	
10/3			6315	850	3395	
15/3	G 1025	3000			6395	
18/3			6428	755	5640	
20/3			6521	850	4790	

The bin card is used to record all inputs and outputs of stock as well as the stock balance. The card helps to control the stock of each item and this will help management to identify stock movements, minimise unnecessary waste, or even stock theft.

39.3 Stock control levels

For the purpose of controlling stock movements, each bin card should indicate the following levels of control:

a) the minimum stock level
b) the maximum stock level
c) the re-order level.

Because the optimum level of stock must be carried for each item, it is important to calculate the re-order, minimum and maximum levels required for each stock item.

The formulae for these are:

a) Re-order level	=	maximum usage × maximum lead time
b) Minimum stock level	=	re-order level less (average usage × average lead time)
c) Maximum stock level	=	re-order level + re-order quantity less (minimum usage × minimum lead time)

Example
A business uses the following data for an item of its stock:

Average usage	100 units per day
Maximum usage	150 units per day
Minimum usage	80 units per day
Minimum lead time	6 days
Maximum lead time	16 days
Annual working days	240 days
Economic re-order quantity	800 units

You are required to calculate the re-order, minimum and maximum levels of stock.

a) Re-order level	=	150 × 16	=	2 400 units
b) Minimum stock level	=	2 400 – (100 × 11)	=	1 300 units
c) Maximum stock level	=	2 400 + 800 – (80 × 6)	=	2 720 units

The economic re-order quantity refers to the optimum order level, that is, the best amount of stock to order at any time the stocks need replenishing to the levels wanted. The formula for the re-order quantity is:

$$Q = \sqrt{\frac{2AC}{H}}$$

Q the economic re-order quantity
A the annual demand of the stock item
C the cost of ordering one consignment
H the cost of holding 1 unit in stock

How was the economic re-order level of 800 units calculated?

A the annual demand: 100 units per day × 240 annual days = 2 400 units
C ordering one consignment: £4 on average
H cost of holding one unit in stock for one year: estimated 0.30p

$$Q = \sqrt{\frac{2 \times 4 \times 24\,000}{0.3}} = \sqrt{\frac{192\,000}{0.3}} = 800 \text{ units}$$

The re-order quantity of 800 units should then be sufficient to bring stocks up to the required levels once it arrives in store.

39.4 Stock valuation

A good purchaser needs to know the market well and have an available list of well-known suppliers that he or she can rely upon. The buyer needs to be fully aware of prices, trends, sources of supply, delivery times and anything else which will assist in procuring materials at the best possible advantage to the business. Stock is an important asset to an organisation and is part of its working capital.

The value of the unused stock at the end of a financial period will be used to calculate profit/loss in both the manufacturing account (for raw materials and work-in-progress) and the trading account (for finished goods). The value of this stock will also be recorded in the balance sheet under current assets and therefore represents part of the business's working capital.

39.4.1 Methods of stock valuation

As in all accounting, there are various ways to measure the cost of something. The most obvious way to value stock is at its cost price. When the manufacturing account was prepared and stock of finished goods required a valuation, the most common method was to use the factory cost per unit. This is recommended practice as seen in SSAP 9 (Statement of Standard Accounting Practice – Stocks and Work-in-Progress), which states that

> 'the value of stock transferred to store should be at the prime cost plus factory overheads at what is considered to be the normal level of output.'

When raw materials or components are purchased, these will be recorded at their cost price. The only problem which may occur, particularly when prices rise during inflationary periods, is at which cost price: the most recent? The average cost price?

Generally speaking, when direct materials have a low unit value of cost such as nuts, bolts, washers, pins, screws, metal bits and pieces etc and purchased in large quantities, it does not really matter which method is applied to value stock, as long as it is calculated on a consistent basis, that is, once a method has been applied, the same method should *always* be used otherwise the calculation of profits will be distorted.

In SSAP 2 (Disclosure of accounting policies), the two critical concepts of accounting – consistency and prudence – should be the essential consideration when stocks of raw materials, work-in-progress, or finished goods, are valued.

The following represents three distinct ways of valuing stocks at their cost price. The purchase of finished goods can also be valued by these methods although it is more associated with the purchase of direct materials for use in production.

39.4.2 FIFO

First in first out method which assumes that the first items of stock in are the first items of stock out. The stock on hand will use the most current prices to value stock.

39.4.3 LIFO

Last in first out method assumes that the stock purchased last, is the first stock out and therefore the stock on hand is valued at the earlier stock prices.

39.4.4 AVCO

The average cost method where the stock on hand is valued at the weighted average of the unit prices of the consignments received.

In physical terms, the actual movement of this stock is unimportant in its valuation. Whether the stock on hand is the first or last purchased, when it is of low unit value, is really irrelevant. Where materials have a large unit price, the purchase of certain components, for example, an electric motor, then it is more correct to count these individually at the price they were purchased for.

A further possibility would be to use a standard cost (pre-determined prices) as the basis of valuation. The problem here is that unless the standard costs are determined very carefully and often reviewed, they may bear little relation to the actual costs incurred.

39.4.5 Lower of cost and net realisable value (NRV)

SSAP 9, Stock and work-in-progress, specifies that stocks should be valued 'at the lower of cost and net realisable value (NRV)'. The NRV is defined as the selling price *less* the costs of getting the goods into a saleable condition (that is, any production, marketing, selling and distribution costs). If the NRV is *less* than its cost value, then the NRV should be used to value a particular stock. Again, the concept of conservatism is adopted to anticipate any possible losses arising from old or obsolete stock.

There are computer programs available to maintain stock records for an infinite number of different stock types. Companies like Wadham Stringer, which deals with motor vehicle parts, require an absolutely effective system of stock control to ensure that all their stock parts are up-to-date in relation to minimum and maximum levels, re-order levels and current balances actually in stock. From time to time, computer records should be checked with physical records of stock to ensure effective stock control and to avoid cases of pilfering or fraud.

The following pages illustrate the stock record cards, using the same item of stock and adopting the three alternative methods of valuation:

Example

Unit:	Code 4235	
	Bracket	
January:	Balance in stock	2000 units @ £1.00
January:	Purchases	1000 units @ £1.00
January:	Purchases	2000 units @ £1.20
February:	Issues of stock	1500 units
March:	Purchases	2000 units @ £1.35
March:	Issues of stock	2000 units

The FIFO method

STOCK RECORD CARD

Unit:	Bracket	Quantity levels:	
Code:	4235	Minimum:	2 000
Supplier:	Johnson's	Maximum:	6 500
		Reorder:	3 500

	RECEIVED			ISSUED			BALANCE		
Date	**Qty.**	**Unit price £**	**Cost £**	**Qty.**	**Unit price £**	**Cost £**	**No. in stock**	**Unit price £**	**Stock value £**
1/1	Balance						2 000	1.00	2 000
10/1	1 000	1.00	1 000				3 000	1.00	3 000
25/1	2 000	1.20	2 400				2 000	1.20	5 400
10/2				1 500	1.00	1 500	1 500	1.00	
							2 000	1.20	3 900
8/3	2 000	1.35	2 700				2 000	1.35	6 600
25/3				1 500	1.00	1 500	1 500	1.20	
				500	1.20	600	2 000	1.35	4 500

In stock: 31/3, 3500 units valued at £4500.

LIFO method

STOCK RECORD CARD

Unit: Bracket
Code: 4235
Supplier: Johnson's

Quantity levels:
Minimum: 2 000
Maximum: 6 500
Reorder: 3 500

	RECEIVED			ISSUED			BALANCE		
Date	**Qty.**	**Unit price £**	**Cost £**	**Qty.**	**Unit price £**	**Cost £**	**No. in stock**	**Unit price £**	**Stock value £**
1/1	Balance						2 000	1.00	2 000
10/1	1 000	1.00	1 000				3 000	1.00	3 000
25/1	2 000	1.20	2 400				2 000	1.20	5 400
10/2				1 500	1.20	1 800	3 000	1.00	
							500	1.20	3 600
8/3	2 000	1.35	2 700				2 000	1.35	6 300
25/3				2 000	1.35	2 700	3 000	1.00	
							5 00	1.20	3 600

In stock: 31/3, 3500 units valued at £3600.

AVCO method

STOCK RECORD CARD

Unit: Bracket
Code: 4235
Supplier: Johnson's

Quantity levels:
Minimum: 2 000
Maximum: 6 500
Reorder: 3 500

	RECEIVED			ISSUED			BALANCE		
Date	**Qty.**	**Unit price £**	**Cost £**	**Qty.**	**Unit price £**	**Cost £**	**No. in stock**	**Unit price £**	**Stock value £**
1/1	Balance						2 000	1.000	2 000
10/1	1 000	1.00	1 000				3 000	1.000	3 000
25/1	2 000	1.20	2 400				2 000	1.200	2 400
							*5 000	1.080	5 400
10/2				1 500	1.080	1 620	3 500	1.080	3 780
8/3	2 000	1.35	2 700				2 000	1.350	2 700
							*5 500	1.178	6 480
25/3				2 000	1.178	2 356	3 500	1.178	4 124

Note

*Calculation of average unit price $= \dfrac{\text{Stock value}}{\text{No. of units}} = \dfrac{£5\,400}{5\,000} = £1.08.$

In stock: 31/3, 3500 units valued at £4124.

Value of stock on 31 March

	£
Using the FIFO method of stock valuation:	4 500
Using the LIFO method of stock valuation:	3 600
Using the AVCO method of stock valuation:	4 124

Clearly, because prices increased between January and March, FIFO's stock value was the highest because the stock in hand was valued at the latest prices. LIFO's stock value was the lowest because the stock in hand used the earlier lower prices in January. AVCO's stock value was somewhere between the two, taking the average cost value in terms of units purchased.

It does not matter which of these methods is adopted as long as the same method is consistently applied from one financial period to the next. Over the accounting periods, the discrepancies between stock valuations arising from the different bases used will be eliminated because the stock value at the end of one financial period becomes the initial stock value in the next period.

For example, if the FIFO method was used as a base, it would have a greater value of stock at the year end, but its opening stock would also be greater, thereby having the effect of increasing the cost of sales. This apparent advantage would then be nullified in the following final accounts at the end of the period.

39.4.6 The effect on the trading account

Assume that sales for the period were £75 000 and that opening stock plus purchases were £64 000. The effect of using these alternative methods in this period would be:

	FIFO	*LIFO*	*AVCO*
	£	£	£
Sales	75 000	75 000	75 000
– Cost of sales:			
Stock (beginning) + purchases	64 000	64 000	64 000
– Stock (31 March)	4 500	3 600	4 124
	59 500	60 400	59 876
Gross profit	15 500	14 600	15 124

As the value of stock under FIFO was of the highest value, it has the highest gross profit. Using LIFO, with its lowest stock value, the gross profit is the lowest. AVCO falls between FIFO and LIFO. On 1 April, in the new financial period, the stock (beginning) values will be the same as on 31 March. LIFO's opening stock value will be £3600 giving it the advantage of a lower opening cost of sales than either FIFO or AVCO. Discrepancies in future calculations of gross profit should therefore cancel each other out.

39.4.7 The lower of cost and net realisable value (NRV)

If the NRV is judged to have a lower value than the cost of some items of stock (because the stock is old, damaged or obsolete), then the NRV will be used to value the stock rather than the cost price. Again, this emphasises accounting's concept of prudence.

Stock valuation at 31 March

Code No.	*Units in stock*	*Cost price* £	*Value at cost* £	*NRV* £	*Lower of cost + NRV* £
DX 421	100	1.5	150	175	150
422	20	5.0	100	25	25
423	120	4.2	504	600	504
424	5	10.0	50	10	10
425	210	1.0	210	252	210
			1 014	1 062	899

For these stocks valued on 31 March, the lower of cost plus NRV, which equals £899, would be taken as the stock end-value. Code numbers 422 and 424 value the stock items as well under the cost price, perhaps because the stock is damaged or out-of-date.

Many different types of businesses have adopted this method of stock valuation as a base for valuing many of their stock items, following the guidelines laid down in SSAP 9, Stock and work-in-progress.

39.5 Stock-taking at year end

At the financial year end the physical stock-take for large organisations may take several days or longer and it may be difficult to coincide its value at exactly the year end date. Large stores or manufacturing companies may have to make some adjustments to the value of stock if they had not completed its stock valuation at the due date.

Example
A manufacturing company, PQR Ltd, had the following information at its year end accounts, 31 October 19–8:
'Unfortunately, the closing value of finished goods stock could not be counted until 5 November 19–8 when it had a total production cost of £13 000 stock. The following transactions took place during the 5 days after the company's year end but BEFORE the physical stock-take for the year'.

Sales to customers (selling prices)	£5 000
Returns by customers (selling prices)	£1 250
Work-in-progress completed at cost	£2 000

Mark up policy is 25 per cent on total production cost.

How much is the value of closing stock of finished goods to be transferred to the company's trading account?

Company's mark up of 25 per cent on cost equals a 20 per cent margin of profit on selling prices:

Value of finished goods at 31 October

	£
Total production cost as per stock-taking	13 000
Less work-in-progress (uncompleted)	2 000
	11 000

Add goods unsold at 31 October at cost	4 000
	15 000
Less returned goods returned at cost	1 000
Value of finished goods as at 31 October	14 000

(Chartered Institute of Management Accountants)

Although the 1985 Companies Act does not outlaw the use of LIFO, SSAP 9 states that it should **not** be used because it would fail to provide an up-to-date valuation of stock. Both FIFO and AVCO methods are recommended.

Summary

The value of stock is an important asset in business. The cost of materials may account for a significant amount of working capital and therefore purchases must be at the optimum level. A system of stock control must be effective and the documentation procedure must ensure that all stock is properly ordered, inspected and stored. The bin cards record the movement and amount of stock held and should be reconciled with stock-taking. Although there are various methods to value stock, once a method is adopted it should be used consistently otherwise profit distortion will occur.

Questions

1 Why is it important to have a system of stock control in a large manufacturing organisation? (39.1)

2 Make a list of all the significant documents used in the acquisition of materials. (39.2)

3 Why is it important to record the details of stock movements on a bin or stock record card? (39.2)

4 The following data refers to an item of direct materials:

Cost of material	£10 per unit
Usage per day *	100 units
Minimum lead time	20 days
Maximum lead time	30 days
Cost of ordering materials	£400 per order
Carrying costs	10% of cost per unit of raw material

* Assume that the daily usage is both the average level of use and is also the maximum and minimum levels of use.

REQUIRED:
a) the re-order level
b) the re-order quantity
c) the maximum level
d) the minimum level. (39.3)

(Association of Accounting Technicians)

5 You are given the following information regarding material stock code Q242:
1 The average demand for the material is 400 kilos per week, 50 weeks for the year
2 The cost of ordering is £150 per order
3 Q242 costs £6.00 per kilo and carrying costs (holding costs) are 33 per cent of this figure for each kilo held

4 The maximum usage in any one week is 600 kilos, the minimum 400 kilos

On average, the orders take between one and three weeks to be delivered. Note that these figures are based on weeks rather than days of use.

REQUIRED:
a) the optimum order quantity to be placed;
b) the re-order level;
c) the minimum stock level;
d) the maximum stock level.(39.3)

(Association of Accounting Technicians)

6 Calculate the normal stock control levels from the following information:

Economic order quantity	12 000 kilos
Lead time	10–14 working days
Average usage	600 kilos per day
Minimum usage	400 kilos per day
Maximum usage	800 kilos per day. (39.3)

(Chartered Association of Certified Accountants)

7 A business has the following information at its year end 31 December 19–8:
Stock-taking was not completed until after the year ended, on 7 January 19–9, valued £17 800 and the following transactions had taken place during the week after the year end 31 December 19–8 but before 7 January 19–9:
Sales £1200 at selling prices
Returns inward £200 at selling prices
Purchases at cost £2750
The mark up policy of the business is one third.

Calculate what the value of closing stock should be as at 31 December 19–8. (39.4)

(Association of Accounting Technicians)

8 The goods listed below were in stock at Jack's Store on 31 December.
Record the items on a stock card/sheet and calculate the value of stock at the end of the year, 31 December. (39.4–5)

Code no.	*Items*	*Quantity*	*Cost per unit*	*NRV per unit*	*Lower of cost or NRV*
			£	£	£
427	Jeans	50	10.50	12.50	525.00
428	Jeans	10	15.20	14.00	
859/1	Sweaters	120	8.75	7.50	
859/2	Sweaters	60	12.50	15.95	
859/3	Sweaters	15	9.95	12.50	
870	Men's socks	50	1.15	1.50	
870/1	Men's socks	5	3.90	1.00	

9 The stock issues of a manufacturer for the months June to August inclusive were as follows:
Stock Issues – June, July, August

		Quantity (units)	*Cost per unit*	*Value of stock*
			£	£
1/6	Balance	200	2.00	400.00
15/6	Purchases	100	1.95	

30/6	Purchases	200	2.10
		500	
30/6	Issues	150	
1/7	Balance	350	
21/7	Purchases	200	2.15
		550	
30/7	Issues	200	
1/8	Balance	350	
10/8	Purchases	150	2.20
21/8	Purchases	100	2.20
		600	
31/8	Issues	250	
1/9	Balance	350	

REQUIRED:
Write up a stock record card for the months June to August and calculate the value of stock on 1 September in terms of both FIFO and LIFO order issues. (39.4)

10 Complete the stock record card by entering the 'balance in hand' figure on the right of the card. Calculate the value of stock end if purchases were £2.50 per ream up to 12/9 and £3.00 after 12/9 (use FIFO method). (39.4)

STOCK RECORD CARD

MONTH: Sept

Item: Typewriting Paper – Size A4
Suppliers: 1 ABC Co Ltd
2 XYZ Ltd

Quantities
MIN: 100 Ream
MAX: 200 Ream
Re-order level:

DATE	ORDERED			RECEIVED			ISSUED		BALANCE
	Supp.	O/No.	Qty	Supp.	O/No.	Qty.	Dept.	Qty	130 Reams
Sept 1	1	347	150						
3	2	348	125						
6							P	36	
6							A	20	
9				1	347	150			
10							T	25	
12				2	348	100			
14							B	55	
14							M	60	
16	2	349	100						
18							A	25	
19				2	349	90			
20							P	79	

11 Use FIFO and LIFO methods to value the following stock:

Jan.	1	Balance	50 units @ £3 unit
	10	Purchased	100 units @ £3
	16	Purchased	100 units @ £3.20
	24	Issued	80 units
Feb.	7	Purchased	200 units @ £3.50
	14	Issued	240 units
	20	Issued	80 units
	28	Purchased	50 units @ £3.40

REQUIRED:

a) Prepare two stock cards to illustrate FIFO and LIFO methods of stock recording.

b) What effect would these methods have in the trading account? (39.4)

12(a) Complete the stock card below by showing the value in the end column. When the stock is sold, it is on the basis of FIFO. This means that for value purposes, the stock first in is assumed to be the first sold out. (39.4)

Type of goods	Stock level Unit 5	150–200 Re-order level	100
Code no.	11/13		
Supplier	Arena, Metro		

Date		*Quantity received*	*Unit value* £	*Sales*	*Stock balance*	*Unit value* £	*Value* £
June	1	Balance			200	4.00	800
	5			80	120	4.00	480
	12	Arena 200	4.25		200	4.25	850
					320		1330
	15			140			
	18			50			
	20	Metro 120	4.00				
	28			145			

Note: As a check, you should have 105 units in stock value on 28 June.

(b) The end of the firm's financial year is 30 June. The value of the unsold stock, Code No. 11/13, is entered on a stock sheet along with other stocks in order to calculate the value of unsold stock at the end of the accounting period.

The firm values its unsold stock at the 'lower of cost or net realisable value'. This basically means that if the expected selling price is less than the cost price, then the lower figure will be used to assess the stock value. (39.5)

Complete the stock sheet as on 30 June:

Code no. and comments	*Stock balance quantity*	*Unit value* £	*Value* £	*Net realisable value* £	£	*Value* £	*Lower of cost net realisable value*
11/13	105			105	5.00	525	
11/27	215	10.00	2150	215	7.00	1505	1505.00

(old stock)					
11/13	150	6.50		150	7.50
11/42	10	8.50		10	2.00
(damaged)					
11/50	85	12.75		85	15.50
					total

(c) Completion of Trading and Profit and Loss account.

Sales for the financial year were	£38 850
Purchases for the financial year were	£27 500
Stock (1/7) commencing	£2 650
Distribution Costs	£3 750
Administration Expenses	£1 225

Prepare the firm's trading and profit and loss account for the period ending 30 June. Use the stock valuation from the stock sheet above.

13 John Gaunt commenced trading on 1 January year 1 as a distributor of the Red Diamond Mark 1 Farm Tractor with an initial capital of £50 000 used to open a bank account.

Upon commencing trading, John Gaunt bought fixtures and fittings costing £10 000 which he installed in his rented premises.

Overhead expenses, including rent of premises but excluding depreciation, have been incurred as follows:

Year ended 31 December, Year 1	£24 000
Year ended 31 December, Year 2	£26 000
Year ended 31 December, Year 3	£31 000

Depreciation on fixtures and fittings is to be provided at the rate of 20 per cent per annum using the reducing balance method.

Purchases and sales of the Red Diamond Mark 1 Farm Tractor up to 31 December Year 3 were as follows:

	Purchases	*Sales*
Year 1	6 at £25 000 each	4 at £30 000 each
Year 2	8 at £25 000 each	3 at £30 000 each 4 at £32 000 each
Year 3		
February		1 at £34 000
March	4 at £28 000 each	
May		3 at £37 000 each
July	5 at £30 000 each	
September		4 at £38 000 each
October	2 at £32 000 each	
December		2 at £38 000 each

John Gaunt has accepted, with some reluctance, his accountant's advice to use the FIFO basis for stock valuation as from 1 January Year 3 instead of the LIFO basis which he claims to have used in earlier years.

All John Gaunt's business transactions are on a cash (non-credit) basis.

John Gaunt does not intend to take any drawings from the business until Year 4.

REQUIRED:

a) Prepare, in as much detail as possible, John Gaunt's trading and profit and loss account for *each* of the years ended 31 December, using:
   the last in first out basis of stock valuation; and
   the first in first out basis of stock valuation.
b) Prepare John Gaunt's capital account for the year ended 31 December Year 3.
c) A concise report to John Gaunt in support of the accountant's advice concerning the stock valuation basis. (39.4–5)

(Association of Accounting Technicians)

40 Accounting for incomplete records

Objectives

On completing this section you should:

- recognise that not all businesses keep formal ledger accounts
- understand that final accounts can be prepared from a trader's documents
- recognise the use of control accounts to establish sales and purchases
- use the business equation to calculate profit
- calculate stock value which has been lost.

40.1 Introduction

The sole trader, in charge of a small business, often does not have the time or expertise to prepare a formal set of accounting books such as ledgers and trial balance.

It is essential however, for tax purposes at least, to keep significant accounting records and documents relating to the business's finances, so that the accountant can prepare the final accounts at the end of the financial year. The business may also have to prepare Vat records and returns if its turnover is greater than a certain level set by the Chancellor each year.

The businessman (or woman) therefore, needs to retain essential information concerning the business, on a day-to-day level. He needs to know the cash resources he has available, how much his customers owe him, how much he owes his suppliers, what his sales figures are, when to pay his Vat and other bills, and many other diverse aspects of the business.

Even if accounting records are not prepared on a formal basis, information still needs to be kept so that an accountant can use it to prepare the final accounts at the financial year-end. From records regarded as 'incomplete' it is still possible to reconstruct certain accounts to enable the financial reports to be prepared.

40.2 Preparation of accounts

In business practice, an accountant would require all the available records kept by the business throughout the financial period, including all relevant documents such as:

invoices to customers and from suppliers,
credit notes to customers and from suppliers,
bank receipts,
bank payments,
bank statements,
Vat returns,
bills paid or unpaid.

The accountant would organise this information in chronological order where necessary, and prepare the following:

a) Establish the owner's capital at the commencement of the financial year (assets less liabilities).
b) Prepare a summary of cash receipts and payments for the year, identifying the monies in and out of the business and calculating the balance of cash in hand.

c) Reconstructing accounts for debtors and creditors, where relevant, to calculate sales and purchases for the year (on credit).
d) Ensure all relevant adjustments are included such as accruals, prepayments and provisions.
e) Prepare the trading and profit and loss account for the financial year ended and a balance sheet as at that date.

Example
Tina Smith is a sole trader in business as a computer engineer and supplier of computer hardware and software. She has a small workshop attached to her residence and most of her business is with local clients. On 1 January, the start of her financial year, her statement of affairs (or balance sheet) was as follows:

	£	£
Assets:		
Workshop (cost)	8 000	
Equipment	2 250	
Motor vehicle	1 500	
Debtors	550	
Bank	800	
Stock	3 350	16 450
Less Liabilities:		
Creditors		1 350
Capital (1/1)		15 100

Owner's capital: £15 100

40.2.1 Preparation of bank/cash summary

From the necessary documents including cheque book records, bank statements, till rolls and other sources, a simplified cash book may be drawn up. Tina Smith's summary was as follows:

Tina Smith – Bank summary

	Receipts	£		*Payments*	£
1/1	Balance (bank)	800		Payments to suppliers	33 400
	Customer receipts	48 575		Drawings by Smith	8 800
	Cash sales	2 400		Wages	4 500
	Commission received	500		Motor costs	1 300
				General expenses	850
				Insurance and rates	595
				Telephone	325
				Light and heat	280
				Advertising	450
				New equipment	285
				Workshop extension	590
			31/12	Balance (bank) c/d	900
		52 275			52 275
	Balance b/d	900			

NOTE
This type of accounting, in its organisation, is similar to that of Chapter 29 – Accounting for clubs and societies. The receipts and payments of monies listed above, are used to help prepare the trading and profit and loss account. The accountant will also need to list further information, including the balance day adjustments.

Other information available on 31 December:

a) Cash discounts: discount allowed to customers, £780.
   discount received from suppliers, £565.
b) Returns inward, £255 and returns outward, £950.
c) Stock valued at cost £4250.
d) Debtors balance, £740; creditors balance, £1855.
e) Provision for depreciation: motor vehicle and equipment, by 20 per cent.
f) A garage bill on the motor vehicle was owing, £211.

40.2.2 Reconstruction of debtors and creditors to establish credit sales and purchases

It may be resonably straightforward to establish cash sales if the owner of the business retains all till rolls or cash receipts. Some traders religiously keep a tally of daily sales records and the accountant has little problem in summing up a total figure. The same may apply for cash purchases.

To arrive at credit sales or credit purchases for the year, the accountant may get his information from invoices sent to customers or received from suppliers. Credit notes will also help to establish details concerning returns inward and returns outward. If cash discount has been taken advantage of, the details are usually found on the invoice.

Debtors: to establish credit sales

	DEBIT			CREDIT	
1/1	Balance b/d	550	31/12	Bank/cash	48 575
31/12	Sales	49 800		Discount allowed	780
				Returns inward	255
				Balance c/d	740
		50 350			50 350
	Balance b/d	740			

NOTE
The sales figure of £49 800 was calculated by deducting the opening debtor's balance of £550 from the total of the credit column, £50 350.

Creditors: to establish credit purchases

	DEBIT			CREDIT	
31/12	Bank/cash	33 400	1/1	Balance b/d	1 350
	Discount received	565	31/12	Purchases	35 420
	Returns outward	950			
	Balance c/d	1 855			
		36 770			36 770
				Balance b/d	1 855

NOTE
The purchases figure of £35 420 was calculated by deducting the opening creditor's balance of £1350 from the total of the debit column, £36 770.

The credit sales and credit purchases figures are then transferred to the trading account.

Preparation of the trading and profit and loss account for Tina Smith, year ended 31 December

	£	£	£
Sales (credit)	49 800		
(cash)	2 400		
	52 200		
– Returns inward	255		51 945
– Cost of sales:			
Stock (1/1)	3 350		
Purchases	35 420		
	38 770		
– Returns outward	950	37 820	
– Stock (31/12)		4 250	33 570
Gross profit			18 375
– Expenses			
Wages		4 500	
General expenses		850	
Motor costs	1 300		
+ Accrued	211	1 511	
Insurance and rates		595	
Telephone		325	
Light and heat		280	
Advertising		450	
Discount allowed		780	

(contiinued)

(continued)

Depreciation: Equipment	507		
Motor	300	807	10 098
			8 277
+ Other revenue			
Commission	500		
Discount received	565		1 065
Net profit			9 342

Preparation of the balance sheet for Tina Smith, as at 31 December

	Cost £	*Depreciation* £	*Net* £
FIXED ASSETS			
Workshop premises	8 000		
+ Extension	590	—	8 590
Equipment	2 250		
+ New	285		
	2 535	507	2 028
Motor vehicle	1 500	300	1 200
	12 625	807	11 818
CURRENT ASSETS			
Stock	4 250		
Debtors	740		
Bank/cash	900		
Prepayments	—	5 890	
– CURRENT LIABILITIES			
Creditors	1 855		
Accruals	211	2 066	
Working capital			3 824
			15 642
FINANCED BY:			
Capital (1/1)	15 100		
+ Net profit	9 342	24 442	
– Drawings		8 800	15 642

NOTE
Tina Smith has increased her net worth by £542 during her financial year. Most of her £9342 profit has been used up because of the owner's personal drawings throughout the year, £8800. Tina's balance sheet is also referred to as her 'statement of affairs' when dealing with incomplete records.

Tina Smith will be assessed for tax. The Inland Revenue will base the tax payable on her profit for the year less the appropriate taxable allowances. For example:

		£
Profit for the year		9 342
– Allowances		4 500
Taxable income	=	4 842
		4 842 × 24 per cent tax rate
	=	1 162.08 tax payable

40.3 The calculation of profit from the owner's net worth

It should be possible to assess a businessman's or woman's financial position at a specific point in time by preparing a statement of affairs, i.e. a balance sheet, to calculate net worth (his or her capital).

The accounting equation to establish capital is:

Capital = Assets – Liabilities

If the net worth of the owner is calculated at both the beginning and end of an accounting period, then it is possible to determine profit or loss for the year.

If net worth has increased (without further investment of capital by the owner), then a profit has been made. If net worth has decreased, the owner has either personally withdrawn too much from the business, or the business has made a loss, or it may be a combination of the two.

In Tina Smith's case, her net worth had increased by £542 over the year:

1/1:				
Capital	=	Assets	–	Liabilities
£15 100	=	£16 450	–	£1 350
31/12:				
Capital	=	Assets	–	Liabilities
£15 642	=	£17 708	–	£2 066

Tina's capital (net worth) was £15 100, this equalled her net assets on 1 January. On 31 December, her net worth was £15 642, an increase in capital of £542.

Information has indicated that her total drawings for the year were £8800 and that she had not invested any further new capital in the business. What is her profit for the year?

Using the business equation, $P = NA + D - NC$, where NA = net asset change; D = Drawings; NC = New capital invested; and P = Profit then

P	=	NA	+	D	–	NC
£9342	=	£542	+	£8800	–	0

40.4 The valuation of stock following loss through fire or theft

If stock is lost because of fire on the premises or is stolen due to theft or burglary, the loss must be assessed as accurately as possible particularly if it is insured and compensation is required for the loss.

If adequate stock records are not kept it is still possible to value the stock loss if the gross profit margin is known and the trading account can be constructed.

Example 1
Jack owns a shop in the local high street and on 18 May there was a fire which destroyed most of his stock. He could salvage about £500 worth and the insurance assessor wanted an accurate assessment of stock loss on the claim form.

At the start of the financial year Jack had an opening stock value of £6000. His purchases to 18 May had been £28 000. His sales to this date were £40 000, Jack having a margin of 25 per cent on sales.

How much stock was lost in the fire? His financial year runs from 1 January to 31 December.

Construction of trading account to value stock loss to 18 May

	£	£
Sales		40 000
less		
Cost of sales:		
Stock (1/1)	6 000	
+ Purchases	28 000	
	34 000	
– Stock (18/5)	4 000	30 000
Gross profit		10 000

Working backwards: 25 per cent of sales = a gross profit of £10 000 therefore cost of sales is £30 000. The difference between £34 000 (stock + purchases) and £30 000 is the stock which should be a value of £4000.

If Jack salvaged £500 stock from the fire, the assessment of loss for the insurance claim must be for £3500.

Answer: Stock loss valued at £3500.

Example 2
You work for a firm of accountants which prepares the accounts for Murry Ltd.

During the night of 2 June, Murry Ltd suffered a fire. The fire destroyed all the company's stock records and a quantity of stock. The stock was covered by insurance against loss by fire. You have been asked by your firm to assist with preparing the insurance claim for Murry Ltd.

Data available;

a)

	On 1/1	On 2/6
	£000	£000
Stock at cost	264	?
Trade debtors	78	94
Trade creditors	90	106

b) The following transactions took place between 1 January and 2 June.

	£000
Cash purchases	34
Payments to creditors	548
Cash received from debtors	628
Cash sales	160
Discount received	20
Discount allowed	16

c) The physical stocktake taken first thing in the morning on 3 June showed the remaining stock (undamaged) to have a cost value of £182 000.

d) Murry Ltd operate a standard margin of 30 per cent, i.e. a gross profit of 30 per cent on selling price.

REQUIRED:

1 Calculate the total value of purchases for the period.

2 Calculate the total value of sales for the period.

3 Use the information in (1) and (2) to calculate the cost of the damaged stock.

1 Value of purchases

Creditors:

	DEBIT	£		*CREDIT*	£
2/6	Bank/cash	548 000	1/1	Balance b/d	90 000
	Discount received	20 000			
	Balance c/d	106 000	2/6	Purchases	584 000
		674 000			674 000
			3/6	Balance b/d	106 000

Credit purchases	=	584 000
Cash purchases	=	34 000
Total	=	618 000

2 Value of sales

Debtors:

		£			£
1/1	Balance b/d	78 000	2/6	Bank/cash	628 000
2/6	Sales	660 000		Discount allowed	16 000
				Balance c/d	94 000
		738 000			738 000
3/6	Balance b/d	94 000			

Credit sales	=	660 000
Cash sales	=	160 000
Total	=	820 000

3

Trading account – Murry Ltd from 1 January–2 June

	£	£	£
Sales			820 000
– Cost of sales:			
Stock (1/1)	264 000		
+ Purchases	618 000	882 000	
– Stock (2/6) (undamaged)		182 000	
		700 000	
Loss of stock		126 000	
			574 000
Gross profit (30%)			246 000

Cost of damaged stock: £126 000

Example 3: finding missing figures
Anthea Jenkins, a client, wants you to prepare her final accounts for the period ended, 31 March 19–8.

The only financial records she has are listed below:

	As at 1 April 19–7	*As at 31 March 19–8*
	£	£
Fixed assets (net)	4000	?
Debtors	3500	5500
Creditors	8000	8500
Stock	10200	12600
Bank	2800	2400
Cash	400	500
Light, Heat due	300	200
Rent in advance	100	180
Bank loan	2500	?

All shop takings from sales are banked after taking out:

Assistant's cash wages	£2800
Stock purchases	£1200
Drawings	?

Anthea is not exactly sure how much she has taken out as cash drawings and wants you to calculate this for her.

She has also taken for her own use, £200 worth of stock (at cost).
There is a 25 per cent margin on sales.
Depreciation for the year is 25 per cent on net value of assets.

From a check of the bank statements and cheques drawn, an analysis of bank payments revealed:

	£	
Purchases	98 400	
Rates	1 480	
Wages	4 400	
General costs	1 450	
Payments on loan	500	(interest charges £350 inclusive)

REQUIRED:

1 The calculation of the owner's capital as on 1 April 19–7
2 The assessment of sales and purchases for the year
3 A bank summary to indicate both cash and bank balances and to include the calculation of cash drawings for the year
4 The preparation of the profit and loss account for the year ended 31 March 19–8 and a balance sheet as on that date.

1 Owner's capital

Capital	=	Assets	–	Liabilities
£10 200	=	£21 000	–	£10 800

2 Sales and purchases

Purchase ledger control account

	£		£
Bank	98 400	Balance b/d	8 000
Cash	1 200	Purchases	100 100
Balance b/d	8 500		
	108 100		108 100
		Balance b/d	8 500

To calculate sales:	£	£
Opening stock	10 200	
Purchases	100 100	110 300
Stock drawings		(200)
Closing stock		(12 600)
Cost of sales		97 500
Add mark up of one third (margin 25%)		32 500
Sales =		130 000

How much from sales has been banked?

Sales ledger control account

	£		£
Balance b/d	3 500	Bank	128 000
Sales	130 000	Balance c/d	5 500
	133 500		133 500
Balance b/d	5 500		

3

Cash book summary

	Cash	Bank		Cash	Bank
	£	£		£	£
Balance b/d	400	2800	Wages	2 800	4 400
Sales	128 000		Purchases	1 200	98 400
Contra (cash)		106 720	Rates		1 480
			Light, heat		890
			General costs		1 450
			Loan repayments		500
			Contra (bank)	106 720	
			Drawings	17 180	
			Balance c/d	500	2 400
	128 400	109 520		128 400	109 520
Balance b/d	500	2 400			

NOTE: calculation of drawings

		£
a)	Credit side of bank	109 520
	– Debit side of bank	2 800
	Therefore banked (as a contra with cash)	106 720
b)	Debit side of cash	128 400
	– Credit side of cash	111 220
	Therefore drawings	17 180

4

Anthea Jenkins –
Trading and profit and loss account year ended 31 March 19–8

	£	£
Sales		130 000
less		
Cost of sales (as above)		97 500
Gross profit		32 500

(continued)

(continued)

less		
Expenses:		
Light, heat	790	
Rates	1 400	
Wages	7 200	
General costs	1 450	
Depreciation	1 000	
Interest on loan	350	12 190
Net profit		20 310

Balance sheet as at 31 March 19–8

	£	£	£
FIXED ASSETS (NET)			3 000
CURRENT ASSETS			
Stock	12 600		
Debtors	5 500		
Bank	2 400		
Cash	500		
Prepayments	180	21 180	
CURRENT LIABILITIES			
Creditors	8 500		
Accruals	200	8 700	
Working capital			12 480
			15 480
LONG TERM LIABILITIES			
Bank loan (2500 – 500 + 350)			2 350
			13 130
Capital	10 200		
+ Profit	20 310		
– Drawings	(17 380)		13 130

The reconstruction of these accounts need not necessarily use control accounts or cash books. The figures could be calculated arithmetically and if you find it easier to do so in an exam, you should choose the method which is easier for you. However, if a question required you to reconstruct a bank summary or control accounts, you need to ensure you can follow these principles.

Summary

Small businesses like sole traders rarely keep a system of ledger accounts, although they do retain essential records for the accountant to piece together to prepare the final accounts. The control accounts can be constructed to find sales and purchases, and missing figures such as drawings can be found from the construction of a cash and bank summary. It is also possible to calculate any loss of stock by constructing the trading account after calculating sales and purchases for the period.

Questions

1 You have just completed a two year Business Studies Course and have been asked by an old school friend, J Starky, to have a look at his books. J Starky has been running a retailing business for the past year and needs to know what his state of affairs is for taxation purposes.
J Starky's summary cash book for the year ended 31 March 19–8 is as follows:

	£		£
1/4 Balance b/f	10 000	Payments to suppliers	157 340
Cash sales	50 000	Cash purchases	7 880
Cash received from debtors	219 500	Rent	22 500
		Rates	900
		Salaries	13 080
		Wages	30 500
		General expenses	22 000
		Drawings	15 000
		31/3 Balance c/f	10 300
	279 500		279 500

His assets and liabilities were:

	1/4/19–7	*31/3/19–8*
	£	£
Creditors for goods	28 400	30 010
Rent owing		500
Stock	54 000	53 000
Debtors	46 600	55 700
Prepaid rates	–	295
Fixtures and fittings	10 000	10 000
Vehicle	7 500	7 500

In preparing the accounts you decide:
i) To depreciate the vehicle by $33\frac{1}{3}$ per cent.
ii) To depreciate the fixtures and fittings by 10 per cent.
iii) To make a provision for bad debts of 5 per cent.
iv) To assume (based on J Starky's estimate) that J Starky has taken £1000 worth of goods from the business for his own use.

REQUIRED:
Prepare the trading and profit and loss account for the year ended 31 March 19–8 and a balance sheet as at that date. (40.2–3)

(BTEC National)

2 D Bazen's assets and liabilities on 1 January 19–8 and 31 December 19–8 were:

	1/1/19–8	31/12/19–8
	£	£
Cash in hand	420	490
Cash at bank		96
Bank loan (repayable in five years)	3 000	3 000
Bank overdraft	6 000	
Stock in trade	2 100	3 600
Trade debtors	3 420	3 561
Trade creditors	2 916	1 696
Equipment	5 000	4 800
Premises	25 000	25 000
Expenses paid in advance	231	360
Rent received in advance	96	89
Expenses accrued	41	52
Rent receivable	67	161

During the year ended 31 December 19–8, Bazen had withdrawn cash £8000, for private use, and had paid the proceeds of selling his private car, £6220, into the business.

REQUIRED:

a) An opening statement of affairs as at 1 January 19–8 to find the opening capital.
b) A closing statement of affairs as at 31 December 19–8, to find the closing capital.
c) A statement showing the calculation of the net profit for the year ended 31 December 19–8. (40.2–3)

(Associated Examining Board)

3 On 30 November 19–8 A Mole's balances were: premises £76 000; fittings £2320; stock £4060; bank overdraft £3515; trade debtors £2500; trade creditors; £5100; capital £?

A Mole does not keep full accounting records, but the following information, relating to the half year ended 31 May 19–9; is available.

Bank account

	£		£
Sales	5 060	Balance b/d	3 515
Debtors	14 021	Drawings	3 610
Balance c/d	23 728	Expenses	2 444
		Creditors	13 240
		Premises	20 000
	42 809		42 809

Cash discount allowed amounted to £52 and cash discount received was £65.

Depreciation on fittings is at the rate of 10 per cent per annum.

On 31 May 19–9 the following figures are available: stock £5012; trade creditors £2341; trade debtors £4323.

REQUIRED:

a) For the six months ended 31 May 19–9:
   i) the trade debtors' total account and the trade creditors' total account, showing the calculation of credit sales and credit purchases;
   ii) the trading and profit and loss account.
b) The balance sheet as at 31 May 19–9.
c) An explanation of the meaning of cash discount. How does cash discount affect the proprietor's capital? (40.2–3)

(Associated Examining Board)

4 Ted Albeury is a retailer who does not keep the appropriate accounting books. He keeps records of receipts and payments through the bank and also other significant documents such as invoices and general bills attributed to his business. He seeks assistance from a firm of accountants where you work as a junior assistant.

At the commencement of his financial year, 1 January 19–8 his statement of affairs showed he had the following balances:

	£	£
Premises	100 000	
Fixtures, fittings and equipment	10 000	
Motor vehicle	3 500	
Debtors	2 750	
Creditors		2 600
Stock	4 780	
Bank loan (10 years) 12% p.a.		40 400
Capital		80 000
Rates in advance	70	
Wages owing		100

His summarised bank statement for the year:

Receipts	£	*Payments*	£
Balance (1 Jan)	2 000	Payments to suppliers	38 550
Receipts from sales	47 250	Light and heat	295
Rent received	1 510	Advertising	300
		Wages to assistant	1 550
		Drawings	2 875
		Rates	250
		Motor expenses	750
		Equipment purchases	1 300
		General expenses	1 705
		Balance (31 Dec)	3 185
	50 760		50 760

NOTES
Discount given to customers, £225.
Discount from suppliers, £550.

Further information at 31 December 19–8:

		£
a)	Debtors	1 800
	Creditors	2 465
	Stock	4 190

b) The motor vehicle is revalued at £3000.
Fixtures to be depreciated by 25 per cent on 1 January 19–8 value.
c) The rates were £90 paid in advance and wages still outstanding were £75.
d) A full year's interest is owing on the bank loan.

REQUIRED:
Prepare the following:
a) A computation of sales and purchases figures for the year.
b) Ted Albeury's trading and profit and loss accounts for the year ended 31 December 19–8.
c) Ted Albeury's balance sheet as at 31 December 19–8, clearly showing working capital and the current ratio in brackets.

d) A brief report to your immediate supervisor including the accounting ratios relating to profit for the financial year ended 31 December 19–8. (40.2–3)

(Institute of Bankers)

5 Julie Jones, a retailer, did not keep proper books of account. However, it had been possible to provide the following financial information on her activities for the year ended 30 September 19–8.

Summarised statements

	Cash	*Bank*		*Cash*	*Bank*
	£	£		£	£
Balances (1/10/19–7	178	2 580	Wages and salaries	1 300	
Rate rebate after appeal		50	Lighting and heating		190
			Advertising	35	
Shop takings (including receipts from credit sales)	1 580	16 990	Rent and rates		550
			Payments to self		2 500
			Creditors for goods	170	12 270
Surrender of private national savings bonds		550	Repairs to shop window		25
			Running expenses motor van	32	170
			Additional shop shelving		350
			Purchase of new motor van		1 700
			Balances at (30/9/19–8) c/d	221	2 415

NOTES
Discounts allowed, £125.
Discounts received, £247.

1 Balances other than cash or bank as at 1 October 19–7 were:

	£
Premises	15 000
Fixtures and fittings	2 580
Rent owing	75
Motor van	350
Trade debtors	750
Prepaid advertising	70
Stock	3 000
Trade creditors	1 433

2 Balances other than cash and bank as at 30 September 19–8:

	£
Trade debtors	1 870
Trade creditors	2 400
Stock	4 350

3 The proprietor took £130 of goods for her own use during the year.

4 The existing motor van was disposed of early in the year for £200; settlement had not been received for this amount. The new van was to be depreciated at 20 per cent on cost.

5 Fixtures and fittings were depreciated at 10 per cent per annum on the reducing balance method including any additions.

6 At 30 September 19–8: rent in arrears, £120; advertising paid in advance, £15.

REQUIRED:
a) Prepare a trading and profit and loss account for the year ended 30 September 19–8.
b) A balance sheet as at that date. (40.2–3)

(AEB)

6 R Smithers runs a retail store in the local village. After a fire on the night of 20 June, he lost most of his stock. He needed to make an assessment of the stock lost in the fire for insurance purposes.

	£
Sales to 20 June	26 800
Margin on sales 20 per cent	
Purchases to 20 June	20 500
Stock salvaged at cost	400
Stock I January	3 850
Returns out	90

REQUIRED:
a) A constructed trading account on 20 June to indicate the stock position at this date.
b) The amount of stock lost in the fire for insurance purposes. (40.4)

7 During the night of 17 June the premises of Match Ltd were damaged by a fire which also destroyed a quantity of stock and all of the company's stock records. The destroyed stock was covered by insurance against loss by fire and the company wishes to calculate the amount to claim. The following information is available:

i)

	(On 1/1)	*(On 17/6)*
	£000	*£000*
Stock at cost	132	
Trade creditors	45	53
Trade debtors	39	47

ii) The following transactions took place between 1 January and 17 June

	£000
Cash purchases	17
Payments to creditors	274
Cash received from debtors	314
Cash sales	80
Discounts received	10
Discounts allowed	8

iii) A physical stock take carried out first thing in the morning on 18 June showed the remaining stock to have a cost of £91 000.

iv) Match Ltd earns a gross profit of 30 per cent of selling price on all of its sales.

REQUIRED:
Calculate the cost of the stock destroyed by the fire. (40.4)

(RSA)

8 You work for a firm of accountants which prepares the accounts for R Powell Ltd. During the night of 2 June the company suffered a fire which destroyed all the company's stock records and a quantity of stock. The stock was covered by insurance against loss by fire. You have been asked by your firm to assist with preparing the insurance claim and have ascertained the following information:

a)

	On 1/1	*On 2/6*
	£	£
Stock at cost	64 500	?
Trade debtors	78 250	94 725
Trade creditors	90 100	106 400

b) The following transactions took place between 1 January and 2 June:

	£
Cash purchases	34 200
Payments to creditors	184 500
Cash received from debtors	282 250
Cash sales	60 900
Discount received	2 000
Discount allowed	1 600

c) The physical stocktake, carried out first thing in the morning on 3 June, showed the remaining stock (undamaged) to have a cost value of £5 000.

d) The company operates a standard margin of 40 per cent on gross profit.

REQUIRED:
Calculate the cost of the stock destroyed by the fire. (40.4)

(BTEC)

9 The assets and liabilities as at the close of business on 31 October 19–8 of J Patel, retailer, are summarised as follows:

	£	£
Motor vehicles:		
At cost	9 000	
Provision for depreciation	1 800	
		7 200
Fixtures and fittings:		
At cost	10 000	
Provision for depreciation	6 000	
		4 000
Stock		16 100
Trade debtors		19 630
Cash		160
		£47 090
Capital – J Patel		30 910
Bank overdraft		6 740
Trade creditors		9 440
		£47 090

All receipts from credit customers are paid intact into the business bank account, while cash sales receipts are banked after deduction of cash drawings and providing for the shop till cash float. The cash float was increased from £160 to £200 in September 19–9.

The following is a summary of the transactions in the business bank account for the year ended 31 October 19–9.

Receipts	£	*Payments*	£
Credit sales	181 370	Drawings	8 500
Cash sales	61 190	Motor van (bought 1 May 19–9)	11 200

		Purchases	163 100
Proceeds of sale of land owned privately by J Patel	16 000	Establishment and administrative expenses	33 300
		Sales and distribution expenses	29 100

Additional information for the year ended 31 October 19–9:

a) A gross profit of $33^1/_3$ per cent has been achieved on all sales
b) Bad debts of £530 have been written off during the year
c) Trade debtors at 31 October 19–9 were reduced by £8 130 as compared with a year earlier
d) Trade creditors at 31 October 19–9 amounted to £12 700
e) Depreciation is to be provided at the following annual rates on cost:
   Motor vehicles 20%
   Fixtures and fittings 10%
f) Stock at 31 October 19–9 has been valued at £23 700

REQUIRED:
A trading and profit and loss account for the year ended 31 October 19–9 and a balance sheet as at that date for J Patel.

(Association of Accounting Technicians)

10 J had the following assets and liabilities on 1 October 19–7

	£
Plant and equipment	6 420
Motor vehicles	4 200
Stock of goods for resale	890
Trade creditors	470
Trade debtors	1 260
Balance at bank	3 520
Cash in hand	80
Accrued electricity	30
Prepaid business rates	1 300

J's summarised cashbook for the year ended 30 September 19–8 was as follows:

	Cash	*Bank*		*Cash*	*Bank*
	£	£		£	£
Balance b/f	80	3 520	Electricity		270
Trade debtors		29 640	Postage/stationery		65
Sales	3 630		Business rates		2 800
Plant disposal		1 735	Wages		1 750
Bank	3 000		Bank charges		120
			Rent		2 400
			Purchases	6 460	
			Trade creditors		12 740
			Van		1 405
			Vehicle expenses		980
			Drawings		6 000
			Cash		3 000
			Balance c/f	250	3 365
	6 710	34 895		6 710	34 895

Other information:

a) The plant disposal occurred on 1 August 19–8. On 1 October 19–7 the net book value of the plant disposed of was £1 420.
b) The amount entered in the cashbook for business rates is made up of two equal payments of £1 400. These occurred on 1 March 19–8 and 1 September 19–8 and were made in respect of the six-month periods ending 30 September 19–8 and 31 March 19–9.
c) The amount entered in the cashbook for the van relates to an acquisition which occurred on 1 April 19–8. The value shown includes

	£
Twelve months' road fund licence (annual vehicle tax)	110
Petrol	20
Twelve-month maintenance warranty	200

d) Wages owing on 30 September 19–8 are estimated to be £180.
e) Closing stock on 30 September 19–8, valued at cost, amounted to £775.
f) Electricity owing on 30 September 19–8 amounted to £345.
g) A full year's depreciation is to be provided on all assets held on 30 September 19–8 at the following rates, using the reducing balance method:

Plant and equipment	15%
Motor vehicle	25%

h) On 30 September 19–8 trade debtors amounted to £1 330 and trade creditors were £265.

REQUIRED:

1 Prepare J's trading and profit and loss account for the year ended 30 September 19–8, in vertical form;
2 Calculate J's capital at 1 October 19–7;
3 Prepare J's balance sheet at 30 September 19–8, in vertical form.

(Chartered Institute of Management Accountants)

41 Accounting for departments

Objectives

On completing this section you should:

- recognise that accounting can be adapted for different organisations
- be aware that a department can be allocated costs as a cost centre
- understand that profit can be identified for each department thereby assisting management decision making.

41.1 Introduction

This particular aspect of accounting is most useful to those retail stores which may have many different departments, each department really a store in its own right. In some of the large departmental stores like Boots, Debenhams and Dingles, the size of some of their departments is far larger than many individual shops, with huge turnovers, numbers of employees and budgets of thousands of pounds.

For such stores, it is an immediate advantage to know how successful or otherwise each of their departments is and, therefore, it is of great value to be able to assess the individual profit or loss of each department as well as for the store as a whole.

Comparisons can be made inter-departmentally to see if each of their activities are up to the targets set for them by the management. Results can then be analysed and evaluated and those departments whose figures are different from the budgeted figures can then be called upon to explain the reasons behind the variances which may have occurred.

Example

A store makes a profit of £35 000 overall, the break-down being as follows:

	Profit	*Loss*
	£	£
Ladies wear	15 000	
Mens wear		(18 000)
Footwear	10 000	
Furnishings	6 000	
Household	22 000	
	53 000	(18 000)

If the total of the store's profit only had been calculated, it would have hidden the significant fact that mens wear had made a loss of £18 000. By calculating individual profit or loss for each of the departments, it becomes easier to analyse the financial performance of separate departments and helps management to make better decision relating to all aspects of the store, sales, purchasing, staff and costs.

41.2 Costs

As far as costs are concerned, a cost incurred by a specific department, directly attributed to it such as wages or materials, is known as an *allocation* of cost.

If a cost is incurred for the benefit of a number of departments and is not so easily traceable to any specific one, it is known as an *apportion* of cost. For example, rent, rates and insurance may cost a store £5000 per month but how should this be apportioned to each of the departments? The size of a department in terms of floor area, the number of staff employed or the value of sales, can be used as the basis for distribution of the cost. This was also discussed in Chapter 36.

Example
The following information relates to the monthly figures of three departments:

	Menswear	*Ladieswear*	*Footwear*	*Total*
	£	£	£	£
Sales	24 000	60 000	12 000	96 000
Cost of sales	16 000	24 000	3 600	43 600
Wages	3 800	4 200	2 600	10 600
Rent, rates, insurance				4 200
Sales and distribution				8 000
Administration				12 000
Total cost				78 400

How much profit did each department make?
The policy of the management is to apportion those costs not specific to any one section, according to the following criteria (or base):

a) Rent, rates, insurance and administration should be distributed in relation to floor area:

Menswear	$^{1}/_{3}$
Ladieswear	$^{1}/_{2}$
Footwear	$^{1}/_{6}$

b) Sales and distribution costs should be distributed in relation to sales value:

Menswear	$^{24}/_{96}$	($^{2}/_{8}$)
Ladieswear	$^{60}/_{96}$	($^{5}/_{8}$)
Footwear	$^{12}/_{96}$	($^{1}/_{8}$)

Departmental trading and profit and loss account, month ending 31 May

	Menswear	*Ladieswear*	*Footwear*	*Total*
	£	£	£	£
Sales	24 000	60 000	12 000	96 000
Cost of sales	16 000	24 000	3 600	43 600
Gross profit	8 000	36 000	8 400	52 400
Wages	3 800	4 200	2 600	10 600
Rent, rates, insurance	1 400	2 100	700	4 200
Sales and distribution	2 000	5 000	1 000	8 000

Administration	4 000	6 000	2 000	12 000
	11 200	17 300	6 300	34 800
Net profit/loss	(3 200)	18 700	2 100	17 600

The outcome of these figures indicate that ladieswear obviously carries the store having the greatest profit of £18 700, against a poor performance by menswear, which suffered a loss of £3200. Footwear had a relatively small profit of £2100.

These figures only relate to the month of May. What has been the trend? Is this just a poor month for mens wear or is the department showing signs of becoming a liability to the store as a whole? Management should investigate and research these performances and try to evaluate what is needed to turn mens wear back into a profitable department.

Because the menswear made such a loss, and perhaps on investigation it has performed poorly in recent times, would it be worth considering closing down this department and concentrate on using the space more profitably? We need to think about this one a little more. Was the apportionment of the overheads, rent, distribution and administration a fair division of costs? Were the bases of apportionment reasonable and logical? If they were and these could not be reduced what would happen if menswear were to close down?

When the existing facilities are available for use, the fixed costs still remain, they do not disappear with the closure. The rent, rates and administration costs would still most probably be the same and would have to be carried by the other departments. If, however, the other departments can more profitably utilise the space, or a new department is opened which is forecast to improve results, then the menswear may have to close.

A further consideration is that departments are often inter-dependent and help promote the store. Having a menswear department may well contribute towards the success of the other sections of the business. Couples doing their shopping together will be more attracted to a store offering a wide range of products and facilities.

Apart from the difficulty of reducing fixed costs when closing down a section of activity, there is the added problem of making some of your staff redundant and perhaps having to make large pay settlements. Unemployment of colleagues may well reduce the motivation and morale of the existing staff which could have a serious knock-on effect on overall productivity.

Summary

Departmental accounting can assist management to identify the performance of each department or product in the organisation. Costs may be allocated to relevant sections according to criteria such as floor area or sales value, making a department a kind of cost centre, accountable for the control of its own costs. As a result, profit or loss can be calculated for each department emphasising those which are more profitable and effective against those which are not.

Questions

1 Jake's Store has two major departments, electrical and furnishings. The financial figures for the month of August were:

	Electrical	*Furnishings*	*Total*
	£	*£*	*£*
Sales	50 000	75 000	125 000
Stock (1/9)	8 400	6 500	14 900
Purchases	34 500	40 000	74 500
Stock (30/9)	10 900	8 500	19 400
Wages	8 000	12 000	20 000
Administration			8 000
Sales and distribution			6 000
Rent and rates			10 000
Depreciation charges			6 000

The apportioning of expenses is as follows:

a) Administration and depreciation costs on the basis of floor area: $^1/_4$ (electrical) and $^3/_4$ (furnishings).
b) Rates, rent and insurance on the basis of floor area and number of employees: $^2/_5$ (electrical) and $^3/_5$ (furnishings).
c) Sales and distribution costs on the basis of sales value.

REQUIRED:

a) Prepare a trading and profit and loss account of Jake's Store for the month of August, in columnar form, to show both gross and net profit for each department as well as the overall total profit.
b) Briefly comment on your findings. (41.1–2)

2 a) What is the basic difference between the allocation of a cost and the apportioning of a cost? Give examples to clarify your answer.
b) On which kind of bases can expenses be apportioned? Suggest on what bases the following expenses could be distributed:
rent and rates
light and heat
advertising and selling
canteen costs
administration
depreciation of motor vehicles (representatives)
depreciation of fixtures and fittings (store). (41.1–2)

3 Carlingford Ltd is a large store and the following information relates to the year ended 31 December:

		£
Sales:		
Department	A	21 400
	B	33 600
	C	24 800
	D	18 600
Purchases:		
Department	A	17 900
	B	24 700
	C	21 100
	D	14 900
Returns outward:		
Department	A	350
	B	560
	C	320

	D	810
Stock (1 Jan):		
Department	A	2 940
	B	3 760
	C	4 100
	D	1 670
Stock (31 Dec):		
Department	A	3 490
	B	1 900
	C	2 880
	D	1 760

Purchases of £1000 were transferred from department A to department C.

REQUIRED:

You are asked to prepare a departmental trading account in columnar form for the period ended 31 December. You should also calculate the gross profit percentage of each department. (41.1–2)

(Royal Society of Arts)

4 Jacksons & Walker is a store which has three departments, A, B and C. The following information relates to the business's financial year ended 31 December:

		£
Stocks on 1/1		
Department	A	4 400
	B	6 000
	C	11 000
Stocks on 31/1:		
Department	A	3 300
	B	4 600
	C	7 500
Purchases:		
Department	A	64 000
	B	84 000
	C	102 000
Wages and salaries:		
Department	A	30 600
	B	33 500
	C	42 000
Light and heat		3 300
Rent, rates, insurance		4 800
General administration		6 000
Distribution costs		8 500
Sales:		
Department	A	120 000
	B	180 000
	C	200 000

Those expenses not directly attributed to any one department are to be apportioned:

a) Light and heat to be borne equally between departments.

b) Rent, rates and insurance and general administration according to space: department A, $\frac{1}{5}$, departments B and C $\frac{2}{5}$ each.

c) Distribution costs to be distributed in relation to the sales value.

REQUIRED:

a) Prepare the trading and profit and loss account for each department in columnar form, including a column for totals.
b) Calculate the gross and net margins of each department and briefly state your findings. (41.1–2)

5 The following information relates to the activities of A Parrish, a wholesaler, selling two distinct products, X and Y, for the year ended 31 March 19–8.

Balances as at 1 April 19–7

	£
Freehold premises at cost	36 000
Capital	118 700
Motor vehicles at cost	20 000
Fixtures and fittings at cost	25 000
Stocks: X	6 500
Y	26 000
Provisions for depreciation:	
Motor vehicles	3 500
Fixtures and fittings	4 500
Balances as at 31 March 19–8	
Purchases: X	35 000
Y	158 000
Sales: X	43 500
Y	201 950
Sales return: X	3 500
Y	11 950
Purchases return: X	4 300
Y	14 900
Drawings	9 000
Trade creditors	21 000
Trade debtors	22 950
Balance at bank	18 900
Cash	3 050
Administration expenses	15 000
Selling expenses	21 500

The following further information had not yet been taken into account:

i) during the year he had taken £450 of good X for his own use; the goods taken were valued at cost price;
ii) depreciation was to be provided as follows:
motor vehicles 20 per cent on cost
fixtures and fittings 10 per cent on cost;
iii) stocks at 31 March 19–8:

	£
X	7 750
Y	31 200

iv) commissions owing to sales team as at 31 March 19–8 were £1350;
v) administration expenses paid for in advance were £1500.

REQUIRED:

a) Separate trading accounts for each of the products X and Y (columnar presentation may be used) for the year ended 31 March 19–8.
b) A profit and loss account for the whole business for the year ended 31 March 19–8
c) A detailed statement of the working capital as at 31 March 19–8. (41.1–2)

(Associated Examining Board)

42 Accounting for payroll

Objectives

On completing this section you should:

- understand different types of payment methods
- calculate gross pay from clock cards or time sheets
- understand the difference between statutory and voluntary deductions
- calculate statutory deductions
- understand the payroll system
- be aware of the major payroll forms provided by the Tax Office.

42.1 Introduction

Wages and salaries are a reward for labour. Most people have to work for a living and the income they earn is a result of having to go to work five or more days a week. Wages are usually paid on a weekly basis whereas salaries are generally associated with staff who are more often than not paid on a monthly basis, by cheque or through the bank, building society or post office. Pay is also referred to as 'remuneration'.

There are two major ways on which remuneration may be calculated:

a) Time rates
b) Payment by results.

42.1.1 Time rates

This is by far the most common way of being paid for most employees. This could be a flat rate where the same sum is paid each week or each month, for example, £200 per week. It could be on an hourly rate for example, 36 hours a week at a basic £4 per hour and a higher rate of pay above the basic rate could be earned for any overtime worked, for example, at time and a third or time and a half.

If the basic week was 36 hours and pay was £4.00 per hour and one and a half for overtime (over 36 hours), how much would you earn working 40 hours?

			£
36 hours basic:	36 × £4.00 per hour	=	144.00
4 hours overtime:	4 × £6.00 per hour	=	24.00
Total gross pay:		=	168.00

42.1.2 Payment by results

This method of remuneration offers an incentive to workers to work harder for more pay. Sales people on commission will earn more if they sell more. Factory workers who can produce more in a certain length of time and increase production will receive more pay. Piecework is a method where a factory worker is paid for greater productivity and is particularly suitable where the work is of a repetitive nature.

Examples:
Say £1.00 is paid for every 100 units produced. If a worker produced 15 000 units in a week, how much would he earn?

$$\frac{15\,000 \times 1.00}{100} = £150$$

A sales representative earns a flat retainer of £ 100 per month and a commission is paid at 2.5 per cent of total sales. If his sales were £18 000 in one month, how much would he earn?

		£
Commission: £18 000 × 2.5%	=	450.00
Basic retainer	=	100.00
Total pay	=	550.00

42.1.3 Gross and net pay

The **gross pay** of an employee refers to the total income earned before any deductions are taken from pay. There are what is called statutory and voluntary deductions.

Statutory deductions are those which must be paid because they are legally required by Government. These are income tax and national insurance contributions (NIC), both are collected using the pay as you earn (PAYE) system.

Voluntary deductions are those agreed to by an employee and may be for a pension fund, trade union subscriptions, social club funds, voluntary savings, or anything else which the employee wants deducted from his gross pay.

A **pension fund** is also referred to as **superannuation**. Most employees contribute towards the Government's own superannuation scheme called SERPS (State Earnings-Related Pension Scheme).

Some employees choose their own pension plans and can 'contract out', that is, find an alternative private pension scheme of their own and pay marginally less NIC.

Example of calculating net pay

	£	£
Gross pay (per week)		188.00
Deductions:		
Income tax	32.55	
NIC	13.70	
Pension fund	6.50	
Trade union	1.25	54.00
Net pay		134.00

42.2 Processing the payroll

Wages are associated with a wage packet and payment in cash, whereas a salary is more in keeping with payment by cheque or through a bank. It is however, becoming far more frequent for all employees to be paid through the bank, building society or post office. This is seen as more efficient and better for security reasons. When employees are paid through the bank by credit transfer, this is known as BACS (Bankers Automatic Clearing System).

However, irrespective of how one is paid, whether in cash or through a bank, the documentation procedure is basically the same. The major documents involved are:

Clock cards or time sheets
Tax table A – free pay
Tax table B – taxable pay
National Insurance Tables 1 and 1A
Tax deduction cards P11
Payslip advice
Payroll sheet
Cash analysis sheet
P6 employee's tax notification number
Employee's Forms P45 and P46

For all employees, the correct procedure for calculating the gross pay and making the correct deductions to arrive at net pay, is of paramount importance, not only to the individual, but also to keep within the legal framework when making statutory deductions from pay.

42.3 Clock cards and time sheets

To record how long an employee is at work, the clock card may be used to time staff coming in and going out of their work place, including the lunch break. The cards will be used to provide the payroll staff the data required to calculate the number of hours worked, including any overtime hours. They will then calculate the gross pay by multiplying the hours by the rate per hour.

The clock card is ideal for those staff on hourly rates of pay or those on what is called 'flexitime', that is, an employee works so many hours a week but is not entirely restricted to a set time of clocking in and out of work.

Example
The following information refers to the clock cards of Jackie Lomas and Roger Pebbles. Jackie works on factory floor 4 on a 40 hours per week basic time. Roger's work place is on floor 7. Any overtime from Monday to Friday is paid at the rate of time and a third. Saturday is at time and a half. Any additional overtime on Sundays is at double time. Each worker is allowed to be late upto just 3 minutes clocking in time. Time lost over 3 minutes means a deduction of a quarter of an hour's basic pay. Over 20 minutes late in any one hour results in an hour's pay lost.

Jackie is paid as a skilled worker at £6.42 per hour basic. Roger is unskilled on the assembly line and earns £4.50 per hour basic.

Study the two clock cards below and check them for accuracy. Jackie's card has been completed. Can you complete Roger's card? (Your answer should be £234.13).

Clock cards

NAME Jackie Lomas WKS NO. 296
FACTORY 4 WK ENDING 9/4

DAY	IN	OUT	IN	OUT	BASIC TIME	OVER TIME
MON	8.30	12.31	1.29	6.02	8	½
TUES	8.28	12.34	1.30	7.03	8	1½
WED	8.25	12.30	1.28	8.05	8	2½
THURS	8.32	12.32	1.27	6.01	8	½
FRI	8.20	12.32	1.28	5.32	8	
SAT	8.30	12.30				4
SUN						-

TOTAL NUMBER OF HOURS WORKED

BASIC TIME	40	OVER-* TIME	9	ADDL O/T	

RATE OF PAY £ PER HOUR

40	Hours @ £ 6.42 per hr	£ 256 - 80
9	Overtime Hours	
5	M - F @ £ 8.56 per hr	£ 42 - 80
4	Sat @ £ 9.63 per hr	£ 38 - 52
	Additional @ £ ____ per hour	£
	GROSS PAY	£ 338 - 12

NAME Roger Pebbles WKS NO. 429
FACTORY 7 WK ENDING 9/4

DAY	IN	OUT	IN	OUT	BASIC TIME	OVER TIME
MON	8.32	12.32	1.30	6.04	8	½
TUES	8.26	12.34	1.31	6.06	8	½
WED	8.35	12.31	1.27	8.06	7¾	2½
THURS	8.30	12.32	1.28	8.07	8	2½
FRI	8.28	12.34	1.27	5.31	8	
SAT	8.30	12.30			3	
SUN						

TOTAL NUMBER OF HOURS WORKED

BASIC TIME		OVER-* TIME		ADDL O/T	

RATE OF PAY £ PER HOUR

39¾	Hours @ £ 4 -50 per hour	£ 177-88
9	Overtime Hours	
	M - F @ £ ____ per hr	£
	Sat @ £ ____ per hr	£
	Additional @ £ ____ per hour	£
	GROSS PAY	£

*(a) Mon-Fri overtime is paid at ordinary time plus one third.
(b) Saturday overtime is paid at ordinary time plus one half.
(c) Sunday overtime is paid at double ordinary time.

Some firms use a time book rather than a card system, where staff would simply sign their names under 'time in' and 'time out', rather than clock in and out. What management do not ever want to see is one member of staff clocking in for another because that person is late, or might not turn up at all! This is fraud and is often seen as a sackable offence.

A time sheet can be used to list the employees on the payroll and indicate the number of hours they have worked in any given week, for example:

JOBSON & LITTLE CO LTD

TIME SHEET (hours)

Department: Cleaning

Week Ending ....

Name	No.	Monday	Tuesday	Wednesday	Thursday	Friday	Saturday
D Amis	010	7	7	9	7	9	3
R Bagshot	011	7	8	7	8	7	0
S Brain	012	7	7	7	7	7	3
P Cash	013	9	9	7	7	7	3

(continued)

(continued)

J Edmond	014	7	7	8	8	7	0
R Jones	015	7	7	7	9	7	3
Total hours		44	45	45	46	44	12
Department Head				Date			

If the basic week was 35 hours (5 × 7 hours per day) and overtime was at time and a third for weekdays, plus time and a half for Saturdays, how much would D Amis earn in the week given that the basic rate is £6.00 per hour?

35 hours × £6 = £210
4 hours × £8 = £32
3 hours × £9 = £27 £269

How much would would J Edmond earn if his basic rate was £4.50 per hour?

35 hours × £4.50 = £157.50
2 hours × £6.00 = £12.00 £169.50

42.4 Calculating statutory deductions

Income tax and national insurance contributions are both statutory deductions from pay. The amount to be deducted is decided by the Chancellor of the Exchequer and is presented to Parliament in his budget speech each year.

42.4.1 Income tax

Income tax in the UK is a progressive tax which means that the more you earn, the more you pay. At the time of writing, there are three tax bands:

a) the lower rate 20% (0 – £3 900)
b) the basic rate 24% (3 901 – £25 500)
c) the higher rate 40% (over £25 500)

The lower rate is levied on a low income band, for example, on the first £3900 per annum tax, would be at 20%. The basic rate is from this figure to the next band, up to £25 500 per annum. The higher rate is then charged at £25 500 plus. The thresholds of these bands may change each year and is on the decision of the Chancellor.

The figures are calculated not on gross pay but on a person's taxable pay, that is, after tax allowances have been deducted from gross pay.

All employees are liable for income tax through the PAYE system (pay as you earn). Your employer deducts income tax and national insurance from your pay and this is sent in total to the Inland Revenue each month along with Form P30B (payslip completed by the employer showing the totals for tax and NIC deducted).

Each person is entitled to tax allowances (free pay) which is deducted from gross pay to arrive at what is called 'taxable pay'. Taxable allowances include:

- single person's allowance
- married couple's allowance
- pension or superannuation allowances
- mortgage interest relief allowance (if it is not already deducted by the lender on monthly payments)
- subscriptions to professional bodies
- some personal expenses at the place of work.

The most significant allowances for most persons is the single and married couple's allowances. For example, if a married man has a tax allowance of £5500 per annum, this is his 'tax free' pay. He would only be liable to pay tax on any earnings above £5500. If he did not earn this amount, he would not be liable for any tax.

Each person's tax code is prepared by the Tax Office on form P6 (T). It lists the allowances you are entitled to and at the foot of the form it states:

Your code for the year to 6 April 199. . . is 376L

The code 376L represents a single person's allowance for that particular year. If a 5 is added to the 3 digits, it indicates the allowance of £3765. The L indicates a single person, H for a married person, P for pensioner, etc. A married person may have a code of say 555H. This would indicate an allowance of £5555 per annum, tax free.

Therefore, the greater the personal allowances you have, the less will be your taxable pay. For example, if a person had an income of £35 500 per annum and his allowances were £5500, his taxable pay = £30 000. How much tax would he be liable to pay? Using the current tax bands as stated below:

						Tax charge (£)
Lower rate	£0	–	£3 900 ×	20%	=	780
Basic rate	£3 901	–	£25 500 (21 600) ×	24%	=	5 184
Higher rate	£ 25 501	–	£30 000 (4 500) ×	40%	=	1 800
			£30 000 taxable pay`		=	7 764

For persons who are self-employed, PAYE does not concern them. Their financial year end accounts, indicating their income less allowable expenses, will be sent with their tax return to the Inland Revenue, who will determine how much tax they will pay, if any.

42.4.2 National insurance contributions (NIC)

This is another form of tax which the employee has to pay but in return, it does provide funds for benefits such as unemployment, sick pay, retirement pension, child support and so forth. Both the employee and the employer are charged. Persons who earn a low income (less than £58 at time of press) do not pay NIC. Those who earn above this figure are subject to pay this tax which is based on gross wages (not net). The figures are:

1st £58 of pay at 2%
£58 to a maximum of £440 weekly at 10%

Therefore, a person earning £220 per week pays NIC:

2% × 58 = £1.16
10% × 162 = £16.20 £17.36

The employers' contribution is normally a little above the employees' rate and there is no maximum limit of £440, the employer is charged on the whole sum earned.

Tax and NIC tables can be used to make these calculations and no wages office is without them. Examples of these tables are shown after the multiple choice questions, pp. 562–67.

42.4.3 Tax tables

The Inland Revenue provide employers with two books of tax tables so that the correct deductions for tax can be calculated.

Tax Table A gives the cumulative tax free pay to date, shown opposite the tax code number. For example, if you look at Table A, week 1, tax code 241 gives £46.52 free pay for the first week. It is based on 52 weekly pays throughout the year. For week 2, the free pay will be double this figure and is cumulative for the 52 weeks.

For those employees on monthly pay, the pay to date is shown after the weekly rates.

Tax Table B gives the tax due to date and is used in conjunction with Table A. The total pay to date, less the cumulative tax free pay to date = the taxable pay to date. From this, the total tax due is given in the column opposite the taxable pay to date. For example, if you look at Table B (tax at 24 per cent), if the taxable income to date was £400, the total tax due should be £96.

When the weekly or monthly taxable pay limits are exceeded, supplementary Tax Tables C and D are used, where the additional higher tax rate of 40 per cent will be charged on the higher earnings.

It sounds rather complicated, but an illustrated example may help you to understand it better:

Graham is an employee at Pearce's and in Week 1 of the tax year commencing on 6 April, he earned £328.17 His tax code for the year is 435L. This represents £4355 allowances. How much tax will Graham pay?
Table A for Free Pay in Week 1 the code 435 = £83.83 tax free pay.

	£
Gross pay	328.17
Less free pay	83.83
Taxable pay	244.34

For tax purposes, this is always rounded down to the pound, £244.

Now using Table B for Taxable Pay at the basic rate of 24 per cent on £244 = £58.56.

In Table B there is also a lower relief table because tax is only 20 per cent on the first tax band. If this was up to £3 900, in Week 1 the lower relief to be deducted would be approximately £3.00 per week (3900 × 4% = 156/52)

Therefore the tax due in Week 1 would be £58.56 – £3.00 = £55.56.

42.4.4 NIC tables

In our example, Graham would pay 2 per cent on the first £58 of his gross pay of £328 and a further 10 per cent on the balance, £270:

		£
2% on 58.00	=	1.16
10% on 270.00	=	27.00
NIC due to pay	=	28.16

However, there are national insurance contribution tables from which these amounts payable are extracted and the figures do vary slightly from the manual calculations.

The NIC Tables 1 are used for 'not contracted out' contributions, that is, those persons who are still in the State Earnings Related Pension Scheme (SERPS), £328 earnings = £28.21 in contributions payable.

Tables 1 include:

Table A	(standard rate) is used for employees over 16 and under pension age and those employees who have their own personal pension from 1 July 1988.
Table B	(reduced rate) is used for married women and widows.
Table C	is used for employees over the pension age, including those previously contracted out and those employees who have made their own arrangements to pay NIC.
Table 1A	are for those persons having 'contracted out' of SERPS and have chosen their own personal pension plans.
Table D	is used for persons who have contracted out and pay the standard rate NIC.
Table E	is used for married women and widows who have contracted out and pay NIC at the reduced rate.

Both employee and employer are charged NIC and the tables will indicate the total of both employee's and employer's contributions and a separate figure for the employee's contributions, based on the earnings on which the contributions are payable, (again in rounded pounds, not pence).

42.5 Pay slips

PAY ADVICE Wk/endg. 12/4
NAME J. LOMAS
WORKS NO. 296 DEPT. F4

Earnings	Basic Time				
	40 hrs @ 6.42			256	80
	Overtime				
	5 8.56			42	80
	4 hrs @ 9.63			38	52
	Additional Overtime				
	hrs @				
	GROSS PAY			£338	12
Deductions	PAYE	65	34		
	NI Contr.	26	50		
	Other Deduct	1	50		
	Pension				
		93	34		
	TOTAL DEDUCTIONS			£ 93	34
Additions	Tax Refund				
	Other Addns.	-	-		
	TOTAL ADDITIONS			£	
	NET PAY			£244	78

PAY ADVICE Wk/endg. 12/4
NAME R. PEBBLES
WORKS NO. 429 DEPT. F7

Earnings	Basic Time				
	39 3/4 hrs @ 4.50			177	88
	Overtime				
	6 6.00			36	00
	3 hrs @ 6.75			20	25
	Additional Overtime				
	hrs @				
	GROSS PAY			£234	13
Deductions	PAYE	27	00		
	NI Contr.	18	81		
	Other Deduct.				
	Pension	10	00		
	TOTAL DEDUCTIONS			£ 55	81
Additions	Tax Refund				
	Other Addns				
	TOTAL ADDITIONS			£	
	NET PAY			£178	32

If you study the pay slips of J Lomas and R Pebbles, they show how the gross and net pay was calculated. This pay is the first in the tax year, 12 April. Check that their gross and net pay calculations are correct. The payslips are then recorded on the payroll sheet below. For simplicity only the two employees are listed.

42.6 Payroll

Once all the employees' pay has been calculated, the payroll is prepared and lists all employees of the organisation, recording the gross pay to date, tax, NIC, pension and other deductions, net pay and also the employers' NIC contributions, taken from the NIC tables. The example simply illustrates how the two employees above would be recorded on the payroll of the company. Note that the employer is also obliged to pay NIC to the tax office. These are known as secondary (or employers') contributions.

PAYROLL SHEET

WEEK NUMBER 1

DATE 10 APRIL . . .

EMPLOYEE	GROSS PAY	PAYE DED	NIC DED	PENSION	OTHER DED	NET PAY	EMPLOYER'S NIC
Lomas J	338.12	65.34	26.50		1.50	244.78	34.53
Pebbles R	234.13	27.00	18.81	10.00		178.32	23.92
Totals	572.25	92.34	45.31	10.00	1.50	423.10	58.45

42.6.1 Recording wages in the nominal ledger

If the details of the two employees were posted to the ledger, the entries would be:

Debit:	Wages account	£572.25 (gross wages)
	Employers' NIC	£58.45

The payments due to the Tax Office are credited under the inland Revenue account:

Credit:	Inland Revenue account	
	Tax	£92.34
	NIC employees'	£45.31
	NIC employers'	£58.45

The bank account is credited with the amounts to be paid:

Credit:	Net pay	£423.10
	Pension fund	£10.00
	Other (subscriptions)	£1.50

Nominal ledger

	Debit	Credit	Balance
	£	£	£
Wages account			
Gross pay	572.25		
Employer's NIC	58.45		630.70 Dr
Inland Revenue account			
Tax		92.34	
Employees' NIC		45.31	
Employers' NIC		58.45	196.10 Cr
Bank account			
Net pay		423.10	
Pension		10.00	
Other (subs)		1.50	434.60 Cr

Debits	=	£630.70		
Credits	=		£196.10	
			£434.60	£630.70

42.6.2 The form P11

This is the tax and NIC deductions card (or sheet) for each individual employee. It records the employee's name, national insurance and work numbers, tax code and the weekly or monthly earnings in pay. Pay is recorded on a cumulative basis, that is, each pay period is added to the previous. Tax is recorded on the right and NIC on the left. Any SSP (statutory sick pay) or SMP (statutory maternity pay) is also recorded in the appropriate columns.

In the example, Roger Pebbles' first four weeks pay commencing on 6 April (the new tax year) is recorded.

42.7 Major payroll forms from the Inland Revenue

Deductions from pay need to be accurate both from the individual's and Tax Office's point of view. The Tax Office produces an Employer's Guide to PAYE which includes a pack of cards as an illustration and guidance on income tax regulations. Card No. 11, for example, is a quick reference to the type of forms in use. The major ones are:

P6 (T) Tax code number notification of the employee to the employer.

P9 Tax code number notification to the employer. P6 and P9 inform you and your employer of your tax code allowances, including any changes to these. The code number is used to calculate your tax free pay to date.

P11 This is the tax deductions working sheet for each individual employee. It records weekly or monthly earnings, income tax, NIC, SSP and SMP.

Deductions Working Sheet P11 Year to 5 April 19 ___

Employer's name	R PEARCE
Tax District and reference	

Complete only for occupational pension schemes newly contracted-out since 1 January 1986.
Scheme contracted-out number

S	4							

Employee's surname *in CAPITALS*	PEBBLES	First two forenames	ROGER, ALLAN
National Insurance no.	Date of birth *in figures* (Day Month Year)	Works no. etc	Date of leaving *in figures* (Day Month Year)
YE, 34, 43, 42, D	14, 08, 68	0007	

Tax code †	Amended code†				
511 H	Wk/Mth in which applied				

National Insurance contributions*

For employer's use	Earnings on which employee's contributions payable 1a	Total of employee's and employer's contributions payable 1b	Employee's contributions payable 1c	Earnings on which employee's contributions at contracted-out rate payable included in column 1a 1d	Employee's contributions at contracted-out rate included in column 1c 1e	Statutory Sick Pay in the week or month included in column 2 1f	Statutory Sick Pay recovered. Only complete this column if you are claiming Small Employer's Relief 1g	Statutory Maternity Pay in the week or month included in column 2 1h
	£	£	£	£	£	£	£	£
23-92	224	42 73	18 81					
12-42	177	25 53	13 11					
11-72	167	23 83	12 11					
21-67	212	38 28	16 61					
	Total c/fwd	Total c/fwd	Total c/fwd	Total c/fwd	Total c/fwd	Total c/fwd	Total c/fwd	Total c/fwd

PAYE Income Tax

Month no	Week no	Pay in the week or month including Statutory Sick Pay/Statutory Maternity Pay 2	Total pay to date 3	Total free pay to date (Table A) 4a	K codes only: Total 'additional pay' to date (Table A) 4b	Total taxable pay to date i.e. column 3 minus column 4a or column 3 plus column 4b 5	Total tax due to date as shown by Taxable Pay Tables 6	K codes only: Tax due at end of current period Mark refunds 'R' 6a	K codes only: Regulatory limit i.e. 50% of column 2 entry 6b	Tax deducted or refunded in the week or month Mark refunds 'R' 7	K codes only: Tax not deducted owing to the Regulatory limit 8	For employer's use
		£		£	£	£	£	£	£	£	£	
6 April to 5 May 1	1	224 13	224 13	98 45		125 68	27 –			27		
	2	177 88	402 01	196 90		205 11	43 20			22 20		
	3	167 88	569 89	295 35		274 54	56 76			13 56		
	4	212 90	782 79	393 80		388 99	81 12			24 36		
6 May to 5 June 2	5											
	6											
	7											
	8											
6 June to 5 July 3	9											
	10											
	11											
	12											
	13											
6 July to 5 Aug 4	14											
	15											
	16											
	17											
6 Aug to 5 Sept 5	18											
	19											
	20											
	21											
6 Sept to 5 Oct 6	22											
	23											
	24											
	25											
	26											
6 Oct to 5 Nov 7	27											
	28											
	29											
	30											

* You must enter the NI contribution table letter overleaf beside the NI totals box - *see the note shown there.*

† If amended cross out previous code.

Ø If any week/month the amount in column 4a is more than the amount in column 3, leave column 5 blank.

P11(1993)

P11 D	Indicates all benefits and expenses paid to an employee.
P14	This is a year end summary of pay for each employee, showing total tax, NIC etc. P60 is a certificate of the same information given to the employee, a copy of P14.
P15	Is used by an employee to claim tax allowances, particularly if on an emergency coding.
P30 B	The payslip to be completed by the employer showing totals deducted from employees for tax and NIC (less refunds, SSP and SMP) for the month, to be paid to the tax office within 14 days after month end. P30BC is the payslip booklet containing payslips.
P32	Employer's payment record, the month's tax and NIC details to be paid to the Inland Revenue.
P35	A summary of all P14's and sent with all P14's to the Inland Revenue totalling all tax and NIC paid for the year.
P45	This is used when an employee either starts or leaves a job. Details of the tax code, total pay and tax due to date and tax paid to date are recorded.
P46	If a new employee is without a P45, (it might be the first job from school), an emergency tax code number 344L is used until a new tax code is provided by the tax office. A P15 (tax allowance claim) will be completed by the employee and sent to the Tax Office.
P47	This is an application to make a tax refund to a new employee if it exceeds £200.
P48	Is the tax office's authority to make the refund on P47.
P60	The certificate of an employee's pay and tax deductions for the year. It is either a separate form, or the third part of P14.

Tables A	The tax free tables.
Tables B	The taxable pay tables.
NIC 268	A quick guide to NIC, SSP and SMP.
CF 391	National Insurance tables (not contracted out). Red Book 1.
CF 392	National Insurance tables (contracted out). Red Book 1a.
SSP 55	Statutory Sick Pay tables. Red Book 2.
SMP 55	Statutory Maternity Pay tables. Red Book 3.

42.8 Payment by cash

When a number of staff are to be paid by cash, it is necessary to obtain the right number of notes and coins in sufficient quantities to enable each wage packet to be made up.

Notes should be of various denominations and sensibly divided into £50, £20, £10 and £5 notes. The right number of coins is also needed. This is the coin or cash analysis, sometimes referred to as 'coining'.

The right sum of money must be collected from the bank in sufficient time to make up the staff pay. Where a considerable sum of money is required, it makes sense to be fully aware of the security procedures involved. There are security organisations like Securicor, which take over the responsibility of handling and controlling the cash from bank to business premises.

If smaller sums of money are needed and members of staff are responsible for obtaining money from the bank, it is only prudent to vary the times and journeys to and from the bank in order to break up established routines.

An example of a cash analysis is as follows:

Employee's Name:	*Net Pay*
	£
Burns, A	87.90
Davies, D	94.00
Fenwick, R	174.14
Follows, B	126.40
Jones, J	160.01
Jackson, P	201.10
Robinson, J	96.55
Total cash required:	940.10

Below is a cash analysis form which shows the notes and coins each staff member will receive.

From the totals of the cash analysis, a cash analysis summary may be drawn up which specifies the denominations in notes and coins required from the bank.

This is given to the bank, along with a cheque for the full amount, £940.10. The cashier will check it for accuracy and prepare the right number of notes and coins which will be used to make up the wage packets of the employees.

Wages cash analysis form
Week number4

Employee's Name	Notes			Coins							NET PAY
	£20	£10	£5	£1	50p	20p	10p	5p	2p	1p	
1) Burns, A	2	3	3	2	1	2					87.90
2) Davies, D	3	2	2	4							94.00
3) Fenwick, R	5	5	4	4			1		2		174.14
4) Follows, B	5	2	1	1		2					126.40
5) Jones, J	5	5	2							1	160.01
6) Jackson, P	8	2	4	1			1				201.10
7) Robinson, J	3	2	3	1	1			1			96.55
8)											
9)											
TOTALS	31	21	19	13	2	4	2	1	2	1	940.10

Summary

There are various methods by which gross pay can be earned. Most people are paid on time rates, that is, working so many hours a week. Others may be paid by results like sales people paid on a commission basis. Wages are made up of gross pay less statutory deductions for tax and NIC and also any voluntary deductions like a pension scheme, to arrive at net pay. Tax and NIC can be calculated either from given data or from tax and NIC tables provided by the Inland Revenue (Tax Office). The Tax Office can provide assistance and documents to help employers make the correct deductions from the pay of their employees.

Questions

1 Calculate the following:

a) Harry Jones has a basic week of 36 hours paid at a flat rate of £4.00 per hour. Overtime is at time and a half. How much will he earn working 39 hours?

b) Calculate the gross pay for Jack working 46 hours and Fred working 43 hours per week, paid at £2.80 per hour. Overtime starts after 38 hours and is at time and a quarter. (42.1)

2 Calculate the gross pay for each employee:

Tom	40 hours
Dick	38.5 hours
Harry	45 hours.

The basic working week is 36 hours, at £3.00 per hour. Overtime is at time and a half. (42.1)

3 Charlie is on piece work where the attendance money is £1.25 hour. The piece rate is:

to 1000 units	2p	unit
1001 to 1500 units	3p	unit
over 1501 units	2.5p	unit

How much will Charlie earn in a 42 hour week in which he produces a total of 1825 units? (42.1)

4 A representative is paid a basic salary of £400 per month. He is also paid 10 per cent commission on sales over £5000. In a month where his sales were £9850, how much was his monthly pay? (42.1)

5 A person earns £150 per week and is paid an additional 8 hours overtime at £4.75 per hour. Statutory deductions for tax and NIC are £32.55 (tax) and £13.70 (NIC). Calculate both gross and net pay. (42.1)

6 On the paysheet of three employees, work numbers 10, 11 and 12, their hours per week plus overtime was recorded as:

No. 10 35 hours basic plus 5 hours week-day and 4 hours Saturday
No. 11 35 hours basic plus 2 hours week-day and 3 hours Saturday
No. 12 35 hours basic plus 6 hours week-day, 3 hours Saturday and 3 hours Sunday.

The rates of pay are £4.2 per hour basic, time and a quarter for week-day, time and a half Saturday and double time for Sunday. Calculate pay for each employee.

7 Calculate the week's net pay for Arthur:

Gross pay:		£226.80
Deductions:		
Pension	£14.00 (tax free)	
NIC	£16.34	
Trade union	£1.10	
Tax	?	

Arthur has £110 tax free allowances on top of his pension. The basic rate of tax is 24 per cent and also the lower rate relief of £3. is deducted. Tax on £s only, not pence. (42.4)

8 What is meant by the term statutory deductions from pay? What is the P11 used for? (42.4,6)

9 How would you record the following payroll information in the nominal ledger (42.6):

Gross pay	3864.63
Employer's NIC	312.28
Employee's NIC	197.76
Income tax	527.50
Net pay	3068.47
Pension fund paid	70.90

10 Jane has a tax code of 344L and earns £5096 per annum. What is her taxable pay and how much would she expect to pay in tax per annum? (use the first £3000 taxable income at the lower rate of 20%). (42.4–5)

11 Peter earns an annual salary of £14 780 and has a tax allowance of 516H. How much tax per month will he expect to pay? (same lower rate as Jane and above this figure, tax at the basic 254). Note: add a 5 to the tax code number to provide the allowance 516H = £5165 per annum. (42.4–5)

12 Jake earns £36 800 per annum; tax free pay is £109.98 per week and he also pays 6 per cent of his gross pay to a pension fund (tax free). Use the lower rate at 20 per cent on first £3000 p.a., the basic rate of 24 per cent up to £23 700 p.a. and the balance at the higher rate of 40 per cent tax p.a. to calculate his weekly tax. (Tax on £s only for basic and higher rates.) (42.4–5)

13 a) Anne earns £308 per week and pays NIC at 2 per cent on the first £60 and 9 per cent on the balance. Calculate her NIC payable in the week.
b) Susie earns £242 per week and pays NIC at the lower rate, 2 per cent on the first £60 and 3.85 per cent on the balance. Calculate her NIC payable in the week. (42.4–5)

14 Jane has a tax code of 344L and earns £108 in Week 1 of the tax year.
a) What is her free pay in Week 1 using Tax Table A?
b) How much is her taxable pay?
c) How much tax is she liable to pay at the lower rate of tax? (Tax on £s only.) (42.4–5)

15 What is the difference between using forms P45 and P46? (42.7)

Multiple-choice questions

Introduction

Many examination boards use this type of technique to test students on their skills and knowledge. It can test a wide range of areas and has the advantage of high speed marking of scripts which is often done by computer. All the candidate has to do is to tick or circle what he or she considers to be the correct response, usually one of four possible answers.

Try these multiple-choice questions and see if you agree with the suggested answers which follow on page 561.

1 Which of the following is not a liability?
A bank overdraft
B supplier's account credit
C bank loan
D prepayment

2 In which category of the balance sheet would you expect to find a provision for bad and doubtful debts?
A fixed assets
B long term liabilities
C current assets
D current liabilities

3 A company needs some large scale financing but does not wish to increase its external debt. The ideal way would be:
A get a mortgage
B arrange for a long-term bank loan
C obtain a lease
D provide a new share issue

4 Which of the following is the incorrect equation?

	Capital	*Assets*	*Liabilities*
A	3000	5000	2000
B	15000	37500	22500
C	2900	12800	9800
D	100	3800	3700

5 Working capital was £43200 and the following transactions occurred:
creditors were paid £3000
bad debts written off were £250
stock valued at £100 was sold for £230 on credit.
Working capital is now:
A £43080
B £46080
C £40080
D £42850

6 The trial balance may best be described as:
A a list of balances taken from the balance sheet
B a list of balances taken from the personal ledgers
C a list of all transactions taken from the books
D a list of balances from the main ledger

7 Which source of finance would be the most appropriate to overcome a temporary shortfall in working capital?
A a bank loan
B a hire purchase agreement
C a bank overdraft
D a debenture issue

8 When a company's profit and loss account is prepared, it shows:
A the net book value of its assets
B revenue expenditure during the year
C capital expenditure during the year
D a mix of both revenue and capital expenditure

9 When the profit and loss account is prepared, all these accounts will be used except:
A light and heat account
B salaries account
C cash account
D depreciation of fixed assets account

10 The balance sheet will indicate to interested parties:
A the net sales for the year
B the cost of production
C the net value of plant and machinery
D the cost of advertising

11 Which of the following would be in a company appropriation account for the current year?
A directors' fees
B proposed preference dividend to be paid in the following year
C the total of the retained profits
D the interest payable

12 A decrease in the provision for bad and doubtful debts would result in:
A an increase in current liabilities
B a decrease in the net profit
C an increase in the net profit
D none of the above

13 The capital of a sole trader could change as a result of:
A paying wages by cash
B equipment purchased by cheque
C purchases on credit terms
D drawings by cheque

14 After the calculation of net profit it is discovered that a fixed asset costing £5000 has been included under purchases. The effect would be:
A to overstate the gross profit
B to overstate the value of fixed assets
C to understate the net profit
D to overstate the net profit

15 From the following information you are to calculate credit sales:
Debtors at 1 January £10 000
Debtors at 31 December £9000
Receipts during the year (including cash sales of £5000) £85 000
A £81 000
B £86 000

C £79 000
D £84 000

16 Rent paid on 1 October 19–5 for the year to the following 30 September 19–6 was £1200. Rent paid on 1 October 19–6 to the following 30 September 19–7 was £1600. The charge to the profit and loss account for the year 31 December 19–6 would be:
A £1200
B £1600
C £1300
D £1500

17 A sales invoice must include the correct calculation for Vat because this will affect:
A the yearly sales
B stock levels
C the gross profit
D the amount owed by the debtor

18 Cheques must be completed accurately. Decide whether each of these statements is true (T) or false (F):
(i) Words and figures must match
(ii) Cheques do not need to be dated.
A (i) T (ii) F
B (i) T (ii) T
C (i) F (ii) F
D (i) F (ii) T

19–20 A company's documents will include the following:
A customer's statement
B purchase requision note
C goods received note
D purchase invoice
Which of these will:

19 Help to monitor outstanding debts?

20 Help to calculate the cost of sales?

21 The cash flow forecast indicates:
A the profit and loss for the year
B the value of cash from projected receipts and payments
C the estimation of fixed asset values
D the financial position of the business

22 A business bought equipment for £10 000 which had an estimated useful life of 5 years and a residual value of £1000. The straight line method of depreciation was adopted and 3 years later, the equipment sold for £4000. The amount to profit and loss account on disposal is:
A profit of £600
B loss of £600
C no profit or loss
D loss of £400

23–25 When the evaluation of a company's accounts is prepared, ratios are used which look at:
A debtors
B profitability
C return on capital employed
D liquidity
Which of these will help monitor:

23 How well the business is performing

24 Check on credit control

25 The ability of the business to pay its debts on time.

26 The acid test ratio is used to measure:
A net assets less current liabilities
B short term solvency
C profitability
D the rate of stock turnover

27 The rate of stock turnover helps to measure:
A the average stock held
B the value of closing stock
C the number of times the average stock is sold
D the working capital minus the closing stock

28 The cash book shows an overdrawn balance of £500. When checking against the bank statement, it is found that: a cheque drawn for £160 has not yet been presented for payment at the bank, the bank has charged interest of £35 on overdraft, a sum of £100 deposited has not yet been credited by the bank. The correct bank figure entered in the balance sheet should be:
A £535 overdrawn
B £595 overdrawn
C £560 overdrawn
D £475 overdrawn

29 The profit and loss account will indicate whether a company can afford to increase its overheads. Which interested party could find this the most beneficial?
A the bank manager considering whether to grant a loan
B the shareholders
C the tax office
D the VAT office

30 A factory has the following costs:

advertising	£500
assembly workers' wages	£4000
raw materials	£3500
factory insurance	£240
foreman's wages	£1200

3000 units are produced
The direct cost per unit is:
A £2.9
B £2.5
C £2.98
D £1.33

31 Which of the following should adversely affect a business's cash budget?
A an increase in cash sales
B a reduction in bank charges
C an increase in the price of goods
D a decrease in debtors

32 Which of the following is a cash outflow?
A sales on a credit basis
B charges for depreciation of vehicles

C commission received
D wages paid

33 Which of the following is a direct cost to a business?
A advertising costs
B factory depreciation
C storemen's wages
D manufacturing wages

34 Decide whether each of the following statements is True (T) or False (F)
i) The cost of raw materials is an indirect cost
ii) Indirect costs include factory light and heat.
A i) T ii) T
B i) T ii) F
C i) F ii) T
D i) F ii) F

35 In the manufacture of a product, direct material cost is £10 per unit, direct labour £5 per unit and factory overheads £5 per unit. 2500 units were produced. What is the prime cost?
A £15
B £50 000
C £37 500
D £20

36 These are the factory costs of a business based on 200 units:
Delivery charges £400
Direct materials £2000
Factory rent and rates £500
Direct wages £8000
Factory power £350
Factory depreciation £150
The factory overheads per unit are:
A £5
B £50
C £7
D £57

37 The trial balance is extracted from the books at the year end. Decide whether the following statements is True (T) or False (F):
i) A transaction that is omitted from the books means that the trial balance will fail to balance
ii) If the trial balance does balance, the ledgers are correct.
A i) T ii) T
B i) F ii) T
C i) T ii) F
D i) F ii) F

38 The trial balance is prepared for which purpose?
A to value the closing stock
B to prepare a cash budget
C to help with credit control
D to prepare the trading and profit and loss account

39 A business is considering obtaining a bank loan. What could a bank manager obtain from its balance sheet?
A the cost of production
B overhead costs

C the business's liquidity position
D the margin of profit the business makes

40 An appropriation account for a limited company will indicate:
A the company's total reserves
B the amount of interest paid to its creditors
C the amount paid or provided for dividends
D the value of the company' shares

Suggested answers to multiple-choice questions

1	D	**2**	C	**3**	D	**4**	C
5	A	**6**	D	**7**	C	**8**	B
9	C	**10**	C	**11**	B	**12**	C
13	D	**14**	C	**15**	C	**16**	C
17	D	**18**	A	**19**	A	**20**	D
21	B	**22**	B	**23**	C	**24**	A
25	D	**26**	B	**27**	C	**28**	A
29	A	**30**	B	**31**	C	**32**	D
33	D	**34**	C	**35**	C	**36**	A
37	D	**38**	D	**39**	C	**40**	C

A bank of further multiple-choice questions, organised by chapter, is contained in the lecturer's pack.

Financial tables for tax and NIC

TABLE A – PAY ADJUSTMENT WEEK 1 Apr 6 to Apr 12

Code	Total pay adjustment to date	Code	Total pay adjustment to date	Code	Total pay adjustment to date	Code	Total pay adjustment to date	Code	Total pay adjustment to date	Code	Total pay adjustment to date	Code	Total pay adjustment to date	Code	Total pay adjustment to date	Code	Total pay adjustment to date
	£		£		£		£		£		£		£		£		£
0	**NIL**																
1	0.37	**61**	11.91	**121**	23.45	**181**	34.99	**241**	46.52	**301**	58.06	**351**	67.68	**401**	77.29	**451**	86.91
2	0.56	**62**	12.10	**122**	23.64	**182**	35.18	**242**	46.72	**302**	58.25	**352**	67.87	**402**	77.49	**452**	87.10
3	0.75	**63**	12.29	**123**	23.83	**183**	35.37	**243**	46.91	**303**	58.45	**353**	68.06	**403**	77.68	**453**	87.29
4	0.95	**64**	12.49	**124**	24.02	**184**	35.56	**244**	47.10	**304**	58.64	**354**	68.25	**404**	77.87	**454**	87.49
5	1.14	**65**	12.68	**125**	24.22	**185**	35.75	**245**	47.29	**305**	58.83	**355**	68.45	**405**	78.06	**455**	87.68
6	1.33	**66**	12.87	**126**	24.41	**186**	35.95	**246**	47.49	**306**	59.02	**356**	68.64	**406**	78.25	**456**	87.87
7	1.52	**67**	13.06	**127**	24.60	**187**	36.14	**247**	47.68	**307**	59.22	**357**	68.83	**407**	78.45	**457**	88.06
8	1.72	**68**	13.25	**128**	24.79	**188**	36.33	**248**	47.87	**308**	59.41	**358**	69.02	**408**	78.64	**458**	88.25
9	1.91	**69**	13.45	**129**	24.99	**189**	36.52	**249**	48.06	**309**	59.60	**359**	69.22	**409**	78.83	**459**	88.45
10	2.10	**70**	13.64	**130**	25.18	**190**	36.72	**250**	48.25	**310**	59.79	**360**	69.41	**410**	79.02	**460**	88.64
11	2.29	**71**	13.83	**131**	25.37	**191**	36.91	**251**	48.45	**311**	59.99	**361**	69.60	**411**	79.22	**461**	88.83
12	2.49	**72**	14.02	**132**	25.56	**192**	37.10	**252**	48.64	**312**	60.18	**362**	69.79	**412**	79.41	**462**	89.02
13	2.68	**73**	14.22	**133**	25.75	**193**	37.29	**253**	48.83	**313**	60.37	**363**	69.99	**413**	79.60	**463**	89.22
14	2.87	**74**	14.41	**134**	25.95	**194**	37.49	**254**	49.02	**314**	60.56	**364**	70.18	**414**	79.79	**464**	89.41
15	3.06	**75**	14.60	**135**	26.14	**195**	37.68	**255**	49.22	**315**	60.75	**365**	70.37	**415**	79.99	**465**	89.60
16	3.25	**76**	14.79	**136**	26.33	**196**	37.87	**256**	49.41	**316**	60.95	**366**	70.56	**416**	80.18	**466**	89.79
17	3.45	**77**	14.99	**137**	26.52	**197**	38.06	**257**	49.60	**317**	61.14	**367**	70.75	**417**	80.37	**467**	89.99
18	3.64	**78**	15.18	**138**	26.72	**198**	38.25	**258**	49.79	**318**	61.33	**368**	70.95	**418**	80.56	**468**	90.18
19	3.83	**79**	15.37	**139**	26.91	**199**	38.45	**259**	49.99	**319**	61.52	**369**	71.14	**419**	80.75	**469**	90.37
20	4.02	**80**	15.56	**140**	27.10	**200**	38.64	**260**	50.18	**320**	61.72	**370**	71.33	**420**	80.95	**470**	90.56
21	4.22	**81**	15.75	**141**	27.29	**201**	38.83	**261**	50.37	**321**	61.91	**371**	71.52	**421**	81.14	**471**	90.75
22	4.41	**82**	15.95	**142**	27.49	**202**	39.02	**262**	50.56	**322**	62.10	**372**	71.72	**422**	81.33	**472**	90.95
23	4.60	**83**	16.14	**143**	27.68	**203**	39.22	**263**	50.75	**323**	62.29	**373**	71.91	**423**	81.52	**473**	91.14
24	4.79	**84**	16.33	**144**	27.87	**204**	39.41	**264**	50.95	**324**	62.49	**374**	72.10	**424**	81.72	**474**	91.33
25	4.99	**85**	16.52	**145**	28.06	**205**	39.60	**265**	51.14	**325**	62.68	**375**	72.29	**425**	81.91	**475**	91.52
26	5.18	**86**	16.72	**146**	28.25	**206**	39.79	**266**	51.33	**326**	62.87	**376**	72.49	**426**	82.10	**476**	91.72
27	5.37	**87**	16.91	**147**	28.45	**207**	39.99	**267**	51.52	**327**	63.06	**377**	72.68	**427**	82.29	**477**	91.91
28	5.56	**88**	17.10	**148**	28.64	**208**	40.18	**268**	51.72	**328**	63.25	**378**	72.87	**428**	82.49	**478**	92.10
29	5.75	**89**	17.29	**149**	28.83	**209**	40.37	**269**	51.91	**329**	63.45	**379**	73.06	**429**	82.68	**479**	92.29
30	5.95	**90**	17.49	**150**	29.02	**210**	40.56	**270**	52.10	**330**	63.64	**380**	73.25	**430**	82.87	**480**	92.49
31	6.14	**91**	17.68	**151**	29.22	**211**	40.75	**271**	52.29	**331**	63.83	**381**	73.45	**431**	83.06	**481**	92.68
32	6.33	**92**	17.87	**152**	29.41	**212**	40.95	**272**	52.49	**332**	64.02	**382**	73.64	**432**	83.25	**482**	92.87
33	6.52	**93**	18.06	**153**	29.60	**213**	41.14	**273**	52.68	**333**	64.22	**383**	73.83	**433**	83.45	**483**	93.06
34	6.72	**94**	18.25	**154**	29.79	**214**	41.33	**274**	52.87	**334**	64.41	**384**	74.02	**434**	83.64	**484**	93.25
35	6.91	**95**	18.45	**155**	29.99	**215**	41.52	**275**	53.06	**335**	64.60	**385**	74.22	**435**	83.83	**485**	93.45
36	7.10	**96**	18.64	**156**	30.18	**216**	41.72	**276**	53.25	**336**	64.79	**386**	74.41	**436**	84.02	**486**	93.64
37	7.29	**97**	18.83	**157**	30.37	**217**	41.91	**277**	53.45	**337**	64.99	**387**	74.60	**437**	84.22	**487**	93.83
38	7.49	**98**	19.02	**158**	30.56	**218**	42.10	**278**	53.64	**338**	65.18	**388**	74.79	**438**	84.41	**488**	94.02
39	7.68	**99**	19.22	**159**	30.75	**219**	42.29	**279**	53.83	**339**	65.37	**389**	74.99	**439**	84.60	**489**	94.22
40	7.87	**100**	19.41	**160**	30.95	**220**	42.49	**280**	54.02	**340**	65.56	**390**	75.18	**440**	84.79	**490**	94.41
41	8.06	**101**	19.60	**161**	31.14	**221**	42.68	**281**	54.22	**341**	65.75	**391**	75.37	**441**	84.99	**491**	94.60
42	8.25	**102**	19.79	**162**	31.33	**222**	42.87	**282**	54.41	**342**	65.95	**392**	75.56	**442**	85.18	**492**	94.79
43	8.45	**103**	19.99	**163**	31.52	**223**	43.06	**283**	54.60	**343**	66.14	**393**	75.75	**443**	85.37	**493**	94.99

Code	Total pay adjustment to date	Code	Total pay adjustment to date	Code	Total pay adjustment to date	Code	Total pay adjustment to date	Code	Total pay adjustment to date	Code	Total pay adjustment to date	Code	Total pay adjustment to date	Code	Total pay adjustment to date	Code	Total pay adjustment to date
	£		£		£		£		£		£		£		£		£
44	8.64	**104**	20.18	**164**	31.72	**224**	43.25	**284**	54.79	**344**	66.33	**394**	75.95	**444**	85.56	**494**	95.18
45	8.83	**105**	20.37	**165**	31.91	**225**	43.45	**285**	54.99	**345**	66.52	**395**	76.14	**445**	85.75	**495**	95.37
46	9.02	**106**	20.56	**166**	32.10	**226**	43.64	**286**	55.18	**346**	66.72	**396**	76.33	**446**	85.95	**496**	95.56
47	9.22	**107**	20.75	**167**	32.29	**227**	43.83	**287**	55.37	**347**	66.91	**397**	76.52	**447**	86.14	**497**	95.75
48	9.41	**108**	20.95	**168**	32.49	**228**	44.02	**288**	55.56	**348**	67.10	**398**	76.72	**448**	86.33	**498**	95.95
49	9.60	**109**	21.14	**169**	32.68	**229**	44.22	**289**	55.75	**349**	67.29	**399**	76.91	**449**	86.52	**499**	96.14
50	9.79	**110**	21.33	**170**	32.87	**230**	44.41	**290**	55.95	**350**	67.49	**400**	77.10	**450**	86.72	**500**	96.33
51	9.99	**111**	21.52	**171**	33.06	**231**	44.60	**291**	56.14								
52	10.18	**112**	21.72	**172**	33.25	**232**	44.79	**292**	56.33								
53	10.37	**113**	21.91	**173**	33.45	**233**	44.99	**293**	56.52								
54	10.56	**114**	22.10	**174**	33.64	**234**	45.18	**294**	56.72								
55	10.75	**115**	22.29	**175**	33.83	**235**	45.37	**295**	56.91								
56	10.95	**116**	22.49	**176**	34.02	**236**	45.56	**296**	57.10								
57	11.14	**117**	22.68	**177**	34.22	**237**	45.75	**297**	57.29								
58	11.33	**118**	22.87	**178**	34.41	**238**	45.95	**298**	57.49								
59	11.52	**119**	23.06	**179**	34.60	**239**	46.14	**299**	57.68								
60	11.72	**120**	23.25	**180**	34.79	**240**	46.33	**300**	57.87								

Pay adjustment where code exceeds 500

Where the code is in the range 501 to 1000 inclusive proceed as follows:

a. Subtract **500** from the code and use the balance of the code to obtain a pay adjustment figure from the table above.

b. Add this pay adjustment figure to the figure given in the box alongside to obtain the figure of total pay adjustment to date **£ 96.16**

A (NIC) 6 April 1995 to 5 April 1996

Weekly table for not contracted-out standard rate contributions

Earnings on which employee's contributions payable Ia	Total of employee's and employer's contributions payable Ib	Employee's contributions payable Ic	Employer's contributions*
£	£	£	£
138	16.13	9.21	6.92
139	16.28	9.31	6.97
140	16.43	9.41	7.02
141	16.58	9.51	7.07
142	16.73	9.61	7.12
143	16.88	9.71	7.17
144	17.03	9.81	7.22
145	17.18	9.91	7.27
146	17.33	10.01	7.32
147	17.48	10.11	7.37
148	17.63	10.21	7.42
149	17.78	10.31	7.47
150	20.94	10.41	10.53
151	21.11	10.51	10.60
152	21.28	10.61	10.67
153	21.45	10.71	10.74
154	21.62	10.81	10.81
155	21.79	10.91	10.88
156	21.96	11.01	10.95
157	22.13	11.11	11.02

Earnings on which employee's contributions payable Ia	Total of employee's and employer's contributions payable Ib	Employee's contributions payable Ic	Employer's contributions*
£	£	£	£
158	22.30	11.21	11.09
159	22.47	11.31	11.16
160	22.64	11.41	11.23
161	22.81	11.51	11.30
162	22.98	11.61	11.37
163	23.15	11.71	11.44
164	23.32	11.81	11.51
165	23.49	11.91	11.58
166	23.66	12.01	11.65
167	23.83	12.11	11.72
168	24.00	12.21	11.79
169	24.17	12.31	11.86
170	24.34	12.41	11.93
171	24.51	12.51	12.00
172	24.68	12.61	12.07
173	24.85	12.71	12.14
174	25.02	12.81	12.21
175	25.19	12.91	12.28
176	25.36	13.01	12.35
177	25.53	13.11	12.42

Earnings on which employee's contributions payable la	Total of employee's and employer's contributions payable lb	Employee's contributions payable lc	Employer's contributions*
£	£	£	£
178	25.70	13.21	12.49
179	25.87	13.31	12.56
180	26.04	13.41	12.63
181	26.21	13.51	12.70
182	26.38	13.61	12.77
183	26.55	13.71	12.84
184	26.72	13.81	12.91
185	26.89	13.91	12.98
186	27.06	14.01	13.05
187	27.23	14.11	13.12
188	27.40	14.21	13.19
189	27.57	14.31	13.26
190	27.74	14.41	13.33
191	27.91	14.51	13.40
192	28.08	14.61	13.47
193	28.25	14.71	13.54
194	28.42	14.81	13.61
195	28.59	14.91	13.68
196	28.76	15.01	13.75
197	28.93	15.11	13.82
198	29.10	15.21	13.89
199	29.27	15.31	13.96
200	29.44	15.41	14.03
201	29.61	15.51	14.10
202	29.78	15.61	14.17
203	29.95	15.71	14.24
204	30.12	15.81	14.31
205	36.87	15.91	20.96
206	37.07	16.01	21.06
207	37.27	16.11	21.16
208	37.48	16.21	21.27
209	37.68	16.31	21.37
210	37.88	16.41	21.47
211	38.08	16.51	21.57
212	38.28	16.61	21.67
213	38.49	16.71	21.78
214	38.69	16.81	21.88
215	38.89	16.91	21.98
216	39.09	17.01	22.08
217	39.29	17.11	22.18

Earnings on which employee's contributions payable la	Total of employee's and employer's contributions payable lb	Employee's contributions payable lc	Employer's contributions*
£	£	£	£
218	39.50	17.21	22.29
219	39.70	17.31	22.39
220	39.90	17.41	22.49
221	40.10	17.51	22.59
222	40.30	17.61	22.69
223	40.51	17.71	22.80
224	40.71	17.81	22.90
225	40.91	17.91	23.00
226	41.11	18.01	23.10
227	41.31	18.11	23.20
228	41.52	18.21	23.31
229	41.72	18.31	23.41
230	41.92	18.41	23.51
231	42.12	18.51	23.61
232	42.32	18.61	23.71
233	42.53	18.71	23.82
234	42.73	18.81	23.92
235	42.93	18.91	24.02
236	43.13	19.01	24.12
237	43.33	19.11	24.22
238	43.54	19.21	24.33
239	43.74	19.31	24.43
240	43.94	19.41	24.53
241	44.14	19.51	24.63
242	44.34	19.61	24.73
243	44.55	19.71	24.84
244	44.75	19.81	24.94
245	44.95	19.91	25.04
246	45.15	20.01	25.14
247	45.35	20.11	25.24
248	45.56	20.21	25.35
249	45.76	20.31	25.45
250	45.96	20.41	25.55
251	46.16	20.51	25.65
252	46.36	20.61	25.75
253	46.57	20.71	25.86
254	46.77	20.81	25.96
255	46.97	20.91	26.06
256	47.17	21.01	26.16
257	47.37	21.11	26.26

* for information only – do not enter on P11

Table B
(Tax at 24%)

Tax Due on Taxable Pay from £1 to £99			
Total TAXABLE PAY to date	Total TAX DUE to date	Total TAXABLE PAY to date	Total TAX DUE to date
£	£	£	£
1	0.24	**46**	11.04
2	0.48	**47**	11.28
3	0.72	**48**	11.52
4	0.96	**49**	11.76
5	1.20	**50**	12.00
6	1.44	**51**	12.24
7	1.68	**52**	12.48
8	1.92	**53**	12.72
9	2.16	**54**	12.96
10	2.40	**55**	13.20
11	2.64	**56**	13.44
12	2.88	**57**	13.68
13	3.12	**58**	13.92
14	3.36	**59**	14.16
15	3.60	**60**	14.40
16	3.84	**61**	14.64
17	4.08	**62**	14.88
18	4.32	**63**	15.12
19	4.56	**64**	15.36
20	4.80	**65**	15.60
21	5.04	**66**	15.84
22	5.28	**67**	16.08
23	5.52	**68**	16.32
24	5.76	**69**	16.56
25	6.00	**70**	16.80
26	6.24	**71**	17.04
27	6.48	**72**	17.28
28	6.72	**73**	17.52
29	6.96	**74**	17.76
30	7.20	**75**	18.00
31	7.44	**76**	18.24
32	7.68	**77**	18.48
33	7.92	**78**	18.72
34	8.16	**79**	18.96
35	8.40	**80**	19.20
36	8.64	**81**	19.44
37	8.88	**82**	19.68
38	9.12	**83**	19.92
39	9.36	**84**	20.16
40	9.60	**85**	20.40
41	9.84	**86**	20.64
42	10.08	**87**	20.88
43	10.32	**88**	21.12
44	10.56	**89**	21.36
45	10.80	**90**	21.60

Tax Due on Taxable Pay from £100 to £25,500							
Total TAXABLE PAY to date	Total TAX DUE to date	Total TAXABLE PAY to date	Total TAX DUE to date	Total TAXABLE PAY to date	Total TAX DUE to date	Total TAXABLE PAY to date	Total TAX DUE to date
£	£	£	£	£	£	£	£
100	24.00	**4600**	1104.00	**9100**	2184.00	**13600**	3264.00
200	48.00	**4700**	1128.00	**9200**	2208.00	**13700**	3288.00
300	72.00	**4800**	1152.00	**9300**	2232.00	**13800**	3312.00
400	96.00	**4900**	1176.00	**9400**	2256.00	**13900**	3336.00
500	120.00	**5000**	1200.00	**9500**	2280.00	**14000**	3360.00
600	144.00	**5100**	1224.00	**9600**	2304.00	**14100**	3384.00
700	168.00	**5200**	1248.00	**9700**	2328.00	**14200**	3408.00
800	192.00	**5300**	1272.00	**9800**	2352.00	**14300**	3432.00
900	216.00	**5400**	1296.00	**9900**	2376.00	**14400**	3456.00
1000	240.00	**5500**	1320.00	**10000**	2400.00	**14500**	3480.00
1100	264.00	**5600**	1344.00	**10100**	2424.00	**14600**	3504.00
1200	288.00	**5700**	1368.00	**10200**	2448.00	**14700**	3528.00
1300	312.00	**5800**	1392.00	**10300**	2472.00	**14800**	3552.00
1400	336.00	**5900**	1416.00	**10400**	2496.00	**14900**	3576.00
1500	360.00	**6000**	1440.00	**10500**	2520.00	**15000**	3600.00
1600	384.00	**6100**	1464.00	**10600**	2544.00	**15100**	3624.00
1700	408.00	**6200**	1488.00	**10700**	2568.00	**15200**	3648.00
1800	432.00	**6300**	1512.00	**10800**	2592.00	**15300**	3672.00
1900	456.00	**6400**	1536.00	**10900**	2616.00	**15400**	3696.00
2000	480.00	**6500**	1560.00	**11000**	2640.00	**15500**	3720.00
2100	504.00	**6600**	1584.00	**11100**	2664.00	**15600**	3744.00
2200	528.00	**6700**	1608.00	**11200**	2688.00	**15700**	3768.00
2300	552.00	**6800**	1632.00	**11300**	2712.00	**15800**	3792.00
2400	576.00	**6900**	1656.00	**11400**	2736.00	**15900**	3816.00
2500	600.00	**7000**	1680.00	**11500**	2760.00	**16000**	3840.00
2600	624.00	**7100**	1704.00	**11600**	2784.00	**16100**	3864.00
2700	648.00	**7200**	1728.00	**11700**	2808.00	**16200**	3888.00
2800	672.00	**7300**	1752.00	**11800**	2832.00	**16300**	3912.00
2900	696.00	**7400**	1776.00	**11900**	2856.00	**16400**	3936.00
3000	720.00	**7500**	1800.00	**12000**	2880.00	**16500**	3960.00
3100	744.00	**7600**	1824.00	**12100**	2904.00	**16600**	3984.00
3200	768.00	**7700**	1848.00	**12200**	2928.00	**16700**	4008.00
3300	792.00	**7800**	1872.00	**12300**	2952.00	**16800**	4032.00
3400	816.00	**7900**	1896.00	**12400**	2976.00	**16900**	4056.00
3500	840.00	**8000**	1920.00	**12500**	3000.00	**17000**	4080.00
3600	864.00	**8100**	1944.00	**12600**	3024.00	**17100**	4104.00
3700	888.00	**8200**	1968.00	**12700**	3048.00	**17200**	4128.00
3800	912.00	**8300**	1992.00	**12800**	3072.00	**17300**	4152.00
3900	936.00	**8400**	2016.00	**12900**	3096.00	**17400**	4176.00
4000	960.00	**8500**	2040.00	**13000**	3120.00	**17500**	4200.00
4100	984.00	**8600**	2064.00	**13100**	3144.00	**17600**	4224.00
4200	1008.00	**8700**	2088.00	**13200**	3168.00	**17700**	4248.00
4300	1032.00	**8800**	2112.00	**13300**	3192.00	**17800**	4272.00
4400	1056.00	**8900**	2136.00	**13400**	3216.00	**17900**	4296.00
4500	1080.00	**9000**	2160.00	**13500**	3240.00	**18000**	4320.00

Tax Due on Taxable Pay from £1 to £99

Total TAXABLE PAY to date	Total TAX DUE to date	Total TAXABLE PAY to date	Total TAX DUE to date
£	£	£	£
91	21.84	**96**	23.04
92	22.08	**97**	23.28
93	22.32	**98**	23.52
94	22.56	**99**	23.76
95	22.80		

Where the exact amount of taxable pay is not shown, add together the figures for two (or more) entries to make up the amount of taxable pay to the nearest £1 below

Tax Due on Taxable Pay from £100 to £25,500

Total TAXABLE PAY to date	Total TAX DUE to date	Total TAXABLE PAY to date	Total TAX DUE to date	Total TAXABLE PAY to date	Total TAX DUE to date	Total TAXABLE PAY to date	Total TAX DUE to date
£	£	£	£	£	£	£	£
18100	4344.00	**20100**	4824.00	**22100**	5304.00	**24100**	5784.00
18200	4368.00	**20200**	4848.00	**22200**	5328.00	**24200**	5808.00
18300	4392.00	**20300**	4872.00	**22300**	5352.00	**24300**	5832.00
18400	4416.00	**20400**	4896.00	**22400**	5376.00	**24400**	5856.00
18500	4440.00	**20500**	4920.00	**22500**	5400.00	**24500**	5880.00
18600	4464.00	**20600**	4944.00	**22600**	5424.00	**24600**	5904.00
18700	4488.00	**20700**	4968.00	**22700**	5448.00	**24700**	5928.00
18800	4512.00	**20800**	4992.00	**22800**	5472.00	**24800**	5952.00
18900	4536.00	**20900**	5016.00	**22900**	5496.00	**24900**	5976.00
19000	4560.00	**21000**	5040.00	**23000**	5520.00	**25000**	6000.00
19100	4584.00	**21100**	5064.00	**23100**	5544.00	**25100**	6024.00
19200	4608.00	**21200**	5088.00	**23200**	5568.00	**25200**	6048.00
19300	4632.00	**21300**	5112.00	**23300**	5592.00	**25300**	6072.00
19400	4656.00	**21400**	5136.00	**23400**	5616.00	**25400**	6096.00
19500	4680.00	**21500**	5160.00	**23500**	5640.00	**25500**	6120.00
19600	4704.00	**21600**	5184.00	**23600**	5664.00		
19700	4728.00	**21700**	5208.00	**23700**	5688.00		
19800	4752.00	**21800**	5232.00	**23800**	5712.00		
19900	4776.00	**21900**	5256.00	**23900**	5736.00		
20000	4800.00	**22000**	5280.00	**24000**	5760.00		

Table B Subtraction Tables (Lower Rate Relief)

Do not use the subtraction tables for code BR.

For all ordinary suffix codes and prefix K codes – When you have used the table to work out the tax at 24% refer to the tables below to give the benefit of the lower rate band. Find the week or month in which the pay day falls (it is the same week or month you have used in Tables A) and subtract the amount shown to arrive at the tax due.

There is an example below

Employee paid at Weekly rates

Week No.	Amount to subtract
	£
1	3.00
2	6.00
3	9.00
4	12.00
5	15.00
6	18.00
7	21.00
8	24.00
9	27.00
10	30.00
11	33.00
12	36.00
13	39.00
14	42.00
15	45.00
16	48.00
17	51.00
18	54.00
19	57.00
20	60.00
21	63.00
22	66.00
23	69.00
24	72.00
25	75.00
26	78.00

Employee paid at Weekly rates

Week No.	Amount to subtract
	£
27	81.00
28	84.00
29	87.00
30	90.00
31	93.00
32	96.00
33	99.00
34	102.00
35	105.00
36	108.00
37	111.00
38	114.00
39	117.00
40	120.00
41	123.00
42	126.00
43	129.00
44	132.00
45	135.00
46	138.00
47	141.00
48	144.00
49	147.00
50	150.00
51	153.00
52	156.00

Employee paid at Monthly rates

Month No.	Amount to subtract
	£
1	13.00
2	26.00
3	39.00
4	52.00
5	65.00
6	78.00
7	91.00
8	104.00
9	117.00
10	130.00
11	143.00
12	156.00

Use of Table B *Example 1*

Employee's code is **376L**
The payment is made in **Week 7**

Pay in the week	£ 200
Previous pay to date	£1200
Total pay to date	£1400
Less free pay in Week 7 (from Table A)	£ 507.43
Total taxable pay to date	**£ 892.57**

The tax is worked out by first looking in Table B for the nearest round figure below £892

		Tax due
It is	£800	£192.00
Look in the shaded columns for the remainder	£ 92	£ 22.08
Totals	£892	£214.08
Then give the Lower Rate Relief by looking in the table on this page for Week 7 and subtract the amount from the tax due. It is		£ 21.00
Total tax due to date		**£193.08**

Answers

Chapter 1 What is accounting?

1 Accounting involves the collection, recording and analysis of financial information for the purpose of better control and organisation of a business.

2 1) Identifying and recording 2) Classifying and measuring; 3) Communicating and explaining.

3 Accounting records all financial transactions including income and expenditure, customers who owe the business money, money owed to suppliers and other creditors, receipts and payments through the bank, etc.

4 a) All parties would want to know whether a business was profitable but especially owners, managers, employees, Government and financial institutions like the banks.
b) The Government; the Customs & Excise for Vat and the Inland Revenue for taxes.
c) Management need accounting information to help them organise and control the business and to enable them to make better, more informed decisions.

5 Book-keeping is the primary part of financial accounting and is concerned with keeping accurate up-to-date records such as sales, purchases, bank, cash, wages, advertising and all other accounts.

6 Financial accounting is concerned with the book-keeping side of business and the communication of it to those interested parties as seen in Fig. 1.1 such as preparing the profit and loss account and balance sheet. Cost and management accounting seeks to analyse, evaluate and interpret data to improve management decision-making.

7 Accountants could work in private practice, preparing accounts for clients, offering tax advice, etc., they could operate within a company helping to manage the organisation, or take up specialised posts in auditing and tax, or work in the private or public sectors of business in a variety of posts.

8 Accounting could be seen as two-fold: financial accounting is to provide historical information, that is, data which is recorded on a day-to-day basis and is used to prepare the financial statements such as the profit and loss account and balance sheet which interests a wide number of users. Secondly, cost and management accounting is aimed at internal management for the purpose of planning, controlling and making decisions, rather than for external users of financial information.

Chapter 2 Types of business organisations

1 The private sector is in the hands of individuals, e.g. sole traders, whereas in the public sector, the activity is in the hands of Government at various levels.

2 a) sole trader; b) plc; c) partnership.

3 Larger input of capital, shared control and responsibility, wider expertise and experience, etc.

4 The initial capital invested. A sole trader is unlikely to have the finances required to set up a plc.

5 a) £m1092.9; b) £m770.9; c) £m1092.9; d) figures in millions;
e) capital 770.9 = assets 1092.9 – liabilities 322.

6 £30 billion on education and science; £69 billion on income tax.

7 This tax is similar to the former rating system where local rates are raised on the basis of the value of the dwelling. Dwellings are residences under different bands, A, B, C, etc.

8 The Conservative Party has largely privatised many former nationalised industries such as gas, electricity, water, etc.

Chapter 3 Sources of finance

1 The owner or owners personal investment capital and borrowed capital from a bank or other source. The accounting equation: C = A – L indicates that the owner is worth the difference between the assets of the business less its liabilities (borrowed capital).

2 Loans, including bank overdrafts, creditors, debentures.

3 An overdraft is usually required for day-to-day running costs whereas a bank loan could serve a specific purpose such as buying a vehicle or equipment.

4 A share is part of the owners' capital; debentures are liabilities and are part of borrowed or loan capital.

5 a) interest £2250 b) yes (not like shares, interest on loans must be paid c) yes, debentures can be bought and sold through the stock exchange.

6 a) It may not have sufficient financial resources to do so or it may have alternative plans to use its funds. By lease/hire it does not need to worry about repairs or maintenance.
b) If customers do not pay quickly enough, the company may become short of funds, this being overcome by a factoring company who will buy its invoices.

7 Difficult to raise large sums of borrowed capital and profits are usually used up by the owners as withdrawals from the business.

8 A plc can ask the public to buy its shares and millions could be raised as share capital. With this larger equity, it is possible for them to raise large sums as borrowed capital from banks or other institutions.

Chapter 4 The basic principles of business accounting systems

1 Identifying and recording, classifying and measuring and communicating and explaining. The journal is the first stage in the process, entering transactions to facilitate posting to the ledgers.

2 a) The five groups of accounts refer to: revenue, expenses, capital, assets and liabilities.
b) Customers recorded in the sales ledger, suppliers in the purchase ledger and all other accounts in the nominal ledger.
c) Revenue and expense accounts.
d) Capital, assets and liability accounts.

3 a) £88 000, b) £24 000, c) £89 800, d) £2 400
a) £3 000, b) £56 000, c) £24 140

4 Because of the accounting equation: C = A-L, whatever the difference between assets and liabilities will be the value of capital. This is a result of the dual aspect of recording.

5

	Capital	=	Assets	–	Liabilities
a)	5000	=	5000	–	0
b)	5000	=	5000	–	0
c)	5000	=	7000	–	2000
d)	4800	=	6800	–	2000
e)	4800	=	10200	–	5400
f)	4800	=	9700	–	4900
g)	4800	=	8950	–	4150

6 a) Capital £17 740, assets £72 875, liabilities £55 135. Capital £15 000 + profit £4 000 – drawings £1 260
b) stock would lose value and profit would fall.

7 a) Capital £30 000, assets £50 050, liabilities £20 050
b) C £30 000 = A £50 050 – L £20 050

8 Capital £40 000, assets £79 745, liabilities £39 745, capital £35 000 + profit £10 000 – drawings £5 000

9 a) Capital £47 000, assets £89 000, liabilities £42 000, capital £40 000 + profit £7 000
b) C = A – L

10 a) Capital (1/1) £2 449 – net loss and drawings £676 = £1 773
b) capital (31/12) £1 773, assets £7 286, liabilities £5 513 = £1 773

11 a) Gross profit £16 430, expenses £15 640, net profit £790
b) Net profit £790 added to capital
c) Capital £10 000 + profit £790 – drawings £500 = £10 290

12 a) Gross profit £74 900, net profit £22 360
b) wages, salaries £28 340
c) C £30 500 = A £52 800 – L £22 300
d) profit £22 360 – drawings £12 360 is an increase of £10 000 in capital

Chapter 5 How transactions are recorded in accounts

1 Place transactions into correct accounts; allocate to correct groups; place into correct debit or credit side of account.

2 Revenue, capital and liabilities: credit increases, debit decreases; assets and expenses: debit increases, credit decreases

3

2	Equipment	+ asset	dr equip	550
	Bank	– asset	cr bank	550
3	Van	+ asset	dr van	2 600
	Bank	– asset	cr bank	2 600
4	Purchases	+ expense	dr purchases	850
	Bank	– asset	cr bank	850
5	Purchases	+ expense	dr purchases	400
	T Jones	+ liability	cr T Jones	400
6	Bank	+ asset	dr bank	250
	Sales	+ revenue	cr sales	250
7	Baker	+ asset	dr Baker	220
	Sales	+ revenue	cr sales	220
8	Rent	+ expense	dr rent	450
	Bank	– asset	cr bank	450

Trial balance totals 5870: bank 800, equipment 550, van 2600, purchases 1250, rent 450, Baker 220 debits;
capital 5000, sales 470, Jones 400 credits.

4 a) Bank 4000 (A) debit, capital 4000 (C) credit
b) Equipment 550 (A) debit, bank 550 (asset) credit
c) Bank 2500 (A) debit, bank loan 2500 (L) credit
d) Van (A) 1000 debit, bank 200 (A) credit, Harry's 800 (L) credit
e) Equipment (A) 2000 debit, Hardwick's 2000 (L) credit
f) Premises 2500 (A) debit, bank (A) 2500 credit
g) Premises 25000 (A) debit, mortgage (L) credit
h) Fixtures 150 (A) debit, bank 150 (A) credit
i) Hardwick 500 (L) debit, bank 500 (A) credit
j) Van 875 (A) debit, bank 875 (A) credit
k) Bank loan 125 (L) debit, bank 125 (A) credit
l) Harry's 100 (L) debit, bank 100 (A) credit
Note: Bank balance 1500

5 a) Purchases 1500 (E) debit, Arrowsmith 1500 (L) credit
b) Purchases 650 (E) debit, bank 650 (A) credit
c) Purchases 880 (E) debit, Jones 880 (L) credit
d) James 420 (A) debit, sales (R) 420 credit
e) Harris 300 (A) debit, sales (R) 300 credit
f) Bank 365 (A) debit, sales (R) 365 credit
g) Purchases 2000 (E) debit, Arrowsmith 2000 (L) credit
h) Rent 250 (E) debit, bank (A) 250 credit

i) Overheads 150 (E) debit, bank (A) 150 credit
j) Arrowsmith 500 (L) debit, bank (A) 500 credit
k) Purchases 850 (E) debit, bank (A) 850 credit
l) Bank loan 125 (L) debit, bank (A) 125 credit
m) Arrowsmith 500 (L) debit, bank (A) 500 credit
n) Bank 150 (A) debit, Harris 150 (A) credit

Note: Bank balance 1010 overdrawn and trial balance totals 38 925.

6 Jones: balance c/d 350 debit, b/d 350 credit (creditor), bank: balance c/d 1510 debit, b/d 1510 credit (overdrawn), sales 4775 credit.

7 Trial balance totals: 27600, credits: sales, creditors, loan, interest, capital, all others debits.

8 Trial balance totals: 7175, debits: bank 2255, Baker 100, purchases 4000, rent 125, gen. exps. 80, light, heat 80, advert. 35, van 500, credits: capital 2000, sales 2175, T Smith 3000.

9 Trial balance totals: 7000, debits: van 1500, bank 1080, cash 200, eqpt. 1800, rent 250, purchases 1600, stat. 40, motor exps. 30, gen. exps. 80, W'barrow 297, Smith 90, ret. in 33, credits: capital 3000, HP 900, sales 1220, Steele 250, Daley 400, Land 1080, ret. out 150.

10 Trial balance totals: 6060, debits van 1800, eqpt. 1750, furn. 150, purchases 1595, ret. in 40, Bright 125, Taylor 150, o'hs 250, drawings 200, credits: capital 2200, bank o/d 50, XYZ 1150, Good, 235, Rawlings 960, sales 1405, ret. out 60.

11 Trial balance totals: 4433, debits: van 750, drawings 160, gen. exps. 115, ret. in 44, light, heat 135, Arrowsmith 275, Jones, 236, eqpt. 750, purchases 1968, credits: capital 1550, bank o/d 365, LC Ltd. 520, ret. out 65, Hardcastle 620, sales 1113, Smith 200.

12 Trial balance totals: 3910, debits: David 580, Jones 460, bank 125, purchases 1500, rent 300, wages 125, o'hs. 70, eqpt. 750, credits: capital 650, Robert 650, sales 1010, Andrew 850, Brown 750.

13 Trial balance totals: 28968, debits: drawings 3100, fixtures 2500, stock 2386, purchases 13255, Gibson 555, bank 1828, gen. exps. 5344, credits: capital 7228, sales 21255, Lowe 485.

14 Trial balance totals: 19300, credits: Wells 500, dis. received 200, sales 13000, capital 5600; all other accounts debit.

Chapter 6 Business accounting systems in practice

1
a) Transactions in the journal are for those on credit whereas the cash book is used for cash transactions.
b) Bank reconciliation is the checking of the cash book figures with those of the bank statement.
c) A petty cash book enables the use of cash for relatively small payments such as incidental sta tionery or window cleaning without resorting to the use of cheques.
d) The journal is used for transactions outside the scope of the other journals, eg correcting errors or making adjustments to the accounts.
e) They are used to analyse different sales or purchase categories, eg washing machines and refrigerators and can assist management with stock control and marketing.
f) The trial balance is an arithmetical check on the accuracy of double entry recording in the ledger. The ETB is a kind of worksheet where extra columns are used alongside the trial balance to make adjustments and to extend them to the profit and loss and balance sheet columns.
g) If the trial balance fails to balance the suspense account will provide a temporary balancing facility until the error(s) are located.
h) Some bills may still be unpaid and need to be included so that a correct assessment of profit is made.

2 Their function is to use them as a cross check with the sales and purchase ledgers. The balances of the two control accounts should equal the total balances of the sales and purchase ledgers. If the control accounts confirm the balances of the two ledgers, then the figures are entered in the trial balance to represent debtors and creditors.

3 Interested parties are those persons or organisations interested in financial statements like managers, investors, creditors, employees, Government and so forth. Financial statements refer to the profit and loss account and balance sheet.

4 a) Sales invoices and monies received from customers
b) Purchase invoices and payments made to suppliers
c) The cashier who may also be responsible for the nominal ledger
d) A computerised system has many software programs for all ledgers, stock control, payroll, etc, which has advantages such as instant up date of records, automatic double entry, printouts of accounts, etc
e) Have an effective credit control system to vet and monitor all customers.

Chapter 7 Sales on credit (1): an introduction

1 Units £783, top £57.38, sink £26.8 – 10% = £780.46, labour £240, Vat £178.58 = £1199.04 total.

2 A sales order and then the invoice is raised with the goods.

3 a) quotation: an offer to sell goods at a certain price; sales order: a formal order for goods; b) statement: a monthly account to customers; bank statement: a summary of banking transactions from the bank; c) trade discount: a sum allowed to buyer off the list price; cash discount: a sum offered to a buyer for prompt payment d) carriage forward – customer pays, carriage paid – supplier pays.

4 An invoice is the bill of sale with copies for sales office, accounts, despatch, stores etc.

5 a) Invoice £79.5, b) £71.55, c) £12.52, total £84.07.

6 A statement is the monthly account sent to customers to inform them of how much they owe.

7 a) £84.07 debit, b) £384.87, £473.62, £457.97, £157.17, c) invoices are debit, credit note and cheque are credits.

8 Credit control is the monitoring of debtors in the sales ledger to ensure that customers are credit worthy and pay on time.

9 An aged debtors list 'ages' debts into monthly categories in order to analyse which debts are old and need chasing up.

Chapter 8 Sales on credit (2): the sales journal

1 a) Sales journal: £2260
b) Sales ledger: debit customer's account
c) Sales account credit side.

2 a) Sales journal: sales £1240, Vat £217, total £1457
b) Sales ledger (debits): Goldney £423, Capel £399.5, Carlton £352.5, Wood £432, total debtors £1607. Nominal ledger: sales £1240 Cr, Vat £217 Cr, sales ledger control £1607 Dr.

3 a) Invoice £2167 – £433.4 = £1733.6 + Vat £303.38 = total £2036.98
b) Sales journal: Creese £2036.98, sales £1733.8, Vat £303.38
c) as a cross-checking device with the sales ledger.

4 a) Sales journal: product A £840, B £220, Vat £185.5, total £1245.5
b) Sales ledger (debits) Jones £532, Smith £721, Brown £1262.5
c) Nominal ledger: each sales a/c credit, s/l control a/c debit £2515.5.

5 a) sales £1600, Vat £280 = £1880, b) Davies £575.5, Smith £352.5, Forbes £508, c) control a/c £1436 debit, Vat and sales a/c credit.

6 a) Vat correct, b) sales £1000, Vat £175 = £1175, c) debit: customers in s/l, credit: sales, Vat, debit control a/cs in nominal ledger.

7 a) Vat incorrect, Faldo, read £91, b) golf £1480, cricket £936, tennis £544, Vat £518 = £3478, c) each sales a/c credited, e.g. golf £1480 credit.

Chapter 9 Vat and Vat returns

1 a) Monthly, annually b) Invoice date c) On form Vat 100 as inputs d) After 12 months and written off e) No, only those for business purposes allowed by Vat Office f) As part of the expense, Vat is not separated g) Vat payable on expenses recorded in Vat account as an input.

2 Vat account: debits: £787.5, £1830.5, balance c/d £544.5, credits: £2165, £997.5 balance b/d = £544.5

3 Vat input claimed (5/6) = £243 333 at standard rate = £42 583.

4 Vat outputs £58 590, Vat inputs £41 860, Vat balance = £16 730 Cr.

5 Vat account: debits: 62, 1687, 140, 147, 126, credits: 1270, 119 = balance £127 Cr, Sales £11600 Cr, Purchases £8960 Dr, Eqpt. £840 Dr, Motor vehicle £8850 Dr, Operating exps. £720 Dr.

6 a) Purchases £17500 Dr, sales £25 000 Cr, Vat due £1312.5, debtors £11 125 Dr, creditors £8562 Cr, b) Gross profit £8550

Chapter 10 Purchases on credit (1): an introduction

1 The grn records incoming goods which must be checked in and signed for what has been supplied; only pay for what you get.

2 Can be used for different purposes such as goods being paid before delivery, usually when goods are sent on approval before delivery.

3 The control grid is stamped on incoming invoices to ensure a thorough check is completed and initialled by those authorised.

4 Value £917, carriage £35, Vat £166.59 = £1118.59.

5 Net value £945.00, Vat £157.11 = £1102.11.

6 Ask for credit note £8.26 (to cover Vat discrepancy) or replace invoice with a new one.

7 Tax point is usually the invoice date, showing when the title of the goods passes from supplier to customer; the date is important for the Vat return F100.

Chapter 11 Purchases on credit (2): the purchases journal

1 a) Purchases journal: purchases £1800, Vat £315, total = £2115
b) Purchases ledger: credit creditors
c) Nominal ledger: purchases £1800 Dr, Vat £315 Dr, P/L control £2115 Cr.

2 Purchases journal: purchases £3117, Vat £444.17, P/L control £3561.17.
Invoices corrected: No. 4367, £60.56, 34420, £60.42, 2321, £29.07.

3 a) Invoice: goods £165, Vat £27.43, total £192.43
b) Purchase ledger: Sports Ltd. £192.43 Cr
c) Nominal ledger: purchases £165 Dr, Vat £27.43 Dr.

4 a) Credited in purchase ledger
b) Each purchase account total debited, e.g. Men's shoes account £855 Dr
c) Correct figures, Vat 15%.

5 a) Purchases journal: purchases £2780, Vat £486.5, total £3266.5
b) Purchase ledger (credits) Metro £1210, Auto £1204, Dunlop £352.5
c) P/L control £2566.5 Cr
d) Purchases £2780 Dr, Vat £486.5 Dr.

6 a) Purchases journal: purchases £3365, Vat £504.75, total = £3869.75
b) Purchase ledger: suppliers credited: £1207.5, £1466.25, £1196
c) Nominal ledger: purchases and Vat Dr, P/L control £3869.75 Cr. [Vat at 15%].

7 a) Purchases £2360, Vat £404.59, total £2764.59 (note Slazenger's 5% cash discount)
b) Purchase ledger (credits) Slazenger £619.59, Metre £525.5 Auto £619.5

c) Nominal ledger (debits) purchases £2360, Vat £404.59, P/L control £1764.59 credit.

8 a) Sales invoice £300, Vat £45 = £345; £540, Vat £81 = £621
purchase invoices £312, Vat £46.8 = £358.8; £110, Vat £16.5 = £126.50
b) Sales £840, purchases £312, fittings £110, Vat £62.70 [Vat at 15%].

Chapter 12 The returns journals

1 a) RI journal: returns in £200, Vat £35, total £235
b) Sales ledger (credits) Lewis £70.5, Smith £141, Taylor £23.5
c) Nominal ledger: returns in £200 Dr, Vat £35 Dr, s/l control £235 Cr

2 a) RI journal: returns in £100, Vat £17.5, total £117.5
b) Sales ledger (debits) Lewis £656.5, Smith £968.3, Taylor £377.7
c) Nominal ledger: returns in £875 Dr, Vat £206.5 Cr, s/l control £2002.5 Dr

3 a) RO journal: returns out £180, Vat £31.5, total £211.5
b) Purchase ledger (debits) Slazenger £70.5, Auto £23.5, Metre £117.5
c) Nominal ledger: returns out £180 Cr, Vat £31.5 Cr, P/l control £211.5 Dr.

4 a) RO journal: returns out £174, Vat £30.45, total £204.45
b) Purchase ledger (credits) £814.5, Auto £251.3, Metre £602.75
c) Nominal ledger: returns out £1154 Cr, Vat £254.45 Cr, p/l control £1668.55 Cr

5 a) Purchases journal: purchases £440, Vat £66, total £506
Sales journal: sales £820, Vat £123, total £943
RO journal: returns out, £40, Vat £6, total £46
RI journal: returns in, £20, Vat £3, total £23
Stationery £120, Vat £18, total £138
Office furniture £320, Vat £48, total £368.
b) Nominal ledger: purchases £440 Dr, sales £820 Cr; returns out, £40 Cr; returns in, £20 Dr, Vat £6 Dr, stationery £120 Dr, office furniture £320 Dr.

6 Sales ledger (all debits): Appleby £230, Shuttleworth £320, Vincent £651.
Purchases ledger: Morton £460 Cr, Pierce £180 Cr.

7 a) Purchases journal: total £9500. Sales journal: total £10200
b) Trial balance totals: £47 480
Debits: cash £2658, bank £16 758, fixtures £6200, advertising £56, rent £6000, wages £170, insurance £400, printing and stationery £38, drawings £500, purchases £9500, Redhill £3100, Shaw £1800, returns in £300
Credits: capital £30 000, sales £11480, Green £3000, Black £2500, returns out £500.
c) To help organise accounts more efficiently, particularly if there are many accounts for debtors and creditors.

Chapter 13 Analysed journals

1 a) Sales A (James, Seymour) £440, Sales B (Forster, Simpson) £800, Vat £217 = total £1457
b) debit each customer (s/l), credit sales, Vat and control (n/l).

2 a) Vat £732.54 b) footwear £1862, leisure £1094, sports £1230 = total £4918.54, c) each purchase account is debited, Vat debited, each supplier credited.

3 a) Vat £623.7, b) golf £1840, cricket £1180, tennis £544, total sales £3564, Vat £623.7 = total £4187.7 c) each sales account and Vat account credited, s/l control £4187.7 Dr

4 Totals £1625.4, Vat £205.6, purchases £606, motors £240.9, stat. 91.1, light, heat 357.8, advert. 124.

5 a) Total sales £5930, Vat £1037.75, s/l control £6967.75
b) Jackson £657, Thomson £1520, Illingworth £901, Rocastle £2803, James £1710 debits, s/l control a/c £7591 Dr

Chapter 14 Banking transactions

1 To keep money for safe-keeping, to lend money for overdrafts and loans; in the middle between savers and borrowers, provides a wide variety of services.
2 Deposit account is an investment earning interest. Current account is a business account, using cheques for payment.
3 Cheque to be paid into a bank account.
4 Cash £480.41, other £165.92, total = £646.33.
5 Safety. Regular trips can be observed with criminal intent.
6 DD suitable for irregular payments which may differ in amount and at intervals which may vary. SO for regular fixed sums paid.
7 BGC (credit transfers) convenient for payments through the bank – bills, wages, suppliers. The payee is credited, the drawer debited.
8 Allows cheques to be paid using the bank's money as credit and can temporarily assist working capital difficulties.
9 Bank is free to decide how to use customers money and has a duty to honour cheques and also act with discretion.
10 Your local bank is a mine of financial information. If you were starting a business, there are starter packs to collect.

Chapter 15 The cash book

1 a) Balances b/d: cash £540, bank £2143, discount allowed £25, discount received £45
b) Sales ledger: bank and discount allowed Cr, (e.g. Barnes).
Bought ledger: bank and discount received Dr, (e.g. Rawlings).
2 a) Balances b/d: cash £305, bank £1490, discount allowed £35, discount received £10
b) Nominal ledger: sales £2800 Cr, general expenses £230 Dr.
3 a) Balances b/d: cash £145, bank £2187, discount allowed £28, discount received £44. b) Sales and purchases ledgers: each personal account would have a nil balance.
4 Balances b/d: cash £28, bank £22 Cr (overdrawn), discount received £7.
5 Balance b/d: bank £195 Cr (overdrawn). Totals: discount allowed £20, debtors £1020, sales £1725, bank £3230 (receipts); discount received £30, creditors £1820, drawings £600, wages £240, other expenses £765, bank £3425 (payments).
6 a) Balances b/d: cash £123, bank £291 Cr (overdrawn), discount allowed £5, discount received £9. b) R/D returned to drawer (person who signed cheque). Account may have insufficient funds, cheque not accepted by bank.
7 a) Analysis: wine £830; beer £1030; spirits £290; other sales £134; total £2284. Vat £342.60; bank £2626.60. b) Each sale account credited. c) Better for control and organisation of stocks.
8 a) Balances b/d: cash £85.31, bank £201, discount allowed £50.65, discount received £28.00. b) Sales £863.30 Cr. Salaries £227, Advertising £42.24, Delivery expenses £25.25 and Petty expenses £8.50, all Dr.
9 Discount recd £40.75, creditors £1249.25, stationery £27.23, light £180, tele. £146.50. Wages £1946, drawings £600, sundries £30.64, Vat £50.16, bank £4229.78.

Chapter 16 The bank reconciliation statement

Note: BRS = bank reconciliation statement
1 Bank b/d £2112. BRS £2592 + £615 – £1110 = £2097 (bank).
2 Bank b/d £11 164. BRS £13236 + £716 – £2788 = £11 164 (bank).
3 Bank b/d £697. BRS £3189 + 0 – £2492 = £697 (bank).
4 Bank b/d £563. BRS £590 + £40 – £10 = £620 (bank).

5 Bank b/d £838. BRS £1270 + £210 – £642 = £838 (bank).
It is necessary to reverse procedure from £838 bank to calculate the £1270 bank statement balance.

6 Bank b/d £213. BRS £203 + £39 – £29 = £213 (bank).

7 Bank b/d £285 Cr (overdrawn). BRS £190 Dr (overdrawn) + £528 = £338 – £623 = £285 (bank Cr) overdrawn.

8 a) Bank b/d £2850. BRS £1935 + £1800 – £1535 = £2200 (bank).
Cash book debits: £600 £420 £122; credits: £79, £1353 £90 £200 and £70. b) To ensure that the cash book and bank statement entries cross-check correctly.

9 a) Bank £630 Cr, BRS £893 (overdrawn) – deposits £1215 + unpresented cheques £952 = £630 (overdrawn). Cash book errors: Debits: 426, 500, credits: 840, 19, 23, 215, 99, 1700.

10 Bank b/d £285 (overdrawn). BRS £479 + £46 – £810 = £285 (o/d).

11 Cash book: Debits 142, 8, credits: 1689, 164, 310, 144, 46, balance b/d £2203. BRS £1784 (overdrawn) – deposits £800, + unpresented cheques £2259 – error £1040 = £2203 cash book.

Chapter 17 The petty cash book

1 a) Cash balance £13.33 b) Totals: cleaning £19.58, travel £8, news £3.5 stat. £34.07, post £21.5, refresh. £4.85, Vat £9.37, sundries £10.8, total £111.67, all debits in ledger.

2 Cash balance £22.16, Vat £8.2, post £29.61, travel £32.8, cleaning £31.5, refresh. £23.49, stat. £18.04, sundries £34.2 = £177.84.

3 a) Cash balance £19.25 b) Totals: Vat £8.7, travel £17.63, stat. £17.63, post £10.25, clean £20, refresh. £15.6, sundries £15.94, total £105.75, reimbursement £105.75 as per cash spent.

4 a) Cash balance £12.05. Totals: cleaning £15.66, refresh. £13.70 travel £34.75, post £21.15, Vat £8.89, sundries £43.80, total £137.95 b) each expense is a debit.

5 a) Cash balance £16 b) Totals: stat. £67.09, Vat £12.14, travel £19.55, refresh. £12.45, sundries £22.77, total £134, all debits in ledger.

6 a) £84.35 b) cash balance £38.54. Totals: Vat £5.02, travel £8.35, clean £16.3, post £13.28, stat. £12.4, refresh. £3.76, sundries £2.35, total £61.46 c) each expense total a debit.

7 Cash balance £17.25, Vat £3.94, post £17.2, stat. £26.61, travel £7, cleaning £22.5, sundries £5.5 = £82.75.

Chapter 18 Computer-based accounts

1 Where businesses have relatively large numbers of repetitive transactions, such as sales and purchases, the computer is ideal because information can instantly be stored in memory, updated, analysed and retrieved when required.

2 Keyboard, monitor (screen), disk drive and printer.

3 The software is the 'brains' enabling programs to operate. In accounting, programs available include ledgers, payroll, stock control, invoicing and job costing.

4 A programs menu system offers a range of functions which an operator can use. For example, a sub-section of the sales program, ledger transactions, would have a number of functions such as posting and accounts update, to enable accounts to be processed.

5 You could use the worked example in Chapter 19 to provide the data you need for journal or cash book entries.

6 Check the options compared to a manual system and note how a computer program offers greater analytical information.

7 Small types of businesses, like retailers, who would benefit more by using a cash book or other system to record their takings and expenditure and those enterprises which do not have a sufficient number of accounts of a repetitive nature.

Chapter 19 The accounting system in action: a worked example

Chapter 20 Control accounts

1 a) S/L control: debits £35 000, £36 000, £200, £100, £50 and £200.
Credits: £400, £500, £200, £30 400, £400 and £1000.
Balance £38650 Dr. Sales ledger £39 050. Discrepancy £600. b) P/L control: debits £200, £600, £100, £11 400 and £400.
Credits: £12 000, £24 000, £20 and £100.
Balance £23 420 Cr agrees with purchases ledger. c) Control accounts are used as a cross-checking device. A measure of control is maintained. Totals of debtors and creditors from the control accounts are posted to the trial balance.

2 a) Sales ledger: Durban £893 Dr, Elliott £2122 Dr.
Nominal ledger: sales £2975 Cr, returns in £32 Dr. b) S/L control balance £51138 Dr. c) To cross-check with the personal ledgers.

3 S/L control: £38 324 Dr, £456 Cr.
Sales ledger £38 124. Discrepancy £200.
P/L control: £12 484 Cr, £150 Dr agrees with the purchases ledger.

4 a) S/L control: debits £18 776, £231 and £55, 130 411.
Credits: £3112, £125 050, £460, £661 and £3150.
Balance £17 040 Dr. Sales ledger £16 940. Discrepancy £100.
P/L control: debits £2097, £139 830, £460, £3227, 23188.
Credits: £13 199, £155 603.
Balance £23 188 Cr agrees with purchases ledger. b) Error of £100 could be from any item posted from the subsidiary books such as the journals or cash book.

5 S/L control: debits £41 220, £37 350, £790, £40 and £300.
Credits £500, £27 800, £950, £675 and £800.
Balance £48 975 Dr. Agrees with the sales ledger.

6 P/L control: debits £58 200, £2450, £11 285.
Credits: £6432, £81 360, £125.
Balance £15 982 Cr. Agrees with purchases ledger.

7 a) S/L control: debits £5000, £103 000, £300.
Credits: £81 000, £1500, £400, £200.
Balance £25 200 Dr. Sales ledger £25110. Discrepancy £90. b) P/L control: debits £74 000, £1200, £600.
Credits: £9000, £72 000.
Balance £5200 Cr. Agrees with purchases ledger.

8 S/l control account:debits, balance £35 740, £249 124, £4 020, credits, £188 125, £4 480, £1 235, £800, £3 200, balance c/d £91 044, totals = £288 884. P/l control account: debits, £391 130, £2 850, £1 235, £1 285, £85, balance c/d £77 215, credits, balance £28 480, £445 320, totals = £473 800.

9 S/l control account: debits, balance £160 387.7, returns £11 376.19, disc. £10 419.76, bad debt rec £421.33, credits, disc £25 404.36, cancel prov for bad debts £20 859.22, contras £99 032.54, returns £6 820.24, sales over £2 291.18, c/note £270, balance c/d £27 927.44 totals = £182 604.98 Debtors: balance £86 476.15, less £8 762.44, £49 516.27, £270 = £27 927.44 as per control.

Chapter 21 Introducing final accounts: sole traders

Note: FA = fixed assets. CA = current assets. CL = current liabilities. WC = working capital. LTL = long-term liabilities.

1 a) Gross profit £785, net profit £200. b) FA £17 000, CA £4535, CL £1435, WC £3100, LTL £10 000 = £10 100.
Capital £10 000 + profit £200 – drawings £100 = £10 100.
WC ratio 3.2:1.

2 a) Gross profit £6285, net profit £5230. b) FA £63 150, CA £4720, CL £1180, WC £3540, LTL £42 000 = £24 690.
Capital £20 000 + profit £5230 – drawings £540 = £24 690.
WC ratio 4:1.

3 a) Gross profit £108 300, net profit £67 570. b) FA £56 500, CA £59 700, CL £4230, WC £55 470, LTL £38 000 = £73 970.
Capital £16 600 + profit £67 570 – drawings £10 200 = £73 970.
WC ratio 14:1.

4 a) Gross profit £7535, net loss £1053. b) FA £6225, CA £7252, CL £3580, WC £3672, LTL £4050 = £5847. Capital £11 000 – loss £1053 – drawings £4100 = £5847. c) WC ratio .2:1. A very sound ratio to meet current debts despite net loss of £1053.

5 a) All entries in trial balance correct. Estimated value of closing stock £800. b) Gross profit £13 925, net profit £11 430. FA £34 290, CA £1515, CL £1525, WC (£10), LTL £12 350 = £21 930. Capital £10 500 + profit £11 430 = £21 930.

6 a) Gross profit £7150, net profit £500. FA £61 900, CA £8830, CL £13 055, WC (£4225), LTL £37 175 = £20 500. Capital £20 000 + profit £500 = £20 500. b) 0.68:1 (insolvent).

7 Gross profit £15 820, net profit £6 780, FA £18 100, WC £3 880 = £21 980. Capital £18 000 + profit £6 780 – drawings £2 800 = £21 980.

8 Gross profit £904.88, net loss £240.29, FA £1 225, WC £2 387.48 – LTL £402.77 = £3209.71.
Capital £4050 – net loss £240.29 – drawings £600 = £3209.71

Chapter 22 Adjustments to final accounts

Note: FA = fixed assets. CA = current assets. CL = current liabilities. WC = working capital. LTL = long-term liabilities.

1 a) Gross profit £15 430, net profit £6590. b) FA £8375, CA £13 425, CL £2710, WC £10 715, = £19 090.
Capital £18 000 + profit £6590 – drawings £5500 = £19 090.

2 Gross profit £7770, net profit £1373. FA £15010, CA £33 750, CL £35 587, WC (£1837), insolvent, = £13 173. Capital £16 000 + profit £1373 – drawings £4200 = £13 173.

3 Gross profit £10 000, net profit £8000. FA £73 000, CA £11 670, CL £2670, WC £9000 = £82 000. Capital £80 000 + profit £8000 – drawings £6000 = £82 000.

4 Gross profit £12 500, net profit £7000. FA £72 500, CA £18 200, CL £3700, WC £14 500 = £87 000. Capital £85 000 + profit £7000 – drawings £5000 = £87 000.

5 Rent account: debit £1275, accured c/d £250, credit prepaid c/d £125, P & L account £1400. Debit prepaid b/d £125, credit accrued b/d £250.

6 Gross profit £29 500, net profit £16 400. FA £50 000, CA £6700, CL £3900, WC £2800, LTL £21 000 = £31 800. Capital £20 850 + profit £16 400 – drawings £5450 = £31 800.

7 Gross profit £32 125, net profit £4250. FA £21 500, CA £25 500, CL £18 100, WC £7400 = £28 900. Capital £29 250 + profit £4250 – drawings £4600 = £28 900.

8 Light, heat account: debit £2 800, accrued £750, credit P & L account £3 550. Credit accrued b/d £750. Adjustment: debit prepaid c/d £1500, correct figure to P & L = £2050 (3550 – 1500)

9 Insurance account: debit £3 000 paid, credit prepaid c/d £200, £333, P & L account £2467.

10 Telephone account: debit paid £2646, accrued c/d £560, credit prepaid c/d £130, p & L account £3076, debit prepaid b/d £130, credit accrued b/d £560

Chapter 23 Bad debts and provision for debtors

Note: FA = fixed assets. CA = current assets. CL = current liabilities. WC = working capital. LTL = long-term liabilities.

1 H Smith: Gross profit £4950, net profit £403, FA £1900, WC £4003 = £5903. Capital £8000 + profit £403 – drawings £2500 = £5903

2 S Waugh: Gross profit £150 100, net profit £57 400, FA £89 000, CA £52 740, CL £14 340, WC £38 400 = £127 400, LTL £25 000 = £102 400. Capital £60 000 + profit £57 400 – drawings £15 000 = £102 400

3 Charcoal: bad debts £6370, provision for bad debts £8418 (2558 + 3780 + 2080). P & L account, bad debts provision £8388. Balance sheet, debtors £88 210 – £8418 = £79 792

4 A Farney: Gross profit £57 600, net profit £28 834, FA £66 500, CA £47 124, (debtors £20 974), CL £7550, WC £39 574 = £106 074, LTL £10 000 = £96 074. Capital £75 740 + profit £28 834 – drawings £8500 = £96 074

5 Bradshaw: a) provision 19–4 £5850, 19–5 £5150 b) Provision account: 19–4, credit P & L account £950, balance b/d £5850. 19–5, debit P & L account £700, balance b/d £5150 c) provision increased by 16% in year 1, reduced by 12% year 2 d) debtors = £17 1353

6 Tip Top: a) provision for bad debts a/c, credit £410, debit £168 balance c/d £242 (2% of £12 100), b) debtors £12 360 – £260 – £242 = £11 858 – £716 cr. = £11 142. Creditors £7348 – £654 dr. = £6694. Note: P & L account credit bad debts prov. £168, (Blaney's bad debt recovered £970 does not affect the total of debtors as it is both a debit and credit entry).

Chapter 24 Capital and revenue expenditure

1 a) Group A errors: filing cabinet, petty cash, office desk, chair, drawings.
Group B errors: carriage outwards, advertising, new staples, gun, dividends, transfer to reserve, new light bulbs.
Pocket calculators and painting of building could be classed as either depending on value and time. Both likely to be revenue expenditure items.
b) Profits would either be over- or understated, having the same effect on the assets of the business.

2 Capital expenditure: vehicle, fittings, seats and covers.
Revenue expenditure: tax, insurance, petrol, maintenance, tyre and exhaust (running expenses).
The vehicle at cost may have included tax and insurance as part of capital expenditure.

3 To ensure that the profit and loss statement is 'true and fair' and an accurate reflection of the business activities. If capital expenditure items were treated as revenue expenditure, profits would be understated as would assets. The reverse would be true if revenue items were treated as capital items.

4 a), d), h) capital expenditure, all the rest revenue expenditure.

5 a), b), c), d), e), h), i), k) all capital expenditure, f), g), j), 1) revenue expenditure.

6 a) So that profits are not distored and fixed assets and expenses are correctly valued.
b) profit and fixed assets are under-stated by £2320.

Chapter 25 The depreciation of fixed assets

Note: FA = fixed assets. CA = current assets. CL = current liabilities. WC = working capital. LTL = long-term liabilities.

1 Gross profit £9787, net loss £28 883, FA £125 320, WC £1907 = £127 227. Capital £170 350 – loss £28 883 – drawings £14 240 = £127 227.

2 i) Gross profit £110 615, net profit £16 667, FA £104 400, CA £54 340, CL £26 020, WC £28 320 = £132 720. Capital £131 653 + profit £16 667 – drawings £15 600 = £132 720
ii) Mitchell has ample working capital and could use some funds to expand or improve her business.

3 Gross profit £55 141, net profit £5888, FA £30 300, CA £27 560, CL £6681, WC £20 879 = £51 179. Capital £53 091 + profit £5888 – drawings £7800 = £51 179.

4 Capital £27 908. Gross profit £65 409, net profit £31 632, FA £43 025, CA £15 495, CL £9400, WC £6095 = £49 120. Capital £27 908 + profit £31 632 – drawings £10 420 = £49 120.

5 Gross profit £32 600. Net profit £20 828. (Depreciation £512.)

6 a) Gross profit £130 000, net profit £57 100. b) FA £65 000, CA £181 100, CL £86 500, WC £94 600 = £159 600. Capital £127 500 + profit £57 100 – drawings £25 000 = £159 600.

7 a) Premises £1 500 000 Dr. Plant and machinery £900 000 Dr. Depreciation of plant and machinery £423 500 Cr. Asset disposal a/c £10 000 (P & L a/c). b) Balance sheet: FA £2 400 000 (cost), depreciation £423 500, net value £1 976 500. c) Details of the revaluation such as name of valuers, date valued, basis of valuation.

8 Balances: a) plant £4500 Dr. b) Depreciation of plant £1350, c) Asset disposal a/c £100 (P & L a/c). d) Balance sheet. FA £4500 (cost), depreciation £1350, net value £3150. e) Revaluation and reducing balance methods.

9 a) Stationery: debits £110, £406; credits £125, £391 (P & L).
Rent: debit £768; credits: £96, £96, £576 (P & L).
Provision for bad debts: debits £49, £200 (P & L); credit £249. b) Profit & Loss a/c: stationery £391, rent £576, provision for bad debts £49 (Cr). c) Balance sheet: prepayments–rent £96, stationery £125. Debtors £4000 – provision for bad debts £200, = £3800. Adjustments must be indicated to give a true and fair picture of the accounts for the accounting period.

10 a) Wear and tear, time, obsolescence, depletion, etc.
b) Obsolescence, wear and tear, depletion, n/a, time.
c) To apply the most appropriate method and use it in the most equitable way in relation to the benefit provided by it.
d) To keep control and monitor the cost, depreciation, movement, etc of fixed assets.
e) Prime book of entry to record the purchase/sale of fixed assets as well as other adjustments, etc.

11 a) Ford £7290, Toyota £6480.
b) Journal: Dr motor vehicle £15 500, Cr disposal £6000, bank £9500, Dr disposal £10 000 Cr motor vehicles £10 000, Dr prov. for depn. £2710, Cr disposal £2710 Dr P & L £2198, Cr prov, for depn. £2198. Dr P & L £1290 (loss) Cr disposal £1290 Ledger balances: Motor vehicle £23 500 Dr, Prov. for depn £3718Cr, Disposal of vehicle, £10 000 Dr, depn. £2710, trade-in £6000, p & L £1290 credits. P & L account: depn £2198, loss on sale £1290. FA: £23 500 – £3718 = £19 782.
c) Ledger balances: Prov. for depn £3201 Cr, Disposal of vehicle, £10 000 Dr, depn £2953, trade-in £6000, P & L £1047 credits. P & L account: Depn Ford £243, Toyota £648, Mercedes £1033 = £1924, loss on sales £1047. FA: £23 500 – £3201 = £20 299.
d) The statement is untrue because depreciation does not set cash aside for replacement, although profits are reduced due to the expense of it.

12 a) In accounting, depreciation in a charge against profits. The cost of an asset is written off over its expected useful life, however, in times of inflation, its replacement cost is likely to be higher than its original cost. Unless some asset replacement reserve is provided, there is a danger that the 'real' capital may also be diminished.
b) 19–8 vehicles account: £15 000 Dr, 19–9 £32 000 Dr, provision for depn account: 19–8 P & L £3328 Cr, balance b/d £5015 Cr, 19–9 P & L £7309 Cr, balance b/d £10 074 Cr. dispossal account: 19–8 P & L loss £1187, (depn £2313), 19–9 P & L gain £650 Dr, (depn £2250).

Chapter 26 Accounting for partnerships

1 i) a) Share of profits £10 415 each. b) Current accounts: Trevalyn £4550 Cr, Curtis £2265 Cr.

Balance sheet: capital £45 000, current accounts £6815 = £51 815. ii) A limited partner has no right to control, only general partners. He is only liable up to the amount of his capital, not personal wealth.

2 a) Share of profits: Robert £9900, Susan £7425, Thomas £2475. b) Current accounts: Robert £81 Cr, Susan £100 Cr, Thomas £328 Dr.

3 Share of profits: Alan £18 000, Bill £12 000, Charles £6000. Current accounts: Alan £13 000 Cr, Bill £5000 Cr, Charles £0.
FA £112 000, CA £47 400, CL £21 400, WC £26 000 = £138 000. Capital £120 000, current accounts £18 000 = £138 000.

4 a) Share of profits £8900 each. Current accounts: Fairway £2500 Cr, Rough £7060 Dr. b) FA £51 500, WC £3940 = £55 440 – LTL £15 000 = £40 440. Capital £45 000, current accounts (£4560) = £40 440.

5 a) Gross profit £10 012, net profit £5690. Share of profits: Smith £3036, Jones £2024. b) Current accounts: Smith £101 Dr, Jones £824 Cr. FA £27 500, WC £3222 = £30 722. Capital £30 000, Current accounts £722 = £30 722.

6 a) Share of profits £2242 each. Current accounts: Stevenson £11 392 Cr, Little £1558 Dr. b) FA £63 790, WC £6044 = £69 834. Capital £60 000, current accounts £9834 = £69 834. c) Employees' salaries an expense in profit and loss account. Partners' salaries in appropriation account to show profit/loss which excludes owners' salaries.

7 a) Share of profits: Wooldridge £6540, James £4360. Current accounts: Wooldridge £7990 Cr, James £2660 Cr. b) FA £114 000, WC £5650, LTL £29 000 = £90 650. Capital £80 000, current accounts £10 650 = £90 650. c) Under Section 24 of the 1890 Partnership Act, profits or losses must be borne equally if no agreement exists in the event of partners in disagreement.

8 i) Gross profit £25 000, net profit £9000. Share of profits £2500 each. Current accounts: Dick £1870 Cr, Tom £2960 Cr. ii) FA £11 250, CA £29 580, CL £6000, WC £23 580 = £34 830. Capital £30 000, current accounts £4830 = £34 830.
Note: £350 purchases lost are deducted from cost of sales and entered as a current asset. iii) NP% 12, ROCE 25.8 returns on profit.

9 i) Share of profits: Smith £2050, Jones £2050, Rogers £1025. Current accounts: Smith £1095 Cr, Jones £1075 Cr, Rogers £370 Dr. ii) FA £30 700, WC £50, LTL £4950 = £25 800. Capital £24 000, current accounts £1800 = £25 800. iii) Working capital very marginal.

10 a) Share of profits £8500 each. Current accounts: French £2100 Cr, Saunders £7160 Dr. b) FA £61 000, WC (£1060), LTL £20 000 = £39 940. Capital £45 000, current accounts (£5060) = £39 940. c) WC ratio = 0.87:1 (insolvent). Insufficient funds to cover debts. Improve by reducing future drawings, particularly Saunders. Increase sales. d) The profit of £19 800 would be reduced to £19 300 and French's current account would be increased by £250. Saunders decreased by £250.

11 Net profit £44 000 + £300 depn. – £100 loss on sale = £44 200. Share of profits: bell £6900, Ring £4140, Gong £2760, FA £74 850, WC £8350 = £83 200. Capital accounts Bell £30 000, Ring £21 200, Gong £22 800, Current accounts Bell (£3100), Ring £3260, Gong £9040 = £83 200

12 Dec. 19–7 Net profit £27 225. Share of profit: £9075 each. Mar. 19–8 £8690. Share of profits: Stone £2995, Pebble £1797, Brick £1198. Capital accounts: Stone £20 000, Pebble £16 000, Brick £10 000. Current accounts: Stone £4120, Pebble £1472, Brick £5323.

Chapter 27 Accounting for limited companies

1 Net profit £108 000 (before tax), £78 000 (after tax) + P&L £22 000 – dividends £64 000 – reserves £20 000 = P&L £16 000. FA £554 000, (depreciation £256 000), WC £16 000 = £570 000. Capital £500 000, premium a/c £20 000, reserves £34 000, P&L £16 000 = £570 000.

2 Gross profit £135 500, net profit £46 500 (before tax), £32 000 (after tax) – dividends £2500

– reserves £25 000 = P & L £4500. FA £135 100, WC £23 900, LTL £52 000 = £107 000. Capital £50 000, premium a/c £10 000, reserves £42 500, P & L £4500 = £107 000.

3 a) Net profit £40 600 (before tax), £30 600 (after tax) + P & L £19 200 – dividends £14 400 – reserves £10 400 = P & L £25 000. b) FA £165 000, CA £39 960, CL £34 560, WC £5400 = £170 400. Capital £130 000, reserves £15 400, P & L £25 000 = £170 400.

4 a) Net profit £10 300 + P & L £9600 – dividends £7200 – reserves £12 000 = P & L £700. b) FA £75 000, WC £2700 = £77 700. Capital £65 000, reserves £12 000, P & L £700 = £77 700. c) Interim dividend: part payment, usually half-yearly. Ordinary shares (equities) true shares, carry greater risk, no fixed dividends. Preference shares paid at fixed rate of dividend, carry less risk.

5 a) Net profit £300 (before tax), £290 (after tax) + P & L £10 – dividends £230 – reserves £40 = P & L £30. b) FA £1380, WC £140 = £1520. Capital £1400, reserves £90, P & L £30 = £1520. Equity £1020.

6 Gross profit £151 800, net profit £43 033 (before tax), £23 833 (after tax) + P & L £7780 – dividends £22 400 – reserves £4000 = P & L £5213. FA £322 330, CA £102169, CL £110 286, WC (£8117) insolvent, LTL £40 000 = £274 213. Capital £240 000, reserves £29 000, P & L £5213 = £274 213.

7 a) Assets: premises £75 000, fittings £14 300, debtors £18 600, stock £6861, bank £13 679 = £128 440. Liabilities: creditors £10 300, dividends £7500 = £17 800. Capital £110 640, (A – L). Capital £100 000 P & L £10 640 = £110 640. b) Insufficient WC, danger of insolvency. Too much WC, funds should be optimised to make best use of resources.

8 a) Net profit £8964 + P & L £3200 – dividends £7200 – reserves £2000 = P & L £2964. b) FA £82 904, CA £25 870, CL £13 810, WC £12 060, LTL £30 000 = £64 964. Capital £60 000, reserves, £2000, P & L £2964 = £64 964.

9 a) Gross profit £121 500, net profit £45 000 (before tax), £29 500 (after tax) – dividends £9000 – reserves £20 000 = P & L £500. FA £156 500, WC £61 500, LTL £40 000 = £178 000. Capital £100 000, reserves £77 500, P & L £500 = £178 000 b) 1.6:1, working capital appears adequate.

10 Net profit £80 000 (before interest and tax), £47 500 (after tax) + P & L £40 000 – dividends £55 000 – reserves £25 000 = P & L £7500. FA £355 000, CA £419 000, CL £296 500, WC £122 500, LTL £100 000 = £377 500. Capital £300 000, reserves £70 000, P & L £7500 = £377 500.

11 Gross profit £157 980, net profit (b/t) £108 480, tax £15 000, profit (a/t) £93 480, P & L account balance c/f £158 175, FA £116 900, CA £270 875, CL £129 600, WC £141 275 = £258 175. (Note: loss on disposal £1000)

12 A provision is seen as any amount retained from profits for the purpose of providing for any liability or loss which is likely to be incurred but the figure is unknown, e.g. provision for depreciation or bad debts, etc. Reserves include amounts to be retained as an integral part of a business's resources or from premiums from share issues or revaluation of fixed assets. Accrued expenses are those due to be paid at the year end, e.g. for light, heat, telephone, etc, as distinct from creditors who are owed for the supply of goods or services.

Chapter 28 Cash flow statements

1 Wexford: inflow £610, divis (£30), tax (£160), FA (£4400), Loans £4400 = + cash £420

2 Rock: inflow £400, divis (£100), tax (£250), FA (£6500), loan/shares £5650 = cash (£800)

3 Jackson: inflow NP £12 750 + £3500 – WC (£7070) = £7180, tax (£5100), FA (£16 000) sale FA £1500, shares £10 000 = cash (£420)

4 Maxpax: inflow NP £37 000 + £12 000, – WC (£19 000) = £30 000, divis (£26 000), tax (£14 000), FA (£40 000), shares £56 000 = cash + £6000

5 Aspen: inflow NP £48 160 + £20 300 – WC (£4140) = £64 320, divis (£10 000), tax (£17 120), FA (£70 400), shares £20 000 = cash (13 200)

6 Francis: inflow NP £10 400 + £8000 – WC (£5600) = £12 800, tax (£12 000), FA (£20 000), sale £4200, shares £10 000, loan (£1000) = cash (9000)

7 XYZ: inflow NP £7500 + £3800 – WC (£800) = 10500, tax (£6000), FA £9000, sale £3500 = cash £1000)

Chapter 29 Accounting for clubs and societies

1 Expenditure £1808, income £1585, deficit £223. FA £10140, CA £1345, (including £1000 bank), CL £68, WC £1277 = £11417. Accumulated fund £11640 – deficit £223 = £11417.
2 Expenditure £4145, income £10145 (bar profit £3400). Surplus £6000. FA £1800, CA £9480, CL £680, WC £8800 = £10600. Accumulated fund £4600 + surplus £6000 = £10600.
3 a) Accumulated fund £36759. b) Expenditure £7386, income £8127, surplus £741. FA £33 850, bank investment £2807, CA £1037, CL £194, WC £843 = £37500. Accumulated fund £36 759 + surplus £741 = £37 500.
4 a) Accumulated fund £15 550. b) R & P a/c: balance £1195 + receipts £2950 – payments £2535 = closing balance £1610. c) Expenditure £2470, income £2950, surplus £480. FA £14 590, WC £1440 = £16 030. Accumulated fund £15 550 + surplus £480 = £16 030.
5 a) Accumulated fund £1220. b) Subscriptions a/c: debits – £65, £37; credits – £10, £1987, £85, balance £1980. Prizes a/c: COS £272. Surplus = £165. c) Expenditure £3249, income £2822, deficit £427. FA £780, CA £131, CL £118, WC £13 = £793. Accumulated fund £1220 – deficit £427 = £793.
6 Accumulated find £1955. Expenditure £2955, income £3020, surplus £65. FA £1460, CA £601, CL £41, WC £560 = £2020. Accumulated fund £1955 + surplus £65 = £2020.
7 a) R & P account bank £111, refreshment account: surplus £499 b) Expenditure £1288, income £1304 = surplus £16. FA £133, CA £328, CL £116, WC £212 = £345. AF £329 + £16 = £345
8 a) Bar a/c: sales £10 243, COS £7149 surplus £3094. Expenditure £6318, income £13269, surplus £6951. Subscriptions a/c £782. (subscriptions £22 w/o: Dr expense, Cr subscriptions).
b) FA = £268 244, CA £4432, CL £176, WC £4256 = £272 500 – LTL £55 000 = £217 500. Accumulated fund £210 549 + surplus £6951 = £217 500.
9 Bar surplus £318, I & E surplus £5577 (subs £17 670), FA £106 200, CA £19 465, CL £2088, WC £17 377 = £123 577. AF £118 000 + £5577 = £123 577
10 Surplus £13 091 (subs £11 900, profit on tools £2900, loss on exhib. £35). FA £8000, CA £8880, CL £545, WC £8335 = £16 335. AF £3244 + £13 091 = £16 335

Chapter 30 The trial balance and its limitations

1 a) Errors of: principle, principle, commission, omission and original entry. b) In each case, a debit has a corresponding credit, not disclosed by the trial balance. c) Drawings £550 Dr, wages £550 Cr, office equipment £180 Dr, purchases £180 Cr, rates and water £85 Dr, accrued expenses £85 Cr, Vat £7.5 Dr, Welland £7.5 Cr.
2 The trial balance is an arithmetical check on the accuracy of the recording of double entry. If each transaction has an equal Dr and Cr any error will not be disclosed.
3 D Brown £211.5 Dr, J Brown £211.5 Cr, office equipment £2250 Dr, purchases £2250 Cr, debtors £27 Dr, sales £27 Cr, light and heat £36 Dr, bank £36 Cr.
4 a) Rawlins £23.5 Dr, returns out £20, Vat £3.5 Cr, Jones £253 Dr, sales £220, Vat £33 Cr, Smith £54 Dr, purchases £54 Cr, drawings £435 Dr, purchases £435 Cr, bank £42 Dr, commission £42 Cr, equipment £200 Dr, purchases £200 Cr, sales £300 Dr, equipment £300 Cr.
b) Each item which affects either revenue or expenses affects the profit of a business.

Chapter 31 The journal and the use of the suspenses account

1 W Brown Dr, Willis & Brown Cr, office equipment Dr, purchases Cr, Elliott Dr, discount allowed

Cr, drawings Dr, delivery expenses Cr, light and heat Dr, bank Cr.

2 a) R Smith £285 Dr, J Smith £285 Cr, sales £600 Dr, equipment £600 Cr, discount allowed £8 Dr, suspense £8 Cr, suspense £200 Dr, sales £200 Cr, suspense £55 Dr, salaries £55 Cr, debtors £275 Dr, sales £275 Cr, insurance £55 Dr, bank £55 Cr. b) Suspense a/c: debits – sales £200 and salaries £55; credits – balance £247 and discount allowed £8.

3 a) Trial balance totals £30105.
Debits: purchases £2960, returns in £98, petty cash £18, discount allowed £45, rates £91, bank charges £14, stock £823, debtors £960, premises £25 000.
Credits: sales £6916, returns out £46, bank overdraft £621, creditors £840, capital £21682.
b) Errors of principle, compensation, etc.

4 a) Sales £220 Dr, suspense £220 Cr, suspense £121 Dr, Wilkinson £121 Cr, vehicle repairs £27 Dr, suspense £27 Cr, Heath £9 Dr, suspense £9 Cr, suspense £240 Dr, discount allowed £120 and discount received £120 Cr. Suspense a/c: debits – Wilkinson £121 and discounts £240; credits – balance £105, sales £220, vehicle repairs £27 and Heath £9. b) Errors of principle, commission, omission and compensation.

5 i) Discount received £100 Dr, suspense £100 Cr, suspense £8 Dr, Stanley £8 Cr, sales £900 Dr, suspense £900 Cr, sales £9 Dr, Purcell £9 Cr, purchases £360 Dr, suspense £360 Cr, Blow £20 Dr, returns in £20 Cr, sales £15 Dr, Vat £15 Cr. ii) Suspense a/c: debits – balance £1352 and Stanley £8; credits – discount received £100, sales £900 and purchases £360. iii) The adjusted profit £12200.

6 i) Purchases £64 Dr, creditors £64 Cr, furniture £82 Dr, repairs £82 Cr, suspense £290 Dr, bank £290 Cr, sales £378 Dr, suspense £378 Cr, interest charges £50 Dr, bank £50 Cr, creditors £100 Dr, suspense £100 Cr. ii) Suspense a/c: debits – balance £188 and bank £290; credits – sales £378 and creditors £100. iii) The adjusted profit £382.

7 a) Equipment £500 Dr, purchases £500 Cr, Light and heat £85 Cr, bank £85 Cr, discount allowed £68 Dr, suspense £68 Cr, suspense £800 Dr, sales £800 Cr, suspense £45 Dr, Smith £45 Cr, returns in £87 Dr, suspense £87 Cr. Suspense a/c: debits – sales £800 and Smith £45; credits – balance £690 discount allowed £68 and returns in £87. b) Trial balance totals £50745.

8 Suspense £315 Dr, sales £315 Cr, general expenses £85 Dr, suspense £85 Cr, suspense £500 Dr, purchases £500 Cr, suspense £90 Dr, discount recedived £90 Cr, suspense £95 Dr, returns out £95 Cr. Suspense a/c: debits – sales £315, discount received £90, purchases £500 and returns out £95; credits – balance £915 and general expenses £85. Adjusted profit £13335.

9 a) Debtors £1200 Dr, sales £1200 Cr suspense £500 Dr, Dodds £500 Cr suspense £752 Dr, discounts £752 Cr discounts £448 Dr, suspense £448 Cr suspense £495 Dr, p/l controll £495 Cr depreciaiton £750 Dr, suspense £750 Cr
Suspense account: debits – s/l control £500, discounts £752, p/l control £495. Credits – balance £549, discounts £448, depn. £750
b) Net profit £9746 + £754 = £10 500 adjusted profit.

Chapter 32 The extended trial balance

1 ABC: Gross profit £9700, net profit £4022, FA £31350, WC £4072, LTL £15 500 = £19 922. Capital £18 000 + profit £4022 – drawings £2100 = £19 922

2 Mitchell: Gross profit £110 615, net profit £16 667, FA £104 400, CA £54 340, CL £26 020, WC £28 320, = £132 720. Capital £131 653 + profit £16 667 – drawings £15 600 = £132 720

3 Yousef: Gross profit £55 141, net profit £5888, FA £30 300, CA £27 560, CL £6681, WC £20 879 = £51 179. Capital £53 091 + profit £5888 – drawings £7800 = 51 179

4 Walker: Gross profit £65 409, net profit £31 632 (depn £875), FA £43 025, CA £15 495, CL £9400, WC £6095 = £49 120. Capital £27 908 + profit £31 632 – drawings £10 420 = £49 120

5 Smith: Gross profit £11 353, net loss (£26), FA £10 030, CA £5584, CL £4840, WC £744, LTL £4500 = £6274. Capital £8860 – loss (£26) – drawings £2560 = £6274

6 a) Suspense account Dr debtors £500, discounts £752, creditors £495, Cr discounts £448, acct fees £750
b) Sales £76 450, debtors £24 700, discounts £96, creditors £16 495, trial balance totals £194 295
c) Gross profit £30 650, net profit £9270, FA £75 800, CA £28 156, CL £23 847, WC £4309 – LTL £10 000 = £70 109.

Chapter 33 Accounting standards

1 Accounts would be prepared far more subjectively and many more anomalies would occur in the final accounts.

2 a) The owner(s) is separate from that of the business,
b Transactions with a monetary value can only be recorded, not human or other vlaues.

3 At original cost, at cost less depreciation, at net relisable value (NRV), at present value, etc.

4 The value of future returns from an asset, discounted at the going interest rate, to bring returns to their present vlaue.

5 Two methods which try to deal with inflation are CPP and CCA. CPP requires recording at cost adjusted by an appropriate index (e.g. RPI) with the problem that there are other indices to use. With CCA, the profit for the year is calculated after allowing for inflation and assets stated at their value to the business. In adjusting asset values for the effect of inflation, profit would be lower and distributions to shareholders lower, protecting capital maintenance.

6 CCA. It is linked to capital maintenance because asset values can be indexed for inflation and 'profit' is thereby reduced with its effect, maintaining net asset values.

7 SSAP 2 outlines the four basic accounting concepts: going concern, accruals, consistency and prudence, which provides the whole basis of preparing of final accounts.

8 Concepts include: historical cost, consitency (depn), prudence (stock and provision for losses), realisation (sales), accruals (interest), going concern (assumption the company does continue).

9 The total cost of purchases and expenses, including Vat, is recording in the final accounts. No Vat account recorded.

10 A registered trader records inputs and outputs of Vat. The income and expenses in the final accounts would exclude Vat charges, any balance of Vat is listed in the balance sheet.

11 In the value of stock, the concepts include: consistency, prudence and accruals (use of same method, using lower of cost and matching revenue with expenses).

12 SSAP 13 and 21 both have items which can be capitalised or 'expensed'. Research is revenue expenditure where development can be capitalised. A finance lease and HP can be capitalised but an operating lease treated as revenue expenditure.

13 If there is evidence which will significantly influence the value of certain accounts such as the loss of value from investments or stocks or an increase in liabilities. (SSAP 17)

14 As a contingent liability (also an an accrued expense in the P & L a/c). (SSAP 18)

Chapter 34 Evaluating business performance: accounting ratios

1 a)

	19–8	**19–9**
Net profit%	15	15
ROCE	30.5	30.1
ROTA	24.1	23.6
WC ratio	1.01	0.98
Acid test	0.5	0.42

b) Profit returns taken before tax. All ratios marginally inferior in 19–9. The company is insolvent in 19–9 and perhaps the dividends should be reduced to ensure solvency.

2 a) WC is the ability of a business to meet its short-term debt. The minimum ratio should be 1:1,

a figure less than this means insolvency. Each business should identify its own margin of safety.
b) WC ratio 1.95, acid test 1.16. These appear adequate as a test of the business's liquidity.

3 a) Profitability: tests returns on profit before or after tax.
Liquidity: tests ability to meet debt.
b) Gross profit %, net profit % (profit to sales).
c) WC ratio, CA/CL
d) 'A' ROCI 10%, ROCE 9.1%, WC ratio 2:1.
d) 'B' ROCI 25%, ROCE 20%, WC ratio 0.5:1.
Business A moderate profitability and sound liquidity.
Business B good profitability but poor liquidity.

4 i)

	Big	**Spiv**
WC ratio	1.8	1.3
Acid test	0.47	0.16
Gearing	9.5%	114%
NP %	12%	15%
EPS	31.3p	83.3p
ROCE	25.2%	33.3%

ii) Big has low gearing and sound liquidity. Spiv has higher gearing and relies more on outside finance and has more attractive returns, especially EPS (earnings per share).

5 a)

	19–3	**19–4**	**19–5**	**19–6**
Gross profit (£)	15 000	18 000	18 000	27 000
Net profit (£)	3 000	4 500	1 500	8 000
GP%	33.33	33.33	25.00	28.00
NP%	6.67	8.33	2.08	8.33

b) The poor year was 19–5. GP% inferior, identify what went wrong with buying or selling. Recovery in 19–6, improving GP return.

6

	Ball Bearings	**Rocco**
Net Profit (a/t)	£1.5m	£1.6m
EPS	15p	80p
Dividend	7p	20p
Cover	2.1	4
WC ratio	0.98	0.95
Acid test	0.5	0.95
Capital gearing	300%	6.67%

The bank is far more profitable and stable, even though its WC ratio is 0.95; as a bank it should not have a liquidity problem.

7

	19–6	**19–7**	**19–8**
Gross profit	36 000	50 000	70 000
Net profit	1 600	7 000	16 000
GP%	30%	33.33%	35%
NP%	1.3%	4.6%	8%
ROCE	2.67	6.67	10
Stock turnover	10.5	11.8	13

Sound improvement although 8% net return in 19–8 still looks low. Stock turnover has gained each year as sales have expanded and the trend looks promising.

8

	A	**B**	**C**
Net profit (b/t)	695 000	695 000	645 000
Net profit (a/t)	451 750	451 750	419 250
Dividends	410 000	420 000	360 000
P & L balance	41 750	31 750	59 250
EPS	13.4p	12.9p	14p
Gearing	16.6%	0%	16.6%

Plan C may be the best to pursue because it has the highest retained profits and marginally better EPS. In times of high interest rates it may be better to opt for Plan A.

9

	Year 1	Year 2	Year 3
	£	£	£
a) Gross profit	10 000	12 000	13 050
Net profit	3 850	5 050	4 675
b) GP%	33.3%	33.3%	29%
NP%	12.8%	14%	10.4%
Dist. %	10%	8.9%	9.1%
Admin. %	10.5%	10.4%	9.5%
Stock turnover	10	9.6	8
Credit days	73	73	89
ROCI	14.5%	16.8%	14.7%

c) Year 3 inferior primarily because of fall in GP% from 33.3% to 29% indicating trading problems. Accounting ratios may fail to reveal the true or realistic situation.

10 a) Although the gross profits per cent of X is far higher than Y, both have the same net returns which suggests that X has far greater operating costs. A key figure is ROCE which reflects a combination of asset turnover and net profit per cent and Y is far more profitable and efficient in its return on investment. Business X has better solvency and carries less stock than Y but has a far slower rate of turnover being only one third of Y. The faster turnover of Y suggests it is like a supermarket with lower prices and the lower acid test should not be a cause of anxiety. X is also more efficient in terms of paying and collecting their debts.

b) Consistency is of importance in accounting and applies to adopting methods/bases when calculating figures for depreciation and stock etc. It applies in this case because when comparing X and Y, it is hoped that ratios have been computed by the use of the same bases, otherwise comparisons become distorted and less meaningful.

11 a) Balance sheet: PB plc, FA £ 10 000, WC £10 000 = £20 000, Capital + profit = £20 000. GB Ltd, FA £3600, WC £400, LTL £2200 = £1800, Capital + profit = £1800.

b) Liquidity ratios: PB plc 3.5, 1.5, GB Ltd, 1.67, 0.67.

c) Return on funds: PB plc, 20%, GB Ltd, 11.1%.

d) Gearing: PB plc 11.1%, GB Ltd 122.2% (with acceptable variations)

e) PB plc has much better short- and long-term liquidity and has a much larger value of employable capital.

12 a) P & L: gross profit £1160, net profit (b/tax) £520, (a/tax) £360, retained profits c/f £580, b) divi. 20p, eps 72p, c) yield 6.35%.

13 a)

	Yr.1	Yr.2	Yr.3
Gross %	33.3	25.	20.
Net %	10.	4.4	2.6
ROCE %	15.	8.	5.8
WC ratio	3.5	2.14	1.73
Acid test	2.3	1.43	1.
Sales/cap empld	1.5	1.8	2.25
Debt collection	79 days	81 days	74 days
Owner's stake%	80.	74.1	68.6
EPS	24p	12.9p	9.3p

b) Turnover has been achieved but at declining profit and liquidity levels. Difficult to justify increased investment. Problem is the high COS, but variabe OHs improved along with asset usage.

14 a)

	Co. A	Co.B
Gross %	25.	25.
Net %	5.63	7.5
Net % (–int)	7.5	7.71

ROCE %	8.2	7.5
ROCE % (–int)	10.9	7.7
WC ratio	4.	4.
Acid test	1.	1.5
Gearing %	37.5	2.1
Interest cover	4 times	37 times
Stock turnover	6 times	3 times
Sales/cap emplyd.	1.45	1
EPS	15p	11.25

b) Profits and liquidity similar although A better ROCE and EPS. Long-term solvency shows B stronger. A has better use of resources. Invest in B, larger company, stronger solvency, 40 per cent a large slice.

Chapter 35 Accounting for manufacturing organisations

1 Prime cost £119 150. Prime cost/unit £23.83. Factory OHs £22 900. Factory cost £142 150. Factory cost/unit £28.43. Gross profit £43 480.

2 a) Prime cost £57549. Factory OHs £11 759. Factory cost £69 308. Factory profit £8692. Total gross profit £34 197. Net loss £389. b) DL/unit £7.75, DM/unit £21.02, FOHs/unit £5.88, FC/unit £34.65. c) Yes, by £4.35 per unit.

3 a) Prime cost £1 096 160. Factory OHs £54 650, factory cost £1 146 000. FC/unit £38.20. b) Gross profit £449 640. Net profit £372 000.

4 a) Prime cost £46 512. Factory OHs £13 335. Factory cost £60 000. b) Gross profit £32 300. Net profit £20 000. c) Prime cost/unit £3.88. FOHs/unit £1.11. FC/unit £5. Value of finished goods £16 250. Mark up 60%.

5 Prime cost £100 958. Factory OHs £14 745. Factory cost £115 703. Gross profit £64 793. Net profit £38 717. FA £43 025, CA £19 672, CL £9400, WC £10 272 = £53 297. Capital £25 000 + profit £38 717 – drawings £10 420 = £53 297.

6 Prime cost £198 623. Factory cost £201 000. FC/unit £4.02. Value of finished goods £18 090. Gross profit £12 590. Net profit £1802. P & L balance £382. FA £91 400, WC (£11 018), insolvent = £80 382. Capital £70 000, premium a/c £7000, reserves £3000, P & L £382 = £80 382.

7 Prime cost £75 000. Factory OHs £40 550. Factory cost £103 250. Manufacturing loss £8250. Gross profit £85 000 – £8250 = £76 750. Net profit £8400.

8

	Star 1	Star 2	Star 3	Total
a) Prime cost	92 400	112 300	131 500	336 200
Factory cost	95 400	115 300	137 500	348 200
b) Gross profit	24 000	44 000	48 000	116 000
c) Gross profit %	20%	27.5%	25.3%	

9 Fairdeal: prime cost £74 000, factory OHs £49 460, factory cost £99 460, m/f profit £540. Trading profit £46 500 + £540 = gross profit £47 040, expenses £35 044 (prov for unrealised profit £54), net profit £11 996. FA £126 750, CA £49 546, CL £14 300, WC £35 246 = £161 996. Capital + profits = £161 996.

Chapter 36 Aspects of costing

1 To provide management with further information about the behaviour of costs and help to forecast what future costs might be in terms of labour, materials and overheads.

2 Absorption costs includes the total cost of making a product with its full share of fixed and variable costs. Hence the cost per unit will be the total costs divided by the output. With marginal costs, the focus is on variable costs only and the variable cost per unit in order to arrive at contribution. Fixed overheads for the period are deducted in total to calculate estimated profits.

3 a) Absorption cost £128 000/8000 = £16 per unit. b) Direct wages and materials c) £28 000 d) Contribution: 20–12.5 = £7.5, break-even: 28 000/7.5 = 3734 units, estimated profit on 8000 units = £32 000.

4 a) Profit £42 000, b) £3.16 per unit, c) Contribution: 4–1.895 = £2.105, d) Profit £45 157.5, check 5100 × 2.105 extra profit, e) Profit £37 790, f) 30 048 units to break-even, g) Marginal stock: 500 × 1.895 = £948, absorption stock: 500 × 2.51 = £1255

5

	A	B	C	Total	
	£	£	£	£	
Indirect materials	1 800	750	450	3 000	Allocated
Indirect labour	27 400	23 100	18 500	69 000	Allocated
Power	1 500	1 000	500	3 000	Floor area
Rent, rates	30 000	20 000	10 000	60 000	Floor area
Insurance (staff)	750	450	300	1 500	Employees
Distribution costs	4 8000	32 000		8 000	Sales
Administration			10 000	10 000	Allocated
Canteen costs	2 250	1 350	900	4 500	Employees
	68 500	49 850	40 650	159 000	
Service centre	24 390	16 260	(40 650)		
	92 890	66 110	159 000		

Chapter 37 Budgets

1 a) and b) Cash budget

	April	May	June	July	Aug	Sept
Balance b/f	5 000	1 000	5 000	1 000	14 000	28 000
Receipts	20 000	30 000	35 000	34 000	36 000	25 000
Payments	24 000	26 000	39 000	21 000	22 000	29 100
Balance c/f	1 000	5 000	1 000	14 000	28 000	23 900

c) Banking limits may be tight during the first three months but improve in last three.

2 a) and b) Cash budget

	July	Aug	Sept	Oct	Nov	Dec
Balance b/f	2 000	4 040	(7 900)	(8 060)	(4 840)	11 680
Receipts	23 200	32 000	24 000	28 000	39 000	31 200
Payments	21 160	43 940	24 160	24 780	22 480	20 660
Balance c/f	4 040	(7 900)	(8 060)	(4 840)	11 680	22 220

c) Small needs overdraft facility for months August to October.

3 Cash budget

	April	May	June	July	Aug	Sept
Balance b/f	120 000	3 500	1 200	(600)	(4 100)	(5 100)
Receipts	—	12 000	15 000	15 000	18 000	21 000
Payments	116 500	14 300	16 800	18 500	19 000	19 500
Balance c/f	3 500	1 200	(600)	(4 100)	(5 100)	(3 600)

4 a) Cash budget

	Dec	Jan	Feb	Mar
Balance b/f	1 000	3 725	1 125	1 700
Receipts	9 750	10 500	8 250	7 500

Payments	7 025	13 100	7 675	10 750
Balance c/f	3 725	1 125	1 700	(1 550)

b) Fixed costs are insensitive to output change, for example, rent, rates, insurance. Variable costs change relative to output and are sensitive to changes in levels of production. Examples, materials and direct labour.

5 a) Cash budget

	July	**Aug**	**Sept**	**Oct**	**Nov**	**Dec**
Balance b/f	10 000	4 800	1 200	2 200	1 700	(540)
Receipts		6 000	13 600	13 600	12 000	10 800
Payments	5 200	9 600	12 600	14 100	14 240	9 740
Balance c/f	4 800	1 200	2 200	1 700	(540)	520

b) Trading a/c: sales £64 000 – cost of sales £36 800 = gross profit £27 200. Net profit £9220. FA £10 500, CA £13 120, CL £4400, WC £8720 = £19 220. Capital £10 000 + profit £9220 = £19 220. Note: value of stock 400 units × £11.5 = £4600.

c) The owner may need a bank overdraft facility as his cash flow reduces to an overdraft in November.

6 a) Cash budget

	July	**Aug**	**Sept**	**Oct**	**Nov**	**Dec**
Balance b/f	12 000	(11 200)	(21 760)	(23 590)	(12 080)	520
Receipts		25 000	35 000	36 000	37 500	40 000
Payments	23 200	35 560	36 830	24 490	24 900	26 475
Balance c/f	(11 200)	(21 760)	(23 590)	(12 080)	520	14 045

b) Trading a/c: sales £203 500 – cost of sales £134 310 = Gross profit £69 190. Net profit £55 490. FA £19 500, CA £61 965, CL £2575, WC £59 390, LTL £10 000 = £68 890. Capital £17 000 + profit £55 490 – drawings £3600 = £68 890.
Note: stock value 240 units x £33 = £7920.

7 a) Prime cost £133 000, factory cost £209 000. FC/unit £5.5. b) Gross profit £87 500. Net profit £11 250. c) Mark-up 45.45%. Margin 31.25%.

8 a) Factory cost £2500. FC/unit 50p. SP/unit 75p. b) Gross profit £1225, expenses £325, net profit £900.

9 a) Prime cost £90 000, factory cost £112 000. FC/unit £5.60. SP/unit £8.40. b) Gross profit £50 400, net profit £14 400. Note: mark-up 50%, margin 33.33%. c) Variable cost: sensitive to output change. Fixed cost: insensitive to output change. Greater output dilutes fixed costs.

Chapter 38 The sale and purchase of a business

1 a) Jackson's (buyer's) journal: debits – premises £30 000, equipment £4000, motor £800, debtors £3500, stock £4500 and goodwill £6550; credits – provision for bad debts £350, creditors £7000, Davies (vendor) £42 000. Totals £49 350. b) Bank £42 000 Dr, capital £21 000 Cr, bank loan £21 000 Cr. On settlement: Davies £42 000 Dr, bank £42 000 Cr. c) Balance sheet: FA £34 800, goodwill £6550, WC £650, LTL £21 000 = £21 000. Capital = £21 000.

2 a) Smith's (buyer's) journal: debits – premises £65 000, equipment £5000, motor £2000, stock £9000, debtors £7500, goodwill £4500; credits – creditors £8000, Donald (vendor) £85 000. Totals £93 000. Bank £68 000 Dr. Loan £68 000 Cr.
On settlement: Donald £85 000 Dr, bank £85 000 Cr. b) Balance sheet: FA £97 000, goodwill £4500, CA £24 500, CL £13 000, WC £11 500 = £113 000, LTL F£68 000 = £45 000. Capital £45 000.

3 a) Donald's (vendor's) journal: debits – realisation £85 000 and creditors £8000; credits – premises £50 000, equipment £8000, van £2000, stock £12 000, debtors £7500 and capital (profit) £13 500. Totals £93 000. Smith £85 000 Dr. Realisation £85 000 Cr. Bank £85 000 Dr. Smith £85 000 Cr. b) Realisation a/c: debits – premises £50 000, equipment £8000, van £2000, stock £12 000, debtors £7500, capital £13 500; credits – creditors £8000 and Smith £85 000. Totals £93 000. c) Capital a/c: debit bank £93 500; credit balance £80 000; profit £13 500.

4 a) Accounting equation Johnson: capital £14 090 = assets £16 890 – liabilities £2800. Taylor: capital £12 580 = assets £14 580 – liabilities £2000. b) Balance sheet: FA £15 000, CA £12 800, CL £4300, WC £8500 = £23 500. Capital: Johnson £11 500, Taylor £12 000 = £23 500.

Chapter 39 Stock valuation

1 To ensure control of stock movements and buying optimum levels of stock.

2 Documents to include: purchase requisition, purchase order, delivery note, GRN, stock requisition voucher, store issue voucher, stock card.

3 To check quantities on any given item and to ensure re-orders are made on time.

4 a) 3000 b) 4382, c) 5382 d) 500.

5 £17 800 + £2750 – £2750 = £15 800.

6 a) 1732 b) 1800 (600 × 3 weeks) c) 1000 d) 3132.

7 11 200 re-order, 4000 minimum level, 19 200 maximum level.

8 Jack's: lower of cost/NRV, £525, £140, £900, £750, £149.25, £57.5, £5, total = £2526.75

9 FIFO: stock value 1/7 £715, 1/8 £745, 1/9 £765 = 100 units × £2.15 = £215, 250 units × £2.20 = £550 = £765 total value. LIFO: stock value 1/7 £700, 1/8 £700, 1/9 £700 = 200 units × £2.00 = £400, 100 × £1.95 = £195, 50 units × £2.10 = £105 = £700 total value.

10 Stock card: 12/9, 299 reams × £2.50 = £747.50, 20/9, 170 reams: using FIFO: 80 × £2.50 = £200, 90 × £3 = £270 = £470 total value.

11 FIFO: 24/1 balance 100 units × £3.20, 70 units × £3 = 170 units total value £530. 28/2, balance 50 units × £3.40, 50 units × £3.50 = 100 units total value £345. LIFO: 24/1 balance 150 units × £3, 20 units × £3.20 = 170 units total value £514. 28/2, balance 50 units × £3, 50 units £3.40 = 100 units total value £320. b) The stock value of LIFO is £25 less than FIFO, gross profit would be £25 less if LIFO used.

12 a) Stock card: 28/6, 105 units × £4 = £420 value, b) Stock sheet total £4003.75, c) Gross profit £7729.

13 a)

		Year 1	Year 2	Year 3
Gross Profit	LIFO	20 000	43 000	80 000
	FIFO	20 000	43 000	96 000
Net Profit (Loss)	LIFO	(6 000)	15 400	47 720
	FIFO	(6 000)	15 400	63 720

b) Capital a/c Year 1 = £44 000, Year 2 = £59 400, Year 3 = £123 120.

c) FIFO identifies more closely with actual stock movement values and stock end will reflect current value of stock. SSAP 9 recommends its use.

Chapter 40 Accounting for incomplete records

1 Sales £278 600, purchases £166 830, gross profit £111 770, net profit £16 300. FA £14 000, WC £86 000 = £100 000. Capital £99 700 + profit £16 300 – drawings £16 000 = £100 000.

2 a) 1/1 FA £30 000, CA £6238, CL £9053, LTL £3000 = capital £24 185. b) 31/12 FA £29 800, CA £8268, CL £1837, WC £6431, LTL £3000 = £33 231. Capital £33 231.

c) Profit = Net asset change + drawings – new capital

£10 826 £9046 £8000 £6220

3 a) Sales £29 956, purchases £10 546, gross profit £11 362, net profit £8699. b) FA £98 088, CA £9335, CL £26 069, WC (£16 734) insolvent = £81 354. Capital £76 265 + profit £8699 – drawings £3610 = £81 354.

4 a) Sales £46 525, purchases £38 965, gross profit £6970, net loss £3848, b) FA £118 800, CA £9265, CL £7388, WC £1877, LTL £40 400 = £73 277. Capital £80 000 – loss £3848 – drawings £2875 = £73 277.

5 a) Sales £19 815, purchases £13 654, gross profit £7641, net profit £4628. b) FA £18 997, CA £9071, CL £2520, WC £6551 = £25 548. Capital £23 000 + profit £4628 – drawings £2630 = £25 548.

6 a) Sales £26 800 COS (before stock loss) £23 860. Stock loss £2420 COS (including stock loss) £21 440. Gross profit £5360. (Margin 20%.) b) Stock loss £2420.

7 Sales £410 000, purchases £309 000. COS (before stock loss) £350 000. Stock loss £63 000. COS (after stock loss) £287 000. Gross profit £123 000. (Margin 30%.)

8 Sales £361 225, purchases £237 000, COS (before stock loss) £296 500. Stock loss £79 765. COS (after stock loss) £216 735. Gross profit £144 490. (Margin 40%)

9 Credit sales £173 770, cash sales £61 190 = £234 960. Credit purchases £166 360. Sales £238 140 (COS £158 760 + 50%) cash drawings (£238 140 – £234 960 = £3180 – £40 = £3140). Gross profit £79 380, net profit £12 530, FA £18 480, CA £42 020, CL £12 700, WC £29 320 = £47 800. Capital £30 910 + £16 000 + profit £12 530 – drawings £8500, £3410 = £47 800.

10 a) Sales (29 640 – 1260 + 1330 + 3630) £33 340, purchases (6460 + 12 740 – 470 + 265) £18 995. Gross profit £14 230, expenses £11 024, profit on disposal £315 = net profit £3521.
b) £17 140, c) FA £8206, CA £7275, CL £790, WC £6485 = £14 691. Capital £17 170 + profit £3521 – drawings £6000 = £14 691.

Chapter 41 Accounting for departments

1 a)

	Electrical	Furnishings	Total
Gross profit	18 000	37 000	55 000
Net profit	100	4 900	5 000

b) The furnishings department carries the store, electrical barely break even. An evaluation is needed as to why profitability is a low £100.

2 a) Allocation: a cost specifically allotted to a department or cost centre, for example, wages and cost of materials. Apportion: a cost incurred for the benefit of two or more sections which must be divided on some basis such as floor space or number of staff.
b) Likely bases: a) floor space; b) meter readings or floor space; c) sales volume or value; d) number of staff; e) floor space or number of staff; f) sales volume or value; g) floor space or value of fixtures in each department.

3

	Dept A	Dept B	Dept C	Dept D
Gross profit	5400	7600	1800	4600
Gross profit %	25.2%	22.6%	7.26%	24.7%

Obviously Dept C requires some evaluation as having a disproportionately low gross margin.

4 a)

	Dept A	Dept B	Dept C	Total
Gross profit	54 900	94 600	94 500	244 000
Net profit	19 000	52 620	43 680	115 300
Gross profit (%)	45.75%	52.60%	47.25%	
Net profit (%)	15.8%	29.2%	21.8%	

Dept B appeared to be the most successful. Was it the most efficient in terms of buying and cost effectiveness? Were the overheads apportioned on a fair basis?

5

	Product X	Product Y	Total
a) Gross profit	11 000	52 100	63 100
b) Net profit			20 250

c) FA £66 500, WC £63 000 = £129 500. Capital £118 700 + profit £20 250 – drawings £9450 = £129 500.

Chapter 42 Accounting for payroll

1 a) Harry £162 b) Jack £134.4, Fred £123.9
2 Tom £126, Dick £119.25, Harry £148.5
3 Charlie £52.5 + £43.12 = £95.62
4 £885
5 Gross £188, net £141.75
6 No. 10: £147 + £26.25, £25.20 = £198.45
No. 11: £147 + £10.50, £18.90 = £176.40
No. 12: £147 + £31.50, £18.90, £25.20 = £222.60
7 Gross pay £226.80 less tax £21.48, pension £14, NIC £16.34, TU £1.10 = £173.88 net pay.
8 Statutory deductions are those legally obligated to be deducted from gross pay such as tax and NIC. The P11 is used to record the employee's pay details – gross pay, tax and NIC.
9 Gross pay and employee's NIC is debited £4176.91, Inland Revenue is credited with £1037.54, and bank with £3139.37
10 Jane: £330.2 p.a. (£5096 – £3445 = £1651 × 20% tax).
11 Peter £182.24 tax per month (£801.25 1st £250 × 20% = £50 tax, 551.25 × 24% = £132.24 basic rate, total tax = £182.24
12 Jake £707.69 per week, – allow. £152.44 = £555.25 taxable pay per week (1st 57.69 × 20% = £11.53, next £398.07 × 24% = £95.52 and balance of £99.49 × 40% = £39.60, total tax for week = £146.65 Note that basic and higher rate tax to nearest £1.
13 a) Anne NIC £23.52, Susie NIC £8.20.
14 a) Jane £66.33, b) £41.67, c) £8.20
15 A P45 is completed for an employee when he leaves a job and 2 copies are given to his new employer. A P46 is used if an employee is without a P45 or is a school leaver on his first job.

Glossary of terms

Account A formal record of one or more business transactions expressed in money and kept in a ledger/journal.

Accrual The accounting treatment of expense incurred in one financial year but paid in the next financial year.

Advice note Note accompanying the delivery of goods.

Asset Any resource owned by a business, tangible or intangible.

Audit An examination of the accounts and supporting records by an independent accountant.

Auditor The person who carries out the audit.

Bad debt An amount receivable but deemed to be uncollectable.

Balance The difference between the debit and the credit entries in an account.

Balance sheet A statement of assets held in a business at a particular time — the Position Statement.

Bank reconciliation A statement explaining the difference between the cash book and the statement issued from the bank.

Book value [NBV] The original cost of an asset less the cumulative depreciation. [Net Book Value]

Book-keeping The process of recording financial transactions in the ledger/journal.

Books of prime entry Books into which transactions are first recorded before transfer to the ledger, that is, the journals and cash books.

Budget The expression of a business plan in money terms.

Capital Usually refers to the owner's net worth: that is, the total capital employed minus long-term liabilities.

Cash book A book in which all the cash/bank receipts and payments are recorded.

Cash discount An amount allowed for prompt settlement of an invoice.

Cash flow statement A statement focusing on inflow and outflow of cash during the financial year and is a link between the balance sheet of two successive period and the profit and loss for the year.

Contra The setting off of matching debit with credit against each other.

Credit note The document which shows the amount and other particulars regarding the reduction or cancellation of the amount originally invoiced.

Creditor One to whom money is owed.

Current asset An asset held for less than one year which can be converted to cash, such as stock, w.i.p., or debtors.

Current liability A short-term debt which must be repaid before the anniversary of the next balance sheet.

Debit note Sent to a customer if an invoice has been undercharged. Some customers send a debit note to their suppliers for goods returned [to debit the supplier's account].

Debtor One who owes money to the business.

Depreciation The estimated loss in value of a fixed asset as a result of wear and tear or obsolescence.

Final accounts The profit and loss account and balance sheet drawn up at the end of the financial year.

Fixed asset An asset held for more than one year, such as land, buildings, plant and machinery, office equipment.

Goodwill The excess paid for a business over the book value of assets minus liabilities being acquired on purchase.

GRN Goods received note; records deliveries once they have been checked into store.

Intangible asset An asset which has no physical substance but possesses a value, such as goodwill or development costs.

Imprest system Most usually associated with petty cash, whereby a fixed amount of money is advanced to the Petty Cashier who is reimbursed on a regular basis for the amounts paid out on petty cash vouchers.

Invoice The document which shows the quantity, price, terms and other particulars regarding goods or services provided.

Journal Used for transactions normally outside the scope of journals (below)

Journals Books of prime entry which list and summarise all goods and services bought and sold on a credit basis including returns. They include: sales, purchases, returns inward and returns outward journals

Ledger The main book of account in which entries are recorded and divided into the purchases, sales and nominal ledgers.

Liability Amount owing to third party.

Margin Profit expressed as a percentage of selling value.

Mark-up Profit expressed as a percentage of cost value.

Nominal accounts Refers to accounts in the nominal ledger for revenue, expenses and capital accounts.

Net assets Assets less liabilities which should equal the net worth of the owner(s); thus C = A – L.

Personal accounts The accounts found in the sales and purchase ledgers for individual debtors and creditors.

Par The nominal or face value of a security.

Personal accounts The accounts found in the sales and purchase ledgers for individual debtors and creditors.

Petty cash book A book kept by the Petty Cashier in which small cash disbursements are recorded. It is a subsidiary of the cash book.

Petty cash voucher Document supporting an entry in the petty cash book.

Posting The act of transferring entries from the books of prime entry to their separate accounts in the ledger or cash book.

Prepayment The accounting treatment of expenses incurred in the current financial year which relates to the next financial year.

Profit and loss account A summary account which nets off all revenue expenditure against income showing as its balance the net profit for the accounting period.

Provision Amount written off or retained out of profits to provide for depreciation or known liability.

Real accounts Refers to asset accounts – premises, equipment, vehicles, stock etc.

Receipt A written acknowledgement of payment for goods or services received.

Statement of account A statement prepared to show the amount due. Usually a statement will show only the amounts and dates of transactions between the two parties since the preparation of the previous statement.

Statement of affairs A report, usually prepared from incomplete records, that show the assets, liabilities and net worth of a business.

Stock in trade Goods held for subsequent sale in the ordinary course of business.

Tangible asset *See* Fixed Asset.

Taxable income Earnings that are subject to tax.

Trade discount A reduction that is allowed to certain customers on a list price. Usually the greater the quantity of items purchased the higher the discount.

Trial balance A list of all the balances in the ledgers of a business to prove the arithmetical accuracy of the debit and credit balances before preparing final accounts.

Turnover Net sales — that is, sales less returns inwards.

Value added tax Tax levied by H. M. Customs and Excise on the supply of some goods and services.

Working capital The difference between current assets and current liabilities, also referred to as net current assets. It should be sufficient to trade comfortably and meet day-to-day costs.

Written down value *See* Book Value.

Index